Chris Madden

Mod 7 Week 1 Chapt 1+2

2 3, 4+8

3 9

4 5

COMMUNICATING AT WORK

Principles and Practices for Business and the Professions

Questions for groups p 239

Meeting Checklists pp 269, 272, 273, 281

COMMUNICATING AT WORK

Principles and Practices for Business and the Professions

FIFTH EDITION

Ronald B. Adler
Santa Barbara City College

Jeanne Marquardt Elmhorst
Albuquerque Technical–Vocational Institute

THE McGRAW-HILL COMPANIES, INC.

New York • St. Louis • San Francisco • Auckland • Bogotá • Caracas • Lisbon • London • Madrid • Mexico City • Milan • Montreal • New Delhi • San Juan • Singapore • Sydney • Tokyo • Toronto •

McGraw-Hill

A Division of The ***McGraw-Hill*** *Companies*

COMMUNICATING AT WORK: Principles and Practices for Business and the Professions

Acknowledgments appear on page 488 and on this page by reference.

This book is printed on acid-free paper.

2 3 4 5 6 7 8 9 0 DOC DOC 9 0 9 8 7 6

ISBN 0-07-000478-1

This book was set in New Aster by Graphic World, Inc.
The editors were Phillip A. Butcher and James R. Belser;
the text designer was Joseph A. Piliero;
the cover designer was Joan Greenfield.
the production supervisor was Kathryn Porzio.
The photo editor was Anne Manning.
R. R. Donnelley & Sons Company was printer and binder.

Photo Credits

Chapters 1 and 2: Joel Gordon; Chapter 3: Bob Daemmrich/Stock, Boston; Chapter 4: David Powers/Stock, Boston; Chapters 5, 6, and 7: Joel Gordon; Chapter 8: Mark Antman/Image Works; Chapter 9: Gale Zucker/Stock, Boston; Chapter 10: Richard Pasley/ Stock, Boston; Chapter 11: Ogust/Image Works; Chapter 12: Susan Lapides/Design Conceptions; Chapter 13: Joel Gordon; Chapter 14: Joseph Schuyler/Stock, Boston; Chapter 15: AP/Wide World.

Library of Congress Cataloging-in-Publication Data

Adler, Ronald B. (Ronald Brian) (date).
Communicating at work: principles and practices for business and the professions / Ronald B. Adler, Jeanne Marquardt Elmhorst. —5th ed.
p. cm.
Includes bibliographical references and index.
ISBN 0-07-000478-1
1. Business communication. 2. Interpersonal communication.
I. Elmhorst, Jeanne Marquardt. II. Title.
HF5718.A33 1996
658.4'5—dc20 95-41256

INTERNATIONAL EDITION

When ordering this title, use ISBN 0-07-114001-8.

About the Authors

Ronald B. Adler is Associate Professor of Communication at Santa Barbara City College, where he specializes in organizational and interpersonal communication. He is the author of *Confidence in Communication: A Guide to Assertive and Social Skills* and coauthor of *Understanding Human Communication, Interplay: The Process of Interpersonal Communication* as well as the widely used text *Looking Out/Looking In.* Professor Adler is a consultant for a number of corporate, professional, and government clients and leads workshops in such areas as conflict resolution, presentational speaking, team building, and interviewing.

Jeanne Marquardt Elmhorst lives in Albuquerque, New Mexico and has been involved in communication studies for over fifteen years. She received her master's degree from the University of Wisconsin–Stevens Point, then travelled and taught in Asia for three years, sparking her interest in intercultural communication. She has taught at the University of Albuquerque and the University of New Mexico. She is currently an instructor at Albuquerque Technical-Vocational Institute, where her courses reflect the variety in the communication discipline: business and professional, organizational, listening, gender, intercultural, and interpersonal. Jeanne also provides training for business and government clients.

Contents

— PART III —
WORKING IN GROUPS
221

— PART IV —
MAKING EFFECTIVE PRESENTATIONS
285

Preface

In an age of downsizing, change, and career insecurity, good communication skills are more important than ever. The fifth edition of *Communicating at Work* aims at retaining the features that have served career-oriented students well in the past while also reflecting changes in the world of work.

Longtime users will recognize the approach that has helped *Communicating at Work* retain its popularity with students and their professors over the past fourteen years:

- A practical approach that presents academic findings in a form that readers can use to launch and advance in their careers
- Examples from a broad range of settings that illustrate how communication principles operate in the "real world"
- A direct, readable style

Features of the New Edition

Along with these familiar characteristics, this new edition contains many changes that should help students become more successful in their studies and careers.

Improved Pedagogy. Each chapter opens with an outline that makes its content and structure clear. Chapter openers also list key terms, which are highlighted when first introduced in the text and are defined in the *Glossary* at the end of the book. Activities are now integrated throughout each chapter and identified by their goals. *Skill Builders* give readers practice in applying newly learned skills. *Invitations to Insight* help readers understand how concepts from the text apply in the everyday world of work. *Ethical Challenges* invite readers to explore the ethical implications of on-the-job communication.

Expanded Consideration of Culture and Gender. The important topics of culture and gender are treated throughout the text, rather than isolated in a single section. For example, Chapter 2 introduces the many dimensions of culture and discusses its importance in an increasingly diverse, interconnected world. Chapter 3 contains discussions of how gender and culture influence language use and nonverbal communication, as well as descriptions of the challenges of communicating with people for whom English is a second language. It also contains a new section on identifying, avoiding, and responding to sexual harassment. Chapter 4 explores gender variables that affect listening and cultural differences in listening style. Chapter 9 explains that meetings can be conducted in a manner that reflects the cultural norms of the people who attend them. Chapters 11 and 15 offer tips on adapting presentations to the cultural backgrounds of the audience.

Focus on New Communication Technologies. Chapter 1 discusses when and how to use new technologies, including e-mail, voice mail, and teleconferencing, as well as traditional channels such as writing, telephone, and face-to-face contact. Chapter 12 offers new advice on using computer-generated graphics in presentations. Chapter 13 provides tips for speaking "on camera" for video presentations.

Clearer Organization. Longtime users will find the overall organization of this edition familiar. The first two chapters have been reorganized for the sake of clarity and space management. Material on using formal and informal communication networks has been tightened up and moved to Chapter 1. Discussion of organizational cultures in Chapter 2 has been retained and updated. The end-of-book Glossary pulls together definitions of key terms in one convenient location.

Other New Material. Throughout the book, new sections offer information requested by users on a variety of topics. For example:

- The discussion of listening in Chapter 4 includes new material distinguishing sincere and "counterfeit" questioning styles and an expanded discussion on types of paraphrasing responses.
- Chapter 5 has new sections on offering both praise and constructive criticism.
- Chapter 7 contains expanded samples of written correspondence accompanying employment and career research interviews.
- Chapter 8 now contains an expanded discussion of self-directed work teams, reflecting the trend toward this style of participative communication.
- Major new sections of Chapter 14 offer advice on two common types of business and professional communication: special-occasion speaking (introductions, tributes, acceptances, etc.) and group presentations.
- Chapter 15 helps readers take advantage of theoretical advances to make their presentations more persuasive.
- The Appendix offers improved examples of business correspondence.

Improvements like these don't happen in a vacuum. We owe a great deal to colleagues around the country whose suggestions have helped shape this edition: Carolyn Clark, Shirley Jones, Loretta Walker, and Roselyn Kirk at Salt Lake Community College; Ellen Bonaguro, Northern Illinois University; Thomas J. Costello, University of Illinois–Urbana; Anne Cunningham, Bergen Community College; Mary Hale, University of Colorado–Boulder; Jeffrey Kellogg, University of Mississippi; Leonard A. McCormick, Tarrant County Junior College; James Quisenberry, Morehead State University; Ted Spencer, Eastern Washington University; Francine Sulinski, University of Maine–Orono; and Edgar B. Wycoff, University of Central Florida.

Ronald B. Adler

Jeanne Marquardt Elmhorst

COMMUNICATING AT WORK

Principles and Practices for Business and the Professions

PART I

Basics of Business and Professional Communication

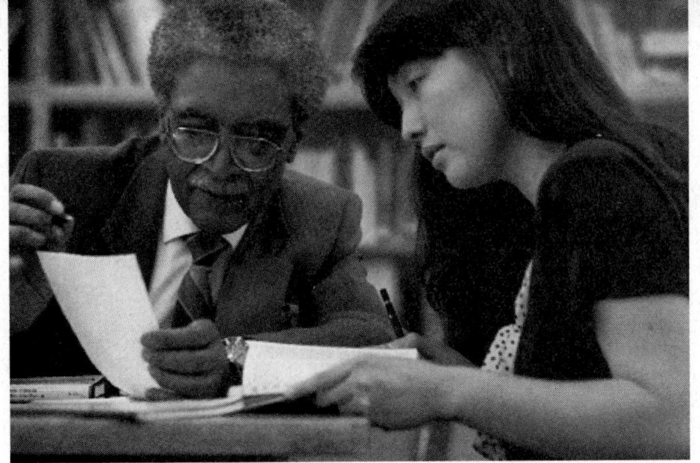

CHAPTER 1

Communicating at Work

KEY TERMS

Audioconferencing / Channel / Chronological context / Communication networks / Content messages / Context / Cultural context / Decoding / Document (computer) conferencing / Downward communication / Electronic mail (e-mail) / Encoding / Feedback / Formal communication networks / Horizontal (lateral) communication / Informal communication networks / Message / Noise / Organizational chart / Physical context / Physical noise / Physiological noise / Psychological noise / Receiver / Relational messages / Sender / Social context / Upward communication / Videoconferencing / Voice mail

THE IMPORTANCE OF COMMUNICATION

Virtually everyone communicates at work. No matter what the field, and no matter how much you know about your job, specialized knowledge alone isn't enough to guarantee success: communication skills are also vital. Table 1-1 lists the results of a survey of 1,000 personnel managers in the United States. The respondents identified the top three skills for job performance as involving communication. Other important attributes—including technical competence, work experience, academic background, and recommendations—all lagged behind.[1] Other surveys support the importance of communication-related skills including working on teams, teaching others, serving customers, leading, negotiating, working with cultural diversity, interviewing, listening, conducting meetings, and resolving conflicts.[2]

Subscribers to the *Harvard Business Review* rated "the ability to communicate" the most important factor in making an executive "promotable," more important than ambition, education, and capacity for hard work.[3] Research spanning several decades has consistently ranked communication skills as crucial for managers.[4] One twenty-year study that followed the progress of Stanford University M.B.A.s revealed that the most successful graduates (as measured by both career advancement and salary) shared personality traits

TABLE 1-1 Factors Most Important in Helping Graduating College Students Obtain Employment

Rank/Order	Factors/Skills Evaluated
1	Oral (speaking) communication
2	Listening ability
3	Enthusiasm
4	Written communication skills
5	Technical competence
6	Appearance
7	Poise
8	Work experience
9	Résumé
10	Specific degree held
11	Grade point average
12	Part-time or summer employment
13	Accreditation of program
14	Leadership in campus/community activities
15	Participation in campus/community activities
16	Recommendations
17	School attended

Source: Dan B. Curtis, Jerry L, Winsor, and Ronald D. Stephens, "National Preferences in Business and Communication Education," *Communication Education* 38 (January 1989): 11.

that distinguish good communicators: a desire to persuade, an interest in talking and working with other people, and an outgoing, ascendant personality. As students, these achievers developed their communication skills by choosing courses in areas such as persuasion, selling ideas, negotiation, and other forms of speaking.[5]

Although the need for face-to-face skills may seem less important in today's high-tech world, the opposite is true. Business consultant Susan Peterson explains how communication can help workers make sense of the avalanche of information that threatens to overwhelm them.

> We have more information, faster than we ever dreamed, but what is happening to our quality of communication? As managers, and business leaders, perhaps our responsibility is to manage this information. To make sure we communicate.[6]

Without human skills, technology will overwhelm an organization. Columbia University researchers discovered that, in the changing workplace, computers and other kinds of sophisticated equipment are now performing routine jobs, leaving workers to handle the human challenges of improving the organization and responding to customers.[7] After studying the needs of four Silicon Valley manufacturing firms, educational psychologist Russell Rumberger discovered that what employees needed was "oral literacy—the ability to communicate, to work in teams and to shift rapidly as the work changed."[8]

Most successful people recognize the role communication skills have played in their career. In a survey of college graduates in a wide variety of fields, most respondents said that communication was vital to their job success. Most, in fact, said that communication skills were more important than the major subject they had studied in college.[9] In one survey of business-school alumni, oral communication skills were judged as "mandatory" or "very important" by 100 percent of the respondents—every person who replied.[10]

The importance of communication is not surprising when you consider the staggering amount of time people spend communicating on the job. Most experts state that the average business executive spends 75 to 80 percent of the time communicating—about forty-five minutes out of every hour.[11] Businesspeople aren't the only ones whose jobs depend on effective communication. The Los Angeles Police Department cited "bad communication" among the most common reasons for errors in shooting by its officers.[12] After two studies indicated that physicians with poor communication skills are more likely to be sued, an editorial in the *Journal*

> The 1990s are proving to be the decade when the soft stuff—like how you listen to employees and customers—finally gets some respect. The new model replaces the top-down military command with a stress on teamwork. In the 1920s IBM chief Tom Watson hung signs saying THINK in every office. . . . Today's signs should read COMMUNICATE.
>
> Jolie Solomon, "The Fall of the Dinosaurs," *Newsweek*

of the American Medical Associaton called for more communication classes for doctors.[13]

The importance of communicating effectively on the job is clear. But this discussion so far hasn't even addressed the fact that communication skills often make the difference between being hired and being rejected in the first place. In a study of the help-wanted sections of 160 Sunday newspapers, nearly 6,300 classified ads specifically asked for applicants with communication skills. A survey of 154 employers who recruit on college campuses showed that one of the three most preferred areas of study was oral and written business communication. (The other two were accounting and personnel management/human behavior in organizations.) When 170 well-known business and industrial firms were asked to list the most common reasons for *not* offering jobs to applicants, the most frequent replies were "inability to communicate" and "poor communication skills."[14]

THE NATURE OF COMMUNICATION

It is easier to recognize the importance of communication than it is to define the term. A close look at what happens when people try to communicate can offer clues about why some attempts succeed and others fail.

The Process of Communication

No matter what the setting or the number of people involved, all communication consists of a few elements. Although the process of communication is more than the total of these elements, understanding them can help explain what happens when one person tries to express an idea to others.

Sender. The communication process begins with a ***sender,*** the person who transmits a message—a sales manager making a presentation to a client, a computer programmer explaining a new program to a co-worker, or an after-dinner speaker introducing a guest.

Message. A ***message*** is any signal that triggers the response of a receiver. Some messages are deliberate, while others (such as sighs and yawns) are unintentional. Messages are not synonymous with meanings. For example, you might remind a co-worker about a deadline with the intention of being helpful, but your colleague could interpret the message as an indication that you were annoyed or mistrustful.

Encoding. The sender must choose certain words or nonverbal methods to send an intentional message. This activity is called ***encoding.*** The words and channels that a communicator chooses to deliver a message can make a tremendous difference in how that message is received. Consider the simple act of a manager's offering feedback to an employee: Whether the words are respectful or abrupt and whether the message is delivered in person or in a memo can make a big difference in how the feedback is received.

Channel. The ***channel*** (sometimes called the *medium*) is the method used to deliver a message. As a business communicator, you can often choose whether to put your message in writing as a letter or memo. You can deliver it by hand or send it via regular mail or use an overnight delivery service. You can send electronically via fax or electronic mail. Or you can communicate it orally, either over the phone or in person.

Receiver. A ***receiver*** is any person who notices and attaches some meaning to a message. In the best of circumstances, a message reaches its intended receiver with no problems. In the confusing and imperfect world of business, however, several problems can occur. The message may never get to the receiver. It might be delivered but lie buried under a mountain of papers on the recipient's desk. If the message is oral, the listener might forget it. Even worse, a message intended for one receiver might be intercepted by another one. A bystander might overhear your critical remarks about a co-worker, or a competitor might see a copy of your correspondence to a customer.

Decoding. Even if a message does get to its intended receiver intact, there is no guarantee that it will be understood as the sender intended it to be. The receiver must still ***decode*** it, attaching meaning to the words or symbols. As we have already seen, decoding is not always accurate. Your friendly joke might be taken as a deliberate offense, or a suggestion might be misinterpreted as an order. The request for "next year's figures" might mean the next fiscal year, not calendar year. It is a mistake to assume that your messages will always be decoded accurately.

Feedback. Receivers don't just absorb messages like sponges; they respond to them. Consider audience questions during a talk or the way a customer glances at the clock during a sales presentation. Imagine the tone of voice an employer might use while saying, "I'll have to think about your proposal." Behaviors like these show that most communication is a two-way affair. The discernible response of a receiver to a sender's message is called ***feedback.*** Some feedback is nonverbal—smiles, sighs, and so on. Sometimes it is oral, as when you react to a colleague's ideas with questions or comments. Feedback can also be written, as when you respond to a co-worker's memo. In many cases, *no* message can be a kind of feedback. Failure to answer a letter or to return a phone call can suggest how the noncommunicative person feels about the sender. When we add the element of feedback to our communication model, we begin to recognize that in face-to-face settings people are simultaneously senders and receivers of information. This explains why these two roles are superimposed in the communication model pictured in Figure 1-1.

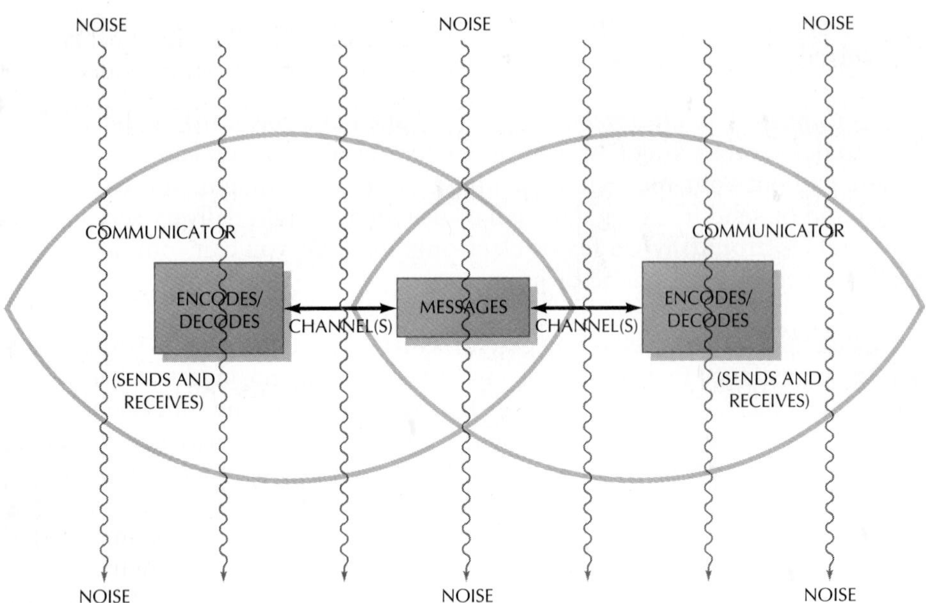

FIGURE 1-1 Communication model.

Noise. It might seem that, with enough feedback, the mental images of sender and receiver will match: the message received will be identical to the message sent. Your own experience probably shows that this doesn't always happen. One of the greatest sources of communication failure is ***noise***—the term communication scholars use for factors that interfere with the exchange of messages. ***Physical noise***—external sounds that distract communicators—falls into this category, but there are other types of external noise that don't involve sound. For example, an overcrowded room or a smelly cigar can disrupt concentration. A second kind of interference is ***physiological noise.*** Hearing disorders fall into this category, as do illnesses and disabilities that make it difficult to send or receive messages. Recall how hard it is to pay attention when

INVITATION TO INSIGHT

Think about a situation you have experienced in which communication went wrong. Diagnose the problem by finding the parts of the communication process that contributed to the trouble:

1. *Sender* Did the wrong person *send* the message?
2. *Message* Was the message unclear? Were there too many messages?
3. *Channel* Was the most appropriate channel chosen?
4. *Receiver* Was there no receiver at all? Was the message poorly formulated for the person(s) at whom it was aimed? Was it received by the wrong person?
5. *Feedback* Was feedback adequate to ensure understanding?
6. *Noise* Did physical, physiological, or psychological noise distort the message?

you are recovering from a night on the town or have the flu. The third type of interference is ***psychological noise,*** consisting of forces within sender or receiver that interfere with understanding. Egotism, defensiveness, hostility, preoccupation, fear—all these and more constitute psychological noise.

Context. Communication is influenced by the ***context*** in which it occurs. There are several dimensions of context, including physical, social, chronological, and cultural. We will now take a brief look at each of them.

Communication always takes place in some setting. This ***physical context*** can influence the content and quality of interaction. You can appreciate how the physical context can influence the quality of interaction by imagining how discussing a problem with your boss or asking for a raise might be received differently in each of the following settings:

In the boss's office

In your work area, with others observing the conversation

Over lunch at a local restaurant

At a company picnic or party

The ***social context*** refers to the nature of the relationship between the communicators, as well as who is present. Imagine, for example, the difference in asking a manager for the raise under a variety of different social contexts:

You and the manager have been friends for several years, *or* you and the manager have no personal relationship.

You are the same age as your manager, *or* she or he is fifteen years older (or younger) than you.

You and the manager have gotten along well in the past, *or* you have had an ongoing personality conflict with the manager.

You and the manager are alone, *or* your only chance to ask for the raise comes with other employees around.

The ***chronological context*** refers to the ways in which time influences interaction. A sample of time-related considerations shows the importance of adapting to the chronological context:

What time of day is it (first appointment in the morning or just before quitting)?

> The best advice I can give about communicating is to have patience. Know at the start that your ideas won't always be accepted or understood the first time around. Keep calm, and figure a better way to deliver the message. And pay special attention to timing. Your idea may get a bad response if you barge into someone's office and demand a hearing; but if you choose a time and place that makes the other person more receptive, you just may get through.
>
> Linn Kastan, president, Red Line Engineering, Inc.

What are the communicator's personal preferences for time (is one a morning person or a late starter)?

Is it before, during, or after work hours?

Is this the busy season (Christmas season, tax time)?

Has there just been a major layoff, downsizing, or profit loss?

You can boost your chances for success by paying attention to chronological factors. When calling someone or requesting a person's help, consider asking, "Is this a good time?" or "Do you have time now, or would another time be more convenient?"

The ***cultural context*** of communication includes both the organizational and the ethnic and/or national backgrounds of the persons communicating. Chapter 2 discusses the role of culture in detail. For now, you can get a sense of the importance of culture by imagining how just a few differences in backgrounds might influence communication between the following people:

Baby boomers and generation X-ers

Euro-Americans and Hispanics

New Yorkers and Californians

Men and women

Americans and Japanese

An interesting application of contextual change occurred during secret negotiations between Israel and the PLO when the hosts, the Norwegian foreign minister and Marianne Heiberg, his wife, changed the context. In their home, away from formal meeting halls, the hosts invited the negotiators to play on the floor with their four-year-old child. After changing the context, impasses were broken and a Mideast peace accord was hammered out.[15]

Communication Principles

The communication model pictured in Figure 1-1 is not yet complete. It is like a still picture of a live event: all the elements are present except action. Several characteristics describe the dynamic nature of the communication process.

Communication Is Unavoidable. A fundamental axiom of communication is "One can't not communicate." As you will learn in Chapter 3, we send a rich stream of nonverbal messages even when we are silent. Facial expression, posture, gesture, clothing, and a host of other behaviors offer cues about our attitudes. The impossibility of not communicating means that we send messages even by our absence. Failing to show up at an event or leaving the room suggests meanings to others. Because communication is unavoidable, it is essential to consider the unintentional messages you send.

Communication Operates on Two Levels. Every time two or more people communicate, they exchange two kinds of messages. The most obvious ones are ***content messages***—information about the topic under discussion. But at a less apparent level, the communicators are also exchanging ***relational messages***—signals indicating how they feel about one another.[16] Relational messages indicate a variety of attitudes. An important one is *affinity*—the degree to which a communicator likes the other person in general or a particular message that is being sent. Another kind of relational message deals with *control*—the amount of influence in that situation. Communication theorists sometimes talk about three self-explanatory distributions of control that can exist between communicators: "one up," "one down," and "straight across." A third type of relational message can reflect a communicator's degree of *respect* for the other person or people. Note that respect and affinity aren't always identical: it is possible to like others without respecting them and to respect them without liking them. In the world of work, respect and liking don't always go hand in hand. As Chapter 3 will explain, most relational messages are expressed nonverbally. Chapters 4, 5, 8, 13, and 15 will emphasize the value of paying attention to your relational messages and those of others.

Communication Is Irreversible. At one time or another, we have all wished we could take back words we regretted uttering. Unfortunately, this isn't possible. Our words and deeds are recorded in others' memories, and we can't erase them. As the old saying goes, people may forgive, but they don't forget. In fact, often the more vigorously you try to erase an act, the more vividly it stands out. This means you should weigh your words carefully. An offhand comment or a critical remark uttered in the heat of conflict can haunt you long afterward.

Communication Is a Process. It is not accurate to talk about an "act" of communication as if sending or receiving a message were an isolated event. Rather, every communication event needs to be examined as part of its communication context, as we described a few pages ago. Suppose, for example, your boss responds to your request for a raise by saying, "I was going to ask you to take a *cut* in pay!" How would you react? The answer probably depends on several factors: Is your boss a joker or a serious person? How does the comment fit into the history of your relationship—have your boss's remarks been critical or supportive in the past? How does the messsage fit with ones you have received from other people? What mood are you in today? All these questions show that the meaning of a message depends in part on what has happened before. Each message is part of a process: it doesn't occur in isolation.

Communication Is Not a Panacea. Although communication can smooth out the bumps and straighten the road to success, it won't always get you what you want. If the quality of communication is poor, the results are likely to be disappointing. This explains why some problems grow worse the longer they are discussed. Misunderstandings and ill feelings can increase when people communicate badly. Even effective communication won't solve all problems: there are some situations in which the parties understand one another perfectly and still disagree. These limitations are important to understand as you begin to study communication on the job. Boosting your communication skill can increase your success, but it isn't a cure-all.

USING COMMUNICATION NETWORKS

When people communicate in organizations, they need a system for managing the flow of information. You can appreciate this need if you consider how confusing unregulated communication would be, even in a small organization with only 17 employees. If each were free to pass information to every other person, each employee would be sending and receiving information—possibly conflicting information— from 16 other people. In fact, there would be 136 possible 2-person combinations. In an organization with 200 members, there would be 19,900 possible combinations—clearly an unwieldy number.

With this degree of complexity, there is some system for structuring who will communicate with whom. These systems are called ***communication networks***—regular patterns of person-to-person relationships through which information flows in an organization.[17] Two kinds of networks exist: formal and informal.

Formal Communication Networks

Formal communication networks are systems designed by management to dictate who should talk to whom to get a job done.[18] In a small organization, networks are so simple that they may hardly be noticeable; in a larger organization, they become more intricate. The most common way of describing formal communication networks is with ***organizational charts*** like the one in Figure 1-2. Organizational charts are more than a bureaucrat's toy; they provide a clear guideline of who is responsible for a given task and which employees are responsible for others' performance. Figure 1-2 is a typical organizational chart. It shows that Henry Muller reports to his boss, Herman Flores, while Terri Kwan reports to Bill North. Organizational charts show that communication can flow in several directions: upward, downward, and horizontally.

Downward Communication. ***Downward communication*** occurs whenever superiors initiate messages to their subordinates. As Table 1-2 shows, there are several types of downward communication:

- *Job instructions.* Directions about what to do or how to do it. "When you restock the shelves, put the new merchandise behind the old stock."
- *Job rationate.* Explanations of how one task relates to other tasks. "We rotate the stock like that so the customers won't wind up with stale merchandise."

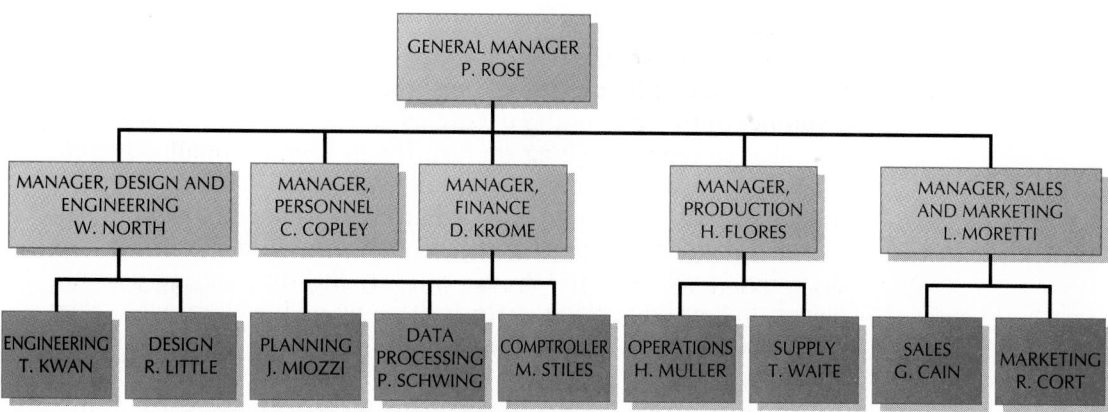

FIGURE 1-2 Dynacom Systems, Inc., organizational chart.

TABLE 1-2 Types of Formal Communication in Organizations

	Downward Communication	Upward Communication	Horizontal (Lateral) Communication
Definition	Superior to subordinate	Subordinate to superior	Between co-workers with different areas of responsibility
Types	Job instructions Rationale for job Organizational procedures and practices Feedback to subordinates Indoctrination to organization culture	What subordinates are doing Unsolved work problems Suggestions for improvement Subordinates' feelings about job and co-workers	Coordinate tasks Solve problems Share information Manage conflicts Build rapport
Potential benefits	Prevention/correction of employee errors Greater job satisfaction Improved morale	Prevention of new problems and solution of old ones Increased acceptance of management decisions	Increased cooperation among employees with different duties Greater understanding of organization's mission
Potential problems	Insufficient or unclear messages Message overload Message distorted as it passes through one or more intermediaries	Superiors may discourage, disregard, or downplay importance of subordinates' messages Supervisors may unfairly blame subordinates for unpleasant news	Rivalry may occur between employees from different areas Specialization makes understanding difficult Information overload discourages contacts Physical barriers discourage contact Lack of motivation

- *Procedures and practices.* Information about rules, regulations, policies, and benefits. "Don't try to argue with unhappy customers. If you can't handle them yourself, call the manager."
- *Feedback.* Information about how effectively a person is performing. "You're really catching on fast. If you keep up the good work, you'll be an assistant manager by the end of the year."
- *Indoctrination.* Information aimed at motivating employees by impressing the organization's mission upon them and specifying how they should relate to it. "People can buy the stuff we sell at other places, but we can bring them in here by giving them what they want quickly and pleasantly. If we do that, we'll all come out ahead."

Most managers would agree—at least in principle—that downward communication is important. It is hard to argue with the need for giving instructions, explaining rationale, describing procedures, and so on. Like their bosses, employees recognize the importance of downward communication. A study at General Electric revealed that "clear communication between boss and worker" was the most important factor in job satisfaction for most people. GE was so impressed with the findings of this study that it launched a program to encourage managers to communicate more and more directly with their employees, including holding informal meetings to encourage interaction.[19]

This desire for feedback is probably so strong because supervisors rarely provide enough of it. As two researchers in the field, Daniel Katz and Robert Kahn, put it: "The frequent complaint . . . by the individual is that he does not know where he stands with his superiors."[20] Many companies do take a more enlightened approach to feedback. Ed Carlson, former president of United Airlines, is generally credited with turning the company from a loser into a winner during his tenure. Part of his success was due to keeping United's employees—all of them—aware of how the company was doing. "Nothing is worse for morale than a lack of information down in the ranks," he said. "I call it NETMA—Nobody Ever Tells Me Anything— and I have tried hard to minimize that problem."[21] True to his word, Carlson passed along to the field staff information on United's operations that was previously considered too important to circulate.

Upward Communication. Messages flowing from subordinates to superiors are labeled ***upward communication.*** Many leading businesses attribute their success to the emphasis on upward communication in their organizations. Sam Walton, founder of Wal-Mart, the fourth-largest retailer in the United States, claimed that "our best ideas come from clerks and stockboys."[22] Industry observers credit the dramatic turnaround of Mattel Corporation to the openness to employee suggestions of its CEO, John Aberman.[23] Upward communication can convey four types of messages:[24]

- *What subordinates are doing.* "We'll have that job done by closing time today."

- *Unsolved work problems.* "We're still having trouble with the air conditioner in the accounting office."
- *Suggestions for improvement.* "I think I've figured a way to give people the vacation schedules they want and still keep our staffing up."
- *How subordinates feel about each other and the job.* "I'm having a hard time working with Louie. He seems to think I'm mad at him." Or "I'm getting frustrated. I've been in the same job for over a year now, and I'm itching for more responsibility."

These messages can benefit both subordinates and superiors, and this explains why one survey showed that organization members find upward communication to be the most important and satisfying kind of on-the-job interaction.[25] Upward communication is especially important for women. Females who engage in more interactions with their supervisors advance in the organizational hierarchy faster than those who do not spend as much time communicating upward.[26] A probable explanation for this fact is that women are less connected to the kinds of informal networks that will be described in a few pages. Given this absence of connections, it makes sense that women would rely on official contacts to work efficiently and effectively.

Despite the importance of upward communication, the survey described in the preceding paragraph produced a second finding: Employees find participation in upward communication extremely difficult. Table 1-2 suggests some reasons why. Being frank with superiors can be risky, especially when the news isn't what the boss wants to hear. Busy superiors can also be too preoccupied or certain of their expertise to pay attention to employees.

Most of the responsibility for improving upward communication rests with managers. They should begin the process by announcing their willingness to hear from subordinates. A number of vehicles facilitate upward messages: an "open-door" policy, grievance procedures, periodic intereviews, group meetings, and the suggestion box, to name a few. Formal channels aren't the only way to promote upward messages. Informal contacts can often be most effective; chats during breaks, in the elevator, or at social gatherings can sometimes tell more than planned sessions. But no method will be effective unless a manager is sincerely interested in hearing from subordinates and genuinely values their ideas. Just talking about this isn't enough. Employees have to see evidence of a willingness to hear upward messages—both good and bad—before they will really open up.

Horizontal Communication. A third type of organizational interaction is ***horizontal communication*** (sometimes called *lateral* communication). It consists of messages between members of an organization with equal power. The most obvious type of horizontal communication goes on between members of the same division of an organization: office workers in the same department, co-workers on a construction project, and so on. In other cases, lateral communication occurs between people from different areas: accounting calls maintenance to get a machine repaired, hospital admissions calls intensive care to reserve a bed, and so on. Horizontal communication serves five purposes:[27]

- *Task coordination.* "Let's get together this afternoon and set up a production schedule."
- *Problem solving.* "It takes three days for my department to get reports from yours. How can we speed things up?"
- *Sharing information.* "I just found out that a big convention is coming to town next week, so you ought to get ready for lots of business."
- *Conflict resolution.* "I've heard that you were complaining about my work to the boss. If you're not happy, I wish you'd tell me first."
- *Building rapport.* "I appreciate the way you got that rush job done on time. I'd like to say thanks by buying you lunch when it's convenient."

Research suggests that people in most organizations communicate horizontally, but the reasons for doing so are different in high-performing groups from those in less effective ones.[28] Low-performing groups are likely to reach out to different parts of the organization to get information on how to follow existing procedures. For example, an engineer might contact the purchasing department to check on the status of an equipment order. By contrast, lateral contacts in high-performing organizations are used to getting the information needed to solve complex and difficult work problems. For instance, before starting design work on a new product, the same engineer might contact the sales manager to find out what features customers want most.

Despite the importance of the five functions of horizontal communication, several forces work to discourage communication between peers.[29] *Rivalry* is one. People who feel threatened by one another aren't likely to be cooperative. The threat can come from competition for a promotion, raise, or other scarce resource. Sometimes rivalry occurs over an informal role. For example, two office comedians might feel threatened each time the other gets a laugh; that could inhibit their cooperation. Another challenge is the *specialization* that makes it hard for people with different technical specialties to understand one another. *Information overload* can also discourage employees from reaching out to others in different areas, and a simple *lack of motivation* is another problem. Finally, *physical barriers* can interfere with horizontal connections.

Informal Communication Networks

So far, we have focused on networks that are created by management. While organizational charts can describe some of the ways people interact in organizations, they don't tell the whole story. Alongside the formal networks, every organization also has ***informal communication networks***—patterns of interaction based on friendships, shared personal or career interests, and proximity between workers. As Figure 1-3 shows, informal relationships operate in ways that have little to do with the formal relationships laid out in organizational charts.

1. The editor of religious books and the publisher both attend the Second Avenue Christian Science Church.

2. The editor of cookbooks is a close personal friend of the publisher of the periodical division and recently influenced her to promote another friend to manager of educational journals.

3. The editor of fiction and the editor of travel books bypass the assistant publishers to enlist the aid of the publisher of the book division in getting raises.

4. The producer of feature films is engaged to the editor of *The College Librarian.*

5. The director of the film division and the publisher of the periodical division disagree with the publisher's fiscal policies and collaborate against her.

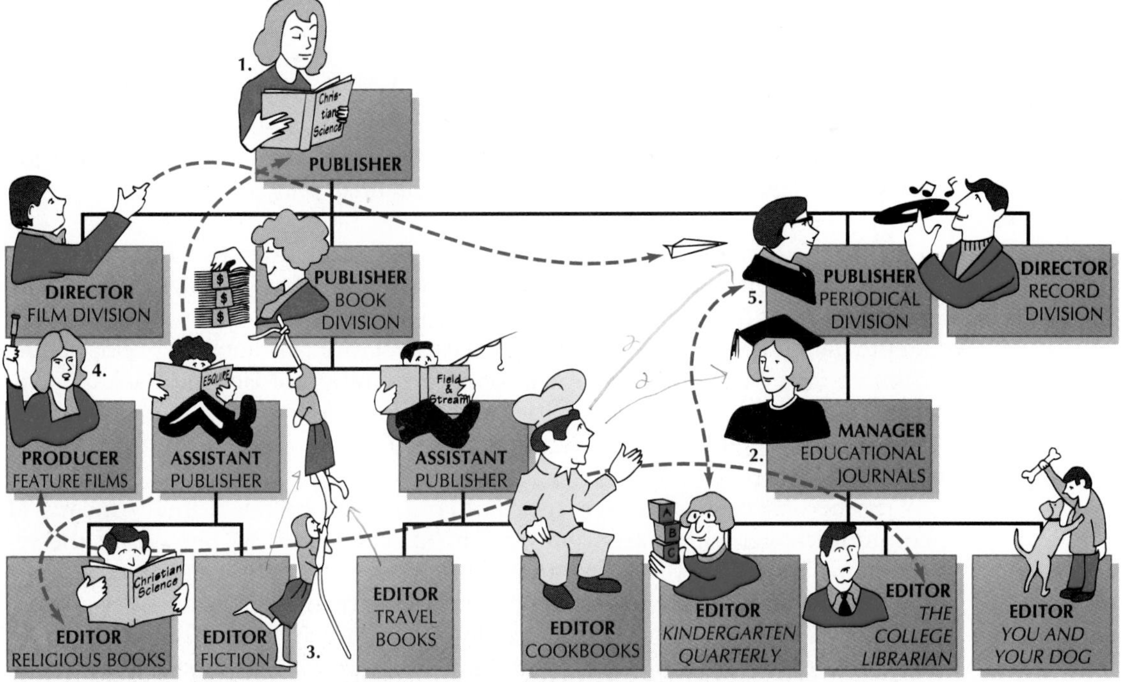

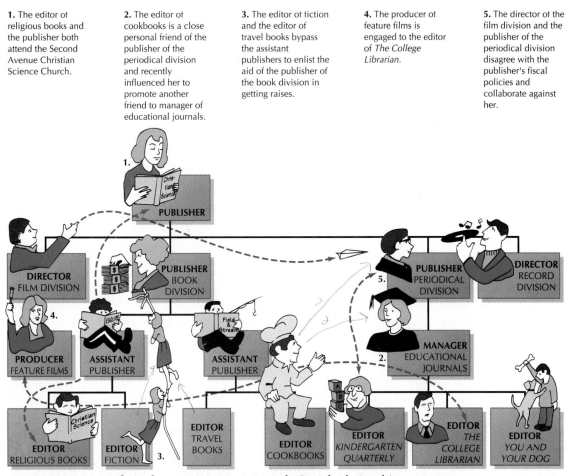

FIGURE 1-3 An informal communication network. Social relationships not recognized by the organization can influence decision making. (Adapted from *Business Today.* New York: Random House, 1979, pp. 102–103.)

Functions of Informal Networks. As the following examples show, not all informal messages are idle rumors. Informal communication can serve several useful functions.

Confirming. Some informal communication confirms formal messages. You have probably heard this sort of confirmation yourself: "The boss is really serious about cutting down on long-distance calls this time. I heard him yelling about it when I walked past his office."

Expanding. Information communication can fill in the gaps left by incomplete formal messages. You might say to an experienced co-worker: "The invitation to the office party says 'casual dress.' What does that mean—jeans and T-shirt or sport coat and tie?"

Expediting. Informal networks can often deliver messages more quickly than official channels can. Canny job hunters, for example, often use personal contacts to learn about openings within an organization long before the vacancies are published.

Contradicting. Sometimes informal networks contradict official messages. You might learn from a friend in accounting that the deadline for purchases on this year's budget isn't as firm as it sounded in the comptroller's recent memo.

Circumventing. Informal contacts can sometimes help you bypass official channels that are unnecessarily cumbersome and time-consuming. Your tennis partner who works in duplicating might sneak in an occasional rush job for you instead of putting it at the end of the line.

Supplementing. Sometimes even management realizes that informal communication can get the job done better than the more formal variety can. Paradoxical as it seems, many companies elevate informal communication to an official policy by encouraging open, unstructured contacts between people from various parts of the organization. A description of Hewlett Packard's approach to problem solving characterizes this style, which has been termed MBWA, "management by wandering around."

Some observers consider informal contacts to be the primary means of communication within an organization. In one survey, 57 percent of the respondents said that the grapevine is "the only way to find out what's really happening" in their organizations.[30] Two well-known analysts flatly assert that as much as 90 percent of what goes on in a company has nothing to do with formal events.[31] Writing in the *Harvard Business Review,* David Krackhardt and Jeffrey Hanson capture the difference between formal and informal networks: "If the formal organization is the skeleton of a company, the informal is the central nervous system."[32]

Like the human nervous system, informal networks are faster, and often more dependable, than formal channels.[33] They also provide a shortcut (and sometimes a way around) for the slower and more cumbersome formal channels, making innovation easier.[34] This fact helps explain why organizational decision makers tend to rely on verbal information from trusted associates.[35] Smart communicators don't just rely on informal contacts with peers for information: they take advantage of sources from throughout the organization. One study revealed that general managers spent a great deal of time with people who were not direct subordinates, superiors, or peers—people with whom, according to the official chain of command, they had no need to deal. Many of these people seemed relatively unimportant to outsiders: secretaries, lower-level subordinates, and supervisors with little power. Despite their unrelated job descriptions and low official status, successful managers all seemed to cultivate these contacts.[36]

Enlightened organizations do everything possible to encourage constructive, informal interaction. Corning Glass deliberately installed escalators in its new engineering building to boost the kind of face-to-face contacts that are less likely in elevators. 3M sponsors clubs for any groups of employees who request them, realizing that this sort of employee interaction is likely to encourage new ideas that will help the company. Other firms mingle workers from different departments in the same office, convinced that people who rub elbows will swap ideas and see themselves as part of a companywide team.

Informal networks don't just operate within organizations. Friends, neighbors, and community members increase their effectiveness by sharing information. In some cities, Chambers of Commerce host networking events to encourage these ties among community businesses. Even without these organized contacts, most people are surprised to realize just how many people they know who can offer useful information.

Cultivating Informal Networks. Developing a strong informal communication network is not all coincidence. Several steps can help you to develop these important links.

Seek Exposure to People at All Levels of the Organization. Sometimes the best informants are people with low official status. A telephone operator or receptionist, for example, may have a better idea of who talks with whom than anyone else in the organization. Secretaries are exposed to most of the information addressed to their bosses, and they usually serve as gatekeepers who can give or deny access to them. Custodial and maintenance people travel around the building and, in their rounds, see and hear many interesting things. Besides, a friendly repair person can fix a broken widget now instead of insisting that you file a work order that probably won't get attention for six weeks.

Treat Everyone in the Organization with Respect. As you will soon read, perhaps the most important factor in an organization's morale is the degree to

SKILL BUILDER

Develop your skill at cultivating informal communication networks by following these instructions:

1. Choose one of the following information goals, or identify a school- or work-related goal of your own.
   a. Identify which instructors and/or courses in an academic department of your institution are worth seeking out and which should be avoided.
   b. Define what qualities the management in a given organization values in employees.
   c. Identify computer users you know to determine which software program best suits your needs for a given application (e.g., word processing, database) and context (e.g. customer tracking, report writing).
2. Identify the people who can help you acquire the information you are seeking. Be sure to seek out people from a variety of positions within the organization to gain the most complete possible perspective.

which its members feel valued. Besides the fact that thoughtfulness and courtesy are simple good manners, they can make the difference between your developing a network of friends or a network of enemies. Remember birthdays. Ask about children. Discuss hobbies. And, above all, be polite and pleasant.

Ask Questions. When you discover a knowledgeable information source, ask for explanations of events. The simple question "What's going on here?" can generate more information than can a stack of policy manuals and managerial briefings. The other key question to ask is "Who can help me?" Your personal contacts can often direct you to the person or persons who can give you the information you need or support your efforts.

Don't Flaunt Informal Shortcuts. Almost no one totally follows the book—even the managers who wrote it. Nonetheless, it's asking for trouble to act in ways that blatantly violate official procedures. You might know that your boss's boss would authorize extra money for you to attend an out-of-town meeting, even though your department's travel budget is shot. If you think the only way to get the trip approved is to go over your immediate boss's head, be discreet. You might, for example, offhandedly refer to your interest in the meeting to the top boss while walking to the parking lot or coming in the front door in the morning, also mentioning that it's too bad the travel funds are gone. If the boss says "No problem," be sure to report the good news to your immediate superior, stressing the luck involved. If your boss thinks you've made an end run around his or her authority you'll soon regret it.

CHOOSING THE OPTIMAL COMMUNICATION CHANNEL

As a business communicator, you often can choose how to deliver a message. Deciding which communication channel to use isn't a trivial matter. Sometimes a written message succeeds where an oral one fails; at other times talking to the recipient in person will produce results that the printed word can't match. An understanding of these two channels will help you make the best choice about how to deliver your important messages.

Face-to-Face Communication

Face-to-face communication comes in many forms. Some are one-to-one meetings, either scheduled or spur of the moment. Others involve small groups of people, gathering spontaneously or in formal meetings. Still other

British prime minister Lloyd George had a low opinion of professional diplomats and their belief that notes and memoranda were the best means of clarifying issues. "Letters are the very devil!" he said on one occasion. "If you want to settle a thing, you see your opponent and talk it over with him. The last thing you do is write him a letter!"

Gordon A. Craig, *Diplomatic Problems of Our Times*

face-to-face communication occurs in large groups, where one or more speakers make presentations to an audience. Whatever the setting and number of people, all types of face-to-face communication possess the same qualities.

One potential advantage of face-to-face communication is its *speed.* Once you make contact with your audience, there is no time lag between the transmission of a message and its reception. This is especially valuable when time is of the essence: if you need a price or have to have the funds in an account released *now,* putting your request in a letter or memo won't be much help.

A second advantage of face-to-face communication is the *control* it gives you as the speaker. You might spend hours drafting a memo, letter, or report only to have the recipient scan it superficially or not read it at all. In a personal contact, however, you have much more command over the receiver's attention. The listener at least has to pretend to pay attention—and if you use the speaking skills described in the following chapters, your messages ought to be clear and interesting enough to capture the attention of your audience.

Another enormous advantage of face-to-face communication is that it permits *instantaneous feedback.* When you speak directly to one or more listeners, you can respond to questions as soon as they arise. You can rephrase or elaborate when your listeners seem confused, and you can speed up if details aren't necessary. You can revise hurriedly if you see you have used the wrong word and offended or confused your audience. Because of the tremendous amount of feedback available in face-to-face communication, it has been termed the "richest" kind of communication channel (see Figure 1-4).[37]

A final advantage of face-to-face interaction is its *personal quality.* When a personal meeting goes well, the relationship that communicators develop can help solve problems that might have been more difficult when handled at a distance. Personal meetings are especially important in some cultures, where failure to visit someone in person is an insult. The same principle can occur

FIGURE 1-4 Richness of communication channels. (Adapted from R. H. Lengel and R. L. Daft, "The Selection of Communication Media as an Executive Skill." *Academy of Management EXECUTIVE* 11, 1988, p. 226.)

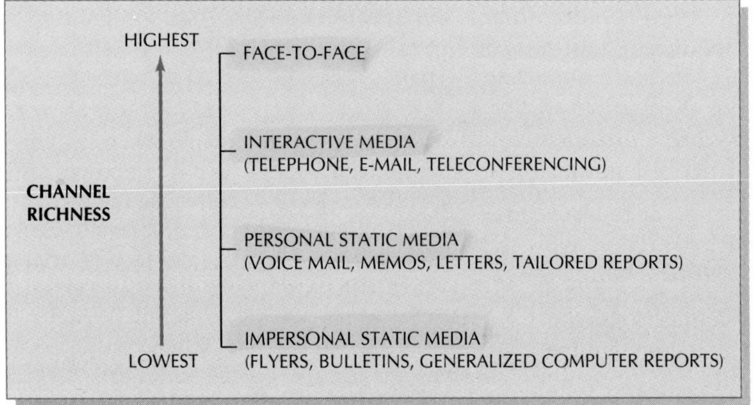

closer to home. People who don't show up for meetings may (intentionally or unintentionally) suggest to others that they are too important or too busy or too apathetic to be present. Comedian Woody Allen once said that 90 percent of success comes from just showing up. Although his claim might be a humorous exaggeration, the point is a good one.

Although it has many advantages, face-to-face communication isn't always the best approach. The biggest drawback of personal contacts is the difficulty in arranging them. Even when communicators are in the same building, scheduling a meeting can be difficult and frustrating. When the people who need to meet are separated by greater distances, personal contact is expensive and time-consuming. Even a crosstown trip for a half-hour meeting can take most of the morning or afternoon when it involves transportation.

A personal encounter might also be unproductive if the contact antagonizes one or more of the participants. If the personalities or the subject is likely to make someone angry or defensive, then less confrontational forms of communication might be better.

Teleconferencing

Face-to-face meetings may be desirable, but distance often makes them impractical. Teleconferencing is billed by its promoters as the next best thing to meeting in person. ***Videoconferencing*** allows participants in two or more locations to see and speak with each other. Until recently, most videoconferencing required elaborate studios at each location, which made the technology unaffordable for all but the largest organizations. New "desktop" conferencing using personal computers is putting the medium in reach of more workers. Market researchers predict that, as videoconferencing becomes an accepted part of buying a PC system, the ability to talk face-to-face over long distances will become common.[38] Even nonnetworked communicators will be able to take part in videoconferences: companies like Kinko's are providing walk-in connections for would-be teleconferencers.

Document or ***computer conferencing*** is another form of teleconferencing. This technology replaces face-to-face meetings by allowing individuals to work on documents that are "shared" via computer. As one person makes suggestions or changes a document, the others can view that change on their own screens. Document conferences can take place in "real" time, with participants

Smile! You're on Corporate Camera

Thanks to teleconferencing, job hunters with the widest of horizons may spend less time circling the globe to meet potential employers. Corporate headhunter Korn/Ferry International is setting up a videoconferencing system that links its U.S. offices with London, Hong Kong, and Tokyo. The new system allows executives in one part of the world to interview job candidates on other continents.

No one expects employers to extend job offers based on a long distance interview. Korn/Ferry and its clients use the conferences to shrink a large pool of candidates down to a short list who will receive face-to-face interviews. The system will save money, even though teleconferencing costs several hundred dollars per hour. This expense is trivial when compared to international airfare, hotels, and meals.

Los Angeles Times (Mar. 1, 1993): D2

interacting via their computers at the same moment, or over different periods of time, with participants working independently but picking up on the comments and input of others in their group. Communication experts have developed computer software (called *group decision support systems,* or "groupware") that facilitates electronic conferencing.

Teleconferencing isn't likely to replace face-to-face meetings completely. Some types of interaction just don't work as well when conducted long-distance: brainstorming, negotiations, and persuasion are a few examples. Still, many executives view teleconferencing as a way to eliminate unnecessary travel and improve long-distance communication.[39] And research suggests that, for many tasks, teleconferences can be just as productive as personal meetings and produce greater consensus among members.[40]

Telephone and Voice Mail

A telephone conversation lacks the visual feedback that often reveals how your message is getting across. The telephone still communicates vocal cues, however—tone of voice, pauses, interruptions, and so on. Telephone conversations also make it harder to hold the attention of your listener. Recall, for instance, all the fingernail cleaning and paper-clip sculpting you have done while unsuspecting speakers have rattled on.

The drawbacks of telephone communication are offset by one tremendous advantage: It often lets you contact a receiver who would be impossible to reach in person. You can touch base with someone halfway around the world in less time than it takes to catch an elevator to the next floor. The telephone can even help you get through to busy people who are nearby. Office hermits who barricade themselves behind closed doors will often drop everything when the telephone rings—or at least answer it grudgingly.

Telephones can be a useful tool for group communication as well as one-to-one contacts. ***Audioconferencing*** allows a group of geographically separated people to speak via telephones. A sales manager in Cleveland, a customer in Cincinnati, and an engineer in Dallas can hash out the details of a problem without ever leaving their respective offices—far better than a time-consuming and expensive face-to-face meeting or a frustrating round-robin series of phone calls in which the customer phones a question to the sales manager, who calls the engineer and then shuttles the answer back to the customer.

Despite its advantages, telephoning has drawbacks. Since many people are moving targets, you might not get through on your first (or even your second or third) try. As more people carry pagers and cellular phones, mobility is becoming less of a challenge, but catching someone on the first call can still be a pleasant surprise.

Even when you are able to "reach out and touch someone" with the phone, making contact can be problematic if you reach the caller at a bad time. Your chances of having a successful conversation will drop if the other person is hurried, angry, or distracted. For this reason, it's smart to ask, "Is this a good time?" before launching into your conversation. Scheduling a second call when you have the best chance of getting what you need is often worth the inconvenience.

Real-time communication isn't the only type of telephone communication. ***Voice mail*** is the 1990s' version of the answering machine. Many communicators hate voice mail, often with justification. Some voice mail menus and submenus can take forever ("If you want information about schedules, press 1 now. For a list of addresses, press 2. For product information, press 3. . . ."), and "clever" greetings can be annoying. But voice mail does have its advantages. It allows you to leave a message at any time of the day or night. You can feel confident that the recipient will actually receive the message in your own voice, just as you spoke it, without the omissions and distortions that come when an intermediary transcribes your message. Sophisticated voice-mail systems "date-stamp" a message, letting the other person know precisely when you called. Many systems also let you set up vocal "mailing lists" and send a spoken "memo" to several people at once, and then the systems notify you when your message has been received.

Even at their best, voice-mail messages might seem inferior to speaking in person to the other party. Sometimes, though, a voice-mail message can be even better than a personal contact. Leaving a recorded message can save you from wasting time swapping formulistic pleasantries with people you'd rather not talk to. Also, delivering your message electronically can keep the other person from responding in ways you don't want to hear. With voice mail you can decline an invitation, express just the right amount of irritation, or offer an excuse—all without having the other person talk back. You can use voice mail most effectively if you follow the tips in Table 1-3.

Some organizations have developed ingenious ways of using voice mail to promote better upward and downward communication. Yellow Freight of Overland Park, Kansas, is a long-distance trucking company. Its drivers spend most of their time on the road, making it difficult for them to pass along to management the kind of detailed ideas that can prevent problems and improve the company's effectiveness. To get around this challenge, drivers are invited to send messages to management via a toll-free long-distance phone number. Many of the ideas sent to the telephone "suggestion box" are adopted by management, which publicizes them in audiotape cassettes distributed quarterly to drivers. Employees report that hearing their own suggestions played back on tape to the entire fleet of drivers is a real morale booster.

Despite its advantages, oral communication isn't a perfect medium. Possibly the greatest disadvantage of speech is its *transience*. All communication is fragile, but the spoken word is especially prone to being forgotten or misunderstood. Listeners quickly forget much of what they hear—half of a message almost immediately and half of the remainder two days later. Thus, a customer might forget three of the five product features you mentioned, or your boss might forget exactly *why* you need more staff support and only recall the dollar amount you requested.

Even if they remember an oral message, listeners are likely to *distort* it. Some details drop out with each telling of a story. Facts and figures change. Receivers may even invent variations on the truth, just to make the story more interesting or to make it fit their own idea of what ought to have happened.

TABLE 1-3 Guidelines for Using Voice Mail

Voice mail can be a useful tool or an annoyance to the receiver, depending on how you use it. The following tips will help you get your message across most effectively when you begin speaking after the beep.

1. *Leave the name of the person for whom the message is directed.* Most home answering machines and some voice-mail boxes in businesses are shared by more than one person. Don't make the recipient guess who you're trying to reach.
2. *Identify yourself.* Unless the recipient knows you well, leave your first *and* last name. You may not be the only John, Kim, Lizzie, or Gus in the receiver's circle of acquaintances. If there's any possibility of misunderstanding, spell your last name.
3. *Leave your phone number,* especially if you want to be called back quickly. Even if you know others have your number, they may not have it with them when they are picking up messages.
4. *Organize your message in advance.* Don't confuse the recipient by sending a rambling message in which you carry on a conversation with yourself, change your mind, or switch ideas in midmessage. This sort of rambling makes you sound muddle-headed, and it is likely to annoy the recipient.
5. *Keep the message as short as possible.* Even a one-minute message can seem endless to the person who receives it. A long message—even if it is well organized—may contain too much information for the listener to digest. If you have a great deal to say, consider alerting your receiver to the main points, and then send the details via fax, memo, or overnight mail.
6. *Speak slowly and clearly.* The vocal fidelity of some voice-mail systems is poor, and you don't want your message to be misunderstood.

The farther the message travels in space and time from its original sender, the greater the chance of distortion.

Written Communication

Written communication comes in a variety of forms. Letters, memos, bulletins, and reports are familiar fixtures in almost everybody's career.

Written messages have a different set of advantages and drawbacks than their spoken counterparts have. Unlike speech, written communication is *permanent.* Once your words are down on paper, they are saved for future reference—either to your delight or to your undying embarrassment and chagrin. While people may have trouble accurately recalling what you said a few hours ago, they can refer to your written remarks years later. Even if the receiver has lost or forgotten your message, you can always supply a copy from your files.

Along with its permanence, written communication can be *easier to understand* than speech. Readers can study complex passages as many times as necessary, a luxury they do not have when the same message is delivered orally. They can take a break if their interest wanes and, after a cup of coffee or a quick stretch, come back to what they were reading refreshed and ready to go on.

Perhaps the greatest advantage of written communication is that you can *compose it in advance*. You can take as much time as necessary to shape a message just as you want it, pondering every word if necessary. You can try out several versions on test readers to anticipate the reactions of your real audience, and you can make changes until you get the desired response.

Finally, written messages are *less prone to errors*. Even the best-rehearsed oral presentations can go awry. You can misplace an important set of papers or forget to mention a key idea. Furthermore, the spontaneity that makes spoken communication so effective can backfire. Your attempt to improvise might sound confusing or lame, and the joke you thought would make the perfect ice-breaker might fall flat. Every speaker has thought, hours after a conversation, "If only I'd said . . ." When you communicate in writing, you have time to choose exactly the right words.

Two kinds of written communication deserve special mention. Facsimiles (most commonly called "faxes") are documents that have been transmitted electronically over telephone lines. They share most of the features of other written documents, but the *speed* with which they can be sent and received makes them more similar to oral messages delivered in person or over the phone. In fact, faxes can be thought of as print versions of voice-mail messages. Because they can put a huge amount of detail in the hands of a receiver almost instantly, faxes can be an ideal complement to phone conversations. You can tell someone (in person or on voice mail) "Let's talk after you've looked over the details I'm faxing you." The faxed document prevents the tedium and inaccuracy of describing the subject over the phone, and the vocal follow-up gives you and the other person the chance to share ideas far more efficiently than you could in an exchange of written messages.

Electronic mail (or ***e-mail***) is another unique communication channel. It allows communicators to send and respond to one another's written messages via computer. Like the telephone and faxes, e-mail is virtually instantaneous: once you push the "send" key on your computer, the message will be waiting for the addressee, usually in a matter of seconds or minutes. E-mail is used as an alternative to telephones and personal contacts within an office, as well as for long-distance communication.

E-mail possesses some characteristics of voice mail: Besides its speed, it allows you to leave messages for others to pick up at their convenience. However, because your ideas appear in writing, e-mail (like letters and faxes) makes it easier to comprehend lengthy, detailed messages.

E-mail differs from most other forms of written communication in one important way: its informal, almost spontaneous nature. Communicators using e-mail have almost no concerns with the kind of formatting that is important in other business correspondence, and the ease of logging on and sending a message increases the frequency and informality of contacts. For this reason, some users have termed e-mail a "conveyor belt for ideas."[41]

The speed and easy-to-use nature of e-mail also make it a tool for improving personal relationships on the job. Speeding up routine communication leaves more time for personal contacts, which the medium also makes more possible. Technology consultant Beau Carr explains: "It may sound backwards, but people who refuse to learn about technology are the ones losing the human touch. . . . Users can focus more energy and attention on relating to other people and at the same time deliver products and services faster, better, and probably less expensively."[42]

Which Channel to Use

As Table 1-4 shows, each communication channel has both advantages and drawbacks. Despite these pros and cons, there are guidelines that will help you decide how to deliver your message most effectively. Following these guidelines can produce dramatic results. In one survey, managers who were identified as "media sensitive"—those who matched the channel to the message—were almost twice as likely to receive top ratings in their performance reviews when compared with less media-sensitive peers.[43]

In general, oral communication is best for messages that require a personal dimension. Oral channels are also best for ideas that have a strong need for visual support—demonstration, photos or slides, and so on. Spoken communication is also especially useful when there is a need for immediate feedback, such as question-and-answer sessions or a quick reply to your ideas.

Written communication (with the exception of e-mail) works best when you want to create a relatively formal tone. Writing is almost always the best medium when you must choose your words carefully. Writing is also better than speaking when you want to convey complicated ideas that are likely to require much study and thought by the receiver. It is also smart to put your message in writing when you want it to be the final word, with no feedback or discussion. Finally, writing is best for *any* message if you want a record to exist. In business and the professions, sending confirming letters and memoranda is common practice, as is keeping minutes of meetings. These steps guarantee that what is said will be a matter of record, useful in case of later

SKILL BUILDER

Use the information on pages 20–27 to decide which communication channel is best for each message:

1. Complaining to your boss about a difficult coworker
2. Asking for a few days of leave from work to attend a special reunion
3. Training a new employee to operate a complicated computer program
4. Notifying the manager of a local business that you still haven't received the refund you were promised
5. Reminding your busy, overworked boss about a long overdue reimbursement for out-of-pocket expenses
6. Apologizing to a customer for a mistake your company made
7. Getting your boss's reaction to the idea of giving you more responsibility

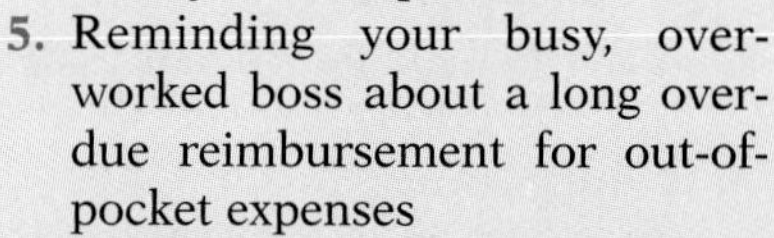

TABLE 1-4 Considerations in Choosing a Communication Channel

	Person-to-Person	Telecon-ferencing	Telephone	Voice Mail	E-Mail	Fax	Hard Copy (Interoffice or Mail)
Speed of establishing contact	Variable	Usually difficult to coordinate	Variable	Fast	Fast	Fast	Slow (dependent on distance)
Time required for feedback	Immediate (once contact established)	Immediate (once contact established)	Immediate (once contact established)	Delayed	Delayed	Delayed	Delayed
Amount of information conveyed	Highest	High	Vocal, but not visual	Vocal, but not visual	Lowest (text only, no formatting)	Low	Low
Control over how message is composed and delivered	Moderate	Moderate	Moderate	Higher	High	High	High
Control over receiver (when and how thoroughly message will be heard)	Highest	High	Less than with visual contact	Low	Low	Low	Low
Personal (off the record) **vs. formal** (on the record)	Personal	Personal	Personal	Personal	Personal	More formal	More formal
Cost	Low or high (depending on distance)	High	Low	Low	Low (after e-mail account is set up)	Low (after equipment is purchased)	Low to modest
Permanent record	None	Usually none, though possible	Usually none	Possible	Yes	Yes	Yes
Effective for detailed messages	Weak	Weak	Weakest	Weak	Better	Good	Good
Effective for immediate, emotional response (motivation, sales, etc.)	Good	Good	Good	Poor	Fair	Poor	Poor

misunderstandings or disputes and in case anyone wants to review the history of an issue.

In many cases, it is wise to send a message using both oral and written channels. This kind of redundancy captures the best of both media, and it works in a variety of settings:

- Distribute a written text or outline that parallels your presentation.
- Follow a letter, fax, or e-mail message with a phone call, or call first and then write.
- Send a report or proposal and then make appointments with your readers to discuss it.

You won't always have the luxury of choosing the communication channel. But when you do, the right decision can make your message clearer and more effective.

SUMMARY

No matter what the job, communication is both a frequent and a critically important process. It occupies more time than any other activity and often makes the difference between success and failure for the organization as a whole and for its individual members.

Communication, as the term is used in this book, is a process in which people who occupy differing environments exchange messages in a specific context via one or more channels and often respond to each other's messages through verbal and nonverbal feedback. The effectiveness of communication can be diminished by physical, physiological, or psychological noise, which can exist within either the sender, receiver, or channel. Communication is an unavoidable, irreversible process. Although it is vitally important, it is not a panacea that can solve every personal and organizational problem.

Attending to the fundamental elements of the communication process can improve the chances of success: choosing the most credible sender, picking the optimal receivers and attending to their needs, developing messages strategically and structuring them clearly, minimizing communication noise, and taking advantage of feedback to clarify confusing messages.

Formal communication networks—which can be pictured in flowcharts and organizational charts—are management's way of establishing what it believes are necessary relationship among people within an organization. Formal communication flows in several directions: downward from superiors to subordinates, upward from subordinates to superiors, and horizontally among people of equal rank. Formal communication structures are necessary as a business grows and its tasks become more complex, but they must be handled carefully to avoid problems.

Unlike formal relationships, informal communication networks consist of interaction patterns that are not designed by management. Informal networks can be based on physical proximity, shared career interests, or personal friendships. An informal network can be quite small or a large grapevine that connects many people. Informal networks serve many purposes: they can confirm, expand upon, expedite, contradict, circumvent, or supplement formal messages. Because these functions are so useful, it is important to cultivate and use informal contacts within an organization.

In business, communicators can exchange messages via a number of channels, some oral and others written. The channel used to deliver a message can have a strong influence on its effectiveness. Each channel has both advantages and drawbacks. The best choice in a given situation depends primarily on the nature of the message and the desired relationship between the sender and receiver.

RESOURCES

Eisenberg, E. M., and H. L. Goodall, Jr., "The Changing World of Work" and "Relational Contexts for Organizational Communication," in *Organizational Communication: Balancing Creativity and Constraint* (New York: St. Martin's Press, 1993), chaps. 1 and 8.

This excellent text on organizational communication begins by illustrating how changing values and priorities in people's lives lead to shifts in how they view their work and their work relationships. Chapter 8 expands the notion of the changing contexts of work relationships, including ideas for communicating with superiors, subordinates, peers, and customers and avoiding some pitfalls of intimacy in office relationships.

Krackhard, D., and J. R. Hanson, "Informal Networks: The Company behind the Chart," *Harvard Business Review* 71 (July 1993): 104–111.

The cross-functional and cross-divisional informal networks in a company often bear little resemblance to formal organizational charts. Yet understanding these informal networks is a key to understanding who really talks to, advises, and trusts others. This article demonstrates how managers can understand various informal networks—advice networks, trust networks, and communication networks—and how this knowledge of networks can be applied to solve some organizational problems and encourage more cooperative and productive interactions.

Nicoll, David C., "Acknowledge and Use Your Grapevine," *Management Decision* 32 (1994): 25–30.

This article gives a thorough and clear explanation of the functions and value of informal communication networks within organizations. It explains that the "grapevine" complements, rather than conflicts with, formal communication channels.

Vesper, J., and V. R. Ruggiero, "Communicating Electronically," *Contemporary Business Communication: From Thought to Expression* (New York: HarperCollins, 1993), chap. 16.

This chapter catalogs numerous new technological tools available to the contemporary business communicator. The authors address the pros and cons (or advantages and disadvantages) of the multitude of tools and follow that with a discussion of three common results of all of this new technology: feeling overwhelmed, overloaded, or overconfident. The chapter concludes with practical advice for meeting these challenges.

CHAPTER 2

Communication, Culture, and Work

KEY TERMS

Co-culture / Collectivist culture / Culture / High-context culture / Individualistic culture / Low-context culture / Organizational culture / Power distance / Uncertainty avoidance

When Carol Teinchek and Bruce Marshall first started Sundown Bakery, the business was fairly simple. Carol ran the shop up front, while Bruce ran the bakery and ordered supplies. When the business began to grow, Carol hired two part-time clerks to help out in the shop. Marina had moved to the country two years ago from El Salvador, and Kim was a newly arrived Korean who was working his way through college. Bruce hired Maurice, a French-Canadian, as an assistant.

The ovens were soon running twenty-four hours a day, supervised by Maurice, who was now master baker, and two assistants on each of three shifts. Marina and Kim were supervising the shop, since Carol was usually too busy managing general sales distribution to spend much time with customers. Bruce still spent three or four hours a day in the bakery whenever he could get out of his office, but spent most of that time coordinating production and solving problems with Maurice.

The expanding size of Sundown led to a change in the personality of the company. The family feeling that was strong when Sundown was a small operation was less noticeable. The new employees didn't know Bruce and Carol well, and, as a result, there was less give-and-take of ideas between the owners and workers. When Bruce and Carol put together a brief employee manual to save time orienting new workers, Maurice was heard muttering sarcastic comments about "the bureaucrats." Bruce and Carol wanted to keep the lines of communication open, but the task was harder.

Another challenge grew out of the changing character of the employees. Sundown now employed workers from seven different countries. José, who was born in Brazil, confessed to Bruce that he felt uncomfortable being managed by Carol. "It's nothing personal," he said. "But where I come from, a man doesn't take orders from a woman." The Sundown employee profile was different in other ways. Two of the assistant bakers were gay; one of the sales clerks got around by wheelchair.

The challenges faced by the owners and employees of Sundown Bakery are similar to those encountered by virtually every organization in the 1990s. The personality of the company—the organizational culture, as it is called—has affected the ways business is conducted and people work together. The different backgrounds and characteristics of the employees have made the potential for communication both more rewarding and more difficult.

This chapter will deal with the same issues faced by Sundown Bakery—and, indeed, by every organization. It will begin by describing the changing nature of the work force and showing how communication can be more effective among an increasingly diverse body of workers. Then it will introduce the notion of organizational cultures, explaining how every organization has a personality and how that character plays an important role in the success and satisfaction of organizational members.

CULTURAL DIVERSITY AND COMMUNICATION

In past generations, most workers—at least most American workers—could spend their entire career without encountering people from different backgrounds. But those days are past. The world is entering a period in which cultural diversity is a fact of everyday life. Consider the statistics. Today, American-born white males constitute only 45 percent of the U.S. work force; over the next few years, that figure will decline to 39 percent. In the period from today until the year 2000, women, minorities, and immigrants will constitute 84 percent of the new entrants into the American work force. By the turn of the century, minorities will make up 25 percent of the population of the United States. English will be the second language for more than half of California's population. Sometime in the next century, whites will become the minority of the population in the United States.[1]

As these figures suggest, the culturally diverse workplace of the 1990s differs from that of earlier generations in two ways. First, it is made up of people from different national backgrounds. Instead of the mostly European ancestry that was the norm in past years, in most places there is an increasing number of workers from around the world, especially from Asia, the Caribbean, and Latin America. In addition to having diverse national backgrounds, more and more managers and employees represent different groups that have always been present, though less visible, in the work force. The most obvious example in this category is women. The percentage of female employees in the United States has skyrocketed in a single generation so that today over 45 percent of all workers and 20 percent of managers are women. The ethnic balance of native-born Americans is also changing. Instead of being concentrated in a few mostly low-status occupations, Hispanic-Americans and African-Americans are far more visible in every field today. Likewise, workers who are physically challenged are entering the work force in greater numbers than ever before.

Changing demographics means that more of us can expect to work with people who come from different backgrounds and thus have different customs and attitudes. This growing cultural diversity has the potential for disaster or benefit. For those companies and individuals who can take advantage of the richness of cultural diversity, the opportunities are great. Stona Fitch, vice-president of manufacturing for Procter & Gamble, says, "The first companies that achieve a true multicultural environment will have a competitive edge. Diversity provides a much richer environment, a variety of viewpoints, greater productivity. And, not unimportantly, it makes work more fun and interesting." Kevin Sullivan, vice-president of human resources at Apple Computer, echoes the idea: "When you are surrounded by sameness, you only get variations on the same."[2]

For those who cannot or will not face the changing scene, the dangers are unavoidable. "Trying to run an international or multinational company in a competitive environment without the creativity, resources, and skills of that size of a workforce is undercutting your company's ability to be successful," says A. Barry Rand, president of U.S. marketing operations for Xerox. Judith Katz, a corporate consultant in San Diego, states flatly, "Managers that haven't learned to manage diversity by the year 2000 will be incompetent."[3]

The Nature of Culture

When most people use the word *culture,* they think of people from different national backgrounds. National cultures certainly do exist, and as you will read in the following pages, they play an important role in shaping the way people communicate. But there are other dimensions of culture too. Within a nation, regional differences can exert a powerful influence on communication. New Yorkers and Alaskans may find one another's styles of behaving so different that they might as well be from different countries. Race and ethnicity can also shape behavior. So can age: the customs, values, and attitudes of a 20-year-old generation X-er may vary radically from those of her parents who were raised in the 1960s, or her grandparents, who lived through the Great Depression and World War II. Still other differences can create distinctive cultures: gender, sexual orientation, physical disabilities, religion, and socioeconomic background are just a few.

All of these factors lead to a definition of ***culture*** as a set of values, beliefs, norms, customs, rules, and codes that lead people to define themselves as a distinct group, giving them a sense of commonality.[4] It's important to realize that culture is learned, not innate. A Korean-born infant adopted soon after birth by American parents and raised in the United States will think and act differently than his or her cousins who grew up in Seoul. An African-American who grew up in the inner city will view the world differently than he or she would if raised in the suburbs—or in a country like France, where African heritage has different significance than it does in the United States. A Jordanian who has lived in the United States since the mid-1980s will probably be more acculturated than his brother-in-law visiting from Amman.

Just because culture is learned doesn't mean it is unimportant. The norms and values we learn as part of our cultural conditioning shape the way people view the world and the way they interact with one another. The book you are reading now is an example of the powerful, almost invisible force of culture. The fact that you are studying business and professional communication from a text rather than learning about it orally from an elder is just one example of a cultural standard. The assumption behind this book—that career advancement is important—is another. All the advice you will read—on how to operate in groups, how to negotiate differences with others, how to organize and present your ideas—embodies cultural assumptions. The overwhelming influence of culture on communication led famous anthropologist Edward Hall to assert that "culture is communication and communication is culture."[5]

Cultural Differences in International Business

With the dramatic increase in international trade and multinational corporations, the chances of interacting with people from different national backgrounds are greater than ever. Communication scholars Larry Samovar and

Richard Porter cite statistics demonstrating that the business world of the 1990s is really a global village: approximately 80 percent of U.S. products compete in international markets; some 3,500 multinational corporations are based in the United States; and a staggering 40,000 U.S. firms do business with overseas customers.[6] Foreign multinational companies are expanding their U.S. operations: some 300 Japanese companies operate in Michigan alone; German, British and Dutch companies have many U.S. sites.[7] In the first eight months after NAFTA's passage, U.S.–Mexico trade increased 20 percent, and there has been a fourfold increase since 1990 in the number of U.S. college graduates going to work in Mexico.[8] Table 2-1 is based on observations made at two Japanese-owned factories operating in the San Diego–Tijuana area, employing both U.S. and Mexican workers. It illustrates some of the challenges communicators face in the international, multicultural 1990s, where working with people from dramatically different backgrounds is a fact of life.

The ability to work effectively with people from other countries is especially important if you plan a career in management, where international experience is rapidly moving from the "desirable" to the "essential." "We'd be blind not to see how critically important international experience is," says Colby H. Chandler, CEO of Eastman Kodak.[9] Whether you are working abroad or working for or with foreign nationals in the United States, understanding cultural differences is an important key to effective communication.

TABLE 2-1 Cultural Traits Influencing Communication on the Job

	U.S.	Japan	Mexico
Social unit	Individual	Group	Family
Authority structure	Egalitarian	Hierarchical	Hierarchical
Basis for authority	Competence	Seniority	Trust
Style of negotiation	Direct	Indirect	Indirect
Decison making	Individualistic	Consensus	Authoritarian
Attitude toward conflict/competition	Seeks	Avoids	Avoids
Importance of personal relationships	Beneficial	Essential	Essential
Basis for status	Money/competence	Title/position	Title/position
Role of formality	Medium/low	High	High
Sense of history	Low	High	High
Importance of time	High	High (in business) Low (in personal matters)	Low

Source: After E. R. McDaniel and L. A. Samovar, "Cultural Influences on Communication in Multinational Organizations: *Maquiladora* Case Study." Paper presented at the Western States Communication Association annual convention, San Jose, California, 1994.

The following categories are not an exhaustive list of differences between countries, but they suggest the importance of learning rules of the cultures in which you will operate. Before going on, though, it is important to keep a sense of perspective about cultural influences on communication. Along with important differences, people from varied backgrounds also share many similarities. For example, computer engineers from Singapore, Lima, Tel Aviv, and Vancouver would find plenty of mutual interests and perspectives. Even when we acknowledge cultural variation, the fact remains that not everyone in a culture behaves identically. Figure 2-1 shows both the overlap in communication practices and the range of behavior within each one. Ignoring cross-cultural similarities and intracultural variation can lead to stereotyping people from different backgrounds, exaggerating and caricaturizing the other culture, and judging its communication practices as radically different and implicitly wrong.

Names and Forms of Address. Americans take pleasure in their informality and their quickness in getting on a first-name basis with others. First names are seen as friendly and indicative of fondness and attachment. With the exceptions of Thailand and Australia, business exchanges with persons from other countries tend to be much more formal.

Understanding the order of names is a first step in communicating effectively in international business. In China and Korea, the family surname comes first and the generational and given names next. The latter two are sometimes hyphenated when written in English, as in Mi-Kyong. Park Sun Hee would indicate a family name of Park, so you would address the person as "Ms. Park." Calling her "Sun Hee" may be taken as a sign of disrespect, not friendliness. In Mexico, both the paternal and maternal family names are often used, but a person is addressed by the paternal surname. The Mexican president, Ernesto Zedillo Ponce de Leon, is addressed as "Presidente Zedillo."

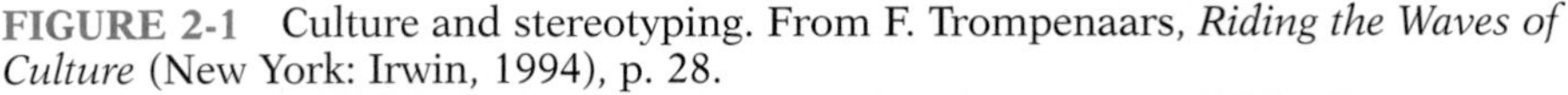

FIGURE 2-1 Culture and stereotyping. From F. Trompenaars, *Riding the Waves of Culture* (New York: Irwin, 1994), p. 28.

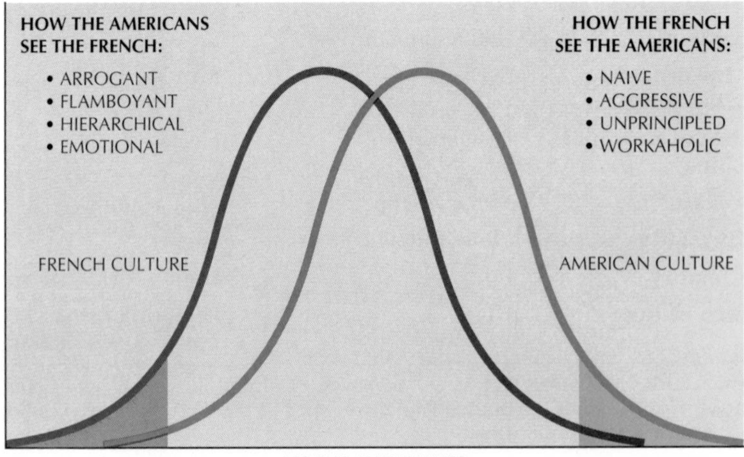

In Portuguese-speaking countries, such as Brazil, it is the reverse, so Jose Lopez Flores is addressed as "Señor Flores." In Japan, the honorific title *san* comes after the person's family name and is used for either males or females. Michiko Higa would be addressed as "Higa-san," although any title more superior would replace *san* at the end of the name. *Kacho* and *bucho* are titles for section or department heads and would be used as "Higa-kacho" or "Higa-bucho."[10]

The use of titles also varies around the world. Other than the custom of addressing physicians and surgeons as "Doctor," not many titles are used in the United States. In many other countries, though, titles are an important way of showing respect. In Mexico the abbreviated titles on business cards require some skill to understand. "Lic," for example, stands for *licenciado/a,* a title used for someone with a general college degree. If handed a business card printed "Lic. Pedro Sedano Gomez," you would address the man as "Licenciado Sedano." Other common title abbreviations are "Ing." for *ingeniero/a,* someone with an engineering degree; "Arq." for a person with an architectural degree, and "Gte. Gral" for *gerente general* (pronounced "hair-enteh hen-eh-ral"), meaning "general manager." A person whose card reads "Gte. Gral. Garcia Gomez" would be addressed as "Gerente General Garcia." The most common are "Sr.," "Sra.," and "Srta." for *señor, señora,* and *señorita,* respectively. If in doubt about a woman's marital status, use *señorita.* As in the U.S. holders of academic doctorates are entitled to be addressed as *"Doctor"* (or the feminine equivalent, *"Doctora"*). This title supersedes any others.[11] Using formal titles until others invite you to be more casual will avoid appearances of disrespect. Titles are also important in many European countries, especially Germany. In Egypt, too, it is discourteous to use first names or ignore titles of persons.[12]

Social Customs. Cultural differences begin as soon as communicators encounter one another. Greetings range from the bow (the lower it is, the more respectful) in Japan, to the *wai* in Thailand (pressed palms together with a head bow), to the handshake in Europe and South America.

In many countries, exchanging business cards is an important ritual. In Japan, especially, give and receive cards with care: use two hands and study the card carefully rather than taking it and one-handedly stuffing it in a pocket. Asian business expert Yeu-Sai Kun suggests that you observe the card-

> The instant use of first names is particularly obnoxious to many foreign business people. Although the Japanese may be an extreme example, it is fair to say that in that country first names are used *only* among family members and intimate friends. Even longtime business associates and coworkers shy away from the use of first names. Small wonder that when a foreign businessman is introduced to Marv, Cedric, Mary, or Bill, his greetings often turn into a muffled and embarrassed silence.
>
> Arthur M. Whitehill, *Business Horizons*

carefully, indicate with a nod that you have understood it, and in general treat the card with the respect you would give its owner.[13] One U.S. businessperson lost a deal in Japan because his inattention to the Japanese businessmen's cards was taken as a measure of the lack of attention he would give to their business.[14]

In China and Japan, a small exchange of well-wrapped gifts (pens, paperweights) is expected at first encounters; in Arab countries and western European countries, gifts are not exchanged initially. Avoid gifts in sets of fours in Japan, as the spoken number four has the same sound as the word for "death." In China, clocks represent a similar bad fate and should not be given as gifts. In a Hindu nation like India, where cows are sacred, avoid gifts of leather. In Arab countries, gifts for a businessman's wife would be inappropriate, but if you are visiting a home in Latin America or Europe, a gift for the family or children is appreciated. Regional gifts, specialties of your area, often make special gifts abroad—Amish handicrafts from Pennsylvania, maple syrup from Vermont, Native American pottery from the Southwest.

Styles of Dress. As travel and communication make the world feel like a smaller place, regional differences in clothing are becoming less pronounced. The standard Western business suit is common in most urban settings. Despite this fact, it is still important to dress carefully. For both men and women abroad, conservative dress will take you much further than the latest fad or fashion. Traditional business suits for men and conservative (skirt, not pant) suits or dresses for women are preferred in many foreign business settings. In Japan, be sure socks or hose are clean and without holes, as you will frequently remove shoes when dining traditionally or visiting a home. In Muslim countries, women should respect and observe modest dress customs, including longer sleeves and skirts than may be fashionable elsewhere.

Time. In international business, the first shock for travelers from the United States is often the way members of other cultures understand and use time. Americans, like most northern Europeans, have what anthropologists term a *monochronic* view of time, seeing it as an almost tangible substance. American speech reflects this attitude when people talk about saving time, making time, having time, wasting time, using time, and taking time. In American culture, time is money, so it is rationed carefully. Appointments are scheduled in datebooks and rigidly adhered to. One thing is done at a time.

This monochronic orientation is not universal. Cultures with a *polychronic* orientation see time as taking a back seat to personal relationships. In polychronic societies, many things can be happening simultaneously. People are less concerned about living by the clock. Meetings go on for as long as they take; they don't abruptly end because "it's time." Most Latin American cultures, as well as southern European and Middle Eastern cultures, have a polychronic orientation. In Mexico, for example, "you make friends first and do business later," according to R. C. Schrader, who heads California's trade office in Mexico City.[15]

International management consultant Fons Trompenaars describes how the difference between monochronic time and polychronic time can make a strong impression when people from different cultures interact:

> I once purchased an airline ticket from a woman who, while making out my ticket (correctly), was talking on the telephone to a friend and admiring her co-worker's baby. People who do more than one thing at a time can, without meaning to, insult those who are used to doing only one thing.
>
> Likewise, people who do only one thing at a time can, without meaning to, insult those who are used to doing several things. A South Korean manager explained his shock and disappointment upon returning to the Netherlands to see his boss:
>
> "He was on the phone when I entered his office, and as I came in he raised his hand slightly at me. Then he rudely continued his conversation as if I were not even in the room with him. Only after he had finished his conversation five minutes later did he get up and greet me with an enthuasiastic, but insincere, 'Kim, happy to see you.' I just could not believe it."
>
> To a synchronic [monochronic] person, not being greeted spontaneously and immediately, even while still talking on the telephone, is a slight. The whole notion of sequencing your emotions and postponing them until other matters are out of the way suggests insincerity. You show how you value people by giving them time, even if they show up unexpectedly.[16]

Because they handle more than one thing simultaneously, members of polychronic cultures are less concerned with punctuality than those raised with monochronic standards. It is not that being punctual is unimportant; it is just that other factors may take priority. This fact helps explain why the notion of being "on time" varies. Extremely monochronic cultures view even small delays as an offense. In polychronic cultures, varying degrees of lateness are acceptable—from roughly fifteen minutes in southern Europe to part or all of the day in the Middle East and Africa.[17]

Tolerance for Conflict. In some cultures, each person is responsible for helping to maintain harmony of a group and of society. The Korean term *kibun* embodies ideas of internal harmony or aura of harmony surrounding each person.[18] The maintenance and pursuit of harmony is expressed in the Japanese term *wa*. In other places—the Middle East and southern Europe, for example—harmony takes a back seat to emotional expression. Figure 2-2 illustrates how the rules for expressing emotions vary around the world.

The cultural avoidance of conflict means a Korean businessperson will probably not say "no" directly to you, fearing that you will lose face and suffer embarrassment. In order to help you maintain your *kibun*, he might spare you unpleasant news or information; it will be softened so that you don't suffer disgrace or shame, especially in front of others. You may be told that he

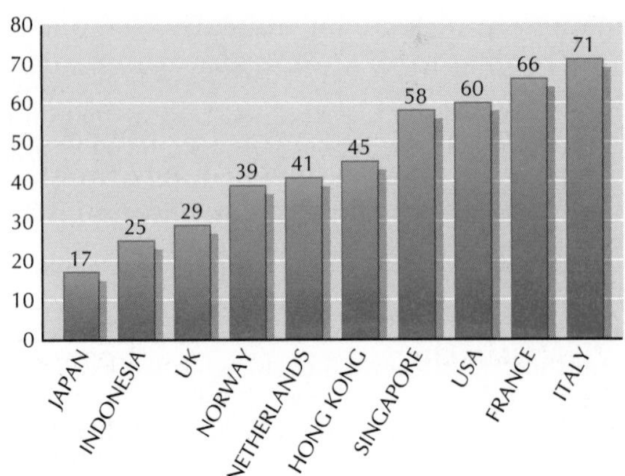

FIGURE 2-2 Percentage of employees who would openly express feeling upset at work. After F. Trompenaars, *Riding the Waves of Culture* (New York: Irwin, 1994), p. 70.

will consider the matter or that it would be very difficult. Mexican business culture also values harmony and discourages confrontation. This attitude creates problems when it clashes with more aggressive standards that U.S. businesspeople usually bring to transactions. As president of Black & Decker Latin America, Jose Maria Gonzales is used to working with colleagues and suppliers from north of the border. Despite that fact, he says that coping with the difference between U.S. and Mexican approaches to conflict doesn't come easily:

> In a meeting Americans can argue, hit the table and leave as if nothing happened, while a Mexican might not forgive you for three months. I have to make sure not to personalize things sometimes.[19]

This sort of accommodation works both ways. Just as people from cultures that seek harmony must learn to adapt to and accept conflict, communicators from more aggressive societies like the United States need to appreciate the importance of harmony when communicating cross-culturally. Once communicators learn to use the same set of rules about how to express and handle disagreements, conducting business becomes much easier.

Gender Roles. Women from the United States and Canada who travel internationally are likely to be astonished and chagrined by the way they are regarded in some overseas cultures, where ideas of appropriate feminine behavior can be quite different. In some countries, a woman who outranks a man may not be treated that way by hosts; they may still speak to and prefer to negotiate with the male, assuming he is her superior. In Asian countries and Muslim countries women may find they are omitted from substantive conversation or overlooked in negotiations because of designated gender roles in those countries. Sometimes, a woman can establish credibility by clarifying her role and responsibilities in writing before a personal visit, but this step will not necessarily produce the desired effect.

INVITATION TO INSIGHT

Either through personal interviews or research, identify the differences in communication practices between your own culture and another one that interests you. What potential problems might arise between communicators who fail to understand these cultural differences?

As galling as it may be to face what feels like blatant sex discrimination, acceptance of different standards may be the best approach, at least in the short run. Asserting oneself and working to change gender roles may be accepted and admired in U.S. culture, but it could backfire in other countries.

Co-cultural Dimensions of a Diverse Society

It isn't necessary to travel abroad to find cultural differences. Diversity at home exerts a powerful effect on communicating at work. Domestic society is made up of a variety of ***co-cultures***—groups that have a clear identity within the encompassing culture. The "melting-pot" metaphor that suggested that people can or should gradually lose their identity is increasingly being viewed as inaccurate. Other metaphors, such as the "tapestry" and "salad bowl," have been suggested as better ways to describe society as a mixture of co-cultures.[20] Whatever the image, the fact is clear: We live in a diverse society, and career success depends on communicating effectively with people whose customs and values are different. As communication scholars Myron Lustig and Jolene Koester put it, "One can no longer assume that clients, customers, business partners, and co-workers have similar cultural views about what is important and appropriate."[21] In the following pages we will take a quick look at how the co-cultural influences of ethnicity and physical disabilities affect communication at work.

Ethnicity. One of the basic challenges facing communicators who deal with ethnic diversity is to choose labels that describe members of various groups. For instance, what do you call someone whose ancestors came to Truchas, New Mexico, from Spain before the founding of either the United States or Mexico as nations? *Mexican-American* doesn't work. *Latino* is often rejected, as is *Chicano*. What do you call someone who is a fifth-generation Chinese, never visited China, doesn't speak Chinese, but "looks" Chinese? This person may not believe he is Chinese any more than a fifth-generation immigrant whose ancestors came from Normandy believes she is French, yet racial features make all the difference.

The 1988 Commission on Minority Participation in Education and American Life looked at four major minority groups and established some common terminology: African-American, Hispanic, Native American and Alaskan Natives, and Asian and Pacific Island Americans.[22] However, many people use other classifying schemes to label others and themselves. Some schemes are religious (Catholic, Jewish); some focus on national roots

(Cuban-American, Vietnamese-American) or geographic roots (Arab-American); and others are primarily cultural (Hopi). To complicate matters further, there is often disagreement about which term is preferred for a specific group (*black* versus *African-American, white* or *Anglo-American*). In some parts of the country anyone who is not black, Hispanic, or Asian is called "Anglo." The issues are complicated, and efforts to discuss them often result in criticism from one group or another.

Even when the issue of labels is settled, other problems remain. Making generalizations about any group is a dangerous matter. It is difficult, for example, to find blanket characteristics that describe both a white executive who grew up in an affluent family and attended exclusive schools and an unemployed janitor who was a high school dropout and lives on public assistance. It is an oversimplification to describe a single "white" or "black" style of communication, just as it is dangerous to claim that all Arabs, baby boomers, Israelis, or women are alike.

Keeping in mind the risks of overgeneralizing, scholars have tried to find some patterns of communication that are common for many, if not all, members of various groups. Understanding how communication is affected by cultural conditioning can help prevent jumping to mistaken conclusions about what a certain kind of behavior means.

The amount of talk and silence that is appropriate can differ from one ethnic co-culture to another. For example, most Native American and many Asian-American cultures value silence more highly than does mainstream U.S. culture. By contrast, African-American and Euro-American cultures place a high value on verbal skills, and their members tend to speak more. It is easy to imagine how the silence of, say, a Japanese-American or Native American employee could be viewed by an African-American or Euro-American colleague as a sign of dislike.

Attitudes toward conflict also differ from one ethnic co-culture to another. Asian cultures place a high value on saving face, so Asian-Americans often display a preference for not disagreeing assertively and directly. A disinclination to deal with conflict is also common among many communicators with strong roots in British, Asian, Scandinavian, or German cultures. As we have already suggested, Native Americans may prefer to deal with conflict through silence rather than direct confrontation. By contrast, many (though certainly not all) people with a Greek, Italian, French, or South American background may prefer a direct, open conflict style.

Even when communicators from different backgrounds speak roughly the same amount, the degree of personal information they reveal can differ dramatically. For example, Euro-Americans disclose more than African-Americans or Puerto Ricans, who in turn reveal more than Mexican-Americans.[23] (Of course, varying social and cultural contexts may create different disclosure patterns.) Communication researcher Thomas Kochman reports an example involving a white woman who went to work with a sling on her arm. Her white co-workers asked questions about her condition, while her black colleagues did not mention the sling. She interpreted the whites' questions as a measure of concern and the blacks' apparent lack of curiosity as indifference about her well-being.[24] Understanding how cultural norms for disclosure vary, we can easily see how misunderstandings led to hurt feelings in this example. The black employees felt they were being considerate of their colleague; they didn't want to be impolite by prying into a personal matter. On the other hand, whites were shown to perceive others as impolite for *not* asking questions or showing interest in the personal lives of co-workers.

The range of acceptable and taboo topics can vary by co-culture. Returning to work after the death of a parent, one Euro-American employee appreciated and valued all of the co-workers who expressed sympathy and asked questions about the deceased parent. Someone of Dine' (Navajo) background could be extremely uncomfortable with the mention of the person who died and discussions of death, burial, and the life of the deceased. Because of cultural taboos, such conversations might produce great anxiety instead of comfort.

Nonverbal standards also vary by co-culture. Most communicators unconsciously assume that their rules for behaviors such as eye contact are universal. Researchers, however, have found that eye behavior can vary significantly. One study found that widely opened eyes are often interpreted in mainstream U.S. culture as a sign of surprise or wonder and in Hispanic culture as a call for help, signifying "I don't understand." To African-Americans, the same kind of gaze is often regarded as a measure of innocence.[25]

Since Euro-Americans often associate eye contact with honesty and respect, it is easy to misjudge others for whom steady eye contact would be a sign of disrespect. There are many cases where attempts by Puerto Ricans and Native Americans to show respect to persons in authority by not looking at them has been interpreted as dishonesty or disrespect by those accustomed to greater eye contact. Hopi and Navajo people generally avoid steady eye contact, as it is considered offensive, disrespectful, and rude. Blacks tend to make more eye contact when speaking but will not have such a steady gaze at someone they are listening to. Whites tend to make more continuous eye contact while listening to someone.[26]

Disabilities. Belonging to a co-culture based on ethnicity or nationality requires years of immersion. By contrast, says columnist Karen Stone, "disability is a club anyone can join, anytime. It's very easy. Have a stroke and be paralyzed. . . . Be in a car wreck and never walk again."[27] The Americans with Disabilities Act of 1990 (ADA) guarantees that people with disabilities receive reasonable accommodations and equal access to employment, buildings, transportation, and services. These legal guarantees are important, but they don't change the fact that, in many ways, having a disability removes one from mainstream culture.

Consider how disabilities change identity. A variety of other important attributes—ethnicity, age, and nationality, for example— can be overshadowed by physical condition. Typical language habits reflect this fact. The tendency is to use labels like "blind," "wheelchair-bound," or "deaf" to describe a person, putting him or her in a category that emphasizes physical condition over all other attributes. Advocates urge terms that treat a disability as one feature, not as a defining characteristic. Describing Mike as "a person who is blind" is both more accurate and less constricting than calling him a "blind person." The difference between "deaf person" and "person who is deaf" might seem subtle—until you imagine which label you would prefer if you lost your hearing.

There are no hard-and-fast rules about communicating with people who have disabilities. After eleven years of research, communication researcher Dawn Braithwaite found that strategies preferred by some were rejected by others.[28] This variability showed up in situations in which an able-bodied person might appropriately offer help. About half of the survey respondents were open to offers of assistance, while others preferred that able-bodied persons wait until they receive a request for help. In either case, though, one message came through clearly: It is important for the self-esteem and safety of a person with a disability to maintain control over if, when, and how help is given. If your offer of help is turned down, accept that fact. If it is accepted, either ask "How can I help?" or ask if your intentions are acceptable: "Would you like me to open the door?"

Despite the lack of specific overall rules, there are some guidelines for interacting with people who have various types of disabilities:

- *Blindness.* When approaching a person who is blind, give your name and those of others with you. When speaking in a group, address the person by name (there are no visual channels to indicate whom your remarks are addressed to). Don't speak more loudly or slowly than you normally would: a vision loss has no effect on hearing! If you are escorting a blind person, let him or her take your arm, rather than trying to hold on to or move the person.
- *Hearing impairments.* Touching or tapping the person on the shoulder or arm may be an acceptable way to get the attention of someone, at least until you find out if other approaches would be more welcome. Writing notes and using e-mail when possible can be a substitute for speech. When you do converse, face the person and speak clearly, especially if she or he reads lips. Speaking loudly or

INVITATION TO INSIGHT

Create an experience in which you are a member of a co-cultural minority. Perhaps you can visit a work setting in which you are outnumbered by members of another ethnic group. You might create conditions in which you temporarily experience a physical disability such as blindness, deafness, or loss of mobility. Be sure you spend enough time in this situation to develop at least some appreciation for what it feels like to be in a nondominant situation. (If being a member of a minority is familiar to you, look for situations in which you are part of a majority and consider the differences that come with this status.)

shouting or overexaggerating articulation will not help. Make eye contact with and speak to the person, not to any interpreter who might be present. The interpreter is trained to watch you, so keep your focus on the person to whom your message is directed.

- *Disabilities requiring use of a wheelchair.* The wheelchair is part of the person's personal territory. Don't lean or sprawl on someone's wheelchair or treat it as a public piece of furniture. When possible, put yourself on the same level as the person in the chair instead of looking down.
- *Speaking difficulties.* Listen attentively without interrupting. If you do not understand, paraphrase what you believe was said and allow the person to verify or clarify your understanding.

So far we have focused on guidelines for able-bodied communicators. People with disabilities also can take steps to improve communication. Braithwaite identified several strategies that can minimize the impact of the disability and help put able-bodied people at ease. They include:

- *Initiating a transaction.* "Excuse me. Would you mind looking up a phone number?"
- *Modeling behavior.* "If you move your lips more like this, I can understand you better."
- *Establishing normalcy.* "Don't you hate waiting in lines like this?"
- *Confronting the issue.* "I may have trouble speaking, but I can understand just fine!"
- *Using humor.* "Tony, they tell me your singing is so awful that even a guy like me who can't hear would hate it!"

Fundamental Dimensions of Cultural Diversity

So far we have discussed obvious differences between cultures and co-cultures. As important as customs and norms are, they are only the tip of the cultural iceberg. Underlying what might appear to be idiosyncrasies in behavior are a number of fundamental values that shape the way members of a culture think, feel, and act. In the following pages, we will look at some of these fundamental differences. Once you appreciate them, you will understand how and why people from different backgrounds behave as they do, and you will have ideas of how you can adapt to improve the quality of your communication with others.

High versus Low Context. Anthropologist Edward Hall identified two distinct ways in which members of various cultures deliver messages.[29] A ***low-context culture*** uses language primarily to express thoughts, feelings, and ideas as clearly and logically as possible. To low-context communicators, the meaning of a statement is in the words spoken. By contrast, a ***high-context culture*** relies heavily on subtle, often nonverbal cues to convey meaning and maintain social harmony. Communicators in these societies learn to discover meaning from the context in which a message is delivered: the nonverbal behaviors of the speaker, the history of the relationship, and the general social rules that govern interaction between people. When delivering difficult or awkward messages, high-context speakers often convey meaning through context rather than plainly stated words to avoid upsetting their listeners.

Mainstream culture in the United States and Canada falls toward the low-context end of the scale. Longtime residents generally value straight talk and grow impatient with "beating around the bush." By contrast, most Asian and Middle Eastern cultures fit the high-context pattern. In many Asian societies, for example, maintaining harmony is important, so communicators avoid speaking directly if that would threaten another person's dignity. For this reason, communicators raised in Japanese or Korean cultures are less likely than Americans to offer a clear "no" to an undesirable request. Instead, they would probably use roundabout expressions like "I agree with you in principle, but . . ." or "I sympathize with you. . . ." One Japanese instructor told his American audience that, in his language, there were over fifty ways to say "no" without actually uttering the word.

The clash between directness and indirectness can aggravate problems between straight-talking, low-context communicators such as Israelis, who value speaking clearly, and high-context communicators such as Arabs, whose culture stresses smooth interaction. It's easy to imagine how the clash of cultural styles could lead to misunderstandings and conflicts between Israelis and their Palestinian neighbors. Israelis might view their Arab counterparts as evasive, while Palestinians might perceive the Israelis as insensitive and blunt.

Even within a single country, co-cultures can have different notions about the value of direct speech. For example, Puerto Rican language style resembles high-context Japanese or Korean more than low-context English. As a group, Puerto Ricans value social harmony and avoid confrontation, which leads them to systematically speak in indirect ways to avoid giving offense.[30] The same holds true for Mexican-Americans, as communication researcher Don Locke explains:

> Whereas members of the dominant culture of the United States are taught to value openness, frankness, and directness, the traditional Mexican-American approach requires the use of much diplomacy and tact when communicating with another individual. Concern and respect for the feelings of others dictate that a screen be provided behind which an individual may preserve dignity. . . . The manner of expression is likely to be elaborate and indirect, since the aim is to make the personal relationship at least appear harmonious, to show respect for the other's individuality. To the Mexican-American, direct argument or contradiction appears rude and disrespectful.[31]

Even the relatively straightforward African-American style of communicating isn't totally direct. In many cases it is "characterized by a speaker's use of innuendoes, insinuations, inferences, implications and suggestions to make the point" so that "the indirect message might not be a result of what is actually said, but of the meaning assigned to it by the hearer."[32] For example, rather than asking for a change of office outright, a person might describe the advantages of a different office, give a history of how long he or she has been in the present office, and add details or stories, taking a circular route to the main point. Table 2-2 illustrates how cultural orientation affects interpretations of an employee's behavior.

A preference for high- or low-context communication isn't the only factor that distinguishes one culture from another. One survey of 160,000 employees in 60 countries revealed several other ways in which the worldviews of one national culture can differ from those of another.[33] We will look at some of them now.

Individualism and Collectivism. Members of ***individualistic cultures*** are inclined to put their own interests and those of their immediate family ahead of social concerns. Individualistic cultures offer their members a great deal of freedom, the belief being that this freedom makes it possible for each person to achieve personal success. ***Collectivist cultures,*** however, have tight social frameworks in which members of a group (such as an organization) are supposed to care for one another and for the group. In collectivist societies, members are expected to believe that the welfare of the organization is as important as their own. The power of collectivist beliefs was illustrated when PepsiCo rewarded one of its managers in China with a bonus of 60,000 yuan—about $12,000 at the official rate of exchange. Rather than pocketing the money himself, as an American manager probably would have done, he divided it equally among his subordinates.[34]

Interestingly, research has disclosed a strong relationship between individualism and a country's wealth. Rich countries like the United States,

TABLE 2-2 Differences in Cultural Orientations Can Affect Interpretation of Employee Behaviors

Behavior	Possible Interpretations
1. Hesitance to take independent initiative on tasks	Respect for authority, fear of loss of face, desire for anonymity, fear of job loss
2. Reluctance to complain or make negative statements	Desire for harmony in relationships, respect for authority, compassion for the other person, fear of a negative reflection on the group, fear of job loss
3. Failure to admit lack of understanding	Fear of loss of face, fear of embarrassment for the speaker, fear of not understanding the material if it is repeated
4. Reluctance to seek or accept promotions	Desire for anonymity, belief in leaving things to fate, desire not to be elevated above the group, respect for informal group hierarchy, fear of loss of face, wishes of family members
5. Reluctance to praise self	Desire for anonymity, desire not to be set apart from the group

Source: After S. Thiederman, *Profiting in America's Multicultural Marketplace* (New York: Lexington, 1991), p. 201.

Canada, Australia, and Great Britain are very individualistic. Poor countries like Pakistan and Colombia are more collectivist.

Power Distance. The term ***power distance*** refers to attitudes toward differences in authority. Cultures with high power distance accept the fact that power is distributed unequally—that some members have greater resources and influence than others. In these cultures, differences in organizational status and rank are clear-cut. Employees have a great deal of respect for those in high positions. Other cultures downplay differences in power. In countries with low power distance, supervisors and managers may have power, but it is not flaunted or emphasized. Employees are more comfortable approaching—and even challenging—their superiors. Egalitarian countries with low power distance include Israel, Denmark, and Austria. Some nations with high power distance are the Philippines, Mexico, and Venezuela.

It is easy to imagine how workers with different notions of power distance might find it difficult to work together. Imagine how a young business school graduate from a U.S. firm might grow frustrated after being transferred to the Guadalajara branch office, where the same relentless questioning that marked him as a free thinker in school is regarded as overly aggressive troublemaking. Likewise, visualize how a Filipino employee, newly arrived in Sydney, might be viewed by his Australian boss as indecisive and weak.

Uncertainty Avoidance. The world is an uncertain place. International politics, economic trends, and the forces of nature make it impossible to predict the future with accuracy. ***Uncertainty avoidance*** is a measure of how accepting a culture is of a lack of predictability. Some cultures (for example, Singapore and Hong Kong) are comfortable with this fact. Their acceptance of uncertainty allows them to take risks, and they are relatively tolerant of behavior that differs from the norm. Other cultures (for example, Japan, Greece, and Portugal) are uncomfortable with change. They value tradition and shun changes. Organizations in these cultures are characterized by more formal rules and less tolerance for different ideas. Employees have relatively low job mobility, and lifetime employment is common.

When these characteristics are compared with those of other cultures, it is easy to see why patterns of communication that have worked well with traditional American organizations don't always succeed with a culturally diverse work force.[35] Consider, for example, the use of work teams. It should come as no surprise that they are successful in highly collectivized countries like Japan; likewise, it is understandable that they have met with mixed results in the United States, the culture of which is more individualistic. On the other hand, the low power distance of U.S. culture suggests that teams composed of people from various levels of authority can work well, while such mixed groups would not work in countries like India, where the gap between members of different social levels is great.

Cultural diversity also suggests that the best approach to leadership will vary from one culture to another. As you will read in Chapter 9, the best leadership style will change according to the situation—and one important situational variable is the cultural background of the people who are to be led. For instance, workers in cultures with high power distance—Latin Americans are a prime example—are likely to respond better to an autocratic top-down approach than those in more egalitarian cultures such as New Zealand, the United States, or Israel.

Cultural differences also explain why techniques that motivate members of one culture might not work in another setting. Traditional motivational theory is based on Abraham Maslow's claim that people are most concerned with satisfying basic physiological needs. Once these basic needs are met, people will, in turn, move on to satisfy higher-level needs in the following order: safety, love, esteem, and self-actualization. Whatever value this theory has with American culture, it does not seem to fit other cultures as well. In cultures that avoid uncertainty, security needs would be among the most basic. Some Scandinavian countries, like Sweden, Norway, and Denmark would view social needs as more important. The stress on achievement (a form of self-actualization) that is so fundamental when motivating U.S. employees makes sense according to Maslow, since it fits neatly with two American cultural characteristics: a willingness to accept a moderate degree of risk and the "hard" orientation of concern for performance. The same stress on achievement would not work in a culture that emphasizes personal needs and avoids uncertainty.

Don't assume that this information is important only in international business. In the changing American work force, the chances are growing that a work team will be composed of members who don't fit the traditional American profile. It's fair to expect new arrivals to the United States to accommodate to the dominant culture; but it's also reasonable to expect mainstream Americans to recognize—and profit from—the different cultural perspectives of new arrivals.

Communicating across Diversity

Communicating with others from different backgrounds isn't always easy. Some of the responsibility for building bridges rests with management, and a growing number of businesses are taking this job seriously.[36] But you don't need to join a corporate training program to benefit from cultural diversity.

INVITATION TO INSIGHT

Choose one set of cultural values described on pages 47–51, and identify the characteristic that is not representative of your own culture. For example, if you are used to a low-context culture, you might focus on high-context communication. Now consider both the advantages and the disadvantages of working in an environment in which this unfamiliar norm is the dominant one. For instance, how might interaction be more effective or otherwise desirable if most people communicated in a high-context manner?

Table 2-3 lists attitudes and behaviors that can promote more satisfying, productive relationships among members of different cultures. These principles can be summarized in four categories.

Learn about Different Cultures and Subcultures. Many cultural problems are not caused by malice but by a lack of knowledge. Trainers in cultural sensitivity cite examples of how mistaken assumptions can lead to trouble.[37] In one West Coast bank, officials were dismayed when Filipino female employees didn't cooperate with the new "friendly teller" program. Management failed to realize that in Filipino culture, overtly friendly women can be taken for prostitutes. A Taiwanese executive who was transferred to the midwestern offices of a large company was viewed as aloof and autocratic

TABLE 2-3 Attitudes and Behaviors That Block or Promote Intercultural Relations

Assumptions That Block Authentic Relations	
Assumptions majority makes	*Assumptions minorities make*
• Differences should not affect performance. • Minorities will always welcome inclusion in the majority culture. • Open recognition of differences may embarrass minorities. • Minorities are using their situation to take advantage of the majority. • "Liberal" members of the majority are free of discriminatory attitudes. • Minorities are oversensitive.	• All members of the majority have the same attitudes about minorities. • There are no majority members who understand minorities. • Majority members are not really trying to understand minorities. • The only way to change the situation is by confrontation and force. • All majority members will let you down in a "crunch."
Behaviors That Block Authentic Relations	
Behaviors of majority culture	*Behaviors of minority cultures*
• Interruptions • Condescending behavior • Expressions of too-easy acceptance and friendship • Talking about, rather than to, minorities who are present	• Confrontation too early and too harshly • Rejection of offers of help and friendship • Giving answers majority members want to hear • Isolationism
Assumptions and Behaviors That Promote Authentic Relations	
• Treating people as individuals as well as members of a culture • Demonstrating interest in learning about other cultures • Listening without interrupting • Taking risks (e.g., being first to confront differences) • Expressing concerns directly and constructively	• Staying with and working through difficult confrontations • Acknowledging sincere attempts (even clumsy ones) • Dealing with others where they are, instead of expecting them to be perfect • Recognizing that interdependence is needed between members of majority and minority cultures

Source: After Philip R. Harris and Robert T. Moran, *Managing Cultural Differences,* 2nd ed. (Houston: Grid, 1987), pp. 245–247.

by his peers, who did not understand that Asian culture encourages a more distant managerial style.

Misunderstandings like these are less likely to cause problems when mainstream workers understand each other's cultural backgrounds. As Paulette Williams, formerly senior manager at Weyerhauser's nurseries in southern California, put it, "If you don't learn how other people feel, you can hurt them unintentionally."[38]

View Diversity as an Opportunity. It is easy to think of cultural differences as an annoyance that makes it harder to take care of business. Dealing with others who have different attitudes or customs takes patience and time—both scarce commodities in a busy work schedule. But with the right attitude, cultural diversity can stop being just a necessary cost of doing business and can become an opportunity.

People with differing backgrounds can bring new strengths to a business. Women, for instance, are generally more skilled than men at reading nonverbal cues.[39] This makes them ideal members of a negotiating team, where they may be especially skilled at interpreting how the other people are feeling. Workers from diverse ethnic groups can offer new insights into how customers or other workers with similar backgrounds can be reached. A Hispanic supervisor, for example, may be especially effective at motivating and training other Hispanics, and a Korean team member can give new insights into how a Korean-managed competitor operates.

INVITATION TO INSIGHT

Barbara A. Walker, manager of international diversity at Digital Equipment Corporation, has learned—along with others at the company—that in order for organizations whose workforces are diverse to be fully effective, people at those firms need to confront and discuss their feelings about diversity in the workforce.

Management realized that the company had an unwritten rule against talking about the issues of race and gender. "The prevailing view," says Walker, "was that open and frank conversation on these issues, particularly in the presence of minorities and women, was taboo in polite conversation. But if people couldn't talk to each other, they couldn't learn from each other."

Once they became aware of the taboo against discussing differences among people, Digital's managers set out to destroy it. Top managers at the company were encouraged to meet in small groups to discuss the "undiscussable." Gradually, employees at other levels of the organization—of both genders and all ethnicities and races— were included in the discussion groups, which came to be known as Core Groups. Together, the employees struggled to acknowledge, understand, and eliminate the stereotypes and prejudices they held about each other.

The work was arduous . . . but the realization came at last: The best way for people to work effectively with each other was to recognize and celebrate, not deny, each other's differences. Stereotypes, they learned, grow out of ignorance; thus learning about their differences was the surest way to eliminate stereotypes.

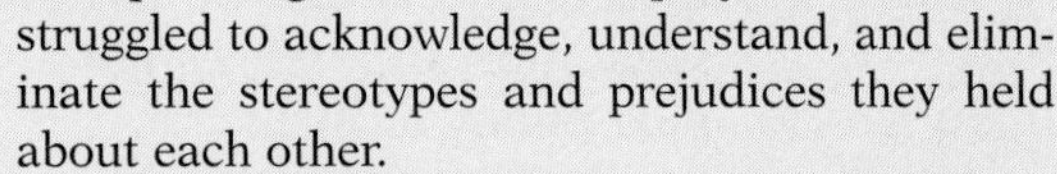

Barbara Mandrell and Susan Kohler-Gray, "Digital Equipment Corporation: A Pioneer in Diversity," *Personnel*

Don't Condescend. It's easy to view people who are different as inferior. A new employee who was hired in part because of his or her ethnic identity might seem less qualified than mainstream workers. Your first reaction to a physically challenged colleague might be sympathy or pity. Immigrants who are learning English as a second language might sound less intelligent than native speakers. Even white males, members of the traditional majority, might seem like members of the "good-old-boy club," undeserving of respect since their success seemingly owes more to personal connections than to merit.

Even excessive efforts to demonstrate an attitude of equality can come across as condescending. One African-American woman listed three statements that white women who want to treat black women with respect and friendship should never utter: (1) "I never even notice that you're black"; (2) "You're different from most black people"; (3) "I understand what you're going through as a black woman, because I'm (Jewish, Italian, etc.)."[40]

In the same way, well-intentioned but misguided efforts to lower expectations for members of some co-cultures can come across as patronizing. Don't insult others by assuming that they are incapable of doing a good job. As one African-American employee of a major American firm put it, "So often, if a black is blowing it, the white manager is afraid to tell him."[41] This sort of kid-glove treatment is not good for anyone, since it generates resentment from other employees and denies the employee in question the chance to learn and to prove that he or she is able to grow.

Talk about Differences. When people from differing backgrounds don't talk to one another, misperceptions can take root. In a study of American corporations, Charles Kelly found that blacks perceived whites as being reserved and ambitious and having an attitude of superiority. He found that whites perceived blacks as being easygoing and ambitious and feeling as if they are owed something.[42] Without open discussion of concerns, attitudes like these are less likely to disappear.

Subjects like cultural, sexual, or ethnic differences can be so threatening that many people try to pretend they don't exist. They fear that bringing up these subjects can be embarrassing or that they will seem prejudiced. But since most differences are apparent, pretending not to notice them may appear phony or insincere.

Experts agree that ignoring differences can be just as dangerous as emphasizing them. The key to success is to recognize that cultural diversity can be positive and that understanding others who are different can enrich you and your organization. If you approach others with this attitude, you are likely to be well received.

The demographic profile of the marketplace is changing dramatically. The percentage of white males entering the work force is declining, while the number of women, ethnic minorities, employees from overseas, and physically challenged workers is on the rise. The diversity of employees and customers increases the diversity of norms and values that every worker is likely to encounter. These changes will require a shift in both attitudes and skills in order to maintain productivity and good working relationships. It will be necessary to learn about different cultures and co-cultures, view diversity as an opportunity, avoid condescension, and discuss differences openly.

ORGANIZATIONAL CULTURE

So far we have explored culture as a matter of geography, ethnicity, and physical condition. But even people with identical personal backgrounds can find themselves in very different cultures, depending on the organizations to which they belong. Just like individuals, organizations have personalities. Some are casual, energetic, even zany; others are formal, slow-moving, and serious. Social scientists call this personality an ***organizational culture***—a relatively stable picture of the organization that is shared by its members. In everyday language, culture is the insiders' view of "the way things are around here."

Like human personalities, organizational cultures that appeal to one kind of person repel others. Many people abhor bureaucracies, with their clearly defined job hierarchies and voluminous rules; others feel most comfortable in that sort of setting. Some people welcome the chaotic disorganization and constant change that often characterize new companies in emerging fields; others feel more at home in organizations with clearly defined jobs and products. Some people like a working environment in which employees are one big family; others prefer to keep their working and personal lives separate.

Belonging to an organizational culture means choosing a way of life. Consider one example of how cultures—and their effects—can differ.

> Take an up-and-coming executive at General Electric who is being wooed by Xerox—more money, a bigger office, greater responsibility. If his first reaction is to grab it, he's probably going to be disappointed. Xerox has a totally different culture than GE. Success (and even survival) at Xerox is closely tied to an ability to maintain a near frenetic pace, the ability to work and play hard, Xerox-style.
>
> By contrast, GE has a more thoughtful and slow-moving culture. The GE culture treats each business activity seriously—almost as though each activity will have an enormous impact on the company. Success at GE is a function of being able to take work seriously, a strong sense of peer group respect, considerable deference for authority, and a sense of deliberateness. . . . But these same values might not be held in high esteem elsewhere.
>
> Bright young comers at GE could, for example, quickly fizzle out at Xerox—and not even understand why. They'll be doing exactly what they did to succeed at GE—maybe even working harder at it—but their deliberate approach to issues large and small will be seen by insiders at Xerox as a sign they "lack smarts."[43]

Cultures aren't limited to large corporations. Every organization has its own way of doing business and treating people. Anyone who has worked for more than one restaurant or retail store, attended more than one college or university, belonged to more than one team, or volunteered for more than one worthy cause knows that even when the same job is being performed, the way of doing business can be radically different. Furthermore, the culture of an organization can make all the difference between a satisfying and a disappointing job. Research shows that employees are more satisfied and committed to their jobs when their values match those of their supervisors and the organization.[44]

When Allen Kennedy, co-author of the landmark book *Corporate Cultures*, was asked what ingredient was used to build and maintain strong cultures, he responded:

> The answer, pure and simple, is through effective communication—to employees, customers, shareholders, public officials, and the public at large. The companies and organizations that do the best job thinking through what they are all about, deciding how and to whom these central messages should be communicated and executing the communication plan in a quality way, invariably build a strong sense of esprit within their own organization and among the many constituents they serve.[45]

Dimensions of Organizational Culture

What elements distinguish one culture from another? Several dimensions distinguish organizations, even those doing the same kind of work. Table 2-4 lists other qualities which some theorists have identified as differences between "modern" and "postmodern" organizations.[46]

1. *Sociability.* Are employees involved with one another on a personal level, or do they limit interaction to job-related tasks? A "one big family" culture isn't necessarily superior to a less personal one, but shared notions about how much sociability is appropriate is an important ingredient of job satisfaction.
2. *Power distribution and job autonomy.* What is the degree of power distance between people at different levels within the organization? What are the demands to report and justify actions to

TABLE 2-4 Some Differences between Modern and Postmodern Organizational Cultures

Modern Organizations	Postmodern Organizations
Specialization of tasks	Diffusion of tasks
Rigid structures	Flexible structures
Top-down flow of information	Information valued from all sources
Employees identify with their occupations	Employees identify with the company
Individual jobs, limited or no retraining	Overlapping teams and constant retraining
Frequent job-hopping	Long-term employment
Top-down management	Self-managing teams

higher management? How much freedom do employees have to make decisions themselves? Some workers are most comfortable when they have both limited authority and responsibility; others prefer more freedom.

3. *Degree of structure.* Are job roles highly defined, with people operating within their own area of responsibility, or is it considered acceptable to get involved in other areas of the organization's work? Does the organization have a large number of policies and procedures, or are issues handled less formally?
4. *Achievement rewards.* How (if at all) are the accomplishments of employees acknowledged and rewarded? Are praise and other types of reinforcement commonplace or infrequent? Is recognition based on true ability or other, less fair reasons? Is the level of reinforcement suitable to meet your personal needs?
5. *Opportunities for growth.* Does the company encourage workers to develop their skills and take on new responsibilities, or does it focus exclusively on employees' handling their present jobs competently? Does it encourage education and training? Are you satisfied with the opportunities for growth provided by the organization?
6. *Tolerance for risk and change.* Does management encourage employees to take well-reasoned chances, or is avoiding risk a high priority? Is change expected and welcomed, or are tradition, predictability, and stability highly valued?
7. *Conflict tolerance.* Does the company believe that disagreement is not necessarily a sign of disloyalty, or is harmony stressed? Are the organizational norms for managing conflict compatible with your personal style?
8. *Emotional support.* Does management show a genuine interest in the well-being of employees by seeking out and responding to their concerns? Do you feel as if you are receiving the emotional support you want and deserve?

Creating and Maintaining Organizational Cultures

Whether the culture is created deliberately or evolves without a grand design, the earliest phase of an organization's life is the best time to set the tone

At HP [Hewlett Packard] it's a tradition that product design engineers leave whatever they are working on out on top of their desk so that anyone can play with it. Walking around is the heart of their philosophy for all employees, and the trust level is so high that people feel free to tinker with the things their colleagues are inventing. . . . HP also talks about the "next bench syndrome." The idea is that you look around you to people working at the next bench and think of things that you might invent to make it easier for them to do their jobs.

T. J. Peters and R. H. Waterman, Jr., *In Search of Excellence: Lessons from America's Best-Run Companies* for its lifelong culture. Early events are enshrined in stories that can take on the quality of legends.[47] One of the most famous of these tales is told at IBM about former chairman of the board Thomas Watson, Jr. Watson was barred from entering a high-security area of one of the company's plants because he was not wearing the proper identification badge. Rather than firing the assertive guard who blocked his entry, Watson acknowledged the policy and waited at the gate until the proper identification was found. The story confirms a policy central to IBM's culture: everybody at the company obeys the rules.

An organization's culture takes on a life of its own. Customs and rituals develop that perpetuate a company's values. Some of these practices are as simple as changing labels. Employees are called "crew members" at McDonald's, "hosts" at Disney Productions, and "associates" at J.C. Penney, reflecting those companies' shared belief that every worker plays an important role in the corporation's success. Caterpillar employees have been known to celebrate the introduction of new earth-moving machines by hosting day-long events in which the huge pieces of equipment are dressed in costume. Company-sponsored events can also foster an organization's culture. At Tupperware, the president and senior managers spend fully one month a year at celebrations honoring top salespersons and managers.[48]

Practices like these both reflect the company's culture and continue to shape it, but they are nothing more than useless gimmicks unless they are backed up by day-to-day policies. The "employees count" orientation at Hewlett Packard has been backed up by a no-layoff policy that began in the 1940s and continued through tough economic times. When business dipped during the 1970 recession, HP personnel—from the founders down—took a 10 percent cut in pay and hours rather than lay off staff. HP's faith in its employees also shows in its "open lab stock" policy, which encourages engineers to take home equipment for their personal use. Enlightened managers are convinced that practices like these build a corporate culture that pays dividends in increased loyalty and productivity.[49]

Not all cultural traditions are so positive. In some organizations, negative customs perpetuate an unhappy state of affairs. Complaining can become a part of a company's culture: bitter employees may spend time over coffee ridiculing management and criticizing the company. So can coercion: supervisors often try to prod unproductive workers by issuing more and more rules, feeding the flames of unhappiness that they are trying to extinguish. Unavailability is sometimes an organizational trait as well: managers who dislike and fear subordinates often barricade themselves in offices, cutting off communication with the rank-and-file employees, who, in turn, feel increasingly alienated.

Organizational Culture and Career Planning

Even if you are not in a position to help shape an organization's culture at this stage in your life, the concept still has major implications for your career. As a prospective employee, you might be tempted to select a company on the basis of its most obvious characteristics. What is the starting salary? How are the working conditions? What are the chances for promotion? If you consider only these factors, you could wind up with an impressive title and income—but miserable.

When you are thinking about going to work for an organization, make an effort to pin down its personality, just as you would if you were choosing a mate. After all, you are likely to spend more hours per year at work than you will with a spouse. You can get a sense of a company's culture in five ways.[50]

Study the Physical Setting. An organization's physical plant says something about its personality. Even though most organizations don't make statements by *building* their environment, they do say something about themselves by *choosing* the space in which they operate. In Chapter 3, you will see that one axiom of personal nonverbal communication is "You can't avoid communicating"—that is, everything one does or does not do sends a message for others to interpret. The same principle holds for organizations. For example, choosing to locate in a high-rent or low-rent district might say something about the prosperity of the organization, its concern with thrift, the public it wants to serve, or even its competence. Likewise, the physical condition of the facilities makes a statement. Is the workplace clean or dirty? Are workers' areas personalized or standardized?

Power relationships can also become apparent when you look at the amount and location of existing space given to various groups. Environmental consultant Fred I. Steele illustrates this point:

> My work as a consultant to personnel departments has made it very clear to me that members of most organizations feel the personnel function to be of low potency and importance. The personnel offices are usually cramped, very inelegantly furnished (read "drab" if you like), and located in out-of-the-way or "leftover" space. The symbolic significance of this is all the greater because in many systems the personnel department is visited more frequently by both current and prospective employees than any other department. The setting of a personnel department should be quite carefully designed; in fact it is usually not, in keeping with its low status in the system.[51]

At Allgemeine Rechtsschutz AG, a West German insurance firm, employees will have unmistakable evidence of their standing on the corporate ladder when a new $2.8 million headquarters opens in Düsseldorf at the end of the year. Each story will be occupied by a progressively higher echelon of workers, from 360 typists and clerks on the ground floor to president Heinz G. Kramberg alone at the top on the twelfth floor. Kramberg says he ordered the staircase design to "encourage ambition and provide a visual image of our organization structure."

"Stairway to Success," *Newsweek*

Read What the Company Says about Itself. Press releases, annual reports, and advertisements can all be revealing. Companies with strong values are proud to publicize them. An emphasis on only profit and loss raises doubts about the company's concern for its personnel. Pride about innovation, service to customers, and commitment to the community—all are clues about an organization's culture. Of course, noble statements may only be lip service to praiseworthy values. Use the other suggestions in this section to see if a company practices what it preaches.

Test How the Company Greets Strangers. How are you treated when you visit a company or deal with its employees? Do they seem happy or grumpy? Are they willing to deal with you promptly, or are you left cooling your heels? Do they seem helpful, or do they seem unconcerned with your needs? A walking tour of the working areas can help give a feel for the organization's personality. "Vibrations" may not be a scientific term, but companies do have them.

Interview Company People. Strike up conversations with employees. See what they say about the company. Even rehearsed answers can be revealing: the apparent enthusiasm and sincerity with which they are delivered offer a clue about whether employees believe in the company line.

An employment interview is probably not the best place to explore these subjects. It's hard to imagine an employer who would do anything but praise the company in this setting. Talking with employees off company premises can yield information not gathered in a job interview. Even if you don't learn much about the organization as a whole, you'll get a good picture of the kind of people you will be working with.

Learn How People Spend Their Time. During your interview and observations, find out what kinds of activities occupy employees' time. A surprising amount of effort might go into activities that are only remotely related to getting the job done: dealing with paperwork, playing office politics, dealing with balky equipment, or attending one meeting after another. The *way* a company goes about its business reveals more about its culture than the kind of work it does.

INVITATION TO INSIGHT

Choose an organization in a field that interests you, or focus on an organization to which you already belong. By analyzing the organization's physical setting and literature, interviewing others, and making your own observations, construct a description of the organizational culture that addresses the dimensions listed on pages 56–57. On the basis of your findings, how would you rate the quality of communication in this organization? What recommendations, if any, would you make about improving communication?

SUMMARY

As American society becomes increasingly diverse, the ability to communicate with members of other cultures becomes a business necessity. Diversity has many dimensions: nationality, physical ability, language, and ethnicity are a few. Diversity manifests itself in a great variety of norms and cultural values, such as high or low context, individualism versus collectivism, power distance, and degree of uncertainty avoidance.

Communicators who succeed in a diverse workplace must educate themselves to different cultures and co-cultures. Viewing diversity as an opportunity instead of a problem is an important attitude. Treating people from different cultural backgrounds with respect is essential. Finally, being willing to acknowledge and discuss cultural differences can help communicators understand and appreciate one another.

Every organization has a distinct culture—a relatively stable picture of the organization's personality shared by its members. Cultures are usually shaped in the organization's early days, often by its earliest leaders. Everyday customs and rituals both reflect the culture and continue to shape it. When evaluating an organization, a prospective employee ought to make sure that the culture is comfortable and positive. Good salary and working conditions are not enough to guarantee job satisfaction if the company's personality doesn't suit the employee. Firsthand observation and informal contact with current employees are good ways to analyze an organization's culture.

RESOURCES

Carnevale, A. P., and S. C. Stone, "Diversity: Beyond the Golden Rule," *Training and Development* (October 1994): 22–39.

This comprehensive article addresses the theory and practice of diversity initiatives from the standpoint of leadership and pragmatic business sense. The authors argue that diversity requires the transformation of organizational culture, and several paradigms for and obstacles to that transformation are addressed.

Kras, E., *Management in Two Cultures: Bridging the Gap between U.S. and Mexican Managers,* rev. ed. (Yarmouth, Maine: Intercultural Press, 1995).

This handbook is based on interviews with Mexican and U.S. managers. It compares the values and behaviors of each culture, and offers suggestions for effective intercultural communication.

Moran, R. T., D. Braaten, and J. Walsh, *International Business Case Studies for the Multicultural Marketplace* (Houston, Tex.: Gulf, 1994).

This book provides over thirty case studies that cover a variety of issues that arise in global business. It discusses the strategies and tactics used by some of the world's most successful international businesses and organizations.

Pepper, G, L., *Communicating in Organizations: A Cultural Approach* (New York: McGraw-Hill, 1995).

This organizational communication text challenges readers to see organizational culture as a pervasive factor that permeates everything else about the organization. Each aspect of organizational communication is viewed through the lens of organizational culture. An excellent immersion into organizational culture issues.

Storti, C., *Cross-Cultural Dialogues: 74 Brief Encounters with Cultural Difference* (Yarmouth, Maine: Intercultural Press, 1994).

This collection of brief conversations (just four to eight lines each) illustrates the hidden assumptions and rules that can challenge communicators from different cultural backgrounds. Each dialogue is accompanied by commentary that helps expose both cultural differences and ways of dealing with them.

Tannen, D., *That's Not What I Meant!: How Conversational Style Makes or Breaks Your Relations with Others* (New York: Morrow, 1986).

This book details how co-cultural communication differences can lead to misunderstandings and problems. Chapters include examination of how age, class, gender, ethnicity, and geography all shape communication, usually in subtle but powerful ways.

PART II

Personal Skills

CHAPTER 3

Verbal and Nonverbal Messages

KEY TERMS

Biased language / Equivocal terms / High-level abstractions / Jargon / Low-level abstractions / Nonverbal communication / Paralanguage / Rapport talk / Report talk / Trigger words

Although they are neighbors and see each other almost every day, Bob and Carolyn rarely speak to each other. Ever since their partnership broke up, the hard feelings have made even casual conversation painful.

"We both should have known better," Bob lamented. "It was such a simple misunderstanding. We went into the partnership agreeing that we would be 'equal partners,' but now I can see that we had different ideas about what being 'equals' meant. I saw each of us taking charge of the areas that we did best: I'm good at marketing and sales, and Carolyn knows product design and production backwards and forwards. So it made sense to me that, while we were each equally responsible for the business and deserving an equal share of the profits, we would each make the final decisions in the areas where we were experts."

"That's not what I meant by 'equal partners,'" stated Carolyn flatly, "Bob wasn't willing to take responsibility for the hard work of production. He kept saying, 'that's where you're the expert.' And he didn't have any faith in my ideas about sales and marketing. He wanted to make those decisions himself, whether or not I agreed. To me, being equal means you have just as much say as the other person in every part of the business."

In hindsight, both Bob and Carolyn realize that there had been signs of trouble from the beginning of their partnership. "Even before we opened for business, I could tell that Carolyn was unhappy," sighs Bob. "I always saw the venture as a chance to make a fortune. But whenever I'd get excited and talk about how much money we could make, Carolyn would clam up and get this grim look on her face."

Carolyn also remembers early, unspoken signs of trouble. "I've always wanted to have a business that my kids could be proud of," she says. "But when I'd talk about that, Bob wouldn't have much to say. Even though he never said so, at times I got the feeling that he was laughing at my high ideals."

This story illustrates the importance of paying close attention to verbal and nonverbal messages. The ill-fated partnership between Bob and Carolyn could have been avoided if they had paid more attention to the unspoken but powerful nonverbal clues that warned of trouble. And examining more carefully just what an "equal" partnership meant could have helped them avoid the clash that finally led to their breakup.

How well you communicate your ideas will make the difference between success and failure. Expressing yourself effectively will boost your chances for a positive reaction, while a bungling delivery will torpedo even the best ideas. This chapter will look at the two channels by which you communicate: your words and your nonverbal behavior. In the following pages, you will gain a healthy respect for the advantages of using these channels effectively and the pitfalls of using them poorly. By the time you have finished this chapter, you should recognize that significant problems can lurk in even the simplest statements, and you will discover some ways of avoiding or overcoming such problems. You will also become more aware of the wordless messages that each of us constantly sends and receives.

VERBAL MESSAGES

Words are the vessels that carry most of our ideas to others. We sometimes forget, though, that they are only vessels and often imperfect ones—they are not the ideas themselves. Sometimes the message they carry is incomplete or even entirely different from our intended meaning. At their least complicated, misunderstandings involve words being interpreted differently from the way we intended them. Even a simple statement like "Let's talk next Tuesday at 1 P.M." can lead to problems. You might mean "Let's meet next Tuesday," while the other person interprets the remark to mean "Let's discuss the matter over the phone." It is easy to see how even a small misunderstanding like this can lead to lost time and feelings of irritation. Some problems with language go beyond simple misunderstanding.[1] As Table 3-1 shows, the listener can understand the meaning of every word perfectly

TABLE 3-1 Even Simple Messages Can Be Misunderstood

What the Manager Said	What the Manager Meant	What the Subordinate Heard
I'll look into hiring another person for your department as soon as I complete my budget review.	We'll start interviewing for that job in about three weeks.	I'm tied up with more important things. Let's forget about hiring for the indefinite future.
Your performance was below par last quarter. I really expected more out of you.	You're going to have to try harder, but I know you can do it.	If you screw up one more time, you're out.
I'd like that report as soon as you can get to it.	I need that report within the week.	Drop that rush order you're working on and fill out that report today.
I talked to the boss, but at the present time, due to budget problems, we'll be unable to fully match your competitive salary offer.	We can give you 95 percent of that offer, and I know we'll be able to do even more for you next year.	If I were you, I'd take that competitive offer. We're certainly not going to pay that kind of salary to a person with your credentials.
We have a job opening in Los Angeles that we think would be just your cup of tea. We'd like you to go out there and look it over.	If you'd like that job, it's yours. If not, of course you can stay here in Denver. You be the judge.	You don't have to go out to L.A. if you don't want to. However, if you don't, you can kiss good-bye to your career with this firm.
Your people seem to be having some problems getting their work out on time. I want you to look into this situation and straighten it out.	Talk to your people and find out what the problem is. Then get together with them and jointly solve it.	I don't care how many heads you bust, just get me that output. I've got enough problems around here without you screwing things up too.

Table from *Organizational Behavior: Theory and Practice* by Steven Altman, Enzo Valenzi, and Richard M. Hodgetts (San Diego: Harcourt Brace Jovanovich, 1985). Copyright © 1985 by Harcourt Brace Jovanovich, Inc. Reproduced by permission of the publisher.

and still interpret a message in a way that is completely different from its intended meaning.

Clarity and Ambiguity

Since the most basic language problems involve misunderstandings, we will begin our study of language by examining how to prevent this sort of miscommunication. We will also look at times when a lack of clarity can actually be desirable.

Use Unequivocal Terms to Avoid Misunderstandings. ***Equivocal terms*** are those with more than one meaning:

> A shipment ordered for Portland goes to Oregon instead of Maine.
>
> Responding to a telephone message, you call the wrong Ms. Jones.
>
> In an employment interview, you respond to the interviewer's question "What are your goals?" by speaking for several minutes about your desire to become a divisional manager within five years, only to find that the interviewer really wanted to know what you are seeking from life.

Sometimes equivocal problems arise because communicators from different fields use the same term in specialized ways. Hollywood agent Jerry Katzman describes just such a problem. In a meeting with representatives of a Silicon Valley software publisher, he used the phrase "in development" to mean a project that was at the rough-idea stage. By contrast, the software people were used to using that phrase to describe a project that had been funded and was being created. Ultimately Katzman had to use a blackboard to define his terms. "It was like when the Japanese first came to Hollywood," he reported. "They had to use interpreters, and we did too."[2]

Equivocation sometimes comes from different cultural values. Compared with U.S. businesspeople, Mexicans are less inclined to express conflict and more relaxed about managing time. The Spanish word *ahorita* means "right now" or "immediately" in English. Despite its clear-cut dictionary meaning, North Americans have found that their Mexican counterparts use the term quite differently:

> When are those photocopies going to be ready?
>
> "Ahorita," answers the secretary who knows the copy machine is broken.
>
> When will that delivery be made?
>
> "Ahorita," answers the salesman who has no truck.
>
> One U.S. financial officer sheepishly admits he finally prohibited his Mexican staff from giving him *ahorita* as an answer.[3]

Sometimes equivocal misunderstandings only become apparent after the fact. But at least some of them can be avoided if you double-check your understanding of terms that might be interpreted in more than one way. When you agree to meet "Wednesday" with someone, mention the date to be sure that you're both thinking of the same week. When your supervisor says that your ideas are "okay," make sure that the term means "well done" and not just "adequate."

Use Lower-Level Abstractions When Clarity Is Essential. Any object or idea can be described at various levels, some very general and others quite specific. Consider the following example:

problem

equipment problem

breakdown of copying machine

automatic paper feeder does not work

sheets jammed in paper path

Low-level abstractions are highly specific statements that refer directly to objects or events that can be observed. By contrast, ***high-level abstractions*** cover a broader range of possible objects or events without describing them in much detail.

High-level abstractions can create problems because they are often subject to a wide variety of interpretations. For example:

"Straighten up the area."	A quick cleanup or a spit-and-polish job?
"We need some market research."	A short questionnaire for a few of our biggest customers or lengthy personal interviews of thousands of potential customers?
"Keep up the good work!"	Which parts of the work are good?
"Bring me a list of your costs on this job."	General categories of costs or an itemization of every expenditure, including postage and my secretary's overtime? A handwritten list for discussion purposes or a formal report?
"Give me your honest opinion."	Speak my mind completely or only answer the questions you have specifically asked? Be diplomatic or blunt?

The confusion created by these examples indicates the value of using low-level abstractions. But there are times when high-level abstractions are handy. For one thing, they are time-savers; they let us describe the "office staff" without naming Gladys, Sidney, Ida, Jerry, and all the others specifically. Or we can refer to "the orders for last month" without detailing each one. In addition, very specific language can sometimes create so many verbal trees that your listeners won't be able to see the forest. For instance, referring to "the eastern-region sales force" saves your listener from having to figure out that that's what Bruce, Emily, Sam, Hilda, George, Fay, and Gary are. Similarly, itemizing each mechanical problem in a plant may obscure the fact that each of these problems is related to outdated, worn-out machines.

Since both abstract language and specific language have their advantages, it is often best to use both. One way to achieve maximum clarity is to begin explaining your proposal, problem, request, or appreciation with an abstract statement, which you then qualify with specifics:

> "I'm worried about the amount of time we seem to be spending on relatively unimportant matters [abstract]. In our last meeting, for instance, we talked for twenty minutes about when to schedule the company picnic and then only had fifteen minutes to discuss our hiring needs [specific]."

> "Management has asked me to encourage you to share any ideas you have about how we could improve our operation [abstract]. We're especially interested in ways to reduce our transportation costs and to reward employees who have made specific contributions [specifics]."

> "I'd like to take on more responsibility [abstract]. Until now, the only decisions I've been involved in are about small matters [still abstract], such as daily schedules and customer refunds [more specific]. I'd like a chance to help decide issues such as buying and advertising [specific requests]."

One common type of overly abstract language is the use of excessively broad terms. Consider a few examples:

all	each	any	never	nothing
every	always	none	no one	nobody

When faced with a statement containing one of these words, an astute communicator will politely question its use by echoing the phrase with stress on the universal quantifier:

A: Our needs never get considered around here.
B: *Never?*

SKILL BUILDER

Practice your skill at using low-level abstractions by describing how each of the following sentences is likely to be misunderstood (or not understood at all). Then translate each into clearer language.

1. "Things are going pretty well."
2. "There are just a few small problems to clear up."
3. "I just need a little more time to finish the job."
4. "I think I understand what you mean."

A: I can't understand anything he's saying.
B: *Anything?*

A: All the staff support the proposal.
B: *All* of them?

Use Jargon Judiciously. Every profession has its own specialized vocabulary, often termed ***jargon.*** People who order office supplies talk about "NCR paper" and "three-up labels." Computer users talk about "32-bit architecture" and "image-compression boards."

In most cases, terms like these serve a useful purpose. For one thing, they save time. It is quicker, for instance, for an accountant to use the term *liquidity* than to say "the degree to which an asset can be converted into cash." In the same way, *CPM* is a handy term that advertisers use to stand for "the advertising cost to make a thousand impressions." A specialized vocabulary is particularly vital when the subject matter is technical and complex. The phrase *sleeping pill* simply won't do for physicians, nurses, and other health professionals because it says nothing about the dosage, the particular drug, or the circumstances under which it should be used. Similarly, geologists can't discuss their findings by talking about "rocks."

Most business professionals agree that it is important to learn the jargon of your field as quickly as possible. Doing so can speed up the exchange of information and make you appear competent and well informed. A certain amount of jargon has its value for outsiders as well. Speakers who sprinkle their comments with jargon will appear more credible to some listeners.[4] While incomprehensible language may *impress* listeners, it doesn't help them to *understand* an idea. Thus, if your goal is to explain yourself (and not merely to build your image), the ideal mixture may be a combination of clear language sprinkled with a bit of professional jargon.

Problems arise when insiders use their specialized vocabulary without explaining it to the uninitiated. A customer shopping for a computer might be

Another nuance of English involves phrases that, if taken literally, can confuse the foreign born. "You can say that again" and "It's just one of those things," for example, are merely *idioms.* Cole Porter, the composer who popularized the latter phrase, never intended for the listener to respond by asking, "What things?" nor would it be appropriate to go ahead and "say it again." . . .

To make matters worse, sometimes the same words have an opposite meaning depending on the context. To say "I believe in this idea" connotes a firm commitment to the concept. On the other hand, to respond "I believe so" to a question connotes some doubt about the matter. The questions "Would you like something to drink?" and "Would you like a drink?" carry with them quite different messages. The first offers any kind of beverage, whereas the second signals the availability of alcohol. . . .

As you can see, there is a great deal more to understanding what is intended than just knowing the vocabulary.

Sondra Thiederman, *Profiting in America's Multicultural Marketplace* mystified by a dealer's talk about RAM and ROM memory, transparent software, and bytes and bits of disk storage capacity. When the same information is translated into language the buyer can understand—number of pages of information that can be stored on a disk, for example—a sale is more likely.[5]

Jargon-free speech is especially important when dealing with people who are not familiar with the English language or the culture. For example, phrases like "getting a handle," "thrown a curve," or "coming from left field" might seem perfectly clear to a native-born American, but they could stump even a fluent speaker who was raised elsewhere.

Use Ambiguous Language When It Is Strategically Desirable. Vague language can be a sign of deliberate deception, as an old joke shows. A reporter warned a state senator, "Sir, your constituents were confused by today's speech." "Good," the senator replied. "It took me two days to write it that way."

While vagueness can signal an ethical lapse and while straight talk and clear language are usually admirable goals, there *are* occasions when deliberate vagueness is the best approach.[6] Vague speech can achieve two useful goals.

To Promote Harmony. A group of workers who have been feuding over everything from next year's budget to funding the office coffee supply can at least reach consensus on abstractions like "the need to work well together" or "finding solutions we all can live with." While vague statements such as these might seem meaningless in light of everyday conflicts, they do provide a point upon which everyone can agree—a small but important start toward more cooperation.

To Soften the Blow of Difficult Messages. Business communicators face the constant challenge of delivering difficult messages: "This work isn't good enough." "You let me down." "We don't want to do business with you anymore." While statements like these may be honest, they can also be brutal. Ambiguous language provides a way to deliver difficult messages that softens their blow and makes it possible to work smoothly with the recipients in the future. For example:

INVITATION TO INSIGHT

Identify jargon terms in your own line of work, or interview a worker in a field that interests you, and identify jargon terms that he or she uses. Then answer the following questions:

1. How does each term make communication more efficient?
2. What confusion might arise from the use of each term with certain listeners? In cases where confusion or misunderstandings might arise, suggest alternative words or phrases that could convey the meaning more clearly.

In his book *Are You Communicating?* author Donald Walton offers examples of how strategic ambiguity can be a tool for delivering unpleasant messages in a palatable way:

Business talk: Your suggestion is very interesting
Translation: You must be kidding.

Business talk: The idea is under active consideration.
Translation: It should be in the files here somewhere; we'll keep searching.

Business talk: We will advise you later.
Translation: Don't count on it.

Business talk: Let's get together sometime.
Translation: You'll never hear from me again.

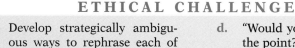

ETHICAL CHALLENGE

1. Develop strategically ambiguous ways to rephrase each of the following statements:
   a. "You've done a sloppy job here."
   b. "I can't understand what you're trying to say in this letter."
   c. "Nobody likes your idea."
   d. "Would you please hurry up and get to the point?"
2. On the basis of your responses here, decide how honest strategically ambiguous statements are. If they are not completely honest, can they be considered ethical? If not, how can they be morally justified?

BRUTE HONESTY	STRATEGIC AMBIGUITY
"This work isn't good enough."	"I think the boss will want us to back up these predictions with some figures."

BRUTE HONESTY	STRATEGIC AMBIGUITY
"You're so disorganized that it's impossible to tell what you're driving at."	"I'm having a hard time understanding that last idea. Can you run it by me again?"
"I don't want to work with you."	"Right now I don't see any projects on the horizon. But if that changes, I'll let you know."

As these examples show, the challenge is to find a way to be ambiguous without being dishonest or misunderstood.

Inflammatory Language

Language has the power to stir intense emotions. It can motivate, inspire, and amuse audiences. Unfortunately, it can also generate negative feelings: antagonism, defensiveness, and prejudice. You can prevent these negative outcomes by following two guidelines.

SKILL BUILDER

Describe a former co-worker three times. In your first account, use positively biased terms. In the second description, discuss the same person, using words with negative connotations. Finally, describe the co-worker in low-level abstractions without using biased language of any sort.

Avoid Biased Language. Emotional problems arise when speakers intentionally or unintentionally use ***biased language***—terms that seem to be objective but actually conceal an emotional bias. Consider, for example, the range of words you could use to refer to a twenty-five-year-old man who disagrees with your proposal: *gentleman, fellow, guy, young man, kid,* or *person.* All of these are denotatively accurate, yet each one paints a different picture in the listener's mind.

When faced with connotatively biased language, it's wise to recognize that the speaker is editorializing. Tactfully restate the term in language that doesn't contain an evaluation:

SPEAKER'S BIASED LANGUAGE	LISTENER'S RESTATEMENT
"It's a *gamble.*"	"So you don't think the idea is a reasonable risk. Is that it?"
"He's *long-winded.*"	"Bill *has* been talking for a long time."
"She's so *wishy-washy.*"	"You think Susan isn't willing to make a decision?"

Beware of Trigger Words. Some terms have such strong emotional associations that they act almost like a trigger, setting off an intense emotional reaction in certain listeners. These ***trigger words*** can refer to specific people (your boss, the president), groups or categories of individuals (union stewards, the personnel department, customers with complaints), issues (right-to-work laws, affirmative action, flexible scheduling), or other topics (sexual harassment, Japanese imports, downsizing).

INVITATION TO INSIGHT

Become more aware of your own emotional triggers by following these instructions:

1. In each category shown, identify two words that trigger positive reactions for you and two other words that make you react negatively:

   A person's name
   The label for a category of people
   A rule or policy

2. How do you react, both internally and observably, when you hear these terms? What might be the consequences of these reactions?
3. Use the same categories to identify words that trigger positive and negative reactions in a person you work with. What are the consequences of using these emotion-laden words with that person? Which of the terms should you continue to use, and which should you replace with more neutral words?

A word that seems innocuous to you can trigger an avalanche of emotions in someone else. Describing a female customer as a "lady" can be taken as a compliment or a sexist remark, depending on the attitude of the recipient. The difference between calling someone "a deaf person" and "a person who is deaf" may seem insignificant to people with normal hearing, but to someone with a hearing loss the former term sounds more like a global label, while the latter is just descriptive. Different ethnic labels may have powerful associations for people to whom they are applied. Which is preferred: Hispanic or Latino? Black or African-American? There is no clear answer to questions like these. Such words usually bring up intense feelings—either good or bad—that transport a listener out of the present into a mental or verbal tirade related to past experiences.

What is the best way to deal with trigger words? The first thing to realize is that, like others, you almost certainly have your own trigger wrods. You therefore ought to begin by recognizing them, so that when one comes up you'll at least be aware of your sensitivity and thus avoid overreacting. If, for example, you are very sensitive about your tendency to make careless errors when calculating even the simplest mathematical problems, you probably ought to think twice before getting defensive over a colleague's remark such as "Let's double-check those figures, just to be safe." It could be an innocent remark.

What about coping with the trigger words of others? If you are aware of the semantic triggers that set off other people, you can sometimes avoid using those terms. It's just as easy to refer to adult females as "women" as to call them "girls," since the latter is so offensive to many people.

Sometimes, however, you will discover too late that an apparently innocent term is a trigger word. The best reaction when faced with such an emotional response is to let the other person get the strong feelings out of his or her system. At that point, you can choose a more agreeable term and proceed with the discussion.

Male and Female Language Use

Chapter 2 described how culture affects communication. Some social scientists have suggested that conversation between men and women is a kind of cross-cultural communication in which members of each sex are not speaking different dialects but "genderlects."[7] They have argued that these different approaches affect the way men and women interact with one another in ways that are powerful but usually unnoticed.

As you read about differences in male and female speech, understand that the descriptions don't characterize all men and women. The relationship between gender and language is like the one between gender and height: men are generally taller than women, but some women are taller than some men. In fact, the difference between the tallest man and the shortest man (or the tallest woman and the shortest woman) is greater than the difference between the average man and the average woman. In the same way, the differences between male and female speech discussed in this section describe many, but not all, communicators. Remember also that gender isn't the only factor that influences conversational style. Cultural, geographical, and occupational influences also play a role. Finally, understand that the differences outlined in this section reflect past communication patterns. As the roles of men and women in society become less separate, we can expect that language differences may diminish.

Women's Speech. From childhood, females learn to use speech for what Tannen and others refer to as ***rapport talk:*** to create connections, establish goodwill, show support, and build community.

For women an important part of building rapport is using language as an *expressive tool:* to articulate emotions ("I'm worried about finishing those reports today"; "I'm glad everybody had a chance to speak") and clarify relationships ("We don't seem to be working well together").

Women's speech often goes beyond just expressing emotions; it also is characteristically *supportive.* Women listen and respond to spoken and unspoken conversational clues about the other person's feelings. One form of support is "troubles talk": sharing one's own problems as a way of showing solidarity. A characteristically female reply to a description of difficulties at work would be "I know what that's like. Last year I had so much trouble with a client on the Bustos case. . . . " This response lets the speaker know that she is not alone, that she is understood.

Another characteristic of women's conversational style is its *tentative* nature. This is reflected in questioning forms ("Could we go now?" "Would you type that for me?"); hedges and disclaimers ("I'm not sure about these figures . . . "; "This might not be a good time to bring this up, but . . . "); and tag questions ("The report is due today, isn't it?"). These speech forms, especially when used by women, can create the impression of less authority, status, certainty, accuracy, or credibility. However, tentative spech doesn't have to be regarded as weak: another interpretation is that it builds rapport by avoiding dogmatism and suggesting equality.

These two interpretations of tentative speech show that language doesn't have any absolute meaning; rather, it is a product of the relationships and expectations of the people who use it. This explains why men who use tag questions may be perceived as more affiliative and cordial (because these forms are not expected), while women who use them may be viewed (especially by men in a business environment) as less self-assured.

Conversational initiation and maintenance are also characteristic of women's speech. Women have long been taught to ask questions to get a conversation going, to find out what others are interested in, and to show interest in a conversational partner. So, typically, women ask questions to start and maintain conversations: "Did you hear about . . . ?" "Are you going to . . . ?" "Did you know that . . . ?" In addition, women use "listening noises" ("Uh, huh," "Oh really?" "Is that right?") to show interest. If women do interrupt, it is often to support or affirm the speaker, not to challenge or threaten.

Men's Speech. As Table 3-2 shows, men's styles of speech differ from women's in some important ways. Whereas women use talk to build rapport,

TABLE 3-2 Differences in Male and Female Language Use

Women's Style	Men's Style
Rapport	Report
Expressive	Instrumental
Supportive	Advising
Tentative	Certain
Conversational initiation and maintenance	Conversational control

men are more comfortable with what linguists have labeled ***report talk:*** speech that focuses less on feelings and relationships and more on information, facts, knowledge, and competence. Men are more inclined to use language to claim attention, assert a position, establish status, and show independence.

Men's speech uses language *instrumentally* (as opposed to expressively) to get things done: report information, solve visible problems, achieve, accomplish, attain, execute, perform. The results are often tangible and the reward visible. ("Fax these reports to accounting." "I'll make reservations at Sara's." "Finish that proposal by Monday.") Language is also used by men to define status.

When dealing with personal problems, a characteristically male approach is to offer *advice* that will lead to a solution. Empathizing to show sympathy and establish solidarity just doesn't seem helpful or appropriate.

Men's speech is more *assertive, certain, direct,* and *authoritative.* Men use statements of fact rather than opinion. ("That deduction belongs on schedule C" rather than "I think that's a Schedule C deduction.") Declarative sentences and dropped pitch at the end create a sense of sureness and authority. Men are more likely to speak directly, giving clear and unambiguous commands or directions rather than couching requests in the form of questions.

Men's speech style includes several characteristics of conversational *dominance* or *control:* verbosity, topic control, and interruptions. Most research

Many women are frequently told, "Don't apologize" or "You're always apologizing." The reason "apologizing" is seen as something they should stop doing is that it seems synonymous with putting oneself down. But for many women, and a fair number of men, saying "I'm sorry" isn't literally an apology; it is a ritual way of restoring balance to a conversation. "I'm sorry," spoken in this spirit, if it has any literal meaning at all, does not mean "I apologize," which would be tantamount to accepting blame, but rather "I'm sorry that happened." To understand the ritual nature of apologies, think of a funeral at which you might say, "I'm so sorry about Reginald's death." When you say that, you are not pleading guilty to a murder charge. You're expressing regret that something happened without taking or assigning blame. In other words, "I'm sorry" can be an expression of understanding—and caring about—the other person's feelings rather than an apology.

Deborah Tannen, *Talking from 9 to 5*

supports the statement that in conversations between men and women, men talk at greater length. Often in response to questions from women, men decide which topic of conversation to pursue and talk longer than the women in the same conversation. Research on interruptions is mixed as to who interrupts more, but it appears that the purpose of men's interruptions is often to gain control of the conversational topic or the conversation itself.

Meeting Gender-Related Language Challenges. Problems can arise when stereotypically male and female language styles clash on the job—often without anyone knowing exactly why. For instance, a woman who says, "I'm having difficulty with the Garcia account," may want to hear her concerns acknowledged and know that others have experienced similar problems. Her goal may be to gain support, establish connection, and seek rapport. Or she may just want to relieve her frustration by talking about the situation. A man, conditioned to use speech to solve problems, might respond, logically, with advice: "Here's one way you could handle it. . . . " If the woman wanted support and connection, being given advice might produce an effect that is just the opposite of the rapport she was looking for: the woman might feel that her male colleague was trying to appear "one-up," coming across as a superior. From his frame of reference, the man *was* being helpful: he offered useful information at the request of someone in need.

Another gender-related problem can arise when a man pays attention to the content of a message while a woman focuses on the relational dimension of the words. If a male supervisor says, "I can't do anything about your hours; the boss says they're set and can't be changed," a woman may hear a relational message of "I don't care" or "I don't want to be bothered." The man, used to dealing with communication at the content level, isn't being unsympathetic: he is just responding to a request.

Both male and female language styles work well—as long as speakers operate by the same rules. Frustrations result when people expect others to use their own style. The following suggestions can help communicators understand and adapt to one another's differing uses of language:

- *Be aware of different styles.* Once you are aware that men and women have been taught to use language differently, there's less likelihood of being dismayed at a style that doesn't match yours. The cultural analogy is apt here: If you were traveling in another country, you wouldn't be offended by the customs of its inhabitants, even if they were different from yours. In the same way, accepting gender differences can lead to smoother relationships—even if members of the other sex behave differently than you do.
- *Switch styles, when appropriate.* Being bilingual is an obvious advantage in a multicultural world. In the same way, using a communication style that isn't characteristic of your gender can be useful. If you routinely focus on the content of others' remarks, consider paying more attention to the unstated relational messages behind their words. If you generally focus on the unexpressed-

feelings part of a message, consider being more task-oriented. If your first instinct is to be supportive, consider the value of offering advice; and if advice is your reflexive way of responding, think about whether offering support and understanding might sometimes be more helpful.

- *Combine styles.* Effective communication may not be an either-or matter of choosing one style. In many situations, you may get the best results by combining typically male and female approaches. Research confirms what common sense suggests: A "mixed-gender strategy" that balances the traditionally male, task-oriented approach with the characteristically female relationship-oriented approach is rated most highly by both male and female respondents.[8] Choosing the approach that is right for the other communicator and the situation can create satisfaction far greater than that which comes from using a single stereotypical style.

SEXUAL HARASSMENT

Verbal and nonverbal sexual harassment on the job has always existed, but in recent decades it has been identified as a problem requiring governmental response. The Civil Rights Act of 1964 and subsequent legislation and court decisions have identified two types of sexual harassment:

- *Quid pro quo* (a Latin term meaning "this for that"). Examples of this form of harassment include directly or indirectly threatening not to promote someone who won't date you or implying that their employment depends on the exchange of sexual favors.
- *Hostile work environment.* This category includes any verbal or nonverbal behavior that has the intention or effect of interfering with someone's work or creating an environment that is intimidating, offensive, or hostile. Unwelcome remarks ("babe," "hunk"), humor, stares ("elevator eyes"), signs, and invasions of physical space all can create a hostile work environment.

Although sexual harassment is often thought of in terms of men targeting women, either sex can be the instigator and either may be the recipient. Men may be offended by hostile remarks that attack every person with both an X and Y chromosome; women may sense a hostile environment when sexual innuendos and explicit comments prevail.

Harassment is more common than many workers might expect. One study by the U.S. Merit System Protection Board found that 42 percent of women who worked for the federal government reported having been sexually harassed, either verbally or physically.[9] In Los Angeles, the harassment was so widespread that the mayor ordered training programs for every city worker.

Avoiding Accusations of Sexual Harassment

As defined by the law, sexual harassment doesn't have to be intentional. If a behavior has the *effect* of creating a hostile work environment, a claim of harassment can be made. Whether or not you agree with this principle, the fact remains that even innocent remarks or actions can get you into trouble. A sincere compliment or a well-intentioned joke can lead to months or years of legal maneuvering. For this reason, it makes sense to avoid even the appearance of harassment.

Since much harassment is in the eye of the receiver, it is smart to avoid behavior that might even risk causing a complaint. Excessive remarks about appearance that don't relate to the job at hand, persistent requests for social contact, staring, or uninvited physical contact is an invitation for trouble. So is language that might be perceived as hostile. For example, people might have been calling the female staff in the front office "the girls" forever, but using the term *women* makes more sense in today's working environment.

Beyond the normal precautions and courtesy, it is smart to be especially aware around people who you know are sensitive to perceived or actual sexual harassment. Look at the situation from the other person's point of view. Could your language be considered offensive? Could your actions lead to discomfort? If you are in doubt about whether your actions might offend a particular person, it might be smart to ask. You might think some people are hypersensitive, but finding out whether the courts support your perspective is probably not worth the effort.

Responding to Sexual Harassment

Most organizations have developed policies prohibiting sexual harassment and procedures for people who feel they are being harassed. In addition to company policy, victims of sexual harassment are entitled to legal protection. The U.S. Equal Employment Opportunity Commission (EEOC), state and local agencies, and the court system all enforce civil rights acts relating to harassment.

Despite the determination of government to protect employees from harassment, fighting sexual discrimination using legal channels takes time and stamina. Victims sometimes experience depression, ridicule, isolation, and reprisal.[10] Even when they do not suffer these consequences, people who file formal grievances with the government can find delays discouraging. For example, a 1993 internal analysis by the EEOC found that the average processing time for a case was 294 days.[11] Even after a wait, the results are often discouraging for those who file complaints. In 1993, for example, the EEOC dismissed or found no discrimination in 84.2 percent of the charges brought to it. For these reasons, taking care of harassment at the lowest, most informal level possible can solve the problem in a way that doesn't punish the victim. Listed below are several options, in escalating order. They aren't meant as a step-by-step guide to how to respond, but they will help you decide which options are best for you.

1. *Consider dismissing the incident.* This approach is appropriate only if you truly believe that the remark or behavior isn't worth worrying about. Pretending to dismiss incidents that you believe are important can lead to self-blame and diminished self-esteem.

2. *Ask the harasser to stop.* Inform the harasser early that the behavior is unwelcome, and ask him or her to cease immediately. Your statement should be firm, but unless the offense is clearly deliberate, it doesn't have to be angry. Remember that many words or deeds that make you uncomfortable may not be deliberately hostile remarks. (See Chapter 5 for details on how to be assertive without being aggressive.)
3. *Keep a diary.* If the harassment persists, keep a record of every incident. Detail the date, time, place, and exactly what happened. Describe how you responded and how you felt.
4. *Write a personal letter to the harasser.* A written statement may help the harasser to understand what behavior you find offensive. Just as important, it can show that you take the problem seriously. Put the letter in a sealed envelope (keeping a copy for yourself). Use information from your diary to detail specifics about what happened, what behavior you want stopped, and how you felt. Keep a record of when you delivered the letter. If you want to be certain that the delivery of the letter will be acknowledged, take a friend along when you present it.
5. *Ask a friend to intervene.* Perhaps a mutual acquaintance can persuade the harasser to stop. The person you choose should be someone who you are convinced understands your discomfort and supports your opinion. Be sure this intermediary is also someone the harasser respects and trusts.
6. *Complain through channels.* Report the situation to your supervisor, personnel office, or a committee that has been set up to consider harassment complaints. Think about what results you are seeking. Usually, having the harasser stop is enough, but decide if you want more action: a transfer, reimbursement for medical bills, and so on.
7. *File a legal complaint.* You may file a complaint with the federal EEOC or with your state agency. You have the right to obtain the services of an attorney regarding your legal options. For example, some victims request a letter from the EEOC authorizing them to pursue a lawsuit on their own.

NONVERBAL COMMUNICATION

Words are not the only way we communicate. You can appreciate this fact by imagining the following scenes:

> Your boss has told the staff that he welcomes any suggestions about how to improve the organization. You take him at his word and schedule an appointment to discuss some ideas you have had. As you begin to outline your proposed changes, he focuses his gaze directly on you, folds his arms across his chest, clenches his jaw muscles, and begins to frown. At the end of your remarks, he rises abruptly from his chair,

says "Thank you for your ideas" in a monotone, and gives you a curt handshake.

You are on a committee interviewing applicants for the job of customer relations representative. You notice one résumé that seems far superior to the others: the candidate received almost perfect grades at a top-flight university, had a similar position with a leading company in a distant city, and came with enthusiastic letters of recommendation. During the interview, you notice that she rarely looks you in the eye.

Despite the expense, you have decided to have a highly regarded CPA handle your tax matters. While waiting for the accountant to appear, you scan the impressive display of diplomas from prestigious universities and professional associations. The accountant enters, and as the conversation proceeds, he yawns repeatedly.

Most people would find these situations odd and disturbing. This reaction would have nothing to do with the verbal behavior of the boss, applicant, or accountant. In each case, though, the person's nonverbal behavior sends messages above and beyond the words being spoken: the boss doesn't really seem to want to hear your suggestions; you wonder whether the job applicant would in fact be good at dealing with customers, despite her credentials, or possibly even whether those credentials are genuine; and despite the CPA's reputation and credentials, you wonder whether he is interested enough in your case to give you the time and attention you want. Nonverbal communication plays an important role in all types of business and professional interaction.

What is nonverbal communication? If *non-* means "not" and *verbal* means "words," then it seems logical that nonverbal communication means communication that does not use words. Actually, this definition is not totally correct. As you will soon learn, every spoken message has a vocal element coming not from *what* we say but from *how* we say it. For our purposes, we will include this vocal dimension along with messages sent by the body and the environment. Our working definition of ***nonverbal communication,*** then, is those messages expressed by other than linguistic means.

Common sense might suggest that most of the messages we send and receive are verbal. Communication researchers, however, have found that nonverbal messages have great impact. Over a quarter century of research suggests that approximately 35 percent of social meaning comes from verbal statements, while the remaining 65 percent comes from nonverbal behavior.[12] Furthermore, when nonverbal behavior seems to contradict a verbal message, the spoken words carry less weight than the nonverbal cues.[13] While the claim that nonverbal cues carry almost twice the weight of speech might seem preposterous, consider as an example how facial, bodily, and vocal behavior could shape the meaning of a statement like "Thanks a lot for your ideas. I'll think about them." The same words could convey sincere appreciation, indifference and dismissal, or sarcasm and anger. This example (and you can think of many others) shows the critical role that nonverbal communication plays in conveying meaning.

Characteristics of Nonverbal Communication

Now that we have defined nonverbal communication and discussed its importance, we need to take a look at some of its characteristics. Nonverbal communication resembles verbal communication in some ways and is quite different in others.

Nonverbal Behavior Always Has Communicative Value. You may not always *intend* to send nonverbal messages, but everything about your appearance, every movement, every facial expression, every nuance of your voice has the potential to convey meaning.[14] You can demonstrate this fact by imagining that your boss has "called you on the carpet," claiming that you haven't been working hard enough. How could you not send a nonverbal message? Nodding gravely would be a response; so would blushing, avoiding or making direct eye contact, or shaking your head affirmatively or negatively. For that matter, so would rolling yourself into a ball or leaving the room. While you can shut off your linguistic channels of communication by refusing to speak or write, it is impossible to avoid behaving nonverbally.

One writer learned this fact from movie producer Sam Goldwyn while presenting his proposal for a new film. "Mr. Goldwyn," the writer implored, "I'm telling you a sensational story. I'm only asking for your opinion, and you fall asleep." Goldwyn's reply: "Isn't sleeping an opinion?"

Nonverbal Behavior Is Ambiguous. Some books claim that "body language" is the key that makes it possible to read a person like a book. While an awareness of nonverbal behavior can certainly boost your understanding of others, it will never transform you into a mind reader.

Nonverbal messages may be constantly available, but they are not always easy to understand. Compared with verbal language, nonverbal behavior is highly ambiguous. Does a customer's yawn signal boredom or fatigue? Are your co-workers laughing with or at you? Is a subordinate trembling with nervousness or cold? Most nonverbal behaviors have a multitude of possible meanings, and it is a serious mistake to assume that you can decide which is true in any given case.

INVITATION TO INSIGHT

Prove to yourself that nonverbal communication is constant and impossible to stop.

1. Observe the nonverbal behaviors of a person you work with. What messages do you get from your observations?
2. Describe an alternative intepretation for each nonverbal behavior you have noticed.
3. Speculate on which of your interpretations is more accurate. Are you certain you are right? How could you find out?

Nonverbal Communication Primarily Expresses Attitudes. While it is relatively easy to infer general interest, liking, disagreement, amusement, and so on, from another's actions, messages about ideas or concepts don't lend themselves to nonverbal channels. How, for instance, would you express the following messages nonverbally?

"Sales are running 16 percent above last year's."

"I need more change at checkstand 2."

"Management decided to cancel the sales meeting after all."

"Let's meet at two to plan the agenda for tomorrow's meeting."

It's apparent that such thoughts are best expressed in speech and writing. It's also apparent, though, that nonverbal behavior will imply how the speaker *feels* about these statements: whether the speaker is pleased that sales are up or worried that they're not as high as expected, how urgently the cashier at checkstand 2 needs change, and so on.

Much Nonverbal Behavior Is Culture-Bound. Certain types of nonverbal behavior seem to be universal. For example, there is strong agreement among members of most literate cultures about which facial expressions represent happiness, fear, surprise, sadness, anger, and disgust or contempt.[15] Many nonverbal expressions do vary from culture to culture, however. For instance, an American's "okay" hand sign has a different and obscene meaning in some other cultures. The nod that means "yes" in some cultures means "no" in others, while in still other cultures it means only that the other person understood the question.

Head shakes are particularly difficult to interpret. People in the United States shake their heads up and down to signify "yes." Many British, however, make the same motions just to indicate that they hear—not necessarily that they agree. To say "no," people shake their heads from side to side in the United States, jerk their heads back in a haughty manner in the Middle East, wave a hand in front of the face in the Orient, and shake a finger from side to side in Ethiopia. . . .

The pointing of a finger is a dangerous action. In North America it is a very normal gesture, but it is considered very rude in many other parts of the world—especially in areas of Asia and Africa. It is therefore much safer to merely close the hand and point with the thumb.

Other forms of communication have also caused problems. The tone of the voice, for example, can be important. Some cultures permit people to raise their voices when they are not close to others, but loudness in other cultures is often associated with anger or a loss of self-control. . . .

A lack of knowledge of such differences in verbal and nonverbal forms of communication has resulted in many a social and corporate blunder. Local people tend to be willing to overlook most of the mistakes of tourists; after all, they are just temporary visitors. Locals are much less tolerant of the errors of business people—especially those who represent firms trying to project an impression of permanent interest in the local economy. The consequences of erring, therefore, are much greater for the corporation.

David A. Ricks, *Big Business Blunders*

In this age of international communication in business, it is especially important to understand that there are cultural differences in the meaning assigned to nonverbal behaviors. Consider the different rules about what distance is appropriate between speakers. One study revealed that the "proper" space between two speakers varied considerably from one culture to another: to Japanese, a comfortable space was 40.2 inches; to Americans, 35.4 inches; and to Venezuelans, 32.2 inches.[16] It's easy to see how this could lead to problems for a native of the United States doing business overseas. To a Latin American, the North American would seem too withdrawn, whereas a Japanese might see the same businessperson as too aggressive.

Types of Nonverbal Communication

We have already mentioned several types of nonverbal messages. We will now discuss each in more detail.

Voice. Your own experience shows that the voice communicates in ways that have nothing to do with the words a speaker utters. You may recall, for instance, overhearing two people arguing in an adjoining room or apartment; even though you couldn't make out their words, their emotions and the fact that they were arguing were apparent from the sound of their voices. Similarly, you have probably overheard people talking in a language you didn't understand; yet the speakers' feelings—excitement, delight, exhaustion, boredom, grief—were conveyed by their voices.

Social scientists use the term ***paralanguage*** to describe a wide range of vocal characteristics, each of which helps express an attitude:

pitch (high–low)
range (spread–narrow)
articulation (precise–imprecise)
rhythm (smooth–jerky)
volume (loud–soft)
resonance (resonant–thin)
tempo (rapid–slow)
dysfluencies (*um, er,* etc.)
pauses (frequency and duration)

The paralinguistic content of a message can reflect a speaker's feelings. For instance, a subordinate who begins to stammer as he says "Everything is going fine here" might sound nervous or doubtful to his manager—as if everything were *not* fine and the subordinate were afraid that the truth would be discovered. A statement such as "I can't make the meeting Friday morning" may be heard as "I'm very sorry" or "I couldn't care less about the meeting"

I've watched people spend literally four minutes trying to leave just the "right" 20-second voice mail message. Are they perfectionists? Neurotics? Narcissists? I don't know. But I do know that voice mail has made people extraordinarily sensitive to the shadings and nuances of tone. The technology sensitizes people as much to the sound of the voice as the content of the message.

Michael Schrage

or even "Everything's getting out of control"—depending on how the speaker says it.

While paralanguage reflects feelings and attitudes, the *emphasis* a speaker puts on certain words can also change the meaning of a statement radically. Notice the differences in this one statement:

"*I* need this job done right now." (Others might not.)

"I *need* this job done right now." (It's important!)

"I need *this* job done right now." (Forget the other jobs.)

"I need this job done *right now.*" (Immediately!)

Generally speaking, variety in the rate, tone, pitch, volume, and other vocal features creates an impression of involvement and enthusiasm. Nonetheless, paralinguistic cues are ambiguous. A subordinate who is speaking very fast may be nervous, although possibly more so about making a presentation to a superior than about the content of the message. A manager who "sounds hostile" when he says "Thank you for your ideas" may not want to hear your ideas, but he may also be distracted and more concerned about another problem, or he may be unaware that his normal manner gives people the impression of hostility. The effect of vocal characteristics also depends in part on whether the speaker is male or female. For example, one researcher discovered that men who used more pitch variety were perceived as dynamic, feminine, and aesthetically inclined, while women were seen as more dynamic and extroverted.[17] Women frequently raise their pitch at the end of a sentence, with the result that others sometimes conclude that the women speaking are less sure of themselves, their position or status, or their message. However, a raised pitch could indicate openness to others' suggestions and invite others to speak.

Appearance. Although we have been warned since childhood not to judge a book by its cover, appearance plays a tremendous role in determining how a communicator's messages will be received in business and elsewhere.[18] As a rule, people who *look* attractive are considered to be likable and persuasive, and they generally have successful careers.[19] For example, research suggests that beginning salaries increase about $2,000 for every 1-point increase on a 5-point attractiveness scale and that more attractive men (but not more attractive women) are given higher starting salaries than their less handsome counterparts.

A number of factors contribute to how attractive a person seems. For instance, potential employers, customers, and co-workers are usually impressed by people who are trim, muscular, and in "good shape." One study, in fact, shows that people who are overweight have more trouble getting job offers.[20] Some aspects of physical appearance cannot be changed very easily. One very significant factor in appearance, though—and one over which you may have the most control—is clothing.

Uniforms of one sort or another are a feature in many, if not most, fields. Some uniforms are obvious: the tailored clothing of airline pilots and flight attendants, the polished boots and helmet of a motorcycle cop, or the scrubs worn by physicians and nurses. Other occupations and organizations have more subtle uniforms, which consist of a clearly defined range of regular clothing that is acceptable. A fifteen-page manual titled *The Disney Look* spells out the rules for everyone from hourly employees to the presidents at all theme parks and company-owned resorts, for example. Taboos include bracelets (except for medical reasons), pants without a jacket, beards and mustaches, and "unnatural hair color." Not all dress codes are spelled out in corporate manuals. A former employee of a major designer of women's clothing described how informal policies operate: "There is an unspoken dress code that requires you to own Lanz dresses. It was put very subtly in my briefing. It was basically: 'You know, it makes our department look good when you wear Lanz dresses'."[21]

Until fairly recently, the businessperson's standard uniform in many organizations—especially for employees dealing with the public—was conservative. At EDS, the multimillion-dollar data processing operation that Ross Perot sold to General Motors Corporation in 1984, the new-employees' handbook spelled out how to dress on the job. Men were expected to wear a "conservative business suit" and "conservative shirt" complemented by "a conservative business tie, color-coordinated with shirt and suit." Acceptable shoes were "all-leather, lace-up, slip-on, or wing-tip." Womens' attire was equally constrained: "a skirted suit, dress, skirt and blouse or skirt and sweater."[22] This type of conservative dress code has not completely disappeared in the 1990s. For example, U.S. attorney Andrew Maloney recently circulated a memo to prosecuters in his Brooklyn office, instructing them to drop their casual attire and "wear dress appropriate for a law office."[23]

Although codes like these may seem like an infringement of freedom of expression, federal law gives employers considerable latitude to enforce them, as long as they don't discriminate. Dress codes must apply uniformly to all workers, regardless of sex or race, and they must make reasonable accommodation for workers' religious or ethnic identification, as well as for physical disabilities.

Attitudes about what clothing is acceptable are changing. Even IBM has abandoned its decades-long policy of requiring employees to wear a dark suit and white shirt. In 1993, the new chairman, Louis Gerstner, appeared publicly in a blue shirt. Not long after, the standard for clothing at some sites even permitted male workers to show up on the job without a suit and tie. A spokesman for IBM explained, "You try to dress like your customers do."[24]

Whether to dress up or dress down depends on the norms of the culture at large and the organization in which you work. In the computer and software industry, for example, casual attire has been common for years. "We're more concerned about what people do than how they look doing it," explained the employee relations manager at Convex Computer Corporation in Dallas.[25]

Despite this open-minded attitude, the smart approach is to dress within the range of what is expected by key people in the industry and company where you work. Wearing a conservative, dark business suit in a freewheeling start-up company where everyone else comes to work in jeans would look just as odd as wearing wrinkled Levis in a Wall Street stock brokerage. Unless you are brilliant and indispensable to the people you work with, the best bet is to wear clothing that they will find acceptable.[26]

The Face and Eyes. On an obvious level, a person's face communicates emotions clearly: a subordinate's confused expression indicates the need to continue with an explanation; a customer's smile and nodding signal the time to close a sale; and a colleague's frown indicates that your request for help has come at a bad time. Facial expressions, like other nonverbal signals, are ambiguous (a co-worker's frown could come from a headache rather than the timing of your request). Nonetheless, researchers have found that accurate judgments of facial expressions can be made.[27]

The eyes themselves communicate a great deal. A skilled nonverbal communicator, for example, can control an interaction by knowing when and where to look to produce the desired results. Since visual contact is an invitation to speak, a speaker who does not want to be interrupted can avoid looking directly at people until it is time to field questions or get reactions.

Eye contact may be the best indicator of how involved a person is in a situation. The advice to "always look people straight in the eye" has been partially contradicted by research: in most two-person conversations, most people seem to look at their partners somewhere between 50 and 60 percent of the time, often alternating short gazes with glances away. Still, a person who makes little or no eye contact seems to have little involvement in the situation. A job applicant who never looks at the interviewer seems to be purposely remaining detached or nervous or to be falsifying his or her credentials. A manager who doesn't make eye contact when she says "I want you to work over in Parts for a few days" may, among other things, give a salesclerk the impression that she doesn't care what *his* feelings are about being moved.

The rules for eye contact vary from one culture to another. In Japanese audiences, people who may appear to be sleeping, with eyes closed and heads nodding, may well be paying the speaker a compliment, indicating intense concentration. In other cultures—Dine' (Navajo), for example—lack of eye contact may indicate respect for elders, not a lack of interest.

Even among communicators who follow the rules of Euro-American culture, eye contact can be deceptive; some people *can* lie while looking you "right in the eye." And even barely perceptible changes in eye contact can send messages that may or may not be accurate. The following story illustrates how eye contact can be misleading—with serious repercussions:

> Discussing his corporation's financial future in front of television cameras, the chief executive officer of a *Fortune* 500 company lowered his eyes just as he began to mention projected earnings. His downcast eyes gave the impres-

> sion—on television—that the executive wasn't on the level. Wall Street observers discounted the CEO's optimistic forecast, and the company's stock price dropped four points over the next few trading days. It took two years to build it up again—even though the projection had proved to be accurate.[28]

Posture and Movement. A person's body communicates messages in several ways. The first is through posture. The way you sit at your desk when you're working can express something about your attitude toward your job or how hard you're working to anyone who cares to look. A less obvious set of bodily clues comes from the small gestures and mannerisms that every communicator exhibits at one time or another. While most people pay reasonably close attention to their facial expression, they are less aware of hand, leg, and foot motions. Thus, fidgeting hands might betray nervousness; a tapping foot, impatience; and clenched fists or white knuckles, restrained anger.

A study on privacy in the workplace by GF Business Equipment Company describes ways in which such gestures can be used to discourage visits from co-workers. In addition to avoiding eye contact with your visitor, the company suggests that you

> shuffle papers or make notes to indicate a desire to return to work . . . keep pen or pencil poised—that communicates an aversion to engage in conversation . . . and if interrupted when dialing a call, don't hang up the receiver.[29]

Good communicators are sensitive to small cues like this and tailor their behavior accordingly. They will notice a forward-leaning position as an indication that their remarks are being well received and will capitalize upon the point that led to this reaction. When a remark results in a pulling back, a smart communicator will uncover the damage and try to remedy it. Awareness of such subtle messages can make the difference between success and failure in a variety of business settings: interviews, presentations, group meetings, and one-to-one interactions.

Body relaxation or tension is a strong indicator of who has the power in one-to-one relationships. As a rule, the more releaxed person in a given situation has the greater status.[30] This is most obvious in job interviews and high-stake situations in which subordinates meet with their superiors—requesting a raise or describing a problem, for example. The person in control can afford to relax, while the supplicant must be watchful and on guard. While excessive tension does little good for either the sender or receiver, total relaxation can be inappropriate for a subordinate. A job candidate who matched the interviewer's casual sprawl would probably create a poor impression. In superior-subordinate interactions, the best posture for the one-down person is probably one that is slightly more rigid than the powerholder's.

Height also affects perceptions of power: tallness usually equates with dominance. Standing up tall can help you appear more authoritative, whereas a slumped posture or slouched shoulders create an appearance of submissive or passive demeanor. Getting your body at the same level as others is a way of nonverbally diminishing status whether speaking with a colleague in a wheelchair or with others shorter than you. To literally have to look up to someone may make the shorter person feel like a subordinate. Sitting down with someone could signal your desire for collegiality rather than status, while standing over or behind someone signals power or status. Since women and persons from some minority co-cultures may not be as tall as the average American male, and since persons in wheelchairs interact at a shorter height, your relative height is a factor worth considering in professional interactions. If you are taller than others or are standing when others are sitting, they may be seeing you as an authority figure or higher-status individual, even if you don't wish to appear as one.[31]

Personal Space and Distance. The distance we put between ourselves and others also reflects feelings and attitudes, and thus it affects communication. Anthropologist Edward Hall has identified four distance zones used by middle-class Americans: intimate (ranging from physical contact to about 18 inches), casual-personal (18 inches to 4 feet), social-consultative (4 to 12 feet), and public (12 feet and beyond).[32]

In some cases the distance zones don't apply at all—or at least the distances aren't flexible enough to reflect the attitudes of the parties. Dentists and barbers, for instance, work within intimate distance—actual physical contact; yet the relationship between dentist and patient or barber and client may be rather impersonal.

In other cases, though, the distance that people put between themselves and others is significant. For example, distance can reflect the attitude of the person who does the positioning. Research shows that a person who expects an unpleasant message or views the speaker as unfriendly takes a more distant position than does someone expecting good news or viewing the speaker as friendly.[33] An observant communicator can thus use the distance others choose with respect to him or her as a basis for hunches about their feelings. ("I get the feeling you're worried about something, Harry. Is there anything wrong?")

Besides reflecting attitudes, distance also creates feelings. In one study, subjects rated people who communicated at a greater distance as less friendly and understanding than those who positioned themselves closer.[34] (Closeness has its limits, of course. Intimate distance is rarely appropriate for business dealings.) Thus, an effective communicator will usually choose to operate at a casual-personal distance when a friendly atmosphere is the goal.

Interpersonal distance is another nonverbal indicator of power. One unspoken cultural rule is that the person with higher status generally controls the degree of approach. As Mehrabian puts it, "It is easy enough to picture an older person in this culture encouraging a younger business partner by patting him or her on the back; but it is very difficult to visualize this situation reversed; that is, with the younger person patting the older and more senior partner."[35] This principle of distance explains why subordinates rarely ques-

INVITATION TO INSIGHT

Demonstrate the impact of nonverbal communication by finding both positive and negative examples of behavior in each of the following categories. Describe in behavioral terms precisely what the difference is between the effective and ineffective examples you have found.

1. Voice
2. Dress
3. Face and eyes
4. Posture and movement
5. Personal space and use of distance
6. Time

tion the boss's right to drop in to their work area without invitation but are reluctant to approach their superior's office even when told "the door is always open."

When a subordinate does wind up in the office of a superior, both tension and distance show who is in charge. The less powerful person usually stands until invited to take a seat and, when given the choice, will be reluctant to sit close to the boss. Wise managers often try to minimize the inhibiting factor of this status gap by including a table or comfortable easy chairs in their offices so that they can meet with subordinates on a more equal level.

Some managers try to promote informal communication by visiting employees in the employees' own offices. David Ogilvy, head of one of the largest advertising agencies in the country, says, "Do not summon people to your office—it frightens them. Instead, go to see them in *their* offices."[36]

Time. The way we use time provides a number of silent messages.[37] Leonard Berlin, senior financial analyst at Exxon, attributes his reputation as a hard worker to the fact that he routinely arrives at work half an hour early. "That's a big thing to my boss," he says. "It doesn't matter that I leave at the regular time; getting here early shows an interest. I think that if I stayed to seven every night it would make less impression."[38]

Many business advisors recommend that you be particularly scrupulous about your use of time during the first few months you are on the job:

> If . . . in that first ninety days, you're late or absent frequently, or seen as a clock watcher, you may earn yourself . . . negative scrutiny for a long time thereafter by your superiors. Rather than excusing any "infractions" of the rules, they'll be looking for slip-ups and a reason potentially to discharge you.[39]

The amount of time we spend on a task or with a problem is also a good indication of how much importance we give it. The manager who never has time to talk over a problem with an employee or who postpones performance reviews because he or she "doesn't have time" is saying something about his or her regard for subordinates—as is the manager who takes time to converse casually with employees every few weeks. The person who cuts one meeting short to attend another is making a statement about the relative importance of the two meetings.

Rules and customs about time vary widely from one culture to another. Whereas most North Americans and northern Europeans value punctuality, other cultures are much more casual about appointments and deadlines. In monochronic cultures, speaking within the allotted time generally shows good planning and concern for the audience. Speaking longer inconveniences the listeners and communicates lack of regard for their schedules. But in some polychronic cultures, speaking only for the allotted time would indicate lack of excitement or actual indifference toward the audience or the issue. Getting down to business quickly can be seen as a rude and insulting move on the part of a potential business associate. In many cultures, the relationship not only is much more important than the business at hand but is the foundation of the business venture and therefore determines whether or not there will be any business conducted. If the personal relationship is not established by "taking time" for dialogue and discussion, there will be no business relationship.

Chris Pagliaro, an American football coach, learned this lesson the hard way when he spent a season leading Milan's team in the Italian league. His realization that time is treated differently began to dawn on him when he arrived for the first practice sessions, scheduled for 8:30 P.M.:

> We got out there at 8:30 P.M. I'm dressed, I've got my whistle, my (American) assistant coach is there, the two American players are there.
>
> And there's no Italians. It's ten 'til nine and I don't see anybody: [not] the owner, nobody. Around 9 o'clock, a couple of them start trickling in.
>
> I had made a practice schedule—typical American coach: at 8:30 we do this, at 8:35 this, at 8:50 this. You might as well throw that one out the window. We got started around 9:20 or 9:30.[40]

The coach was smart and flexible enough to realize that he couldn't fight against a lifetime of cultural conditioning. He developed a compromise between the American need for punctuality and the casual Italian attitude about time:

> By Friday, I knew it was useless. So what I did, I made a schedule and waited around. While the team ran laps, we set our watches back to 8:30. That's the only way I could do it. So we were always starting at 8:30, regardless of what time it was.

Physical Environment. So far we have discussed how personal behavior sends nonverbal messages. The physical environment in which we operate also suggests how we feel and shapes how we communicate.

Consider the way space is allocated in an organization. Power locations become apparent when we look at the amount and location of existing space given to various employees and groups. In many organizations, for instance, an employee's status may be measured by whether his or her office is next to the boss's or is in a dark alcove. An office with a window or an office on the corner often indicates higher status than an inside office with no window. Sometimes lower-ranking employees who do the same job, such as processing orders, are all located in a single large room, while the supervisors have private offices.

In addition to reflecting status and power, the physical layout of an organization also shapes the ways its members interact with one another. For example, the temperature and humidity of a room can have profound effects on the success of communication. One study revealed that as temperatures and humidity increase, impressions of a speaker's attractiveness decline.[41] Understanding this fact can help you avoid scheduling presentations or meetings in hot, stuffy rooms, where the results may be doomed before a word is spoken.

Another way in which environments shape communication is proximity. The distance that separates people is perhaps the most important factor in shaping who talks with whom. Other things being equal, officemates will talk with one another more than with the people next door, and workers in the same area deal with one another more than with similarly employed people in another area. Researcher Thomas J. Allen studied workers in research facilities, medical laboratories, and business schools. He found that the frequency with which a person spoke to colleagues was a direct function of the distance between their desks.[42] In addition to the simple distance separating people, the difficulty of navigating that distance can also reduce interaction.[43] Corners that must be turned, doors that have to be wrestled open, and counters that block access keep people apart. One manager described the obstacle course that separated him from his boss's office:

> I go from my office past the receptionist and down the hall to the other end of the building. I take the elevator to twelve, get off, and take another one to twenty-one. I get off and walk to the other end of the building, and pass through three doors, and I'm at his office—about a hundred feet straight above where I started![44]

Furniture arrangement also plays a big role in the way people communicate. For example, in one study of a medical office, only 10 percent of the patients were "at ease" when conversing with a doctor seated behind a desk, while the figure rose to 55 percent when the desk was removed.[45] Even when the location of furniture is fixed, choices about seating can influence interaction. Dominant, high-status persons often select the position at a table where

The size of the office is only the beginning of a system that is as intricate as ranks in the German army. High-level employees qualify for Venetian blinds and drapes; lower-level employees have to adjust the light with shades. A water carafe and cups are assigned to employees of a certain rank and above. Employees of certain lower rankings have desks of plastic and steel, while those of higher station have desks of oak or walnut. The number of chairs in one's office is a clear sign of grade, just like the number of windows. Some of the steerage-class employees are apparently not expected to have visitors at all, because the only chair they are entitled to is the one behind their desks.

George Lee Walker, *The Chronicles of Doodah*

they can see and be seen. This allows more interaction and more influence over the interactions at the table. Not surprisingly, the person who is seated at the "head" of a table is more often perceived as a leader. Persons who want to diminish their potential for interaction and leadership often seat themselves in less visible spots along the sides of a table.[46]

This sort of information can be useful on the job. You may be able to relocate your work to an area that will give you the interaction you want. Beyond this, realize that several places in your working environment will probably allow you to interact informally with desirable communication partners. Employee lounges, elevators, and dining areas are a few examples. Even rest rooms can be handy places to establish contact, though you will probably want to continue your business in a more congenial spot. If you are interested in making your bosses more aware of your work, it's important to be visible to them. On the other hand, if you would just as soon be left alone, the old axiom "Out of sight, out of mind" applies here.

If you are a manager, think about arranging your subordinates' working areas to increase communication between people who should interact and to separate those who don't need to talk to one another. You can encourage communication between groups of workers by arranging gathering spots where congregation is easy. A good setting for informal contact needs to meet three criteria.[47] First, it ought to be centrally located so that people have to pass through it on their way to other places. Second, it should contain places to sit or rest, to be comfortable. Finally, it must be large enough so that the people gathered there won't interfere with others passing through or working nearby. Of course, if you want to discourage contact at a central spot (the copying machine, for example), simply change one or more of these conditions.

When it comes to managing interaction between members of an organization and its public, you can create the most desirable degree of accessibility by use of space and barriers. Proximity and visibility encourage contact, while distance and closure discourage it.

SUMMARY

Whatever the goal and whatever the context, business and professional communication involves both verbal and nonverbal messages. Verbal messages are most clear when they contain unequivocal and nonabstract language and a minimum of unfamiliar jargon. While clarity is usually the goal, ambiguous messages are sometimes useful ways of promoting harmony, facilitating change, and softening the blow of difficult messages.

Language can sometimes communicate and generate undesirable emotions. Biased terms seem to be objective but actually convey the speaker's attitudes. Trigger words arouse strong emotional reactions in a listener. Effective communicators avoid unintentionally biased language and trigger words.

Social scientists have discovered that men and women typically use speech for different purposes and in different ways. Female language emphasizes rapport, the creation and maintenance of relationships, to a greater degree than male speech, which is focused more on the "report" function of communication: accomplishing the task at hand and asserting control over the situation.

Sexual harassment is a combination of verbal and nonverbal behavior that has been recognized as illegal and inappropriate in the workplace.

What counts as harassment depends in great part on the perceptions of the person who sees himself or herself as the victim. This means that communicators must be sensitive to others' reactions, since their good intentions are not enough to avoid accusations of harassment. People who perceive themselves as victims of harassment in the workplace have a number of options available, ranging from informal to formal.

Nonverbal communication also carries a great deal of meaning, but where words normally express ideas, nonverbal behavior conveys attitudes and emotions. Nonverbal messages are always available, since it is impossible to avoid communicating nonverbally. These messages should be interpreted with caution, however, since they are usually ambiguous and are often culture-bound. Nonverbal messages can be expressed vocally, through appearance (physical stature and clothing), and through the face, eyes, posture, gesture, distance, and time.

The physical environment in which an organization operates also has an important effect on communication, both internal and external. The location and design of a building often makes a statement to employees and the public about the organization's philosophy and power structure. In addition, the spatial arrangement of units can make interaction beween them easy or difficult, and it can also indicate their relative perceived importance. The type and arrangement of space and objects within a given area also have a strong effect on communication, affecting who talks with whom, the amount of interaction, and the quality of that interaction.

RESOURCES

DePaulo, P. J., "Applications of Nonverbal Behavior Research in Marketing and Management," in R. S. Feldman (Ed.), *Applications of Nonverbal Behavioral Theories and Research* (Hillsdale, N.J.: Erlbaum, 1992).

This chapter describes how advertisers and salespeople have used the findings of nonverbal researchers to promote the products they represent. The chapter also discusses how nonverbal cues have been applied to hiring and job assignments, performance appraisal, leadership, and job security.

Kreps, G. L. (Ed.), *Sexual Harassment: Communication Implications* (Cresskill, N.J.: Hampton Press, 1993).

Nearly twenty different articles by leading scholars provide a varied and comprehensive analysis of sexual harassment. Policies are discussed, case studies are included, and the reader is presented with strategies for personal and organizational responses to reduce and eliminate harassment in the workplace.

Richmond, V. P., and J. C. McCroskey, *Nonverbal Behavior in Interpersonal Relations,* 3rd ed. (Boston: Allyn and Bacon, 1995).

This text has very practical readable chapters on nine different nonverbal codes. In addition, business and professional communicators will find the chapter on supervisor-subordinate relationships especially applicable.

Tannen, Deborah, *Talking from 9 to 5: How Women's and Men's Conversational Styles Affect Who Gets Heard, Who Gets Credit, and What Gets Done at Work* (New York: Morrow, 1994).

In this popular follow-up to her best-seller, *You Just Don't Understand,* Tannen analyzes the effects of conversational style differences in the workplace. This very readable book is packed with insights which affect how we evaluate each other as we talk on the job.

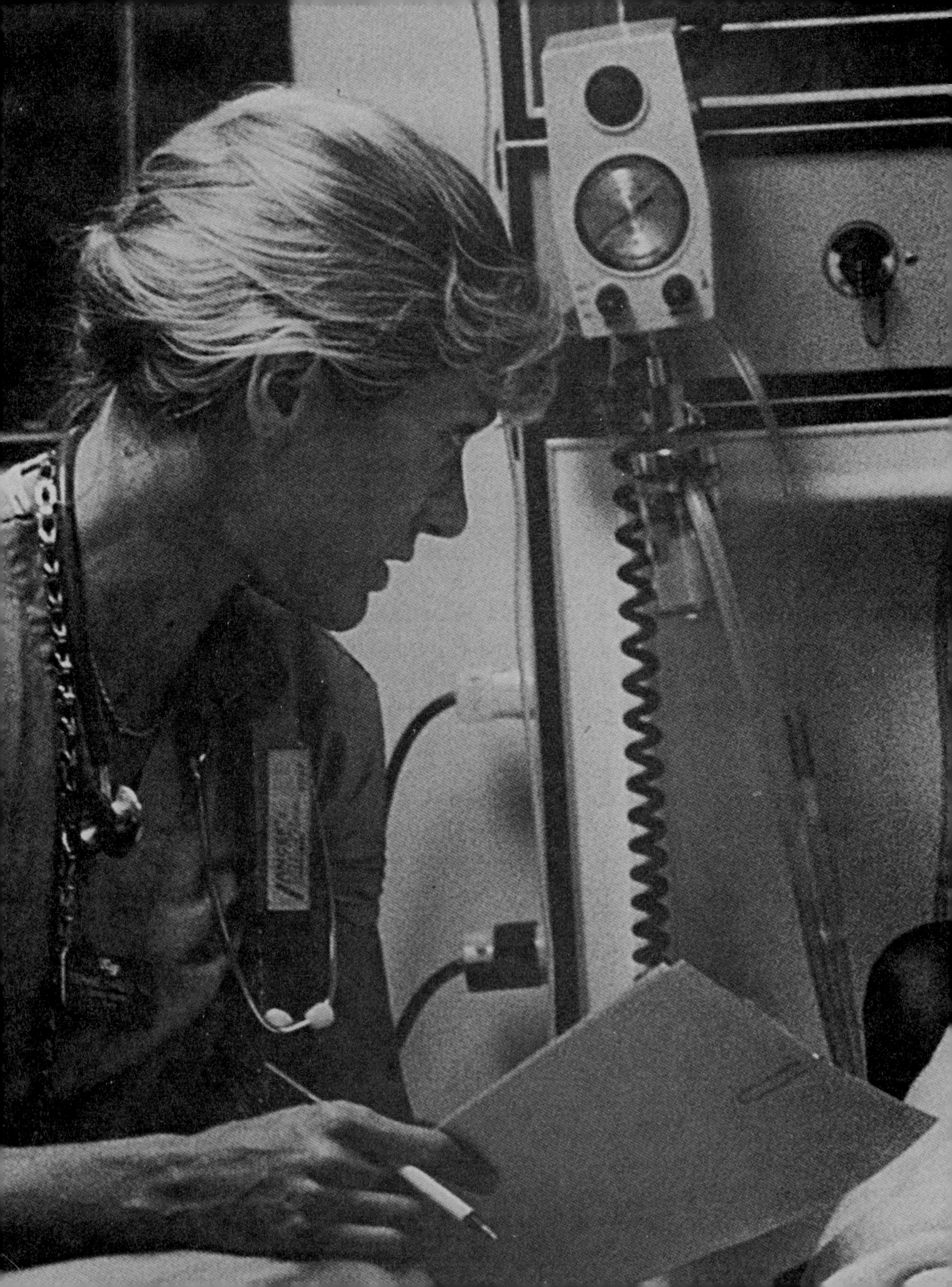

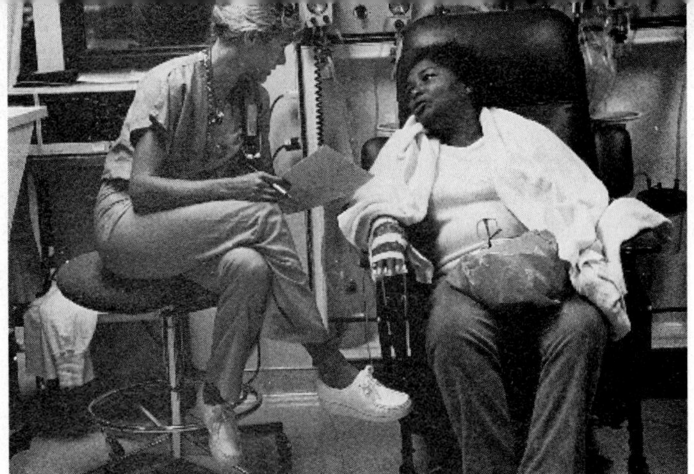

CHAPTER 4

Listening

KEY TERMS

Advising / Analyzing / Counterfeit questions / Paraphrasing / Passive listening / Questioning / Sincere questions / Supporting

> "I told him we were meeting *this* Tuesday, not *next* Tuesday. Now we have to reschedule the meeting. It'll cost us a week's time, and we may not make the deadline."
>
> "He said he was listening, but he'd obviously made up his mind before I started. He didn't give me a minute to talk before he started interrupting. That's the last time I'll try to present a better way to do anything around here!"
>
> "Something went wrong down the line. I warned those people to watch the temperature carefully, but they don't listen. Now a whole batch is spoiled. What does it take to get them to understand?"

Situations like these are disturbingly common in business. They show how frequent listening failures are and how costly they can be. You may not be able to make others listen better, but you *can* boost your own ability to listen carefully to the scores of important messages you are likely to hear every business day.

As you will learn in the following pages, listening effectively is hard work. It involves far more than sitting passively and absorbing others' words. It occurs far more frequently than speaking, reading, or writing and is just as demanding and important.

THE IMPORTANCE OF LISTENING

Business experts agree that listening is a vitally important skill. In his best-selling book, Stephen Covey identifies it as one of the "seven habits of highly effective people."[1] Tom Peters, business consultant and co-author of *In Search of Excellence* and *A Passion for Excellence,* is sometimes called the "guru of excellence." He emphasizes that one key to business success is careful listening: "Find out what the customers really care about, and then act. Listening—that's the key."[2] Betty Harragan, a business consultant and job counselor who has written two career-strategy books, states, "Good managers have always sought, or listened to the opinions of their staff and key subordinates."[3] Business writer Kevin Murphy sums up the opinion of most business professionals when he says, "The better you listen, the luckier you will get."[4]

Why is listening so important? One major reason is time: listening is the most frequent—and, arguably, the most important—type of on-the-job communication. Studies conducted over sixty years ago indicated that adults spent

> My correspondence occupies many a file cabinet after years of dealing with managers in turbulent conditions. The most moving letters by far are the hundreds about "simple listening." In fact, if I had a file labeled "religious conversion"—that is, correspondence from those whose management practices have truly been transformed—I suspect that 50 percent of its contents would deal with just one narrow topic . . . listening to customers.
>
> Tom Peters, "Learning to Listen."

an average of 29.5 percent of their waking hours listening. This is almost a third more time than they spent talking and virtually twice as much time as they spent reading.[5] A more recent study focused on listening in business settings. Personnel at all levels—including top-, middle-, and lower-level managers as well as workers with no managerial responsibilities—were asked to note the time they spent engaged in various types of communication during a typical week.[6] The results were impressive:

Listening	32.7%	Writing	22.6%
Speaking	25.8%	Reading	18.8%

Top executives spend even more time listening than other employees. Researchers have found that executives spend between 65 and 90 percent of the working day listening to someone.[7] Another piece of research revealed that effective managers almost constantly ask questions of their subordinates; in a half-hour conversation, some ask literally hundreds.[8]

Listening on the job is not only frequent; it is important as well. When 282 members of the Academy of Certified Administrative Managers were asked to list the skills most crucial for managerial ability, "active listening" was rated number one and was placed in the "supercritical" category.[9] In another survey, 170 businesspeople were asked to describe the communication skills that they considered most important and that they wished had been taught in college; in each category, listening was the number-one response.[10] Listening is vital to organizations. It can improve quality, boost productivity, and save money. Poor listening can have the opposite effect. As one consultant says:

> With more than 100 million workers in this country, a simple $10 listening mistake by each of them, as a result of poor listening, would add up to a cost of a billion dollars. And most people make numerous listening mistakes every week.
>
> Because of listening mistakes, letters have to be retyped, appointments rescheduled, shipments rerouted. Productivity is affected and profits suffer.[11]

Listening skills can play a major role in career success. Job hunters can often find leads and succeed in employment interviews by keeping their ears open.[12] Listening is just as important once you are on the job. A study of employees in the insurance industry revealed that better listeners occupied higher levels in their company and were more upwardly mobile.[13] The ability to listen well was highly related to the ability to argue persuasively, which helps explain the success of good listeners. Supervisors who were rated as "open" communicators displayed a surprising number of behaviors that indicate good listening.[14] They were likely to ask for suggestions, listen to complaints, and invite personal opinions of both their superiors and subordinates.

Listening skills are important in a variety of careers. Salespeople who listen to their customers can discover their needs and build rapport. As one consulting team says, "Showing a real interest in what prospective customers are saying is one of the simplest ways of getting them to listen to you."[15] Health-care providers are more effective at gathering accurate information from patients and creating positive climates when using "patient-centered" listening instead of "caregiver-centered" listening.[16] From hotels to high-tech computer services, from auto repair to financial institutions, service industries are the fastest-growing segment of the U.S. economy. "Good service, in many respects, is good listening," according to Judi Brownell of Cornell University. "In order to thrive in highly competitive, rapidly changing environments, service employees must learn to listen well."[17]

BARRIERS TO EFFECTIVE LISTENING

Despite the importance of understanding others, the quality of listening is generally poor in most organizations. Research suggests that misunderstandings are the rule, rather than the exception. Conversational partners typically achieve no more than 25 to 50 percent accuracy in interpreting each other's remarks.[18] Listening expert Ralph Nichols echoes this dismal assessment. He estimates that the average white-collar worker listens at about a 25 percent efficiency level.[19] This dismal figure is supported by research showing that immediately after a ten-minute presentation, a normal listener can recall only 50 percent of the information presented. After forty-eight hours, the recall level drops to 25 percent.[20]

Despite the widespread problem of poor listening, most business communicators don't see themselves as lacking in this skill. (You can begin to evaluate your own listening skill by completing the questionnaire in Table 4-1). In one study, subordinates were asked to rate the listening ability of their bosses. More than half put their managers in the "poor" category. When the same managers were asked to rate themselves, 94 percent described themselves as "good" or "very good" listeners! A number of studies have revealed reasons why people listen poorly, despite the advantages of doing just the opposite.[21]

Posted beside the water fountain or the copy machine or mounted in the cafeteria or inside the boss's office in companies small and large throughout America is this little industrial ditty: "I know you believe you understand what you think I said, but I am not sure you realize that what you heard is not what I meant."

There's supposed to be a lesson here, something like: "Listen better." It's meant to cause employees to evaluate themselves and to improve their listening. Trouble is, the single person per month who actually stops and evaluates his/her listening concludes that he/she is an OK listener. It's all those other numskulls that need to learn how to listen.

The message also is obscured by the clear fact that you don't know that you are a poor listener because you've never heard what you've missed. That is, you are unaware of what you haven't heard for the simple reason that you've never heard it.

John Tschohl, "Hot Service Tip: Just Listen!"

TABLE 4-1 Listening-Skill Questionnaire

How well do you listen on the job? How do others rate you? You can compare your answers to these questions to the way others view you by first completing the questionnaire yourself and then having others use the same questions to rate you. Low answers (UF, AAF) can indicate problem areas, as can instances in which your response differs significantly from others' ratings.

KEY:

AAT	The statement is almost always true.
UT	The statement is usually true.
UF	The statement is usually false.
AAF	The statement is almost always false.

AAT	UT	UF	AAF	**1.** I consider all evidence carefully before coming to a conclusion.
AAT	UT	UF	AAF	**2.** I am sensitive to the speaker's unstated feelings as well as to what he or she says explicitly.
AAT	UT	UF	AAF	**3.** I take notes when listening in order to remember information or better understand a complex idea.
AAT	UT	UF	AAF	**4.** I concentrate on what the speaker is saying instead of dwelling on unrelated thoughts.
AAT	UT	UF	AAF	**5.** I listen openly when others disagree with me. I may not accept what they say, but I'm willing to consider their opinions.
AAT	UT	UF	AAF	**6.** I encourage others to express their ideas instead of hogging the stage myself.
AAT	UT	UF	AAF	**7.** I am able to extract key ideas from others' comments, even when their remarks are disorganized.
AAT	UT	UF	AAF	**8.** I am curious about people and ideas. Nobody could accuse me of valuing only my own ideas.
AAT	UT	UF	AAF	**9.** I let others speak instead of interrupting them or changing the topic of conversation to suit my agenda.
AAT	UT	UF	AAF	**10.** I make other speakers feel comfortable and at ease when they are talking.
AAT	UT	UF	AAF	**11.** I remember important ideas others have told me, even when I'm busy.
AAT	UT	UF	AAF	**12.** I let others know when I'm confused about what they are saying instead of pretending that I understand when I really don't.
AAT	UT	UF	AAF	**13.** I recognize that people change over time, and I accept new information instead of judging others only by their past beliefs and actions.
AAT	UT	UF	AAF	**14.** I help others find solutions to their problems by being a good listener.
AAT	UT	UF	AAF	**15.** I can cut through overly emotional appeals and judge the soundness of a speaker's thoughts.
AAT	UT	UF	AAF	**16.** I am good at knowing when to speak and when to listen.

Source: After Judi Brownell, "Perceptions of Listening Behavior: A Management Study," SHA Research Workshop (December 1987).

Physiological Barriers

Hearing Problems. For some people, poor listening results from actual hearing deficiencies. Once recognized, they can usually be treated. An undetected hearing loss may cause employees to get annoyed about the boss's ignoring them or cause a supervisor to get angry when her instructions are bungled. Other people may have auditory processing difficulties, such as auditory discrimination, sequencing, or memory, which create the appearance of not listening or paying attention to what is said but are actually the result of physiological involvement, not intentional disregard.

Rapid Thought. Listeners can process information at a rate of about 500 words per minute, while most speakers talk at around 125 words per minute. This difference leaves us with a great deal of mental spare time. While it is possible to use this time to explore the speaker's ideas, we most often let our minds wander to other matters—from the unfinished business just mentioned to romantic fantasies.

Environmental Barriers

Physical Distractions. A stuffy room, noisy machinery, the cold you feel developing, or a conversation going on nearby are only a few of the distractions that can make listening difficult. Next time you decide not to listen to a speaker, use the spare thinking time to notice all the distractions in the environment.

Message Overload. It is hard to listen carefully when the phone rings every few minutes, people keep dropping in to give you quick messages, a coworker has just handed you cost estimates on a new product line, and your computer continuously beeps to let you know you have incoming mail or scheduled appointments. Coping with a deluge of information is like juggling—you can keep only a few things going at one time.

Attitudinal Barriers

Preoccupation. Business and personal concerns can make it difficult to keep your mind on the subject at hand. Even when your current conversation is important, other unfinished business can divert your attention: the call to

ETHICAL CHALLENGE

Most business experts agree that listening is a vital communication skill. But realists acknowledge that it is impossible to give equal attention to every message and still accomplish the multitude of tasks that occupy every workday.

How can you, as a busy worker, respond to nonessential messages without alienating the people who deliver them?

an angry customer, the questions your boss asked about your schedule delays, the new supplier you heard about and want to interview, and the problems you have with the baby-sitter or the auto mechanic.

Egocentrism. One common reason for listening poorly is the belief—usually mistaken—that your own ideas are more important or valuable than those of others. Besides preventing you from learning useful new information, this egocentric attitude is likely to alienate the very people with whom you need to work. Self-centered listeners are rated lower on social attractiveness than communicators who are open to others' ideas.[22] While a certain amount of self-promotion can be helpful in career advancement, advancing your own ideas at the expense of others' can cause you to slip down a rung or two as you climb the career ladder. As an old saying puts it: "Nobody ever listened themselves out of a job."

Faulty Assumptions

Some of the biggest obstacles to listening don't involve physiological or environmental problems. Instead, they come from inaccurate and unproductive assumptions.

Assuming That Effective Communication Is the Sender's Responsibility. Management expert Peter Drucker recognized that communication depends on the receiver as well as the sender when he wrote: "It is the recipient who communicates. The so-called communicator, the person who emits the communication, does not communicate. He utters. Unless there is someone who hears . . . there is only noise."[23]

As Drucker suggests, even the most thoughtful, well-expressed idea is wasted if the intended receiver fails to listen. The clearest instructions won't prevent mistakes if the employee receiving them is thinking about something else, and the best of products will never be made if the client or the manager isn't paying attention to the presentation. Both the speaker *and* the listener share the burden of reaching an understanding.

Assuming That Listening Is Passive. Some communicators mistakenly assume that listening is basically a passive activity in which the receiver is a sponge, quietly absorbing the speaker's thoughts. In fact, good listening can be hard work. Sometimes you have to speak while listening—to ask questions or paraphrase the sender's ideas, making sure you have understood them. Even when you remain silent, silence should not be mistaken for passivity. Famous attorney Louis Nizer described how he would often emerge

> We can communicate an idea around the world in seventy seconds, but it sometimes takes years for an idea to get through ¼ inch of human skull.
>
> Charles Kettering, inventor and General Motors executive

dripping with sweat from a day in court spent mostly listening. Sperry executive Del Kennedy, commenting on his company's well-known listening training program, says "Most people don't know how exhausting listening can be."[24]

Assuming That Talking Has More Advantages than Listening. At first glance, it seems that speakers control things while listeners are the followers. Western society seems to correlate listening with weakness, passivity, and lack of authority or power.[25] The people who do the talking are the ones who capture everyone's attention, so it is easy to understand how talking can be viewed as the pathway to success.

Despite the value of talking, savvy businesspeople understand that listening is equally important, especially in a fast-moving, high-tech age. Communication expert Susan Peterson explains:

> Back to basics. Actually, the best basic of all; the ability to listen . . . is a vital communication tool that's endangered, in my humble opinion, by all this technology. Too many times, whether it's with e-mail, voice mail or Internet, we are concentrating on the art of telling, not listening. Yet good listening, in my opinion, is 80 to 90 percent of being a good manager and an effective leader. One CEO who has 54,000 employees says he concentrates on what he calls organizational listening. . . . Listening is one of the best ways to keep high touch in your organization. In your day-to-day meetings with customers, clients, or employees, if you listen—really listen with full eye contact and attention, you can own the keys to the communication kingdom.[26]

Writer and management professor David J. Schwartz makes the point more succinctly:

> In an office recently I noticed a sign which said, "To sell John Brown what John Brown buys, you've got to see things through John Brown's eyes." And the way to get John Brown's vision is to listen to what John Brown has to say.[27]

Schwartz goes on to stress the value of listening:

> In hundreds of interviews with people at all levels I've made this discovery: The bigger the person, the more apt he is to encourage *you* to talk; the smaller the person, the more apt he is to preach to you.

I have known some of the most powerful minds who found it difficult to influence their surroundings, to influence their companies, and to gain influence in proportion to their abilities because they could not listen. . . . I can think of two right off the bat and they were both in key jobs in the company. Neither of them is here right now. The reason they left and the reason they couldn't influence the company to the extent they should have is that they both had this crazy defect: They couldn't listen.

They were articulate. They were eloquent. They were brilliant. They were knowledgeable, but they talked and talked. And they never listened. As a result they found it difficult to get across to management.

Jack E. Goldman, senior vice-president and senior scientist, Xerox Corp.

Big people monopolize the *listening.*

Small people monopolize the *talking.*[28]

Sociocultural Differences

Some listening problems come from the differing styles of each communicator. Some arise from cultural communication styles, while others come from differences between typically male and female communication styles.

Cultural Differences. Accent is often the most obvious difference when people from different cultures communicate. A different accent can be a source of psychological noise when it interferes with your ability to understand and appreciate the words of someone whose pronunciation differs from yours. Some communicators mistakenly assume that accented speakers are less intelligent and less able to understand them.[29] Differing accents aren't just a problem in international communication. They can also interfere with communication between speakers from different co-cultures. For example, researchers have found that African-American and Euro-American women hear very different things when speaking to each other.[30] White women tend to hear their own speech as being "normal or universal," and focus on African-American women's pronunciation and grammar (instead of focusing on the message itself), whereas African-American women (who are more used to hearing different styles of speech) find it easier to accept each accent as legitimate.

Some cultural differences are much more subtle than accent. The amount of time that should be spent listening is an example of one such difference. Euro-Americans tend to put great value on time, often measuring status by how much time someone of higher status "spends" on them. Anything perceived as a waste of time is viewed negatively. Time is often treated as a commodity, as evidenced by such terms as "make time," "use time," "have time," and "waste time." Euro-Americans also have a cultural bias toward doing rather than being. They measure accomplishments in terms of things produced. Communicators raised with these orientations may view listening as wasting time, because it is not immediately clear what has been produced by taking the time to hear out another person. When interacting with Asians, U.S. businesspeople may find it very difficult to listen, as much time is spent engaging in small talk or having tea, rather than "getting down to business."[31] The same issues may arise in U.S. business relationships with Latin Americans and Middle Easterners, who also value time spent on speaking and listening to information about families before business. However, time spent on listening in this way is of great importance to the overall relationship.

Culture also influences a communicator's attitude about silence—a big part of listening. African-Americans and Euro-Americans tend to value speaking over listening and talk over silence.[32] Westerners often feel uncomfortable with long silences and want to fill them in with speech. By contrast, Native Americans and Japanese and other Asians regard silence as an important part of communication.[33] It is easy to imagine how a Westerner, uncomfortable with an Asian's silence, would fill in conversational gaps that seemed perfectly normal to a Korean or Navajo. In the same way, an Asian who wants to communicate successfully with a Euro-American would need to spend more time vocalizing.

Gender Differences. Popular magazines are fond of asking, "Who listens better, men or women?" This question is not as helpful as asking, "Do men and women listen differently?" Research shows that, to at least some degree, the answer is yes.[34] By understanding the differences, men and women can do a better job of listening to and understanding one another.

Women often pay more attention to the kinds of relational messages described in Chapter 1, while men often pay more attention to information on the content level. Both men and women may not recognize important messages because they listen for different purposes. Consider a simple example: A computer programmer, when asked by two users if a particular software package will work, may reply, "Sure." The male user may focus on the content of the answer and take the statement at face value. The female user may tune in to the speaker's vocal tone and hear some hesitation or annoyance. Later on, the two users might disagree about what the programmer meant because they listened to different aspects of the response.

Another gender-related difference involves "listening noises"—vocalizers such as "uh-huh" and "ummm" that signal attention. Researchers have discovered that men and women often use and interpret listening noises differently.[35] Women may use them to signal attention, men to signal agreement. Thus, a woman who says "uh-huh" may mean "I'm listening," while a man hearing this utterance would think that his female partner agrees. Once communicators are aware of differences like these, they can clarify the meaning of ambiguous vocal cues: "You seem interested in the idea I'm presenting. Do you agree that we should get started on it?"[36]

Men and women may hear different parts of a message because they listen for different purposes. Women are more likely to catch the feelings behind a speaker's words, while men tend to listen for the facts.[37] For example, at a committee meeting, a colleague is asked to redo a report. He says, "Sure." After the meeting, a female colleague may comment on how upset the person was and his reluctance to redo the report. She "heard" the feelings. A male colleague may respond, "What's the problem? He said he'd do it." Communicators who recognize this difference may choose to make any important feelings explicit when they are speaking to one or more men.

Gender differences don't just affect *how* we listen to one another; they also influence *whether* we listen at all. Well-known sociolinguist Deborah Tannen states: "All else being equal, women are not as likely to be listened to as men, regardless of how they speak or what they say."[38] In business meetings, it is not uncommon for an idea presented by a woman to be ignored or downplayed, while the same idea presented by a man receives more attention. Listeners who are aware of this tendency can train themselves to give equal attention to

INVITATION TO INSIGHT

1. Recall three on-the-job incidents in which you had difficulty listening effectively. For each incident, describe which of the following factors interfered with your listening effectiveness:

   Physiological barriers
   - Hearing problems
   - Rapid thought

   Environmental barriers
   - Physical distractions
   - Message overload

   Attitudinal barriers
   - Preoccupation
   - Egocentrism

   Faulty assumptions
   - Assuming that effective communication is the sender's responsibility
   - Assuming that listening is passive
   - Assuming that talking has more advantages than listening

   Sociocultural differences
   - Culture
   - Gender

   Lack of training

2. Develop a list of ways you could overcome the greatest barriers that prevent you from listening more effectively.

the messages of every communicator regardless of sex. One way to be more attentive to the ideas of everyone in a meeting is to systematically give equal time and attention to each person or to post the ideas in writing.

Lack of Training

Listening may seem like a natural ability—like breathing. "After all," you might say, "I've been listening since I was a child." We could all say the same thing about talking; but even though almost everyone does it, this doesn't mean most people do it well.

Some businesses spend thousands of dollars on training, yet they fail to include training on listening in their workshops.[39] Most organizations, including major corporations such as 3M, American Telephone and Telegraph, General Electric, and Dun and Bradstreet, know better. They have included listening skills in their training programs.[40] Xerox Corporation's program for improving listening has been used by over 1.5 million employees in 71,000 companies, and Sperry Corporation invested more than $4 million to advertise its message: "We know how important it is to listen." In addition, Sperry set up listening seminars for its 87,000 employees in an effort to make its advertising campaign more than a string of empty slogans.

> I only wish I could find an institute that teaches people how to *listen*. After all, a good manager needs to listen at least as much as he needs to talk. Too many people fail to realize that real communication goes in both directions. . . .
>
> You have to be able to listen well if you're going to motivate the people who work for you. Right there, that's the difference between a mediocre company and a great company. The most fulfilling thing for me as a manager is to watch someone the system has labeled as just average or mediocre really come into his own, all because someone has listened to his problems and helped him solve them.
>
> Lee Iacocca with William Novak, *Iacocca: An Autobiography*

APPROACHES TO LISTENING

Just as a carpenter or chef uses different tools to tackle a job, listeners can take advantage of several skills for listening and responding to messages at work. This section will examine each one.

Passive Listening

Sometimes the best approach to listening is to stay out of the way and encourage the other person to talk. ***Passive listening*** involves a mixture of silence and prompts that invite the speaker to keep going: "Uh-huh," "Really?" "Tell me more," and so on. Nonverbal cues that indicate a genuine interest are an important part of passive listening. Eye contact, attentive posture, and appropriate facial expressions show that you are tuned in to the other person.

Passive listening is often the best approach when the spotlight is on the speaker, especially in formal presentations and in those attended by a large audience. You probably can recall feeling annoyed when a speaker's prepared remarks were interrupted constantly by a questioner who was oblivious to the desire of every other audience member to keep quiet and hear what the speaker had to say.

In one-to-one settings passive listening might seem both easy and obvious . . . until you reflect on how often communicators interrupt to insert their own position. You can prove the value and difficulty of passive listening by consciously trying this approach the next time someone approaches you with an important topic.

Questioning

Sincere questions are genuine requests for information. They can be a terrific way to gather facts and details, clarify meanings, and encourage a speaker to elaborate. Not all questions, however, reflect a genuine desire to understand a speaker. ***Counterfeit questions*** are really a disguised attempt to send a message, not receive one. Counterfeit questions come in several forms:[41]

- *Questions that make statements or offer advice.* "Isn't that pretty expensive?" Or "Did you think that it might be cheaper to hire a consultant?"
- *Questions that trap or attack the speaker.* "Are you sure there are no mistakes in this report?" (when the speaker knows there are). Or "Didn't I tell you it wouldn't work?"

> Silence has so many different selling applications. If you stop talking and start listening, you might actually learn something, and even if you don't you'll have a chance to collect your thoughts. Silence is what keeps you from saying more than you need to—and makes the other person want to say more than he means to.
>
> Mark McCormack, *What They Don't Teach You at Harvard Business School*

My first boss . . . is one of the smartest people I know. He was smart enough and comfortable enough with himself to ask really elementary (some would say dumb) questions. The rest of us were scared stiff; we assumed that since we were being paid an exorbitant fee, we shouldn't ask dumb questions. But the result was we'd lose 90 percent of the strategic value of the interview because we were afraid to display our ignorance.

Mostly, it's the "dumb," elementary questions, followed up by a dozen more elementary questions, that yield the pay dirt.

Tom Peters, *Thriving on Chaos*

- *Questions that carry hidden agendas.* "Are you caught up with your work?" (If the answer is "Yes," the next sentence is "Good. Then you could give me a hand with this job.")
- *Questions that seek "correct" answers.* "You don't have any problems with that, do you?"

No question is inherently counterfeit. Each of the examples above could be a sincere request for information. Furthermore, indirect questions can be a face-saving way to avoid embarrassing confrontations. But when the speaker's motive doesn't seem genuine, or if it doesn't seem to be in the receiver's best interests, counterfeit questions can pollute a communication climate just as quickly as any direct attack.[42]

Paraphrasing

Paraphrasing occurs when you restate a speaker's ideas in your own words, to make sure that you have understood them correctly and to show the other person that fact. Paraphrasing makes the usually private process of decoding a message explicit. Paraphrasing is often preceded by phrases such as "Let me make sure I understand what you're saying . . ." or "In other words, you're saying. . . ." When you are paraphrasing, it is important *not* to become a parrot, repeating the speaker's statements word for word. Understanding comes from translating the speaker's thoughts into your own language and then playing them back to ensure their accuracy.

The following conversations illustrate the difference between effective and ineffective paraphrasing:

Print supervisor:	I'm having trouble getting the paper to run that job. That's why I'm behind schedule.
Plant manager:	I see. You can't get the paper to run the job, so you're running behind schedule.
Print supervisor:	Yeah. That's what I said.

After this exchange, the plant manager still doesn't have a clear idea of the problem—why the print supervisor can't get the paper, or what he means when he says he can't get it. Effective paraphrasing, however, could help to get to the root of the problem:

Print supervisor:	I'm having trouble getting the paper to run that job. That's why I'm running behind schedule.
Plant manager:	In other words, your paper supplier hasn't shipped the paper you need for this job.
Print supervisor:	No, they shipped it, but it's full of flaws.
Plant manager:	So the whole shipment is bad.
Print supervisor:	No, only about a third of it. But I've got to get the whole batch replaced, or the dye lots won't match—the paper won't be exactly the same color.
Plant manager:	No problem—the colors can be a little off. But I have to have at least half of that order by Tuesday; the rest can wait a couple of weeks. Can you print on the good paper you have now, then do the rest when the new paper comes in?
Print supervisor:	Sure.

At first glance, questioning and paraphrasing may seem identical, but a closer look reveals that they are different tools. Questions seek new, additional information ("How far behind are we?" "When did it begin?"), while paraphrasing clarifies what a speaker has said. This is an important difference. Your personal experience probably shows that we often think we understand another person only to find later that we were wrong. Paraphrasing is a practical technique that can highlight misunderstandings. People who practice paraphrasing are astonished to find out how many times a speaker will correct or add information to a message that had seemed perfectly clear.

There are three types of paraphrasing. Although each of them reflects the speaker's message, each focuses on a different part of that statement.

Paraphrasing Content. The example above illustrates this most basic kind of paraphrasing, which plays back the receiver's understanding of the explicit message. It is easy to think you understand another person only to find later that you were wrong. At its most basic level, paraphrasing is a kind of safety check that can highlight and clarify misunderstandings. People who practice paraphrasing are astonished to find out how many times a speaker will correct or add information to a message that had seemed perfectly clear.

Paraphrasing Intent. Besides helping you understand *what* others are saying, paraphrasing can help you learn *why* they have spoken up. Imagine that, at a staff meeting, the boss announces, "Next week, we'll start using this display board to show when we're out of the office and where we've gone." It's easy to imagine two quite different reasons for setting up this

SKILL BUILDER

Practice your skill at questioning and paraphrasing by trying the following activity:

1. Choose a person who will talk about one of the following topics:

   How to perform a task
   How to advance in your career
   How to defend a co-worker whose behavior you disapprove of

2. In each conversation, use both questioning and paraphrasing to *understand* the speaker. The measure of your understanding should be your ability to restate the speaker's position in your own words to his or her satisfaction.
3. Now answer the following questions:
   a. Was paraphrasing difficult? Why?
   b. Did you learn any useful information in the conversations? Would you have gained as much by responding in your more usual manner?
   c. How could you use paraphrasing and sincere questioning to help in your everyday work?

procedure: (1) to help keep customers and colleagues informed about where each person is and when he or she will return, or (2) to keep track of employees because the boss suspects that some are slacking off on company time. Paraphrasing intent can help you understand what people mean when they make statements that can be interpreted in more than one way.

Paraphrasing Feeling. Often, the speaker's feelings are the most important part of a message. Despite this fact, most people don't express—or even recognize—their emotions. Ask yourself what emotions might be contained in these statements:

1. "That's the third time he canceled an appointment on me—who does he think he is?"
2. "Whenever a deadline comes, I get excuses instead of results—this can't go on much longer."
3. "One minute she says we have to spend money to make money, and the next minute she talks about cutting costs—I can't figure out what she really wants."

In each example there are at least two or three possible emotions:

1. Anger, hurt, and self-doubt
2. Anger, frustration, and worry
3. Anger and confusion

Paraphrasing the apparent emotion can give the speaker a chance to agree with or contradict your interpretation: "Yeah, I guess it did hurt my feelings," or "I'm more worried than mad." In either case, this sort of response can help the other person to clarify how he or she is feeling and to deal with the emotions.

REASONS FOR LISTENING

There are several reasons why communicators listen. Sometimes you listen for information. In other circumstances, you need to evaluate others' arguments critically. Finally, from time to time, you need to listen as a way of helping others solve their problems.

Listening for Information

This is the most common type of listening in most occupations. We use informational listening to understand a wide variety of messages accurately: a caller's phone number, a supervisor's instructions, a subordinate's problems, a customer's needs. The following strategies can improve your ability to understand informational messages.

Withhold Judgment. It is often difficult to try to understand another person's ideas before judging them, especially when you hold very strong opinions on the matter under discussion. For example, you might ask for a customer's reaction to your company's product or service and then spend your mental energy judging the answer instead of trying to understand it. ("Doesn't this guy have anything better to do than make petty complaints?" "Yeah, sure, he'd like us to deliver on a tighter schedule, but he'd scream his head off if we billed him for the overtime.") Or you might find yourself judging the ideas of a boss, co-worker, or subordinate before he or she has finished explaining them. ("Uh-oh. I hope this doesn't mean I have to spend a week in the field, trying to get market information." "These college kids come in and want to take over right away.") Listen first. Make sure you understand. Then evaluate.

Be Opportunistic. Sometimes a speaker's ideas are so boring or irrelevant that it's hard to stay awake, let alone pay close attention. Still, in situations like this, you can often find reasons to listen by asking yourself how you can use the information. One trainer described this opportunistic approach:

> At a convention recently I found myself in an extremely boring seminar (on listening, ironically enough). After spending the first half-hour wishing I had never signed up, I decided to take advantage of the situation. I turned my thought, "This guy isn't teaching me how to run a seminar on listening," into a question: "What is he teaching me about how *not* to run a seminar?" While providing a negative example was not the presenter's goal, I got a useful lesson.

> Be interested in the topic under discussion. Bad listeners usually declare the subject dry after the first few sentences.
>
> We ought to say to ourselves: "What's he saying that I can use? What worthwhile ideas has he? Is he reporting any workable procedures? Anything that I can cash in, or with which I can make myself happier?"
>
> Ralph Nichols, "Listening Is a 10-Part Skill"

You can use the same technique in your life. Ask yourself the question "What's a better way of explaining this?" Your answer will often clarify your understanding. Similarly, asking yourself what you *don't* understand about a topic can help you formulate questions that will improve your knowledge. Perhaps the best question to ask in boring settings is "What does this have to do with me, anyhow?" You can probably find an answer and in doing so learn some valuable information.

Look for the Main and Supporting Points. "What are you getting at?" We are often tempted to ask this of a long-winded speaker, but it's also an ideal question to consider when you're listening for information. Sometimes it is appropriate to ask—politely—for the speaker's thesis: "I'm trying to pull together what you've been telling me about the problems you've been having meeting your quotas. Could you summarize for me?" "I'd like to be sure the procedure we work out meets your needs as fully as possible. Could you tell me, briefly, which of these problems are the most damaging?" Sometimes, however, it isn't appropriate to ask for the speaker's thesis outright. When you're one of five hundred employees sitting in a darkened banquet room while senior executives try to promote corporate unity by giving short descriptions of what each of their divisions has done that year, you probably shouldn't ask, "Overall, then, would you say your division is losing its market share?" You can still do your own mental job of organizing and looking for patterns in this kind of situation.

Take Notes. Students know they need notes to recall important information for a test. Note taking can be just as valuable in business settings.[43] You are unlikely to remember every deadline, every comment, or even every topic in a meeting or conversation unless you jot it down. This doesn't mean that you have to scribble every word in every setting, but when the topic is important, put it in writing.

Repeat What You Heard. It isn't always possible to take notes, and repetition works well in such cases. Remember that untrained listeners remember only about half of what they hear immediately after hearing it and then only half of that after forty-eight hours. One way to minimize this loss is to go over the important parts of a message as soon as possible. For best results, restate these ideas aloud—to a co-worker, your secretary or assistant, or a friend. Some businesspeople who have access to a typing and dictation pool describe important ideas into a Dictaphone and get a typed record the next day.

Which is better, taking notes or repeating ideas aloud? Notes work reasonably well when they are taken on the spot, especially for recording specific facts such as dates, figures, or people to contact. They aren't especially helpful for recalling ideas or plans, though. When you describe aloud the ideas you've heard, you will find yourself bringing in details that don't come up or seem important when you try to construct an outline on paper.

Evaluative Listening

When faced with a speaker who is trying to persuade you, the proper attitude is one of evaluation. What are the speaker's motives? How accurate are the speaker's facts? Predictions? Do you need what the speaker is trying to "sell"?

The most obvious type of persuasion involves selling in the literal sense. But selling goes on in many other contexts as well. When you try to persuade your boss to adopt an idea, you are selling. When subordinates make requests of you, they are selling. The following pointers can help you to listen effectively as an evaluator.

Seek Information before Evaluating. As obvious as this might seem, it is tempting to begin judging an idea before you know enough. A consultant on business information systems recently described this behavior. "A lot of small businesses are buying computers these days," he said. "Even though they pay me good money to help them decide on the best product, many of them seem to have their minds made up before we begin. Some want PCs, some Macs, and so on. They get their opinions in the oddest ways—from advertising or because a friend uses one for an entirely different purpose. People like this aren't really interested in the facts. They have their minds made up in advance."

Consider the Speaker's Motives. An argument carries more weight when the speaker doesn't have a personal stake in the outcome of your decision. The statement "The Xerox 6100 is the most reliable machine on the market" is easier to accept from *Consumer Reports* magazine than from a Xerox sales representative, for example.

Similarly, reports from customers that they are having no problems getting replacement parts are probably more credible than the same report from the manager of the order fulfillment department—who may feel that any problem could threaten his job. This does not mean you should disregard every statement from an interested party; it means only that you should look closely at the evidence for the statement.

Examine the Speaker's Supporting Data. As an evaluative listener, you need to ask yourself several questions about the evidence a speaker gives you to support her or his statements. First, does it exist at all? What evidence does the order fulfillment manager give that the current computer system is causing problems or that a new one will be better? Does a sales representative back up the claim that a product will pay for itself in less than a year?

Once you have identified the evidence, you need to make sure it is valid. The success of the flexible-hours program instituted in the New York office doesn't mean that the same program will work as well in the factory in West Virginia, where a certain number of people have to be operating the machinery at any given time. The two or three employees unhappy with the new office furniture might be the exceptions rather than representative of the majority, while the one or two satisfied customers you hear about could be the only happy ones. Carefully researched statistics that look at more than a few isolated cases are a much stronger form of proof than a few random examples.

The following questions can help you to examine the overall validity of supporting material:

Is the evidence given true?

Are enough cases cited?

Are the cited cases representative of the whole being considered?

Are there any exceptions to the points the speaker is making?

Do these exceptions need to be considered?

Consider the Speaker's Credentials. A statement that has value when made by a qualified speaker might not be worth considering when uttered by someone else. Your attorney's legal advice on whether a client has grounds for a lawsuit, for instance, is probably better than a co-worker's or your brother-in-law's ideas on the subject. Competence is not universal: a person can be an expert in one area and less qualified in others. Your comptroller could be a whiz at finding ways to cut costs, for example, but be totally ignorant of the market demands that determine what you need to spend to sell your product.

Examine Emotional Appeals. Sometimes emotional reactions are a valid basis for action. The sympathy we feel for underprivileged children is a good reason for donating money to their welfare. The desire to cut down on your own fatigue may be a good reason to hire an assistant.

In some cases, though, emotional appeals can obscure important logical considerations that might dissuade you from accepting a proposal. We can see this by thinking about fund-raisers who seek money for underprivileged children. Your sympathy might not justify allowing a fund-raiser to wander around your building soliciting funds from employees: your employees could resent being asked to give money to *your* favorite cause rather than one of theirs, especially if they have just been asked to donate to another cause. The particular agency asking for your donation might not be the best vehicle for helping underprivileged children: it may have excessive overhead so that much of your contribution never reaches any children, or other organizations might serve needier people.

Listening to Help

We listen informationally and critically for our own benefit. At other times, though, we listen to help the speaker in some way. Sometimes the help is personal, as when a friend asks advice about career planning or managing a conflict with a co-worker. At other times, the help meets organizational goals, as when a subordinate asks you for advice about a technical problem or a sales representative asks you how to persuade a particular customer.

Most helping responses fall into five categories. The most common is ***advising:*** ""Here's what I think . . . ," "You ought to . . . ," "If I were in your position. . . ." Sometimes advice is appropriate, especially when someone asks you for help with a problem on which you have particular expertise. In other cases, though, this kind of help is not helpful. For instance, your career advice to a new employee might be wrong if you're not aware of the person's background and skills or if you're not sure how promotions are made in her department.

In other cases, the advice might be right for you but wrong for the other person. For example, you may find that the best way to react to a supervisor's bad moods is to kid him out of it, but a co-worker may only make the same supervisor angrier if he tries humor. If your advice doesn't prove useful, the other person may blame you for his or her failure. Finally, people who ask for advice often don't really want it. Instead, they are looking for someone to confirm a decision they have already reached.

Another helping style involves ***analyzing*** the speaker's problem: "The real problem seems to be . . . ," "Here's what I see going on. . . ." Analysis is especially helpful when you have more experience or insight than the speaker. For instance, a product manager might be able to help a new sales representative analyze a tricky situation.

Analysis is not a productive response when you are unsure of your analysis or when your goal is to show off your brilliance at the expense of confusing the help seeker. Analysis is also inappropriate when the person is looking for a sympathetic friend, not a calculating machine or a psychiatrist. A co-worker who has just heard that she's been passed over for a promotion would probably rather hear "Oh, I'm sorry—I know you wanted that job" than "You know why that happened? It's your attitude."

A third kind of helping response involves ***questioning*** the speaker: "Exactly how much money is missing?" "When did you start getting complaints about orders being filled incorrectly?" "Why does it bother you that Bob has taken over that end of operations?" The right questions can help you analyze a problem and offer good advice and help the other person recognize important facts that were previously buried. In other cases, though, questions can do more harm than good. Irrelevant questions ("Couldn't we have installed an automatic verifying system and avoided this problem?") can leave the person more confused than ever. Some questions are also disguised forms of advice or subtle traps: "Have you ever considered offering more money to get experienced keypunchers?" "Why haven't you told me about this?"

Helping also takes the form of ***supporting,*** either as reassurance or comfort: "I know you'll make the best decision." "We're all behind you." Such support can sometimes provide a morale boost, giving someone added strength to face a tough situation. At other times, it is not helpful at all. For instance, telling someone who is filled with self-doubt that no problem exists can have a bad impact even when your intentions are good. The person might interpret your remark to mean any competent person could handle the problem easily. Discouraging the help seeker from facing a problem ("Don't worry, things will work themselves out") might just prolong or compound it.

Another response style is ***paraphrasing.*** Just as in informational settings, empathic paraphrasing involves restating the speaker's message in your own language. Here, however, the restatement should include both the speaker's thoughts and the speaker's feelings, whether or not they were explicitly stated: "It sounds like you're confused [feeling]. You can't decide whether to take the risk of a new job or stick with the safe one [thoughts]." "You sound angry at Jess [feeling], but you're afraid to confront him [thought]. Is that it?"

Paraphrasing responses like these can be a useful way to help someone explore a problem. They take you off the hook of giving advice, since help seekers can often make the best decisions for themselves once they have considered all the alternatives. Even when no perfect answer to the problem exists, paraphrasing can let the troubled person blow off steam and feel understood. But this style of listening is usually not appropriate for information-seeking questions ("I can't figure out how to amortize this loan"), and it rarely works when you are itching to give advice. But when you have the time and the problem is a complex personal one, it can be a useful way of responding.

The following suggestions can improve your helpfulness as an empathic listener.

Use a Variety of Response Styles, as Appropriate. It is usually a mistake to rely heavily on one style of responding. From the full repertoire of response styles just described, choose the one that is most appropriate.

Avoid Being Judgmental. You may sometimes be tempted to judge the behavior of an advice seeker: "If you kept your records up to date, you would have noticed that the shipments were going out late." If your goal is to be truly helpful, though, this sort of evaluation is probably out of place. Most people receive all the judgments they need. Far more rare is a sympathetic listener who will let them express thoughts and feelings without fear of criticism.

Sometimes it is impossible to approve of others' behavior. Being nonjudgmental does not mean that you approve of others; it just means that you haven't evaluated their behavior one way or another. You can help coworkers or subordinates to solve a problem, for instance, without telling them it's their own fault that it happened. They probably know that already anyway.

Take Time. As author Stephen Covey puts it, helping others "takes time, but it doesn't take anywhere near as much time as it takes to back up and correct misunderstandings when you're already miles down the road, to redo, to live with unexpressed and unsolved problems."[44] If you are not willing to take

SKILL BUILDER

Practice your helpful listening skills by following these steps:

1. Imagine that a co-worker approaches you with one or more of the following messages:

"The boss keeps telling me crude sexual jokes. I think it's a come-on, and I don't know what to do."
"I never have enough time to do my work. Every time I solve one problem, another one comes up. And the phone never stops ringing. I'm going crazy!"
"This job looks like a dead end to me. I'd like to quit, but it's a tight job market. I don't know what to do."

2. Decide how you would respond to such comments. Identify your response as advice, analysis, questioning, support, or paraphrasing. Which of these styles do you most commonly use when others seek your help?
3. Continuing with whatever situation you have chosen, write out responses for each of the styles you did not originally use.
4. Now decide which of the five responses would be most helpful.
5. Use your insights from the steps above to consider how you could become a more effective empathic listener by broadening your range of response styles.

time to listen, it is better to say, "I'm really preoccupied with this budget. It's due by 4:00 this afternoon, but I do want to listen to you. Could we meet for coffee at 4:30?" Then be sure you do.

SUMMARY

For most workers, listening is the most frequent type of communication on the job, occupying more time than speaking, writing, or reading. Effective listening is important for several reasons. First, it aids the organization in carrying out its mission. In addition, effective listening helps individuals to advance in their careers. It provides information that helps them to learn about important happenings in the organization, as well as assisting them in doing their own jobs well. Listening also helps build strong personal relationships.

Despite these advantages, most workers are poor listeners for a variety of reasons, physiological, environmental, attitudinal, sociocultural, and educational.

There are three approaches to listening. The first is passive. The second involves sincere questioning, which differs from several types of counterfeit questioning. Paraphrasing is the third type of listening.

Despite their superficial similarity, questioning and paraphrasing are different.

During their careers, people listen to accomplish three different goals. The first involves information seeking. Success in this area comes from avoiding premature judgments, being opportunistic, listening for the speaker's main and supporting ideas, taking notes, and repeating what has been heard soon after hearing it.

A second type of listening occurs when the goal is to evaluate the quality of a message. Skill in this area comes from seeking adequate information before forming judgments, considering the speaker's motives, examining the speaker's supporting data, considering the speaker's credentials, and examining emotional appeals dispassionately.

Empathic listening involves responding in a way that helps others resolve their problems. Most people rely excessively on one or two of the following styles of empathic listening: advising, analyzing, questioning, supporting, and paraphrasing. Listeners can increase their helpfulness by using a variety of styles instead of just one or two and avoiding judgmental responses.

RESOURCES

Borisoff, Deborah, and M. Purdy (Eds.), *Listening in Everyday Life: A Personal and Professional Approach* (Lanham, Md.: University Press of America, 1991).

This book includes specific sections on gender and cultural issues in listening and presents separate sections on listening in various occupations: education, business, service industries, legal, medical, and the helping professions. For business and professional readers who want career-specific help, these chapters are lively and practical.

Covey, Stephen R., *The 7 Habits of Highly Effective People* (New York: Fireside Books, 1989).

Stephen Covey is noted for his principle-centered approach to personal and professional communication, and the book describes seven habits that can lead to dynamic personal change. "Habit 5: Seek First to Understand, Then to Be Understood" demonstrates how using empathic listening to understand others can enable us to more effectively communicate our point of view.

O'Brien, Patricia, "Why Men Don't Listen . . . and What It Costs Women at Work," *Working Woman* 18 (March 1991): 56–60.

This article builds on the research of communication scholars who have found that women's remarks generally receive less attention than men's on the job. Men may react defensively to this argument, but those who take it seriously can at least check their own behavior to make sure they are not guilty of the habits O'Brien describes.

Rogers, Carl R., and F. J. Roethlisberger, "Barriers and Gateways to Communication," *Harvard Business Review* 69 (November– December 1991): 105–112.

This classic article argues that the primary barrier to communication is the tendency to evaluate another person's statements instead of first attempting to understand them. The authors urge readers to develop a habit of listening openly to ideas.

Steil, Lyman K., Joanne Summerfield, and George DeMare, *Listening: It Can Change Your Life. A Handbook for Scientists and Engineers* (New York: Wiley, 1983).

Most people think of scientists and engineers as dealing with "hard" information: facts and figures. This book shows that listening can be just as important in technical fields as it is in "softer" businesses. The advice here is useful for every communicator, regardless of his or her job.

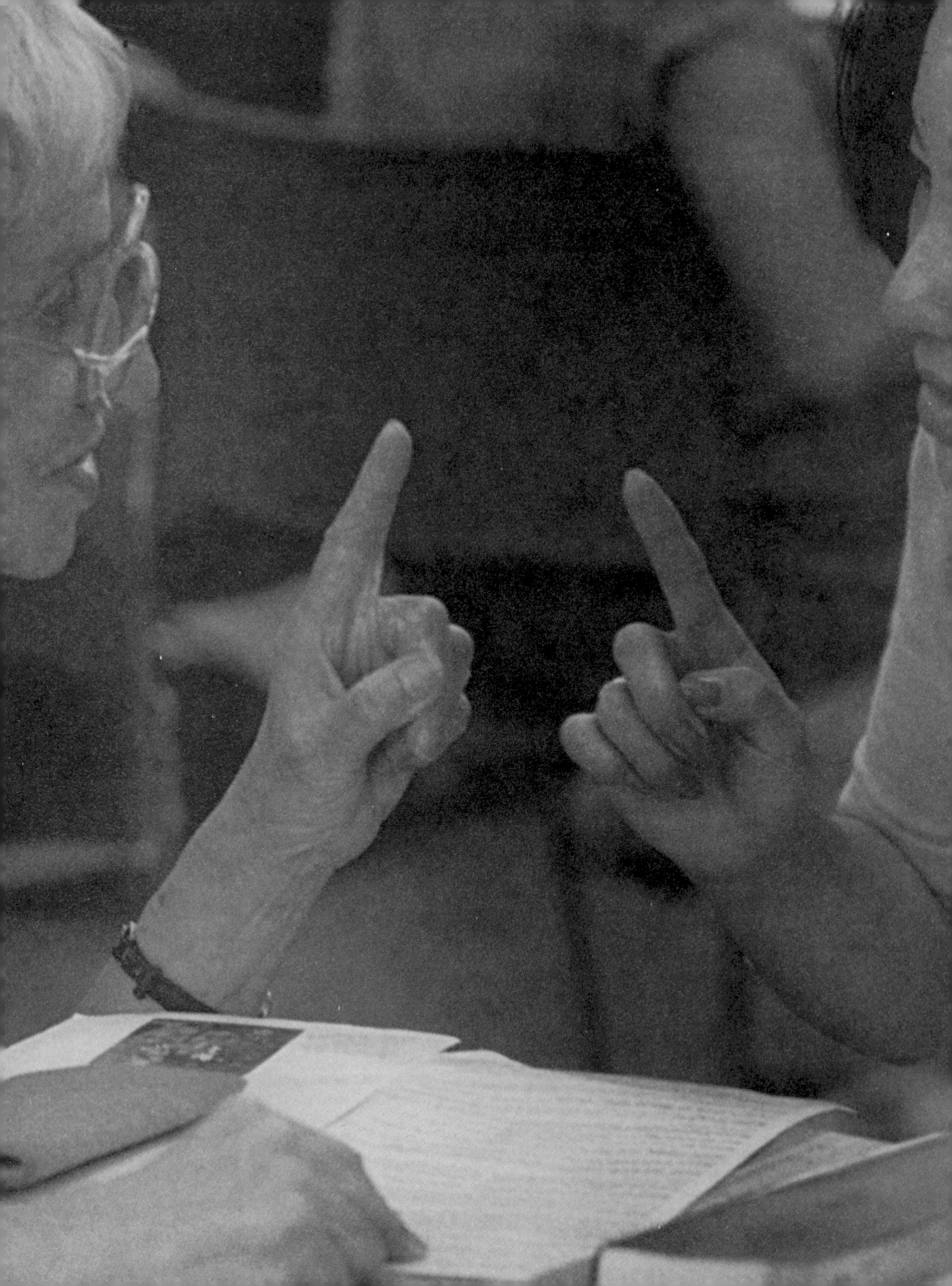

CHAPTER 5

Interpersonal Skills

KEY TERMS

Bargaining orientation / Communication climate / Compromise / Confirming messages / Descriptive statements / Disconfirming messages / "I" language / Lose-lose orientation / Negotiation / Problem-oriented messages / Win-win orientation / "You" language

What does it take to succeed in your career? Talent, good ideas, a good education, technical expertise, skills, hard work, motivation, initiative—all of these are important. In addition, because all jobs require you to get things done through other people—co-workers, customers, managers, people in other departments in the company—career success also depends on your ability to communicate effectively. That ability, often called "people skills," is the ability to work with other people, solve problems, negotiate differences, and handle conflicts so that you can do your job effectively.

BUILDING POSITIVE RELATIONSHIPS

A recent survey of 1,000 personnel directors in the United States revealed just how important communication skills are in a career.[1] When asked to describe the "ideal management profile," the number-one characteristic was "ability to work well with others one-on-one." The personnel managers understood clearly that communication is at the heart of people skills: all three of the top characteristics that were identified as necessary for successful job performance were communication skills. Former Chrysler chairman Lee Iacocca summed up the importance of maintaining good interpersonal working relationships when he said:

> There's one phrase I hate to see on any executive's evaluation, no matter how talented he may be, and that's the line: "He has trouble getting along with other people." To me that's the kiss of death.[2]

Many businesspeople at many levels are greatly concerned about their relationships with other people on the job. Andrew Grove, president of Intel Corporation, discovered the extent of that concern when he began writing a weekly question-and-answer newspaper column on management:

> I couldn't overlook the fact that the overwhelming majority of writers asked for help with interpersonal relationships at work. People wanted ideas on how to deal with the boss who never gives feedback, with the employee who doesn't care about her work, with the customer who propositions them, with coworkers who steal or who crack their gum loudly. In other words, people wanted ideas on how to *manage* better at their workplace, manage as in "the

A company with whom we work has agonized over the past 20 years over the fate of one of its senior managers, a brilliant man seriously lacking in interpersonal skills. Although he currently holds a high-ranking position, he got there by upsetting just about everyone in the 1,000 person firm. Business has fallen off significantly, and now the question is: What to do with him? After numerous failed consultations and training courses designed to boost his skills, the general manager decided to lay him off, and the rest of management was shocked. How could someone with such good ideas be fired? The answer is simply this: In management today, relational skills are not a desirable add-on to the job; they are a big part of the job. Valuing relationships is central.

Eric M. Eisenberg and H. H. Goodall, Jr., *Organizational Communication* boss manages his employees," and also manage as in "make do" or "get along."[3]

This chapter focuses on how to develop and improve the personal communication skills that are so important for individuals and organizations. It describes the ingredients that foster a positive communication climate between people, and then it goes on to offer advice about how to communicate in a variety of important person-to-person situations: giving praise, delivering and receiving criticism without defensiveness, managing conflict constructively, and negotiating in a manner that delivers the best possible outcome.

Communication Climate

Social scientists use the term ***communication climate*** to describe the quality of personal relationships in an organization. Do people feel respected? Do they trust one another? Do they believe that they are appreciated? The weather metaphor suggested by the term *climate* is apt. Your own experience shows that the mood of a workplace can be described as sunny and calm, cold and stormy, or in similar terms. Organizations create an overall climate, which can be healthy or polluted; but within that environment individual relationships have their own microclimates. For example, your interactions with one colleague might be described as icy, while you and another person enjoy a warm relationship.

The climate of an organization comes not so much from the specific tasks that members perform as from the feelings they have about those tasks and each other. In fact, a positive climate can exist under the worst working conditions: in a cramped, poorly furnished, understaffed office; during the graveyard shift of an urban newspaper; or even in a road gang cleaning up trash by the highway. Conversely, the most comfortable, prestigious settings can be polluted by a hostile climate. Table 5-1 provides a tool for diagnosing the communication climate of a working group.

While communication climates are created by a variety of messages, they do share a common denominator. Positive climates result when people believe they are valued, and negative climates occur when they don't believe they are appreciated. Scholars have labeled messages that express feelings of value as ***confirming*** and those that fail to express valuing—or those that explicitly show a lack of valuing—as ***disconfirming.***[4] Psychologist Jack Gibb described six types of supportive statements that are likely to promote a confirming climate.[5] Gibb's supportive categories provide a list of ways to promote positive, confirming relationships.

Use Descriptive "I" Language. Many communicators unnecessarily attack the other person when delivering a message:

"Your report is too sloppy. You'll have to retype it."

"This is the third time this month that you've been late for work. You'll have to be more punctual."

TABLE 5-1 Managerial Communication Climate Questionnaire

KEY:

AAT	The statement is almost always true.
UT	The statement is usually true.
UF	The statement is usually false.
AAF	The statement is almost always false.

To indicate your response, draw a circle around *one* of the four symbols preceding each item.*

AAT	UT	UF	AAF	**1.** It's easy to find out what's going on; there are few secrets around here.
AAT	UT	UF	AAF	**2.** People feel free to say what's on their minds when they're talking to their bosses.
AAT	UT	UF	AAF	**3.** You can count on the truth and accuracy of what company management says about such matters as profits and losses, long-range plans, and impending changes of policy.
AAT	UT	UF	AAF	**4.** Other managers at my level in the company are people with whom I can easily and frankly discuss mutual problems.
AAT	UT	UF	AAF	**5.** My superiors keep me informed on what's expected of me—of what I must do to get ahead.
AAT	UT	UF	AAF	**6.** Managers encourage subordinates to come up with new ideas, and they protect them when they stick their necks out by making suggestions.
AAT	UT	UF	AAF	**7.** Company statements are noted for their clarity and freedom from bureaucratic prose.
AAT	UT	UF	AAF	**8.** Management treats everyone with respect—as mature adults rather than as children.
AAT	UT	UF	AAF	**9.** Management is candid in disclosing bad news; the rule is, "We tell it like it is."
AAT	UT	UF	AAF	**10.** Performance appraisals are conducted in such a way that the subordinate knows where he or she stands and participates in setting his or her own goals for continued progress.
AAT	UT	UF	AAF	**11.** The underlying assumption in the company is that just about everybody has good ideas, and that these ideas should contribute to all major decision making.
AAT	UT	UF	AAF	**12.** When you send messages to higher management, you get a prompt and honest response.
AAT	UT	UF	AAF	**13.** When you see a crisis building up, it's easy to alert higher management about it.
AAT	UT	UF	AAF	**14.** Generally speaking, I receive all the information I need to perform my job effectively.
AAT	UT	UF	AAF	**15.** People representing different departments and different specialties have ample opportunity to consult with each other.
AAT	UT	UF	AAF	**16.** This company plays down status differences between superiors and subordinates.
AAT	UT	UF	AAF	**17.** Managers at all levels are encouraged to be their own bosses—hence, to take risks.
AAT	UT	UF	AAF	**18.** In this company, we stress that managers should act more as counselors and helpers than as order givers and watchmen.
AAT	UT	UF	AAF	**19.** Although I am treated with consideration at all times, I am "stretched" to achieve high performance goals.

TABLE 5-1 Managerial Communication Climate Questionnaire ***(continued)***

AAT	UT	UF	AAF	**20.** The general spirit around here is: "We're all in this boat together, and we sink or swim together" (rather than: "The way to get ahead is to outmaneuver your rivals").
AAT	UT	UF	AAF	**21.** I find it relatively easy to get feedback from my subordinates about their problems, feelings, and accomplishments.
AAT	UT	UF	AAF	**22.** I find it relatively easy to get feedback from my superiors when I send messages asking for information, answers to questions, and so on.
AAT	UT	UF	AAF	**23.** Our publications, for both managers and employees, are known for candor, for completeness, and for providing "gutsy" information.
AAT	UT	UF	AAF	**24.** Higher management is willing to listen to criticism; it approaches new ideas with an open mind, even when these ideas imply criticism.
AAT	UT	UF	AAF	**25.** The company provides a systematic and safe means for anyone to raise questions or criticisms; and questions are answered promptly, fully, and accurately by appropriate line managers.
AAT	UT	UF	AAF	**26.** When someone offers an idea or makes a proposal in decision-making conferences, my approach is: "Let's see why this might be a good idea" (rather than: "What's wrong with it?").
AAT	UT	UF	AAF	**27.** In this company, people feel that managers are sincerely interested in their welfare and progress.
AAT	UT	UF	AAF	**28.** If I am making a major proposal to higher management, I know that I'll get a fair hearing; I'll be subjected to searching questions, but I can talk back without fear of the consequences.
AAT	UT	UF	AAF	**29.** When one of my own subordinates is making a major proposal, I give him or her a fair hearing; I subject the proposal to searching questions, but I encourage the subordinate to talk back without fear of the consequences.
AAT	UT	UF	AAF	**30.** When important news about the company is announced, both managers and employees hear it first before it's released to the general public.

*Potential problems can be identified by false answers (UF, AAF).

Source: W. Charles Redding, *The Corporate Manager's Guide to Better Communication* (Glenview, Ill.: Scott, Foresman, 1984). Copyright © 1984 by Scott, Foresman and Company. Reprinted by permission.

> "That was a dumb promise you made. We can never have the job done by the end of the month."

Statements like these are often called ***"you" language*** because they point a verbal finger of accusation at the receiver: "You're lazy." "You're wrong." By contrast, ***descriptive statements*** are often termed ***"I" language*** since they focus on the speaker instead of judging the other person. Notice how each of the evaluative statements above can be rephrased in descriptive "I" language:

> "I'm afraid the boss will get angry at both of us if we turn in a report with this many errors. We'll get a better reaction if it's retyped."

> "Since you've been coming in late, I've made a lot of excuses when people call asking for you. I'm uncomfortable with that, and that's why I hope you'll start showing up on time."

Treat people as adults. Treat them as partners; treat them with dignity; treat them with respect. Treat *them*—not capital spending and automation—as the primary source of productivity gains. These are fundamental lessons from the excellent companies research. In other words, if you want productivity and the financial reward that goes with it, you must treat your workers as your most important asset.

Thomas J. Peters and Robert H. Waterman, Jr., *In Search of Excellence*

"I'm worried about the promise you made. I don't see how we can get the job done by the end of the month."

Statements like these show that it's possible to be nonjudgmental and still say what you want without landing any verbal punches. In fact, descriptive statements like the ones you just read are *more* complete than are typical everyday complaints since they express both the speaker's feelings and the reason for bringing up the matter—things most evaluative remarks don't do.

Focus on Solving Problems, Not Controlling Others. Some messages try to force others to do something they don't agree with or understand. If you're up against a tight deadline, for example, it's easy to say, "Look, I don't have time to explain—just do it my way." Because control shows a lack of regard for the other person's needs, interests, or opinions, however, it can cause problems in the relationship even if it gets you what you want now.

In contrast, ***problem-oriented messages*** aim at solving both persons' needs. The goal isn't to solve a problem "my way" or "your way" but rather to develop a solution that meets everyone's needs. You will learn more about how to achieve problem-oriented solutions when we discuss win-win negotiating strategies later in this chapter.

Be Honest: Don't Manipulate. Once people discover that they have been manipulated, a defensive reaction is almost guaranteed. For example, if workers are surveyed on their preferences for the layout of new offices and then discover that the plan was completed without tabulating their responses, they will resent being "set up as suckers"—a label nobody likes to accept.

By contrast, simple honesty is less likely to generate defensiveness, even when the news isn't welcome. Telling your subordinates outright that the new office plan was designed by an executive planning committee may not make then ecstatic, but they won't feel that they've been used to justify a closed decision. Even though others might sometimes dislike what you have to

A little bit of dishonesty can create a lot of distrust. If one statement of mine in a hundred is false, you may choose not to rely on me at all. Unless you can develop a theory of when I am honest and when I am not, your discovery of a small dishonesty will cast doubt over everything I say and do.

Roger Fisher and Scott Brown, *Getting Together*

say, your reputation for candor can earn you the respect of subordinates, co-workers, and management.

Honesty doesn't require you to be blunt or cruel, and it doesn't require you to volunteer information that others don't request. You may know that the design committee for the new office layout was told to put as many people in as little space as possible to allow room for an executive dining room, but you also might wisely choose not to pass that information on to your own employees.

Show Concern for Others. Indifference—lack of acknowledgment or concern for others—is a strong disconfirming message. By contrast, a genuine message of interest can make a tremendous difference. A simple apology for making you wait can do wonders. The secretary who takes the time to find the right person to answer your questions can leave you feeling grateful and worthwhile, encouraging you to do business with that company again. The manager who seems genuinely concerned with your opinions—even if she doesn't agree with them—is easier to work with than one who brushes your concerns aside.

Demonstrate an Attitude of Equality. People who act in a superior manner imply that others are inferior—clearly a disconfirming message. Nobody likes to feel less valuable than another person, and an air of superiority communicates this sort of message.

The kind of superiority that arouses defensiveness isn't based as much on intelligence, talent, or skill as on dignity and respect. Talent doesn't justify arrogance. You have probably encountered sales representatives and clerks who acted as though their product knowledge made them superior to their customers, physicians who couldn't be bothered to explain test results to you, and employers who felt their subordinates were stupid. This sort of superior attitude causes defensiveness. Al Neuharth, founder of *USA Today,* has earned a reputation as a tough, abrasive boss. His superior, evaluative comments like the following one suggest why: "When I criticize a female or when I criticize a grossly overweight person or anybody else, it's because, damn it, I think they ought to do better, just as I do."[6]

INVITATION TO INSIGHT

Answer the following questions after explaining to a co-worker the types of confirming and disconfirming behaviors outlined in the preceding pages and asking which ones characterize your on-the-job communication.

1. What kinds of behaviors were identified? In what situations do they occur?
2. What are the results of these behaviors for you and the other people involved?

On the basis of the answers you received, describe specifically how you could behave in a more confirming manner.

Listen with an Open Mind. Listening with an open mind makes good sense. Whether the people you're dealing with are in your department or another, subordinates or customers, they probably have knowledge that you don't. Hearing them out may teach you something useful.

Besides providing useful information, listening open-mindedly can promote good relationships. Consider how you would feel if you had carefully researched a proposal to avoid raising the price on a product line, only to be told, "I see no evidence that we should keep the price down." Suppose, instead, that your supervisor had said, "I have strong reasons for raising the price, but maybe you'll change my mind," or had at least listened carefully to your idea and promised to give it some thought. Even if your supervisor eventually decides against your proposal, you will probably feel that your ideas are heard and respected—provided that the supervisor gives you good reasons for rejecting your plan.

Giving Praise

There's truth to the old saying, "You can catch more flies with honey than with vinegar." Sincere praise, delivered skillfully, can produce dramatic results and leave you and the other person feeling better as well.

Communication consultants Peter and Susan Glaser offer several tips about how to take advantage of the power of praise.

Make Praise Specific. Almost any sincere praise will be appreciated, but describing exactly *what* you appreciate makes it easier for the other person to continue that behavior. Notice how the following specific compliments add clarity:

BROAD	SPECIFIC
"Good job on handling that complaint."	"You really kept your cool when that customer complained."
"I appreciate the support you've given me lately."	"Thanks for being so flexible with my schedule while I was sick."
"You've really been on top of your work lately."	"You've finished every job this month within two days."

Being specific doesn't mean you have to avoid giving broad comments like the ones above. But along with giving general praise, consider the value of

Praise is a very special form of feedback. Although I heard many men and women mention that they got more thanks and praise from women than from men, I never heard anyone say they resented receiving praise. . . . When they had a boss who praised them often, they always said they liked it. "It's a problem," one man joked, "because it's habit-forming. The more praise you get, the more you want!"

Deborah Tannen, *Talking from 9 to 5*

adding enough particulars to help the other person understand exactly what you appreciate.

Praise Progress, Not Just Perfection. You might wonder whether some people do much of anything that deserves sincere praise. If you look for outstanding performance, the answer may be no; but you can still deliver genuine compliments by looking for progress. Consider a few examples:

> "This draft of the report is a lot clearer. Adding a detailed budget really helps explain where the money will go. I think the same kind of detail would help make the schedule clearer."

> "I know we still see things differently, but I'm glad we were able to work so well together on the Baretti job."

Praise Intermittently. Too much praise can become as uncomfortable as too much rich food or too many jokes. Constant praise is also likely to sound insincere. In addition, social scientists have discovered that it isn't even as effective as occasional compliments. Praise others from time to time, when your remarks will have the best effect. But don't go overboard.

Relay Praise. If you already believe that complimenting someone sincerely can improve the communication climate in your relationship, wait until you see the benefits of singing their praises to others who deserve to know. You will win the undying gratitude of the person you are complimenting; you will show your own sense of security and team spirit; and you will be informing others about information they will probably find valuable. Praising others takes little time, and it benefits everyone.

You can also become a "praise messenger" by letting people know that you've heard others saying complimentary things about them. They will be more likely to continue the behavior, and they will feel better both about the person who praised them and about you for delivering the good news.

Praise Sincerely. Insincere praise is worse than no praise at all. It casts doubt on all your other compliments. It suggests that you can't think of anything the other person has done that deserves genuine acknowledgment. And it suggests that you think the recipient is naive enough to believe in your phony compliments.

ETHICAL CHALLENGE

The value of praise is clear, and the guidelines in this section offer advice for when and how to compliment others. But what can you do when you cannot think of anything about another person's performance to praise?

As you consider when and how to praise, it is important to be aware of the cultural rules that may influence both the person receiving compliments and the audience to whom you are delivering them. In some collectivist cultures, it can be embarrassing to be singled out for praise, especially in front of others. In such cases, giving private reinforcement is probably wiser than lavishing compliments publicly.

DEALING WITH CRITICISM

Praise is a pleasure to give and receive, but it isn't always possible. In the real world of work, criticism is a fact of life. Sometimes you have to deliver a complaint, and other times you are on the receiving end of others' gripes. Either way, criticism can start a cycle of defensiveness that pollutes the communication climate between people or working groups. But despite their risks, critical messages don't have to create problems. With enough skill, you can learn to both deliver and respond to them in ways that can maintain—or even improve—working relationships.

Offering Constructive Criticism

Despite its faultfinding nature, criticism doesn't have to trigger a defensive reaction. You can maximize the chances of your comments' being understood and accepted by carefully considering how they can be expressed.

Consider the Content. The first concern is to edit your remarks so that they follow some important guidelines:

- *Limit the criticism to one topic.* You may have several complaints, but it is smart to focus on only one at a time. Your respondent may be able to handle a single problem, but he or she could grow understandably defensive if you pile on one gripe after another.
- *Make sure the criticism is accurate.* Be absolutely sure you get the facts straight before speaking out. If even a small detail is out of line, the other person can argue about that, sidetracking the discussion from the real problem at hand.
- *Define the problem clearly.* Just list the facts, in enough detail so that the recipient knows exactly what you are talking about. Don't overwhelm the other person with an avalanche of complaints, but be prepared to give examples to back up your point.
- *Show how your criticism can benefit the recipient.* Whenever possible, describe the payoffs for responding to your remarks. At the very least, the other person will get you off his or her back by heeding your complaints!

Consider the Sender. Who delivers the criticism can be as important as the content of the remarks. Two guidelines will help you in this area:

- *Choose the most credible critic.* Sometimes the recipient will be more receptive to one person than to another. If a choice is avail-

able, make sure that the message comes from whoever can deliver it most effectively.
- *Make sure the criticism is appropriate to the critic's role.* Even accurate criticism is likely to be rejected if you have no business delivering it. For example, most comments about someone's personal life are out of place unless they affect a working relationship. Job-related comments should be appropriate for your relationship to the other person.

Consider the Context. The framework in which your remarks are delivered can have an important impact on how they are received. Paying attention to three context-related factors can boost the odds of getting the desired reaction:

- *Deliver remarks as part of a positive relationship.* Let the other person know that your specific criticism doesn't diminish your respect or appreciation for the person in other areas. Sincerely acknowledging the positives can make the negatives easier to accept.
- *Accept partial responsibility for the problem.* If possible, show that you may have contributed in some degree to the issue. If nothing else, you might be able to say, "I probably should have brought this up sooner."
- *Accompany your criticism with an offer to help.* You can earn the goodwill of the other person by offering to play a role in solving the problem at hand.

Consider the Delivery. How you express a criticism can make a big difference in the way it is received. Two delivery-related guidelines can help:

- *Deliver criticism in a face-saving manner.* Probably the most important consideration is to make sure your remarks are delivered privately. Criticizing someone in front of others is likely to trigger resentment and embarrassment.
- *Avoid sounding judgmental.* Avoid using the kind of emotive language described in Chapter 3. Don't call names or use inflammatory labels, and don't attribute motives to the other person. Try to use the kind of descriptive "I" language described earlier in this chapter instead of defense-arousing "you" statements.

Responding Nondefensively to Criticism

Receiving criticism can be tougher than giving it. When people are faced with criticism, the two most common responses are "fight" and "flight." Fighters react by counterattacking. "It's not my fault," they might protest. Another fighting response is to blame others: "I'm not the only one who's at fault here. I could have done better if I had gotten more support." Your own experience probably shows that fighting with your critics seldom persuades them to back down.

> My advice to college students is to expect a *lot* of criticism on the job, both from people within your organization and from the public. Much of that criticism will be less fair and more rude than anything you've received during your education. Don't resent or tune out these attacks. If you listen to them carefully, you'll be amazed by the benefits. Your critics will respect you more, and you will learn a tremendous amount of helpful information—about yourself, your job, and human nature.
>
> John Post, marketing manager, Fidelity Investments

Flight is a second reaction to criticism. Most businesspeople are too mature to run away physically from a critic, but there are other ways of evading negative remarks. Sometimes you *can* physically avoid critics—steering clear of their offices or not returning their phone calls, for example. Even when you can't escape unpleasant remarks, you can mentally disengage by refusing to listen thoughtfully to the criticism. While keeping quiet can work in the short run, it seldom is a satisfying way to deal with an ongoing relationship in which you are constantly under attack.

Since neither fighting nor fleeing is likely to satisfy your critics or help you understand legitimate criticism, you need alternatives that allow you to listen nondefensively without losing face. Fortunately, two such alternatives exist.

Seek More Information. Asking your critic to explain the problem gives you a constructive option to fighting or fleeing. By asking your critic for more information, you are showing that you take the criticism seriously but, at the same time, you aren't accepting blame for the problem. There are several ways to seek more information:

- *Ask for examples or clarification.* "You've said I'm not presenting a good attitude to customers. Can you describe exactly what I'm doing?"
- *Guess about details of the criticism.* Even if the critic isn't willing or able to offer specifics, you can guess: "Was it the way I handled Mr. Tyson when the bank sent back his check for insufficient funds?"
- *Paraphrase the critic.* "When you say I have a bad attitude toward customers, it sounds like you think I'm not giving them the service they deserve."
- *Ask what the critic wants.* "How could I behave in a better way around customers?"

Agree with the Criticism. An obvious but often overlooked way of responding nondefensively is to agree with the criticism. Although this approach might seem like a form of self-punishment, it can be extremely effective. There are two ways to agree with a critic:

- *Agree with the facts.* Sometimes you are confronted with facts that can't be disputed. In these cases, your best approach is probably to face up to the truth: "You're right. I *have* been late three times this week." Notice that agreeing with the facts doesn't mean that you are accepting responsibility for every imaginable fault. In the case of being late to work, you might go on to point out that your lateness is a fluke in an otherwise spotless work record; but arguing with indisputable information isn't likely to satisfy your critic, and it will probably make you look bad.

- *Agree with the critic's perception.* Sometimes you can't honestly agree with the criticism. For example, a customer might unjustly accuse you of not caring about good service. After asking for more information to find out the basis of the criticism (a shipment didn't arrive on time, for example), you can acknowledge how the other person might view you as being at fault: "I can understand why it might seem that I don't care about your needs. After all, you did tell me that you absolutely had to have that shipment by last Friday, and I told you that it would be there. I'd be mad too if I were you."

  Notice that agreeing with the perception doesn't require you to *accept* your critic's evaluation as accurate, although you might indeed find that it does have some merit. What you are doing is acknowledging the other person's right to view the issue in a way that may differ from yours. To see the value of this approach, consider how offensive the alternative would be. To say or imply "Your view of the issue is completely wrong and mine is right" isn't likely to satisfy the other person—nor is it a reasonable position in most cases.

MANAGING CONFLICT

Like it or not, conflict is part of every job. Even the most competent, intelligent, ethical people will disagree from time to time. Sometimes conflict involves work-related issues: scheduling, funds, work assignments, and so on. Other times, it focuses on personal issues: sexual harassment, the amount of socializing appropriate during working hours, or whether a shared assistant is doing his or her work efficiently. The dispute may be loud and argumentative, calm and rational, or so indirect that it is never mentioned outright.

SKILL BUILDER

Practice your ability to respond nondefensively to criticism by joining with a partner and rehearsing the kinds of critical messages you are likely to receive on the job.

1. Designate one person as "A" and the other as "B."
2. A begins by describing the kinds of critical messages he or she is likely to receive and identifying who would express them.
3. B then takes the role of the critic and delivers the critical message. A uses the skills described on pages 131–133 to respond nondefensively.
4. After the role-playing session, A and B discuss how the nondefensive listening skills could be used in a real-life situation.
5. A and B change roles and repeat the procedure.

Conflict may be equated with the common cold—unavoidable, unpleasant, and counterproductive. To most people, the fewer conflicts the better. The problem isn't conflict itself, however, but rather *the way in which it is handled.* With the right approach, conflict can produce good results. The Chinese language represents this fact well; in Chinese, the ideogram for the word *crisis* is made up of two characters: danger and opportunity. A poorly handled organizational conflict certainly can be dangerous; relationships suffer and productivity declines. On the other hand, a skillfully handled conflict can result in several benefits.[7] It can function as a safety valve, letting people ventilate frustrations that are blocking their effective functioning. It can lead to solving troublesome problems. James Baldwin said it best: "Nothing can be changed until it is faced." Problems seldom go away just because they are ignored; they usually grow worse. Facing them can promote group loyalty and cohesiveness. People who overcome conflicts successfully often feel that together they have made progress toward their mutual goals. Such experiences often draw people closer.

Approaches to Conflict

When faced with a conflict, you have several choices about how to respond. Each of these approaches has different results.[8]

Avoiding. One way to deal with conflict is to avoid it whenever possible and withdraw when confronted. In some cases, avoidance is physical: refusing to take phone calls, staying barricaded in the office, and so on. In other cases, however, avoidance can be psychological: denying that a problem exists or that it is serious, repressing emotional reactions, and so on. In the workplace, a communicator who avoids conflicts might accept constant schedule delays or poor-quality work from a supplier to avoid a confrontation or might cover up for a co-worker's frequent absences even if it means doing the other person's work. As these examples suggest, avoidance may have the short-term benefit of preventing a confrontation, but there are usually long-term costs, especially in ongoing relationships.

Despite its drawbacks, avoidance is sometimes a wise choice. Table 5-2 lists some circumstances in which keeping quiet may be the most appropriate course of action. For example, when standing up for your rights would be hopeless, silence might be the best policy. You might simply tolerate a superior's unreasonable demands while you look for a new job, or you might steer clear of an angry co-worker who is out to get you. In many cases, however, avoidance has unacceptable costs: you lose self-respect, you become frustrated, and the problem may only get worse.

Accommodating. Whereas avoiders stay away from conflicts, accommodators give ground as a way of maintaining harmony. In many cases, accommodating is hard to defend. It can be equivalent to appeasement, sacrificing one's principles, and putting harmony above dealing with important issues. In her fascinating book *Talking from 9 to 5,* sociolinguist Deborah

Tannen describes an extreme case in which accommodating led to disaster.[9] On January 13, 1982, Air Florida Flight 90 crashed shortly after takeoff from Washington D.C.'s National Airport, killing sixty-nine passengers. The cause of the disaster was excessive ice on the airplane's wings. An analysis of cockpit recordings made on the heavily armored "black box" recovered after the accident revealed that the co-pilot had hinted about excessive ice several times to the pilot before takeoff but that his suggestions went unheeded. The command structure of aircraft operations dictates that the pilot has the final word on whether or not a plane is fit to fly; but it is easy to imagine that a less accommodating approach might have caused the pilot to recheck the situation before making what turned out to be a catastrophic decision.

Despite the obvious drawbacks of accommodating, Table 5-2 shows that this approach does have merit in some circumstances. If you are clearly wrong, then giving up your original position can be a sign of strength, not weakness. If harmony is more important than the issue at hand—especially if the issue is a minor one—then accommodating is probably justified. For example, if you don't care strongly whether the new stationery is printed on cream or gray paper and fighting for one color might be a big concern for others, then giving in is probably smart. Finally, you might accommodate if satisfying the other person is important enough to your welfare. You might, for example, put up with an abusive customer to make an important sale.

Competing. A competitive approach to conflicts is based on the assumption that the only way for one party to reach its goals is to overcome the other. This bargaining approach is common in many negotiations, as you will see later in this chapter. Sometimes a power-based approach to conflict is based on simply disregarding the other person's concerns. Unsympathetic management might turn a deaf ear to the request of employees to make provisions for on-site exercise facilities, implying—or even stating outright—that the physical condition of employees is not the concern of the employer and that providing easy access to exercise would require a cash outlay and reduce time spent on the job.

In many cases, a competitive attitude is unnecessary. As the section of this chapter on win-win negotiating shows, it often *is* possible for both sides in a conflict to reach their goals (see pages 144–150). For instance, an employer might find that the cost of providing on-site exercise equipment is more than offset by reduced absenteeism and greater appeal when recruiting new employees. Furthermore, a competitive orientation can generate ill will that is both costly and unpleasant. In our physical-fitness example, workers whose needs are ignored are likely to resent their employer and act in ways that ultimately wind up costing the company a great deal.

Despite its drawbacks, competition isn't always a bad approach. In some cases, an issue isn't important enough to spend time on working it out. In other instances, there isn't time to collaborate on solutions. Finally, if others are determined to gain advantage at your expense, you might compete out of self-defense.

TABLE 5-2 Factors Governing Choice of a Conflict Style

Consider Avoiding

1. When an issue is genuinely trivial, or when more important issues are pressing
2. When you have no chance of winning
3. When the potential for disruption outweighs the benefits of resolution
4. To let others cool down and regain perspective
5. When the long-term costs of winning may outweigh short-term gains
6. When others can resolve the conflict more effectively

Consider Accommodating

1. When you find you are wrong
2. When the issue is important to the other party and not important to you
3. To build social credits for later issues
4. To minimize loss when you are outmatched and losing
5. When harmony and stability are more important than the subject at hand
6. To allow others to learn by making their own mistakes

Consider Competing

1. When quick, decisive action is vital (e.g., emergencies)
2. On important issues where unpopular actions need implementing (e.g., cost cutting, enforcing unpopular rules)
3. When others will take advantage of your noncompetitive behavior

Consider Collaborating

1. To find solutions when both parties' concerns are too important to be compromised
2. When a long-term relationship between the parties is important
3. To gain commitment of all parties by building consensus
4. When the other party is willing to take a collaborative approach

Consider Compromising

1. When goals are important but not worth the effort or potential disruption of more assertive modes
2. When opponents with equal power are committed to mutually exclusive goals
3. To achieve temporary settlements of complex issues
4. To arrive at expedient solutions under time pressure
5. As a backup, when collaboration is unsuccessful

Source: After Kenneth W. Thomas, "Toward Multi-dimensional Values in Teaching: The Example of Conflict Behavior," *Academy of Management Review* 2, no. 3 (1987): 487.

Collaborating. Rather than taking a competitive approach, collaborative communicators are committed to working together to resolve conflicts. Collaboration is based on the assumption that it is possible to meet one's own needs and those of the other person. This approach is reflected in Rabbi Hillel's statement, "If I am not for myself, who will be? If I am only for myself, what am I? If not now, when?"

Whereas avoiding and accommodating are based on the assumption that conflict should be avoided, and competing is based on the belief that conflict is a struggle, collaboration assumes that conflict is a natural part of life and that working with the other person will produce the best possible solution.

The benefits of collaboration are clear: not only can the issue at hand be resolved, but the relationship between the parties is improved.

Despite its advantages, collaborative communication isn't a panacea. It takes time to work with others, and mutally satisfactory outcome isn't always possible. Furthermore, collaboration requires the cooperation of everyone involved. If the other party isn't disposed to work with you, then you may be setting yourself up for exploitation by communicating openly and offering to work cooperatively.

Compromising. In a compromise, each party sacrifices something he or she is seeking to gain an agreement. On one hand, this approach is cooperative, recognizing that both parties must agree to resolve a conflict. On the other, compromise is self-centered, since the parties act in their self-interest to get the best possible deal.

Compromise is a middle-range approach. It is more assertive than avoiding and accommodating yet less aggressive than competing. It is cooperative yet less so than collaboration. While it does not give any one of the parties in a dispute everything he or she seeks, it provides an outcome that, by definition, everyone involved can live with. As Table 5-2 shows, compromise may not be the perfect approach, but under many circumstances it produces the best possible outcome.

Handling Conflicts Assertively

When you accommodate another's demand or avoid a conflict, few communication skills are necessary. But if you decide to address an issue directly—either to collaborate, to compete, or to seek a compromise—the way you present yourself can make a big difference. An aggressive approach is likely to antagonize the other person. But an assertive style of communicating allows you to present your own concerns in a way that shows respect for the other person. Showing this sort of respect isn't only right as a matter of principle; it also is likely to improve the communication climate and thus make it easier to produce the outcome you are seeking. You stand the best chance of getting your message across in the most effective way when you follow some simple guidelines.

SKILL BUILDER

Describe an avoiding, accommodating, competing, collaborating, and compromising response to each of the following situations:

1. At 4:30 P.M. a boss asks her secretary to work late in order to retype a twenty-five-page report due the next morning. The secretary has an important date that evening.
2. A worker finds the smoke from a colleague's cigarettes offensive.
3. The assistant manager of a bookstore is faced with a customer demanding a refund for a book he claims was a gift. The book has several crumpled pages and a torn cover.
4. A supervisor is faced by an irate employee complaining about another worker's "unfair" promotion to a position the employee had sought.

The first thing to remember about raising a delicate issue is to *stop and think* before you do so. Flying off the handle may be the easiest way to express yourself and feel satisfied in the short run, but the defensive, hostile reaction you get is likely to create more problems than it solves. Before you say anything, do the following three things.

Identify the Goal You Are Seeking. What do you want to happen after you have spoken up? Do you want to change the other person's mind or explain your position, or are you simply interested in blowing off steam? The approach you take will differ according to your goal.

Choose the Best Time to Speak. Timing may not be everything, but it is among the most important factors in getting (or not getting) results. Raising a delicate issue when the other person is tired, grumpy, or distracted by other business will lower the odds of getting the results you are seeking.

Rehearse the Statement. Think over what you want to say and how you can best say it. Preparing your thoughts in advance will help make your point quickly and clearly, and it will prevent you from blurting out an angry statement you'll regret later. When planning your remarks, be sure to think about how you can use "I" language instead of delivering defense-arousing "you" messages. Rehearsing your statement doesn't mean you should memorize your remarks word for word; this approach would sound canned and insincere. Think about your general ideas and perhaps a few key phrases you'll use to make your ideas clear.

When the time comes actually to deliver your delicate message, follow the four guidelines discussed below.

Pinpoint the Specific Behavior You Want to Discuss. Describe the delicate issue in neutral terms without using the kind of emotive language you read about in Chapter 4. The best descriptions are *specific* and *objective.* They avoid accusations or mind reading about the other person's motives, both of which provoke defensiveness even when they are correct.

ACCUSATION	SPECIFIC DESCRIPTION
"You're wasting time on the job."	"The last three status reports have been a week or more late."
"You're being too critical of my work."	"The last few times we've met, you've complained about my work."
"You've been gossiping about me lately."	"Yesterday I couldn't help overhearing you tell Terry you thought I was padding my expense account."

Explain Your Reaction to the Behavior. Your explanation should include both your *interpretation* of the behavior—what you thought it meant—and your *feelings* about the action. It is vital to identify both the interpretation and feelings as yours. It is here that the difference between assertive "I" language and attacking "you" language is clearest.

JUDGMENT	DESCRIPTION
"You're not trying as hard as you could."	"I'm disappointed because it seems to me the reports ought to be ready on time."
"You've gotten awfully critical lately."	"It seems to me you've been awfully critical lately, and I'm confused. I don't know why you've changed so much."
"Why don't you trust me?"	"It sounds as if you think I'm ripping the company off, and that upsets me."

Notice the provisional nature of these statements. They say "Here's how it looks to me" instead of claiming that a personal perception is absolute fact. Besides minimizing defensiveness, such tentative statements are more accurate. Your interpretation might be mistaken, and a provisional description leaves the door open for a correction without any loss of face.

Make a Request. The third part of an assertive message asks for some action from your listener. The best requests are specific and are limited to one or two changes at a time. They also ask for responses that are within the ability of the other person to give.

DEMAND	REQUEST
"Try to be more punctual from now on."	"I'd like your promise that the reports will be ready on time from now on."
"Get off my case!"	"I want to know whether you think my work has changed for the worse lately."
"Quit talking about me behind my back."	"If you have any complaints about how I handle my expense accounts, let's talk about it privately."

Describe the Consequences. The consequence statement should discuss the payoffs (both for you and the other person) of reaching accord. These payoffs can be tangible (money, time) and intangible (psychological comfort, friendship).

THREAT	DESCRIPTION OF CONSEQUENCES
"You'd better speed up before it's too late!"	"If the reports are on time, neither of us will have to hassle with this anymore."
(No consequence statement.)	"Once I understand how you feel, I can do a better job. I want the new product line to succeed as much as you do!"
"If you don't stop your gossiping, you'll be sorry!"	"Both of us have better things to do than feel bad about each other. I know we can work out any problems."

After reading this far, an assertive approach to conflict management may seem ideal. It is clear, honest, and respectful. Indeed, most communicators raised in the mainstream cultures of the United States, Canada, or western Europe would agree that assertiveness is an admirable trait. But other cultures don't view directness with such unqualified admiration, and their members are more likely to take less direct approaches to solving problems. As Chapter 2 explained, *low-context* cultures regard directness as a threat to harmony. People from these backgrounds prize the ability to give and detect hints. In this sense, a competent communicator is one who can adjust his or her style to suit the cultural expectations of others.

Even in high-context cultures that value directness, an assertive approach isn't always the best one.[10] People in less powerful positions need to be sure their assertions won't have punishing results. Employees are usually smart enough to learn whether they can trust their bosses before engaging in straight talk. Businesspeople also need to consider the consequences before asserting themselves with customers. Assertiveness can be a power communication tool, but it isn't one that can be used indiscriminately.

SKILL BUILDER

Sharpen your skill at knowing when and how to communicate assertively by following these steps:

1. Develop an assertive message for each of the following situations in your professional life:
   a. Making a request
   b. Describing a problem involving the recipient of your message
   c. Offering a suggestion
2. Practice each message with a partner until you are confident that it is organized and delivered as effectively as possible. Recording your rehearsal can provide valuable feedback.
3. Now discuss with your partner the potential benefits and drawbacks of delivering each assertive message.

NEGOTIATING SKILLS

Even the clearest and most positive communication doesn't guarantee a positive response. Whenever two parties do not initially agree about an issue, they have three choices:

1. They can accept the status quo:

   "I've tried to talk with him, but it doesn't work. There's nothing more I can do."

   "We can't agree on a price, so there's no deal."

2. The more powerful side can try to impose a solution:

   "I'm the manager. I'll decide how the job will be done."

   "Either you give me the transfer, or I'll file a grievance."

3. The parties can reach an agreement by negotiating:

   "Let's figure out a schedule we can both live with."

   "We'd both like to make the deal. Let's see if we can work out some terms."

Negotiation occurs when two or more parties—either individuals or groups—discuss specific proposals in order to find a mutually acceptable agreement. Negotiation is a common way of settling conflicts in business. Individuals use negotiation to reach agreement on everything from the price of a used car to who will handle an unpleasant job. Managers and workers use it to reach agreements on such issues as how much responsibility a worker should take and what an employee needs to do to be promoted. As one consultant explains, "Negotiations are seldom formal, sit-around-the-table affairs. In fact, almost any form of business problem or disagreement—from scheduling work shifts to 'Who's going to pay this $500 expense?'—is resolved by some form of negotiation."[11]

There is nothing magical about negotiation. When poorly handled, it can leave a problem still unsolved and perhaps worse than before. ("I tried to work things out with him, but he just tried to railroad me. I'm going to the EEOC this time.") When negotiation is handled skillfully, though, it can improve the position of one or even both parties. In the remainder of this chapter, we outline four negotiating styles, showing methods that you can use to resolve your own problems.

Negotiation Styles and Outcomes

Negotiations can be approached in four ways. Each of these approaches produces a different outcome.

Bargaining Orientation. This is the approach taken by competitive communicators. The ***bargaining orientation*** is based on the assumption that only one side can reach its goals and that any victory by that party will be matched by the other's loss.

Despite the fact that it produces losers as well as winners, a bargaining orientation can sometimes be the best approach to negotiating. If the other party is determined to take advantage of you and cannot be convinced that collaboration is possible, then you probably need to adopt a competitive stance out of self-defense. You also may need to bargain if your interests truly conflict with those of the other party and collaborating or compromising is not a satisafactory option. For example, in a one-time commerical transaction (the sale of a car, for instance), your concern for helping the other party may take a back seat to getting the best possible deal for yourself––without violating your ethical principles, of course.

When you are bargaining, information about the other party is perhaps the most powerful asset you can possess. For example, imagine how much stronger your position would be when negotiating a salary with a potential employer if you knew the answers to such key questions as:

What is the financial condition of the company?

How much is management paying people in equivalent positions?

Who else are they considering for the position?

What salary would these people be willing to pay?

How much does management want you?

Likewise, if you and a buyer are dickering over the price of an item, your knowledge of the buyer and the marketplace would give you an advantage:

How much does the buyer want or need the item you are selling?

Are there alternative sources available? Is the buyer aware of them?

How much is the buyer prepared to pay?

Before and during a negotiating session, you should do everything possible to collect such information. You can gather intelligence through personal observations and contacts with people who are familiar with your opponent. Reading about your negotiating partner's situation, his or her business, and the industry at large is also a valuable way to gather information. Finally, you can ask your opponent for information: "How much do other department heads earn in salary and bonuses?" "What would it take to get your signature on the contract?" Of course, there is no guarantee that the answers you get will always be honest. In a salary negotiation, the employer would probably refuse to answer rather than lie, but in sales negotiations, bluffing can be part of the game: "I couldn't possibly pay more than $17.50 per unit," when in reality the buyer would go as high as $20.

While a bargaining approach to negotiations is sometimes obvious and appropriate, there are also cases when it is less apparent and destructive. For example, working groups often set themselves up for bargaining outcomes by following the principle of majority rule. If 51 percent of the group members vote for a proposal, then 49 percent are losers—hardly a prescription for future harmony. Whenever the parties approach a problem by taking positions—that is, by stating specific outcomes they are seeking—they are forcing negotiations toward a bargaining outcome. For example, if an employee who wants to spend more time with his child approaches his boss with a specific request such as asking for a seven-hour day, the stage is set for a bargaining outcome. If the boss doesn't like the proposal, someone will be disappointed. Either the employee will get the time he needs with his child and the boss will have a staff shortage, or the boss will prevail and the employee will have to settle for the current schedule or quit.

Lose-Lose Orientation. With a ***lose-lose orientation,*** a conflict plays out in a way that damages both parties to such a degree that everyone feels like a loser. Nobody starts out seeking a lose-lose outcome, of course; but sometimes when people feel that a negotiating partner is blocking them, they wind up seeking revenge. If the boss denies a request for a special day off, a resentful employee might not work his or her hardest. If customers feel cheated, they are likely to tell others about their dissatisfaction, costing the company future business.

Some lose-lose outcomes occur when negotiating partners ignore one another's needs. Like armies that take mortal losses while trying to defeat their enemies, disputants who go for a bargaining victory often find that they have hurt themselves as much as their opponents. Consider our example of the working parent who insists on a seven-hour workday. By forcing the issue, he may wind up having his request denied and then quitting or being fired as a result of his nonnegotiable demand. In this case, everyone suffers: the employer loses a talented worker, and the employee's career and bank balance suffer. Lose-lose outcomes occur on larger issues as well: unreasonable worker demands can drive employers into bankruptcy, and employers can destroy their workers' effectivness by taking advantage of them. Mutual destruction can also arise from personal disputes; both parties in a feud may ruin their own careers, finding themselves characterized as "unable to get along with others" or as "poor team players."

Compromise. Sometimes it seems better to compromise than to fight battles in a bargaining manner and risk a lose-lose outcome. There certainly are cases in which compromise is the best obtainable outcome—usually when disputed resources are limited or scarce. If two managers each need a full-time secretary but budget restrictions make this impossible, they may have to compromise by sharing one secretary.

While compromises may be necessary, by definition the outcome of a ***compromise*** approach is that both parties lose at least some of what they were seeking. Buyers, for instance, may pay more than they can afford, while sellers receive less than they need. Sometimes a series of compromises can leave neither party getting what he or she really wants. For example, if a supplier and a purchasing officer start out from a "horse-trading" perspective, the purchasing officer might end up with more supplies than the company needs at a higher total expenditure than his business can afford, while the supplier might be getting a lower price than her firm would like. In the case of the employee who wants extra time with his child, a compromise wouldn't be of much help to either party. There might still be times when the employee couldn't be with his child, and the boss would still be short of help. Compromises clearly aren't the best kind of outcome.

Win-Win Orientation. The collaborative approach to negotiation, known as the ***win-win orientation,*** assumes that solutions can be reached that satisfy the needs of all parties. As Table 5-3 shows, a win-win approach differs significantly from the preceding negotiating styles. Most important, it looks beyond the conflicting *means* of both parties (my way versus your way) and focuses on satisfying the *ends* each is seeking.

The key to finding win-win solutions is to take the kind of problem-solving, noncontrolling approach described earlier in this chapter. Instead of viewing your negotiating partner as an adversary who needs to be defeated (a bargaining attitude), seek ways to satisfy both your needs and those of the other party. Win-win outcomes are possible in the many cases when the parties' needs aren't incompatible—just different. Consider again the case of the employee seeking a reduced workday. The employee needs care for his child before and after school. The boss needs to have a certain amount of work done. While these needs appear to conflict, they are not necessarily mutually exclusive. Sometimes the parties' needs are not only compatible but *identical.* In our example, both parties want the employee to continue on the job, and both want to maintain a happy relationship.

TABLE 5-3 Characteristics of Negotiating Styles

Bargaining	Compromise	Win-Win
Controlling orientation exists (us versus them).	Recognition that it is impossible to control other party.	Problem orientation exists (we versus the problem).
One party's gains are viewed as other party's losses.	Recognition of linkage between one's own goal and satisfaction of other party.	Mutual gain is viewed as attainable.
Argument over positions leads to polarization.	Parties accept one another's positions, however grudgingly.	Seeking various approaches increases chances for agreement.
Each side sees issue only from its own point of view.	Partial understanding of other party's position.	Parties understand each other's point of view.
Short-term approach focuses only on immediate problems.	Recognition of need for civil outcome.	Long-term approach seeks good relationship.
Only task issues are usually considered.	Focus on task issues.	Both task and relationship issues are considered.

When the goals of the negotiating parties are compatible or similar, a win-win solution in which everyone is satisfied becomes possible. In this case, a number of win-win solutions are possible, for example:

- The employee could do some work at home during nonbusiness hours.
- The employee could share his full-time position with another worker, giving the boss the coverage the boss needs and the employee the free time. If the employee needs additional income, he could take part-time work that could be done at home at his convenience.
- The boss could help the employee locate a source of child care, possibly providing additional work time for the employee to earn the funds necessary to pay for it.

This list of solutions wouldn't work for everyone. The specific solutions that will work for a problem differ in each case. As you will soon read, the parties actually involved in a dispute should develop a list of possible solutions, and this list will differ according to the situation. The important point is that parties working together *can* find no-lose solutions to their problems.

Research shows that a win-win approach is superior to other problem-solving styles. In one study, researchers compared the problem-solving styles used in six organizations. They found that the two highest-performing organizations used a win-win approach to a greater degree than did the less effective companies, while the lowest-performing organizations used that style less than the others.[12]

The win-win approach is most successful when it follows the five steps described below.

Identify the Needs of Both Parties. The key here is to avoid taking polar positions (arguing over means) and instead to identify the *ends* or goals of both parties. In their excellent book *Getting to Yes,* Roger Fisher and William Ury suggest two questions that can help to identify needs.[13] First, *ask why.* Put yourself in the other person's shoes, and ask yourself why the issue is so important to the other person. Once you have identified his or her needs, try to

SKILL BUILDER

Identify the compatible and identical needs in each of these conflicts:

1. A landlord-tenant dispute over who should pay for an obviously necessary painting job.
2. A disagreement between two co-workers over who should deliver a proposal to an important client.
3. A disagreement between a sales manager and the sales representatives over the quota necessary to earn bonuses.
4. A disagreement between a marketing manager and a product development manager about the kind of advertising that should be used for a new product.

find answers that satisfy the other party. Second, *ask why not.* Try to discover what makes the other party unwilling to meet your request. Then try to find an answer that eliminates this objection.

It is important to identify personal, relational needs as well as task-related ones.[14] Common personal needs include the desire to be understood by the other party, to be appreciated and respected, to have a sense of control over one's work, and to have one's needs acknowledged as important. Unless these are recognized, you are unlikely to gain the cooperation of the other party.

The case of Roseanne, a senior manager, and Kurt, her assistant, shows how win-win problem solving begins with the identification of task and relational needs.

Kurt learned that his department was about to launch a particularly ambitious project and asked Roseanne if he could be in charge of it. They each explained their needs:

> "I'm sorry," she said, "but that's a major project. I need someone with more experience, especially in public relations, to handle that job. I've asked Greta to handle it."
>
> "I guess I understand," Kurt said doubtfully. "But I'd really like to take on more responsibility. This is the second time a big job went to somebody else, and I'm starting to wonder whether I'll get a shot at proving myself."
>
> "Well," Roseanne said, "I don't blame you for wanting to know where you stand. Your work has been good, though you still need some experience before you take on jobs like the one Greta will tackle. Let's try to figure out a way that you can have the responsibility and recognition you want and I can feel confident that the job is the right size."

Brainstorm a List of Possible Solutions. In this step, the goal is to work *with* the other party to develop a large number of solutions that might satisfy everyone's needs. Recall the problem-oriented approach introduced earlier in this chapter: instead of working against one another (How can *I* defeat *you*?), the parties work together against the problem (How can *we* beat the *problem*?).

The key to success here is to avoid evaluating any possible solutions for the time being. Nothing deflates creativity and increases defensiveness as much as evaluation. You can judge the quality of each idea later; but for now, the key is quantity. Perhaps one person's unworkable idea will spark a productive suggestion.

Kurt and Roseanne worked together to brainstorm several possible ways to meet their goals:

> "You could put me in charge of a major project—one not quite as big as this one," Kurt said, "and I could just check everything with you along the way."

"Or," Roseanne said, "I might be able to team you up with someone who has experience in areas where you're weak, and you could run the project together."

"What if I took on a less important project," Kurt proposed, "one that called for me to figure out problems in these areas?"

"Or I could get you to assist Greta on this project, so you could get some experience under her supervision and see how the aspects all fit together."

"Maybe you could assign me to handle the public relations on someone else's project, so I could concentrate on doing it right."

Evaluate the Alternative Solutions. Now is the time to decide which solutions are most promising. During this stage, it is still critical to work for an answer that meets the important needs of all the parties. Cooperation will come only if everyone feels satisfied with the solution.

Kurt and Roseanne's evaluation covered all the possibilities they had previously developed:

"All of these are possibilities," Roseanne said. "Let's see which of them will best suit us both. I could put you in charge of a major project, I guess, but you would need a lot of support, and I'm afraid I don't have enough time to give it to you."

Kurt agreed. "Plus it would drive us both crazy if I had to check every detail with you. But I don't really want to team up with someone, either. The whole idea is for me to get some experience where I need it, and a person who has that experience will just handle those concerns—which gets me nowhere."

"On the other hand," Roseanne said, "I don't want to just put you on your own. How would you feel about handling the public relations on Greta's project? She could use some extra help, and having that help would give her time to train you. It would also help you get a sense of the whole project—not just part of it."

Implement the Solution. Once the best plan is chosen, make sure everyone understands it; then give it a try. Kurt agreed to the idea of handling Greta's public relations:

"Just one thing," he insisted. "I want Greta to know that my job is to be responsible for that part of the project—not just to be her assistant."

"Sounds fair to me," Roseanne replied. "I'll talk to Greta and make sure she's agreeable. I do think she has a lot of good advice to offer, though. You'd be foolish not to consider her opinions. And, of course, both she and I will have to support your decisions. But I'll be sure both of us give you the freedom to come up with your own plan—and the responsibility that goes with the freedom."

Win-Win Negotiating in Action

Creative thinking and a collaborative attitude can transform potential lose-lose situations into win-win outcomes. Consider these examples:

Shorter working hours. As part of their job, teachers at a preschool were expected to keep school equipment clean and organized. Since there was never enough time during the school day to do this job, the director asked the teachers to come in over weekends. Even though they were paid for their time, the teachers resented giving up part of a Saturday or Sunday. A brainstorming session between the teachers and director produced a solution that satisfied everyone's needs: substitutes were hired to cover for the teachers during regular school hours while the teachers sorted and cleaned equipment. This approach had several benefits. Not only were the teachers' weekends left free, but the teachers got a welcome break from child care during the regular week. Furthermore, the director was happy because paying the substitutes cost less than having the teachers work overtime.

Increasing employee compensation. The employees of a contractor wanted a raise. The owner agreed that they deserved one, but he opened his books to the workers to show that he was not financially able to provide the increase that they deserved. After considering alternatives together, the boss and employees came up with a plan that pleased everyone. Workers were allowed to use company vehicles during nonworking hours, saving them the expense of purchasing an extra car or truck. The owner made his vacation home in a popular mountain resort available for employees at a bargain rental rate. Finally, the boss negotiated arrangements with local merchants for his employees to buy home furnishings and appliances at favorable prices. Taken together, these benefits amounted to a solid increase in the employees' buying power—provided at little cost to the boss.

Follow Up on the Solution. Even the most appealing plans may need revision when put into action. After a reasonable amount of time, plan to meet with the other parties and discuss how the solution is working out. If necessary, return to step 1, and identify the needs that are still unmet; then repeat the problem-solving procedure.

Roseanne, Kurt, and Greta met several weeks after developing their plan to check its progress:

> "I'm feeling pretty good about the arrangement," Kurt began. "I appreciate the chance to be responsible for one part of such a big project. Just one thing, Greta. When we agree on the way I'll do a job, I feel uncomfortable when you keep checking on how I'm doing. It makes me wonder whether you think I'll mess it up."
>
> "Not at all, Kurt," Greta replied. "I thought you'd want to know that I'm available for support. Of course, I do want to keep posted, but I don't have any intention of being a snoop. What do you suggest?"
>
> "How about letting me come to you," Kurt suggested. "I promise to keep you on top of things, and I do appreciate your advice. I'd just like to have a little more operating room."
>
> "Sounds like a good arrangement," Roseanne said. "Let's give it a try and get together next week at this time to see how it works."

Since a win-win approach has so many advantages when compared with other negotiating methods, it is hard to imagine why a person would reject it. Despite this, some people do seem unwilling to cooperate. Most such rejec-

> Behaviors in negotiation are often reciprocated. When you scream at people, they tend to scream back. When you apologize . . . they tend to apologize too. Likewise, when you give them some information, they tend to return some information. Just by providing some knowledge, you can stimulate the information sharing you need to create mutually beneficial agreements.
>
> Max H. Bazwrman and Margaret A. Neale, *Negotiating Rationally*

tions come from the other person's inability to imagine how both parties could succeed. When you suspect this is the case, a selling job is in order. Begin by paraphrasing your understanding of the other's ends: "It sounds to me that what you need is...." Once you have clarified these ends, point out the possibility of achieving the other person's goals and your own and sharing the beneficial consequences of such a win-win outcome. For instance, if Kurt had refused to accept Roseanne's decision to assign the project to Greta, the negotiation between them might have gone this way:

> "I just can't accept your saying that the job is too big for me," Kurt said. "I've been here over a year now, and I'm starting to wonder if I'll ever have a chance to show what I can do. I *know* I can handle this one."
>
> "It sounds like you need to know you have a future with us, Kurt, and that you want a chance to prove yourself," said Roseanne. "I'm with you on both counts. I'm just not comfortable turning you loose on this job, but let's see if we can work out some other arrangement that will give you the responsibility and visibility you're after."

There are also cases in which an unwillingness to cooperate comes from malice. The other person may have a personal goal that involves trying to punish you by denying what you seek. For example, if Roseanne disliked Kurt and wanted to force him out of the company by refusing to let him grow in his job, her success would depend on his disappointment. In such instances, it is often difficult to get the other person to admit to such an ignoble goal. You can, however, increase the chances of identifying and sidetracking progress toward that goal by using the assertive-message format described earlier in this chapter: "When you refuse even to discuss my ideas about how we could both get what we want [description], I get the idea that it's important to you that I wind up unhappy, which leaves me confused and worried [explanation]. I'd like to know if you are mad at me and, if you are, why [request]." You can then go on to outline the positive consequences of cooperating for both of you ("I'd be more valuable to you if I could get more experience") and perhaps the negative consequences of failing to reach agreement ("I hope we can settle this between us before management starts asking what's going on"). Success here depends on persuading the other person that he or she will be better off (in terms of money, time, self-respect, friendships, stress) with a solution that satisfies you both than with one that fails to meet the needs of either of you.

Which Negotiating Style to Use

The fundamental decision that negotiators face is whether to adopt a win-win approach or to use bargaining tactics. The other two options are rarely first choices: no rational person would seek a lose-lose outcome, and compromises are usually a second choice when it is impossible to win everything one wants.

Win-win and bargaining negotiating styles are fundamentally incompatible: the behaviors that enable one style to work make the other one impossible. As Table 5-4 shows, there are some times when a bargaining approach may be necessary or justified. The differences between these approaches fall into four categories.

Cooperation versus Competition. Parties in bargaining negotiations view one another as opponents. They assume that one side's gain is the other's loss. On the other hand, win-win negotiators cooperate. They believe that it is possible for both sides to get what they want. The decision about whether the other party is an ally or an opponent can be a self-fulfilling prophecy. If you treat someone like an enemy, the person is likely to behave that way. Cooperating with a negotiating partner, however, increases the odds of getting cooperation in return. Nonetheless, there are some times when it is unrealistic to expect cooperation—when the other side will lose in proportion to your gains, for example.

Power versus Trust. Power is the name of the game in a bargaining contest. Parties fear—often justifiably—that the other side will take advatnage of any weaknesses they show. In a win-win situation, however, parties do not take advantage of each other. Power is replaced by trust.

Distorted versus Open Communication. Although it is impossible to justify telling deliberate lies, negotiators who bargain may withhold information, exaggerate, and bluff. You might, for example, flinch and complain about a price that you really would be willing to pay in order to get a further con-

TABLE 5-4 When to Use Bargaining and Win-Win Negotiating Styles

Use a Bargaining Approach	Use a Win-Win Approach
When your interests and the other party's clearly conflict	When you and the other party have common interests
When the other party insists on taking a win-lose approach	When the other party is willing to consider a win-win approach
When you do not need a long-term harmonious relationship	When a continuing, harmonious relationship is important
When you are powerful enough to prevail	When you are weaker or power is approximately equal

SKILL BUILDER

Decide which negotiating style is most appropriate in each of the following situations. Supply details as necessary to explain your choice.

1. Your boss wants you to work during a time you have planned for an out-of-town vacation.
2. You are not satisfied with the quality of a recent shipment of metal fasteners, which you use in assembling a product.
3. You want to rent office space for your small business at a rate that is 5 to 10 percent less than the advertised price.
4. You need an extra week to complete a long, complex assignment.

cession, and you could act cool toward an offer that really excites you in the hope that your adversary will sweeten it. In a win-win situation, however, honesty is the best policy. Both parties place all their cards on the table, trusting that their openness won't be exploited.

Self-Centered versus Mutual Concern. In bargaining, each party focuses on its own goal. Parties give ground only when forced to. By contrast, parties that use a win-win approach listen openly to each other and come to understand each other's position. Furthermore, they try to help each other achieve satisfaction.

SUMMARY

"People skills" are an essential ingredient for success in any career. These skills create a positive communication climate in which people feel valued. The key to building a positive climate is confirming communication, which conveys respect for the other person, even during a conflict. Confirming messages are phrased in descriptive "I" language. They focus on solving problems, not imposing solutions. They are honest, show concern for the other party, demonstrate an attitude of equality, and reflect the communicator's open-mindedness.

One way to create and maintain a positive communication climate is to offer praise. The chapter presented several guidelines for praising effectively. Since praise is not always possible, the chapter also included guidelines for delivering and receiving criticism nondefensively.

The climate of a relationship can be enhanced by offering criticism in the most constructive manner. The chances for acceptance of criticism are best when a critical message is framed in a way that considers the content by limiting remarks to one topic, making sure they are accurate, defining the problem clearly, and showing how attending to the criticism can benefit the recipient. Choosing the most credible critic and making sure the remarks are appropriate to the critic's role can also maximize the beneficial effects of the criticism. Attention to the context is another way to maximize the chances that criticism will be well received: delivering remarks as part of a positive relationship, accepting partial responsibility for the problem, and accompanying criticism with an offer to help. Finally, delivering the criticism in a face-saving manner and a nonjudgmental tone can lead to a nondefensive response.

When on the receiving end of another person's criticism, several responses can prevent a communicator from becoming defensive. One approach is to seek more information from the critic before deciding if his or her remarks are valid. Asking for examples or clarification, guessing about details when necessary, paraphrasing the critic, and asking what the critic wants are all ways of gaining more information. Agreeing with the facts of the criticism or with the critic's perception are also potentially effective.

On-the-job conflicts are inevitable. The goal should be to handle them constructively. There are five ways to handle conflict: avoiding, accommodating, competing, collaborating, or compromising. Each of these approaches has both advantages and drawbacks, so situational factors will usually govern which one to use at a given time.

Negotiations occur when two or more parties discuss specific proposals to find a mutually acceptable agreement. Negotiations can take four forms: bargaining, lose-lose, compromise, and win-win. The approach that parties take during negotiations often determines the type of outcome that will result. The chapter outlined when to use bargaining and win-win negotiating methods. Win-win outcomes arise when parties identify their needs clearly, brainstorm, and evaluate a variety of possible solutions before choosing the best one and following up on the solution after implementing it.

RESOURCES

Covey, Stephen R., *The 7 Habits of Highly Successful People* (New York: Simon & Schuster, 1989).

As its title suggests, Covey identifies the qualities of people who have led successful lives. "Habit 4: Think Win-Win" expands on the win-win approach to negotiating that we presented in this chapter and shows how it operates in a variety of contexts. Covey's description makes it clear that win-win problem solving and career success are compatible.

Fisher, Roger, and William Ury, *Getting to Yes: Negotiating Agreement without Giving In* (Boston: Houghton Mifflin, 1981).

In this readable, realistic introduction to what they call "principled negotiation," Fisher and Ury discuss communication skills that offer the prospect of accomplishing one's own goals in ways that preserve, or even improve, relationships with the other party.

Hocker, Joyce L., and William W. Wilmot, *Interpersonal Conflict,* 4th ed. (Madison, Wis.: Brown & Benchmark, 1995).

This summary of scholarly research on interpersonal conflict explains what researchers have learned about a variety of topics that are important to business communicators: styles and tactics, types of power, negotiation, and interventions by third parties.

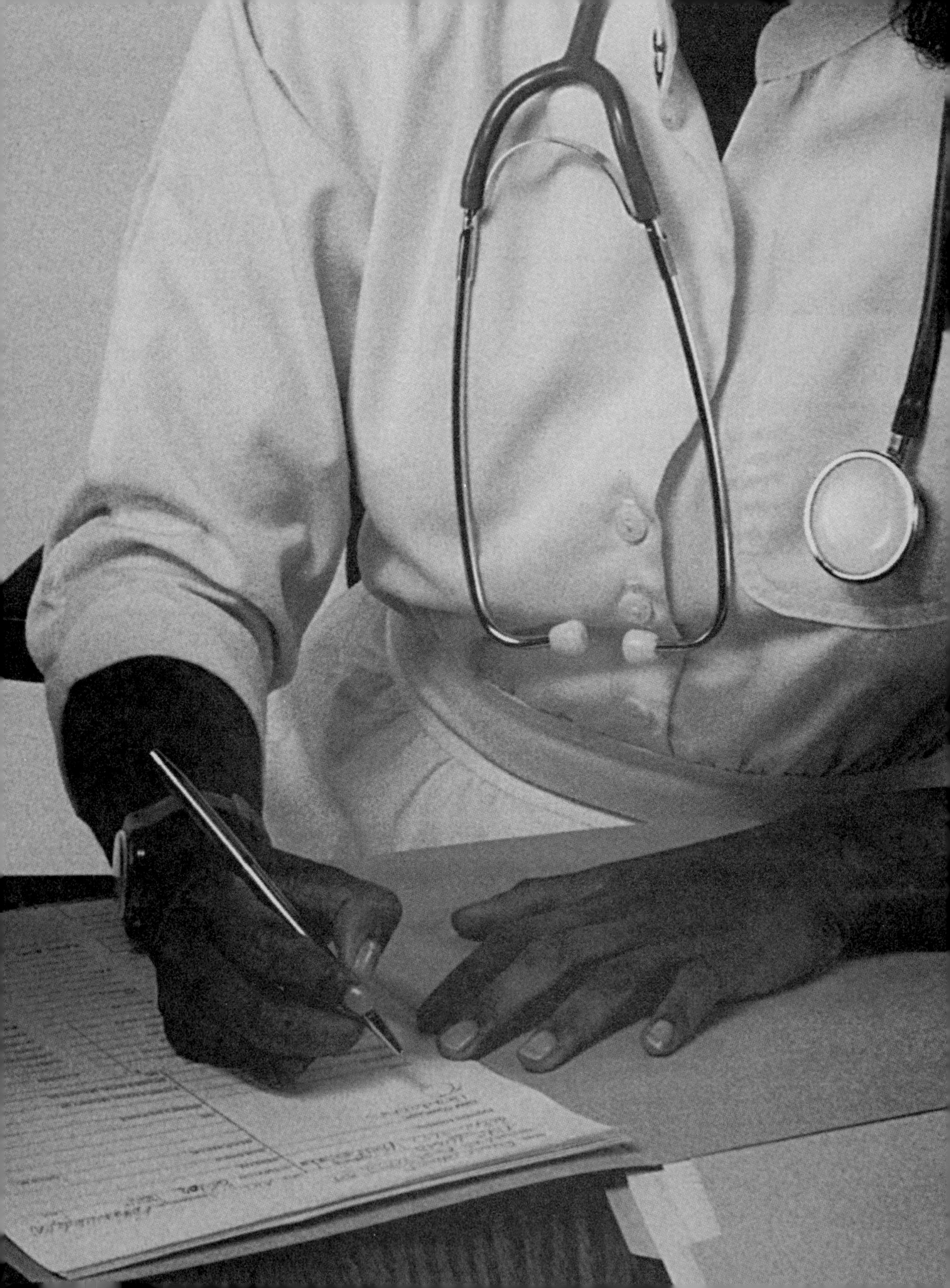

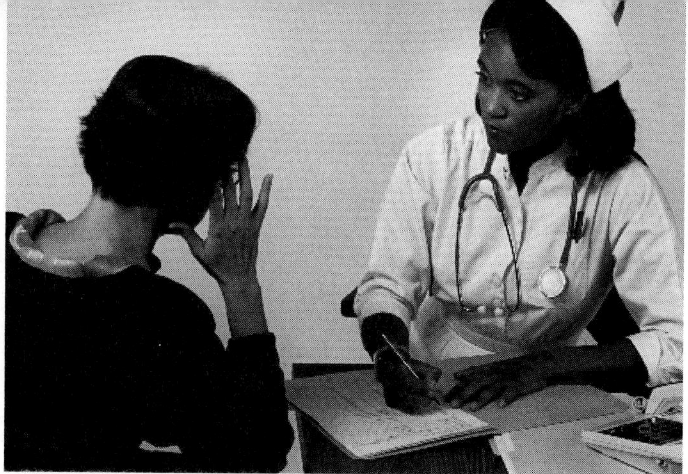

CHAPTER 6

Principles of Interviewing

KEY TERMS

Closed questions / Direct questions / Factual questions / Funnel sequence / Highly scheduled interview / Hypothetical questions / Indirect questions / Interview / Inverted funnel sequence / Leading questions / Moderately scheduled interview / Nonscheduled interview / Open questions / Opinion questions / Primary questions / Secondary questions / Tunnel sequence

Daniel and Cecilia Leon are owners of a small bookstore. A large national chain has opened one of its stores in a nearby mall and is drawing away business. The Leons think adding a small café to their store could recapture customers. They decide to travel around the state, asking other independent booksellers with cafés how well their plan has worked.

Sharon, a marketing manager for a building-supplies manufacturer, is preparing for a trade convention. Although her firm produces more than a thousand products, she can show only a few at the convention. She calls the convention coordinator and asks questions that will help her plan the exhibit: Are the builders who attend the convention mostly concerned with large public buildings, mostly with private homes, or a combination of both? How large will her exhibit space be? Will electrical outlets be available, and can they handle large power demands?

Carol has just been appointed as new manager of a restaurant that has dropped from the leading producer in the chain to the bottom of the list in just over a year. Her job is to figure out where the problem lies and turn the situation around. She begins by talking with virtually every employee, from shift managers to dishwashers.

Susan has worked in the accounting department for three months when Lloyd, her supervisor, calls her into his office. "Is there a problem?" she asks nervously. "No, no," Lloyd replies. "I wanted to let you know we've been pleased with your performance and to find out how you feel about your work in the last three months. I'd also like to know more about how you see yourself in the company in the future."

Each of these conversations is an ***interview,*** a two-party conversation in which at least one person has a specific, serious purpose. This definition makes it clear that interviewing is a special kind of conversation, differing from other types in several ways. Most important, interviewing is always *purposeful.* Unlike more spontaneous conversations, an interview includes at least one participant who has a serious, predetermined reason for being there. Interviews are also more *structured* than most conversations. As you will soon learn, every good interview has several distinct phases and always involves some sort of question-and-answer format. Interviews also have an element of *control* not present in more casual interaction. The interviewer's job is to keep the conversation moving toward a predetermined goal. Interviews are also *bipolar,* always involving just two parties. While there may be several interviewers (as sometimes occurs in employment situations) or multiple respondents (as in a "meet the press" journalistic format), there are always two parties: interviewer and respondent. A final difference between interviewing and other conversation involves the *amount of speaking* by each party. While the speakers in most informal conversations speak equally, experts suggest that participation in most interviews (with the possible exception of sales and information-giving types) ought to be distributed in roughly a 70 to 30 percent ratio, with the interviewee doing most of the talking.[1]

Some people in business spend much of their time in interviews. For example, salespeople spend a great deal of time in sales interviews to assess a customer's needs. Health-care professionals, including nurses, doctors, dental hygienists, and emergency-room receptionists, interview patients to learn about their problems. Most managerial jobs also require some interviews. Many consultants recommend that managers practice "management by walking around" and regularly interview their subordinates about progress, problems, and concerns. In fact, communication authorities claim that interviews are the most common form of planned communication.[2]

There are many kinds of interviews, each of which requires some special skills. Many common principles, however, apply to planning and conducting most interviews.

PLANNING THE INTERVIEW

A successful interview begins before the parties face each other. Whether you are the interviewer or the respondent, background work can mean the difference between success and disappointment.

Define the Goal

Sometimes the purpose of an interview isn't as obvious as it seems at first. For instance, if you are a hotel manager and have received several complaints about the surly manner of a desk clerk, you would certainly speak to the employee. What would your purpose be?

An obvious answer would be to change the clerk's behavior, but this goal isn't precise enough. Will you reprimand the clerk, insisting on a change in behavior? Will you act as a counselor, trying to correct the problem by understanding the causes of the employee's rudeness? Or will you take the role of an explainer, teaching the clerk some new customer-relations skills? While the general goal of each approach is identical (changing the clerk's behavior), the precise goal influences your approach.

The same principle operates in other types of interviews. In a selling situation, is the goal to get a single order or to build a long-term relationship? Is your goal in a grievance interview to ask for specific changes or simply to have your past concerns acknowledged?

INVITATION TO INSIGHT

You can appreciate the frequency and importance of interviewing by realizing how this form of communication is used on the job. Choose a person whose work interests you and who spends much of his or her time interviewing in the course of a typical week. Ask your interview subject what kinds of interviews are common and what role they play in making his or her work successful.

In any interview, you should make your goal as clear as possible, as in the following examples:

Vague: Improve clerk's behavior.
Better: Teach clerk how to handle registration problems.
Best: Teach clerk what to tell guests when rooms are not ready.

Vague: Turn prospect into a customer.
Better: Show customer features and benefits of my product.
Best: Identify prospect's needs and show how my product can satisfy them, resulting in trial order.

The interviewee should also have a clear purpose. Notice, for example, the interviewee's purposes in regard to grievance and employment interviews:

Vague: Complain about unfair supervisor.
Better: Protest unfair scheduling of assignments.
Best: Have supervisor develop fair method of scheduling future assignments.

Vague: Get job offer.
Better: Get job offer by demonstrating my competence.
Best: Get job offer by describing my work experience, referring to my favorable references, and describing my ideas for the position.

Identify and Analyze the Other Party

Whether you are the interviewer or the interviewee, your interviews will be more useful and successful if you select the right person to talk to whenever you have a choice. If you are looking for information, the person you select to interview may greatly influence the quality of the information you get. For example, if you want to know more about the safety procedures in a manufacturing area, the plant manager or foreman can tell you more about them than, say, publicity staff—who probably get their information from the plant manager anyway. Identifying the decision maker can be vital for many interviews. For example, if you want to find out how you can coordinate your efforts with another department's, it may be useful to talk to the person who coordinates that department before you talk to anyone in your own department.

The Other's Concept of Self. The self-image of the other party can have a strong effect on what goes on in an interview. Imagine yourself as the interviewee, and consider the self-image of the interviewer.

For example, if your boss is interviewing you about a project that isn't going well, consider whether she sees herself as a colleague who might be able to help you, an authority whose advice you should take, or an employee who will be in trouble if she has to defend a failure to her own superiors. Likewise, if you are the interviewer, the interviewee's self-concept should influence how you approach the session. A subordinate who feels personally responsible for a failure will need to be treated differently from one who feels that the failure was not his or her fault.

Identifying the appropriate interviewee, the person who makes purchasing decisions, is vital in sales. Mark H. McCormack, owner of a sports promotion agency, describes the situation:

"One of the biggest problems we have had as a sales organization is figuring out who within another company will be making a decision on what. Very often in our business we don't know if it's the advertising department, the marketing department, or someone in PR or corporate communications. It may very well turn out to be the chairman and CEO of a multibillion-dollar corporation if the subject is of personal interest to him."

"In certain companies, particularly multinational, multisegmented operations, it is almost impossible to figure out the decision-making process, or to find any sort of central authority. . . . In most companies, however, the decision-making process is not only there somewhere, it is discernible—as are the names of the decision makers. To find them, it is mostly a matter of doing your homework and asking the right questions."

Mark H. McCormack, *What They Don't Teach You at Harvard Business School*

Knowledge Level. Your questions and answers should be tailored to the information the other person has. A sales representative who bombarded a prospective client with overly technical information would probably be making a mistake, as would a supervisor who sought managerial advice from an employee who has no experience in leading others.

Your Image. Who you are isn't as important as who the other party *thinks* you are. In an employment interview, a knowledgeable applicant who *appears* uninformed is in trouble. In the same way, an employee may want to discuss constructively a problem with the boss, but if the boss thinks the subordinate only wants to complain, the employee's chances for success are limited.

Attitude. Even if the other party has a favorable image of you, his or her feelings about the topic might require careful planning on your part. One interior designer learned this fact the hard way. She was interviewing the partner of a nationally recognized architectural firm about various areas of professional specialization. While discussing the merits of publicly versus privately funded jobs, she asked about requirements for handicapped access. The architect launched into a half-hour tirade about the irrationality of "dumb bureaucratic rules," leaving no time for the designer to cover several important areas.

You may find three sources of information particularly useful. First, you can listen to *what people say.* Co-workers, friends, and even the media can be sources for learning about the other person. "I'm going to ask for a raise," you might tell a friend with whom you work. "How do you think I should bring it up?" If you interview an executive about career opportunities, knowing your subject's career history or education might help you build rapport and ask useful questions.

If you have known the other person before the interview, *what that person has said* can be a good source of information. For instance, you may have once heard your boss comment favorably about an employee who "really had facts and figures to back up what he said." If you are asking for a raise, this information could give you an important clue about how to present your arguments.

Finally, you can discover a great deal about the person you will interview by *observation.* If you have seen the other party dress casually, use informal language, or joke around, you might behave differently than if you had observed more straight-laced behavior. Does he or she seem to encourage drop-in visits or prefer prearranged appointments?

Even if you are meeting the person for the first time, you can still learn something from observation. One sales authority recommends:

> Be observant. Many times there are clues all around the office that will give you ideas that may assist you in talking the prospect's language and, thus, making the sale. Look for trophies, pictures, books, decor, awards, and plaques. It's a safe bet that the prospect is very proud of anything that is on display in the office.[3]

Prepare a List of Topics

Sometimes the topics an interview should cover will become clear as soon as you've listed your objectives. An insurance-claims investigator, for example, usually covers a standard agenda when collecting data on an accident: road conditions, positions of the vehicles, nature and extent of injuries, and so on. In other cases, however, some background research is necessary before you can be sure an agenda is complete. An office manager who is considering the purchase of a new computer might need to do some reading and talk with her staff before she can know what questions to ask the sales representatives who will be calling on her. She will probably want to learn about the topics listed below:

OBJECTIVE

To purchase an affordable desktop publishing system that will be easy to learn and use

LIST OF TOPICS

Attitudes of the staff toward computers

Funds available to allocate for computer use

The general price range of the product

SKILL BUILDER

Imagine that you are interviewing an employee of a company where you might like to work. Develop a list of topics that you will need to cover to get a complete picture of the organization.

Whether software vendors have fixed or negotiable prices

Interviewees, too, should have goals and agendas. A job seeker approaching an employment interview might have a program like this:

OBJECTIVE

To have the interviewer see me as a bright, ambitious, articulate person who knows about and can serve the company's needs

LIST OF TOPICS

Discuss my short-term and long-term career goals.

Answer all questions completely and in an organized way.

Share my knowledge of the company's products and financial condition.

Choose the Best Interview Structure

There are several types of interview structures. Each calls for different levels of planning and produces different results.

A ***highly scheduled interview*** consists of a standardized list of questions. In its most extreme form, it even specifies their precise wording and the order in which they are asked. Highly scheduled interviews are most common in market research, opinion polls, and attitude surveys. Most of the questions allow only a limited range of answers: "How many televisions do you own?" "Which of the following words best describes your evaluation of the company?" The answers to closed questions such as these are easy to tabulate, which makes this approach convenient for surveying large numbers of respondents. Because of their detailed structure, highly scheduled interviews call for less skill by the questioner.

Highly scheduled interviews have drawbacks, however, that make them unsuitable for most situations. The range of topics is limited by a predetermined list of questions, and there is no chance for the interviewer to follow up intriguing or unclear answers that might arise during the conversation.

The ***nonscheduled interview*** stands in contrast to its highly scheduled counterpart. It usually consists of a topical agenda without specific questions. Many managers make a point of regularly "dropping in" on their employees. The conversation may be generally directed at finding out how the employees are doing with their work, whether they are satisfied with their jobs, whether they have any problems—personal or work-related—that the manager should know about, but there are no specific, planned questions. Nonscheduled interviews allow considerable flexibility about the amount of time and nature of the questioning in the various content areas. They permit the conversation to flow in whatever direction seems most productive.

Nonscheduled interviewing looks easy when it's done with skill, but it's actually very difficult. It's easy to lose track of time or to focus too much on one topic and neglect others. When you're worried about what to ask next, you may forget to listen closely to the interviewee's answer and may miss clues to ask for more information.

The ***moderately scheduled interview*** combines features of the other types. The interviewer prepares a list of topics to be covered, anticipates their probable order, and lists several major questions and possible follow-up probes. These make up a flexible plan, which the interviewer can use or adapt as circumstances warrant. The planned questions ensure coverage of important areas, while allowing for examination of important but unforeseen topics.

Consider Possible Questions

After clarifying your purpose, setting an agenda, and deciding on a format, you are ready to think about specific questions. As you might expect, the type and quality of questions are the biggest factor in determining the success or failure of an interview.

The proper questions to ask might seem to be obvious once an agenda is finished, but this is not always the case. An interviewer should consider several types of questions when planning an interview.

Open versus Closed Questions. ***Closed questions*** restrict the interviewee's response. Some ask the respondent to choose from a range of answers: "Which of the three shifts would you prefer to work on?" "Do you think Mary, Dave, or Leonard would be best for the job?" "Would you rather stay in this department or have a transfer?" Other closed questions ask for specific data: "How long have you worked here?" "When do you think the order will be ready?"

Open questions invite a broader, more detailed range of responses. "What makes you interested in working for this company?" "Start at the beginning, and tell me about the problem." "What would you do if you were in my position?"

As an interviewee, you may sometimes want to turn a closed question into an open one so that you can share more information:

Question: Do you have any experience as a manager?

Answer: Not on the job, but I've studied management in several college courses, and I'm looking forward to developing the skills I learned there. I'm especially excited about using the situational leadership approach I learned in my business communication course. I understand you've sent several of your people to workshops on the subject.

As Table 6-1 shows, both open and closed questions have their advantages.

Factual versus Opinion Questions. ***Factual questions*** investigate matters of fact: "Have you taken any courses in accounting?" "Are you willing to relocate if we have an opening in another city?" "Can we apply lease payments to the purchase price, if we decide to buy?" ***Opinion questions,*** as their name implies, ask for the respondent's judgments: "Which vendor do you

TABLE 6-1 Advantages of Open and Closed Questions

When to Use Open Questions	When to Use Closed Questions
1. To relax the interviewee (if the question is easy to answer and nonthreatening)	1. To maintain control over the conversation
2. To discover the interviewee's opinions	2. When specific information is needed and you are not interested in the interviewee's feelings or opinions
3. To evaluate the interviewee's communication skills	3. When time is short
4. To explore the interviewee's possession of information	4. When the interviewer is not highly skilled
5. To discover the interviewee's feelings or values	5. When a high degree of standardization between interviews is important

Source: After Gerald L. Wilson and H. Lloyd Goodall, Jr., *Interviewing in Context* (New York: McGraw-Hill, 1991), pp. 75–80.

think gives the best service?" "Do you think Al is being sincere?" "Is the investment worth it?"

Whether you approach a topic seeking facts or opinions can greatly influence the results. A manager trying to resolve a dispute between two employees could approach each one subjectively, asking, "What's the source of this problem?" "This is a broad opinion-seeking question that invites disagreement between the disputants. A more factual question would be "Tell me when you first noticed the problem, and describe what happened."

This doesn't mean that it is always better to ask factual questions. Opinions are often precisely what you are seeking. A client seeking financial advice from an investment counselor would be making a mistake by asking "How have energy stocks done in the past?" when the real question is "How do you expect they'll do in the future?" Your decision about whether to seek facts or opinions has to be based on your reason for asking the question.

Primary and Secondary Questions. ***Primary questions*** introduce new topics or areas within topics: "How did you hear about our company?" "Do you have any questions for me?" "How often do you use the transit system?" ***Secondary questions*** aim at gathering additional information about a topic that has already been introduced: "Tell me more about it." "What do you mean by 'commitment'?" "Does that price include shipping costs?"

Secondary questions are useful in several circumstances:

- When a previous answer is *incomplete.* "What did Marilyn say then?"
- When a previous answer is *superficial* or *vague.* "What do you mean, you *think* the figures are right?"
- When a previous answer is *irrelevant.* "I understand that the job interests you. Can you tell me about your training in the field?"

- When a previous answer seems *inaccurate.* "You said everyone supports the idea. What about Herb?"

Direct and Indirect Questions. The best way to get information is usually to ask ***direct questions:*** "What area of our business interests you most?" "I hear you've been unhappy with our service. What's the problem?"

Sometimes, however, a straightforward approach won't work. One such case occurs when the respondent isn't *able* to answer a direct question accurately. This inability may come from a lack of information, as when a supervisor's "Do you understand?" gets a "Yes" from employees who mistakenly believe that they do. In another case, a respondent may not be *willing* to give a direct answer that would be risky or embarrassing. A boss who asks a subordinate "Are you satisfied with my leadership?" isn't likely to get a straight answer if the employee thinks the boss is incompetent or unfair. In these instances, an indirect approach would be better. ***Indirect questions*** elicit information without directly asking for it, as the following comparisons show:

DIRECT QUESTION	INDIRECT QUESTION
"Do you understand?"	"Suppose you had to explain this policy to other people in the department. What would you say?"
"Are you satisfied with my leadership?	"If you were manager of this department, what changes would you make?"

Sometimes even the most skillful indirect questions won't generate a good response. But there is another indirect way of judging a response—the interviewee's nonverbal behavior. Facial expressions, posture, gestures, eye contact, and other nonverbal behaviors offer clues about another person's emotional state. Here is a description of how one attorney uses people's nonverbal behaviors as a guide when selecting members of a jury:

> To gauge nonverbal clues, Fahringer may ask the potential juror, "Mr. Jones, I'm going to ask you to do me a favor. Will you look at my client, Billy Williams, right now, and tell me whether you can think of him as being innocent." At that instant, Fahringer concentrates on the juror's face. "If he has difficulty looking at my client, or, when he glances at him, drops his eyes, rejecting him, he has told me all that I need to know."[4]

The same technique can work in the business world. For example, a manager who thinks an employee may be afraid to admit problems with a project can watch how the employee reacts nonverbally to a question such as "Is everything still on schedule for the September 15 opening?"

Hypothetical Questions. ***Hypothetical questions*** seek the respondent's answer to a "what-if" question. They can be a useful way of indirectly getting a respondent to describe beliefs or attitudes: "If we were to take a poll about the morale level around here, what do you think the results would be?"

Hypothetical questions are also a useful way of learning how people would respond in certain situations. A bank manager might test candidates for promotion by asking, "Suppose you became assistant operations manager and you had to talk to one of the tellers about her manner toward customers. What would you do if she accused you of acting bossy and forgetting your friends since your promotion?" Again, there is no guarantee that hypothetical answers will reflect a person's real behavior, but their specificity and realism can give strong clues.

Leading Questions. ***Leading questions*** force or tempt the respondent to answer in one way. They frequently suggest the answer the interviewer expects: "How committed are you to our company's philosophy of customer ser-

SKILL BUILDER

1. Identify the problem with the following leading questions, and rephrase each question so that it is more effective:
   a. In a problem-solving interview: "If everyone is willing to work one Saturday morning per month, we can catch up on our backlog by the end of the quarter. How does that sound to you?"
   b. In a selection interview: "You don't mind traveling once or twice a month, do you?"
   c. In a survey interview: "We think the best features of our product are its price and durability. What do you think?"
   d. In a performance appraisal interview: "Are you still bothered by not getting that promotion?"
   e. In a problem-solving interview: "We're really optimistic about the new job-sharing plan. What do you think?"
2. For each of the following situations, describe whether an open or closed question would be more appropriate, explaining your choice. If you think more than one question is necessary to discover the essential information, list each one.
   a. You want to find out whether your boss would support your request to attend a convention in a distant city.
   b. A manager wants to know whether a project will exceed its projected budget.
   c. An insurance sales representative wants to determine whether a customer has adequate coverage.
   d. An employer wants to find out why an applicant has held four jobs in five years.
3. For each of the following situations, write one factual and one opinion question. Decide which of these questions is most appropriate for the situation, and write two secondary questions as follows-ups for the primary question you have chosen:
   a. You want to know if you are justified in asking your boss for a raise, and you decide to question a co-worker.
   b. A supervisor wants to discover whether an employee's request for a one-month personal leave of absence to visit a sick parent is essential.
   c. You are planning to buy an electronic typewriter or a portable computer. You want to decide whether the computer is worth the extra $500 it will cost.
4. For each of the following direct questions, create an indirect question that could elicit the same information:
   a. "How hard a worker are you?" (Selection)
   b. "Do you agree with my evaluation?" (Appraisal)
   c. "Does the product have any drawbacks?" (Sales)
   d. "Are you telling me the real reason you're leaving?" (Exit)
   e. "Do you really believe my idea is a good one, or are you just going along?" (Problem solving)

vice?" "You aren't really serious about asking for a raise now, are you?" Leading questions may have their place in persuasive interviews when the goal is to sell a product, but they are rarely appropriate in other types of interviews.

Some questions are only mildly leading: "I came across this idea yesterday in the *Wall Street Journal.* It looks interesting. What do you think of it?" In other cases, questions are highly leading. Using emotionally charged words and name-calling, they indicate the only acceptable answer: "You haven't fallen for those worn-out arguments, have you?" Other highly loaded questions rely on a bandwagon effect for pressure: "Do you agree with everyone else that it's best to put this incident behind us and forget the whole thing?"

Organize Questions Effectively

Besides planning individual questions, the interviewer needs to consider the arrangement of groups of questions. There are three basic types of arrangements.

Funnel Sequence. A ***funnel sequence*** begins with a broad, open question and proceeds to seek increasingly specific information, as illustrated by the following example from a problem-solving interview:

Manager: We've lost several good workers in the past year, and we'd hate to lose any more. What do you think is going on?
Employee: Well, a couple of people mentioned pay, but I don't think that's the biggest problem.
Manager: What do you think it is?
Employee: I think it comes down to being bored—not challenged or appreciated.
Manager: What kinds of challenges? What kinds of appreciation?
Employee: Well, I know that Smith and Jones both talked about having some good ideas about how to do the job better, but they complained that nobody seemed interested in listening.
Manager: If you were the manager, how would you listen better?

A funnel sequence is useful when the interviewer is not sure what information she or he is seeking. In the example above, the manager knew that good people were leaving the company, but he didn't know why. His open questions let the employee offer some suggestions. Funnel sequences work best when the respondent knows the topic well or when the interviewer wants to encourage the expression of feelings. They also avoid predisposing the respondent to give a certain type of answer. Imagine, for example, how the conversation might have differed if the manager had started by asking, "Do you think we're paying our people well enough?"

Inverted Funnel Sequence. An ***inverted funnel sequence*** begins with closed questions and gradually broadens the range of possible answers:

Colleague A: I'd like to get your ideas about how I should approach the boss. Do you think I ought to send her a memo about my idea or talk to her about it first?
Colleague B: If I were in that position, I'd mention it briefly and then send her a memo. Then you could go over it together after she's read the memo.
Colleague A: How much detail do you think I ought to go into in the memo?
Colleague B: I'd keep it to a page or two at the most. She's busy, and she gets impatient sometimes.
Colleague A: Here's a rough draft. What do you think of it?

An inverted funnel sequence works well when the subject might be reluctant to offer information at first. The early closed questions are relatively easy to answer, and the answers they provide can lead to more revealing open questions later.

Tunnel Sequence. A ***tunnel sequence*** consists of a series of questions that are similar in depth. They are usually primary in nature, requiring little follow-up. An interviewer surveying consumer attitudes might use a tunnel sequence by asking the following:

"What, if any, magazines do you subscribe to?"

"Which ones do you read thoroughly on a regular basis?"

"Have you stopped subscribing to any magazines within the past year?"

"Can you tell me the names of any other magazines you would enjoy reading regularly?"

Arrange the Setting

A manager at a major publishing company regularly interviews subordinates over lunch at a restaurant where company employees frequently eat together. The manager explains:

> The advantage of meeting here is we're both relaxed. They can talk about their work without feeling as though they've been called on the carpet to defend themselves. They're also more inclined to ask for help with a problem than if we were in the office, and I can ask for improvements and make suggestions without making it seem like a formal reprimand. We also have time to talk without people dropping in or the phone ringing. Of course, if I'm not happy with the person, or if I'm about to fire them, I certainly wouldn't do it over lunch. If that happened, or if they had a serious, confidential problem to discuss, I'd take them in my office, close the door, and have my secretary hold all calls.

The physical setting in which an interview occurs can have a great deal of influence on the results. With some planning of time and place, you can avoid the frustrations of trying to discuss a confidential matter with a co-worker within earshot of people who would love to overhear your conversation or of trying to stop your boss in the hall to ask for a raise when she's on her way to a meeting and the easiest way to get free of you is to say no.

Time. When you plan an interview, give careful thought to how much time you will need to accomplish your purpose, and let the other person know how much time you expect to take. If you ask a co-worker in another department to spend half an hour with you to answer some questions about a mutual project, he can schedule his time so that you won't have to cut the session short or try to cram an important discussion into fifteen minutes.

Other things to consider are the time of day and what the people involved have to do before and after the interview. For example, if you know your boss has an important meeting this afternoon, you can reasonably assume she will be too preoccupied or too busy to talk to you right before it and perhaps immediately afterward. You may also want to avoid scheduling an important interview right before lunch so that neither person will be more anxious to eat than to accomplish the goal of the interview.

Place. The right place is just as important as the right time. The first consideration here is to arrange a setting that is free of distractions. The request "Hold all my calls" is a good sign that you will have the attention of your interviewing partner. Sometimes it's best to choose a spot away from the normal habitat of either person. Not only does this lessen the chance of interruptions, but people often speak more freely and think more creatively when they are in a neutral space, away from familiar settings that trigger habitual ways of responding.

The physical arrangement of the setting can also influence the interview. Generally, the person sitting behind a desk—whether interviewee or respondent—gains power and formality. On the other hand, a seating arrangement in which the parties face each other across a table or sit with no barrier between them promotes equality and informality. Distance, too, affects the relationship between interviewer and respondent. Other things being equal, two people seated 40 inches apart will have more immediacy in their conversation than will the same people discussing the same subject at a distance of 6 or 7 feet.

Isn't it usually desirable to create a casual atmosphere in an interview? As with other variables, the choice of closeness or distance depends on your goal. A medical interviewer who wants to seek personal information without embarrassing the respondent or a supervisor who wants to assert his authority during a reprimand session might choose to increase distance and sit behind a desk. On the other hand, a sales representative who wants to gain the trust of a customer would probably avoid the barrier of a desk.

CONDUCTING THE INTERVIEW

After careful planning, the interview itself takes place. An interview consists of three stages: an opening (or introduction), a body, and a closing. We will now examine each one in detail.

Opening

A good introduction can shape the entire interview. Research suggests that people form lasting impressions of one another in the first few minutes of a conversation. Dave Deaver, a national management recruiter, describes the importance of first impressions in a job interview this way: "The first minute is all-important in an interview. Fifty percent of the decision is made within the first 30 to 60 seconds. About 25 percent of the evaluation is made during the first 15 minutes. It's very difficult to recover the last 25 percent if you've blown the first couple of minutes."[5] These initial impressions shape how a listener regards everything that follows.

A good introduction ought to contain two parts: a greeting and an orientation. The opening is also a time for motivating the interviewee to cooperate and giving a sense of what will follow.

Greeting and Building Rapport. The interviewer should begin with a greeting and a self-introduction, if necessary. In formal situations—taking a legal deposition or conducting a highly scheduled survey, for example—it is appropriate to get right down to business. But in many situations, building rapport is both appropriate and useful. If the interviewer and interviewee are comfortable with one another, the results are likely to be better for both. This explains why a few minutes of informal conversation are often part of the opening of an interview. This small talk tends to set the emotional tone of the interview—whether it is formal or informal, nervous or relaxed, candid or guarded.

The most logical openers involve common ground. A mutual friend or acquaintance is a good example: "How's Mary's new job working out?" "Did you hear that Charlie's wife had a little boy?" Shared interests are also a good starting point: "How was your skiing trip?" "I understand you just bought a new house. We're thinking about moving ourselves. Were you happy with your real-estate agent?" A third type of common ground involves job-related topics, though usually unrelated to the subject of the interview itself. An employee whose goals is to discuss a problem with a co-worker might begin the talk with his boss by asking, "How's the new parking plan we proposed last month working out?" In other cases, noteworthy current events can provide a good starting place: "Did you hear about the fire last night?" "I just read that the prime rate went up again."

Conversation in this rapport-building stage should be sincere. A phony-sounding compliment ("Are those pictures of your family? They certainly are attractive!") will make you sound obsequious and will create the opposite reaction from what you want. On the other hand, you should be able to come up with genuine remarks: "What a great view!" "I hear you're from New York; so am I."

Orientation. In this stage of the opening, the interviewer gives the respondent a brief overview of what is to follow. This orientation helps put the interviewee at ease by removing a natural apprehension of the unknown. At the same time, it helps establish and strengthen the interviewer's control, since it is the interviewer who is clearly setting the agenda. In the orientation, be sure to do the following things.

Explain the Reason for the Interview. A description of the interview's purpose can both put the interviewee at ease and motivate him or her to respond. If your boss called you in for a "chat" about "how things are going," curiosity would probably be your mildest response. Are you headed for a promotion? Are you being softened up for a layoff? Did somebody complain about you? Sharing the reason for an interview can relieve these concerns: "As you know, we're thinking about opening a branch office soon, and we're trying to plan our staffing. I'd like to find out how you feel about your working situation now and what you want so we can consider your needs when we make the changes."

Explain What Information Is Needed and How It Will Be Used. A respondent who knows what the interviewer wants will have a greater likelihood of supplying it. In our example, the boss might be seeking two kinds of information. In one case, a statement of needed information might be "I'm not interested in having you name names of people you like or dislike. I want to know what parts of the business interest you and what you'd consider to be an ideal job." A quite different request for information might be "I'd like to hear your feelings about the people you work with. Who would you like to work with in the future, and who do you have trouble with?"

A description of how the information will be used is also important. In our current example, the boss might explain, "I won't be able to tell you today exactly what changes we'll be making, but I promise you we'll do the best we can to give you what you want." In many situations, it's important to define the confidentiality of the information you are seeking: "I promise you that this talk will be off the record. Nobody else will hear what you tell me."

Mention the Approximate Length of the Interview. An interviewee who knows how long the session will last will feel more comfortable and give better answers.

SKILL BUILDER

With a partner, role-play how you, as an interviewer, could follow the guidelines in this section as you conduct the opening stages of each of the following interviews:

1. You are a real-estate broker meeting a potential home-buying client for the first time.
2. You are considering opening a new restaurant in town (you choose the kind), and you are interviewing the owner of a similar type of establishment in another city about how you can be successful.
3. You are thinking about taking a specific college course (you choose which one), and you are meeting with the professor to get a better idea of what is involved.

Motivation. In some situations, such as a job interview, both people feel the interview is important to them personally. Sometimes, however, you need to give interviewees a reason that will make them feel the interview is worthwhile for them. In some cases, you can simply point out the payoffs: "If we can figure out a better way to handle these orders, it will save us both time." "We'd like to know what you'd like in the new office building so we can try to make everyone as comfortable as possible." If the interview won't directly benefit the other person, you might appeal to his or her ego or desire to help other people: "I'd like to try out a new promotional item, and you know more about them than anyone." "Although you're leaving the company, perhaps you can tell us something that will make it a better place for other people to work."

Body

It is here that the questions and answers are exchanged. While a smooth interview might look spontaneous to an outsider, you have already learned the importance of preparation.

It's unlikely that an interview will ever follow your exact expectations, and it would be a mistake to force it to do so. As an interviewer, you will think of important questions—both primary and secondary—during the session. As a respondent, you will probably be surprised by some of the things the interviewer asks. The best way to proceed is to prepare for the general areas you expect will be covered and do your best when unexpected issues come up.

Responsibilities of the Interviewer. The interviewer performs several tasks during the question-and-answer phase of the discussion.

Control and Focus the Conversation. If an interview is a "conversation with a purpose," it is the interviewer's job to make sure that the discussion focuses on achieving the purpose and doesn't drift away from the agenda. A response can be so interesting that it pulls the discussion off track: "I see you traveled in Europe after college. Did you make it to Barcelona?" Such discussion about backgrounds might be appropriate for the rapport-building part of the opening, but it can get out of control and use up time that would better be spent achieving the interview's purpose.

A second loss of control occurs when the interviewer spends too much time in one legitimate area of discussion, thereby slighting another. Difficult as it may be, an interviewer needs to allot rough blocks of time to each agenda item and then to follow these guidelines during the interview.

Listen Actively. Some interviewers—especially novices—become so caught up in budgeting time and planning upcoming questions that they fail to hear what the respondent is saying.

Use Secondary Questions to Probe for Important Information. Sometimes an answer may be incomplete. At other times, it may be evasive or vague. Since it is impossible to know in advance when probes will be needed, the interviewer should be ready to use them as the occasion dictates.

An interviewer sometimes needs to *repeat* a question before getting a satisfactory answer:

Interviewer: Your résumé shows you attended Arizona State for four years. I'm not clear about whether you earned a degree.
Respondent: I completed all the required courses in my major field of study, as well as several electives.
Interviewer: I see. Did you earn a degree?

When a primary question doesn't deliver enough information, the interviewer needs to seek *elaboration:*

Interviewer: When we made this appointment, you said Bob has been insulting you. I'd like to hear about that.
Respondent: He treats me like a child. I've been here almost as long as he has and I know what I'm doing!
Interviewer: Exactly what does he do? Can you give me a few examples?

Sometimes an answer will be complete but unclear. This requires a request for *clarification:*

Respondent: The certificate pays 11 percent interest.
Interviewer: Is that rate simple or compounded?

A *paraphrasing* probe restates the answer in different words. It invites the respondent to clarify and elaborate upon a previous answer:

Interviewer: You've been with us for a year now and already have been promoted once. How do you feel about the direction your career is taking?

Salespeople don't just pitch products to customers. In order to be effective, they need to find out what the customer needs or wants. Art Parrish, president of Parrish Power Products, explains this process:

"This is how a potential supplier begins to determine your needs. This process can be called many things, but it amounts to communication.

"To determine your needs, the salesman must ask some questions, some subtle, some not so subtle. He is looking for information that will uncover a need as well as potential pitfalls. Is there a need for technical support from the supplier? Are there delivery problems? Are there features about this product that wil reduce your inventory? Is price an obstacle?"

Art Parrish, "A Little Understanding Goes a Long Way"

Respondent: I'm satisfied for now.
Interviewer: So far, so good. Is that how you feel?
Respondent: Not exactly. I was happy to get the promotion, of course. But I don't see many chances for advancement from here.

Often *silence* is the best probe. A pause of up to ten seconds (which feels like an eternity) lets the respondent know more information is expected. Depending on the interviewer's accompanying nonverbal messages, silence can indicate interest or dissatisfaction with the previous answer. *Prods* ("Uh-huh," "Hmmmm," "Go on," "Tell me more," and so on) accomplish the same purpose. For example:

Respondent: I can't figure out where we can cut costs.
Interviewer: Uh-huh.
Respondent: We've already cut our travel and entertainment budget 5 percent.
Interviewer: I know.
Respondent: Some of our people probably still abuse it, but they'd be offended if we cut back more. They think of expense accounts as a fringe benefit.
Interviewer: (silence)
Respondent: Of course, if we could give them something in return for a cut, we might still be able to cut total costs. Maybe have the sales meeting at a resort—make it something of a vacation.

The Interviewee's Role. The interviewee can do several things to help make the interview a success.

Give Clear, Detailed Answers. A piece of obvious advice interviewees often ignore is *answer the question the interviewer has asked.* An off-the-track answer suggests that the respondent hasn't understood the question, is a poor listener, or might even be evading the question. Put yourself in the interviewer's position, and think about what kind of information you would like to have. Then supply it.

Correct Any Misunderstandings. Being human, interviewers sometimes misinterpret comments. Most interviews are important enough for the respondent to want to be sure that the message given has been received accurately. Obviously, you can't ask the interviewer "Were you listening carefully?" but two strategies can help get your message across. First, you can *orally restate* your message. This can be done either in the body or conclusion phase of the interview. For instance, in the body phase, while reporting on a list of exhibit preparations, the interviewee might mention that the brochures will have to be hand-carried; the following exchange could come later in the body phase or at the conclusion:

Interviewer: So, everything will be at the exhibit booth when we get to the convention, and all we have to do is set up the exhibit.

Interviewee: Not quite. The brochures won't be ready in time to ship to the convention, so you'll have to carry them with you on the plane.

Second, you can *put your ideas in writing.* It is sometimes wise to summarize important ideas in a memo that can be delivered before, during, or after the session. This enables the recipient to have a permanent record of your message.

Cover Your Own Agenda. Interviewees often have their own goals. In a selection interview, the employer's goal is to pick the best candidate, while the applicant's aim is to prove that his or her qualifications make him or her the best. This may involve redefining the concept of *best.* For instance, a relatively inexperienced candidate might have the goal of showing the employer that experience isn't as important as education, enthusiasm, or social skills.

Closing

An interview shouldn't end with the last answer to the last question. As with most other types of communication, certain functions need to be performed to bring the interview to a satisfactory conclusion.

Review and Clarify the Results of the Interview. Either party can take responsibility for this step, though in different ways. The person with the greater power (usually the interviewer) is most likely to do so declaratively. For example, in an interview exploring a grievance between employees, a manager might say, "It sounds like you're saying that both of you could have handled it better." When the party with less power (usually the interviewee) does the reviewing and clarifying, the summary often takes the form of a question. A sales representative might close by saying, "So the product sounds good to you, but before you make your final decision you'd like to talk to a few of our clients to see how it has worked out for them. Is that right?"

Establish Future Actions. When the relationship between interviewer and respondent is a continuing one, it is important to clarify how the matter under discussion will be handled. A sales representative might close by saying, "I'll put a list of our customers in the mail to you tomorrow. Then why don't I give you a call next week to see what you're thinking?" A manager might clarify the future by saying, "I'd like you to try out the arrangement we discussed today. Then let's all get together in a few weeks to see how things are going. How does the first of next month sound?"

Conclude with Pleasantries. A sociable conclusion needn't be phony. You can express appreciation or concern, or you can mention future interaction:

"Your ideas were terrific. I know I can use them."

"I appreciate the time you've given me today."

"Good luck with the project."

"Let me know if I can help."

"I'll see you Thursday."

THE ETHICS OF INTERVIEWING

The exchange of information that goes on between interviewer and interviewee should be guided by some basic ethical guidelines and responsibilities.[6] In addition to the moral reasons for following these guidelines, there is often a pragmatic basis for behaving ethically. Since the interview is likely to be part of an ongoing relationship, behaving responsibly and honorably will serve you well in future interactions. Conversely, the costs of developing a poor reputation are usually greater than the benefits of gaining a temporary advantage by behaving unethically or irresponsibly.

Obligations of the Interviewer

A conscientious business communicator will follow several guidelines when conducting an interview.

Make Only Promises You Are Willing and Able to Keep. Don't make offers or claims that may later prove impossible to honor. For example, an employer should not encourage a job applicant about the chances of receiving an offer until she is sure an offer will be forthcoming. To make this sort of promise and then be overruled later by the boss or find out that the budget doesn't permit hiring at this time would be both dishonest and unfair. Likewise, a candidate should not indicate a willingness to start work immediately if she cannot begin work until she has sold her home and moved to the town where her new job is located. Despite the temptations, avoid making any commitments that sound good but are not firm.

Keep Confidences. Interviewers should not reveal confidential information to interviewees, nor should they disclose any private information gained during a session to people who have no legitimate reason to have it. For example, a supervisor who learns about an employee's personal problems should reveal them only with the employee's permission. Likewise, employees who learn confidential information in the course of their jobs—income levels, company plans, and so on—are obliged to make sure that such information stays private.

Allow the Interviewee to Make Free Responses. An interview that coerces the subject into giving unwilling answers is a charade of an honest conversation. For example, a supervisor conducting a performance appraisal who asks a subordinate "Who do you think is responsible for the problems in your area?" should be willing to accept whatever answer is given and not automatically expect the employee to accept the blame. Trying to *persuade* an interviewee is a normal part of doing business, but coercing one is not ethical.

Treat Every Interviewee With Respect. With rare exceptions, the interviewer's job is to help the interviewee do well. This means making sure that the interviewee feels comfortable and understands the nature of the session. It also means the interviewer must design questions that are clear and must help the interviewee answer them as well as possible.

Obligations of the Interviewee

The interviewee is also obliged to behave in an ethical and responsible way during a session. Several guidelines apply here.

Don't Misrepresent the Facts or Your Position. Whether the setting is an employment interview, a performance review session, or an information-gathering survey, it can be tempting to tell interviewers what they want to hear. The temptation is especially great if your welfare is at stake. But besides being unethical, misrepresenting the facts is likely to catch up with you sooner or later and harm you more than telling the truth in the first place would have.

Don't Waste the Interviewer's Time. If the choice exists, be sure you are qualified for the interview. For example, it would be a mistake to apply for

ETHICAL CHALLENGE

1. It is October, and you see conducting regular performance reviews as part of your job. One of the employees you supervise confides that she plans to resign immediately after the company's year-end bonuses are paid. She asks you to keep this news to yourself. You know that your boss will be asking you about the results of the performance reviews and that one of his questions will be about the future prospects of the people you supervise. How will you respond to the employee who has confided in you? To your boss?
2. You know that an employee has been leaving work early for the past several months. You hope he will volunteer this information, without your having to confront him. How can you approach the employee in an interview?
3. As part of a market research project for your employer, you are conducting a series of half-hour interviews with consumers, exploring their attitudes toward a variety of social issues. In the first few minutes of one session, the interviewee makes several racist comments. How do you respond?
4. You are interviewing for a job you really want. The employer asks about your experience with database software. You don't know much about this type of program, but you are confident that you can teach yourself before the job begins. How do you reply to the interviewer?

a job you have little chance of landing or to volunteer for a customer survey if you aren't a member of the population being studied. If preparation for the interview is necessary, be sure to do your homework. Once the interview has begun, be sure to stick to the subject in order to use the time most wisely.

SAMPLE INTERVIEW PLAN

The following plan shows the kind of work that should go on before an interviewer and interviewee sit down to or even schedule a meeting. Every important interview requires the kind of planning exhibited here in order to achieve its goals. As you read this account, notice that it follows the advice outlined in this chapter.

[*Analysis and research*] I know that I'll never build the kind of financial security I am seeking by relying only on the income I earn from my job. Investing successfully will be the path to financial success. I also know that I'm very unsophisticated when it comes to investing, so I want to get myself a financial advisor who can teach me about the world of finance and who can help me set up and follow a plan.

Picking a financial advisor is like choosing a doctor. Skill is important, but it's not the only thing that matters. I need to find someone who has a personal style that I'm comfortable with and whose philosophy matches mine. I also need to find someone who is willing to devote time to me even though I don't have a great deal of money to invest . . . yet!

I've compiled a list of possible advisors from friends, newspaper articles, and listings in the phone directory. I will call several of the people on this list to set up appointments for interviews.

[*Goal*] Based on my needs, the goal for my interviews will be to identify a financial planner with expertise in the field, whose investment philosophy matches mine, and who has a personal style that I am comfortable with.

[*Interview strategy*] I definitely want to conduct these interviews in the offices of each financial planner. Seeing where and how they do business will probably give me a good idea of my comfort level before asking any questions. For instance, seeing a shabby or disorganized office would cause me to doubt the competence of an advisor. On the other hand, a very plush office might make me wonder if I was being charged too much just to support a lavish lifestyle.

I'll also be interested in seeing how much time each person gives me for the interview. If the person is rushed when trying to get a new client, this could mean I won't get the time or attention I need once my money is in the planner's hands.

It will be interesting to see how much each person lets me explain my concerns and how much each controls the conversation. I'm no financial expert, but I don't like the attitude "I'm the expert, so don't waste time asking too many questions." Since I *would* like someone who is willing to explain investing to me in a way that I can understand, I'll be looking for a good teacher.

[*Topics and questions*]

As my goal suggests, I want to explore three topics. The following list shows the questions I'm planning to ask in each topic area as well as follow-up questions I can anticipate asking. I'm sure there will be a need for other secondary questions, but I can't predict all of them. I'll have to think of them on the spot.

TOPIC A: EXPERTISE IN INVESTMENTS AND FINANCIAL PLANNING

[*This series of questions follows an inverted funnel sequence, beginning with a closed question and following with increasingly open ones.*]

1. What credentials do you have that qualify you as a financial planner? How important are credentials? If they aren't important, what is the best measure of a financial planner's qualifications?

[*Again, the questioner uses an inverted funnel sequence to move from a narrow to a broader focus.*]

2. Do you have any areas of specialization? How and why did you specialize in this area?

[*These indirect questions are a way of finding out whether the advisor's performance has been satisfactory.*]

3. How many clients have you served in the last five years? What is the length of the relationship with your clients? How many have you retained, and how many are no longer with you?

[*The average portfolio size is one measure of the advisor's expertise.*]

4. What's the average amount of money you have managed for your clients?

[The first question is a broad, open one. The second, closed question will produce a specific answer that can be compared with those of other potential advisors.]

5. May I see a list of your past and current clients and call some of them for references?

6. How would you describe your track record in terms of investment advice? Specifically, what has been the ratio of successful to unsuccessful advice?

TOPIC B: INVESTMENT PHILOSOPHY

[This broad, open question gives the advisor a chance to describe his or her approach.]

1. How would you describe your investment philosophy?

[This hypothetical question will provide specific information about how a client-advisor relationship might operate.]

2. If I became your client, what steps would you recommend to start and maintain a financial program?

[This inverted funnel sequence of questions moves from specific to broad topics in a logical order.]

3. What kind of products do you like to deal in? Which specific ones might you recommend for me? Why?

[This two-question sequence again follows an inverted funnel sequence. The most important information for the client is contained in the second question.]

4. I've read that some financial advisors make their income from commissions earned when their clients buy and sell investments. Other advisors charge a fee for their time. What approach do you take? Can you explain how this approach is in my interest as well as yours?

[*Although this sounds like a closed question, it is likely to generate a long answer.*]

5. How much should I expect to pay for your advice?

TOPIC C: PERSONAL STYLE

[*This indirect question really asks, "Would we work well together?"*]

1. What kind of clients do you like to work with? What kinds don't you work well with?

[*The first question here is really an indirect way of discovering how much attention the advisor has paid to the potential client.*]

2. Have you looked over the papers I sent you about my financial condition? What did you think of them?

[*This clever hypothetical question has a better chance of generating a useful answer than the more direct "What can* you *tell me about the kind of service I can expect?"*]

3. If I were to call one of your clients at random, what would he or she tell me about the type of service and frequency of communication I can expect with you?

[*This is a straight-forward, open question.*]

4. If we were to develop a relationship, what would you expect of me?

[*This hypothetical question anticipates an important issue.*]

5. Suppose I were to disagree with your advice. What would you say and do?

SUMMARY

Interviewing is a face-to-face conversation in which at least one party has a specific, serious purpose. As such, it is perhaps the most common form of planned communication. Interviewing differs from other types of conversation in its purposeful nature, its degree of structure, its imbalance of control and speaking by one party, and its bipolarity.

A good deal of planning should occur before an important interview begins. The first step involves defining the objective as clearly as possible. At the same time, each party should analyze the other, tailoring the interview to the other's self-concept, knowledge level, image of the interview partner, and attitude toward the topic. The best way to obtain this information is through what others say, what the person in question says, and what you observe.

Having defined the objectives, both interviewer and respondent should prepare agendas, listing the areas they want to cover during the meeting. The interviewer should decide whether a highly scheduled, moderately scheduled, or nonscheduled structure is most desirable. It is also important to plan important primary and secondary questions in advance of the interview. When forming questions, the interviewer should consider desired depth, open versus closed nature, direct or indirect approach, whether fact or opinion is sought, and whether hypothetical or actual inquiries will be most productive. Leading and loaded questions ought to be avoided. It is also important to decide whether questions ought to be organized in funnel, inverted funnel, tunnel, or mixed sequences. Finally, the interviewer and interviewee ought to choose a setting that promotes the best possible outcome.

The interview itself consists of three parts. The opening establishes rapport, orients the respondent, and offers motivation for contributing. During the body, the interviewer should keep the conversation focused, listen actively, and probe for additional information when necessary. The respondent should give clear and detailed answers, correct any misunderstandings, and cover his or her own agenda. The clos-ing ought to review and clarify what has occurred, establish what actions will occur in the future, and conclude with pleasantries.

Besides attending to practical considerations, participants in an interview are obliged to behave in an ethical manner. Interviewers should treat every interviewee with respect, keep confidences, make only promises they are prepared to honor, and avoid coercing the respondent. Interviewees should prepare for the session to avoid wasting the interviewer's time and should represent both facts and their positions honestly.

RESOURCES

Mahoney, F. E., "Adjusting the Interview to Avoid Cultural Bias," *Journal of Career Planning and Employment* 52 (Spring 1992).

Imagine an interview in which limited eye contact, much silence, and no exaggerated claims about one's abilities are valued. This article tries to help interviewers see how the cultural framework creates a paradigm for a successful interview which might be in direct conflict with other (than U.S. mainstream) cultural values.

Ober, Scot, "Collecting Primary Data through Interviews," in *Contemporary Business Communication* (Boston: Houghton Mifflin, 1992), pp. 341–345.

This section of Chapter 11, "Collecting the Data," describes how to conduct personal interviews for research surveys. Guidelines for remaining a clear and unbiased interviewer give readers valuable tips on open versus closed and direct versus indirect questions.

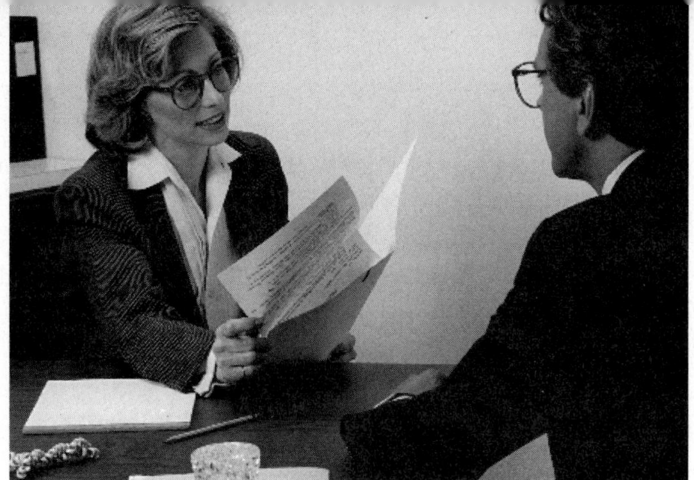

CHAPTER 7

Types of Interviews

KEY TERMS

Bona fide occupational qualification (BFOQ) / Diagnostic interview / Employment interview / Exit interview / Investigative interview / Listen-and-tell performance appraisal style / Performance appraisal interview / Problem-solving performance appraisal style / Research interview / Survey interview / Tell-and-listen performance appraisal style / Tell-and-sell performance appraisal style

The range of interviews you are likely to encounter in the course of your work can be surprisingly broad. Consider these situations:

> Your company is trying to decide whether to convert to a new voice-mail system for handling telephone messages. You sit down with the sales representative from one firm to see what her company's system can offer.
>
> Your boss calls you in for a meeting to rate your performance over the last few months.
>
> One of your best customers is angry with the job your company has done. In an effort to get to the bottom of the problem, you invite him to meet with you.
>
> You are interested in a new job. After making some inquiries, you are invited to meet with the potential employer to discuss your future with that company.

All of these situations call for some sort of interview. Different jobs call for different kinds of interviews. Three kinds of interviews, however, are required for almost any job or career: information-gathering interviews, selection interviews (usually called job interviews), and performance appraisal interviews. In this chapter, we will focus on the particular skills required for each of these three special types of interview.

THE INFORMATION-GATHERING INTERVIEW

Interviewers seek information for a variety of purposes. ***Survey interviews*** gather information from a number of people. They are used to provide information from which to draw conclusions, make interpretations, and determine future action. Manufacturers and advertisers use them to assess market needs and learn consumer reactions to new products. Employers use them to gather employees' ideas about how space should be allotted in a new location or how much a new benefits program might be needed. ***Diagnostic interviews*** allow health-care professionals, attorneys, counselors, and other business and pro-

INVITATION TO INSIGHT

Choose the three types of interview most common in your experience. For each of these types, identify a specific interview you have taken part in in the past or will encounter in the future.

1. Describe the stakes in the situations you have identified. Is money involved? Self-esteem? The future of a career?
2. For the past interviews, describe how satisfied you were with your behavior. For future interviews, predict how satisfied you expect to be with your behavior, given your present level of interviewing skill.

fessional workers to gather information that helps them to respond to the needs of their clientele. ***Research interviews*** provide information upon which to base future decisions. An entrepreneur who is thinking about opening a chain of restaurants might interview others with related experience when developing the concept and question people familiar with the target area to collect ideas about locations and clientele. On a more personal level, an employee thinking about a career change might interview several people who work in the field she is considering to seek advice about how to proceed. ***Investigative interviews*** gather information to determine the causes of an event, usually a problem. Finally, ***exit interviews*** help to determine why an employee is leaving an organization. Since research is the most common type of information-gathering interview for most businesspeople, we will examine it in depth.

Collect Background Information

In many cases, preinterview research is well worth the effort. Suppose, for instance, that you are interested in proposing a job-sharing plan—a system in which two people would share the responsibilities and salary of one full-time job. You decide you need to interview several people in your company before presenting your idea formally. Before conducting these interviews, however, you need to research the answers to some basic questions: How common is job sharing? In what industries does it occur? What forms does it take? Has it been tried by any firms in your field? What have the results of such arrangements been? Until you know at least the rough answers to these questions, you won't be ready to bring up the idea in your company.

Besides conducting traditional library research, you can get answers to questions like these by interviewing knowledgeable people. In this sense, talking about a single information-gathering interview is really an oversimplification, for you will usually conduct several during various stages of a task. You might, indeed, collect some fundamental background information during your first round of interviews. Perhaps you know someone who worked for a company that already has a job-sharing policy. An acquaintance might have mentioned a recent newspaper article on the subject, and you can get the reference that will help you locate it. During this phase, your questions will be necessarily vague, similar to the request you might make of a reference li-

INVITATION TO INSIGHT

Select a person in your chosen career who plays a role in hiring new employees. Conduct an information-gathering interview to discover the following:

1. What methods are used to identify job candidates?
2. What format is used to interview applicants?
3. What formal and informal criteria are used to hire applicants?
4. What personal qualities impress your subject, both positively and negatively?

brarian: "I'm looking for information about job sharing. How do you think I ought to go about it?"

Once you have collected the necessary background information, you can use this knowledge to plan an intelligent approach to your second round of interviews—perhaps with people suggested by your earlier research or with the key decision makers who are your ultimate target.

Define Interview Goals and Questions

Defining the specific goal of your interview is always a key step. Your goal ought to be as specific as possible and be worded in a way that will tell you whether you have the answers you were seeking. Here are examples of how you might define a goal for an information-gathering interview:

VAGUE	SPECIFIC
I want to learn about tax-free municipal bonds.	Will tax-free municipal bonds give me liquidity, appreciation, safety, and tax shelter better than my present investments?
What happened at the accident yesterday?	What caused the accident, and could it have been prevented?
Should I buy a database management system?	Will a database management system be affordable and easy to use? Will it improve my efficiency enough to justify the purchase?

Once you have identified your purpose, you must develop questions that will help you achieve it. For example:

PURPOSE

To learn what steps I need to take to have a job-sharing arrangement approved by management

QUESTIONS

Whom should I approach first?

Who will be the key decision maker on this issue?

Should I present my formal proposal first, or should I start by mentioning the subject informally?

What objections might management have to the proposal?

Is anyone else in the company (nonmanagement personnel) likely to oppose or support the idea?

What arguments (such as precedent, cost savings, employee morale) will most impress management?

What influential people might support this idea?

SKILL BUILDER

For each of the following topics, identify at least two people you could interview to gather information, and give one or more specific objectives for each interview:

1. Learning more about a potential employer (Name a specific organization.)
2. Deciding whether to enroll in a specific class (You choose which one.)
3. Deciding whether to purchase a personal computer (or a piece of software, if you already own a computer)
4. Exploring the career opportunities in a city of your choice
5. Determining the best savings or investment vehicle for you at this time

As you develop your questions, use the guidelines in Chapter 6. Make sure you gather both facts and opinions—and recognize which is which. Be prepared to follow up your primary questions with secondary queries as necessary.

Choose the Right Interviewee

The ideal respondent within an organization will be part of an informal communication network and may have no official relationship with you on the organizational chart. It might be naive to talk with your boss about the job-sharing proposal until you have consulted other sources who could suggest how to broach the subject: perhaps a politically astute co-worker, someone who has experience making proposals to management, or even the boss's secretary, if you are friends, will be helpful.

After you have established the purpose and the appropriate person to interview, follow the guidelines in Chapter 6 to plan and conduct the interview.

THE EMPLOYMENT INTERVIEW

An ***employment interview*** is designed to judge the qualifications and desirability of a candidate for a job. The few minutes spent facing a potential employer can be the most important interview of a lifetime. Consider the stakes. Most workers spend the greatest part of their adult lives on the job—roughly 2,000 hours per year or upward of 80,000 hours during a career. The financial difference between a well-paid position and an unrewarding one can also be staggering. Even without considering the effects of inflation, a gap of only $200 per month can amount to almost $100,000 over the course of a career. Finally, the emotional results of having the right job are considerable. A frustrating job not only makes for unhappiness at work; these dissatisfactions have a way of leaking into non-working hours as well.

How important is an interview in getting the right job? The Bureau of National Affairs, a private research firm that serves both government and industry, conducted a survey to answer this question. It polled 196 personnel executives, seeking the factors that were most important in hiring applicants. The results showed that the employment interview is the single most important factor in landing a job.[1] Further research revealed that the most important factor during these critically decisive interviews was communication skills. Employers identified the ability to communicate effectively as more important in shaping a hiring decision than grade-point average, work experience, extracurricular activities, appearance, and preference for job location.[2]

The best candidate does not necessarily get the job. In most situations, *the person who knows the most about getting hired usually gets the desired position.* "Chemistry is the paramount factor in hiring," states Wilhelmus B. Bryan III, executive vice-president of William H. Clark Associates, a New York recruiting firm.[3] While job-getting skills are no guarantee of qualifications once the actual work begins, they are necessary to get hired in the first place.

Preinterview Steps

Scanning the newspaper for openings and then filing an application with the company's personnel department is one way of looking for a job but often not the most effective. Many employers never advertise jobs, and one study reveals that between 75 and 85 percent of employers in typical U.S. cities did not hire *any* employees through want ads during an entire year.[4]

Even when a company does advertise, the odds are against an applicant who replies with an application and résumé. Since most job announcements attract many more applicants than an employer needs, the job of the personnel department becomes *elimination,* not selection. The goal is to reduce the pool of job seekers to a manageable number by rejecting as many applicants as possible. Given this process of elimination, any shortcoming becomes welcome grounds for rejecting the application and the applicant. Many consultants, therefore, suggest identifying and contacting the person who has the power to hire you *before* an opening exists. The process has several steps.

Conduct Background Research. The first step is to explore the types of work and specific organizations that sound appealing to you. This involves doing library research, reading magazines and newspaper articles, taking classes, and simply fantasizing about jobs you might find interesting. The result of your research should be a list of organizations and names of people who can tell you more about your chosen field.

Develop a Personal Network. The old phrase "It isn't what you know, it's who you know" is certainly true when it comes to getting a job. The results of one survey, pictured in Table 7-1, show the important role of personal contacts in looking for new jobs.

The nature and value of personal networks were demonstrated when researcher Mark Granovetter surveyed over 280 residents of a Boston suburb who had taken a new job within the past year. While only 17 percent of the people surveyed found their jobs through close friends or relatives, the majority learned about their new positions from people who were only distant associates—old college friends, former colleagues, parents of child's playmate,

TABLE 7-1 Success Rates of Sources for Job Opportunities

Source	Success Rate (in %)
Professional associates, former colleagues, friends	75
Fellow students	60
People holding a similar job	50
Professional association placement services	40
Former teachers	30
Newspaper or magazine advertisements	25
Relatives	25
University placement offices	10
Social acquaintances	10
Letters to corporate officers	5
Leads from former employers	5
Mass mailings to employers	5
State placement offices	2
Professional placement agencies	1

Source: After C. J. Stewart and W. B. Cash, Jr., *Interviewing: Principles and Practices,* 4th ed. (Dubuque, Iowa: Wm. C. Brown, 1985), p. 213.

and so on.[5] Weak ties are often more useful than close acquaintances in finding jobs because your close associates rarely know more than you do about career opportunities. Distant acquaintances, however, are connected to other, less familiar communication networks, networks that often contain valuable information about new jobs.[6]

The key to finding the wealth of unadvertised positions is to cultivate a network of contacts who can let you know about job opportunities and pass along your name to potential employers. You can build this network by conducting a series of what is most easily remembered as "three-R" interviews. These interviews get their name from their three goals:

To conduct research that helps you learn more about the field and specific organizations that interest you.

Networking! Isn't that kind of sleazy, like asking people you don't know for a favor when you have no intention of paying them back? The kind of approach a used-car salesman would use?

No. There's nothing sleazy or even manipulative about networking. It's simply a process in which you turn to others for help, just as they have in their careers. Sure, someone may tell you to buzz off. But for every person who has a negative reaction, there'll be ten others willing to lend a hand.

Richard Fein, "Why Networking Isn't Sleazy," *National Business Employment Weekly*

To be remembered by making contacts who will recall you at an appropriate time and either offer you a position or suggest you to a potential employer.

To gain referrals to other people whom you might contact for help in your job search. As Figure 7-1 shows, the referrals from an initial three-R interview can easily lead to meetings with six more useful contacts, all of whom might mention you to *their* friends and associates.

You might wonder why the kind of important person you would like to see in a three-R interview would be willing to meet with you. There are actually several reasons. First, if you have made contact through a referral, your subject will probably see you in deference to your mutual acquaintance. If you can gain a referral, you are most likely to get a friendly reception. Second, interviewees might be willing to see you for ego gratification. It is flattering to have someone say "I respect your accomplishments and ideas" and difficult for even a busy person to say no to a request that accompanies such a comment. A third reason is simple altruism. Most successful people realize they received help somewhere along the line, and many will be willing to do for you what others did for them. Finally, you may get an interview because the person recognizes you as ambitious, someone who might have something to offer his or her organization.

Whenever you approach a three-R interviewee, you ought to accompany your oral communication with some important written correspondence. It's usually wise to make your first contact in a letter. A telephone call runs the risk of not getting through; and even if you do reach the interviewee, your call may come at a bad time. Your first letter, like the one in Figure 7-2, should introduce you, explain your reason for the interview (stressing that you are *not* seeking employment), state your availability for a meeting, and promise a follow-up telephone call. A second letter should precede the interview and confirm its date, place, and time. Finally, a postinterview letter should express thanks for the interviewee's time and mention how helpful the information was. Besides demonstrating common courtesy, these letters become a tangible reminder of you and provide a record of your name and address that will be

FIGURE 7-1 A personal network can grow quickly through referrals.

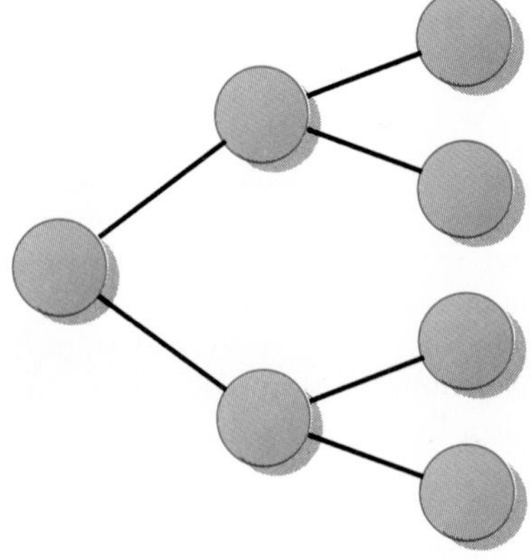

2311 Fernwood Ave.
Knoxville, TN 37995
(615) 505-9361

February 21, 1996

Mr. Ted Dubbels, Chief Engineer
Avrey-Hudson Corp.
121 Industrial Parkway
Knoxville, TN 37991

Dear Mr. Dubbels:

As an amateur musician and electronics tinkerer, I have admired Avery-Hudson's product design philosophy for quite a while. I am the proud owner of an A-H Model 21 amplifier, and am saving to upgrade to a Model 35.

Over the past three years I have been working to turn what I enjoy most into a career by taking courses in electronics at the University of Tennessee with the ultimate goal of entering the field of musical instrument amplifier design. As important as the coursework leading to a B.S.E.E. is, I know there is much to learn outside of the classroom from individuals such as you who have succeeded in this field.

My neighbor, Mr. Tim Rice, has spoken highly of your generosity in helping people in the early stages of their careers. I would be grateful for the opportunity to meet with you to learn how I can best prepare myself for a career in musical instrument amplifier design.

Please rest assured that I am not seeking employment at this time. Your advice is the best payoff I can imagine.

I will be phoning your office within the next few days in hope of planning a meeting time. I am looking forward to talking with you then.

Sincerely,

Christopher Morales

FIGURE 7-2 Sample letter requesting "three-R" interview.

useful if the interviewee wants to contact you in the future. Of course, all correspondence should be typed neatly: your letters are a reflection of you.

Contact Potential Employers. At some point, your research and networking will uncover one or more job leads. You might read a newspaper story about the need of a local employer for people with interests or training like yours. Perhaps a three-R interview subject will say, "I know someone over at ______ who is looking for a person like you." You might learn through a friendly contact that a desirable firm is about to expand its operations. In such a case, it is time to approach the person who has the power to hire you and explore how you can help meet the company's needs.

Whether the job lead comes from a formal announcement or a contact from your personal network, your first step is to let the organization know about your interest in a job. In most cases, the best way to do this is with written correspondence, usually a cover letter and a copy of your résumé. The Appendix of this book has advice on constructing and formatting résumés. A cover letter like the one in Figure 7-3 that takes the following approach will serve you well:

- In the first paragraph, introduce yourself to the reader. Clearly state your purpose for writing (e.g., in response to an advertisement, at the suggestion of a mutual acquaintance, as a result of your research), and describe your ability to meet the company's needs.
- In the second paragraph, highlight one or two of your most impressive accomplishments that are *relevant to the job at hand.* Don't just say you can help the organization: offer some objective evidence that backs up your claim.
- In the closing paragraph, describe the next step you hope to take—usually requesting an interview. Detail any information about limits on your availability (though you should keep these to an absolute minimum). Supply any other information that the prospective employer may have requested.
- Finally, close with a cordial expression of gratitude.

Most career counselors recommend directing your request for an interview to the person who has the ability to hire you, rather than to the company's personnel department. There are several reasons to avoid personnel. First, this department accepts applications only for jobs that have formally been announced. It will reject inquiries about positions that you have learned are soon to be announced, and it may not direct you to other possible jobs that would suit you. Since personnel staff usually don't know about upcoming jobs,

> I know too many stories about people who have been turned down by a particular company's personnel department, who then went back to square one, found out who, in that very same company, had the power to hire for the position they wanted, went to that woman or man, and got hired—ten floors up from the personnel department that had just rejected them.
>
> Richard Bolles, *What Color Is Your Parachute?*

387 Blythe St.
Aurora, CO 80017
(303) 654-7909

April 17, 1996

Mr. John Waldmann, Executive Director
Boulder Arts Council
2987 Seventh St.
Boulder, CO 80302

Dear Mr. Waldmann:

I am writing to express my interest in the position of Events Coordinator for the BAC. I would welcome the chance to use skills acquired over the past 12 years planning events for a variety of community organizations in the Denver area to help the Council extend its reach in the community.

As a person who has coordinated a wide range of community events for nonprofit organizations, I can bring the Arts Council demonstrated ability to motivate and coordinate the work of volunteers and to generate widespread publicity for events on a limited budget. Most recently, I was chairperson for Aurora's Earth Day festival, and I was the public information coordinator for last year's Halloween auction and dance to benefit Denver's Shelter Services for Women. The enclosed résumé details a variety of other activities that have helped prepare me for the position of Events Coordinator.

I would welcome the chance to discuss how I might help the Boulder Arts Council. I will be available any time in the next month, except for the weekend of April 28-29.

I look forward to hearing from you soon.

Sincerely,

Kristina Dudley

Kristina Dudley

FIGURE 7-3 Sample letter requesting an employment interview.

they will generally turn away people who might impress a manager who isn't officially looking for a new employee. We have already discussed another reason why personnel departments aren't the best avenue for getting hired: employees there usually are screening large numbers of applicants, so they are looking for reasons to reject as many as possible to arrive at a manageable number of finalists to interview. Finally, personnel screeners usually are not familiar with the position, so they may reject candidates for superficial or mistaken reasons. The mechanical nature of this screening function is illustrated by reports that computers are beginning to take over the first stages of the application screening process.[7] A software program called Computer Employment Applications serves as the job candidate's first evaluator. The process is a private encounter between applicant and machine, with no interviewer present. The candidate reads questions on the computer screen and types answers into the computer, which then prints out a profile of the applicant as compared with job criteria. It is obvious that programs like this are likely to reject applicants whose experience does not precisely fit the job description even if the applicants might be capable of doing an excellent job in the new position.

Conducting the Interview

If your fate in the selection process was determined by a skilled, objective interviewer, the need for strategic communication might not be essential. Research, however, shows that the rating you are likely to receive from an interviewer can be influenced by a variety of factors as varied as the time of day, the sex of the interviewer and interviewee, whether the candidates before you did well or poorly, and the employer's mood.[8] Since the interview is not a scientific measure of your skills, it is especially important to do everything possible to make the best impression. Interviewing expert Anthony Medley describes one memorable example that illustrates the importance of first impressions:

> A candidate I once interviewed for a secretarial position could type 90 words per minute and take shorthand at 120 words per minute. She was attractive, presentable, and had good references. But after showing up ten minutes late, she called me "Mr. Melody" throughout the interview.
>
> The two things I remembered about her were that she had kept me waiting and constantly mispronounced my name. I finally offered the position to someone whose typing and shorthand skills were not nearly so good.[9]

Dress Appropriately. The information from employers summarized in Table 7-2 confirms the common belief that first impressions are lasting ones.[10] Once an interviewer forms a general impression of you—whether positive or negative—that image will influence his or her perceptions of everything you say in the remainder of the conversation. For this reason, it is essential to present a professional image.

Looking good when you meet a potential employer is vitally important. In one survey, recruiters ranked clothing as the leading factor in shaping their initial impressions of applicants (ahead of physical attractiveness and

TABLE 7-2 Most Frequent Interviewer Complaints about Interviewees

1. Poor personality, manners; lack of poise, confidence; arrogant; egotistical; conceited
2. Poor appearance, lack of neatness, careless dress
3. Lack of enthusiasm, shows little interest, no evidence of initiative, lack of drive
4. Lack of goals and objectives, lack of ambition, poorly motivated, does not know interests, uncertain, indecisive, poor planning
5. Inability to express self well, poor oral expression, poor habits of speech
6. Unrealistic salary demands, overemphasis on money, more interested in salary than opportunity, unrealistic concerning promotion to top jobs
7. Lack of maturity, no leadership potential
8. Lack of extracurricular activities, inadequate reasons for not participating in activities
9. Failure to get information about our company, lack of preparation for the interview, inability to ask intelligent questions
10. Lack of interest in security and benefits, "what can you do for me" attitude
11. Objects to travel, unwilling to relocate

Source: Victor R. Lindquest, *The Northwestern Endicott Report 1988* (Evanston, Ill.: The Placement Center, Northwestern University, 1988).

résumé). Furthermore, 79 percent of the recruiters stated that their initial impressions influenced the rest of the interview.[11] While the best attire to wear will depend on the job you are seeking, it is always safest to dress on the conservative side if you have any doubts.

Know the Organization and the Job. Your background research will pay dividends during the employment interview. One criterion most interviewers use in rating applicants is "knowledge of the position," and a lack of information in this area can be damaging. One example illustrates the advantages that come from knowing even a small amount about a position:

> When I first took a job as a young attorney for Litton Industries, I was interviewing for the position as an assistant division counsel for their Guidance Control Systems Division. That name alone was enough to boggle my mind. A scientist I was not. After a little research, I found that they made something called an inertial navigation system. That was worse than the name of the division. What was an inertial navigation system?
>
> Finally I went to a fraternity brother who had majored in engineering and asked him if he knew what it was all about. He explained to me that inertial navigation was a method of navigating whereby the system allows you, if you know your starting point, to measure speed and distance and therefore know where you are at all times. He also explained the components of the system.
>
> When I went into my interview with the division counsel, I astounded him by my ability to talk the jargon of inertial navigation. . . .
>
> He later told me that I was the first person he had interviewed for the job to whom he did not have to explain inertial navigation. Since he didn't under-

It is easy to get the impression during an interview that the subject of the interview, the *star* (so to speak) of the interview is, well, you. After all, you're the one in the hot seat. You're the one whose life is being dissected. Don't be too flattered. The real subject of the interview is the company. The company is what the interviewer ultimately thinks is important.

Of course, *you* will be very concerned about what opportunities and skills the company has to offer you, but if you're smart, you'll keep that to yourself. It's not that it isn't proper to be interested in advancement and money—in fact, that's a given. What is not a given is your ability to put the interests of your company ahead of your own from time to time; to make personal sacrifices for the good of an important project. The interviewer will be extremely interested in these things if you can find a way to communicate them.

Geoff Martz, *How to Survive without Your Parents' Money*

stand it any better than I did, his being relieved of this obligation was a big plus in my favor. Also he said that he knew that it was not an easy task for me to find someone who could explain the subject and understand it well enough to have the confidence to discuss it. My initiative and interest in going to this extent to prepare for the interview had impressed him.[12]

Respond to the Employer's Needs. While you may need a job to repay a college loan or finance your new Porsche, these concerns won't impress a potential employer. Companies hire employees to satisfy *their* needs, not yours. Although employers will rarely say so outright, the basic question that is *always* being asked in an employment interview is "Are you a person who can help this organization?" Your approach in an interview, then, should be to show your potential employer how your skills match the company's concerns. Background research will pay off here, too: if you have spent time learning about what the employer needs, you will be in a good position to show how you can satisfy company needs and concerns.

Prepare for Important Questions. Most employment interviewers ask questions in five areas:

Educational background. Does the candidate possess adequate training for a successful career? Do the candidate's grades and other activities predict success in this organization?

Work experience. Do any previous jobs prepare the candidate for this position? What does the candidate's employment history suggest about his or her work habits and ability to work well with others?

Career goals. Does the candidate have clear goals? Are they compatible with a career in this organization?

Personal traits. Do the actions and attitudes of the candidate predict good work habits and good interpersonal skills?

Knowledge of organization and job. Does the candidate know the job and organization well enough to be certain that he or she will feel happy in it?

TABLE 7-3 Commonly Asked Questions in Employment Interviews

Educational Background

Why did you choose your major field of study?

How do you feel about your education?

How has your education prepared you for a career?

Why did you choose your college or university?

Describe your greatest success (biggest problem) in college.

What subjects in school did you like best? Why?

What subjects did you like least? Why?

What was your most rewarding college experience?

Work Experience

Tell me about your past jobs. (What did you do in each?)

Which of your past jobs did you enjoy most? Why?

Why did you leave your past jobs?

Describe your greatest accomplishments in your past jobs.

What were your biggest failures? What did you learn from them?

How have your past jobs prepared you for this position?

What were the good and bad features of your last job?

This job requires initiative and hard work. What in your experience demonstrates these qualities?

Have you supervised people in the past? In what capacities? How did you do?

How do you think your present boss (subordinates, co-workers) would describe you?

How do you feel about the way your present company (past companies) is (were) managed?

Career Goals

Why are you interested in this position?

Where do you see yourself in five years? Ten years?

What is your eventual career goal?

Why did you choose the career you are now pursuing?

What are your financial goals?

How would you describe the ideal job?

How would you define success?

What things are most important to you in a career?

Self-Assessment

In your own words, how would you describe yourself?

How have you grown in the last _____ years?

What are your greatest strengths? Your greatest weaknesses?

What things give you the greatest satisfaction?

How do you feel about your career up to this point?

What is the biggest mistake you have made in your career?

Do you prefer working alone or with others?

Continued.

TABLE 7-3 Commonly Asked Questions in Employment Interviews—Continued

Self-Assessment ***Continued***
How do you work under pressure?
What are the most important features of your personality?
Are you a leader? (a creative person? a problem solver?) Give examples.
Knowledge of the Job
Why are you interested in this particular job? Our company?
What can you contribute to this job? Our company?
Why should we hire you? What qualifies you for this position?
What do you think about _____ (job-related topic)?
What part of this job do you think would be most difficult?
Other Topics
Do you have any geographical preferences? Why?
Would you be willing to travel? To relocate?
Do you have any questions for me?

While the specifics of each job are different, many questions will be the same for any position. Table 7-3 lists the most common questions asked by interviewers. In addition, knowledge of the company and job should suggest other specific questions to you.

It is important to realize that some questions are indirect, seeking information that goes beyond their literal and obvious intent. For example, the question "Where do you see yourself five years from now?" most likely asks, "How ambitious are you? Do you have clear, realistic goals? Do your goals fit in our organization?"

Since most employers are untrained in interviewing, you can't expect them to ask every important question.[13] If your interviewer doesn't touch on an important area, look for ways of volunteering information that he or she probably would want to have. For instance, you could show your knowledge of the industry and the company when you respond to a question about your past work experience: "As my résumé shows, I've been working in this field for five years, first at Marston-Keenan and then with the Evergreen Company. In both jobs we were constantly trying to keep up with the pace you set here. For example, the VT-17 was our biggest competitor at Evergreen. . . ."

Be Honest. Whatever else an employer may be seeking, honesty is a mandatory job requirement. If an interviewer finds out that you have misrepresented yourself by lying or exaggerating about even one answer, then everything else you say will be suspect. Emphasize your strengths and downplay your weaknesses, but always be honest.

Emphasize the Positive. Although you should always be honest, it is also wise to phrase your answers in a way that casts you in the most positive light. Consider the difference between positive and negative responses to this question:

Interviewer: I notice you've held several jobs, but you haven't had any experience in the field you've applied for.

Negative answer: Uh, that's right. I only decided that I wanted to go into this field last year. I wish I had known that earlier.

Positive answer: That's right. I've worked in a number of fields, and I've been successful in learning each one quickly. I'd like to think that this kind of adaptability will help me learn this job and grow with it as technology changes the way the company does business.

Notice how the second answer converted a potential negative into a positive answer. If you anticipate questions that have the ability to harm you, you can compose honest answers that present you in a favorable manner.

Another important rule is to avoid criticizing others in an employment interview. Consider the difference between the answers below:

Interviewer: From your transcript, I notice that you graduated with a 2.3 grade-point average. Isn't that a little low?

Negative answer: Sure, but it wasn't my fault. I had some terrible teachers during my first two years of college. We had to memorize a lot of useless information that didn't have anything to do with the real world. Besides, professors give you high grades if they like you. If you don't play their game, they grade you down.

Positive answer: My low grade-point average came mostly from very bad freshman and sophomore years. I wasn't serious about school then, but you can see that my later grades are much higher. I've grown a lot in the past few years, and I'd like to think that I can use what I've learned in this job.

ETHICAL CHALLENGE

Think of a job which you are probably capable of handling well but for which you would most likely not be the candidate hired. Develop a list of questions you would probably be asked in an interview for this position. Then develop a list of answers that show you in the best possible light while being honest.

Most job candidates have been raised to regard modesty as a virtue, which makes it hard to toot their own horns. Excessive boasting certainly is likely to put off an interviewer, but experts flatly state that showcasing your strengths is essential. Florida State University management professor Michele Kacmar found that job seekers who talked about their good qualities were rated higher than those who focused on the interviewer.[14] Preinterview rehearsals will help you find ways of saying positive things about yourself in a confident, non-boastful manner.

Back Up Your Answers with Evidence. Making claims without evidence can sound self-serving. But if you offer evidence to support your answers, the objective facts will confirm your strengths. Compare the two answers below:

Interviewer:	What strengths would you bring to this job?
Weak answer:	I'm a self-starter who can work without close supervision.
Stronger answer:	I'm a self-starter who can work without close supervision. In my last job, I spent roughly two weeks of every month on the road. I was responsible for organizing my own schedule, calling on customers, keeping records, and sending in reports to the home office. In my most recent performance review, my manager wrote that I handled responsibility well without needing close supervision. I have a copy of the evaluation form here, if you'd like to see it.

Keep Your Answers Brief. It is easy to rattle on in an interview out of enthusiasm, a desire to show off your knowledge, or nervousness, but in most cases long answers are not a good idea. The interviewer probably has a lot of ground to cover, and long-winded answers won't help. A good rule of thumb is to keep your responses under two minutes. An interviewer who wants additional information can always ask for it.

Have Your Own Questions Answered. Any good employer will recognize that you have your own concerns about the job. After you have answered the interviewer's questions, you should be prepared to ask a few of your own. Realize that your questions make indirect statements about you just as your answers to the interviewer's inquiries did. Be sure your questions aren't all greedy ones that focus on salary, vacation time, benefits, and so on. Table 7-4 lists some questions to consider asking when you are invited to do so.

Postinterview Follow-up

Without exception, every employment interview should be followed immediately by a thank-you letter to the person who interviewed you. As Figure 7-4 shows, this letter serves several purposes:

TABLE 7-4 Questions to Consider Asking the Interviewer during an Employment Interview

Why is this position open?
How often has it been filled during the past five years?
What have been the reasons for people leaving in the past?
Why did the person who most recently held this position leave?
What would you like the next person who holds this job to do differently?
What are the most pressing issues and problems in this position?
What support does this position have (people, budget, equipment, etc.)?
What are the criteria for success in this position?
What might be the next career steps for a person who does well in this position?
What do you see as the future of this position? This organization?
What are the most important qualities you will look for in the person who will occupy this position?

- It demonstrates common courtesy.
- It reminds the employer of you.
- It gives you a chance to remind the interviewer of important information about you that came up in the interview and to provide facts you may have omitted then.
- It can correct any misunderstandings that may have occurred during the interview.

SKILL BUILDER

You can develop your skill and gain appreciation for the value of the "three-R" interview by doing one of the following activities:

1. Conduct a three-R interview with a person who can help you learn more about how to do your current job better or someone who can inform you about a field that interests you. Follow these steps:
   a. Identify a promising interviewee.
   b. Write a letter requesting an interview.
   c. Follow up your letter with a phone call to arrange a date.
   d. Develop a list of questions that will achieve your stated purpose. Be sure that these questions follow the guidelines in Chapter 6.
   e. Conduct the interview, and report your results.
   f. Write a thank-you letter to your subject.
2. Identify a specific organization you would like to work for, and do the following preinterview steps:
   a. Identify the person—by title and name, if possible—who has the power to hire you.
   b. Using research and the results of three-R interviews, analyze the requirements for the position you would like to hold.
   c. Develop a list of questions a potential boss might ask in a selection interview.
   d. Prepare answers to these questions.

For even more practice, role-play an actual interview, with a companion filling the role of your potential employer.

8975 Santa Clarita Lane
Glendale, CA 90099
(818) 214-0987

March 30, 1996

Ms. Leslie Thoresen
The Think Tank
23262 Wilshire Blvd.
Los Angeles, CA 90076

Dear Ms. Thoresen:

I left our meeting yesterday full of excitement. Your remarks about the value of my experience as a student journalist and volunteer writer of newsletters were very encouraging. I also appreciate your suggestion that I speak with Mr. Leo Benadides. Thank you for promising to tell him that I'll be calling within the next week.

Since you expressed interest in the series of articles I wrote on how Asian women are breaking cultural stereotypes, I am enclosing copies with this letter. I hope you find them interesting.

Your remarks about the dangers of being typecast exclusively as a writer on women's issues were very helpful. Just after we spoke I received an assignment to write a series on e-mail romances. I'll be sure you receive a copy when these articles are published.

Thank you again for taking time from your busy day. I will look forward to hearing from you when the job we discussed is officially created.

Sincerely,

Susan Mineta

Susan Mineta

FIGURE 7-4 Sample thank-you letter.

- It can tactfully remind the interviewer of promises made, such as a second interview or a response by a certain date.

Unlike most business correspondence, a thank-you letter doesn't have to be typewritten. Because it is a personal expression of gratitude, handwriting is considered acceptable. Depending on the formality of your relationship and the image you want to create, you may still choose to use a regular business-letter format. Whatever style you choose, the letter should be neat, error-free, and carefully composed.

Interviewing and the Law

Many laws govern what questions are and are not legal in employment interviews, but the general principle that underlies them all is simple: Questions may not be asked for the purpose of discriminating on the basis of race, color, religion, sex, disabilities, national origin, or age. Employers may still ask about these areas, but the U.S. government's Equal Employment Opportunity Commission (EEOC) permits only questions that investigate a ***"bona fide occupational qualification"*** (***BFOQ*** in bureaucratic jargon) for a particular job. This means any question asked should be job-related. The Supreme Court has said that "the touchstone is business necessity."[15] Table 7-5 lists questions that are generally not considered as BFOQs as well as those that are legitimate.

The Americans with Disabilities Act of 1990 (ADA) requires equal access to employment and provision of "reasonable accommodations" for persons with disabilities. It defines *disability* as a "physical" or "mental impairment" that "substantially limits" one or more "major life activities." As with any

TABLE 7-5 Questions Interviewers Can and Cannot Legally Ask

Federal law restricts employer interviewer questions and other practices to areas clearly related to job requirements. The following are some questions and practices that are generally considered legitimate and others that are not.

Subject	Unacceptable	Acceptable
Name	Maiden name	Name "Have you ever used another name?" *or* "Is any additional information relative to change of name, use of an assumed name, or nickname necessary to enable a check on your work and education record? If yes, please explain."
Residence	"Do you own or rent your home?"	Place of residence
Age	Age Birth date Dates of attendance or completion of elementary or high school Questions that tend to identify applicants over age forty	Statement that hire is subject to verification that applicant meets legal age requirements "If hired, can you show proof of age?" "Are you over eighteen years of age?" "If under eighteen, can you, after employment, submit a work permit?"

Continued.

TABLE 7-5 Questions Interviewers Can and Cannot Legally Ask—Continued

Subject	Unacceptable	Acceptable
Birthplace, citizenship	Birthplace of applicant, applicant's parents, spouse, or other relatives "Are you a U.S. citizen?" *or* citizenship of applicant, applicant's parents, spouse, or other relatives Requirement that applicant produce naturalization, first papers, or alien card *prior to employment*	"Can you, after employment, submit verification of your legal right to work in the United States?" *or* statement that such proof may be required after employment
National origin	Questions as to nationality, lineage, ancestry, national origin, descent, or parentage of applicant, applicant's parents, or spouse "What is your mother tongue?" *or* language commonly used by applicant How applicant acquired ability to read, write, or speak a foreign language	Languages applicant reads, speaks, or writes, if use of a language other than English is relevant to the job for which applicant is applying
Sex, marital status, family	Questions that indicate applicant's sex Questions that indicate applicant's marital status Number and/or ages of children or dependents Provisions for child care Questions regarding pregnancy, childbearing, or birth control Name or address of relative, spouse, or children of adult applicant "With whom do you reside?" *or* "Do you live with your parents?"	Name and address of parent or guardian, if applicant is a minor Statement of company policy regarding work assignment of employees who are related
Race, color	Questions as to applicant's race or color Questions regarding applicant's complexion or color of skin, eyes, hair	
Physical description, photograph	Questions as to applicant's height and weight Requirement that applicant affix a photograph to application Request that asks applicant, at his or her option, to submit a photograph Requirement that calls for a photograph after interview but before employment	Statement that photograph may be required after employment
Physical condition, handicap	Questions regarding applicant's general medical condition, state of health, or illnesses Questions regarding receipt of workers' compensation "Do you have any physical disabilities or handicaps?"	Statement by employer that offer may be made contingent on applicant's passing a job-related physical examination "Do you have any physical condition or handicap that may limit your ability to perform the job applied for? If yes, what can be done to accommodate your limitation?"

TABLE 7-5 Questions Interviewers Can and Cannot Legally Ask—Continued

Subject	Unacceptable	Acceptable
Religion	Questions regarding applicant's religion Religious days observed *or* "Does your religion prevent you from working weekends or holidays?"	Statement by employer of regular days, hours, or shifts to be worked
Arrest, criminal record	Arrest record *or* "Have you ever been arrested?"	"Have you ever been convicted of a felony?" Such a question must be accompanied by a statement that a conviction will not necessarily disqualify an applicant from employment
Military service	General questions regarding military service such as dates and type of discharge Questions regarding service in a foreign military	Questions regarding relevant skills acquired during applicant's U.S. military service
Organizations, activities	"List all organizations, clubs, societies, and lodges to which you belong."	"Please list job-related organizations, clubs, professional societies, or other associations to which you belong—you may omit those that indicate your race, religious creed, color, national origin, ancestry, sex, or age."
References	Questions of applicant's former employers or acquaintances that elicit information specifying the applicant's race, color, religious creed, national origin, ancestry, physical handicap, medical condition, marital status, age, or sex	"By whom were you referred for a position here?" Names of persons willing to provide professional and/or character references for applicant

other job-related issue, the key question is what is "reasonable." The law clearly states, however, that disabled candidates can be questioned only about their ability to perform "essential functions" of a job and that employers are obligated to provide accommodations for disabled candidates and employees. If a person indicates a need for reasonable accommodation during the application process, the company is required to provide it. For example, a person who is deaf can request an interpreter at company expense for the interview.[16]

There are several ways to answer an unlawful question:[17]

1. *Acceptance without comment.* Answer the question, even though you know it is probably unlawful. "I'm forty-seven."
2. *Acceptance with comment.* Point out that the question is probably unlawful but answer it anyway. "I don't think the law allows you to ask my age, but I'm forty-seven."
3. *Confrontation.* Meet the interviewer head-on by asking about the question's appropriateness. "Why did you ask me that?" "Does my age have anything to do with whether I will be hired?"

4. *Rationalization.* Ignore a direct response to the question and point out your qualifications for the position. "My age has nothing to do with my ability to perform the job as described. As you have presented it to me, I have the education, experience, track record, attitude, and desire to excel in this position."
5. *Challenge.* Make the interviewer tell you why this question is a BFOQ. "Please explain to me why age is a criterion for this job."
6. *Redirection.* Refer to an antecedent (something that has come before) to shift the focus of the interview away from your age toward the requirements of the position itself. "What you've said so far suggests that age is not as important for this position as is willingness to travel. Can you tell me more about the travel requirement?"
7. *Refusal.* Say that you will not provide the information requested. "I'm not going to answer that question now, but if I'm hired, I'll be happy to tell you."
8. *Withdrawal.* Physically remove yourself from the interview. End the interview immediately and leave.

Choosing the best response style depends on several factors.[18] First, it is important to consider the probable intent of the interviewer. The question may, indeed, be aimed at collecting information that will allow the employer to discriminate, but it may just as well be a naive inquiry with no harm intended. Most interviewers are unsophisticated at their job. A study reported in the *Wall Street Journal* revealed that over 70 percent of 200 interviewers in Fortune 500 corporations thought that at least five of twelve unlawful questions were safe to ask.[19] Results like these suggest that an illegal question may be the result of ignorance rather than malice. The interviewer who discusses family, nationality, or religion may simply be trying to make conversation.

A second factor when considering how to respond to an illegal question is your desire for the job at hand. You may be more willing to challenge the interviewer when a position isn't critical to your future. On the other hand, if your career rides on succeeding in a particular interview, you may be willing to swallow your objections. A third factor to consider is your feeling of comfort with the interviewer. For example, a female candidate with school-age children might welcome the chance to discuss child-care issues with an interviewer who has identified herself as a single mother who faces the same challenges. A fourth item to consider is your own personal style. If you are comfortable asserting yourself, you may be willing to address an illegal question head-on. If you are less comfortable speaking up, especially to authority figures, you may prefer to respond more evasively.

If you choose to take an aggressive approach to illegal questioning, you have the right to file a charge with the EEOC and your state Fair Employment Practices Commission within 180 days of the interview. In practice, the EEOC will withhold its investigation until the state commission has completed its inquiry. Federal and state agencies have a backlog of cases, however, so it may take years to complete an investigation. A quicker but potentially more expensive course is to sue the employer. Realize, however, that a suit is not likely to make you an attractive candidate to other employers who hear of your action. Blacklists may be unfair, but they are often a fact of business life.

SAMPLE EMPLOYMENT INTERVIEW

The following transcript is based on a real interview. As you read it, pay attention to both the interviewer's questions and the applicant's responses. In both cases, notice the strengths and the areas needing improvement. What parts of this interview would you like to incorporate in your style? What parts would you handle differently?

Interviewer: Monica Hansen? I'm Chris Van Dyke. Welcome.

Applicant: It's good to meet you.

Interviewer: Did you have any trouble finding us?

Applicant: The directions were perfect. And thanks for the parking pass.

Interviewer: Oh, yes. That's a necessity. The garage costs $12 per day if you don't have one. We'll have about a half hour this morning to talk about the personnel administrator's position you've applied for. I'd like to learn about you. And, of course, I want to answer any questions you have about us.

Applicant: Great. I'm looking forward to it.

Interviewer: Good. Let's begin by having you tell me about your most recent position. Your résumé says you were at ITC in Springfield; is that right?

Applicant: That's right. My official job title was personnel assistant, but that really doesn't describe the work I did very well. I recruited nonexempt employees, processed the payroll, oriented new employees, and maintained the files.

Interviewer: Were you involved with insurance?

Applicant: Yes. I processed workers' compensation claims and maintained the insurance reports for our health-care plans.

Interviewer: And you said you were involved in hiring?

Applicant: Yes. I was responsible for recruiting and interviewing all the clerical and secretarial people.

Interviewer: How did that go?

Applicant: It was tough in Springfield. There's actually a shortage of talented secretarial people there. It's an expensive town to live in, and there aren't a lot of people who can afford living there on a secretary's salary. It's not like Atlanta, where there's plenty of good secretarial help.

Interviewer: What did you learn about hiring from your experiences at ITC?

Applicant: I learned to look further than the résumé. Some people seem great on paper, but you find there's something wrong when you hire them. Other people don't have much experience on paper, but they have a lot of potential.

Interviewer: How did you get beyond paper screening?

Applicant: Well, if someone looked at all promising, I would phone the former employers and talk to the people the applicant actually worked for.

Interviewer: What would you do if this was the person's first job?

Applicant: I found that almost everyone had done some kind of work—part time or vacation. And I could check up on that. Or I would even ask for the names of a few teachers and phone them up, if the person was just graduating.

Interviewer: Didn't that take a lot of time?

Applicant: Yes, it did. But it was worth it in the long run, since we got much better employees that way. We almost never had to dismiss someone whom we'd done a phone check on.

Interviewer: You were promoted after a year. Why?

Applicant: I was lucky to be in the right place. The company was growing, and we were very busy. I tried to take advantage of the situation by offering to do more and by taking classes at night.

Interviewer: What classes did you take?

Applicant: I took an applied human relations class last spring. And before that, a couple of computer classes: one in Lotus 1-2-3 and one in desktop publishing. Our department was thinking about starting an employee newsletter, and I wanted to see if we could produce it in-house.

Interviewer: It sounds like you've done very well at ITC. Why do you want to leave?

Applicant: In some ways I *don't* want to leave. The people are great . . . most of them . . . and I've enjoyed the work. But I'm looking for more challenges, and there isn't much chance for me to take on more responsibility there.

Interviewer: Why not?

Applicant: Well, my boss, the personnel director, is very happy in her job and has no plans to leave. She's young, and there's very little chance I'll be able to advance.

Interviewer: I see. Well, that is a problem. And what kind of responsibilities are you looking for?

Applicant: I'd say the biggest one is the chance to help make policy. In my past jobs, I've been carrying out policies that other people—management—have made. That's been fine, but I'd like to be involved in setting some policies myself.

Interviewer: What kinds of policies?

Applicant: Oh, there are several. Designing benefits packages. Coming up with a performance review system that people will take seriously. Teaching our supervisors how to interview and hire more systematically.

Interviewer: I see. Well, the position you've applied for certainly does have those sorts of responsibilities. Let me ask you another question. What do you enjoy most about personnel work?

Applicant: Well, I really enjoy the chance to work so much with people. Of course, there's a lot of paperwork, too, but I especially like the chance to work with people.

Interviewer: When you say "people," what kinds of work are you thinking of?

Applicant: I guess the common denominator is making people happy. Lots of employees get involved with the personnel department—once they've been hired, that is—because they have problems. Maybe it's an insurance claim or a problem with their performance review. It makes me feel good to see them leave feeling satisfied, or at least feeling better after they've come in so upset.

Interviewer: Are you always able to help them?

Applicant: No, of course not. Sometimes a person will want the impossible, and sometimes there just won't be any answer.

Interviewer: Can you give examples of these times?

Applicant: Well, one example of an impossible request comes up a lot with health insurance. At ITC we could choose from two plans. With one plan you could use any doctor you wanted. You had to make a co-payment with that one. With the other plan, you had to choose a doctor from a list of "preferred providers," but there was no co-payment. If an employee chose the preferred-provider plan and later decided he or she wanted to use a doctor that wasn't on the list, we just couldn't do anything about it.

Interviewer: We've had that problem here, too. How did you handle it?

Applicant: Being sympathetic helped a little. Even if I couldn't give them what they wanted, at least saying I was sorry might have made it seem less like a total rejection. I also pointed out that they *could* switch plans during the open-enrollment period, which comes every year. I've also suggested to my boss that we do a better job of informing people about the restrictions of the preferred-provider plan before they sign up and maybe even getting them to sign a statement that says they understand them. I think that would reduce the surprises that come up later.

Interviewer: That's a good idea. Monica, what qualities do you think are important for a personnel officer?

Applicant: Knowing the job is definitely important, but I'd say getting along with people might be even more important.

Interviewer: And how would you describe your ability to get along?

Applicant: Sometimes I think I deserve an Academy Award for acting the opposite of the way I feel.

Interviewer: Really? Tell me about it.

Applicant: Every so often people will come in with an attitude problem, and I try to calm them down by acting more pleasant than I feel. For example, we've had people who think they're entitled to take six months off for a workers' compensation claim, when the doctor has said they're ready to come back after a few weeks. They come in and yell at us, and it's tough to be pleasant at times like those. But I don't think there's any point in being blunt or rude. It just makes them more angry.

Interviewer: I see what you mean. Let's shift gears, Monica. If you were to pick a boss, what are the important traits that he or she should have?

Applicant: Let me see . . . certainly lots of follow-up—letting people know where they stand. The ability to give criticism constructively and to compliment good work. Giving people a task and then leaving them alone, without nagging.

Interviewer: But still being there to help if it's needed, right?

Applicant: Sure. But also giving me the space to finish a job without staying *too* close.

Interviewer: Anything else?

Applicant: Being available for help, as you said. Being consistent. And being willing to train employees in new jobs, letting them grow. And considering the personal goals of employees.

Interviewer: In personnel work, there's a need for confidentiality. What does that mean to you?

Applicant: That's an important area. You see lots of personal information, and it's easy to make offhand remarks that could upset someone.

Interviewer: What kinds of things do you have to be careful about?

Applicant: Oh, even something as simple as a person's birthday. Most people wouldn't care, but some people might be offended if their birthdays got out. I've learned to be constantly on guard, to watch what I say. I'm a private person anyway, so that helps.

Interviewer: Monica, I've been asking you a lot of questions. Let me ask just one more; then it can be your turn. What are the factors that motivate you?

Applicant: Well, I like to be busy. If things aren't busy, I still work, but I like to be stimulated. I seem to get more work done when I'm busy than when there's plenty of time. It's crazy, but true. I'm also motivated by the chance to grow and take on as much responsibility as I can handle.

Interviewer: Monica, what questions do you have for me? What can I tell you about the job or the company?

Applicant: What kind of growth do you see for the company?

Interviewer: Well, we have 155 employees now. As I think you know, we're five years old, and we started with five employees. Our sales were up 14 percent last year, and it looks like we'll be expanding more.

Applicant: How many employees do you think will be added?

Interviewer: Well, we hired twenty new people last year, and we expect to hire almost the same number this year.

Applicant: And what's the turnover like?

Interviewer: That's a good question for a personnel person to ask! We've been growing so much, and people have been able to move into more responsible jobs, so they've been satisfied for the most part. Our turnover has been pretty low—about 15 percent annually.

Applicant: Will the person you hire be involved in making policy?

Interviewer: Yes, definitely. We're still trying to catch up with ourselves after growing so fast. A big project for this year is to put together an employee handbook. Too many of our policies are verbal now, and that's not good. Developing that handbook would mean working directly with the president of the company, and that definitely involves developing policy.

Applicant: Of course, I'm interested in learning about the benefits and salary . . .

Interviewer: Of course. Here's a copy of our benefits summary for you to study. We can talk about salary later. Right now I'd like you to meet a couple of our managers. After you've spoken with them, we can get back together to discuss salary and other matters.

We will definitely be making our decision within the next ten days, so I promise you you'll have an answer before the first of next month.

It's been a real pleasure talking to you, Monica. You certainly express yourself well. I'll talk with you again soon.

Applicant: Thanks. I've enjoyed the talk, too. I'll look forward to hearing from you.

THE PERFORMANCE APPRAISAL INTERVIEW

A working group is like an athletic team: even the best players need the guidance of a coach to help them do their individual best and work with other members. Managers are the coaches in most organizations, and the performance appraisal interview is one way they help their team members.

Definition and Importance

Performance appraisal interviews are scheduled regularly between superior and subordinate to discuss the quality of the subordinate's performance. More specifically, these interviews have several functions, including the following:

- *Letting the employee know where he or she stands.* This kind of feedback includes praising good work, communicating areas that need improvement, and conveying to the employee his or her prospects.
- *Developing employee skills.* The review can be a chance for the employee to learn new skills. Among their other roles, managers and supervisors should be teachers. The performance appraisal interview can be a chance to show an employee how to do a better job.

Some bosses and employees complain that performance reviews are a nuisance. Management guru Robert Townsend agrees—to a point. "Printed forms for performance appraisal and MBOs are used by incompetent bosses in badly managed companies," he claims. Loews Corporation executive Alan Momeyer agrees. He states that an obsession with developing the perfect evaluation form is misguided.

Despite these criticisms, authorities on communication agree that most managers and supervisors need to give employees *more* feedback, not less. "Day-to-day coaching is the most overlooked step of the performance process," says *One Minute Manager* co-author Kenneth Blanchard. Townsend agrees. "Real managers manage by frequent eyeball contact," he insists, quoting one good boss's description of the process: "Half our meetings are held in the hall, the other half in the washroom."

Perhaps these management experts have a point. If bosses spent more time giving employees informal feedback and setting goals on a day-to-day basis, there might be less need for quarterly or semiannual formal meetings. But one way or the other, performance review is one of the most important responsibilities a manager has.

Robert Townsend, *Further Up the Organization;* Alan Momeyer, *Training;* and Kenneth Blanchard, "Rating Managers on Performance Reviews," *Today's Office*

- *Improving employment relationship.* Performance reviews should improve superior-subordinate relationships and give employees a sense of participation in the job. Ideally, employees should leave the interview feeling better about themselves and the organization.
- *Helping management learn the employee's point of view.* Performance appraisal should include upward communication as well as downward. It provides a chance for subordinates to explain their perspective to managers.
- *Counseling the employee.* An appraisal interview provides the chance for managers to learn about personal problems that may be affecting an employee's performance and to offer advice and support.
- *Setting goals for the future.* One result of every performance appraisal interview should be a clear idea of how both the superior and the subordinate will behave in the future.

Despite the potential threat of being evaluated, performance appraisals can be welcomed by employees. One of the greatest hungers that workers have is to know where they stand with management. Researchers have found that receiving "personal feedback" correlates highly with job satisfaction,[20] and appraisal interviews offer a periodic session dedicated to providing just that feedback. Despite this fact, 40 percent of all employees report that they don't receive a regular performance review.[21]

Just because employees want feedback doesn't mean that they are always satisfied with the performance appraisals they do receive. Sometimes performance reviews can be contaminated by organizational politics, generating resentment and undermining morale.[22] Intentionally or not, many unskilled managers turn appraisal sessions into criticisms of past shortcomings that do little besides arouse resentment and defensiveness in employees. The interviewing skills outlined in this section can help make sure that a performance review meets the needs of both management and employees.

Performance review should be an ongoing process, not something that happens only at infrequent intervals during a scheduled interview.[23] The functions of performance appraisal listed on pages 212–213 can and should be performed constantly in the kind of process pictured in Figure 7-5. This doesn't mean that formal interviews are useless, for they provide a chance to focus on how well the ongoing job of judging and improving performance is proceeding. The value of a formal review is captured by former Chrysler chairman Lee Iacocca, who describes how the procedure works in his company:

FIGURE 7-5 The performance appraisal process.

> Every three months, each manager sits down with his immediate superior to review the manager's past accomplishments and to chart his goals for the next term. Once there is agreement on these goals, the manager puts them in writing and the supervisor signs off on it. . . . [T]he discipline of writing something down is the first step toward making it happen. In conversation, you can get away with all kinds of vagueness and nonsense, often without even realizing it. But there's something about putting your thoughts on paper that forces you to get down to specifics. That way, it's harder to deceive yourself—or anybody else.[24]

Styles of Appraisal Interviewing

In his near-classic book, Norman R. F. Maier identifies three styles of appraisal interviewing: "tell and sell," "tell and listen/listen and tell," and "problem solving."[25]

Tell and Sell. A ***tell-and-sell*** performance appraisal style can range from a friendly persuasive style to an authoritarian approach. In any case, the manager who tells and sells believes that his or her evaluation is correct and aims at passing along this assessment to the subordinate.

This style has its drawbacks. First, it can be unfair and unproductive if the manager's evaluation is incorrect. If, for instance, a worker's lack of productivity is due to outside factors and not a lack of effort, as the supervisor suggests, then the evaluation will be unfair and any increase will be in the employee's resentment and defensiveness, not in productivity.

Despite its drawbacks, tell-and-sell interviewing can work well in certain situations: (1) with inexperienced employees who are unable to evaluate themselves; (2) with employees who have much lower status than their bosses and, as a result, are willing to accept the superior's judgments; (3) with employees who are very loyal to the organization or who identify strongly with the manager; and (4) with employees who are not willing to evaluate themselves and who appreciate direction.

Tell and Listen/Listen and Tell. This approach adds a new element to the performance appraisal interview—namely, the manager's willingness to hear the employee's point of view. In a ***tell-and-listen*** interview, the boss offers his or her assessment, and then lets the subordinate react to it. During the final part of a tell-and-listen interview the manager again takes control, identifying future goals for the employee.

Despite its increased two-way communication, a pure tell-and-listen approach is still basically persuasive. The manager's motive for listening is to let the employee have a say, but there is no guarantee that the subordinate's comments will change the boss's ideas.

A more employee-oriented variation of this style is the ***listen-and-tell*** approach. Here the boss lets the subordinate begin the session by describing his or her beliefs, after which the manager has a turn. This structure has three advantages: First, it makes the subordinate's contribution more than just a defensive reaction to the interviewer's evaluation. Second, it lets the manager adjust the evaluation, if the employee's remarks so warrant. Finally, it gives the manager an idea of how well the employee knows his or her own strengths and weaknesses.

Listen-and-tell interviews work best when the interviewer is sincerely interested in the employee's point of view. If the listening phase is just a device to let employees think that they are important, the defensive results will be worse than those from a straightforward tell-and-sell session. The listen-and-tell approach is most successful with employees who fit at least one of the following categories: feeling misunderstood by management, having a high need for participation, or having the ability to understand their jobs and their own behavior.

Problem Solving. A ***problem-solving*** performance appraisal interview involves the employee to a greater degree than the previous two approaches. In it, the manager and employee work together to define areas of concern and to develop appropriate solutions. Thus, the problem-solving manager becomes less of a judge and more of a helper.

Problem-solving interviews are built on the idea of mutual interest and win-win problem solving described in Chapter 5. Both boss and employee realize that their best interests are served by having the employee succeed, and they have the attitude that approaches are possible that leave both parties satisfied. While the interviewer still retains the power that comes with a managerial position, boss and employee cooperate so that neither orders nor threats are necessary.

Steps in the Appraisal Process

Whatever approach is taken, an appraisal session should begin with an opening. After an initial exchange of pleasantries—usually brief—the manager should provide a rationale for the interview, an outline of what information will be covered and how it will be used, and a preview of the interview's probable length. After the preliminaries, the body of an appraisal interview should go on to cover three areas: a review of the criteria established in past meetings, a discussion of the employee's performance, and a setting of goals for the future.

A review is the most onerous task a manager has to perform, because she has to be both judge and jury. The most important thing I can suggest is that the content of a performance review shouldn't be a surprise. It should be a summary of feedback you have given over time and a thoughtful attempt to put that feedback into the larger perspective of what the job is about. Ask yourself: "What have I been telling my employee over the past six months? What was I really trying to say? Can I say it better? What does it mean in the context of what he did over the past months on the job?" Don't look for flashes of revelation; just stick to reality.

Andrew Grove, president, Intel Corporation

Review Progress. The first step in the body of any appraisal interview should be to identify the criteria by which the employee is being evaluated. Ideally, these criteria will already be clear to both the manager and employee, but it is wise to restate them. A manager might say:

> "Bill, as I'm sure you remember, we decided at our last meeting to focus on several targets. We agreed that if you could reach them, you'd be doing your present job very well and you'd be setting yourself up for an assistant sales manager's position. Here's the list of targets we developed last time [shows employee list]. So these are the areas we need to look at today."

Discuss Successes, Problems, and Needs. After the criteria have been defined, the discussion can focus on how well the employee has satisfied them. The nature of the discussion will depend on the style of interview that has been chosen. In a problem-solving format, there will be a give-and-take discussion between superior and subordinate. In a tell-and-sell interview, the evaluation will be dominated by a one-way, top-down style. A tell-and-listen (or listen-and-tell) meeting will combine elements of persuasion and problem solving.

Whatever the interview style, discussion will be easiest when the goals are measurable: Are sales up 15 percent? Have jobs been completed on time? If the employee has explanations for why targets were not reached, it is the manager's job to consider these fairly. Some goals are subjective, so the evaluation of their performance will be a matter of judgment as well. Even seemingly vague goals like "being more patient with customers" can be at least partially clarified by turning them into simple behavioral descriptions such as "letting customers talk without interrupting them."

When evaluating past performance, it is important to maintain a balance among the points under consideration. Without meaning to let it happen, a manager and employee can become involved in discussing (or debating) a relatively unimportant point at length, throwing the overall look at the employee's performance out of perspective. A skillful interviewer will focus only on the most important criteria, usually dealing with no more than three areas that need work. Even the most demanding manager will realize upon reflection that changing old habits is difficult and that it is unrealistic to expect dramatic improvement in too many areas within a short time.

Even when an appraisal is conducted with the best of intentions, its evaluative nature raises the odds of a defensive response. Feedback will be best received when it meets several criteria. Observing these guidelines can boost the chances of keeping the interview's tone constructive:

- *Feedback should be accurate.* Perhaps the worst mistake an evaluator can make is to get the facts wrong. Before you judge an employee, be sure you have an accurate picture of his or her performance and all the factors that affected it. A tell-and-listen approach can help the manager understand an employee's performance more fully.

- *Feedback should be relevant to the job.* For example, it may be legitimate to comment on an employee's appearance in a job that involves contact with the public, but it is probably out of line to be critical about the way he or she handles personal matters after business hours.

The best chances of success occur when the review offers a balance of praise and constructive suggestions for improvement. Both everyday experience and research have demonstrated the power of positive reinforcement. One study revealed that the commitment level of employees dropped when their behavior was identified as only "satisfactory."[26] A manager who uses praise in appraisal interviews should remember the tips for praising outlined in Chapter 5 (pages 128–129).

Sooner or later, even the most outstanding employee will need to hear criticism about his or her work. Delivering negative information is one of the biggest challenges a manager or supervisor can face. The guidelines in Chapter 5 (pages 130–131) offer tips on how to offer negative feedback supportively. Handling critical situations well isn't just the boss's responsibility; the subordinate needs to behave responsibly too. The guidelines for coping nondefensively with criticism outlined on pages 131–133 should be helpful when it is your turn to receive critical messages. While following these guidelines won't guarantee a successful performance review, it can increase the chances that the meeting will be genuinely constructive and serve the interests of both the superior and the subordinate.

Set Goals. Once the employee and manager have discussed past successes, problems, and needs, the task becomes defining goals for the future. The goals should meet several criteria:

- They should focus on the most important aspects of the job. The tried-and-true 80:20 rule applies here: changing 20 percent of a worker's behavior will usually solve 80 percent of the problems.
- The goals should be described as specifically as possible so that both manager and employee will know what actions constitute the target.
- A time period should be stated for each target. People often work best when faced with a deadline, and setting dates lets both parties know when the results are due.
- The targets ought to provide some challenge to the worker, requiring effort yet being attainable. A manageable challenge will produce the greatest growth and leave workers and managers feeling pleased with the changes that occur.

SKILL BUILDER

Imagine that a supervisor or instructor is preparing an evaluation of your performance. Four areas will be covered:

1. Quality of work
2. Productivity
3. Communication skill
4. Attitude

On the basis of your actual behavior on the job, translate these terms into behavioral descriptions of your performance during the last month and behavioral objectives for the coming month.

The Written Record. The appraisal process commonly has a written dimension in addition to the interview itself. Before the meeting, the manager often completes an evaluation form listing characteristics or behaviors important to the job. Ideally, the information on this form is taken from the goals set at the previous interview. In some organizations, the subordinate also fills out a self-rating form covering similar areas. In most companies, a performance review is summarized and documented with a written evaluation. In most cases, the manager completes a final report that summarizes the results of the session. The employee usually has the option of adding his or her own response to the manager's report. This document then becomes part of the employee's records and is used as a basis for future evaluations and as a source of information for decisions about promotions. (See Table 7-6.)

TABLE 7-6 Checklist for Performance Appraisal Interviewing

- *Interview covers key areas*
  - ___ Orients employee
  - ___ Establishes positive climate
  - ___ Reviews past achievement of goals
  - ___ Identifies successes, problems, and needs in employee's area of responsibility
  - ___ Establishes new goals with employee
- *Feedback delivered constructively*
  - ___ Information accurate
  - ___ Feedback appropriate to critic's role
  - ___ Balance of praise and constructive criticism
- *Praise delivered effectively*
  - ___ Praise sincere
  - ___ Specific behaviors identified
  - ___ Emphasis on progress, not perfection
  - ___ Praise communicated by deeds as well as by words
- *Criticism expressed constructively*
  - ___ Criticism limited to key areas
  - ___ Criticism delivered in face-saving manner
  - ___ Criticism accompanied by offer to help
  - ___ Benefits of cooperating emphasized
- *Interview accomplishes all necessary functions*
  - ___ Lets employee know where he or she stands
  - ___ Develops employee skills
  - ___ Improves communication climate, boosts morale
  - ___ Helps management understand employee's point of view
  - ___ Counsels employee as appropriate
  - ___ Sets goals for future

SUMMARY

This chapter focused on three important types of interviews: information gathering, selection, and performance appraisal. The most common type of information-gathering interview aims at conducting research. The research interviewer should begin by collecting background information on the subject and the interviewee. This information is used to define the general goals of the interview and identify the specific questions that should be asked. Equally important is identifying whom to interview to get the desired information.

Selection interviews are critically important for even the most qualified job applicant, for the person who receives a job offer is often the one who knows the most about how to get hired. Since many positions are never advertised, a job seeker should begin the selection process long before an official job interview. The first step involves building a network of personal contacts by conducting a series of "three-R" interviews to research potentially interesting fields, to be remembered by the interviewee, and to gain referrals for other helpful contacts. When these three-R interviews or other sources lead to a job interview itself, candidates should constantly focus on showing how they can help the organization reach its goals. Effective behavior for the interviewee includes looking good, being honest, answering questions briefly, and finding common ground with the interviewer. Every employment interview should be followed by a letter of thanks from the applicant to the interviewer.

Federal and state laws restrict interviewers from asking questions that are not related to the bona fide occupational qualifications of a job. In this chapter, we listed both acceptable and unacceptable questions and practices and suggested strategies for responding to illegal questions.

Performance appraisal interviews give superiors and their subordinates a structured way to look at the quality of the subordinate's performance. When conducted skillfully, these sessions are welcomed by most employees as a chance to learn how they are viewed by management.

Three styles can be used in performance appraisal interviews: tell and sell, tell and listen/listen and tell, and problem solving. The best style varies from one type of employee to another. Whatever the approach, all appraisal interviews should begin with a definition of the criteria used to evaluate the employee. Next, the employee's performance should be evaluated according to these criteria. Finally, manager and employee should set goals for the next evaluation period.

RESOURCES

Boone, L. E., D. L. Kurtz, and J. R. Block, "Effective Employment Interviewing" in *Contemporary Business Communication* (Englewood Cliffs, N.J.: Prentice-Hall, 1994), pp. 555–592.

This chapter presents a thorough look at the range of topics surrounding the hiring process, including the screening interview, in-depth interview, multiple interview, and stress interview. Also covered are cultural differences in international interviews, strategies for negotiating salary and benefits, pre-employment tests, and interview follow-up letters.

Canning, M. B. (Ed.), *Read, Aim, Hire! How to Master the Hiring Process: An Anthology by 12 of the Nation's Top Experts* (Oak Brook, Ill.: PerSysCo, 1992).

Two things make this volume interesting: a great collection of employment and interview cartoons and a look at the employment interview from the other side of the desk. Written by experts who conduct interviews, readers discover how one author spots exaggerations and falsehoods during employment interviews and how another describes his interviewing methods, which, he claims, are better than lie detectors.

Mahoney, F. E., "Adjusting the Interview to Avoid Cultural Bias," *Journal of Career Planning and Employment* 11 (Spring 1992).

This brief article describes how many of the characteristics that are traditionally considered desirable for employment interview candidates are alien to people from many non-Euro-American cultures. While it is written to sensitize employers to recognize the strengths of culturally diverse interviewees, it is also useful for job seekers who want to understand how ways of behaving that are considered strengths in their own cultures can be misunderstood in employment interviews.

Murphy, Kevin R., and Jeannette Cleveland, *Understanding Performance Appraisal* (Newbury Park, Calif.: Sage, 1995).

Murphy and Cleveland present a thorough summary of scholarship on this important type of interview. Topics include environmental and organizational influences on the interview, standards for judging performance, and measures of error and accuracy, and advice is given on setting up and evaluating a goal-oriented evaluation system.

Shingleton, J. D., *Successful Interviewing for College Seniors* (Lincolnwood, Ill.: VGM Career Horizons, 1992).

In this slim publication, the soon-to-be college graduate can find the answers to many questions about job searching and employment interviewing. In addition to chapters on the concept of the interview, including preparation and follow-up suggestions, one chapter addresses the special context of the campus recruiting process.

Stewart, C. J., and W. B. Cash, Jr., *Interviewing: Principles and Practices,* 7th ed. (Madison, Wis.: Brown & Benchmark, 1995).

Chapter 7, "The Selection Interview," describes this event from the perspective of both interviewer and interviewee. It also contains detailed information on what is and isn't legal in employment interviews.

PART III

Working in Groups

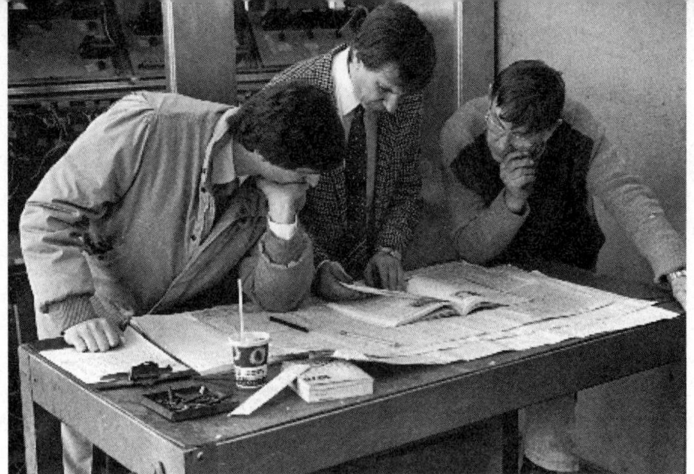

CHAPTER 8

Working in Teams

KEY TERMS

Authoritarian leadership style / Authority role / Brainstorming / Coercive power / Cohesiveness / Conflict phase / Connection power / Consensus / Contingency approaches to leadership / Democratic leadership style / Designated leader / Emergence phase / Emergent leader / Expert opinion / Expert power / Functional roles / Groupthink / Hidden agenda / Information power / Laissez-faire leadership style / Legitimate power / Life-cycle theory of leadership / Norms / Orientation phase / Referent power / Reflective-thinking sequence / Reinforcement phase / Relational roles / Reward power / Risky shift / Roles / Self-directed work teams / Style approach to leadership / Task roles / Team / Trait approach to leadership / Work group

Working with others is a vital part of almost every job. Regardless of the business, you can expect to coordinate tasks and schedules with others, share information, solve problems, and make decisions. In all but the smallest companies, employees work on project teams, task forces, production crews, and committees—all groups of one sort or another. The pervasiveness of groups helps explain why the ability to work as a team player is often regarded as more important than an employee's individual brilliance. Gary Kaplan, owner of a Pasadena, California, executive recruiting firm, explains: "The single-combat warrior, that bright, purposeful worker, tends to suck up a lot of oxygen in an organization. And now they're often seen as too innovative and too difficult."[1]

In his book *Tales of a New America,* Robert Reich describes the importance of teamwork in an increasingly technological age:

> Rarely do even Big Ideas emerge any longer from the solitary labors of genius. Modern science and technology is too complicated for one brain. It requires groups of astronomers, physicists, and computer programmers to discover new dimensions of the universe: teams of microbiologists, oncologists, and chemists to unravel the mysteries of cancer. With ever more frequency, Nobel prizes are awarded to collections of people. Scientific papers are authored by small platoons of researchers.[2]

Teams are not just important in scientific endeavors; in more familiar fields, working with others is as common and as important. In a national survey of architects and landscape architects, over 75 percent of these professionals reported that they "always" or "often" worked in teams.[3] Motorola, Ford, 3M, and General Electric have used teams to become leaders in their fields.[4] Business consultants Thomas J. Peters and Robert H. Waterman, Jr., discovered that many successful companies rely on "skunk works," which they described as "eight or ten zealots off in a corner."[5] At one $5-billion company, Peters and Waterman discovered that three of the five most recent new product ideas came from one skunk works, located in a dingy second-story loft 6 miles from the corporate headquarters. A senior executive at Digital Equipment Company endorsed the importance of small creative groups: "When we've got a big problem here, we grab ten senior guys and stick them in a room for a week. They come up with an answer *and* implement it."[6]

Teams are especially important in large organizations, where people from various parts of the company have to keep in touch in order to handle complicated jobs. Hewlett Packard used cross-functional teams—members from several departments—during the design and production of the DeskJet 1200C, HP's full-color, high-speed inkjet printer. Engineers, manufacturers, marketers, salespeople, and technical writers all met to iron out technical problems, cut production costs, and make sure that the product would meet customers' needs.[7]

Just because groups *can* be effective doesn't guarantee that they always *will* succeed. Some groups are monumental time-wasters, and others produce poor results. But when a group is well conceived and managed, it has several advantages over the same number of individuals working alone.[8] One of these advantages is *productivity*. Research shows that the old saying "Two heads are better than one" can be true: well-conceived and efficiently operating groups produce more solutions than individuals working alone, and the solutions are likely to be better.

Along with greater productivity, the *accuracy* of an effective group's work is higher than that of individuals. Consider the task of creating a new product. A group of people from sales, marketing, design, engineering, and manufacturing is likely to consider all the important angles, while one or two people without this breadth of perspective would probably miss some important ideas.

Teams don't only produce better products; they also generate more *enthusiasm* from the members who created them. People are usually more committed to a decision if they have had a part in making it. Recognizing this principle, many American companies create participatory management programs and quality circles that involve employees in important decisions. For example, William Deardon, chief executive officer of Hershey Foods Corporation, established a corporate planning committee to make the major plans and decisions for the company. "I figured that if we worked it out together," he explained, "the members of the group would feel that it was their plan and our plan—not my plan—and they'd work harder to implement it."[9]

Working effectively in groups calls for many of the skills described in earlier chapters of *Communicating at Work*. Chapter 1 discussed when to meet face-to-face and when to use other communication channels—telephone, electronic mail, and so on. Chapter 2 emphasized the importance of adapting to cultural norms when working with others. Chapter 3 offered tips on using language effectively and being sensitive to nonverbal cues. The listening skills outlined in Chapter 4 are essential when working in teams, as are the interpersonal skills described in Chapter 5. The fundamental communication skills described so far in this book are important, but there are also special characteristics that distinguish communication in groups. In the following pages you will learn about those characteristics and how to apply them when you work in groups and teams.

CHARACTERISTICS OF WORK TEAMS

The word *group* is often used to refer to any assembly of people—the commuters on the morning train, the sightseers gathering for a walking tour of the downtown area, the rock band at a local nightspot. When we talk about people interacting at work, we use the label differently. For our purposes, a ***work group*** or ***team*** is a small, interdependent collection of people with a common identity who interact with one another, usually face to face over time, in order to reach a goal. Using this definition, we can single out several significant characteristics of work-centered groups that can help you develop ways to work more effectively with others on the job.

Size

Most experts say that a twosome is not a group since the partners do not interact in the same way that three or more people do. For instance, two people working together can resolve disputes only by persuading one another, giving in, or compromising. In groups, however, members can form alliances and outvote or pressure the minority.

Although less agreement exists about when a collection of people becomes too large to be considered a group, virtually every small-group expert argues that any collection much larger than twenty people loses many of the properties that define groups—at least effective ones.[10] Research on a number of companies has found that ten-person teams often produce better results at a quicker rate and with higher profits than do groups of several hundred.[11] There are several reasons why size doesn't translate into effectiveness: People begin to act in formal ways. Members have fewer chances to participate, since a few talkative members are likely to dominate the group. Quieter members lose their identity and become less committed to the team. Coalitions also can form, leading members to become more concerned with having their side win than with tackling the challenge at hand.

Most communication experts suggest that the optimal size for small decision-making groups is either five or seven members.[12] The odd number of participants eliminates the risk of tie votes. Teams with fewer than five members lack the resources to come up with good ideas and to carry them out, while larger groups suffer from the problems of anonymity, domination, and lack of commitment.

Interaction

A collection of people working at their desks is merely coacting until the individuals begin to exchange information with one another. In fact, such lack of interaction could even be a problem. A project manager and a marketing manager who don't communicate enough, for example, might find that they are duplicating each other's efforts, with both conducting market research.

Interdependence

Group members don't only interact; they depend on one another. A roomful of telephone salespeople who are working on commission have little effect on one another, and thus they can hardly be called a group, let alone a team. By contrast, consider the workers in a restaurant: If the kitchen crew fails to prepare orders promptly or correctly, the servers' tips will decline. If the em-

One manager let employees know how valuable they are with the following memo:

You Arx a Kxy Pxrson

Xvxn though my typxwritxr is an old modxl, it works vxry wxll-xxcxpt for onx kxy. You would think that with all thx othxr kxys functioning propxrly, onx kxy not working would hardly bx noticxd; but just onx kxy out of whack sxxms to ruin thx wholx xffort.

You may say to yoursxlf–Wxll I'm only onx pxrson. No onx will noticx if I don't do my bxst. But it doxs makx a diffxrxncx bxcausx to bx xffxctivx an organization nxxds activx participation by xvxry onx to thx bxst of his or hxr ability.

So thx nxxt timx you think you arx not important, rxmxmbxr my old typx-writxr. You arx a kxy pxrson.

ployees who clear tables don't do their jobs quickly and thoroughly, the servers will hear complaints from their customers. If the waiters fail to take orders accurately, the cooks will have to fix some meals twice. In a restaurant, as in any real team, the employees are part of an interdependent system.

Duration

A group that interacts over a period of time develops particular characteristics. For example, a group will tend to develop shared standards of appropriate behavior that members are expected to meet. Typical expectations involve how promptly meetings begin, what contribution each member is expected to make to certain routine tasks, what kind of humor is appropriate, and so on.

Goal-Directedness

Many informal gatherings of people may develop the characteristics we have just described. For example, a group of secretaries who meet regularly for lunch, the project managers who go bowling together on Thursday nights, the noontime runners in a department, a therapy group, a group of friends, and even a family are all, in a sense, groups. In our study of business and professional communication, however, we are principally concerned with *decision-making* and *problem-solving* groups—people who are meeting to accomplish a common task.

APPROACHES TO WORKING IN GROUPS AND TEAMS

Throughout most of the history of organizations, the importance of centralized leadership in groups went unquestioned. The common thinking was that one ingredient in effective group functioning was the presence of a leader who could motivate members and make final decisions. Recently, however, experts in business and professional communication have come to recognize another approach to group functioning that puts most or all of the power into the hands of members. Since both of these approaches—centralized and decentralized—are common in today's workplace, the following pages will look at how communication operates in each one.

Centralized Leadership

The difference between effective and ineffective leaders can be dramatic: a losing team gets a new coach and, with the same players, begins winning against the same opponents; a demoralized division gets a new sales manager, and orders increase; a production crew gets a new supervisor, and workers who once spent their time complaining find new enjoyment and productivity. Whatever the nature of the organization, we count on the person "in charge" to make the enterprise work.

What qualities make leaders effective? Sometimes that question is difficult to answer. Many effective leaders seem to perform their role effortlessly, and people seem to follow them naturally; others seem to rule by sheer force.

Scholars and researchers have studied leadership from many perspectives. Following are some leadership approaches.

Trait Approach. The ***trait approach*** is based on the belief that all leaders possess common traits that lead to their effectiveness. The earliest research sought to identify these traits, and by the mid-1930s scores of studies pursued this goal. Their conclusions were contradictory. Certain traits did seem common in most leaders, including physical attractiveness, sociability, desire for leadership, originality, and intelligence.[13] Despite these similarities, the research also showed that these traits were not *predictive* of leadership. In other words, a person possessing these characteristics would not necessarily become a leader. Another research approach was necessary.

Style Approach. Beginning in the 1940s, researchers began to consider the ***style approach,*** that is, to ask whether the designated leader could choose a way of communicating that would increase effectiveness. This research identified three managerial styles. Some leaders are ***authoritarian,*** using legitimate, coercive, and reward power at their disposal to control members. Others are more ***democratic,*** inviting members to help make decisions. A third leadership style is ***laissez-faire:*** the designated leader gives up the power of that position and transforms the group into a leaderless collection of equals.

Early research seemed to suggest that the democratic style produced the best results,[14] but later experiments showed that matters weren't so simple. For instance, groups with autocratic leaders were more productive in stressful situations, while democratically led groups did better when the conditions were nonstressful.[15]

One of the best-known stylistic approaches is the *Leadership Grid®* by Robert Blake and Jane Mouton (see Figure 8-1),[16] which shows that good leadership depends on skillful management of the task and social functions described later in this chapter, on pages 251–253. The horizontal axis of the grid measures a manager's concern for task or production—getting the job done. The vertical axis measures the leader's concern for people and relationships. Blake and Mouton's grid counteracts the tendency in some naive managers to assume that if they focus solely on the task, good results will follow. They argue that the most effective leader is one who adopts a 9,9 style, showing high concern for both product *and* people.

Contingency Approaches. Unlike the style approach, ***contingency approaches*** are based on the idea that the "best" leadership style is flexible—it changes from one situation to the next. For instance, a manager who successfully guides a project team developing an advertising campaign might flop as a trainer or personnel officer. Psychologist Fred Fiedler conducted extensive research in an attempt to discover when a task-oriented approach works best and when a relationship-oriented style is most effective.[17] He found that a decision about whether to emphasize task or relationship issues in a situation

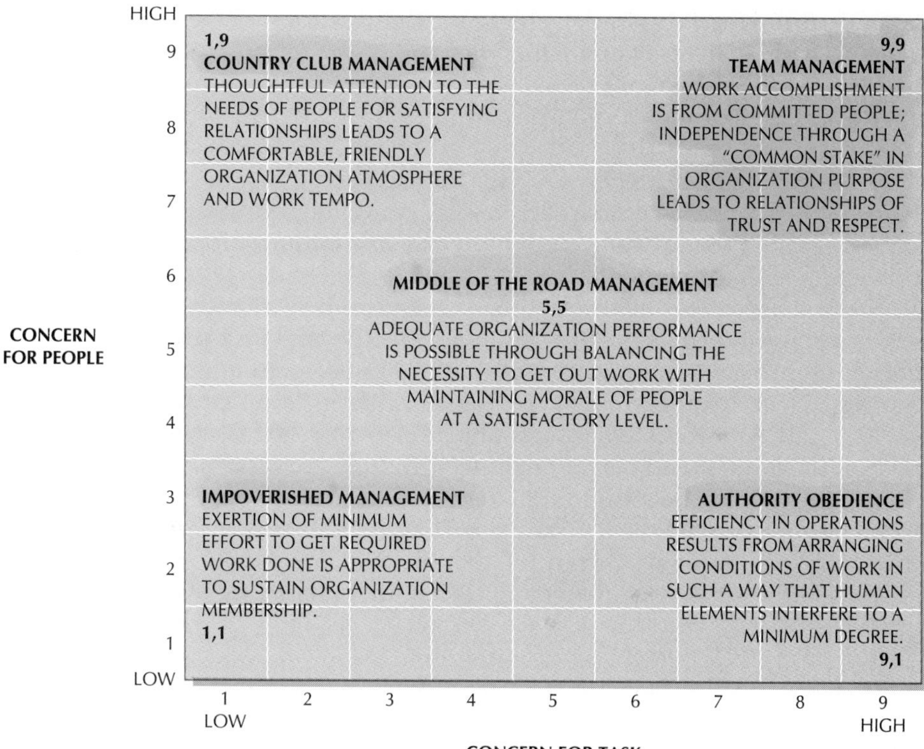
HIGH
9
8
7
6
5
4
3
2
1
LOW
CONCERN FOR PEOPLE
1,9
COUNTRY CLUB MANAGEMENT
THOUGHTFUL ATTENTION TO THE NEEDS OF PEOPLE FOR SATISFYING RELATIONSHIPS LEADS TO A COMFORTABLE, FRIENDLY ORGANIZATION ATMOSPHERE AND WORK TEMPO.
9,9
TEAM MANAGEMENT
WORK ACCOMPLISHMENT IS FROM COMMITTED PEOPLE; INDEPENDENCE THROUGH A "COMMON STAKE" IN ORGANIZATION PURPOSE LEADS TO RELATIONSHIPS OF TRUST AND RESPECT.
MIDDLE OF THE ROAD MANAGEMENT
5,5
ADEQUATE ORGANIZATION PERFORMANCE IS POSSIBLE THROUGH BALANCING THE NECESSITY TO GET OUT WORK WITH MAINTAINING MORALE OF PEOPLE AT A SATISFACTORY LEVEL.
IMPOVERISHED MANAGEMENT
EXERTION OF MINIMUM EFFORT TO GET REQUIRED WORK DONE IS APPROPRIATE TO SUSTAIN ORGANIZATION MEMBERSHIP.
1,1
AUTHORITY OBEDIENCE
EFFICIENCY IN OPERATIONS RESULTS FROM ARRANGING CONDITIONS OF WORK IN SUCH A WAY THAT HUMAN ELEMENTS INTERFERE TO A MINIMUM DEGREE.
9,1
1 2 3 4 5 6 7 8 9
LOW
HIGH
CONCERN FOR TASK

FIGURE 8-1 The Leadership Grid® figure from *Leadership Dilemmas—Grid Solutions* by Robert R. Blake and Anne Adams McCanse (Formerly the *Managerial Grid* by Robert R. Blake and Jane S. Mouton). Houston: Gulf Publishing Company, p. 29. Copyright 1991 by Scientific Methods, Inc. Reproduced by permission of the owners.

depends on three factors: (1) *leader-member relations,* including the attractiveness of the manager and the loyalty of the followers; (2) *task structure,* involving the degree of simplicity or complexity of the job; and (3) *the leader's power,* including job title and the ability to coerce and reward.

Generally, Fiedler's research suggests that a task-oriented approach works best when circumstances are extremely favorable (good leader-member relations, highly structured tasks) or extremely unfavorable (poor leader-member relations, unstructured task, weak leader power). In moderately favorable or unfavorable circumstances, a relationship-oriented approach works best. While these findings are useful, it is important not to overstate them. In most cases, good leadership requires a mixture of relationship and task concerns. The question is not which dimension to *choose,* but which one to *emphasize.*

A more sophisticated model of situational leadership is the life-cycle approach developed by Paul Hersey and Kenneth Blanchard.[18] As Figure 8-2 shows, the ***life-cycle theory*** suggests that a leader's concern for tasks and relationships ought to vary, depending on the maturity of the subordinate or subordinates. As Hersey and Blanchard use it, the term *maturity* has little to do with chronological age. Instead, maturity involves three factors: the employee's level of motivation, the employee's willingness to take responsibility, and the amount of knowledge and experience the employee has in a given situation.[19] A young, ambitious, well-trained recruit might be more mature than a bored, complacent worker who is ready for retirement. It is also important to note that a worker might have a low maturity rating in one situation and a high rating in another.

According to the life-cycle theory, an extremely immature subordinate needs a style of leadership that is highly directive and task-related, with little concern for social issues. As the group member becomes more competent and motivated, the manager ought to offer rewards in terms of social reinforcement. As the subordinate becomes able to perform the task without the guidance of the boss, the manager ought to withdraw the task-related supervision even more, while encouraging the employee's new ability. Finally, when the worker's ability to handle a task is superior, the boss can withdraw socioemotional support in this area, knowing that the worker is functioning at the highest level and that any reinforcements are now primarily internal.

FIGURE 8-2 Life-cycle leadership theory. (Reprinted by permission of Paul Hersey, Center for Leadership Studies. All rights reserved.)

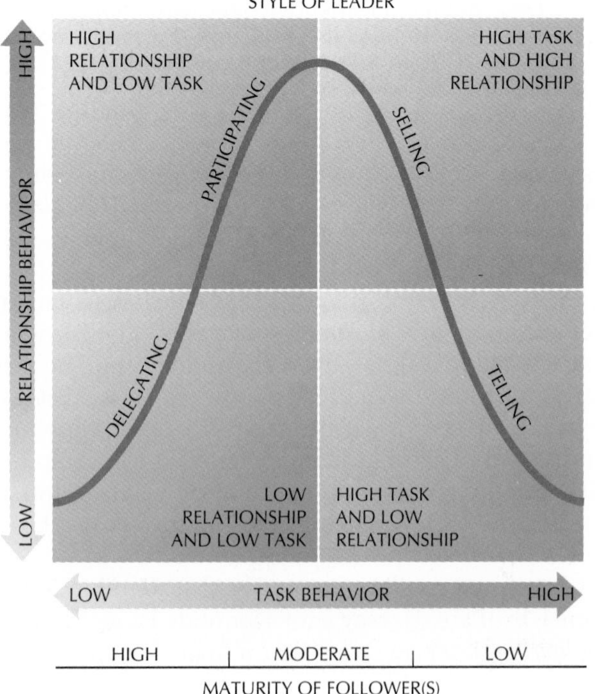

Although withdrawal of social support for mature employees might seem like a kind of punishment, Hersey and Blanchard would say it is not. Reducing the frequency of social reinforcement doesn't mean eliminating it altogether. Thus, an appreciative boss might signal pleasure by an occasional comment and punctuate that satisfaction with a yearly bonus. Also, social reinforcement isn't as scarce as it might seem because employees function at different maturity levels in different areas of their jobs. Thus, while a new systems analyst might be receiving little immediate social reinforcement from the boss for his work on one project, he would probably be getting a great deal of attention in other areas where he is less mature.

Self-Directed Work Teams

When most people think of leadership, they visualize a single person with an official title—what social scientists call a ***designated leader.*** That person's title varies from one setting to another: boss, chairperson, coach, manager, and so on. Designated leaders may be appointed by some higher authority (a single boss, hiring committee, board of directors), they might be chosen by the group (as when a committee elects a chairperson), or they may earn their title because they have started up a business themselves.

Designated leaders aren't the taken-for-granted fixture of groups that they were in the past. In the 1990s, many organizations have moved away from an exclusive focus on working groups managed closely by higher-ups in the chain of command. Instead of depending on this authoritarian model, they have come to rely on ***self-directed work teams***—groups who are responsible for managing their own behavior in order to get a task done.[20]

Self-directed work teams fit well into the way organizations operate in the 1990s. As companies reduce the ranks of middle managers, the ability of teams to work independently becomes more important. As tasks become more complex, groups of workers from different areas need to work together to solve problems, without going through the cumbersome chain of command to coordinate their actions. These trends help explain why more than half of the companies contacted in a 1990 survey intended to rely heavily on self-managed teams in the near future.[21]

Some organizations take shared leadership so seriously that they have formed teams that operate without a designated leader.[22] For example, at one General Mills cereal plant, teams schedule, operate, and maintain machinery so effectively that the plant runs with no managers present during night shifts.

> Many American companies are discovering what may be *the* productivity breakthrough of the 1990s. Call the still-controversial innovation a self-managed team, a cross-functional team, or, to coin a phrase, a superteam. . . .
>
> What makes superteams so controversial is that they ultimately force managers to do what they had only imagined in their most Boschian nightmares: give up control. Because if superteams are working right, *mirabile dictu,* they manage themselves. No boss required.
>
> Brian Dumaine, "Who Needs a Boss?" *Fortune*

How Effective Is Your Team?

What makes some teams effective and others failures? Communication researchers Carl Larson and Frank LaFusto spent nearly three years interviewing members of over seventy-five groups that were clearly winners. The groups came from a wide range of enterprises including a Mount Everest expedition, a cardiac surgery team, the presidential commission that studied the space shuttle *Challenger* accident, the group that developed the IBM personal computer, and two championship football teams. Although the groups pursued widely different goals, they all shared eight important characteristics.

You can understand both why your team functions as it does and how to improve its effectiveness by analyzing how well your group fits the profile of these winning teams. For each factor below, rate your group as follows:

5 The group fits this description perfectly.
4 The group usually resembles the characteristics in this area.
3 The group occasionally fits the characteristics described in this area.
2 The group rarely matches this description.
1 The group does not fit this description at all.

The number of points scored by your team will probably confirm what you already know about your group's effectiveness. The analysis is more useful as a tool for diagnosing how ineffective groups can improve their functioning. Characteristics with low scores suggest areas that need to be changed.

— **1.** *Clear and inspiring team goals*
Members of a winning team know why the group exists, and they believe that the purpose is important and worthwhile. Ineffective teams have either lost sight of their purpose or do not believe that the goal is truly important.

— **2.** *A results-driven structure*
Winning teams are organized in a way that allows them to get the job done in the most efficient manner. Members know what is expected of them. They do whatever is necessary to accomplish the task. Poor teams either are not organized at all or are structured in an inefficient manner.

— **3.** *Competent team members*
Members of winning teams have the skill necessary to accomplish their

The company reports that productivity at plants that rely on self-managed teams is as much as 40 percent higher than at traditional factories. Teams at 3M were so creative that they tripled the number of new products in their division. A group of Federal Express clerks spotted and solved a billing problem, saving the company $2.1 million in just one year.

When to Use Self-Directed Teams. Self-directed teams work best for relatively complex jobs that require a variety of perspectives. For example, a group that is developing a new product can profit from the perspectives of representatives from every part of the business: engineers know what it takes to make the item work, financial types understand costs and budgets, salespeople can represent the customers' needs, and marketing experts know how to promote the product. By contrast, self-management has less value for simple, repetitive tasks like assembly-line work or day-to-day data processing.

Characteristics of Self-Directed Teams. Calling a collection of people a self-directed team doesn't make them one. As Table 8-1 shows, self-directed goals. Less effective groups lack people possessing one or more key skills.

__ 4. *Unified commitment*
People in successful groups share a commitment to the job and to one another. They put the group's goals above their personal interests. While this commitment might seem like a sacrifice to others, for members of winning teams the personal rewards are worth the effort. Members of unsuccessful teams are lukewarm or indifferent about getting the job done.

__ 5. *Collaborative climate*
Another word for collaboration is *teamwork.* People in successful groups trust and support one another. Members of unsuccessful groups look out for themselves before they consider teammates.

__ 6. *Standards of excellence*
In winning teams, doing outstanding work is an important norm. Each member is expected to do his or her personal best. In less successful groups, getting by with the minimum amount of effort is the standard.

__ 7. *External support and recognition*
Successful teams need an appreciative audience that recognizes their effort and provides the resources necessary to get the job done. The audience may be a boss, or it may be the public the group is created to serve. In any case, without recognition and support, the group is likely to become handicapped and demoralized.

__ 8. *Principled leadership*
Winning teams usually have leaders who can create a vision of the group's purpose. They are able to create the changes that are necessary to get the job done. Finally, they have the ability to unleash the talent of group members. Unsuccessful teams either lack leaders or have leaders who do not possess one or more key skills.

The research described above was originally reported in Carl Larson and Frank LaFusto, *TeamWork: What Must Go Right/What Can Go Wrong*

work teams possess qualities that are quite different from hierarchical working groups with designated leaders that are overseen by outside managers. This approach calls for a revolution in the organizational culture of a company that is accustomed to working from an authoritarian model. Sometimes the use of language reflects how well the change has taken root. The policy at Domino's Pizza states that there are no "employees," only "team members." Domino's Jeff DeGraff explains: "If you get annoyed at a team leader, you'd call him a 'boss'." This sort of language usage makes terminology a barometer of organizational attitudes. Domino's conducts monthly surveys of team members, looking for references to "boss." If the term appears too often, team spirit may be faltering.[23]

Besides having the right blend of responsibilities, effective self-directed teams consist of members who possess some important personal qualities:[24]

- *Technical or functional expertise.* Members can't succeed unless they have the specific knowledge to solve the challenge at hand. Consider, for example, a team whose job is to develop an improved medical insurance package. Unless the members understand the details

TABLE 8-1 Some Characteristics of Self-Directed Work Teams

- They set their own goals and inspect their own work.
- They plan, control, and improve their own work processes.
- They often create their own schedules and review their performance.
- They may prepare their own budgets and coordinate their work with other departments.
- They frequently are responsible for acquiring any new training they might need.
- They may hire their own replacements or assume responsibility for disciplining their own members.
- They—not people outside the teams—take responsibility for the quality of their products or services.

Source: After R. S. Wellins, W. C. Byham, and J. M. Wilson, *Empowered Teams: Creating Self-Directed Work Groups That Improve Quality, Productivity, and Participation* (San Francisco: Jossey-Bass, 1991), pp. 4–5.

of HMOs, PPOs, indemnity plans, and so on, they won't be able to get the job done.

- *Problem-solving and decision-making skills.* Raw knowledge is important, but knowing what to do with facts and figures is also essential. The material in this chapter on pages 238–246 offers guidelines for making decisions and solving problems in an effective way. Unless the members use skills like these, their chances for working efficiently and effectively aren't good.
- *Interpersonal skills.* Becoming friends isn't necessary, but knowing how to treat one another with respect and how to handle personal differences skillfully can make the difference between a smoothly functioning team and a group of temperamental individuals.

Types of Power. One key to understanding groups is recognizing that every member of a group has power to shape events. Power comes in several forms, and in most groups each member possesses one or more types.[25]

ETHICAL CHALLENGE

Your company, a mail-order retailer, is committed to using self-directed work teams. You have been assigned to a team whose task is to develop a faster method for enabling customers to return their products and receive refunds.

After one meeting, it becomes clear to you that some members of your group are liabilities: some don't have the talent to figure out a good solution, and others lack the personal skills to work in a group. With this roster of players, the team doesn't seem up to the job. You know that a strong manager directing a group of two or three top performers could accomplish the job better and more quickly.

Your performance review is coming up soon, and you are certain that your boss will ask you how things are going on the team. You don't want to sound too critical, and you know the company's belief in self-directed teams. On the other hand, you think this team is a disaster. What will you say?

Legitimate Power. ***Legitimate power*** is the ability to influence that comes from the position one holds. We often do things for the boss precisely because he or she holds that title. While legitimate power usually belongs to nominal leaders, people in lesser positions sometimes possess it, often depending on circumstances. In some cultures, legitimate power often comes with age. The eldest members have the right to make decisions and speak first. In many organizations, the same principle holds: members who have been with a company the longest gain power by virtue of their longevity.

Coercive Power. The power to punish is known as ***coercive power,*** since we often follow another's bidding when failure to do so would lead to unpleasant consequences. Nominal leaders have coercive power: they can assign unpleasant tasks, deny pay raises, and even fire us. Other members have coercive power, too, though it is usually subtle. A committee member or officemate who acts as a blocker when things don't go his way is coercing others to take his views into account, implying, "If you don't follow at least some of my suggestions, I'll punish the group by continuing to object to your ideas and refusing to cooperate with you."

Reward Power. The flip side of coercive power is ***reward power***—the ability to reward. Nominal leaders control the most obvious rewards: pay raises, improved working conditions, and the ability to promote. But, again, other members can give their own rewards. These come in the form of social payoffs, such as increased goodwill and task-related benefits like voluntary assistance on a job.

Expert Power. ***Expert power*** comes from the group's recognition of a member's expertise in a certain area. Nominal leaders aren't always the experts in a group. In a manufacturing firm, for example, a relatively low-ranking engineer could influence management to alter a project by using her knowledge to declare that a new product won't work. Problems can arise either when management doesn't recognize a knowledgeable member as an expert or when unqualified people are granted expert status.

Referent Power. The term ***referent power*** refers to the influence members hold due to the way others in the group feel about them: their respect, attraction, or liking. It is here that the greatest difference between nominal leaders and members with true influence occurs. An unpopular boss might have to resort to his or her job title and the power to coerce and reward that comes with it to gain compliance, while a popular person, with or without a leadership title, can get others to cooperate without threatening or promising. Mike Zugsmith, co-owner of a commercial real-estate brokerage, captures the importance of referent power, even for a boss: "When I started this company in 1979, I was 28. I was supervising salespeople who were 20 to 30 years my senior. It readily became apparent that simply because your name is on the door doesn't mean you'll get respect. You have to earn it."[26]

Information Power. ***Information power*** is the ability of some members to influence a group because of the information they possess. This information is different from the kind of knowledge that gives rise to expert power. Whereas an expert possesses some form of talent based on training or education, an information-rich group member has access to otherwise obscure knowledge that is valuable to others in the group. A new employee who was hired away from a competitor, for example, is likely to play a key role in the decisions of how his new company will compete against the old one. Likewise, a member who is well connected to the organizational grapevine can exert a major influence on how the group operates: "Don't bring that up now. Smith is going through a divorce and he's saying no to everything." "I just heard there's plenty of money in the travel and entertainment budget. Maybe this is the time to propose that reception for the out-of-town distributors we've been thinking about."

Connection Power. In the "real world" of business, a member's influence can often come from the connections he or she has with influential or important people inside or outside the organization—hence, the term ***connection power.*** The classic example of connection power is the son or daughter of the boss. While the official word from the top may be "Treat my kid just like any other employee," this is easier said than done. Not all connection power is harmful. If one member sees a potential customer socially, he is in a good position to help the business. If another one knows a government official, she can get off-the-record advice about how to handle a government regulation.

If we recognize the influence that comes with connection power, the old saying "It isn't what you know that counts, it's who you know" seems true. If we look at all the types of power described in this section, we can see that a more accurate statement is "What counts is *whom* you know (connection power), *what* you know (information and expert power), who *respects* you (referent power), and who you *are* (legitimate power)." This range of power bases makes it clear that the power to influence a group is truly shared among members, all of whom have the ability to affect how well a group works as a unit and the quality of the product it turns out.

Leadership Emergence

Sometimes leaders are appointed by higher-ups, but in many cases they emerge from a group. ***Emergent leaders*** may be chosen by the members of a

INVITATION TO INSIGHT

Analyze the types of power that exist in your class or some other working group. Which members use each type of power? Who exerts the most influence? What kinds of power do you possess?

group either officially or informally. An athletic team may elect a captain. The owners' association of a condominium chooses a head. Union members pick a team to represent them in contract negotiations with management. Volunteers organizing a fund-raising drive for the local school or church nominate a chairperson.

Emergent leaders don't always have official titles. A group of disgruntled employees might urge one person to approach the boss and ask for a change, for example. A team of students assigned to develop a class project might agree that one person is best suited to take the lead in organizing and presenting their work. Sometimes emergent leaders are officially recognized, but other times their role is never acknowledged overtly. In fact, there are often cases where the designated leader may be the titular head, while an emergent leader really runs the show. Fans of late-night movies recall how the young, inexperienced lieutenant learns to defer to the grizzled, wise sergeant. This pattern often repeats itself in everyday working situations, when new managers or supervisors recognize the greater knowledge of old-timers who are subordinates on the organizational chart. In cases like these, the new manager is smart to defer to the unofficial, emergent leader—at least until he or she gains some experience and wisdom.

Communication researcher Ernest Bormann has studied how emergent leaders gain influence, especially in newly formed groups.[27] According to Bormann, a group selects a leader by the *method of residues*—a process of elimination in which potential candidates are gradually rejected for one reason or another until only one remains. This process of elimination occurs in two phases. In the first, members who are clearly unsuitable are rejected. The surest path to rejection is being quiet: untalkative members were never chosen as leaders in the groups Bormann studied. Failing to participate verbally in a group's work leaves the impression of indifference and lack of commitment. Another ticket to early rejection is dogmatism: members who express their opinions in strong, unqualified terms are usually perceived as being too extreme and inflexible to take a leading role. A third cause of elimination as leader is a lack of skill or intelligence: competence is obviously a necessary condition for successful leadership, and members who lack this quality are rejected early.

Quietness, dogmatism, and incompetence are almost always grounds for disqualification. Beyond these factors, a communication style that members find irritating or disturbing is likely to knock a member out of consideration as a leader. A variety of behaviors fall into this category, depending on the composition of the group. In one case being too serious might be grounds for rejection, while in a different situation a joker would earn disapproval. Using inappropriate language could be a disqualifier. In a group with biased members, gender or ethnicity might be grounds for rejection.

After clearly unsuitable members have been eliminated, roughly half of the group's members may still be candidates for leadership. This can be a tense time, since the jockeying for a role of influence may pit the remaining candidates against one another. In some groups, the contenders for leader acquire what Bormann calls "lieutenants," who support their advancement. If only one candidate has a lieutenant, his or her chances of becoming leader are strong. If two or more contenders have supporters, the process of leader emergence can drag out or even reach a stalemate.

One way to stand out among competitors for leadership is to provide a solution in a time of crisis. How can the group meet a deadline? Gain the sale? Get the necessary equipment? Members who find answers to problems like these are likely to rise to a position of authority.

If you are interested in seeking a leadership position—and you almost certainly will be at one time or another—Bormann's research suggests several steps to take:[28]

- *Participate early and often.* Talking won't guarantee that you will be recognized as a leader, but failing to speak up will almost certainly knock you out of the running.
- *Demonstrate your competence.* Make sure your comments identify you as someone who can help the group succeed. Demonstrate your expert, connection, and information power.
- *Don't push too hard.* It's fine to be assertive, but don't try to overpower other members. Even if you are right, your dogmatism is likely to alienate others.

PROBLEM-SOLVING COMMUNICATION

In the past decades, researchers have developed several methods for helping groups solve problems and make decisions effectively. By taking advantage of these methods, groups can come up with the highest-quality work possible.

Systematic Problem Solving

The range of problems that groups face on the job is almost endless. How can we cut expenses? Increase market share? Reduce customer complaints? Offer a better employee-benefits program? Not all groups approach problems like these systematically,[29] but most researchers agree that groups have the best chance of developing high-quality solutions to problems like these when they follow a systematic method for solving problems.[30] Table 8-2 offers one set of questions a group needs to consider when taking on a job. Without clear answers to these questions, the group can't be sure it has the resources necessary to get the job done.

The best-known problem-solving approach is the ***reflective-thinking sequence,*** developed over eighty years ago by John Dewey and used in many forms since then.[31] In its most useful form, the reflective-thinking sequence is a seven-step process.

1. Define the Problem. A group that doesn't understand the problem will have trouble finding a solution. Sometimes the problem facing a group is clear. It doesn't take much deliberation to understand what's necessary when

TABLE 8-2 Ten Questions for Effective Groups

Groups are often given a task without having enough information to get the job done—or even knowing whether it's possible to work effectively. Seeking answers to the following before starting work can save time and frustration.

1. Exactly what is this group being asked to accomplish?
2. When is the group expected to finish the job?
3. What has already been decided about the topic (e.g., goals and budgets), and how do these decisions affect the group's ability to act?
4. Who will decide whether this group's recommendation is adopted or whether its ideas will be carried out?
5. What criteria are being used to choose group members and/or leaders, and who are the initial members?
6. What other individuals or groups should know about this group's existence and purpose?
7. With whom is this group expected to communicate while it is doing its job? How often, and by what means?
8. What resources does the group have to help accomplish its task? What is the source of this group's organizational authority to use these resources?
9. How will group members be compensated for their time and effort?
10. To whom should this group turn for clarification as it goes about its work?

Source: After B. Stump, "Guidelines for Groups," *Training & Development* (October 1994): 14.

the boss tells you to work out a vacation schedule for the next six months. On the other hand, some problems need rewording because they are too broad as originally presented:

TOO BROAD	BETTER
"How can we reduce employee turnover?"	"How can we reduce turnover among new employees?" (This suggests where to look for the nature of the problem and solutions.)
"How can we boost the morale of the office staff?"	"How can we solve the secretaries' complaints about too much work?"

The best problem statements are phrased as probative questions, ones that encourage exploratory thinking:

POOR	BETTER
"Should we phone people to boost participation in the blood drive?"	"What's the best way to boost participation in the blood drive?"
"Should we increase our advertising budget?"	"What's the best way to publicize our product?"
"Should we prohibit business flights of less than 300 miles?"	"How can we cut our travel expenses?"

By avoiding questions with either-or answers, the group is most likely to consider a large number of possible solutions instead of arguing over one or two options.

2. Analyze the Problem. At this stage, the group tries to discover the causes and extent of the problem, probably by doing some research between meetings. Questions that are usually appropriate in this stage include "How bad is that problem?" "Why does it need to be resolved?" "What are its causes?" It can be just as useful to focus on the positive aspects of the situation during this phase in order to consider how they can be strengthened. Questions in this area include "What forces are on our side?" "How do they help us?" "How can we strengthen them?"

A group analyzing the question "How can we solve the secretaries' complaints about too much work?" might find that the problem is especially bad for certain secretaries. It might discover that the problem is worst when the secretaries have to type long reports at the last minute. It might learn that the major complaint doesn't involve hard work as much as it does resentment at seeing other typists apparently having a lighter load. Positive research findings might be that the secretaries understand the importance of their role, that they view being chosen to do important jobs as a sign of respect for the quality of their work, and that they don't mind occasional periods of scrambling to meet a deadline.

3. Establish Criteria for a Solution. Rather than rushing to solve the problem, it's best to spend some time identifying the characteristics of a good solution. Who would it have to satisfy? What are the cost constraints? What schedule needs to be met? Sometimes criteria like these are imposed from outside the group. Other requirements come from the members themselves. Regardless of the source of these requirements, the group needs to make them clear before considering possible solutions. Without defining the criteria of a satisfactory solution, the group may waste time arguing over proposals that have no chance of being accepted.

The office group dealing with the problem of unhappy secretaries might define three criteria for a solution to its problem:

No hiring of new employees (company policy)

Fair distribution of work among staff (from the unhappy secretaries)

On-time completion of last-minute jobs (from the managers assigning tasks)

4. Consider Possible Solutions to the Problem. This is the time for using the creative thinking techniques described later in this chapter. A major hazard of group problem solving is that it may get bogged down in arguing over the merits of one or two proposals without considering all the other solutions that might exist. Besides limiting the quality of the solution, such squabbling also leads to personal battles between members.

The most valuable feature of brainstorming is the emphasis on generating many ideas before judging any of them. This sort of criticism-free atmosphere encourages people to volunteer solutions that, in turn, lead to other ideas.

A brainstorming list for the overworked typists might include the following:

- Instead of having one typist reporting to two or three people, make arrangements for everybody to have his or her own secretary.
- Assign a typist to report to two or three people only if those people are in a single line of command; the senior person will decide whose project has priority.
- To cut down on the number of jobs that have to be done over, create a company style book that shows how letters are to be set up, contract clauses phrased, and so on.
- Have typists help each other out—someone with too much work to do can ask someone else to take over a project.
- Establish a typing pool: instead of assigning a typist to a specific person or group, turn over all typing tasks to a group leader who will distribute them. Since the typists will be working as a group, they can train new typists themselves.

5. Decide on a Solution. Once the group has considered all possible solutions to a problem, it can go back and find the best answer to the problem. This is done by comparing each idea to the list of criteria developed earlier by the group. In addition to measuring the solution against its own criteria, the group should judge any potential solutions by asking three questions: First, will the proposal bring about all the desired changes? If it solves only part of the problem, it isn't adequate without some changes. Second, can the solution be implemented by the group? If the idea is good but is beyond the power of this group to achieve, it needs to be modified or discarded. Finally, does the idea have any serious disadvantages? A plan that solves one set of problems while generating another probably isn't worth adopting.

In the case of the overworked typists, the first solution is rejected since it doesn't meet the criterion of not adding staff. The second has possibilities, but it is rejected after discussion; among other problems, most higher-level managers already have their own secretaries working overtime, and using more executive time to organize and establish priorities on secretarial work doesn't seem practicable. The third solution seems to have possibilities, but it doesn't solve most aspects of the problem. The fourth seems good. The fifth is even better since it will systematize distribution of work and the group leader can be a head typist. The committee agrees to recommend the fifth solution as essential and the third as an additional step to solve some problems.

6. Implement the Solution. Inventing a solution isn't enough. The group also has to put the plan into action. This probably involves several steps. First, it's necessary to identify the specific tasks that must be accomplished. Second, the group must identify the resources necessary to make the plan work. Third, individual responsibilities must be defined: Who will do what, and when? Finally, the group should plan for emergencies. What will happen if someone is sick? If the project runs over budget? If a job takes longer than expected? Anticipating problems early is far better than being caught by surprise.

In reorganizing the typists, the committee needs to appoint someone to oversee the change. It needs to consider how much time it will take to switch to the new system and what delays are likely to occur with the changeover. A team leader must be chosen to delegate jobs once the typing pool is created. The group must decide how to respond if some supervisors still act as if particular secretaries "belong" to them.

7. Follow Up on the Solution. Even the best ideas don't always work out perfectly in practice. For this reason, the group should check up on the implementation of the solution to see if any adjustments are needed. In the case of the secretarial pool, for example, it might be necessary to remind some managers that their former secretaries no longer work just for them.

Stages in Group Problem Solving

The systematic problem-solving approach described above is certainly sensible, but it doesn't consider how the relationships between individual members can make it difficult for them to follow this kind of rational approach faithfully.[32] As groups conduct business, their discussions are likely to move through several phases characterized by different types of communication. Aubrey Fisher identified four of these stages: orientation, conflict, emergence, and reinforcement.[33]

The first stage in a group's development is the ***orientation phase.*** This is a time of testing the waters. Members may not know one another very well and so are cautious about making statements that might offend. For this reason, during the orientation stage team members aren't likely to take strong positions even on issues they regard as important. It is easy to mistake the lack of conflict during this phase as harmony and assume that the task will proceed smoothly. Peace and quiet, however, are often a sign of caution, not agreement. Despite the tentative nature of communication, the orientation stage is

SKILL BUILDER

Along with three to six of your classmates, use the guidelines for problem solving in this chapter to develop a money-making product or service that could be marketed by students in your class.

important since the norms that can govern the group's communication throughout its life are often formed at this time.

After the team members understand the problem and have a feel for one another, the group typically moves to the ***conflict phase.*** This is the time when members take a strong stand on the issue and defend their positions against others. Disagreement is likely to be greatest during this phase, as are bruised egos. The norms of politeness that were formed during orientation may weaken as members debate with one another, and there is a real risk that personal feelings will interfere with the kind of rational decision making described on pages 238–242. Sometimes the members keep arguing about one solution or another without ever resolving the issue satisfactorily. Other times, conflicts take on a more personal tone as members find fault with one another's behavior. Conflicts may be openly discussed, or they can be conducted more subtly under a thin cover of politeness. In either case, struggle is the main theme.

Some groups never escape from the conflict stage. Their interaction—at least about the problem at hand—may end when time pressures force a solution that almost no one finds satisfactory. The boss may impose a decision from above, or a majority might overrule the minority. Time may even run out without any decision being made. Not all groups suffer from such unhappy outcomes, however. Productive teams manage to work through the conflict phase and move on to the next stage of development.

The ***emergence phase*** of problem solving occurs when the members end their disagreement and solve the problem. The final decision may be enthusiastically supported by every member. In some cases, though, members may compromise or settle for a proposal they didn't originally prefer. In any case, the key to emergence is acceptance of a decision that members willingly (if reluctantly) can support. Communication during the emergence phase is less polarized. Members back off from their previously held firm positions. Comments like "I can live with that" and "Let's give it a try" are common at this point. Even if some people have doubts about the decision, there is a greater likelihood that they will keep their concerns to themselves. Harmony is the theme.

The fourth stage of discussion is the ***reinforcement phase.*** At this point, members not only accept the decision but actively endorse it. Members who found arguments against the decision during the conflict stage now present evidence to support it. In school, the reinforcement stage is apparent when students presenting a group project defend it against any complaints the instructor might have. On the job, the same principle applies: if the boss finds fault with a team's proposals, the tendency is to band together to support them.

In real life, groups don't necessarily follow this four-step process neatly. In an ongoing team, the patterns of communication in the past can influence present and future communication.[34] Teams with a high degree of conflict might have trouble reaching emergence, for example, whereas a group that is highly cohesive might experience little disagreement.

Sometimes a group can become stuck in one phase, never progressing to the phases that follow. Members might never get beyond the superficial, polite interaction of orientation. If they do, they might become mired down in conflict. Ongoing groups might move through some or all of the stages each time they tackle a new problem, as pictured in Figure 8-3. In fact, a group that deals with several issues at one time might be in different stages for each problem.

Knowing that a group to which you belong is likely to pass through these stages can be reassuring. Your urge to get down to business and quit wasting time during the orientation phase might be tempered if you realize that the cautious communication is probably temporary. Likewise, you might be less distressed about conflict if you know that the possibility of emergence may be just around the corner.

Decision-Making Methods

Disagreement may be a healthy, normal part of solving problems on the job, but sooner or later it becomes necessary to make a decision as a group. Whether the issue is who will work over the weekend, how to split the year-end bonus money among members, or what approach to advertising is best, there usually has to be one answer to a problem. There are a number of ways to make business decisions like these.

Consensus. ***Consensus*** is a collective group decision that every member is willing to support. The purest form of consensus is unanimous, unequivocal support: the belief of every member that the decision reached is the best possible one. An entire employee search committee might, for instance, agree

FIGURE 8-3 Cyclical stages in an ongoing group. (From John K. Brilhart and Gloria J. Galanes, *Effective Group Discussion,* 6th ed. Copyright © 1989 Wm. C. Brown Communications, Inc. Reprinted by permission of Times Mirror Higher Education Group, Inc., Dubuque, Iowa. All Rights Reserved.)

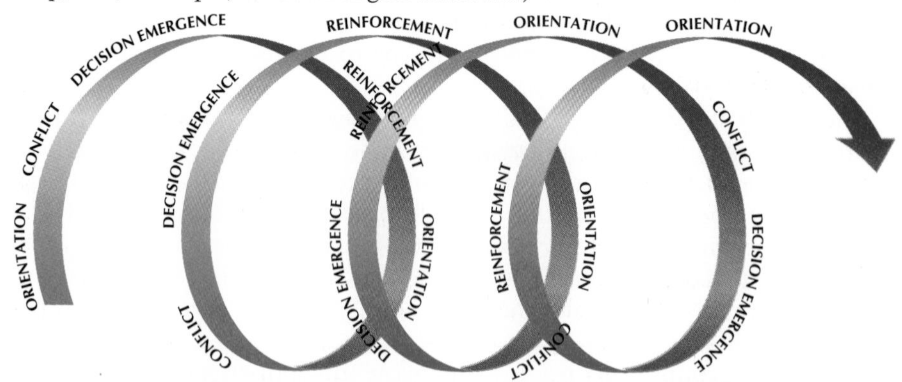

that a particular candidate is perfect for a job. This state of unanimity isn't always possible, however, and it isn't necessary for consensus. Members may support a decision that isn't their first choice, accepting the fact that it is the best one possible for the group at that time. In the case of the new employee, the committee members might agree on a candidate who is the second choice of some members since the people who will actually be working with her are her most enthusiastic supporters.

Consensus is valued more highly in some cultures than others. For example, British and Dutch businesspeople value the "team must be aboard" approach. On the other hand, Germans, French, and Spanish communicators depend more on the decision of a strong leader and view a desire for consensus as somewhat wishy-washy.[35]

Cultural norms aside, consensus has both advantages and drawbacks. While it has the broadest base of support from members, reaching consensus takes time. It requires a spirit of cooperation among group members, a willingness to experience temporary disagreements, a commitment to listening carefully to other ideas, and a win-win attitude. While consensual decisions are often superior to other types, the cost in time and frustration isn't always worth the effort, especially for relatively minor issues. Furthermore, there are times when it simply isn't possible to reach consensus.

Majority Vote. Whereas consensus requires the agreement of the entire group, deciding by a ***majority vote*** needs only the support of a plurality of the members. Thus, majority voting decisions are much quicker and easier to reach. A ten-person staff choosing a decorating scheme for the new office might talk almost endlessly before reaching consensus, but with a majority vote, the decision would require the agreement of only six members. While majority vote works well on relatively minor issues, it is usually not the best approach for more important decisions (at least not in small groups), since it can leave a substantial minority unsatisfied and resentful about being railroaded into accepting a plan they don't support.

Minority Decision. In a ***minority decision,*** a few members make a decision affecting the entire group. This is frequently the case in business situations. For instance, the executive committee of a corporation often acts on behalf of the board of directors, which, in turn, represents the shareholders. Minority decisions are also made in less exalted circumstances. A steering group responsible for planning the company picnic might delegate tasks like publicity, entertainment, and food to smaller collections of members. As long as the minority has the confidence of the larger group, this method works well for many decisions. While it doesn't take advantage of the entire group's creative thinking, the talents of the subgroup are often perfectly adequate for a task.

Expert Opinion. When a single person has the knowledge or skill to make an informed decision, the group may be best served by relying on his or her ***expert opinion.*** As one observer puts it, "If you want a track team to win the high jump, you find one person who can jump seven feet, not seven people who can jump one foot." Some group members are experts because of specialized training: a structural engineer working with a design team on a new building, a senior airline mechanic who decides whether a flight can depart safely, or a systems analyst involved in the development of a new data control system. Other people gain their expertise by experience: the purchasing agent who knows how to get the best deals or a labor negotiator seasoned by years of contract deliberations.

Despite the obvious advantages, following an expert's suggestions isn't always as wise an approach as it might seem. First, it isn't always easy to tell who the expert is. Length of experience isn't necessarily a guarantee, since the business world abounds with old fools. Even when a member clearly is the expert, the other members must *recognize* this fact before they will willingly give their support. Unfortunately, some people who are regarded as experts don't deserve the title, while some geniuses may be ignored.

Authority Rule. In many business groups, decision making is often a matter of ***authority rule:*** the designated leader makes the final decision. This doesn't mean that such leaders must be autocratic: they often listen to the ideas and suggestions of members before making the decisions themselves. The owner of a family business might invite employees to help choose a new company logo, while selecting the final design after hearing their opinions. A store manager might consult with employees about scheduling work hours, while reserving the final decisions to herself. The input from group members can help an authority to make higher-quality decisions than would otherwise be possible. One major risk of inviting suggestions from subordinates, however, is the disappointment that might follow if these suggestions aren't accepted.

Choice of a Decision-Making Method. Each decision-making method has its advantage and disadvantages. The choice of which one to use depends on several factors.

What Type of Decision Is Being Made? If the decision can best be made by one or more experts or if it needs to be made by the authorities in charge, then involving other group members isn't appropriate. If, however, the task at hand calls for creativity or requires a large amount of information from many sources, then input from the entire group can make a big difference.

How Important Is the Decision? Trivial decisions don't require the involvement of the entire group. It's a waste of time and money to bring everyone together to make decisions that can easily be made by one or two people.

How Much Time Is Available? If time is short, it simply may not be possible to consult everyone in the group. This is especially true if the members are not all available—if some are away from the office or out of town, for

SKILL BUILDER

With three to six of your classmates, decide which method of decision making would be most effective for your group in each of the following situations:

1. Choosing the safest course of action if you were lost in a dangerous area near your city or town
2. Deciding whether and how to approach your instructor to propose a change in the grading system of your course
3. Designing the most effective campaign for your school to recruit minority students
4. Duplicating for distribution to your instructor and classmates the solutions to this exercise that your group developed
5. Hiring an instructor for your department
6. Choosing the name for a new brand of breakfast cereal
7. Selecting a new computer system
8. Deciding which of three employees gets the desirable vacant office
9. Planning the weekend work schedule for the upcoming month
10. Deciding whether the employees should affiliate with a labor union

example. Even if everyone is available, the time-consuming deliberations that come with a group discussion may be a luxury you can't afford.

What Are the Personal Relationships among Members? Even important decisions might best be made without convening the whole group if members are on bad terms. If talking things out will improve matters, then a meeting may be worth the emotional wear and tear that it will generate. But if a face-to-face discussion will just make matters worse, then the decision might best be made in some other way.

EFFECTIVE COMMUNICATION IN GROUPS AND TEAMS

Whether you are in a group with centralized leadership or one with shared decision-making power, you can communicate in ways that help a group work effectively and make the experience satisfying. For the group to function well, each member must take into account the issues and problems that may arise whenever people try to communicate.

Recognize Both Group and Personal Goals

Every business and professional group operates to achieve some specific goal: selling a product, providing a service, getting a job done, and so on. In addition to pursuing a group's goals, members usually also have their own *individual* goals. Sometimes an individual's goal in a group is identical (or nearly identical) to the shared goal of the group. For example, a retailer might join the community Christmas fund-raising campaign out of a sincere desire to help the needy. In most cases, however, people also have more personal motives for joining a group. The retailer, for instance, might realize that working on the fund-raising campaign will improve both his visibility and his image in the community—and ultimately lead to more business. Notice the relationship between some common group and individual goals:

GROUP GOAL	INDIVIDUAL GOAL
Athletic team wants to win league championship.	Athlete wants to be star for social rewards.
Sales department wants to meet annual sales target.	Sales representative wants to earn bonus and receive promotions.
Retailer wants to expand hours to attract new business.	Employees want to avoid working nights and weekends.
Company wants employee to attend seminar in Minneapolis.	Employee wants to visit family in Minneapolis.

As some of these examples show, personal goals aren't necessarily harmful to a group or an organization if they are compatible with the group's objectives. In fact, under these circumstances they can actually help the group to achieve its goals. For instance, sales representatives who want to increase their commissions will try to sell more of the company's products. Similarly, an otherwise reluctant employee might volunteer to attend a January seminar in Minneapolis to see her family during the visit.

Only when an individual's goals conflict with the organization's or group's goals do problems occur. If Lou and Marian hate each other, their arguments could keep the group from getting much done in meetings. If Bill is afraid of losing his job because of a mistake that has been made, he may concentrate on trying to avoid being blamed rather than on solving the problem.

The range of personal goals that can interfere with group effectiveness is surprisingly broad. One or more team members might be concerned with finishing the job quickly and getting away to take care of personal business. Others might be more concerned with being liked or appearing smart than with doing the job as quickly or effectively as possible. Someone else might want to impress the boss. All these goals, as well as dozens of others, can sidetrack or derail a group from doing its job.

Groups will be happiest and most efficient when the members are reaching their personal goals. You can boost the effectiveness of your group by doing everything possible to help members satisfy those goals. If the people in your group are looking for fun and companionship, consider ways to tackle the job at hand that also give them what they want. On the other hand, if they are in a hurry because of busy schedules, concentrate on keeping meetings to a minimum. If some members like recognition, stroke their egos by offering compliments whenever you can sincerely do so. The extra effort that you spend catering to the individual needs of members will pay dividends in terms of the energy and loyalty that the group gains from happy members.

In some cases, group members announce their personal goals. In other cases, though, stating a personal, goal outright could be embarrassing or counterproductive. A committee member wouldn't confess, "I volunteered to serve on this committee so I could find new people to date." An employee would never say openly, "I'm planning to learn everything I can here and then quit the firm and open my own business." Personal goals that are not made public are called ***hidden agendas.***

Hidden agendas are not necessarily harmful. The dating goals of a member needn't interfere with group functions. Similarly, many other personal motives are not threatening or even relevant to a group's business. Some hidden agendas are even beneficial. For instance, an up-and-coming young worker's desire to communicate competence to the boss by volunteering for difficult jobs might well help the group. Other hidden agendas, however, are harmful. Two feuding members who use meetings to disparage each other can only harm the group, and the person collecting ideas to go into business himself will most likely hurt the organization when he takes its ideas elsewhere.

There is no single best way to deal with harmful hidden agendas. Sometimes the best course is to bring the goal out into the open. For example, a manager might speak to feuding subordinates one at a time, let them know she recognizes their problem, and work with them to solve it directly and constructively (probably using the conflict management skills described in Chapter 5). When you do decide to bring a hidden personal goal into the open, it's almost always better to confront the member privately. The embarrassment of being unveiled publicly is usually so great that the person becomes defensive and denies that the hidden goal exists.

At other times, it is best to treat a hidden personal goal indirectly. For example, if a member's excessive talking in meetings seems to be a bid for recognition, the best approach might be to make a point of praising his valid contributions more frequently. If two feuding subordinates continue to have trouble working together, the manager can assign them to different projects or transfer one or both of them to different groups.

Promote Desirable Norms

Norms are informal, often unstated rules about what behavior is appropriate in a group. Some norms govern the way tasks are handled, while others shape the social interaction of the group. A group's norms often are shaped by the culture of the organization to which it belongs. For example, 3M's success

INVITATION TO INSIGHT

Although it may be larger than most of the groups discussed in this chapter, your class is a good model of the principles described here. Answer the following questions about your class:

1. What are the stated goals of the class?
2. What are your individual goals? Which of these goals are compatible with the group's goals, and which are not compatible? Are any of your individual goals hidden agendas?
3. What are your instructor's individual goals? Were these goals stated? If not, how did you deduce them? How compatible are these goals with the official goals of the class?
4. How do the individual goals of other class members affect the functioning of your group?

has been attributed to its "bias for yes": when in doubt, employees are encouraged to take a chance instead of avoiding action for fear of failure.[36] Likewise, Motorola's turnaround has been attributed to its changing norms for conflict. The company's culture now makes it acceptable to disagree strongly (and loudly) in meetings, instead of keeping quiet or being overly diplomatic.[37] As Table 8-3 shows, the norms in some groups are constructive, while other groups have equally powerful rules that damage their effectiveness.

Whatever a group's norms may be, members who violate them create a crisis for the rest of the team, who respond in a series of escalating steps.[38] Consider, for example, a worker who violates the norm of not following up on her obligations between group meetings. Her teammates might react with increasing pressure:

- *Delaying action.* Members talk among themselves but do not approach the deviant, hoping that she will change without pressure.
- *Hinting about the violation.* Members tease the violator about being a "flake" or about being lazy, hoping that the message behind the humor will cause her to do her share of work.
- *Discussing the problem openly.* Members confront the nonconformist, explaining their concerns about her behavior.
- *Ridiculing and deriding the violator.* Persuasion shifts to demands for a change in behavior; the group's pressure tactics may well trigger a defensive response in the nonconforming member.
- *Rejecting or isolating the deviant.* If all other measures fail, the team member who doesn't conform to group norms is asked to leave the group. If she cannot be expelled, other members can effectively excommunicate her by not inviting her to meetings and by disregarding any attempts at communicating she might make.

There are two ways in which an understanding of norms can help you to function more effectively in a group.

Create Desirable Norms Early. Norms are established early in a group; and once they exist, they are difficult to change. This means that when you participate in a group that is just being established, you should do whatever you can to create norms that you think will be desirable. For example, if you

TABLE 8-3 Typical Constructive (and Destructive) Norms for a Working Group

- Handle (Ignore) business for co-workers who are away from their desks.
- Be willing (Refuse) to admit your mistakes.
- Occasional time off from work for personal reasons is (isn't) O.K., as long as the absence won't harm the company.
- Do (Don't) be willing to work overtime without complaining when big, important deadlines approach.
- Say so (Keep quiet) if you disagree. Don't (Do) hint or go behind others' backs.

expect members of a committee to be punctual at meetings, it's important to begin each session at the appointed time. If you want others to be candid about their feelings, it's important to be frank yourself and encourage honesty in others at the outset.

Comply with Established Norms Whenever Possible. In an established group, you have the best chance of reaching your goals if you handle the task and social relationships in the group's customary manner. If your co-workers are in the habit of exchanging good-natured insults, you shouldn't be offended when you are the target—and you will be accepted as one of them if you dish out a few yourself. In a group in which the norm is never to criticize another member's ideas directly, a blunt approach probably won't get you very far. When you are entering an established group, it's wise to learn the norms by personal observation and by asking knowledgeable members before plunging in.

It may not always be possible to follow established norms. If a group is in the habit of cracking racist jokes, doing shabby work, or stealing company property, for example, you probably would be unwilling to go along just to be accepted. This sort of conflict between personal values and group norms can lead to a major crisis in values. If the potential for conflict is great enough and the issue is sufficiently important, you may decide to do whatever you can to join a different, more compatible group.

Make Sure All Necessary Functional Roles Are Filled

Whereas norms define what standards are acceptable in groups, ***roles*** are patterns of behavior expected of individual members. Some roles are formal and commonly recognized: chairperson, secretary, treasurer, and so on. Other roles are not chosen officially and are rarely acknowledged. These ***functional roles*** have earned their name because they involve functions that are necessary for the group to do its job. Table 8-4 lists these functional roles, as well as noting some dysfunctional behaviors that reduce the effectiveness of a group. As the table shows, there are two types of functional roles. ***Task roles*** play an important part in accomplishing the job at hand. ***Relational roles*** help keep the interaction between members running smoothly.

SKILL BUILDER

What task, social, and procedural norms would be most desirable for each of the following groups? How could you promote development of these norms as the group's leader? As a member?

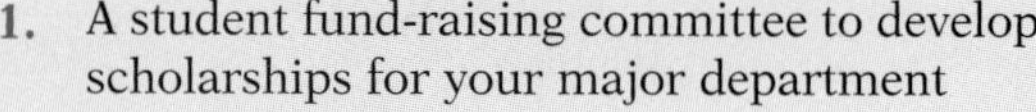

1. A student fund-raising committee to develop scholarships for your major department
2. The employees at a new fast-food restaurant
3. A group of new bank tellers
4. A company softball team

Table 8-4 is a valuable diagnostic tool. When a group isn't operating effectively, you must determine which functions are lacking. For instance, you might note that the group has several good ideas but that no one is summarizing and coordinating them. Or perhaps the group lacks a crucial piece of information, but no one realizes this fact.

TABLE 8-4 Functional Roles of Group Members

Task Functions

1. *Information giver.* Offers facts, evidence, personal experience, and other knowledge relevant to group task.
2. *Information seeker.* Asks other members for task-related information.
3. *Opinion giver.* States personal opinions, attitudes, and beliefs.
4. *Opinion seeker.* Solicits opinions, attitudes, and beliefs of other members.
5. *Starter.* Initiates task-related behavior (e.g., "We'd better get going on this").
6. *Direction giver.* Provides instructions regarding how to perform task at hand.
7. *Summarizer.* Reviews what has been said, identifying common themes or progress.
8. *Diagnoser.* Offers observations about task-related behavior of group (e.g., "We seem to be spending all of our time discussing the problem without proposing any solutions").
9. *Energizer.* Encourages members to work vigorously on task.
10. *Gatekeeper.* Regulates participation of members.
11. *Reality tester.* Checks feasibility of group ideas against real-world contingencies.

Maintenance Functions

1. *Participation encourager.* Encourages reticent members to speak, letting them know that their contribution will be valued.
2. *Harmonizer.* Resolves interpersonal conflicts between members.
3. *Tension reliever.* Uses humor or other devices to release anxiety and frustration of members.
4. *Evaluator of emotional climate.* Offers observations about socioemotional relationships between members (e.g., "I think we're all feeling a little defensive now," or "It sounds like you think nobody trusts you, Bill").
5. *Praise giver.* Reinforces accomplishments and contributions of group members.
6. *Empathic listener.* Listens without evaluation to personal concerns of members.

Dysfunctional Roles

1. *Blocker.* Prevents progress by constantly raising objections.
2. *Attacker.* Aggressively questions the competence or motives of others.
3. *Recognition-seeker.* Repeatedly and unnecessarily calls attention to self by relating irrelevant experiences, boasting, and seeking sympathy.
4. *Joker.* Engages in joking behavior in excess of tension-relieving needs, distracting members.
5. *Withdrawer.* Refuses to take stand on social or task issues; covers up feelings; does not respond to others' comments.

Source: After Kenneth D. Benne and Paul Sheats, "Functional Roles of Group Members," *Journal of Social Issues* 4 (1948): 41–49.

In other cases, your diagnosis of a troubled group might show that all the necessary task functions are being filled but that the social needs of members aren't being met. Perhaps members need to have their good ideas supported ("That's a terrific idea, Neil!"). Maybe personal conflicts need to be acknowledged and resolved ("I know I sound defensive about this. I've worked on this idea for a month, and I hate to see it dismissed in five minutes"). When social needs like these go unfilled, even the best knowledge and talent often aren't enough to guarantee a group's smooth functioning.

Having too many people fill a functional role can be just as troublesome as having nobody fill it. For example, you might discover that several people are acting as opinion givers but that no one is serving as an opinion seeker—like a series of radio stations broadcasting but no one receiving. If two or more people compete for the role of direction giver, the results can be confusing. Even social roles can be overdone. Too much tension relieving or praise giving can become annoying.

Once you have identified the missing functions, you can fill them. Supplying these missing roles often transforms a stalled, frustrated group into a productive team. Other members probably won't recognize what you're doing, but they will realize that you somehow know how to say the "right thing" at the right time.

Promote an Optimal Level of Cohesiveness

Cohesiveness can be defined as the degree to which members feel themselves part of a group and want to remain with that group. You can think of cohesiveness as a magnetic force that attracts members to one another, giving them a collective identity. As you might suspect, highly cohesive groups have happier members than less closely knit groups. Workers who belong to cohesive groups are likely to have higher rates of job satisfaction and lower rates of tension, absenteeism, and turnover than those who belong to less cohesive groups.[39]

Not all cohesive work groups are productive—at least not in terms of the organization's goals. In strikes and slowdowns, for example, highly cohesive workers can actually shut down operations. (Of course, the workers' cohesiveness in such cases may help them to accomplish other group goals, such as higher pay or safer working conditions.) In less dramatic cases, cohesiveness in observing antiorganization norms ("Don't work too hard," "Go ahead and report our lunch as a business expense—we always do that," "If you need some art supplies for your kids, just take them from the supply closet") can leave group members feeling good about each other but

INVITATION TO INSIGHT

Which of the functional roles in Table 8-4 do you generally fill in groups? Do you fill the same role in most groups at most times, or do you switch roles as circumstances require? How could you improve the functioning of one group you belong to by changing your role-related behavior?

harm the interests of the organization. A manager, therefore, should try to develop group cohesivenss that focuses on norms and goals desirable to the organization.

Cohesiveness develops when certain conditions exist in a group. Once you understand these conditions, you can apply them to groups on or off the job. You can also use them to analyze why a group's cohesiveness is high or low and choose ways to reach and maintain a desirable level of cohesiveness. Here are seven factors that promote an optimal level of cohesiveness.[40]

Shared or Compatible Goals. Group members draw closer together when they have a similar aim or when their goals can be mutually satisfied. For instance, the members of a construction crew might have little cohesiveness when their pay is based on individual efforts, but if the entire crew receives a bonus for completing stages of the building ahead of schedule, the members are likely to work together better.

Progress toward Goals. When a group makes progress toward its target, members are drawn together; when progress stops, cohesiveness decreases. Members of the construction crew just mentioned will feel good about each other when they reach their target dates or can reasonably expect to do so. But if they consistently fall short, they are likely to get discouraged and feel less attraction to the group; when talking to their families or friends, there will be less talk about "us" and more about "me."

Shared Norms or Values. Although successful groups tolerate or even thrive on some differences in members' expressed attitudes and behaviors, wide variation in what members consider appropriate behavior reduces cohesiveness. For example, a person who insists on wearing conservative clothes in a business where everyone else dresses casually probably won't fit in with the rest of the group.

Minimal Feelings of Threat among Members. In a cohesive group, members usually feel secure about their status, dignity, and material and social well-being. When conflict arises over these issues, however, the results can be destructive. If all of the junior executives in a division are

Certainly [unified commitment] is "team spirit." It is a sense of loyalty and dedication to the team. It is an unrestrained sense of excitement and enthusiasm about the team. It is a willingness to do anything that has to be done to help the team succeed. It is an intense identification with a group of people. It is a loss of self. "Unified commitment" is very difficult to understand unless you've experienced it. And even if you have experienced it, it is difficult to put into words.

Carl E. Larson and Frank M. J. LaFusto, *TeamWork: What Must Go Right/What Can Go Wrong* competing for the same senior position—especially if senior positions rarely open—the cohesiveness of the group is likely to suffer, at least until the job is filled.

Interdependence among Members. Groups become more cohesive when members need one another to satisfy group goals. When a job can be done by one person alone, the need for unity decreases. An office team in which each member performs a different aspect or stage of a process will be less cohesive than one in which members rely on one another.

Competition from Outside the Group. When members perceive an external threat to their existence or dignity, they draw closer together. Almost everyone knows of a family whose members seem to fight constantly among themselves until an outsider criticizes one of them. The internal bickering stops for the moment, and the group unites against the common enemy. An uncohesive work group could draw together in a similar way when another group competes with it for such things as use of limited company resources or desirable space in a new office building. Many wise managers deliberately set up situations of competition between groups to get tasks accomplished more quickly or to generate more sales dollars.

Shared Group Experiences. When members have been through an experience together, especially an unusual or trying one, they draw closer together. This is why soldiers who have gone through combat together often feel close for the rest of their lives. Work groups that have accomplished difficult tasks are also likely to be more cohesive. Some organizations also provide social events such as annual "retreats" for their executives; retreats might include workshops to discuss particular aspects or problems of members' jobs, sports events, and parties. Annual sales meetings are often partially intended to increase group cohesiveness, since these meetings are not the most cost-efficient way to distribute sales information.

SKILL BUILDER

1. Use the skills you learned in Chapters 6 and 7 to interview one member of a work-related group. Identify the following:
   a. What is the level of the group's cohesiveness? Is this level desirable, too high, or too low?
   b. Which of the factors on pages 253–255 contribute to the level of cohesiveness in this group?
2. On the basis of your findings, develop a report outlining specific steps that might be taken to improve the degree of cohesiveness in this group.

Avoid Excessive Conformity

Bad group decisions can also come about through too much agreement among members. Irving Janis calls this phenomenon ***groupthink,*** an unwillingness, for the sake of harmony, to examine ideas critically.[41] Janis describes several characteristics of groups that succumb to groupthink:

- *Illusion that the group is invulnerable.* "We can afford to raise the price on our deluxe-model kitchen appliances because they're so much better than anything else on the market. Even if our competitors could develop comparable models, we'd still outdo them on style."
- *Tendency to rationalize or discount negative information.* "I know the market research says people will buy other brands if our prices go up any more, but you know how unreliable market research is about things like that."
- *Willingness to ignore ethical or moral consequences of the group's decision.* "The waste we're dumping in the river may kill a few fish, but look, this company provides jobs and a living for all the people who live in this town."
- *Stereotyped views of other groups.* "The only thing those people at the head office care about is the bottom line. They don't give a damn about what we think or what we need."
- *Group pressure to conform.* "Come on, none of the rest of us is interested in direct-mail marketing. Why don't you forget that stuff?"
- *Self-censorship.* "Every time I push for an innovative ad campaign, everybody fights it. I might as well drop it."
- *Illusion of unanimity.* "Then we all agree: cutting prices is the only way to stay competitive."
- *"Mindguards" against threatening information.* "They're talking about running the machines around the clock to meet the schedule. I'd better not bring up what the supervisor said about how her staff feels about working more overtime."

A second type of harmful conformity has been labeled ***risky shift:*** the likelihood of a group to take positions that are more extreme than the members would choose on their own.[42] A risky shift can work in two directions. When members are conservative, their collective decisions are likely to be more cau-

> Alfred P. Sloan, the man who revitalized General Motors in the 1920s when it was close to bankruptcy, appreciated the value of dialogue versus monologue. At a meeting of one of his top committees, everyone agreed to his proposal under consideration. "Gentlemen," observed Sloan, "I take it we are all in complete agreement on the decision here." Everyone around the conference table nodded. "Then," he continued, "I propose we postpone further discussion on this matter until our next meeting, to give ourselves time to develop disagreement and perhaps gain some understanding of what the decision is all about."
>
> *Executive Speechwriter* newsletter

tious than their individual positions. More commonly, groups are prone to taking positions that are riskier than the choices members would have taken had they been acting separately. Thus, risky shift results either in taking risks that aren't justified and suffering the costs or avoiding necessary steps that the team needs to take to survive and prosper.

Paradoxically, cohesive teams are most prone to groupthink and risky shift. When members like and respect one another, the tendency to agree is great. The best way to guard against this sort of collective blindness—especially in very cohesive groups—is to seek the opinions of outsiders who may see things differently. In addition, leaders who are highly influential should avoid stating their opinions early in the discussion.[43]

Encourage Creativity

One advantage of broadly based participation in groups is the greater chance for creativity. As more members bring their different perspectives to a task, the chances of coming up with a winning solution increase.

Of course, the quantity of people involved doesn't guarantee the quality of their contributions. One way to boost the creativity of the group is through ***brainstorming***—an approach that encourages free thinking and minimizes conformity. The term was coined by advertising executive Alex Osborn, who noticed that groups were most creative when they let their imaginations run free.[44] He also realized that creativity was stifled when members began criticizing either their own ideas or those of others. Out of these observations came a series of steps that, with variations, are now used widely.

Conduct a Warm-up Session. During this phase the group is reminded of brainstorming's cardinal rules:

All evaluation and criticism of ideas is forbidden during the early phases of the process.

Wild and crazy ideas are encouraged.

Quantity—not quality—of ideas is the goal.

New combinations of ideas are sought.

Once members understand these rules, they practice them with some nonsense issue, such as uses for a paper clip (high-tech tie clip, lightning rod for an anthill) or a brick (heat and use as a foot warmer in bed, freeze and use as a beer cooler on picnics). This sort of wild thinking loosens the group up to approach the real problem creatively.

Generate Possible Solutions. Now the group applies the brainstorming rules, as described above, to the task at hand. During this stage, a recorder lists all the ideas generated by the group on a chalkboard or flip chart that everyone can see. The leader encourages "hitchhiking" on previous ideas, so

SKILL BUILDER

With four to six classmates, develop a table of contents for a new book entitled *Fifty Things to Do When There's Nothing to Do in (name of your town).* Use the guidelines in this chapter to ensure that the ideas in the book are creative and interesting.

that one suggestion leads to variations. The leader should also keep the level of enthusiasm high to spur more contributions.

Eliminate Duplicate Ideas. After the brainstorming session is completed, duplicate suggestions are eliminated. No evaluation of ideas is made at this stage; the group simply clarifies and simplifies the list of ideas it has developed.

Evaluate Ideas. Once the group has generated all the ideas it can think of, it can begin to decide which are worth considering seriously. Unless only one or two ideas stand out as winners, it's usually best to prune the unworkable ones in several passes. Begin by scratching the clearly unworkable ideas, leaving any that have even some merit. After discussing the remainder, the group can pick the top two or three ideas for serious consideration and then decide which one is best.

SUMMARY

When used effectively, small groups are superior to individuals working alone: small groups are more productive, their results can be more accurate, and members will support decisions more enthusiastically.

Many work groups are still accountable to organizational higher-ups and are organized around a designated leader. The best approach to leading a group varies according to the circumstances, and this chapter outlined the conditions under which a variety of styles can be used. In the 1990s, many groups are defined as self-directed work teams and are responsible for managing their own behavior. Leadership in these groups is often shared among members, who are recognized as possessing several types of power that can affect the group's functioning. In groups without a designated leader, a predictable process occurs in which a single leader often emerges.

A variety of communication concepts can improve the effectiveness of working teams. The reflective-thinking sequence is a means of effective problem solving that produces high-quality results. Recognizing that working groups often go through predictable stages of orientation, conflict, emergence, and reinforcement can help members tolerate the inevitable frustrations of group problem solving. Carefully choosing the method of making a decision can use time effectively and generate an outcome that members are most likely to support.

The chapter made several suggestions about how groups can operate more successfully. These include recognizing and trying to fulfill both personal and group goals, promoting desirable norms, ensuring that functional roles are filled, promoting an optimal level of cohesiveness, avoiding excessive conformity, and boosting creativity.

RESOURCES

Larson, C. E., and F. M. J. LaFusto, *TeamWork: What Must Go Right/What Can Go Wrong* (Newbury Park, Calif.: Sage, 1989).

This brief, useful book outlines eight important characteristics shared by successful groups and shows how they can be applied to any working team.

Hackett, D. H., and C. L. Martin, *Facilitation Skills for Team Leaders* (Menlo Park, Calif.: Crisp Publications, 1993).

Part of a "Fifty-Minute Series," this workbook is loaded with activities, exercises, checklists, and assessments. The interactive format encourages readers to become involved in learning facilitation skills.

Rees, F. *How to Lead Work Teams: Facilitation Skills* (San Diego: Pfeiffer, 1991).

This book describes the move toward teams and the changing skills needed by managers, with an emphasis on skills needed to facilitate team processes. The chapters "Encouraging Participation" and "Getting to Consensus and Closure" feature explanations and examples of the requisite verbal and nonverbal communication skills that proficient group leaders will want to possess.

Scholtes, P. R., *The Team Handbook: How to Use Teams to Improve Quality* (Madison, Wis.: Joiner Associates, 1988).

This book shows how teams can lead to more effective organizations. Chapter 6, "Learning to Work Together," describes the stages of team growth and expands a multitude of ideas for building a successful team. Ten common group problems are identified, along with recommendations and guidance for handling them.

CHAPTER 9

Effective Meetings

KEY TERMS

Agenda / Direct question / Meeting / Nominal group technique (NGT) / Overhead questions / Relay questions / Relevancy challenge / Reverse questions

> As they do every week, the agents of a real-estate firm meet to discuss the latest trends in the market and to share information that will help them increase their sales.
>
> The tenants in an apartment building gather to discuss the need for better maintenance and security.
>
> A group of employees meet with top management to discuss a list of important issues, including the need for child care, a potential series of layoffs, and health benefits.
>
> The owner of a small business meets over lunch with the director of a local advertising agency, who outlines how her firm can increase the client's market share.

Examples like these show that meetings are a fact of life on the job. Sociolinguist Deborah Tannen's definition of the term helps explain why we so often hear that someone we want to contact is "in a meeting." She characterizes a ***meeting*** as any focused conversation that has a specific agenda, especially but not only if it has been set up in advance.[1] This definition shows that *group* and *meeting* are not identical terms. A team of assembly-line workers or of firefighters fits our description of a group, but these people spend very little time in meetings. The members of some groups work in separate offices, separate buildings, or separate cities; they communicate with one another about their group efforts, but only occasionally do they meet all at once, face-to-face, to discuss shared concerns. In this chapter, we will focus specifically on how groups operate in meetings—that is, on those occasions when their members gather to discuss common concerns.

Meetings really are ubiquitous. In one study of fifteen corporations, researchers gave pocket recorders to a wide range of key workers—from sales representatives to vice-presidents—and asked these workers to list what they were doing every twenty minutes on the job. An analysis of almost 90,000 working days showed that an impressive 46 percent of the time was spent in meetings of one sort or another.[2] Other estimates confirm this figure.[3] The number of times people meet as they do business is staggering: approximately 20 million business meetings take place each day in the United States, and businesspeople spend an average of half their time attending them.[4] Table 9-1 shows that the time spent in meetings costs businesses a considerable amount of money. If you include the time spent planning and following up on face-to-face interaction, the costs are even higher.

> My first grade arithmetic primer asked, "If it takes two ditch diggers two days to dig a ditch, how long would it take four ditch diggers?" In the first grade, the correct answer is "one day." In executives' work, however, the right answer is probably "four days," if not "forever."
>
> Peter Drucker

TABLE 9-1 Hourly Costs of Meetings

	Number of People Attending Meeting					
Annual salary	*2*	*4*	*6*	*8*	*10*	*20*
$62,500	$125	$250	$375	$500	$625	$1,250
$50,000	100	200	300	400	500	1,000
$37,500	75	150	225	300	375	750
$25,000	50	100	150	200	250	500
$12,500	25	50	75	100	125	250

Source: After *Six Secrets to Improve Your Future Business Meetings* (Austin, Tex.: 3M Visual Systems).

Just because meetings are common doesn't mean that they are always productive. A survey by one marketing research company showed that executives consider one-third of the gatherings they attend to be unnecessary.[5] Inefficient use of meeting time led one skeptic to pen this poem:

Let's fingertap together
In a dedicated way,
and postpone all decisions
Until another day.

Let's orchestrate and dialogue
In words that we adore,
The words that we've all mumbled
A million times before.

Let's shuffle all our paper,
And fuzzify our minds;
Let's wrap our brains in cobwebs,
And love red tape that binds.

Let's regulate the people
With rules, reports, and forms;
Inspire true innovation
As long as it conforms.

Let's optimize the status quo,
And sit right where we are,
For if we keep our profile low,
We'll get no battle scar.

Let's cut our red tape lengthwise,
Pronunciate our words,
And build great stacks of paper
The stuff that undergirds.

Yes, let's fingertap together
In a dedicated way,
And postpone all decisions
Until another day.[6]

Since meetings are so common and so prone to inefficiency, it's important to take a closer look at them. By the time you have finished reading this chapter, you should understand some methods for planning and participating in meetings that will produce efficient, satisfying results.

TYPES OF MEETINGS

People meet for many reasons. In most business and professional settings, meetings fall into three categories: information sharing, problem solving, and ritual activities.

Information Sharing

In many organizations, people meet regularly to exchange information. Police officers and nurses, for example, begin every shift with a meeting in which the people going off duty brief their replacements on what has been happening recently. Members of a medical research team experimenting with a new drug may meet regularly to compare notes on their results. In many office groups, the Monday morning meeting is an important tool for informing group members about new developments, emerging trends, and the coming week's tasks. Perkin Elmer Corporation, a producer of scientific measuring instruments and precision optical equipment, is a typical example. The firm schedules a weekly meeting of all corporate and top executives to keep them up to date on the activities of the more than twenty divisions the company has around the world.

Problem Solving or Decision Making

In other meetings, a group may decide to take some action or make a change in existing policies or procedures. "Which supplier should we contract?" "Should we introduce a new product line?" "Should we delay production so we can work out a design flaw in our new typewriter?" "Where can we cut costs if sales don't improve this year?" "How can we best schedule vacations?" All these are questions that might be discussed in problem-solving meetings. Because problem-solving and decision-making meetings are the most challenging type of group activity, the bulk of this chapter discusses how to conduct them effectively.

INVITATION TO INSIGHT

You can gain an appreciation for the importance of meetings by interviewing one or more people in a field that is important to you. You should have these people give you answers to each of the following questions:

1. How frequent are meetings in your work?
2. What is the length of time that these meetings take?
3. What kinds of topics are covered in your meetings?
4. How effective are meetings? What factors contribute to their effectiveness or ineffectiveness?

Meetings in Corporate America

Over 900 people from 36 small, medium, and large companies in the public and private sectors completed surveys describing the last meeting they attended. The results help paint a profile of on-the-job meetings:

- The *typical meeting* in corporate America
  - Lasts one and a half hours
  - Is attended by nine people
  - Is called with two hours' notice (unless it is regularly scheduled)
  - Has a written agenda less than half the time
  - Covers the agenda completely only half the time
- *Major topics* of meetings are
  - Organizational updates
  - Project management
  - Product or service issues
- *Major purposes* of meetings are
  - To resolve a conflict
  - To reach a group decision
  - To communicate information
- *Satisfaction with a meeting* is correlated with satisfaction with
  - Meeting leaders
  - Who attends the meeting
  - The agenda
  - The meeting's outcome

P. R. Monge, C. McSween, and J. Wyer, "A Profile of Meetings in Corporate America," Annenberg School of Communications, University of Southern California, 1989

Ritual Activities

In still other meetings, the social function is far more important than any specific task. In one firm, Friday afternoon "progress review sessions" are a regular fixture. Their apparently serious title is really an insider's tongue-in-cheek joke: the meetings take place in a local bar and to an outsider look like little more than a T.G.I.F. party. Despite the setting and apparently unbusinesslike activity, however, these meetings serve several important purposes.[7] First, they reaffirm the members' commitment to one another and to the company. Choosing to socialize with one another instead of rushing home is a sign of belonging and caring. Second, the sessions provide a chance to swap useful ideas and stories that might not be appropriate in the office. Who's in trouble? What does the boss really want? As you read in Chapter 1, this sort of informal communication can be invaluable, and the meetings provide a good setting for it. Finally, ritual meetings can be a kind of perk that confers status on the members. "Progress review committee" members charge expenses to the company and leave work early to attend. Thus, being invited to join the sessions is a sign of having arrived in the company.

Some meetings serve more than one function. In fact, the functions we've been describing are often dependent on one another. A production team deciding on what suppliers to use will share information about the quality of materials and service from past jobs. In a meeting in which a project team works out a plan to produce a new line of office furniture, a sales manager might discuss market demands in terms of functionality, appearance, and costs; a designer might suggest some ways that those needs might be met; a production manager could present information on various materials and their costs; and an engineer might provide some technical information about the strength of materials and the capacity of the manufacturing division to work with those materials. Drawing on the knowledge and skills of all the members, the group would try to work out a general plan that would take into account all of the factors involved.

Whatever your career or profession, chances are you will be expected to participate in and even lead meetings. Your skills in planning, conducting, and participating in meetings may be vital to your job success.

PLANNING A PROBLEM-SOLVING MEETING

Successful meetings are just like interviews, presentations, letters, and memos: they must be planned.

When to Hold a Meeting

Given the costs of bringing people together, the most fundamental question is whether to hold a meeting at all. There are many times when a meeting probably isn't justified:[8]

- The matter could be handled just as well over the phone.
- You could send a memo, e-mail, or fax and achieve the same goal.
- Key people are not available to attend.
- There isn't enough time to handle the business at hand.
- Members aren't prepared.
- The meeting is routine, and there is no compelling reason to meet.

Keeping these points in mind, a planner should call a meeting (or appoint a committee) only when the answers to the following questions are yes.

Is the Job beyond the Capacity of One Person? A job might be too much for one person to handle for two reasons: First, it might call for more *information* than any single person possesses. For example, the job of improving health conditions in a food-processing plant would probably require the medical background of a physician or other health professional, the first-hand experience of employees familiar with the work, and a manager who knows the resources available for developing and implementing the program.

Not all meetings are ineffective—but many are. When asked what can go wrong in meetings, a group of managers and professionals gave 1,305 examples. Sixteen of them accounted for 90 percent of all the problems:

- No goals or agenda
- No premeeting orientation
- Starting late
- Poor or inadequate preparation
- Getting off the subject
- Too long
- Disorganized
- Inconclusive
- Ineffective leadership
- Irrelevant information discussed
- Time wasted
- Interruptions
- Ineffective at making decisions
- Rambling, redundant, digressive discussions
- Individuals dominate discussions
- No published results or follow-up action

Roger K. Mosvick and Robert B. Nelson, *We've Got to Start Meeting Like This*

Second, a job might take more *time* than one person has available. For instance, even if one employee were capable of writing and publishing an employee handbook, it's unlikely that the person would be able to handle the task and have much time for other duties.

Are Individuals' Tasks Interdependent? Each member at a committee meeting should have a different role. If each member's share of the task can be completed without input from other members, it's better to have the members coacting under the supervision of a manager.

Consider the job of preparing the employee handbook that we just mentioned. If each person on the handbook team is responsible for a separate section, there is little need for the group to meet frequently to discuss the task: meetings would be little more than "show-and-tell" sessions. A more efficient plan might be for the group to meet at the outset to devise an outline and a set of guidelines about style, length, and so on, and then for a manager or group leader to see that each person completes his or her own section according to those guidelines.

There are times when people who do the same job can profit by sharing ideas in a group. Members of the handbook team, for example, might get new ideas about how the book could be made better from talking to one another. Similarly, sales representatives, industrial designers, physicians, or attorneys who work independently might profit by exchanging experiences and ideas. This is part of the purpose of professional conventions. Also, many companies schedule quarterly or annual meetings of people who do similar but independent work. While this may seem to contradict the requirement for interdependence of members' tasks, there is no real conflict. A group of people who do the same kind of work can often improve their individual performance through meetings by performing some of the complementary *functional roles.* For example, one colleague might serve as reality tester. ("Writing individual notes to each potential customer in your territory sounds like a good idea, but do you really have time to do that?") Another might take the job of being information giver. ("You know, there's a printer just outside Boston who can do large jobs like that just as well as your regular printer, but he's cheaper. Call me, and I'll give you the name and address.") Others serve as diagnosers. ("Have you checked the feed mechanism? Sometimes a problem there can throw the whole machine out of whack.") Some can just serve as empathic listeners. ("Yeah, I know. It's tough to get people who can do that kind of work right.")

Is There More than One Decision or Solution? Questions that have only one right answer aren't well suited to discussion in meetings. Whether the sales force made its quota last year or whether the budget will accommodate paying overtime to meet a schedule, for instance, are questions answered by checking the figures, not by getting the regional sales managers or the department members to reach an agreement.

Tasks that don't have fixed outcomes, however, are appropriate for committee discussion. Consider the job facing the members of an advertising agency who are planning a campaign for a client. There is no obvious best way to sell products or ideas such as yearly physical examinations, office equipment, or clothing. Tasks such as these call for the kind of creativity that a talented, well-chosen group can generate.

Are Misunderstandings or Reservations Likely? It's easy to see how meetings can be useful when the goal is to generate ideas or solve problems. But meetings are often necessary when confusing or controversial information is being communicated. Suppose, for instance, that changing federal rules and company policy require employees to document their use of company cars in far more detail than was ever required before. It's easy to imagine how this sort of change would be met with grumbling and resistance. In this sort of situation, simply issuing a memo outlining the new rules might not gain the kind of compliance that is necessary. Only by talking out their complaints and hearing why the new policy is being instituted will employees see a need to go along with the new procedure. "I can write down the vision of the company a thousand times and send it out to people," says Dennis Stamp, chairman of Vancouver's Priority Management Systems, Inc. "But when I sit with them face-to-face and give them the vision, for some reason it is much more accepted."[9]

Setting an Agenda

An ***agenda*** is a list of topics to be covered in a meeting. A meeting without an agenda is like a ship at sea without a destination or compass: no one aboard knows where it is or where it's headed. A good agenda contains several kinds of information, all illustrated in Figure 9-1.[10]

Time, Length, and Location. To avoid problems, all three of these details need to be present on an agenda. Without the *starting time,* you can expect to hear such comments as "I thought you said ten, not nine," or "We always started at three before." Unless you announce the *length,* expect some members to leave early, pleading, "I have another meeting," or "I didn't realize we'd run this long—I've got a doctor's appointment." Failure to note the *loca-*

SKILL BUILDER

Use the information in this chapter to decide which of the following tasks would best be handled by a problem-solving group and which should be handled by one or more individuals working separately. Be prepared to explain the reasons for each choice.

1. Developing procedures for interviewing prospective employees
2. Tabulating responses to a customer survey
3. Investigating several brands of office machines for possible purchase
4. Choosing the most desirable employee health insurance program
5. Organizing the company picnic
6. Researching the existence and cost of training programs for improving communication among staff members

AGENDA

Date:	March 19, 1996
To:	Pat Rivera, Fred Brady, Kevin Jessup, Monica Flores, Dave Cohn
From:	Ted Gross
Subject:	Planning meeting for new Louisville office.
Time/Place:	Tuesday, April 2, from 9:30 to 11:00 A.M. in the third-floor conference room.
Background:	We are still on target for an August 10 opening date for the Louisville office. Completing the tasks below will keep us on schedule—vital if we're to be ready for the fall season.

We will discuss the follow items:

1. Office Equipment

   Please come with a list of business machines and other equipment you think will be needed for the office. At the meeting we'll refine this list to standardize our purchases as much as possible. Let's try to start out with compatible equipment!

2. Office Decoration

   Ellen Tibbits of the Louisville Design Group will present a preliminary design for our reaction. She will come up with a final plan based on our suggestions.

3. Promotion

   Kevin wants to prepare a series of press releases for distribution to Louisville media a month or so before the office opens. Please come with suggestions of items that should be mentioned in these releases.

FIGURE 9-1 Format for a comprehensive agenda.

tion results in members' stumbling in late after waiting in the "usual place," wondering why no one showed up.

Participants. The overall size of the group is important: When attendance grows beyond seven members, the likelihood of some members' falling silent increases. If the agenda includes one or more problem-solving items, it's best to keep the size small so that everyone can participate in discussions. If the meeting is primarily informational, a larger group may be acceptable.

Be sure to identify on the agenda the people who will be attending. By listing who will attend, you alert all members about whom to expect in the meeting. If you have overlooked someone who ought to attend, a member who received the agenda can tell you. It is frustrating and a waste of time to call a meeting and then discover that the person with key information isn't there.

Background Information. Sometimes participants will need background information to give them new details or to remind them of things they may have forgotten. Background information can also provide a description of the meeting's significance.

Items and Goals. A good agenda goes beyond just listing topics and describes the goal for the discussion. "Meetings should be outcome- rather than process-driven," says Anita Underwood, Dun and Bradstreet's vice-president of organizational management.[11] Most people have at least a vague idea of why they are meeting. Vague ideas, however, often lead to vague meetings. A clear list of topics and goals like the ones in Figure 9-1 will result in better-informed members and more productive, satisfying meetings.

The best goals are *result-oriented, specific,* and *realistic.* Notice the difference between goals that do and don't meet these criteria:

POORLY WORDED	BETTER
"Let's talk about how we can solve the sales problems in the northwestern region."	"We will come up with a list of specific ways our product can be shown to be useful in the special climate conditions of the Northwest."
"We're going to talk about the new income-savings plan."	"We will explain the advantages and disadvantages of our two income-savings plans so that employees can decide which best suits their needs."
"Joe Fishman will tell you about his trip to the new supplier's plant."	"Joe will explain the facilities of our new supplier and how we can use them to cut costs."

Goals like these are useful in at least two ways: First, they help to identify those who ought to attend the meeting. Second, specific goals also help the people who do attend to prepare for the meeting, and they help to keep the discussion on track once it begins.

The person who calls the meeting isn't the only one who can or should set goals. There are many times when other members have important business. The planner is often wise to use an "expectations check" to identify members' concerns.[12] Members can be polled before the meeting, so that their issues can be included in the agenda, or at the start of the meeting. The fact that a member wants to discuss something does not mean that the topic should automatically be considered. If the issue is inappro-

SKILL BUILDER

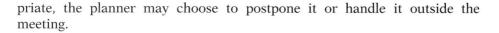

Your institution is considering restructuring its general-education requirements. You have been selected by the administration to chair a committee to present the students' point of view. Decide whom to include on the committee, and draft an agenda for the group's first meeting.

priate, the planner may choose to postpone it or handle it outside the meeting.

Premeeting Work. The best meetings occur when people have done all the necessary advance work. The agenda is a good place to tell members how to prepare for the meeting by reading information, developing reports, preparing or duplicating documents, or locating facts or figures. If all members need to prepare in the same way (for example, by reading an article), adding that fact to the agenda is advised. If certain members have specific jobs to do, the meeting organizer can jot these tasks on their individual copies: "Sarah—be sure to bring last year's sales figures"; "Wes—please duplicate copies of the annual report for everyone."

The order of agenda items is important. Some experts suggest that the difficulty of items should form a bell-shaped curve, with items arranged in order of ascending and descending difficulty (see Figure 9-2). The meeting ought to begin with relatively simple business: minutes, announcements, and the easiest decisions. Once members have hit their stride and a good climate has developed, the group can move on to the most difficult items. These should ideally occupy the middle third of the session. Then the final third of the meeting can focus on easier items to allow a period of decompression and goodwill. (Table 9-2 is a checklist for planning a meeting.)

CONDUCTING THE MEETING

To the uninitiated observer, a well-run meeting seems almost effortless. Time is used efficiently, the tone is constructive, and the quality of ideas is good. Despite their apparent simplicity, results like this usually don't just happen: they grow from some important communication skills. (Table 9-3 is a checklist for conducting a meeting.)

Beginning the Meeting

Effective openings get the meeting off to a good start. First, they give everyone a clear picture of what is to be accomplished. Second, they define how the group will try to reach its goal. Finally, they set the stage for good teamwork and, thus, good results. The first few remarks by the person who called the meeting can set the stage for a constructive session. They should cover the following points.[13]

TABLE 9-2 Checklist for Planning a Meeting

- Is membership well chosen?
  Is the size of group appropriate?
  Are the necessary knowledge and skills represented?
- Have unproductive members been excluded (if practical)?
- Is enough time allotted for tasks at hand?
- Is the meeting time convenient for most members?
- Is the location adequate?
  Is the size appropriate?
  Are the facilities appropriate?
  Is there freedom from distractions?
- Is a complete agenda circulated?
  Is it distributed far enough in advance of the meeting?
  Does it include particulars (meeting data, time, length, location, attendees)?
  Does it contain background information as necessary?
  Does it list goals for each item supplied?

Identify the Goals of the Meeting. This means repeating the information listed in the agenda, but mentioning it here will remind everyone of the meeting's goals and help to focus the discussion. For example:

> "We're faced with a serious problem. Inventory losses have almost doubled in the last year, from 5 to 9 percent. We need to decide what's causing these losses and come up with some ideas about how to reduce them."

Provide Necessary Background Information. Background information explains the context of the meeting and gives everyone the same picture of the subject being discussed. It prevents misunderstandings and helps members to understand the nature of the information the group will consider. Clarifying key terms is often helpful:

> "By 'inventory losses,' we mean materials that are missing or damaged after we receive them. These losses might occur in the main warehouse, en route to the stores, or within the stores themselves."

Show How the Group Can Help. Outline the contributions that members can make during the meeting. Some of these contributions will come from specific people:

> "Tom's going to compare our losses with industry figures, so we can get an idea of how much of the problem is an unavoidable cost of doing business. Chris will talk about his experiences with the problem at Sterling, where he worked until last year. That firm had some good ideas we may be able to use."

Other contributions can be made by everyone present. This is the time to define specifically how each member can help make the meeting a success:

> "We're counting on everybody here to suggest areas where we can cut losses. Once we've come up with ideas, I'll ask each of you to work out a schedule for putting the ideas to work in your department."

TABLE 9-3 Checklist for Conducting a Meeting

- *Opening the meeting*
  Have goals for the meeting been identified?
  Has necessary background information been reviewed?
  Are expectations for members' contributions clear?
  Has the sequence of events for the meeting been previewed?
  Have time constraints been identified?
- *Encouraging balanced participation*
  Have leader and members used questions to draw out quiet members?
  Are off-track comments redirected with references to the agenda and relevancy challenges?
  Do leader and members suggest moving on when an agenda item has been dealt with adequately?
- *Maintaining positive tone*
  Are questioning and paraphrasing used as nondefensive responses to hostile remarks?
  Are dubious comments enhanced as much as possible?
  Does the meeting reflect the cultural norms of attendees?
- *Solving problems creatively*
  Is the problem defined clearly (versus too narrowly or broadly)?
  Are the causes and effects of the problem analyzed?
  Are clear criteria for resolving the problem established?
  Are possible solutions brainstormed without being evaluated?
  Is a decision made based on the previously established criteria?
  Are methods of implementing the solution developed?

Preview the Meeting. If you have not already done so, outline how the meeting will run. For instance:

> "We'll begin by hearing the reports from Tom and Chris. Then we'll all work together to brainstorm a list of ways to cut losses. The goal here will be to get as many ideas as possible. Once we've come up with a list, we can decide which ideas to use and how to make them work."

Identify Time Constraints. Clarifying how much time is available helps to prevent time wasting. In some cases, it's only necessary to remind the group of how much time can be spent in the meeting as a whole ("We can develop this list between now and eleven o'clock if we keep on track"). In other cases, it can be useful to preview the available time for each agenda item:

> "Tom and Chris have promised to keep their remarks brief, so by ten o'clock we should be ready to start brainstorming. If we get our list put

Some meetings should be long and leisurely. Some should be mercifully brief. A good way to handle the latter is to hold the meeting with everybody standing up. The meetees won't believe you at first. Then they get very uncomfortable and can hardly wait to get the meeting over with. If you have more than one comfortable chair for office visitors, move to a smaller office.

Robert Townsend, *Further Up the Organization*

together by ten-thirty, we'll still have a half hour to talk about which ideas to try and how to put them into action."

Following these guidelines will get your meeting off to a good start. Even if you are not in charge of the meeting, you can still make sure that the opening is a good one by asking questions that will get the leader to share the kind of information just listed:

"How much time do you expect we'll need?"

"How far do you expect we'll get today?"

"What can we do to help solve the problem?"

And so on.

Conducting Business

No meeting will be successful without committed, talented participants. But even the best attendees do not guarantee success. Someone—either the leader or a responsible member—has to be sure that all important business is covered in a way that takes advantage of the talents of everyone present. A number of approaches are available that use meeting time effectively (see Table 9-3).

Encouraging Participation. Loosely structured, informal meetings may appear to give everyone an equal chance to speak out, but because of gender, culture, and style differences, every member may not, in fact, have the same access.[14] Group members' relative status or rank, ages, gender, and cultural backgrounds all influence interaction patterns in groups. Unbalanced participation can cause two sorts of problems: First, it discourages people who don't get a chance to talk. Second, it prevents the group from considering potentially useful ideas. There are several ways to improve participation at meetings.

Use the Nominal Group Technique. One method for giving every member's ideas an equal chance to be considered is the ***nominal group technique (NGT).***[15] (The method's name comes from the fact that, for much of this process, the participants are a group in name only, since they are working independently.) The NGT method consists of five phases:

1. Each member writes down his or her ideas on paper, which is then collected by a discussion leader. This method ensures that good ideas from quiet members will have a chance for consideration.
2. All ideas are posted for every member to see. By keeping the authorship of ideas private at this point, consideration is less likely to be based on personal factors such as authority or popularity.
3. Members discuss the ideas to understand them better, but criticism is prohibited. The goal here is to clarify the possibilities, not to evaluate them.

4. Each member privately rank-orders the ideas from most to least promising. Individual ranking again prevents domination by a few talkative or influential members.
5. Items that receive the greatest number of votes are discussed critically and thoroughly by the group. At this point, a decision can be made, using whichever decision-making method described in Chapter 8 (e.g., consensus, majority rule) is most appropriate.

The NGT method is too elaborate for relatively unimportant matters but works well for important issues. Besides reducing the tendency for more talkative members to dominate the discussion, the anonymity of the process lessens the potential for harmful conflicts.

Have Members Take Turns. Another approach is to give every member a turn to speak. While it probably isn't wise to conduct an entire meeting this way, the technique can be useful at the beginning of a meeting to start members off on an equal footing, or in the middle if a few people are dominating the discussion, or at the end if some people have not been heard.

Use Questions. Questions are another way to encourage participation. Lawrence Loban, writing in *Supervision* magazine, suggests that the answer lies in using questions to draw members out.[16] He describes four types of questions.

Overhead questions are directed toward the group as a whole, and anyone is free to answer:

"Sales have flattened out in the western region. Can anybody suggest what's going on?"

"We need to find some way of rewarding our top producers. I'd like to hear your ideas."

As long as overhead questions draw a response from all members, it's wise to continue using them. When a few people begin to dominate, however, it's time to switch to one of the following types.

Direct questions are aimed at a particular individual, who is addressed by name:

"How would that suggestion work for you, Kim?"

"Greg, how's the new plan working in your department?"

Direct questions are a useful way to draw out quiet members, but they must be used skillfully. Never start a discussion with a direct question. This creates a "schoolroom atmosphere" and suggests the rule "Don't speak until you're called on"—hardly a desirable norm in most meetings. It's also important to give respondents a way out of potentially embarrassing questions. For example, a chairman might ask, "Tony, can you give us the figures for your department now, or will you need to check them and get back to us?"

Reverse questions occur when a member asks the leader a question and the leader refers the question back to the person who originally phrased it:

"Suppose the decision were up to you, Gary. What would you do?"

"That's a good question, Laurie. Do you think it's a practical idea?"

Reverse questions work well when the leader senses that a member really wants to make a statement but is unwilling to do so directly. It's important to use reverse questions with care: the member could be asking for information, in which case a direct answer is appropriate.

Relay questions occur when the leader refers a question asked by one member to the entire group:

"Cynthia has just raised a good question. Who can respond to it?"

"Can anyone offer a suggestion for Les?"

Relay questions are especially useful when the leader wants to avoid disclosing his or her opinion for fear of inhibiting or influencing the group. Relays should usually be rephrased as overhead questions directed at the entire group. This avoids the suggestion that one member is smarter than the others. Of course, if a particular person does have special expertise, it is appropriate to direct the inquiry to him or her:

"Didn't you have a problem like that once with a distributor, Britt? How did you work things out?"

Members Can Be Leaders, Too

Good leadership promotes successful meetings, but members can also play an important role in making a meeting successful. The following tips can be used by every person involved in a meeting:

- Ask that an agenda be sent out before the meeting, or agree on an agenda at the beginning of the meeting.
- Ask for help at the beginning of the meeting. Seek clarification on the meeting's goal. Is it to present information? To make a decision?
- Be "tactfully bold" and suggest canceling an unnecessary or badly planned meeting. Convene it when there is a need and an agenda.
- Volunteer to be a record keeper. A written set of minutes reduces the chance for misunderstandings, and keeping notes yourself leads to a record that reflects your perception of events.
- Suggest that a time keeper be appointed, or volunteer yourself. This person advises the group when time for addressing each issue—and the meeting itself—is nearly over and alerts the group when time runs out.
- Ask for help before the meeting closes. Ask "Exactly what have we decided today?" "What do we need to do before our next meeting?"

Adapted from Ana M. Keep, *Moving Meetings.*

Keeping Discussions on Track. Sometimes the problem isn't too little discussion but too much. Groups often waste time, conducting leisurely discussions when time is short. Even when time is plentiful, members often talk on and on without moving any closer to accomplishing a goal. In other cases, someone may bring up a topic that is unrelated to the task at hand. When problems like these occur, the leader or some other member needs to get the discussion back on track by using one of the following techniques.

Remind the Group of Time Pressures. When the group is handling an urgent topic in a leisurely manner, you can remind everyone about the importance of moving quickly. But when doing so, it is important to acknowledge the value of the comments being made:

> "Radio ads sound good, but for now we'd better stick to the newspaper program. John wanted copy from us by noon, and we'll never make it if we don't get going."

Summarize and Redirect the Discussion. When members ramble on about a topic after the job is done, you can get the discussion moving again by tactfully summarizing what has been accomplished and mentioning the next task:

> "It seems as if we've come up with a good list of the factors that might be contributing to absenteeism. Can anybody think of more causes? If not, maybe we should move on and try to think of as many solutions as we can."

Use Relevancy Challenges. When a discussion wanders away from the business at hand, summarizing won't help. Sometimes the unrelated ideas are good ones that just don't apply to the group's immediate job. In other cases, they are not only irrelevant but worthless. In either situation, you can get the group back on track by questioning the idea's relevancy. In a ***relevancy challenge,*** the questioner tactfully asks a member to explain how an apparently off-the-track idea relates to the group's task.[17] Typical relevancy challenges sound like this:

> "I'm confused, Tom, How will leasing new equipment instead of buying it help us to boost productivity?"

> "Fran asked us to figure which word processing package to buy. Does the graphics package you mentioned have something to do with the word-processing decision?"

At this point the member who made the original remark can either explain its relevance or acknowledge that it wasn't germane. In either case, the advantage of this sort of challenge is that it isn't personal. It focuses on the *remark* and not on the *person* and thus reduces the chance of a defensive response.

Promise to Deal with Good Ideas Later. Another way to keep the goodwill of a member who has brought up an irrelevant idea is to suggest a way of dealing with it at the appropriate time:

> "That equipment-leasing idea sounds promising. Let's bring it up to Jeff after the meeting and see what he thinks of it."
>
> "A graphics package seems important to you, Lee. Why don't you look into what's available, and we can decide whether the change would be worth the cost."

As with relevancy challenges, your suggestion about dealing with an idea later has to be sincere if the other person is going to accept it. One way to show your sincerity is to mention exactly when you would like to discuss the matter. This might be a specific time (after lunch), or it might be when certain conditions are met ("after you've worked up the cost"). Another way to show your sincerity is to inquire about the idea after the meeting: "How's the research going on the graphics package?"

Keeping a Positive Tone. Almost everyone would agree that "getting along with people" is a vital ingredient in a successful career. In meetings, getting along can be especially tough when others don't cooperate with your efforts to keep the meeting on track—or, even worse, attack your ideas. The following suggestions can help you handle these irritating situations in a way that gets the job done and keeps potential enemies as allies.

Ask Questions and Paraphrase to Clarify Understanding. Criticizing an idea—even an apparently stupid one—can result in a defensive reaction that will waste time and generate ill will. It's also important to remember that even a seemingly idiotic remark can have some merit. Given these facts, it's often

SKILL BUILDER

Use the skills introduced on pages 277–278 to describe how you would respond to the following comments in a meeting:

1. "There's no way people will work Sundays without being paid double overtime."
2. "No consultant is going to tell me how to be a better manager!"
3. "I don't think this brainstorming is worth the time. Most of the ideas we come up with are crazy."
4. "Talking about interest rates reminds me of a time in '79 when this story about Carter was going around. . . ."
5. "Sorry, but I don't have any ideas about how to cut costs."

wise to handle apparently bad ideas by asking for some clarification. And the most obvious way to clarify an idea is to ask questions:

> "Why do you think we ought to let Marcia go?"
>
> "Who would cover the store if you went skiing next week?"
>
> "What makes you think we shouldn't have a Christmas party this year?"

You can also paraphrase to get more information about an apparently hostile or foolish remark:

> "It sounds as if you're saying Marcia's doing a bad job."
>
> "So you think we could cover the store if you went skiing?"
>
> "Sounds as if you think a Christmas party would be a waste of money."

This sort of paraphrasing accomplishes two things: First, it provides a way to double-check your understanding. If your replay of the speaker's ideas isn't accurate, he or she can correct you: "I don't think Marcia's doing a bad job. I just don't think we need so many people up front." Second, even if your understanding is accurate, paraphrasing is an invitation for the other person to explain the idea in more detail: "If we could find somebody to work a double shift while I was skiing, I'd be willing to do the same thing for him later."

Enhance the Value of Members' Comments. It's obvious that you should acknowledge the value of good ideas by praising or thanking the people who contribute them. Surprisingly, you can use the same method with apparently bad ideas. Even the most worthless comments often have some merit. You can take advantage of such merits by using a three-part response:[18]

1. Acknowledge the merits of the idea.
2. Explain any concerns you have.
3. Improve the usefulness of the idea by building on it or asking others for suggestions.

Notice how this sort of response can enhance the value of apparently worthless comments:

> "I'm glad you're so concerned about the parking problem, Craig [acknowledges merit of comment]. But wouldn't requiring people to carpool generate a lot of resentment [balancing concern]? How could we encourage people to carpool voluntarily [builds on original idea]?"
>
> "You're right, Pat. Your department could use another person [acknowledges merit of comment]. But Mr. Peters is really serious about this hiring freeze [balancing concern]. Let's try to come up with some ways we can get you more help without having to hire a new person [builds on original idea]."

Pay Attention to Cultural Factors. Like every other type of communication, the "rules" for conducting productive, harmonious meetings vary from one culture to another. For example, in Japan problem-solving meetings are usually preceded by a series of one-to-one sessions between participants to iron out issues, a process called *nemawashi.*[19] The practice arises from the Japanese cultural practice that two people may speak candidly to one another, but when a third person enters the discussion, they become a group, requiring communicators to speak indirectly to maintain harmony. By contrast, in countries where emotional expressiveness is the norm, volatile exchanges in meetings are as much the rule as the exception. "I've just come back from a meeting in Milan," stated Canadian management consultant Dennis Stamp. "If people acted the same way in North American meetings you'd think they were coming to blows."[20]

Concluding the Meeting

The way a meeting ends can have a strong influence on how members feel about the group and how well they follow up on any decisions that have been made or instructions that have been given.[21]

When to Close the Meeting. There are three times when a meeting should be closed.

When the Scheduled Closing Time Has Arrived. Even if the discussion has been a good one, it's often best to close on schedule to prevent members from drifting off to other commitments one by one or losing attention and becoming resentful. It's wise to press on only if the subject is important and the members seem willing to keep working.

When the Group Lacks Resources to Continue. If the group lacks the necessary person or facts to continue, adjourn until the resources are available. If you need to get cost figures for a new purchase or someone's approval for a new idea, for example, it is probably a waste of time to proceed until the data or go-ahead has been secured. In these cases, be sure to identify who is responsible for getting the needed information, and set a new meeting date.

When the Agenda Has Been Covered. It seems obvious that a meeting should adjourn when its business is finished. Nonetheless, any veteran of meetings will testify that some discussions drag on because no one is willing to call a halt. Unless everyone is willing to socialize, it's best to use the techniques that follow to wrap up a meeting when the job is completed.

How to Conclude a Meeting. A good conclusion has three parts. In many discussions, the leader will be responsible for taking these steps. In leaderless groups or in groups with a weak leader, one or more members can take the initiative. (Table 9-4 is a checklist for concluding a meeting.)

Signal When Time Is Almost Up. A warning allows the group to wrap up business and gives everyone a chance to have a final say:

> "We have about fifteen minutes before we adjourn. We still need to hear Bob's report on the Kansas City conference, so let's devote the rest of our time to that."

> "It's almost time for some of you to leave for the airport. I'd like to wrap up our meeting by putting the list of suggestions Mr. Moss has asked us to send him into its final form."

Summarize the Meeting's Accomplishments and Future Actions. For the sake of understanding, review what information has been conveyed and what decisions have been made. Just as important is reminding members of their responsibilities:

> "It looks like we won't have to meet again until the sales conference next Tuesday in San Juan. We'll follow the revised schedule that we worked up today. Chris will have copies to everyone first thing tomorrow morning. Nick will call the hotel to book the larger meeting room, and Pat will take care of having the awards made up. Let's all plan to meet over dinner at the hotel next Tuesday night."

Thank the Group. Acknowledging the group's good work is more than just good manners. This sort of reinforcement shows that you appreciate the group's efforts and encourages good performance in the future. Besides acknowledging the group as a whole, be sure to give credit to any members who deserve special mention:

> "We really got a lot done today. Thanks to all of you, we're back on schedule. Bruce, I appreciate the work you did on the specifications. We never would have made it without you."

TABLE 9-4 Checklist for Concluding a Meeting

- *Concluding the meeting*
  - Does the meeting run the proper length of time (versus ending prematurely or continuing after excessive length or wasted time)?
  - Is a warning given shortly before conclusion to allow wrap-up of business?
  - Is a summary of the meeting's results and a preview of future actions given?
  - Does the leader acknowledge contributions of group members?
- *Follow-up activities*
  - Does the leader build an agenda for the next meeting upon results of the previous one?
  - Does the leader follow up on assignments of other members?
  - Do members follow through on their own assignments?

"You were all great about coming in early this morning. The extra rehearsal will make a big difference in the presentation. Those charts are terrific, Julie. And your suggestion about using the slide projector will make a big difference, Lou. Let's all celebrate after we get the contract."

Following Up the Meeting

It's a mistake to assume that even a satisfying meeting is a success until you follow up to make sure that the desired results have really been obtained. A thorough follow-up involves three steps.

Build an Agenda for the Next Meeting. Most groups meet frequently, and they rarely conclude their business in one sitting. A smart leader plans the next meeting by noting which items need to be carried over from the preceding one. What unfinished business must be addressed? What progress reports must be shared? What new information should members hear?

Follow Up on Other Members. You can be sure that the promised outcomes of a meeting actually occur if you check up on other members. If the meeting provided instructions—such as how to use the new long-distance phone service—see if the people who attended are actually following the steps that were outlined. If tasks were assigned, check on whether they're being performed. You don't have to be demanding or snoopy to do this sort of checking. A friendly phone call or personal remark can do the trick: "Is the new phone system working for you?" "How's it going on those sales figures?" "Did you manage to get hold of Williams yet?"

Take Care of Your Own Assignments. Most homework that arises out of meetings needs continued attention. If you wait until the last minute before tackling it, the results are likely to be sloppy and embarrassing.

SUMMARY

Meetings are a common event in most organizations. They occupy large amounts of time and cost the business a great deal of money. Some meetings are aimed at sharing information; others are of a problem-solving nature; still others serve a ritual function that confers status on members, builds cohesiveness, and provides an informal channel of communication.

Meetings should be held only when the job at hand is beyond the capacity of one person to handle, requires a division of labor, and has more than one right answer. If misunderstandings or resistance to a decision is likely, it is also wise to hold a meeting to overcome those hazards. Well in advance of each meeting, members should receive an agenda that announces the time, length, and location of the session; those who will attend; background information on the topic; goals for the meeting; and any advance work members need to do.

Once the meeting is called to order, the chairperson should announce the goals of the session, review necessary background information, show how members can help, preview how the session will proceed, and identify any time constraints. The participation of quiet members can be encouraged by using the nominal group technique, giving everyone a chance to speak, and using questions. When discussions wander off track, the chairperson and other members can regain focus by referring to time pressures, summarizing and redirecting the remarks of the members who have digressed, using relevancy challenges, and promising to deal with tangential issues after the meeting. The tone of meetings can be kept positive if members make an attempt to understand one another by asking questions and paraphrasing and if they enhance the value of one another's comments. Effective meetings are conducted in a manner that reflects the rules of the cultural norms of the participants.

The meeting should be closed when its scheduled time is completed, when the group lacks resources to continue, or when the agenda has been completed—whichever comes first. The chairperson should give the group warning that time is almost up and then summarize the meeting's accomplishments and future actions. Group members should also be thanked for their contributions. The chairperson's activities after the meeting has concluded include building an agenda for the next session, following up on other members, and honoring his or her own commitments.

RESOURCES

Finley, Michael, "Subduing the Loudmouth: How to Keep Dominating People from Dominating Meetings," *Manage* 44 (January 1993): 7–9.

In this article, various meeting experts from the corporate world offer their suggestions for handling loudmouths.

Keep, Ana M., *Moving Meetings* (New York: Irwin, 1994).

This book is a practical guide for leading and participating in meetings.

Matejka, Ken, and Romania Julian, "Meeting Is Such Sweet Sorrow," *Management Decision* 32 (1994): 62–64.

This humorous article shows how some meetings resemble a dramatic performance with a cast of stereotypical characters, including the bungling idiot, the multiple personality, the genius, the martyr, the hero, the victim, and the bully. The article also explains five common myths about meetings that often lead to using 100 pounds of energy to produce 3 ounces of results.

Meeting Management News (St. Paul, Minn.: 3M Meeting Management Institute).

3M publishes this occasional newsletter as a service to business communicators. In addition to *Meeting Management News,* 3M publishes a variety of resources, including bibliographies, tips for making presentations and leading meetings, and information on grants and research.

PART IV

Making Effective Presentations

NORTH
WESTERN
REPORTER
2d Series
280
281
300
301
319
320

CHAPTER 10

Developing the Presentation

KEY TERMS

General purpose / Specific purpose / Thesis statement

Whatever your field, whatever your job, speaking to an audience is a fact of life. Sales representatives and account executives deliver presentations to potential customers. Brand managers propose ideas to management and explain new product lines to the sales force. Department heads and supervisors brief superiors on recent developments and subordinates on new company policies. Computer specialists explain new systems and software to the people who will use them. Accountants give financial reports to their superiors and explain paperwork requirements to everyone else. Even engineers and research scientists report on their methods, progress, and results. Presentations are so pervasive that some experts have estimated that speakers address audiences an astonishing 33 million times each day.[1] According to one survey, businesspeople give an average of twenty-six presentations a year.[2] Table 10-1 offers a sample of the kinds of presentations that most people deliver sooner or later in their careers.

While some business and professional presentations are formal, full-dress performances before large audiences, most are comparatively informal talks to a few people or even a single person. If you drop into your boss's office and say, "Do you have a few minutes? I have some information that may help us cut down our travel expenses," you're arranging a presentation. You're also delivering a presentation when you teach the office staff how to use the new phone system, explain the structure of your department to a new employee, or explain to management why you need a larger budget.

As your career progresses, presentational speaking skills become even more important. As one automobile executive explained:

> As an executive rose in management, he had to rely less on his technical training and more on his ability to sell his ideas and programs to the next level of management. When I was just an engineer somewhere down the line working

TABLE 10-1 Common Types of Presentational Speaking

Type of Presentation	Example
Briefing and informational announcements	Announcing new health-insurance procedure
Orientation sessions	Conducting new-employee orientation
Training programs	Explaining how to operate new computer software
Research and technical reports	Describing a market research survey
Progress reports	Giving a status report on monthly sales
Civic and social presentations	Making a speech at a local service club
Convention and conference presentations	Reporting on company's technological breakthroughs
Television and radio interviews	Describing company's position on industrial accident or injury
Introductions	Introducing new employee to other workers
Sales presentations	Presenting product to potential customer
Project and policy proposals	Proposing new travel policy to management
Ceremonial occasions	Speaking at retirement celebration for longtime employee

> on a technical problem, everything affecting me was in my grasp. All I had to do was solve this particular problem, and I was doing my job. But now, as head of advanced engineering, I have to anticipate and predict product trends and then sell my programs for capitalizing on those trends.[3]

Most people who work in organizations eventually find that their effectiveness and success depend on their ability to organize their ideas and present them effectively. Sometimes a written memo or report will do the job, but there are often important reasons for presenting your ideas in person. For example, if people don't understand a point in a proposal, they may put it aside for weeks or simply veto it. Delivering your message in person provides immediate feedback that helps you clarify points and answer questions. Oral presentations are often more persuasive as well. A speaker's knowledge, enthusiasm, and apparent confidence can influence people to accept or reject an idea in a way that a written document cannot.

In practice, you'll rarely get approval for an important idea without explaining it in person. As one executive put it:

> The people who have the power and responsibility to say *yes* or *no* want a chance to consider and question the proposal in the flesh. Documents merely set up a meeting and record what the meeting decided. Anyone serious about an idea welcomes the chance to present it himself—in person. We wisely discount proposals whose authors are unwilling to be present at the launching.[4]

Presentations aren't delivered only to internal audiences. Many people also give work-related addresses to listeners outside their organizations. Realizing that effective speakers carry their message to the public in ways that print and electronic media can't match, companies send representatives into the community to deliver speeches in a wide variety of settings.[5] Western Electric Company has over 100 speakers who make some 2,000 presentations each year. Standard Oil has between 50 and 100 representatives delivering some 500 speeches annually. Dow Chemical employees face 1,000 audiences each year, and 300 Georgia Pacific speakers made approximately 1,500 appearances in one twelve-month period. Don't get the idea that all these speakers are smooth-talking public relations experts. Over 90 percent of the 2,200 talks General Motors employees give each year are delivered by middle managers. Organizations realize the need to help their employees learn to give presentations. Some of the world's biggest corporations sponsor training. Toastmasters International, a group dedicated to helping businesspeople present their ideas effectively, now has 1,700 members around the world.[6] Research confirms that speakers can become more effective with training.[7]

Even people who seem to work in fairly solitary jobs give speeches to clubs, professional organizations, and community groups. The botany researchers at a national plant nursery regularly give speeches to garden clubs; textbook and journal editors speak to college and professional seminars about the requirements of writing for publication; and computer programmers conduct classes for small-business owners and individuals who buy computers.

Different kinds of presentations make different demands on the speaker. For example, a sales presentation to one customer may often seem more like a conversation because the customer may interrupt with questions, while a speaker addressing an audience of several hundred people may delay questions until the end. In spite of the differences, all presentations make many of the same demands on the speaker. The planning, structure, supports, and strategy of each of them are very important, and a good speaker follows approximately the same steps in planning and developing almost any presentation. The material in the next five chapters applies to almost any presentation you will give in your career or profession.

ESTABLISHING A PURPOSE

The first step in planning any presentation should be to define your purpose. A statement of purpose describes what you want to accomplish. Then, after you have spoken, the same statement helps you know whether you have achieved your goal. There are two kinds of purposes to consider: general and specific.

General Purpose

As the name implies, a ***general purpose*** is a broad indication of what you're trying to accomplish. There are three general purposes.

To Inform. The goal of an informative presentation is either to expand your listeners' knowledge or to help them acquire a specific skill. Teaching a group of product managers about new developments in technology, training a new sales representative, or giving a progress report on regional sales to a senior sales manager are all typical examples of informative talks.

To Persuade. Persuasion focuses on trying to change what an audience thinks or does. Selling is the most obvious example, but there are others as well. A union organizer will try to persuade a group of employees to vote for a union, while a management representative might try to persuade them not to. An accountant might try to convince management to adopt a different procedure for reporting expenditures. A marketing manager might try to convince sales representatives to be more enthusiastic about a product that has not sold well.

> Giving a presentation without recognizing, focusing on, and remembering your objective is the equivalent of dumping the contents of your briefcase all over your boss's desk. You don't speak to fill time by reeling off fact after unorganized fact, nor to show beautiful pictures that take the breath away, nor to impress the audience with your wit and skill as a dramatic speaker. You don't give speeches to win speech-making awards. You are there to make the best of an opportunity, just as you do in every other aspect of your business activities.
>
> Sandy Linver, *Speak and Get Results*

To Entertain. Sometimes a speaker's goal is to help the audience have a good time. The welcoming speaker at a convention might concentrate on getting the participants to relax and look forward to the coming events. After-dinner speakers at company gatherings or awards dinners usually consider themselves successful if their remarks leave the group in a jovial mood.

Specific Purpose

If you think of a speech as a journey, your specific purpose is your destination. Stating the ***specific purpose*** tells you what you will have accomplished when you have "arrived." A good specific-purpose statement usually answers three questions:

Whom do I want to influence?

What do I want them to do?

How, when, and *where* do I want them to do it?

Your purpose statement should combine the answers to these questions into a single statement: "I want (who) to (do what) (how, when, where)." Here are some examples of good purpose statements:

> "I want the people who haven't been participating in the United Way campaign to sign up."
>
> "I want at least five people in the audience to ask me for my business card after my talk and at least one person to schedule an appointment with me to discuss my company's services."
>
> "I want at least five people in the department to consider transferring to the new Fort Worth office."
>
> "I want the boss to tell the committee that he's in favor of my proposal when they discuss it after my presentation."

Like these examples, your purpose statements should do three things: describe the reaction you are seeking, be as specific as possible, and make your goal realistic.

Describe the Reaction You Are Seeking. Your purpose statement should be worded in terms of the reaction you want from your audience. You can appreciate the importance of specifying the desired results when you consider a statement that doesn't meet this criterion: "I want to show each person in this office how to operate the new voice-mail system correctly."

What's wrong with this statement? Most important, it says nothing about the desired audience response. With a purpose such as this, you could give a detailed explanation of the whole system without knowing whether anyone learned a thing! Notice the improvement in this statement: "I want everyone in this group to show me that he or she can operate the voice-mail system correctly after my talk." With this goal, you can get an idea of how well you've done after delivering your presentation.

Be as Specific as Possible. A good purpose statement identifies the who, what, how, when, and where of your goal as precisely as possible. For instance, your target audience—the who—may not include every listener in the audience. Take one of the statements we mentioned earlier: "I want the boss to tell the committee that he's in favor of my proposal when they discuss it after my presentation." This statement correctly recognizes the boss as the key decision maker. If you've convinced him, your proposal is as good as approved; if not, the support of less influential committee members may not help you. Once you identify your target audience, you can focus your energy on the people who truly count.

The best purpose statements describe your goals in *measurable terms*. Consider these examples:

VAGUE	SPECIFIC
"I want to collect some donations in this meeting."	"I want to collect at least $15 from each person in this meeting."
"I want to get my manager's support for my idea."	"I want my manager to give me one day per week and the help of a secretary to develop my idea."

Knowing exactly what you want to accomplish dramatically increases the chances that you will reach your goal. Suppose you need to convince a group of subordinates to stay within their budgets. You already know that the following statement is no good: "I want to talk about the importance of our new budget limitations." (If you're not sure why, take another look at the preceding section on describing reactions.) A more result-oriented goal would be "I want this group to stay within their budgets." But even this purpose statement has problems. Whom are you going to encourage: people who are already holding the line on expenses or those who look like they might overspend? How many people do you hope to persuade?

SKILL BUILDER

Write a specific-purpose statement for each of the following situations:

1. A farewell speech honoring a not-too-popular manager at his retirement dinner
2. A training session introducing a new telephone intercom system
3. A kickoff speech for the United Way payroll deduction campaign
4. An appeal to the boss for a new person in your department
5. A proposal to your department head for changing course requirements for the major
6. A banker's speech to an economics class on the topic "The Changing Banking Industry"
7. A request to your landlord for new carpeting

How will you appeal to them? (Each group might require a different approach.) When do you want them to do it: beginning immediately or when they get around to it? The latter may not be until after the fiscal year is over—too late to save this year's profits in your department. A comprehensive specific-purpose statement can take care of questions such as these: "I want to convince the four people who had spent more than half their year's budgets by May 1 that the department's solvency depends on their cutting expenses and have them show me a revised plan by the end of the week that demonstrates how they intend to trim costs for the rest of the year." This statement gives you several ideas about how to plan your presentation. Imagine how much more difficult your task would be if you had settled for the first vague purpose statement.

Make Your Goal Realistic. Presentational speaking is like most other aspects of life: you usually don't get everything you want. The available time, the characteristics of your audience, and the subject itself can limit what you can realistically hope to accomplish. Thus, your purpose statement should be attainable. For example, a sales representative selling expensive office equipment shouldn't expect to make a sale the first time she calls on a purchasing officer; instead, her purpose might be simply to get an appointment to make a presentation. Similarly, a department head training a group of new employees shouldn't expect to teach them the operations of the whole department in the first half hour (unless the operations are very simple); at the outset, he might select a few basic principles that he could expect them to learn and use for the first few days or weeks.

DEVELOPING THE THESIS

The ***thesis statement***—sometimes called the *central idea* or *key idea*—is a single sentence that summarizes your message. Table 10-2 offers some tips for formulating this sort of statement. Once you have a thesis, every other part of your talk should support it. The thesis gives your listeners a clear idea of what you are trying to tell them:

> "We're behind schedule for reasons beyond our control, but we can catch up and finish the job on time."
>
> "Our new just-in-time order system helps us make sure that our supplies are not dated or shelf-worn, but we must monitor the inventory daily."

Presentations without a clear thesis leave the audience asking, "What's this person getting at?" And while listeners are trying to figure out the answer, they'll be missing much of what you're saying.

The thesis is so important that you will repeat it several times during your presentation: at least once in the introduction, probably several times during the body, and again in the conclusion.

TABLE 10-2 Methods for Defining a Thesis Statement

1. Imagine that you met a member of your audience at the elevator and had only a few seconds to explain your idea before the doors closed.
2. Imagine that you had to send a one- or two-sentence telegram that communicated your main ideas.
3. Ask yourself, "If my listeners heard only a small portion of my remarks, what is the minimum they should have learned?"
4. Suppose that a friend asked one of your listeners what you were driving at in your presentation. What would you want the audience member to say?

Beginning speakers often confuse the thesis of a presentation with its purpose. Whereas a purpose statement is a note to *yourself* outlining what you hope to accomplish, a thesis statement tells your *audience* your main idea. Sometimes the two can be virtually identical. There are other cases, however, where purpose and thesis differ. Consider a few examples:

THESIS	PURPOSE
"Switching to Sun Valley Bread will increase your sales."	"I want Krakos Grocery to order Sun Valley bread."
"Our preschool curriculum may look like nothing but play, but it is based on sound educational theory and research."	"Parents will be confident that their children are being prepared for later schooling."
"You don't have to accept sexual harassment."	"Audience members will be able to respond to sexual harassment instead of accepting it."
"Recent advances have changed my field dramatically in the past few years."	"I want to acquire new customers seeking state-of-the-art technology."

It may seem unethical to avoid mentioning your purpose to an audience, but sometimes the omission is a matter of common sense and not deception. Mr. Krakos already knows the Sun Valley representative wants to sell him bread, but he's most interested in hearing *why* he should change suppliers. Similarly, an after-dinner speaker at a local service club might have the pur-

ETHICAL CHALLENGE

Sometimes it is legitimate to withhold your purpose from an audience, while doing so at other times is unethical. Check your ability to distinguish the difference by identifying three situations for each of the following:

1. When it is legitimate to withhold your purpose
2. When withholding your purpose would be unethical

pose of getting the audience to relax, but sharing that goal would probably seem out of place.

There are other times, however, when hiding your purpose would clearly be unethical. A speaker who began his presentation by saying "I don't want to sell you anything; I just want to show you some aspects of home safety that every homeowner should know" and then went on to make a hard-sell pitch for his company's home fire alarms would clearly be stepping out of bounds. It usually isn't necessary to state your purpose as long as you are willing to share it with your audience, if asked. It's very rare, however, not to state the thesis at the beginning of a presentation.

ANALYZING THE SITUATION

A purpose statement describes the end you want to achieve, but it doesn't describe how you can reach your goal. The means is the presentation itself—the ideas you use and the way you express them.

Before you plan even one sentence of the actual presentation, you have to think about the situation in which you'll speak. A presentation that might fascinate you could bore or irritate the audience. You can make sure that your approach is on target by considering three factors: yourself as the speaker, the audience, and the occasion. Figure 10-1 shows how each of these factors narrows and focuses all the ways you could present a topic into the approach that best suits a particular situation.

Analyzing the Audience

The saying "Different strokes for different folks" is never more true than when you are delivering a presentation. Having good ideas isn't enough. You have to present those ideas in a way that your listeners will understand and

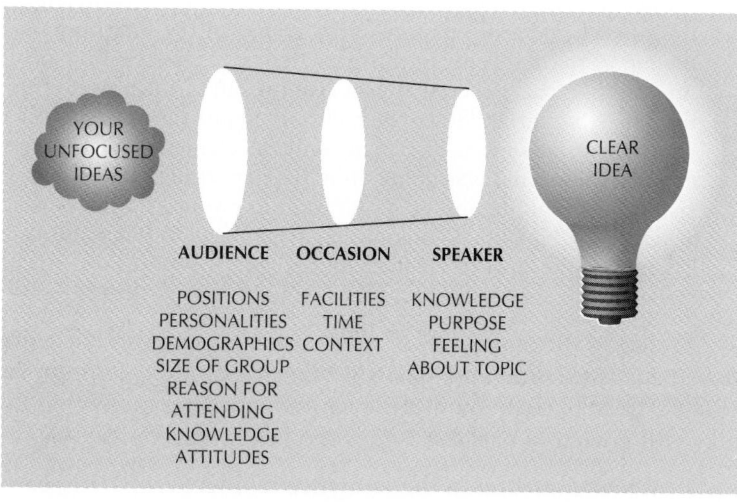

FIGURE 10-1 Analyzing the speaking situation.

appreciate.[8] A number of factors will shape the way you adapt your material to a particular audience.

You should ask yourself a number of questions about your audience members.

What Are Their Positions? Begin by considering the job titles of the members of your audience. If audience members are specialists—in engineering, finance, or marketing, for example—they'll probably be interested in the more technical aspects of your talk that pertain to their specialties. On the other hand, an audience of nonexperts or generalists would probably be bored by a detailed talk on a subject they don't understand. Surprisingly, most managers fall into this category. Even an executive who came up through the ranks as an engineer takes a different perspective upon becoming responsible for an entire job. The details that might once have been fascinating are now less important—perhaps still interesting, but not suitable for an overall view of a project. "Just give me a quick description, a schedule, and the dollar figures" is a common attitude.

What Are Their Personal Preferences? The personal idiosyncrasies of your listeners are just as important as their job titles. Some people insist on a formal presentation, while others are much more casual. Some audiences appreciate humor, while others are straitlaced. Some people hate to waste time on casual conversation and digressions, while others are willing to work at a more leisurely pace. Knowing these preferences can make the difference between success and failure in a presentation. One business consultant described how attitudes can vary from one set of listeners to another:

> We found . . . that in the same corporation engineers giving reports to different department heads were required to go about it in a totally different manner. One department head wanted every detail covered in the report. He wanted analyses of why the report was being done, complete background on the subject under discussion, and a review of the literature, and he expected the report to run twenty or thirty written pages. In addition, he wanted an oral presentation that covered almost every detail of the report. The man who ran the department right down the hall wanted just the opposite. He wanted short, comprehensive reports discussing only the elements that were new. He said he already knew what was going on in his department. He didn't want an analysis of the situation, and he didn't want any young engineer wasting his time. The reports that got an A in one department got an F in another and vice versa. Therefore, the first rule for anyone giving a report is to ask those who requested the report what form they would like it to take.[9]

Violating the standards of what your listeners find acceptable can antagonize your audience and destroy your credibility. Humor can be especially tricky. The joke that you find clever and amusing may offend your audience. A joke will probably backfire under the following conditions:

- When someone in the audience will feel embarrassed
- When one or more listeners' feelings are hurt

- When someone's weakness provides the laugh
- When profanity is needed to make the remark funny
- When everyone present can't join in the laughter

Entertainer Ted Danson learned these principles the hard way when he participated in a roast of his good friend Whoopi Goldberg at a Friar's Club event. Appearing in blackface, Danson repeatedly used racial slurs in what he and Goldberg both viewed as a harmless display of humor. Most audience members and the public at large were offended, however.[10]

What Demographic Characteristics Are Significant? A number of measurable characteristics of your listeners might suggest ways to develop your remarks. One such characteristic is *sex*. What is the distribution of men and women? Even in this age of relative enlightenment, some topics must be approached differently, depending on your audience's sex. For instance, if you were trying to promote an equal opportunity program in your company, you might have to prove to male management that there was discrimination against women; the women in the company would probably already be aware of it.

A second demographic characteristic is *age*. A life insurance salesperson might emphasize retirement benefits to older customers and support for dependent children to younger ones with families. A speaker promoting a company health plan would discuss different activities with listeners in their twenties and thirties than she would with employees who were nearing retirement.

Cultural background is often an important audience factor. You would use a different approach with blue-collar workers than you would with a group of white-collar professionals. Likewise, the ethnic mix of a group might affect your remarks. The points you make, the examples you use, and even the language you speak will probably be shaped by the cultural makeup of your audience.

Another demographic factor is the *economic status* of your audience. This factor is especially important in sales, where financial resources "qualify" potential customers as prospects for a product or service as well as suggest what features are likely to interest them. In real estate, for example, well-to-do customers would certainly be interested in different properties than less affluent

SKILL BUILDER

Imagine that you have been asked to give a fifteen-minute description of your department's functions. How would your purpose and approach differ for each of the following audiences:

1. A group of new employees from all over the company
2. New employees within the department
3. A group of managers from other departments
4. Several of your superiors
5. A supplier who is helping you update equipment
6. A group of customers touring the company

ones. They might also be more concerned about the tax consequences of a sale and less concerned with monthly payments than with the interest rate at which the mortgage is written.

Not every variable is important in planning every speech. For instance, an engineer speaking about recent advances in the field should consider her audience's level of knowledge (about engineering and those advances) and occupations (that is, what those advances have to do with her listeners' work), but matters such as sex, age, and economic status probably wouldn't be important. On the other hand, a representative from Planned Parenthood speaking to a community organization would have to consider sex, age, and economic status as well as listeners' religious backgrounds and their attitudes toward the medical profession. The first step to good audience analysis is to recognize which dimensions of your listeners' background are important and to profile those dimensions accurately.

What Size Is the Group? The number of listeners will govern some very basic speaking plans. How many copies of a handout should you prepare? How large must your visuals be to be seen by everyone? How much time should you plan for a question-and-answer session? With a large audience, you usually need to take a wider range of audience concerns into account; your delivery and choice of language will tend to be more formal; and your listeners are less likely to interrupt with questions or comments. A progress report on your current assignment would look ridiculous if you delivered it from behind a podium to four or five people. You would look just as foolish speaking to a hundred listeners while reclining in a chair.

Why Is the Audience There? Just like speakers, audiences have reasons for attending a presentation. Sometimes these reasons are straightforward; for example, the members of a sales force will attend a sales meeting to learn about the company's new products and how to sell them and so increase their commissions. Not all audience purposes are as clear, though. If the sales meeting is being held in Miami or Hawaii, some attendees could be most interested in the idea of an expense-paid vacation. Many attendees might assume that all the information presented at the meeting will also be provided in written form and will not listen carefully to the presentation.

This doesn't mean that you should give up when you face an audience with ulterior motives. Rather, it means you need to find creative ways to achieve both the audience's goal and yours. If the computer service representatives you're addressing are hostile to the new computer system, they may attend the training sessions only because they're required to do so. You will need to convince them that the system has advantages for them, such as saving them time and making their jobs easier, before they'll listen to your instructions on how to operate the system. If you don't do this, they may eventually make errors and blame them on the system.

Sometimes you can develop an approach that satisfies all your listeners. Like those teachers who reach the greatest number of students, you can learn to be entertaining and informative at the same time. But you can't please everyone all the time. If some of your listeners want to hear about the new product line and some want to hear, in detail, why last year's line failed, you will probably have to make a choice. At such times, your decision should be based on who you are most concerned about reaching.

What Does the Audience Know? A group of experts doesn't need the background information that other audiences would require. In fact, these people would probably be bored and offended by your basic explanation. Likewise, people who are familiar with a project don't need to be brought up to date—unless they have missed some late-breaking developments. It's also important to ask yourself what your listeners do *not* know: uninformed people or nonexperts will be mystified (as well as bored and resentful) unless you give them background information.

Also ask yourself what misconceptions your listeners might have about the topic you're discussing. A potential customer might think that his current insurance coverage is perfectly adequate. Your boss may think that the obsolete equipment that's slowing your productivity is perfectly fine. When misconceptions like these exist, be sure to clear them up early in your presentation—or even beforehand, if possible.

One way to discover the attitudes of your audience—and to gain the audience's approval of your idea—is to meet with listeners before your presentation. With this sort of preparation, you can make whatever adjustments are necessary to win over the key decision makers before you begin your formal presentation. A communication expert describes the value of this kind of advance work:

"At one of the largest publicly-owned utilities in the United States, senior officers of both Human Resources and Management Information Systems had prepared new program proposals for car pooling and a pilot electronic mail program. The research and development stages for each of these proposals had taken between four and six months. After extensive presentations, covering timeliness, costs both direct and indirect, and benefits to department heads and customers, the meeting participants were called upon for comment.

"Nearly everyone present at the meeting—between eight and ten other department heads—had suggestions for improvements and modifications. Why? Because they had not been given an opportunity to study the proposals in advance. Consequently, the discussion on these proposals alone took two or three times the allotted time for the entire meeting. So many changes were suggested by the other participants that the makers of the original proposals had to spend months revising them.

". . . Obviously, if the chairman of the meeting (the chief executive officer) had been consulted before this meeting to help "bless" the projects, and other department heads had been briefed prior to the presentation to help buy them in, better results in a shorter period of time would have been achieved. My friend can attest to the effectiveness of this method because it's what he did before his own later presentation. The result was so fast that he had to hold himself back from suggesting that his proposal be further discussed before final acceptance."

Milo Frank, *How to Have a Successful Meeting in Half the Time*

What Are the Listeners' Attitudes? You need to consider two sets of attitudes when planning your presentation. The first is your audience's attitude toward *you as the speaker*. If listeners feel hostile or indifferent ("Charlie is such a bore"), your approach won't be the same as the one taken if they are excited to hear from you ("I'm glad he says he's going to simplify the paperwork; last year, he did a great job of speeding up the process for getting repairs done"). You'll read more about how to deal with hostile audiences in Chapter 15.

In addition to listeners' feelings about you, the audience's attitude about *your subject* should influence your approach. Do your employees think the benefits of the new pension plan are too far in the future to be important? Does the sales force think the new product line is exciting or just the same old line in a new package? Do the workers think the new vice-president is a genius or just another figurehead? Attitudes such as these should govern your approach.

Analyzing Yourself as the Speaker

No two presentations are alike. While you can learn to speak better by listening to other speakers, a good presentation is rather like a good hairstyle or sense of humor: what suits someone else might not work for you. One of the biggest mistakes you can make is to try to be a carbon copy of some other effective speaker. When developing your presentation, be sure to consider several factors.

Your Purpose. The very first question to ask yourself is why you are speaking. Are you especially interested in reaching one person or one subgroup in the audience? What do you want your key listeners to think or do after hearing you? How will you know when you've succeeded?

Your Knowledge. It's best to speak on a subject about which you have considerable knowledge. This is usually the case, since you generally speak on a subject precisely because you *are* an authority. Regardless of how well you know your subject, you may need to do some research—on the last three years' sales figures, the number of companies that have used the flexible-hours program you're proposing, the actual maintenance costs of the new equipment your company is buying, and so on.

If you do need to gain more information, don't fool yourself into a false sense of security by thinking you know enough. It's better to overprepare now than to look like a fool later. Kenneth Clarke, Britain's finance minister, embarrassed himself due to faulty knowledge. While visiting the northern England town of Consett, he praised its success as an industrial center, saying it had "one of the best steelworks in Europe." But the steel mill had closed down fifteen years earlier, putting 3,000 employees out of work. To redeem himself of that gaffe, Clarke cited another Consett factory as a major competition in the world of disposable diapers. The town's diaper plant had closed down two years before.[11]

[Public speaking] . . . requires a lot of preparation. There's just no way around it—you have to do your homework. A speaker may be very well informed, but if he hasn't thought out exactly what he wants to say *today, to this audience*, he has no business taking up other people's valuable time.

It's important to be able to talk to people in their own language. If you do it well, they'll say "God, he said exactly what I was thinking." And when they begin to respect you, they'll follow you to the death. The *reason* they're following you is not because you're providing some mysterious leadership. It's because you're following them.

Lee Iacocca with William Novak, *Iacocca: An Autobiography*

Your Feelings about the Topic. An old sales axiom says, "You can't sell a product you don't believe in." Research shows that sincerity is one of the greatest assets a speaker can have.[12] When you are excited about a topic, your delivery improves: your voice becomes more expressive, your movements are more natural, and your face reflects your enthusiasm. On the other hand, if you don't care much about your topic—whether it's a report on your department's sales, a proposal for a new program, a product you're selling, or a new method you're explaining—the audience will know it and think, "If the speaker doesn't believe in it, why should I?" A good test for your enthusiasm and sincerity is to ask yourself if you really care whether your audience understands or believes what you have to say. If you feel indifferent or only mildly enthusiastic, it's best to search for a new idea for your proposal or a new approach to your subject.

Analyzing the Occasion

Even a complete understanding of your audience won't give you everything you need to plan an effective presentation. You also need to adapt your remarks to fit the circumstances of your presentation. Several factors contribute to the occasion.

Facilities. Will you be speaking in a large or small room? Will there be enough seating for all the listeners? Will the place be brightly or dimly lit? Will it be well ventilated or stuffy? Are chairs movable or fixed to the floor? Will there be distracting background noises?

Questions like these are critical, and failure to anticipate facility problems can trip you up. For example, the absence of an easel to hold your charts can turn your well-rehearsed presentation into a fiasco. Lack of a convenient electrical outlet can replace your slide show with an embarrassing blackout. Even the placement of doorways can make a difference. Most experienced speakers won't settle for others' assurances about facilities; they check out the room in advance and come prepared for every possible disaster.

Time. There are two considerations here. The first is the time of day you'll be speaking. A straightforward, factual speech that would work well with an alert, rested audience at 10 A.M. might need to be more entertaining or emphatic to hold everyone's attention just before quitting time.

Besides taking the hour of day into account, you also need to consider the length of time you have to speak. Most business presentations are brief. One director of a Los Angeles shopping mall typically gives prospective vendors twenty minutes to make their pitch. "I automatically x-out anyone who is late or exceeds their time allotment. My experience has shown that people who have trouble adhering to parameters and deadlines are unreliable.[13] Alan Brawn, national sales manager for Hughes-JCC, reinforces the importance of keeping your remarks within the preset time limit. "Typically, if major points aren't made in about six minutes, a person's time in the sun is done."[14]

Despite an absolute claim like this, the amount of time you have to speak will vary. In any case, it's your job to find out what your time constraints are and stick within them. If you have only a little time to give a progress report to management, for example, you can only outline the major aspects of your most recent product; whereas if you have half an hour, you might be expected to go into more detail and discuss some of the alternatives you have considered along the way. Sometimes the length of your talk won't be explicitly dictated, but that doesn't mean you should talk as long as you like. Usually, factors in the situation suggest how long it's wise for you to speak. Notice, for example, how well speaker Hugh Marsh adapted his remarks to the after-dinner setting of his summary business report to a group of association members:

> Good evening, ladies and gentlemen. Whenever I get on a podium this late, after a long day at the office, I remind myself of several immutable laws.
>
> First. There is Marsh's First Law of Oratory—on any platform, any speech will grow in length to fill the time available for its delivery. Well, take heart. I only have fifteen minutes.
>
> Then there is Marsh's *Second* Law of Oratory—the farthest distance between two points is a speech. Or, as we used to say in Texas, speeches too often are like a Longhorn steer—a point here and a point there and a lot of bull in between. Well, again, take heart. I will try to keep my two points close together.
>
> Another law I remind myself of is Marsh's *Third* Law of Oratory—no speech ever sounds as good at 7:00 P.M. as it did at noon.

SKILL BUILDER

List the most important factors to consider when planning a presentation to:

1. Ask your boss for a raise
2. Give instructions to a trainee
3. Interview for a job
4. Announce a cost increase in employee health-care benefits
5. Brief a new supervisor on standard but informal operating procedures within your group

And, finally, there is Marsh's First Law of Meeting Attendance—everybody's gotta be someplace.

As long as we're here, let's be friends. I'll be brief. You be attentive. I'll make my few points and get off so we can get back to the fun part of the meeting—socializing.[15]

Context. Events surrounding your presentation also influence what you say or how you say it. For example, if others are speaking as part of your program, you need to take them into account. ("I had originally planned to discuss the technical aspects of our new express delivery system, but I think Carol has covered them pretty thoroughly. Let me just bring your attention to two things.") Preceding speakers may have left your audience feeling bored or stimulated, receptive or angry, thoughtful or jovial. Since that state of affairs will affect how the audience receives your presentation, you should try to adjust to it.

Current events could also affect what you say or how you say it. For example, if you're presenting your new budget proposal just after the company has suffered a major financial loss, you should be prepared to show how your budget will cut costs. As you'll read in Chapter 11, one effective way to begin a speech is to talk about a recent occurrence: beginning your talk to the sales force by mentioning Steve's major new account, for instance, is a good way to get attention and motivate your audience.

SUMMARY

At one time or another, almost everyone makes on-the-job presentations. Some are formal and others informal, and some are directed at audiences within the firm, while others are aimed at external audiences. Even if presentations are not as frequent as other types of communication, they are important: the audience usually includes influential people, and the stakes are frequently high. In addition, the reputation you acquire as a good or bad speaker can affect the success of your career.

Presentations are often superior to written messages in several respects: Presentations generate a quick response, allow the sender to adapt the message to the interests of an audience, and frequently are a more effective means of persuasion.

The first step in planning a presentation is to define your purpose. Is your general goal to inform or persuade? Specifically, you should define whom you want to reach, what you want them to do, how you want them to do it, and when and where it should be done. Your purpose statement should be worded in terms of the desired audience reaction, and it should be specific and attainable.

A second fundamental step in planning a presentation is to define your thesis, phrased as a single-sentence statement of your message. Your purpose and thesis should be based on an analysis of the speaking situation. This analysis consists of three parts: First, analyze yourself as a speaker. Consider your purpose for speaking, your knowledge of the subject, and the sincerity you can bring to the topic. Second, analyze the audience: who the listeners are, why they are listening to you, what they know, and what their attitudes are about you and your topic. Finally, analyze the speaking occasion. Consider the facilities in which you will be speaking, the time of day and length of time you have to speak, and the context in which your remarks will occur.

RESOURCES

"In Search of Enlightenment: A Guide to Presentation Resources," *Presentations* (November 1994): 31–39.

This is a compendium of helpful resources for designing and delivering presentations. The directory includes lists of organizations, books, videotapes, courseware, seminars, and trade shows that offer support for presentational speakers.

Jaffe, C., "Speakers and Pluralistic Audiences," in *Public Speaking: A Cultural Perspective* (Belmont, Calif.: Wadsworth, 1995), chap. 5.

An asset for analyzing increasingly pluralistic audiences, this chapter focuses on cultural variables that influence how speakers and audiences see themselves and each other. The dialogical approach toward the speaker-audience relationship also gets attention.

Sant, T., *Persuasive Business Proposals: Writing to Win Customers, Clients and Contracts* (New York: American Management Association, 1992).

Although this book is primarily about writing business proposals, at the core of the author's thinking is the importance of audience analysis. The first part of the book deals with understanding the source, message, channel, and receiver; central to understanding the receiver are excellent clues for analyzing your audience, whether for writing proposals or giving oral presentations.

Walters, L., *Secrets of Successful Speakers* (New York: McGraw-Hill, 1993).

This book stresses choosing objectives, developing a theme, and customizing your presentation. It also includes ways to build rapport with cross-cultural audiences.

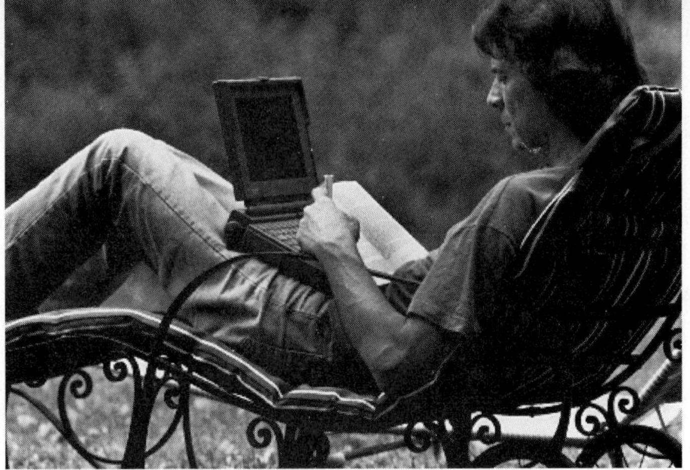

CHAPTER 11

Organizing Your Ideas

KEY TERMS

Cause–effect pattern / Chronological pattern / Claim / Problem–solution pattern / Rhetorical question / Spatial pattern / Topical pattern / Transition

Merrill Snyder, office manager of a midsize corporation, had assigned Tom Byrd, an assistant manager, the task of researching a new telephone system for the company. She asked Tom to report on his progress at the Monday morning personnel department meeting.

Tom arrived with a stack of letters, sample policies, and literature from several suppliers and spread them out on the table as he began to speak.

"If we want to be able to transfer calls to our offices in Dayton and Carlisle, we should take a close look at Centrex. Some people say that AT&T has a better service record, though, which means we should probably consider the Merlin system, but I don't know about that for sure. Intertalk may be better for calls within the building than some other systems, and we can either buy or rent sets from them, although that doesn't do anything for our long–distance requirements. Any of the systems I've looked at will handle modem communication, but we really have to look at fax machines from different suppliers before we can make a decision about whether we also want to use them. Centrex offers a number of services, like call forwarding and call hunting. Although other systems do that, too, they don't all have the same services for the same price. Some other systems I think might be good are—"

"Wait a minute," Merrill said, "I'm having trouble following you. What's Intertalk? Do they offer the same system Centrex does, and how do they compare in price?"

"Intertalk is an intercom system," Tom explained. "If we go with that, it will be in addition to a phone system. But if we pick a phone system that includes intercom, we won't need Intertalk."

"Is Centrex the only system that offers call transferring? Surely not."

"I didn't say it *was*," Tom retorted. "Most systems offer that, but with Centrex you can do it with a regular no–frills phone. Merlin is good, though, and they'll replace sets if they break down so we won't lose time while they try to repair them on the spot."

"Tom," Merrill said, "the only way this will make sense to the rest of us is if you go back to your office and organize your material so that we can see all the features of each system, including prices and options, and how they compare. Draw up a chart. At our next meeting, I hope you'll be prepared to do that." By the tone of her voice, Tom understood that he had been reprimanded.

As this story shows, the organization of a message affects the listener's comprehension of the content. A garbled message isn't easy to follow—and it damages the speaker's credibility. By the time Merrill stopped Tom, she had serious doubts about how carefully he had thought about the systems; and when he finally makes a recommendation, she isn't likely to have much faith in his expertise unless his next presentation is much clearer. A poorly organized message is also frustrating to listeners—and probably the last thing Tom wants to do is frustrate Merrill, whose evaluation of him is likely to influence his future success in the company.

THE IMPORTANCE OF CLEAR ORGANIZATION

Most people will agree that clarity is important, but few realize just how critical it is. A substantial body of research indicates that organizing your remarks clearly can make your messages more understandable, keep your audience happy, and boost your image as a speaker.[1]

Despite the benefits of good organization, most presentations suffer from a variety of problems in this area:

- *Taking too long to get to the point*. Many speakers ramble, gush, or drone on about their topic long after their audience has lost interest. Tom Byrd's long-winded explanation of the telephone system was a waste of Merrill Snyder's time. Most businesspeople are in a hurry and have little patience for nonessential information. "What's the bottom line?" is their spoken or unspoken demand.
- *Including irrelevant material*. Tom Byrd has immersed himself in the topic of telephone service providers and wanted to tell his boss everything on the subject. It's often hard to remember that your audience isn't likely to care as much about your topic as you do. Therefore, you need only include information that your listeners must know.
- *Leaving out necessary information*. It's paradoxical that, in addition to talking too much about unimportant details, some speakers leave out the essentials. How much will a system cost? How much disruption would be involved in switching from the present carrier? How reliable will the new provider be? If you don't answer critical questions, your listeners won't be informed or impressed.
- *Getting ideas mixed up*. Poor speakers haven't taken the time to decide how to present their ideas in the clearest, most logical order. Byrd's disjointed summary was impossible for Snyder to sort out. When your audience isn't as familiar with the topic as you are, you must develop ideas in a way that leads audience members clearly from what they do know to the new information.[2]

Problems like these can lead to organizational chaos. Even experienced speakers can get into trouble when they speak without preparing their ideas. Former president George Bush was an effective speaker when working from

> If you want to "get in touch with your feelings," fine—talk to yourself, we all do. But if you want to communicate with another thinking human being, get in touch with your thoughts. Put them in order, give them a purpose, use them to persuade, to instruct, to discover, to advise.
>
> William Safire, *Words of Wisdom*

prepared notes but was infamous for garbling ideas when speaking off the cuff. The following example illustrates the problem:

> Somebody said to me, "You know, we prayed for you over there." That was not just because I threw up on the prime minister of Japan either. Where was he when I needed him? But—but I—I said, "Let me tell you something." And I say this—I don't know whether any ministers from the Episcopal church are here. I hope so. But I said to him this. You're on to something here. You cannot be President of the United States if you don't have faith. Remember Lincoln, going to his knees in times of trial in the Civil war and all that stuff? You can't be. And we are blessed.[3]

Most speakers would find that some of their own remarks would look equally disjointed. The key to avoiding these lapses of organization is to organize your ideas before speaking.

No matter what the subject or the goal, most effective presentations follow a well–known pattern: "First, tell them what you're going to tell them; then, tell them; then, tell them what you told them." In outline form, the format looks like this:

INTRODUCTION
- I. Attention getter
- II. Thesis

BODY
- I.
- II.
- III.
- etc.

(I.–etc.: no more than five main points)

CONCLUSION
- I. Review
- II. Closing statement

This linear, logical approach to organization isn't the only way to structure a presentation. Researchers have found that it works best with Euro–American audiences or listeners receptive to the Euro–American cultural standard. Listeners from other backgrounds may use less linear patterns, which have been given labels including "star," "wave," and "spiral."[4] Despite the value of these patterns in certain situations, the standard format is probably the safest approach with most business audiences who are part of Euro–American culture.

You have probably encountered this format many times. Despite its familiarity, many speakers act as if they have never heard of it. Like Tom Byrd and President Bush, they launch into their subjects without any prefatory remarks about what they're about to say. Some finish their main ideas and then stop speaking without any summation or closing. Still others deliver what seems to be a model three–part talk but don't stop there; they continue tacking on new information after you have closed your mental files: "Did I mention that . . . ," "We had the same problem, by the way, last year when . . . ," or "Oh, another thing I should have mentioned. . . ." Even worse, many speakers don't seem to have *any* organizational plan in mind. Their remarks sound as if the speakers had dropped their note cards and shuffled them together in random order before addressing the group.

Chapter 10 described the first steps in developing a presentation: analyzing the situation, defining a thesis, and establishing a purpose. Once you have completed these steps, you need to decide what points you'll cover in your presentation and how to arrange them. You can do so by using the guidelines discussed in this chapter.

GATHERING IDEAS AND MATERIAL

Once you have figured out your thesis, you are ready to develop the information that will get your audience to accept it. Collecting this material usually requires research. If, for example, you want to sell potential customers on your product, you'll want to find out which competing products they are using now and how they feel about them. You'll also want to discover whether they are familiar with your product and what attitudes they have about it.

In other cases, the material you'll need to discuss may appear to be obvious. If you're giving a report on last month's sales, the figures might seem to form the bulk of your remarks. If you are explaining how to use a new piece of equipment, the operating steps appear to be the obvious body of your talk. Even in these cases, though, you'll probably need to do some digging. Last month's sales may take on more meaning if you compare them with those recorded in the same period in previous years, and getting those numbers may be worth the effort. Your instructions on the new equipment will be most successful if you find out whether and how accustomed your listeners are to operating similar equipment.

As these examples show, some research is almost always necessary. You should consider several sources for the information that will go into your presentation. The company's files—whether on paper or computerized—are often a good source of information. Interviews with knowledgeable people can provide both facts and insights. Library research is another source of

SKILL BUILDER

What kinds of material would you gather for a presentation on each of the following topics? Where would you find your information?

1. How changes in the telephone industry will affect consumers
2. How to begin an investment program
3. Changing trends in the popularity of various academic courses over the last ten years
4. Why students should (should not) buy a personal computer
5. Career opportunities for women in the field of your choice

information. Formal or informal surveys are often a good source of information. Your research will produce a list of material from which you'll build your presentation. For example, suppose that you have been asked to address a group of employees about why you want them to use Mercury Overnight for letters and packages that need to be delivered quickly. Using your research on Mercury Overnight, you might make up a list that looks something like the one in Figure 11–1.

Notice that this list is a random assortment of points. In fact, your own collection of ideas probably won't even be neatly listed on a single piece of paper. More likely it will be scribbled on an assortment of index cards, check stubs, message pads, or whatever you had at hand when you came across a piece of promising information. Once you've assembled what seems like enough raw material, you're ready to organize it.

FIGURE 11–1 Selling points produced by a brainstorming session.

1. Mercury Overnight will pick up the package at your office instead of you having to go through the mailroom.
2. It will also deliver right to your office if the label is marked properly, so you don't have to wait for the mailroom to process and deliver it to you.
3. When we experimented with different delivery services, Mercury delivered every single package we gave them within twenty-four hours.
4. Some of the companies we tried took two days or more about 25 percent of the time.
5. One company we tried got the package in on time about 90 percent of the time.
6. Other companies we've tried have held up packages for as much as a week for no good reason.
7. Mercury will deliver into the rural areas where many of our customers are, while some of the other companies only deliver in the urban areas.
8. Mercury will bill the departmental accounts, saving bookkeeping time.
9. Some companies charge a lot of extra money for the odd-sized packages we send sometimes, but Mercury just charges by weight.
10. Because we can't always count on overnight delivery with the delivery service we're using now, we often have to take time off to run a package across town.
11. Mercury charges less for heavy packages.
12. If we send several things at once to the same place, Mercury will give us a lower "group rate."
13. Mercury will come out at any time to pick up a package.
14. Other companies will only make a regular daily stop, which doesn't do you much good if your package isn't ready when they come.
15. Mercury will make pickups from seven in the morning until midnight, which is nice if you're working early or late.
16. If you send the package through the post office and don't put enough postage on it, they'll send it back and the package won't get there in time.
17. The packages that we've sent through some other shippers sometimes get so badly damaged that the contents have to be replaced. The shipper will pay for the contents if you insure the package, but that doesn't get it there in time.
18. Sometimes you have to ship a one-of-a-kind item, like a prototype for an advertisement, and if it gets lost or damaged it can take weeks to make a new one.
19. Mercury's basic shipping fee includes insurance.
20. it isn't easy to figure out which delivery service is best.
21. When the company was smaller, we used to just send things by mail.
22. We researched the idea of setting up our own delivery service, but management vetoed it because it cost too much.

ORGANIZING THE BODY

Inexperienced speakers make the mistake of starting to plan a talk by beginning at the beginning, by first writing an introduction. This is like trying to landscape a piece of property before you've put up a building. Even though it doesn't come first in a presentation, the body is the place to start your organizing. Organizing the body of a talk consists of two steps: identifying the key points that support your thesis, and then deciding what organizational plan best develops those points.

Identify Main Points and Subpoints

The list of ideas you've compiled by research and brainstorming probably contains more material than you'll want to use in your talk. So the next step is to figure out what key points best support your thesis and help you achieve your purpose. Your analysis of the speaking situation will also help you to pinpoint your key ideas.

On the basis of this analysis, you might decide that the major reasons that would convince listeners to sign up to use Mercury are:

I. Mercury is more reliable.
II. Mercury is more convenient.
III. Mercury is more economical.

None of these points was on the brainstorming list in Figure 11–1, but they emerge as themes from that list. Each of the points that did appear on that list will fit into one of these categories, so the speech can be organized around these three points.

How do you identify your main points? One way is by applying the "one–week–later" test: ask yourself what main points you want people to remember one week after the presentation. Since most listeners won't recall much more than a few ideas, your one–week–later points logically should be emphasized during your talk.

The basic ideas that grow out of your audience analysis or brainstorming list might work well as the main points of your talk, but this doesn't always happen. As with the Mercury delivery–service example, there may be better ways to organize your material. Before you can decide, you need to think about the different ways the body of a presentation can be organized.

Once you have identified main points, you can fill in your plan with the subpoints that expand on each of them. These subpoints can be added to a standard outline like the one in Figure 11–3 on page 328. A more visual way to represent the relationship between a thesis, main points, and subpoints is by drawing a "logic tree" like the one in Figure 11–2.[5]

Choose the Best Organizational Pattern

There are five basic ways to organize the body of a presentation. You should choose the one that best develops your thesis and thus helps you to achieve your purpose.

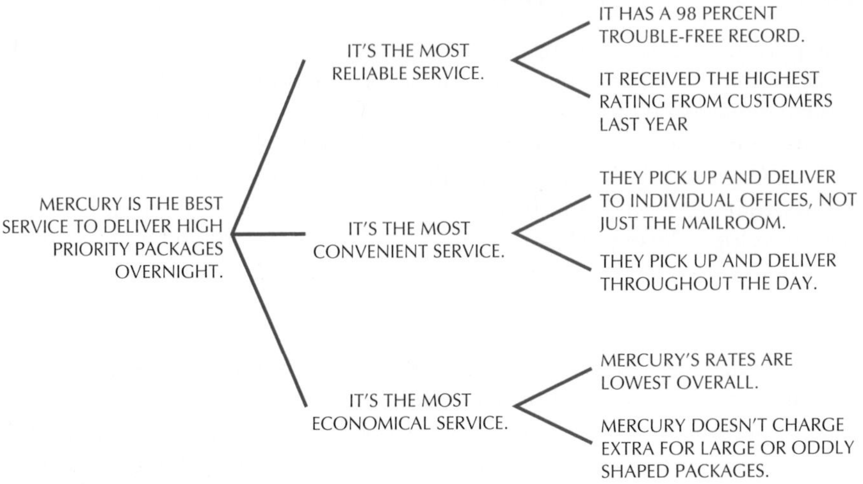

FIGURE 11–2 A "logic tree" illustrates the relationship between the thesis, main points, and subpoints in a presentation.

Chronological. A ***chronological pattern*** arranges your points according to their sequence in time. You can use it to explain a process, such as the steps in putting an order through the order fulfillment and shipping departments or the schedule for developing a new product. One of its most common uses is to give instructions:

Thesis: Logging onto the e-mail system is easy.

- **I.** Click on the Networks line under the Servers menu.
- **II.** Enter your password in the pop-up box that appears.
- **III.** Click on the e-mail icon in the same pop-up box.
- **IV.** When the e-mail window appears, click on either Read messages or Send a message, depending on what you want to do.

Chronological patterns are also useful for discussing events that develop over time:

Thesis: We need to stay on schedule if we're to get the catalog out in time for the holidays.

- **I.** A product list must be ready by March 1.
- **II.** Photography and catalog copy have to be completed by May 6.
- **III.** Page proofs have to be read and corrected by July 30.
- **IV.** Final proofs have to be reviewed by department heads by August 30.
- **V.** Catalogs have to be shipped no later than October 5.

Chronological patterns may be used for discussing history:

Thesis: A review of the last five years shows that we've been moving toward empowering our entire work force to make decisions.

I. Five years ago, management introduced the Employee Advisory Council.
II. Four years ago, we started using project teams that include people from every level of the company.
III. Two years ago, the company started allowing department supervisors to make purchases within their areas without getting the approval of their managers.
IV. Over the last year, the company has followed the suggestions of several workers at the field level in making changes in our billing process.

Spatial. ***Spatial patterns*** organize material according to how it is put together or where it is located physically. You might use a spatial pattern to show the parts in a model for a new product, the location of various departments in your building, or the safety requirements of a piece of equipment—where safety shields should be placed, the support required in the floor, and so on. You might sell a piece of real estate with a spatially organized presentation like this:

Thesis: This home provides all the space you need.
I. The upstairs has enough bedrooms for every member of the family plus a private study.
II. The main floor is spacious, with a large living room, a formal dining room, and an eat-in kitchen.
III. The basement has a finished playroom for the children and a utility room.
IV. The yard has large trees and lots of space for a garden.

You can also show the geographical nature of a subject by citing examples from many places:

Thesis: Business is better in some areas than in others.
I. Northeast regional sales are 50 percent ahead of last year's.
II. Mid-Atlantic regional sales are 10 percent ahead of last year's.
III. Southern regional sales are about the same as last year's.
IV. Midwest regional sales are down about 25 percent from last year's.

Topical. A ***topical pattern*** groups your ideas around some logical themes or divisions in your subject. For example, you might organize a proposal for simplifying the expense–accounting procedures around the reasons for the change or a sales presentation for photocopiers around the three major types of copiers you think a customer might be interested in. An accountant might organize a proposal for a new inventory system this way:

Thesis: A just-in-time inventory system has three major benefits.
I. It eliminates excess inventory that may result from long-term ordering.

II. It cuts down on waste resulting from supplies becoming outdated or shopworn.
III. It saves on storage and computer–records costs.

The topical approach is sometimes termed a "catchall approach" because people occasionally describe a list of points as *topical* if they can't think of another pattern that will work. However, a jumbled list of ideas isn't organized just because you call it "topical." A genuine topical approach has elements that are logically related according to some scheme an audience can easily recognize.

Cause–Effect. A ***cause–effect*** pattern shows that certain events have happened or will happen as a result of certain circumstances. For example, you might show prospective life insurance customers how certain clauses will provide extra coverage if they are hospitalized or demonstrate how a new advertising program will help a product reach a wider market. You might also use it to demonstrate how certain circumstances are creating a problem:

Thesis: Redecorating the offices before raising salaries (*cause*) will damage morale and affect productivity (*effect*).
I. When employees see the offices being redecorated without having received a cost–of–living raise over the past year, they'll be discouraged.
II. Discouraged employees aren't as likely to give the company their best efforts during the upcoming season.

An alternative form of the cause–effect structure is an *effect–cause* structure. When you use this structure, you focus more on results: you begin with the result and how it came to pass or how you think it can be made to happen. For example, you might use an effect–cause pattern to explain why a company has a strict policy about absenteeism or to explain how you expect to accomplish a sales goal you have set. It may also be used to explain how a problem has been created:

Thesis: The decline in our car–rental profits (*effect*) is the result of several problems (*cause*).

SKILL BUILDER

Which organizational plan (chronological, spatial, and so on) would you use for each of the following presentations?

1. Instructions on how to file a health insurance claim form
2. A request for time and money to attend an important convention in your field
3. A comparison of products or services between your organization and a competitor
4. A report on an industrial accident
5. Suggestions on reducing employee turnover

I. Our profits have decreased 35 percent.
II. Several factors are responsible.
  A. Our competitors are offering better service at lower prices.
  B. Our maintenance costs have nearly doubled on newer cars.
  C. Our advertising is not effective.

Problem–Solution. A ***problem–solution*** pattern is usually used when the speaker is proposing some kind of change. When you use this pattern, you describe the problem and then show how your plan will solve it. You might use a problem–solution pattern to show a customer how your service contract will keep her from losing time and paying for expensive repairs when her personal computer breaks down or to demonstrate to management how a new procedure will avoid the problems of the current program. Here is an example:

Thesis: The new method I propose is better than the present method of partially automated machine drilling.
I. There are many problems with the current system.
  A. The handling time is almost five minutes per part.
  B. The rate of errors is about 4 percent.
  C. Our accident rate is very high.
II. The new system will solve these problems.
  A. The handling time is almost eliminated.
  B. The error rate is less than 1 percent.
  C. Workers are no longer involved in the most dangerous part of the process.[6]

Rules for Main Points

Whichever pattern of organization you use, your main points should meet the following criteria.

Main Points Should Be Stated as Claims. A ***claim*** is a statement asserting a fact or belief. By stating your claims in full, grammatical sentences, they will probably satisfy the one–week–later test and be remembered by your listeners. Notice how describing main points as claims in complete sentences is clearer and far more effective than using simple three– or four–word statements.

FRAGMENT	CLAIM
Choosing a physician	It's essential to choose a health-care provider from the list of approved doctors.
Sexual and ethnic discrimination	Allowing sexual or ethnic considerations to intrude into our hiring decisions isn't just bad judgment; it's illegal.

Demographic changes in the market	Due to demographic changes, we can expect our market to shrink in the next ten years.

All Points Should Develop the Thesis. Consider the following outline:

Thesis: Allowing employees more latitude in choosing their work hours is good for the company and for the workers.
- **I.** Flexible scheduling is a relatively new idea.
- **II.** Flexible scheduling improves morale.
- **III.** Flexible scheduling reduces absenteeism.

The first point may be true, but the newness of flexible scheduling doesn't say anything about its value and, therefore, ought to be dropped.

A Presentation Should Contain No More than Five Main Points. Your main points are, after all, what you want your listeners to remember, and people have difficulty recalling more than five pieces of information when it is presented orally.[7] Even when you have a large amount of material, it's usually possible to organize it into five categories or less. For example, if you were preparing an analysis of ways to lower operating expenses in your organization, your brainstorming list might include these ideas:

Reduce wattage in lighting fixtures.

Hire outside data processing firm to handle seasonal billing rather than expand permanent in–house staff.

Sell surplus equipment.

Reduce nonbusiness use of copying machines.

Reduce temperature in less–used parts of the building.

Pay overtime rather than add new employees.

Retrofit old equipment instead of buying new machinery.

Your outline could consolidate this list into three areas:

Thesis: We can reduce operating costs in three areas: energy, personnel, and equipment.
- **I.** We can reduce our energy costs.
  - **A.** Reduce wattage in lighting fixtures.
  - **B.** Reduce temperature in less–used parts of the building.
- **II.** We can save money by not hiring new employees.
  - **A.** Hire outside data processing firm for seasonal billing.
  - **B.** Encourage overtime instead of adding employees.
- **III.** We can reduce our purchase and maintenance costs on equipment.
  - **A.** Retrofit old equipment.

B. Sell surplus equipment.
C. Reduce personal use of copying machines.

This outline contains all the items in your list, but the three broad categories make your presentation much easier to comprehend than a seven–point presentation would be.

Each Main Point Should Contain Only One Idea. Combining ideas or overlapping them will confuse audiences. Consider this outline:

Thesis: Many local businesses continue to discriminate against some job applicants.
I. Businesses discriminate on the basis of ethnic background.
II. Businesses discriminate on the basis of disability.
III. Businesses discriminate on the basis of age and sex.

Since discrimination can be related to either age or sex, there's no logical reason to put age and sex in the same category.

Main Points Should Be Parallel in Structure whenever Possible. Parallel wording can reflect your organization and dramatize your points. Consider how the repetition of "Businesses discriminate" in the last outline helps drive the point home far more forcefully than does the following, less effective wording of your main points:

I. Most businesses discriminate against minorities.
II. Disability is another reason for discriminating against some job applicants.
III. Some businesses even refuse to hire employees who are over sixty–five.
IV. Women often have extra trouble finding a job.

You won't always be able to state your main points using parallel construction, but a look at many of the examples in this chapter shows you that it can be used often.

PLANNING THE INTRODUCTION

The body of a presentation is important, but the introduction that precedes it needs just as much attention. Your introduction should take between 10 and

SKILL BUILDER

Develop outlines for three of the following topics, applying the rules for main points given in this section:

1. When to use small claims court
2. The importance of creativity in advertising
3. Renting versus leasing a car
4. The proper format for a business letter
5. Types of sexual harassment
6. The fastest growing jobs in the 1990s

15 percent of the speaking time. During this short time—less than one minute of a five-minute talk—your listeners form their initial impression of you and your topic. That impression, favorable or not, will affect how they react to the rest of your remarks. To be most effective, an introduction should accomplish several purposes.

Functions of the Introduction

As you have already learned, an introduction should have two parts: an attention getter and a thesis statement and preview. These two parts should accomplish five things.

Capture the Listeners' Attention. As you learned in Chapter 4, audiences don't always approach a presentation ready to listen. The topic may not seem important or interesting to them. Your listeners may have been ordered to attend your presentation. Even when the presentation is obviously important, your listeners will usually have other matters on their minds. It's vital, therefore, to begin by focusing attention on you and your topic if there is any chance that the listeners' minds are elsewhere.

Give Your Audience a Reason to Listen. The best way to grab and hold your listeners' attention is to convince them that your message will be important or interesting to them. For example, if company employees are generally satisfied with the insurance program the company has been using, they won't be interested in hearing about a new health plan that will be cheaper for the company unless you can begin by enumerating its advantages to them—for instance, that it will provide them with better emergency services. Similarly, management will be more interested in hearing your new ideas if you first say that the plans you're proposing will yield higher profits.

Set the Proper Tone for the Topic and Setting. If you want potential customers to buy more fire insurance, your opening remarks should prepare them to think seriously about the problems they would encounter if they had a fire in the house. If you want to congratulate your subordinates about their recent performance and encourage them to perform even better on the next assignment, your opening remarks should put them in a good mood—not focus on the problems you must face. In any case, your introduction should establish rapport with your listeners. Robert Moran accomplished this goal when he began his remarks to a Japanese audience:

> If I were an American and you were an American audience, I would probably begin my speech with a joke. If I were Japanese speaking to a Japanese audience, I would probably begin with an apology. Since I am neither American nor Japanese, I will begin with an apology for not telling a joke.[8]

Establish Your Qualifications. If the audience already knows that you are an expert on the subject, if a previous speaker has given you an impressive introduction, or if your authority makes it clear that you're qualified to talk, establishing credibility isn't necessary. In other cases, however, you need to demonstrate your competence quickly so that the listeners will take your remarks seriously. Nonverbal behaviors will also help boost (or diminish) your credibility. Recall the information on nonverbal communication in Chapter 3, and see additional advice on building credibility through nonverbal behavior in Chapters 13 and 15.

Introduce Your Thesis and Preview Your Presentation. In most cases, you need to state your main idea clearly at the beginning of your remarks so that your listeners know exactly what you're trying to say. In addition to your thesis statement, a preview of your main points tells your listeners where you're headed.

Accomplishing these five goals in less than one minute isn't as difficult as it might seem because you can accomplish several functions at the same time. For example, notice how an insurance agent introduced a thirty–minute talk on an admittedly difficult topic:

[*Sets desired tone by establishing a bond with audience in a humorous way*] Being an insurance agent gives me a lot of sympathy for tax collectors and dog catchers. None of us has an especially popular job. After all, it seems that with life insurance you lose either way: If the policy pays off, you won't be around to enjoy the money. On the other hand, if you don't need the policy, you've spent your hard–earned savings for nothing. Besides, insurance isn't cheap. I'm sure you have plenty of other things you could use your money for: catching up on bills, fixing up your house, buying a new car, or even taking a vacation.

[*Establishes qualifications*] With all those negatives, why should you care about insurance? For that matter, why am I devoting my career to it? For me, the answer is easy: Over the years, I've seen literally hundreds of people—people just like you and me—learn what a difference the right kind of insurance coverage can make. And I've seen hundreds more suffer from learning too late that insurance is necessary.

[*Thesis*] Well, tonight I want to give you some good news. I'll show you that you can win by buying insurance. [*Preview*] You can win by gaining peace of mind, and you can even win by buying insurance that works like an investment, paying dividends that you can use here and now.

Types of Opening Statements

Of all parts of a presentation, the opening words are the hardest for many speakers. You have to be interesting. You have to establish the right tone. Your remarks have to relate to the topic that's being discussed. And, finally, the opening statement has to feel right for you.

The kind of opening you choose will depend on your analysis of the speaking situation. With familiar topics and audiences, you may even decide to skip the preliminaries and give just a brief background before launching into the thesis and preview:

> "We've made good progress on Mr. Boynton's request to look into cost cutting steps. We've found that it is possible to reduce operating expenses by almost 10 percent without cutting efficiency. We'll be introducing six steps this morning."

In most cases, you will want to preface your remarks with some sort of opening statement. Following are seven of the most common and effective ways to begin a presentation.

Ask a Question. Asking the right question is a good way to involve your listeners in your topic and establish its importance to them.

Many speakers try to capture attention by asking the audience a ***rhetorical question:*** one to which the answer is obvious, and which does not really call for a response. For example, a manager who wants to whip up employee enthusiasm for a proposal that will reduce paperwork might ask, "Is it just me, or does anybody else feel like we've spent too much time filling in forms?" Rhetorical questions work well when you can be sure the audience's reaction is the one you want.

Rhetorical questions can be risky, especially when the answer is obvious ("How many of you hate to pay taxes?") or uninteresting ("Have you ever wondered what the Sherman Antitrust Act means to you?"). Other rhetorical questions can be so thought–provoking that your audience will stop listening to you: "If you had to fire three of the people who report to you, how would you decide which ones to let go?" When you decide to begin with a rhetorical question, be sure to avoid mistakes like these.

Other questions call for an overt response: "How many people here are from out of state?" "Who has had trouble meeting deadlines for sales reports?" "What do you see as the biggest threat facing the company?" If you *are* seeking an overt reaction from your listeners, be sure to let them know: "Let me see a show of hands by the people who. . . . " "Hold up your program if you're among those who. . . . " If you want them to respond mentally, let them know: "Answer this question for yourself. Are you sure that all of your expense reports would pass an Internal Revenue audit?"

Tell a Story. Since most people enjoy a good story, beginning with one can be an effective way to get audience attention, set the tone, and lead into the topic. This example, from the introduction to a speech on time management, accomplishes all these functions in a few sentences:

> Jean Fabre, the French naturalist, was one day observing processionary caterpillars. These are little fellows, about an inch long, that form up into long

> strings and move over trees eating leaves and insects. Fabre was able to get them onto the rim of an old red flower pot and had them close up their circle. As they moved around the rim in an unbroken circle, he figured that they would soon realize that they were going around in circles and would stop. Yet they starved to death within reach of food. They confused activity with accomplishment. They were as active as they could be, moving along staying busy. They just weren't getting anywhere.[9]

Give a Quotation. Quotations have two advantages: First, someone else has probably already said what you want to say in a very clever way. Second, quotations let you use a source with high credibility to back up your message.

Not every quotation has to come from a distinguished person. As long as the character you quote is appropriate for the audience and the topic, he or she can be almost anyone—even a fictional character:

> One of America's best-known philosophers—Charlie Brown of the comic strip Peanuts—once said—"There is no problem so big—no challenge so awesome—no dilemma so frustrating or complicated—that one cannot simply walk away from it." The problems of agriculture *are* big—awesome—frustrating *and* complicated . . . and can't be walked away from.[10]

Make a Startling Statement. An excellent way to get listeners' attention is to surprise them. Sales presentations often include startling facts in their openings: "Do you know that half of all business calls never reach the intended party?"

This approach will work only if your startling statement bears a clear relationship to your topic. Stephen Gardner, the assistant attorney general of Texas, used this approach in an exposé of the abuses of credit bureaus:

> The whole credit system is frighteningly out of control. Not only are your financial matters virtually an open book, but it is an open book with a couple of pages missing, some lines crossed out, and some pieces in backwards![11]

You won't achieve the desired result if your startling statement offends your audience. The remarks that might work perfectly at a football banquet could flop miserably in a church sermon. Illinois Bell spokesperson John R. Bonée succeeded in staying on the right side of appropriateness when he spoke to a group of administrators:

> You may have noticed that the title of my remarks this evening is "Making Love in Public" and you may have found it somewhat facetious. Believe me, it is not. Public relations is a widely misunderstood concept. It has been said that some people know so little about it that they think public relations means making love in public. In a certain sense, they are perfectly correct. It does mean, at the very least, making love *to* the public. That's what public relations is all about.[12]

Refer to the Audience. Mentioning your listeners' needs, concerns, or interests clarifies the relevance of your topic immediately and shows that you understand your listeners. For example, "I know you're all worried by rumors of cutbacks in staff. I called you here today to explain just what the budget cuts will mean to this department."

Former California governor George Dukmejian used the technique of referring to the audience in a talk to the Los Angeles Rotary Club. Dukmejian acknowledged the fact that people who listen to after–lunch speakers—even famous ones—appreciate brevity:

> I promise not to speak for too long this afternoon. It's worth noting that the Lord's Prayer is only 56 words long. The Gettysburg Address is 226. The Ten Commandments are 297. But the U.S. Department of Agriculture's order on the price of cabbage is 15,269 words. I'll try to finish somewhere in between.[13]

Refer to the Occasion. Sometimes the event itself provides a good starting point: "We're here today to recognize some very important people."

Sometimes you can begin by referring to some other aspect of the situation—for example, by relating your remarks to those of a previous speaker: "I was very interested in what Larry had to say about the way our expenses will rise in the next couple of years. Let's look at one way we can keep that increase as small as possible."

David M. Roderick of United States Steel used the technique of referring to a previous speaker in the introduction of his remarks to the National Press Club:

> Thank you, Don, for your introduction. I feel privileged to have this renowned forum as a platform for stating the case for our nation's steel industry—its plight and the importance of its survival.
>
> I just hope this issue is not too drab when compared to your two most recent luncheon presentations by gourmet James Beard and economist Arthur Laffer—pie on the plate and pie in the sky. And now steelmaking.
>
> Certainly what happens to the nation's fourth largest industry has to be important. Its demise would certainly be news—bad news for almost everyone. I think, then, its struggle to survive and regroup and prosper should be equally newsworthy.[14]

Use Humor. The right joke can be an effective way to get attention, make a point, and increase your audience's liking for you. The vice-president of an advertising agency, for example, might begin an orientation session for new management trainees with the following tale:

> "I'm sure everyone has heard the story about the guy who smells awful all the time. When asked the reason for this he explains that it's because of his job—working in a circus giving enemas to elephants. The listener asks, "Why don't you get another job?" and the guy replies hotly, "What! And get out of *show business?*"

> "Well, that story has some truth in our business too. Lots of people view advertising as glamorous: three-hour expense-account lunches and big commissions. Advertising is certainly a kind of show business, but along with all the glamour comes a lot of hard, messy work. I want to begin this orientation program by telling you about both the clean, easy parts and the tough, grubby ones. Then you'll have a better idea what to expect in the next months and years."

Jokes aren't the only kind of humorous opener. Sometimes you can make an amusing remark that will set the tone perfectly for your message. For instance:

> Some people say that problems are not problems, but rather, they are opportunities. If that's the case, then given the present situation, we are faced with a hell of a lot of opportunities.[15]

Any humor you use should be appropriate to your topic and to the occasion. Telling a few knock-knock jokes before you launch into your financial report will draw attention— but not to your topic. The tone of your presentation could be ruined by a joke. For instance, you probably shouldn't tell a few jokes about smog and then say, "But seriously, folks, I want to talk about what we're doing to curb air pollution from our own factories."

Your jokes should also be appropriate for your audience. The in-jokes that work well with your office staff, for example, are likely to alienate clients at a contract negotiation because outsiders won't understand them. Jokes that are off color or in any way make light of sexism, racism, or disabilities are likely to offend or embarrass someone in your audience. The risks of telling them aren't worth the laughs they might generate.

PLANNING THE CONCLUSION

The conclusion of your presentation should be even shorter than the introduction: not much more than 5 percent of your total speaking time. Within those few moments, though, you must accomplish two important things.

Functions of the Conclusion

A conclusion should have two parts: a review and a closing statement. Let's look at each of these parts in detail.

The Review. Your review should contain a restatement of your thesis and a summary of your main points. Sometimes these two elements will be presented almost exactly as they appear on your outline:

> "This afternoon, I've suggested that our merchandising approach needs changing to become more profitable. I've suggested three such changes: first, to increase our newspaper advertising; second, to fea-

SKILL BUILDER

Prepare an introduction and a conclusion for each of the following presentations:

1. A talk to employees announcing personnel layoffs
2. The last in a day-long series of talks to a tired audience on maintaining and operating equipment
3. An appeal to co-workers for donations to the Community Christmas Relief Fund
4. A talk to your class by the president of the local chamber of commerce, whose topic is "What Employers Look For in a College Graduate" (Plan your concluding remarks to follow a question-and-answer period.)

ture higher-quality merchandise; and third, to expand our product line in all areas."

Your review can also be a subtler rewording of the same information:

"By now I hope you agree with me that some basic merchandising changes can improve our balance sheet. When people find out that we have a broad range of high-quality products, I'm convinced that we'll have more customers who will spend more money."

The Closing Statement. A strong closing will help your listeners to remember you favorably; a weak ending can nullify many of your previous gains. Besides creating a favorable impression, the closing statement will give your remarks a sense of completion. You shouldn't leave your audience wondering whether you've finished. Finally, a closing statement ought to incite your listeners, encouraging them to act or think in a way that accomplishes your purpose. Let's look at several varieties of closing statements.

Types of Closing Statements

Several of the techniques used for getting attention in your introduction will also work well as closing statements. To refresh your memory, they are:

Ask a question.

Tell a story.

Give a quotation.

Make a startling statement.

Refer to the audience.

Refer to the occasion.

Use humor.

In addition, there are several other types of closing statements you might use.

Return to the Theme of Your Opening Statement. Coming back to the place you started gives a sense of completeness to your presentation. With this approach, you should refer to your opening statement but add a new insight, further details, or a different ending:

> "At the beginning of my talk, I asked whether you might not be paying more tax than you need to. I suspect you discovered that you've been overly generous with Uncle Sam. I hope I have helped you to understand your real liability and to take advantage of some of the tax shelters available to you."

Appeal for Action. When your goal involves getting the audience to act in a certain way, you can sometimes close your presentation by asking for your desired result:

> "So now that you know what these workshops can do, the only question is when you ought to enroll. We have openings on August 19 and on September 23. I'll be available in a moment to sign you up for either date. I'm looking forward to seeing you soon."

End with a Challenge. Whereas an appeal asks for some action, a challenge almost demands it:

> "You can go on as before, not failing completely but not doing the best possible job. Or you can use the ideas you've heard this morning to become more creative, more productive, and more successful. Why be average when you can be superior? Why settle for a few hopes when you can reach your dreams? It's up to you."

ADDING TRANSITIONS

Transitions are words or sentences that connect the segments of a presentation. As Figure 11–3 shows, they work like bridges between the major parts of your remarks and tell your listeners how these parts are related. Transitions should occur between the introduction and the body, between the main points within the body, and between the body and the conclusion. The examples below illustrate each of these instances:

> "Those are big promises. Let me talk about how we can deliver on them."

> "Not all the news is bad, however. Let me tell you about some good things that happened at the conference."

> "After hearing about so many features, you may have trouble remembering them all. Let's review them briefly."

Functions of Transitions

Transitions like the preceding examples serve three important purposes.

```
Purpose:      After hearing this talk, the prospective customer will sign up to use Mercury
              as our exclusive overnight delivery service.

Thesis:       Mercury is the best service to deliver your high-priority packages on time.

INTRODUCTION
     I. Overnight delivery services aren't cheap, but they are worth the expense if they
        do the job of getting important materials into the right hands quickly
        (Attention-getter).
    II. After comparing Mercury with the other delivery services, you'll see that we are
        the best one to do the job (Thesis). As I'll explain in the next few minutes,
        mercury is quickly, more convenient, and more reliable than the competition
        (Preview).

Transition: Let me start by explaining why Mercury is best with the most important feature
of any delivery service: reliability.

BODY
     I. Mercury is more reliable than other services
                A. Mercury's 98 percent trouble free record beats every other service.
                B. Other services have held up deliveries for as much as one week.
                C. Other services have damaged packages.
                D. In some cases, other services have even lost packages.

Transition: Besides being reliable, Mercury is the best service in another important way...
    II. Mercury is more convenient than other services.
                A. They pick up and deliver items to individual offices, not just the mail
                     room like ABC Overnight.
                B. They'll pick up or deliver packages any time between 7:00 a.m. and
                     midnight, instead of only coming by once a day like International Air
                     freight.
                C. They're the only service that will bill departmental accounts separately,
                     saving you bookkeeping time.

Transition: Because it's so convenient and reliable, you might think that Mercury is more
expensive than other services, but it's not.
   III. Mercury is more economical than others services.
                 A. They don't charge extra for oddly shaped packages.
                 B. They charge less than every other service for heavy packages.
                 C. The shipping fee includes insurance.

Transition: By now you can see why it's worth considering Mercury as the provider of
your overnight mail service . . .
CONCLUSION
          I. Mercury is reliable, convenient, and economical (thesis/review).
         II. With Mercury you won't just pay for the best service . . . you'll get it.
```

FIGURE 11–3 A complete presentation outline.

They Promote Clarity. Clarity in speech—especially one-way speech like presentations—is more difficult to achieve than clarity in writing. The format of a letter, memo, book, or report makes its organization of ideas clear. Paragraphs, lists, different typefaces, and underlining can all emphasize how ideas are related to one another. In a presentation, however, listeners don't have the benefit of any of these aids to figure out how your ideas are put together. They have only what the verbal cues provide—transitional words and phrases.

They Emphasize Important Ideas. Transitions within presentations highlight important information the way italics and bold type emphasize it in print:

"Now let's turn to a third reason—perhaps the most important of all—for equipping your field representatives with electronic pagers."

"That's what company policy says about the use of expense accounts. Now let's take a look at how things *really* work."

They Keep Listeners Interested. Transitions give momentum to a presentation. They make listeners want to find out what comes next:

"So we gave them the best dog–and–pony show you've ever seen. And it was perfect—just like we planned. What do you think they said when we were finished?"

"By now you're probably asking yourself what a product like this will cost. And that's the best news of all. . . ."

Characteristics of Effective Transitions

Transitions that promote clarity, emphasize important ideas, and keep listeners interested possess two characteristics. First, they refer to both preceding and upcoming ideas. A transition is like a bridge: to get listeners from one point to another, it must be anchored at both ends. By referring to what you just said and to what you'll say next, you are showing the logical relationship among those ideas. Notice the smooth connections between the ideas in these transitions:

"Those are the problems. Now let's see what can be done about solving them."

"Now you see that the change makes sense financially. But how will it be received by the people that have to live with it?"

If you have trouble planning a transition that links preceding and upcoming material smoothly, the reason may be that the ideas aren't logically related and the organizational plan you've chosen is flawed. Review the organizing patterns on pages 314–316 and the rules for main points on pages 317–319 to be sure that the structure of your presentation's body is logically suited to the topic.

Transitions should also call attention to themselves. You should let listeners know that you're moving from one point to another so that they will be able to follow the structure of your ideas easily. Notice how the examples you have read so far all make it clear that the presentation is shifting gears. This sort of highlighting is often due to the use of key words:

"The *next* important idea is . . ."

"*Another* reason we want to make the change . . ."

"*Finally*, we need to consider . . ."

"To *wrap things up* . . ."

Phrases like these are not in themselves good transitions, since they do not refer to both previous and upcoming material strongly enough. But when used as part of a transition like the ones illustrated in these pages, they do signal listeners that you are moving to a new part of your presentation.

A presentation checklist, covering transitions and the other organizational concepts discussed in this chapter, is presented in Table 11–1.

TABLE 11-1 Checklist for Organizing and Supporting a Presentation

- *Introduction*
  Captures attention of audience.
  Gives audience reasons to listen.
  Sets appropriate tone.
  Establishes speaker's qualifications, if necessary.
  Introduces thesis and previews content.
- *Body*
  Body uses clear, most effective organizational pattern:
    Chronological
    Spatial
    Topical
    Cause–effect
    Problem–solution
  Main points should be stated in complete sentences.
  All points help develop thesis.
  Body contains no more than five main points.
  Each main point contains only one idea.
  Main points should be parallel in structure.
- *Transitions*
  Refer to both recent and upcoming material, showing relationship between the two.
  Clarify structure of speaker's ideas:
    Exist in all necessary parts of presentation
    Between introduction and body
    Between main points within body
    Between body and conclusion
- *Conclusion*
  Reviews thesis and main points.
  Concludes with effective closing statement.

SUMMARY

Presentations must be clearly organized for several reasons: Well-organized presentations are more understandable; they boost the speaker's credibility; they are more persuasive; and they reduce listener frustration.

All presentations ought to follow the same basic structure, containing an introduction, body, and conclusion. After developing a purpose and thesis, the first step in organizing a presentation is to compile a list of all the ideas that might possibly fit into the talk. The purpose statement and audience analysis then serve as devices for choosing the items that are appropriate for this specific presentation. These items ought to be arranged into a series of main points and subpoints, following one of the patterns described in this chapter.

After the body of the presentation has been developed, the introduction, conclusion, and transitions should be added. The introduction should capture the attention of the audience, give the members a reason to listen, set the proper tone, establish the speaker's qualifications, and state the thesis and a preview of the main discussion points. The conclusion should review the thesis and main points and close with a strong statement. Transitions connect the parts of the speech, helping the material flow smoothly and keeping listeners oriented.

RESOURCES

Dreyer, J., and G. H. Patton, *Speech Preparation Workbook* (Englewood Cliffs, N.J.: Prentice-Hall, 1994).

Brief information guides preface the many worksheets and outline forms included in this slim workbook. The authors walk you through the speech preparation process from audience analysis to a postdelivery self-analysis.

Jaffe, C., *Public Speaking: A Cultural Perspective* (Belmont, Calif.: Wadsworth, 1995).

Chapter 9, "Organizing the Speech," shows that the traditional linear organizing pattern that dominates Western communication isn't the only way to present material. The chapter discusses other, non-Euro-American organizational styles, such as the wave, spiral, and star patterns.

Wilder, C., "Concluding with Conviction," in *The Presentations Kit: 10 Steps for Selling Your Ideas* (New York: Wiley, 1994).

Conclusions are vital to the overall impact of a presentation. Wilder offers some forceful ideas that will help you pack all the punch you can into your conclusion. The book includes tips for organizing and delivering your conclusion.

CURRENT MK

VS STRIKE

EXECUTI

101

OUT OF

100

At MO

Option EQ

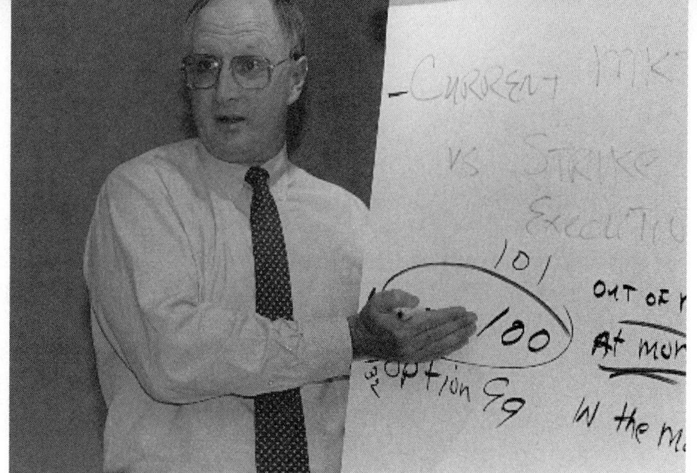

CHAPTER 12

Verbal and Visual Support in Presentations

Functions of Supporting Material
- Clarity
- Interest
- Proof

Verbal Support
- Examples
- Stories
- Statistics
- Comparisons
- Citations

Visual Aids
- Types of Visual Aids
- Media for Presenting Visual Aids
- Computer-Assisted Design of Visual Aids
- Rules for Using Visual Aids

Summary / Resources

KEY TERMS

Bar chart / Citations / Column chart / Comparisons / Examples / Flip chart / Graph / Pictogram / Pie chart / Statistics / Stories / Supporting material / Transparency

Tom Sutcliffe was frustrated. "I know I deserve that raise," he said firmly to his friend and co-worker Tina Agapito. "I laid out all the reasons to the boss as clear as day. I've been doing the work of two people ever since Tran left. My productivity is higher than anybody else's in the place. My salary is way behind the industry average. And all my clients are happy. What else does he want?"

Tina tried to be supportive. "I know you deserve the raise, Tom. And I just can't believe the boss doesn't see that too. Did you back up your claims?"

"What do you mean?" Tom replied.

"Did you give him evidence about your productivity or about how your salary compares with the industry? And did you give him some proof about all your happy clients?"

"I guess not," said Tom. "But I shouldn't have to sell myself around here. The boss ought to appreciate a good employee when he has one!"

"Maybe so," Tina answered. "But the boss hears a lot of requests for money and resources. And he's really busy. Maybe if you can make your case clearer and more interesting, you've still got a chance."

Tina's advice to Tom was good. Solid ideas won't always impress an audience. Most listeners are busy and preoccupied, and they usually don't care nearly as much about your message as you do. The kind of clear organization described in Chapter 11 will help make your presentations a success, but you often need to back up your well-organized points in a way that makes your audience take notice, understand you, and accept your message. In other words, you need to use plenty of supporting material.

FUNCTIONS OF SUPPORTING MATERIAL

Supporting material is anything that backs up the claims in a presentation. You can see the relationship between these claims and supporting material in the following examples:

Claim: We could increase sales by staying open until 10 P.M. on weekday evenings.

Support: An article in *Modern Retailing* cites statistics showing that stores with extended evening hours boost profits by more than 20 percent of the direct overhead involved with the longer business day.

Claim: Replacing the toner cartridge on the laser printer isn't as complicated as it seems.

Support: Here's a diagram that shows how to do it.

Claim: Taking the time to help customers will boost their loyalty and increase your commissions.

Support: Let me read you a letter written by one satisfied customer just last week.

As these examples show, a presentation without supporting material would still be logical if it followed the organizational guidelines in Chapter 11. But it probably wouldn't achieve its goal because it would lack the information necessary to develop the ideas in a way that the audience would understand or appreciate. Carefully selected supporting material can make a presentation more effective by adding three things: clarity, interest, and proof.

Clarity

Supporting material can make abstract or complicated ideas more understandable. Notice how the following example clarifies why computer operating systems that use the "point and click" method make more sense than ones that rely on arcane keyboard commands:

> Imagine driving a car that has no steering wheel, accelerator, brake pedal, turn signal lever, or gear selector. In place of all the familiar manual controls, you have only a typewriter keyboard.
>
> Any time you want to turn a corner, change lanes, slow down, speed up, honk your horn, or back up, you have to type a command sequence on the keyboard. Unfortunately, the car can't understand English sentences. Instead, you must hold down a special key with one finger and type in some letters and numbers, such as "S20:TL:A35," which means, "Slow to 20, turn left, and accelerate to 35."
>
> If you make typing mistakes, one of three things will happen. If you type an unknown command, the car radio will bleat and you will have to type the command again. If what you type happens to be wrong but is nevertheless a valid command, the car will blindly obey. (Imagine typing A95 instead of A35.) If you type something the manufacturer didn't anticipate, the car will screech to a halt and shut itself off.
>
> No doubt you could learn to drive such a car if you had sufficient motivation and determination. But why bother, when so many cars use familiar controls? Most people wouldn't.
>
> Most people don't bother to use a personal computer for the same reasons they wouldn't bother with a keyboard controlled car. Working on a computer isn't a natural skill, and the benefits hardly seem worth the hassle of learning how to get work done in an unfamiliar environment. If you make a typing mistake, the computer may do nothing, tell you it doesn't understand, do the wrong thing, shut itself down, or destroy all the work you've done and then shut itself down. Who cares if the machine is theoretically thousands of times more efficient than pencil and paper? If using the machine rattles you so much that you can't get anything done, it is in fact less efficient and may waste more time than it saves.[1]

Interest

Supporting material can enliven a presentation by making your main points more vivid or meaningful to the audience. Notice how one attorney added interest to a summary aimed at discrediting his opponent's restatement of evidence:

> It seems that when Abe Lincoln was a young trial lawyer in Sangamon County, Illinois, he was arguing a case with a lawyer whose version of the facts came more from his imagination than the testimony. Lincoln, in his argument, turned on him and said:
>
> "Tell me, sir, how many legs has a sheep got?" "Why, four, of course," the fellow answered. "And if I called his tail a leg, then how many legs would that sheep have?" Lincoln asked. The answer came, "Then he'd have five." "No!" Lincoln roared, pounding the jury rail; "he'd still have just *four* legs. *Calling* his tail a leg won't make it a leg. Now let's look at the actual testimony and see how many tails you've been calling legs."[2]

Proof

Besides adding clarity and interest, supporting material can provide evidence for your claims and make your presentation more convincing. A speaker might use supporting materials this way to back up the claim "Employer-sponsored day care can boost productivity as well as help parents":

> A survey of Union Bank employees in California showed the value of on-site, employer-sponsored day care. Turnover of employees using the bank's on-site center was only 2.2 percent, less than one quarter of the 9.9 percent turnover for workers who used other forms of day care. And that's not all: Employees using the day care center were absent from work an average of 1.7 days a year less than other parents of young children. This sort of center can even get parents back to work more quickly after a new baby is born: Mothers who used the bank's center took maternity leaves that were 1.2 weeks shorter than other parents.[3]

VERBAL SUPPORT

As Table 12-1 shows, many kinds of supporting material can be used to add interest, clarity, or proof to a presentation. The most common supports for business and professional presentations are examples, stories, statistics, comparisons, citations, and visual aids.

Examples

Examples are brief illustrations that back up or explain a point. A speaker arguing for an enhanced package of employee benefits could cite examples of companies that already provide a variety of perks:

- Gasket maker Fel-Pro of Skokie, Illinois, contributes $3,500 annually for up to four years of college tuition for employees' children, along with a $1,000 savings bond for the birth of a baby and free income tax preparation.
- Anheuser-Busch employees take home two free cases of beer a month.

- Employees of Ben & Jerry's take home three free pints of ice cream a day.
- G.T. Water Products of Moorpark, California, has opened a tuition-free Montessori-based school for the children of its employees.
- Apple Computer gives its employees six-week paid sabbaticals every five years.
- Mary Kay Cosmetics decorates its cafeteria tables with fresh flowers and white tablecloths, and provides perfume and makeup in its restaurants.[4]

Likewise, a marketing consultant explaining how the name of a business can attract or repel customers could back up the claim by citing examples of clever names:

- Absolute Rubbish, an Oregon waste disposal and recycling company
- Totally Twisted, a Maryland pretzel company
- Rent-a-Nerd computer consultants of Virginia
- Now Showing, a movie theater turned lingerie shop in Oklahoma
- Access/Abilities, a California firm that helps people with disabilities
- Holy Cow Vegetarian Foods in Oregon[5]

The same consultant could show how poor names can discourage business:

- Coffin Air Service
- Big Bill's Plumbing

TABLE 12-1 Types of Verbal Support

Type	Definition	Use	Comments
Example	Brief reference that illustrates a point	Clarify Add interest (if sufficient number given)	Usually best in groups of two or more Precede or follow with story
Story	Detailed account of an incident	Clarify Add interest Prove (factual only)	Adapt to audience Must clearly support thesis Tell at appropriate length
Statistics	Numerical representations of point	Clarify Prove Add interest (when combined with other forms of support)	Link to audience's frame of reference Use sparingly Round off Supplement with visuals, handouts
Comparisons	Show how one idea resembles another	Clarify Add interest (figurative) Prove (literal)	Tailor familiar item to audience Make sure comparison is valid
Citations	Opinion of expert or articulate source	Clarify Add interest (sometimes) Prove	May be paraphrased or read verbatim Cite source Use sources credible to audience Follow up with restatement or explanation

- Bland Farms, a mail order food company
- Poo-Ping Thai restaurant[6]

In many cases you don't need to look outside your own experience for examples to back up a point. Union members claiming that "management cares more about buildings and grounds than employees" might back up their claim by offering examples:

> "We keep hearing that 'employees are our most important asset,' yet we don't see dollars reflecting that philosophy. In the two and a half years since our last pay raise, we have seen the following physical improvements at this site alone: a new irrigation system for the landscaping, renovation of the corporate offices, expansion of the data processing wing, resurfacing of all the parking lots, and a new entrance to the building. Now all those improvements are helpful, but they show that buildings and grounds are more important than people."

When they are used to prove a point, examples are most effective when several are given together. If you are supporting the claim that you are capable of taking on a more challenging job, it is best to remind your boss of several tasks you have handled well. After all, a single example could be an isolated instance or a lucky fluke.

Stories

Stories illustrate a point by describing an incident in some detail. They come in two categories: hypothetical and factual. *Hypothetical stories* are fictional accounts that might easily have happened. They allow you to create material that perfectly illustrates the point you want to make. C. J. Silas, president of Phillips Petroleum Company, used this hypothetical story to illustrate his thesis that government regulation of natural gas is unfair:

> Put yourself in the place of a small gas producer. Imagine that you have an Uncle Harry who dies and leaves you a couple of gas wells in Kansas. If those are old wells—discovered before 1977—you might only be getting 40 cents an mcf for your gas.
>
> Your neighbor, on the other hand, might have a new well right across the fence—drilled just last year. Even though he's producing gas identical to yours, he can probably sell it for ten times as much. Both you and your neighbor may want to drill for more gas. But only one of you is in a good economic position to do so. That's how government controls discourage exploration.[7]

Hypothetical stories like this one are useful because they get the audience involved in the idea you are developing: "Imagine yourself . . . ," "Suppose that you were . . . ," "What would you do if. . . ." Besides being involving, hypothetical stories allow you to create a situation that illustrates exactly the point you are trying to make. You can adjust details, create dialogue, and use figures that support your case. But your account will be effective only if it is believable.

Factual stories can also add interest and clarity. The story below, from a frustrated consumer, illustrates the thesis that many businesses are more interested in making a sale than in supporting their products after the deal is closed. Notice how the last sentence restates the main idea so that the point of the story is clear:

> Last Tuesday I decided to call the automobile dealership. There were two numbers listed in the phone book, one for "Sales," the other for "Service." I asked the service manager if I could bring my car in the following Saturday. Service managers always have a way of making you feel unwanted, and he seemed pleased to be able to tell me that they were closed Saturday and wouldn't be able to take me until a week from Thursday.
>
> I didn't make a date. Instead I called the other number, under "Sales." "Are you open Saturday?" I asked. "Yes, sir," the cheery voice said at the other end of the phone. "We're here Saturdays from eight in the morning till nine in the evening, and Sundays from noon until six."
>
> Now, if I can *buy* a car on Saturday, why can't I get one *fixed* on Saturday? What's going on here anyway? I think I know what's going on, of course. We're *selling* things better than we're *making* them, that's what's going on.[8]

While both factual and hypothetical stories can make a presentation clearer and more interesting, only the factual type can prove a point:

> "Cutting the payroll by using temporary employees sounds like a good idea, but it has problems. Listen to what happened when we tried it at the place I used to work. . . ."
>
> "I'm sure Wes can handle the job. Let me tell you what happened last year when we assigned him to manage the Westco account. . . ."
>
> "You might think life insurance isn't necessary for a young, healthy person like you, but remember Dale Crandall, the linebacker from State? Well, he was about as healthy as they come, but. . . ."

Both hypothetical and factual stories gain effectiveness because they are interesting. You can add interest to your accounts by following several guidelines. First, the story should be suited to your audience members. Will they be familiar with the situation you're describing? Will they care about it? Second, your story should support your point. An amusing story that doesn't support your thesis will just distract your listeners. Finally, be sure the story is the right length. Don't spin out a five-minute yarn to make a minor point, and don't rush through a story that will win your audience over.

Statistics

Statistics are numbers used to represent an idea. Most statistics are collections of examples reduced to numerical form for clarity. If you were arguing that there was a serious manufacturing problem with a new product line, describing one or two dissatisfied customers would not prove that the problem went beyond the usual "acceptable" rate of error in manufacturing. The following statement, though, would constitute proof: "Our return rate on the new line is just over 40 percent—as opposed to the usual rate of 5 percent—and of all those returns, four-fifths are related to a flaw in the gear assembly."

Statistics are probably the most common form of support in business presentations. They are used to measure the size of market segments, sales trends, decreasing or increasing profits, changes in costs, and many other aspects of business. When handled well, statistics are especially strong proof because they are firmly grounded in fact and because they show that the speaker is well informed. John D. Ong of the B. F. Goodrich Company used statistics to back up his claim that the industrial capability of the United States is being overtaken by other countries:

> The rise of competition from Japan, Europe, Asia and Latin America has been so pervasive that I think many of us have lost sight of just how dramatic it's been. Less than 20 years ago, the United States manufactured about 50 percent of the world's television sets, 90 percent of the world's radios, 76 percent of the automobiles, and 47 percent of the world's steel. Now we produce barely 6 percent of the world's TV sets and radios combined, 28 percent of the cars, and 20 percent of the world's steel.[9]

Despite their potential effectiveness, poorly used statistics can spoil a presentation. One common mistake is to bury an audience under an avalanche of numbers like this speaker did at an annual stockholders' meeting:

> Last year was an exciting one for our company. We earned $6.02 per share on a net income of $450 million, up from $4.63 per share on income of $412 million in the preceding year. This increase came in part from a one-time gain of $13 million from the sale of common stock to New Ventures group, our research and development subsidiary. Excluding this one-time gain, we increased our earnings per share 5.8 percent in the recent year, and we increased our net income 6.5 percent.

These numbers would be very appropriate in a printed annual report, but when a speaker rattles them off to an audience one after another, there is little chance of following them. Rather than smothering your listeners with detail, you can provide a few key numbers. (If backup information is important, you can supply it in written materials accompanying your presentation.) Notice how the following appeal uses figures to highlight the most persuasive reasons for extending a business trip, while making details available for anyone who might be interested:

> "Believe it or not, it's actually $600 cheaper for us to spend the weekend in San Francisco than to fly home on Friday after the conference. We'd save more on airfare by staying over Saturday night than the cost of meals and hotels. The difference comes from the plane tickets: $598 per person if we return on Friday versus $249 if we stay over until Sunday. Coupled with cheaper weekend rates at the hotel, we come out ahead. I've worked out the details on this fact sheet, which I'll circulate now."

In addition to restricting the amount of statistical information you convey, it is usually best to simplify that information by rounding off numbers. It's easier to understand "almost two-thirds" than it is to absorb "64.3 percent," and "almost twice the cost" is easier to grasp than is "Item A costs $65.18, while item B runs $127.15."

Besides having too many numbers, statistic-laden presentations are too dry for all but the most dedicated and involved audiences to handle. When you are speaking to a group of nonspecialists, it's important to link your figures to a frame of reference the group will understand. Notice how the following statistics (presented in the form of examples) give new impact to the old principle that "time is money":

> For a manager who is earning $30,000 a year, wasting one hour a day costs the company $3,750 a year. For a secretary at $20,000, fifteen minutes at each of two coffee breaks costs $1,427.50. And for a $100,000-a-year executive, a two-hour lunch costs the company an extra $12,500 annually.[10]

When a presentation contains more than a few statistics, you will probably need to use visual aids to explain them: numbers alone are simply too confusing to understand. The material on pages 346–364 offers guidelines about how to present statistical data graphically.

Comparisons

Comparisons can make a point by showing how one idea resembles another. Some comparisons—called analogies—are *figurative.* They compare items from an unfamiliar area with items from a familiar one. By considering a few examples, you can appreciate the value of figurative comparisons to add clarity and interest to a presentation:

> We think that sending people to one company for loans, another for insurance, and a third for brokerage services makes about as much sense as sending them to one store for eggs, a second for meat, and a third for bread.[11]

> The cheap special fares advertised by some airlines are misleading, since the "mouse print" at the bottom of the page lists so many restrictions. No food chain could get away with advertising prime rib at $3 a pound, limited to six roasts per store, available only when bought in pairs Tuesday through Thursday afternoons.[12]

> The general-purpose home computer is a quaint anachronism and a totally bogus idea. It's like a Swiss Army knife. It may do a lot of things, but it does none of them very well.[13]

By linking the familiar with the unfamiliar, figurative analogies can help listeners understand concepts that would otherwise be mystifying. Consider how a series of familiar concepts can explain the potentially arcane differences between computer networks:

> The physical layout of a computer network—the way various systems are connected—is called its topology. The most common network topologies are bus, ring, and star.

> A bus topology is like a freeway with many on and off ramps. It has a common path (the bus) on which all data travels. Each device on the network can tap into this bus.
>
> Ring topologies are similar to bus configurations, but the ends are tied together so that data travels in a circle unless it's diverted to one of the devices attached to the network.
>
> Star configurations resemble a spider. The wires connecting the various devices with a central point represent the legs of the spider. The phone company's central office concept is an example of a star configuration.[14]

Other comparisons are *literal,* linking similar items from two categories. An account executive might use this sort of comparison to argue, "We need to spend more of our advertising budget on direct mail. That approach worked wonders on the NBT campaign, and I think it can do the same for us here." One critic of the banking industry used literal comparisons to show the abysmal compensation for most bank tellers:

> If the tellers at your local bank seem a little surly these days, they've got a good reason. A comparison of their wages with those of other workers shows that they are among the worst paid workers around, according to a recent survey by the local consulting firm of Towers Perrin Foster and Crosby. Tellers earn about $16,200 annually: about $900 less than the take-home pay for mail clerks, $1,700 less than what the average custodian earns, and it's more than $6,000 less than what a computer operator brings home. When compared to secretaries, bank tellers' pay is pathetic: almost half of the $31,800 the average executive secretary earned in the 90 companies surveyed.

Whenever you propose adopting a policy or using an idea because it worked well somewhere else, you are using comparisons as proof. The strength of this proof depends on how clearly you can establish the similarity between the items you are comparing.

Comparisons are often an ideal way to clarify a potentially confusing idea. Kathryn Kelly, an environmental toxicologist, used this approach to convince residents of a small Alaskan community that the dioxin emissions of a garbage incinerator her company wanted to build weren't harmful. The risks of dioxin exposure are usually compared with the chances of getting cancer from smoking or from carcinogens in foods like peanut butter or charbroiled steaks. But Kelly didn't think the townspeople would relate to these examples, so she used a comparison that struck closer to home. In her presentation she pointed out that the 400 wood stoves in town were emitting dioxins equivalent to 1,200 incinerators—and that her company wanted to build only one.[15]

Whether their purpose is to add clarity, interest, or proof, comparisons should possess two characteristics: First, the familiar part of comparisons should be well known to the audience. For instance, it would be a mistake to say "Jumbo certificates of deposit are similar to treasury bills in several ways" if your listeners do not know anything about treasury bills. Second, you should be sure your comparisons are valid. You would be stretching a point if you tried to discourage employee abuse of the copying machine by claiming,

"Using the machine for personal papers is a crime, just as much as robbery or assault." A closer match is both more valid and effective: "You wouldn't help yourself to spare change from a cash register; everybody with a conscience knows that would be a case of petty theft. But using the copying machine for personal papers costs the company, just as surely as if the money came out of the cash register."

Citations

Citations are a way to let others who are authoritative or articulate make a point more effectively than you could do on your own. Some citations add clarity and impact. You might, for example, add punch to a talk explaining the difficulties of cutting advertising costs by citing the famous remark of Alex Osborne, founder of one of the nation's largest advertising agencies: "Only half my advertising budget does any good. I just don't know which half." Likewise, you could emphasize the importance of getting agreements in writing by quoting movie producer Sam Goldwyn: "A verbal contract isn't worth the paper it's written on."

Other citations help build a persuasive case: "Nancy told me yesterday that we ought to add another 10 percent to our projected expenses," or "The June 28 issue of *Forbes* ran an article stating that the demand for home videotape rentals will triple in the next six years."

You can use citations most effectively by following the guidelines below.

Cite the Source in a Way That Adds to the Credibility of Your Presentation. Notice how each of the citations in this section introduces the source, and consider how much less effective they would be without this sort of introduction.

Cite Sources That Have Credibility with Your Audience. Citing Karl Marx about the abuse of workers won't impress an audience of Republican manufacturers, while a similar message from a *Wall Street Journal* article might be effective.

SKILL BUILDER

What types of support introduced so far in this chapter would you use to add interest, clarity, and proof to the following points?

1. Tuition costs are keeping promising students out of college.
2. Textbooks are (are not) overpriced.
3. Timely payment of bills is in the customer's best interest.
4. Companies are helping themselves as well as employees by sponsoring and subsidizing exercise programs during work hours.
5. A liberal-arts education can benefit one's career—better in many ways than technical training.

Paraphrase Lengthy or Confusing Citations. Some citations are too long, boring, or confusing to read word for word. In these cases, you can still take advantage of the material by paraphrasing it, as in this example:

> "Before we go overboard on the idea of flexible scheduling, it's important to consider the research conducted recently by Professors Graham Staines of Rutgers University and Joseph Pleck of Wellesley College. In a survey of over a thousand employees, they found that people who worked modified schedules were not as happy with their family lives as were people who worked a traditional Monday through Friday, nine-to-five shift."

Restate the Point of Long Citations. If your citation has taken a minute or two to deliver, summarize the point it makes before moving on:

> "After hearing Roberta's figures, you can see that our advertising dollars are well spent."
>
> "You can see from this research that there are hidden costs in this proposal."
>
> "Customer letters like those make it clear that we need to improve our service."

VISUAL AIDS

The old cliché is true: A picture often *is* worth a thousand words. That is why charts, diagrams, and other graphic aids are part of most business presentations.

> Researchers have verified what good speakers have always known intuitively: Using visual aids makes a presentation more effective. In a recent study, two groups of business students watched videotaped presentations describing upcoming time management seminars. One group saw a version of the talk with no visual support, while the other saw the same talk with a number of high quality visuals. After the presentation, the audience was asked about their willingness to enroll in the time management course and about their opinion of the speaker they had just viewed.
>
> Audiences who saw the presentation with visuals were clearly more impressed than those who saw the same talk with no visual support. They planned to spend 16.4 percent more time and 26.4 percent more money on the time management seminar being promoted. They also viewed the speaker as more clear, concise, professional, persuasive, and interesting.[16]

Well-designed graphics are also easier to understand than words alone. A chart listing a point-by-point comparison of two products is easier to follow than a detailed narrative. A plummeting sales curve tells the story more eloquently than any words. You can appreciate the value of visuals to make a point quickly and clearly by reading the following text alone and then seeing how the chart in Figure 12-1 makes the information so much clearer:

> "The power of tax-free accumulation is tremendous. Suppose you invested $10,000 at 10 percent. If you were taxed at a rate of 33 percent, your investment would grow to $35,236 over twenty years. If you were in the 28 percent tax bracket, your original nest egg would grow to $40,169. But with a tax-free investment, the original $10,000 would appreciate to a value of $67,275."

Visuals can help make complicated statistics easier for you to explain and easier for your listeners to understand. Besides increasing the clarity of your material, visuals will make your presentations more interesting. For example, investment brokers often use an array of well-prepared charts, tables, models, and so on, to add variety to information that would be deadly dull without it.

Visuals can also boost your image in ways that extend beyond the presentation itself. A professional display of visuals labels you as a professional person—a candidate for recognition in the future by superiors and the public. Finally, visuals can make your information more memorable. Researchers have discovered that audiences recall far more information when it is presented both verbally and visually than when it is presented in only one way:[17]

Method	Recall after 3 Hours (in %)	Recall after 3 Days (in %)
Verbal only	70	10
Visual only	72	20
Verbal and visual	85	65

FIGURE 12-1 A visual aid is often clearer and more dramatic than words alone.

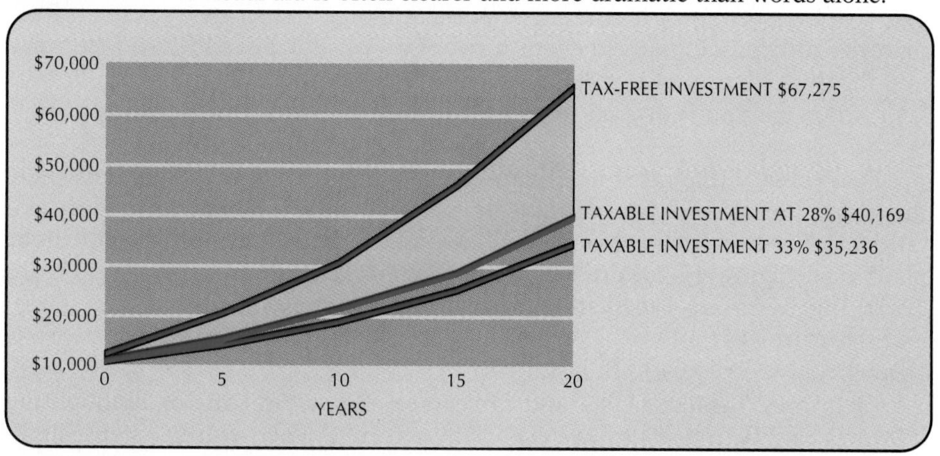

Visual aids perform many useful functions:

- They can *show how things look.* An architect might use a model or an artist's sketch to describe a project to potential clients, and an advertising director could use photographs of a new product as part of a campaign.
- They can *show how things work.* An engineer could include diagrams as part of the instructions for a piece of equipment, and a sales representative could use a model to show how a boat is designed for speed and safety.
- They can *show how things relate to one another.* An organizational chart provides a clear picture of the reporting relationships in a company; a flowchart pictures the steps necessary to get a job done.
- They can *emphasize important points.* You might use a chart to show customers the features of a new product or develop a graph to show the performance of a stock.

Types of Visual Aids

As a speaker, you can choose from a wide array of visual aids to make your presentations more effective. You won't use them all every time you speak, but sooner or later you will, in your presentations, use almost every type described in the following pages.

Objects and Models. Sometimes the object you are discussing or a realistic model is the best kind of support. This is especially true in training sessions and in some types of selling, where hands-on experience is essential. It's difficult to imagine learning how to operate a piece of equipment without actually giving it a try, and few customers would buy an expensive, unfamiliar piece of merchandise without seeing it demonstrated.

Photographs. Photographs can be the most effective means of illustrating a variety of images that need literal representation: an architectural firm's best work, a corporation's management team, or a stylish new product. Photographs also provide an excellent form of proof. For instance, an insurance investigator's picture of a wrecked auto may be all that exists of a car months later, when a claim is argued in court.

Diagrams. Diagrams are abstract, two-dimensional drawings that show the important properties of objects without being completely representational. Types of diagrams you might use in presentations include floor plans (see Figure 12-2), drawings (see Figure 12-3), and maps (see Figure 12-4). Diagrams are excellent for conveying information about size, shape, and structure.

Lists and Tables. Lists and tables are effective means of highlighting key facts and figures. They are especially effective when you list steps, high-

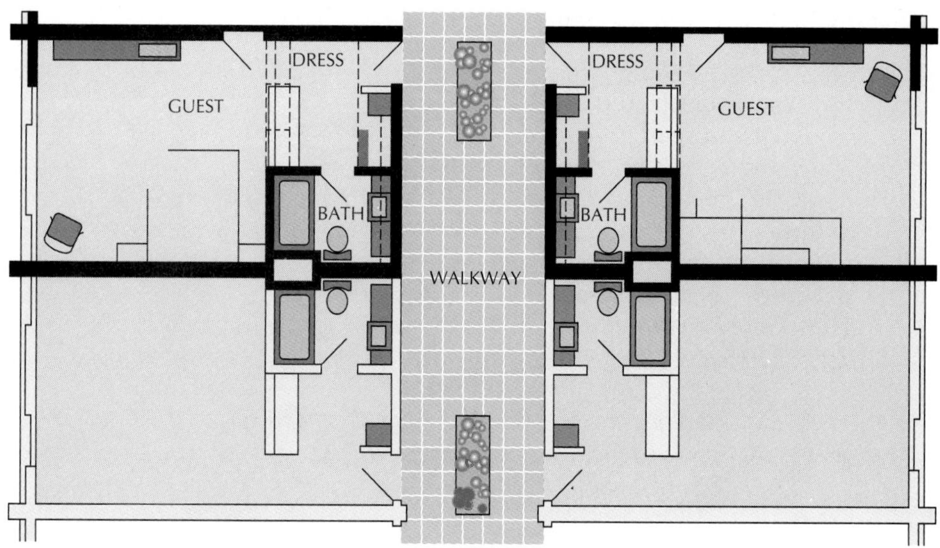

FIGURE 12-2 Floor plan.

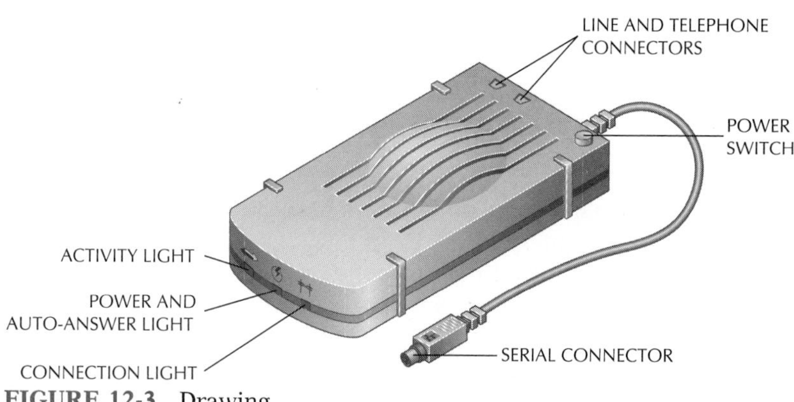

FIGURE 12-3 Drawing.

light features, or compare related facts: advantages and disadvantages, current and past performance, your product versus a competitor's, and so on. The table in Figure 12-5 clearly lists the rate of return for several certificates of deposit offered by one bank. A sales manager might use a similar chart to compare this year's sales performance and last year's in several regions. A personnel officer explaining the advantages and disadvantages of two different health insurance plans available to employees might use a list or table to help individual employees decide which plan might work best for them.

Amateur speakers often assume they need only enlarge tables from a written report in an oral presentation. In practice, this approach rarely works. Most written tables are far too detailed and difficult to understand to be use-

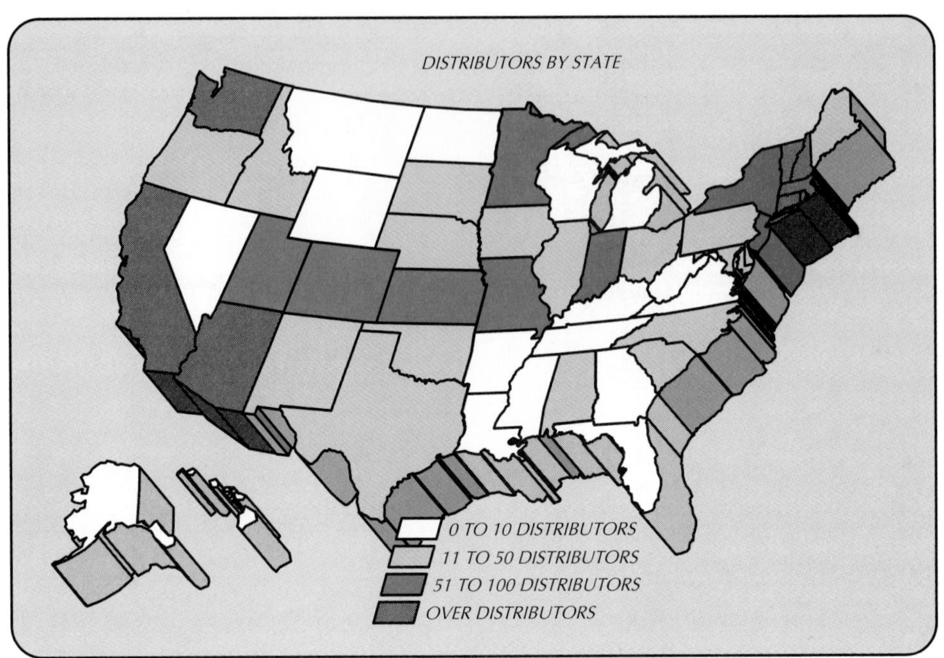

FIGURE 12-4
Map.

ful to a group of listeners. As you design lists and tables, remember the following points:

- *Keep the visual aid simple.* List only highlights. Use only key words or phrases, never full sentences.
- *Use numbered and/or bulleted lists to emphasize key points.* Numbered lists suggest ranking or steps in a process, while bulleted lists work best for items that are equally important.

FIGURE 12-5
Table.

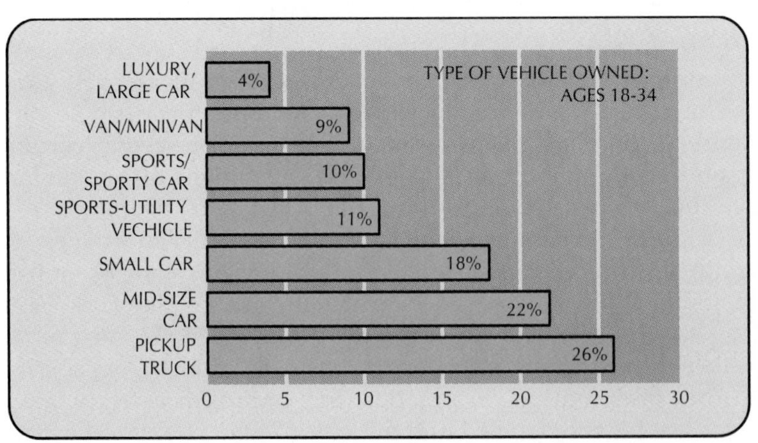

- *Use text sparingly.* If you need more than eight lines of text, create two or more tables. Lines of text should never exceed twenty-five characters across, including spaces.
- *Use large type.* Make sure that the words and numbers are large enough to be read by everyone in the audience.
- *Enhance the list's or table's readability.* Careful layout and generous use of white space will make it easy to read.

Pie Charts. ***Pie charts*** like the one in Figure 12-6 illustrate component percentages of a single item. Frequently, they are used to show how money is spent. They also can illustrate the allocation of resources. For example, a personnel director might use a pie chart to show the percentage of employees who work in each division of the company.

Many computer graphics programs make it easy to produce attractive and dramatic pie charts by tilting the figure or removing one segment. While this highlighting can attract interest, it also risks distorting the data.

Follow these guidelines when constructing pie charts:

- *Place the segment you want to emphasize at the top-center,* twelve o'clock position on the circle. When you are not emphasizing any segments, organize the wedges from largest to smallest, beginning at twelve o'clock with the largest one.
- *Label each segment,* either inside or outside the figure.
- *List the percentage for each segment* as well as its label.

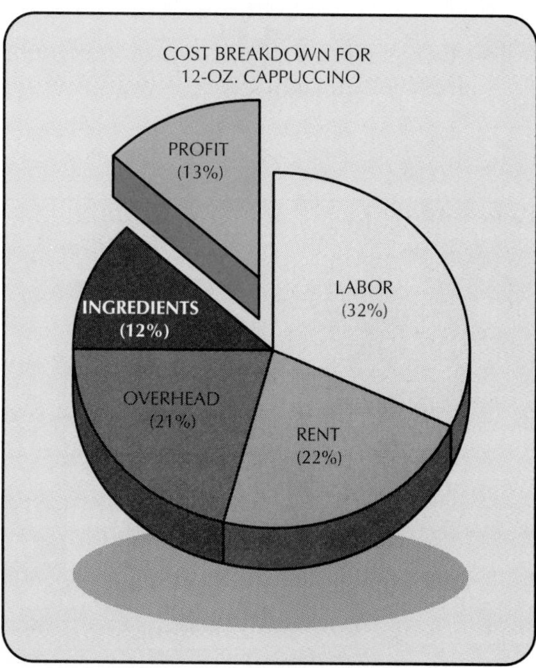

FIGURE 12-6
Pie chart.

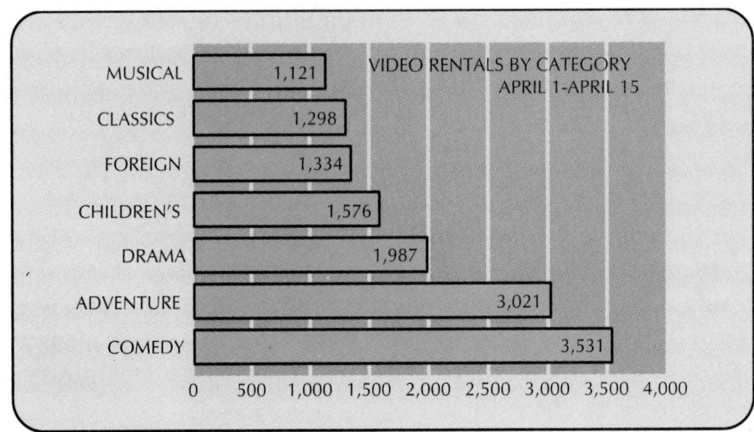

FIGURE 12-7
Simple bar chart.

Bar and Column Charts. Simple ***bar charts*** like the one shown in Figure 12-7 compare the value of several items: the productivity of several employees, the relative amount of advertising money spent on different media, and so on. Subdivided charts like the one in Figure 12-8 compare the component amounts of several items, such as the relative amounts of profit and cost for several products.

Simple ***column charts*** like the one in Figure 12-9 reflect changes in a single item over time. Multiple-column charts like the one in Figure 12-10 compare several items over time.

Several tips will help you design effective bar and column charts:

- *Always represent time on the horizontal axis of your chart,* running from left to right.

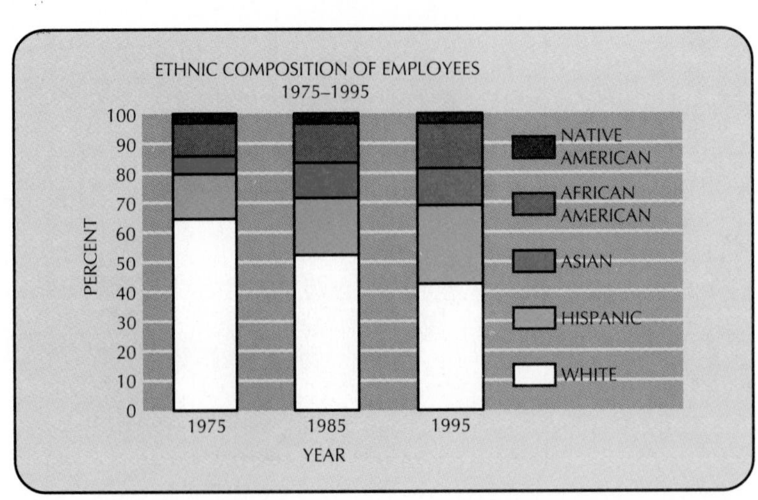

FIGURE 12-8
Subdivided column chart.

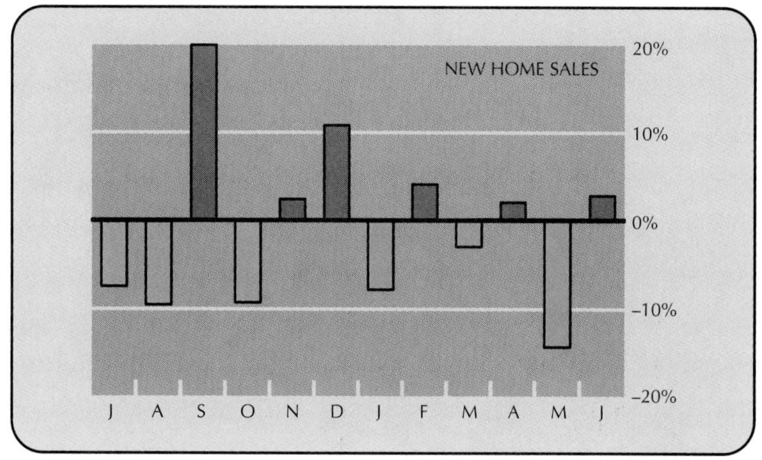

FIGURE 12-9 Simple column chart.

- *Arrange the bars in a sequence that best suits your purpose.* You might choose to order them from high to low, from low to high, in alphabetical order, or in order of importance.
- *Make sure the numerical values represented are clear.* This may mean putting the numbers next to bars or columns. In other cases, the figures will fit inside the bars. In a few instances, the scale on the axes will make numbering each bar unnecessary.

Pictograms. ***Pictograms*** are artistic variations of bar, column, or pie charts. As Figure 12-11 shows, pictograms are more interesting than ordinary bars. This makes them useful in presentations aimed at lay audiences such as the general public. Pictograms are often not mathematically exact, however, which makes them less suited for reports that require precise data.

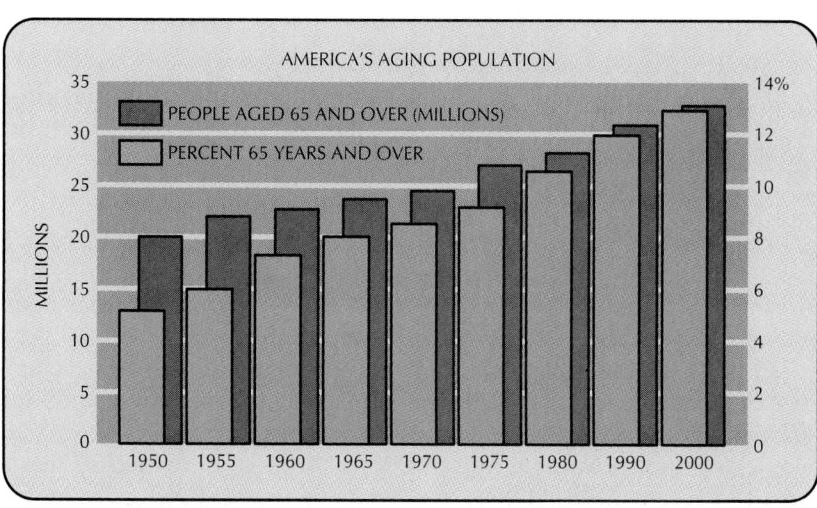

FIGURE 12-10 Multiple-column chart.

FIGURE 12-11
Pictogram.

Graphs. ***Graphs*** show the correlation between two quantities. They are ideally suited to showing trends, such as growth or decline in sales over time. They can also represent a large amount of data without becoming cluttered. Single-line graphs like the one in Figure 12-12 show trends. Multiple-line graphs like the one in Figure 12-13 show relationships among two or more trends. Notice in Figure 12-14 how identical data can be manipulated by adjusting the horizontal and vertical axes.

Media for Presenting Visual Aids

Choosing the most advantageous way to present your visual aids is just as important as picking the right type. The best photograph, chart, or diagram will flop if it isn't displayed effectively.

Flip Charts and Poster Board. ***Flip charts*** consist of a large pad of paper attached to an easel. You reveal visuals on a flip chart one at a time by turning the pages. You can also produce visuals on rigid poster board, which you can display on the same sort of easel.

Flip charts and poster board are commonly used to display visuals in business presentations. In fact, most conference and meeting rooms in business offices and convention hotels are equipped with an easel to show them. Salespeople use them to make presentations to clients. Marketing managers use them to present new plans to upper management. Production managers use them to map out schedules.

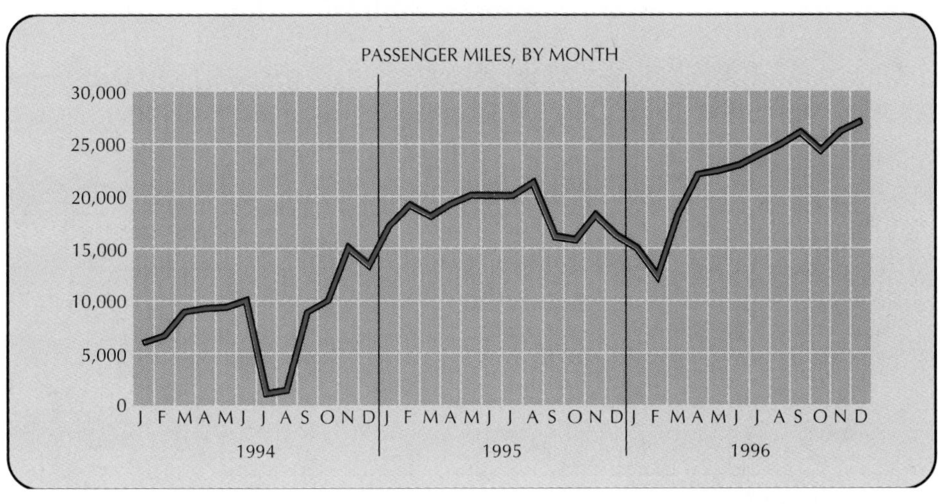

FIGURE 12-12 Single-line graph.

A major advantage of flip charts and poster displays is that they are relatively simple to prepare and easy to use. You can create them with familiar materials: pens, rulers, and so on. They are relatively portable (most easels collapse into a carrying case) and easy to set up. They don't require electrical equipment, which can break down.

Despite these advantages, flip charts and poster boards have several potential drawbacks: First, they may be too small for some members of a large audience to see easily. Second, they are relatively fragile and can become shabby after being handled in presentations. Finally, posters and large charts are clumsy. They do not fit in a briefcase or under an airplane seat, and they make it awkward to perform simple maneuvers like shaking hands or catching a taxi.

SKILL BUILDER

Practice your skill at developing visual aids by doing one of the following activities:

1. Develop a chart or graph showing the overall changes in the demographic characteristics (age, sex, and so on) of your student body over the past ten years.
2. The local chamber of commerce has hired you to compile graphic exhibits that will be used in presentations to encourage people to visit and settle in your area. Design materials reflecting the following information:
   a. Average monthly rainfall
   b. Month-to-month variations in temperature
   c. Days with sunshine

   If you believe that these figures would *discourage* an audience, you may choose data that paint an appealing picture of a different area.
3. Develop three visual aids that could be used to introduce new students to registration procedures used in your school.
4. Collect examples of each type of verbal and visual support described in this chapter. Comment on how effectively each example follows the guidelines in the text. Describe how each one should be adapted for use in an oral presentation.

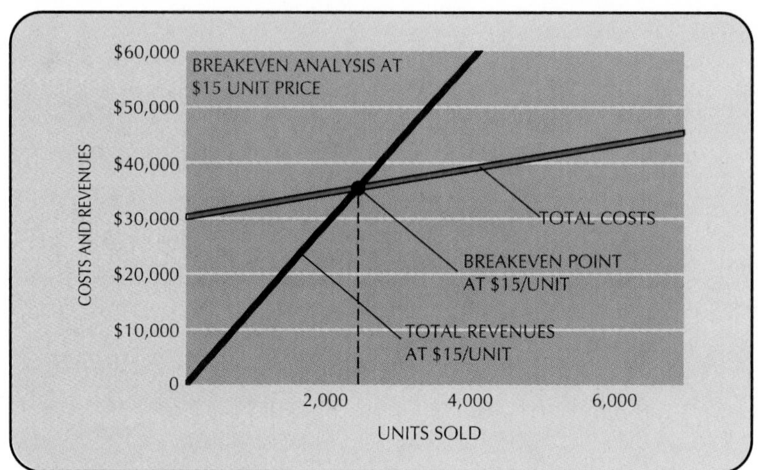

FIGURE 12-13 Multiple-line graph.

Transparencies. ***Transparencies*** are clear sheets that are used with an overhead projector to cast an image on a screen. They are frequently the visual aid of choice when the audience is too large for flip charts or poster displays. You can create original images with special pens or reproduce visuals from other sources by using a standard office copying machine equipped with special acetate sheets. (Most copy shops are equipped for this job.) Color copying machines can even transform a glossy magazine photo or slide into an 8½-by 11-inch transparency, allowing you to mix photos and other types of print exhibits without forcing you to use a slide projector as well as an overhead machine.

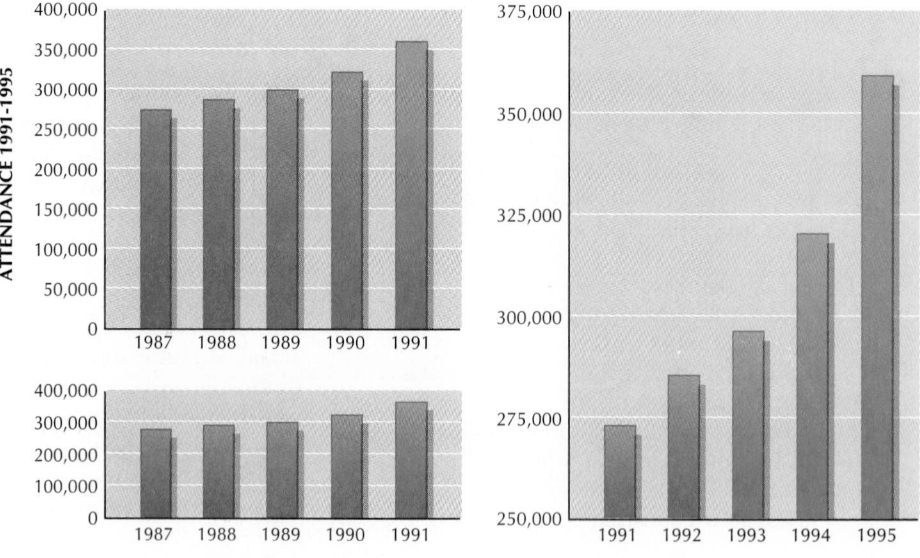

FIGURE 12-14 The same data can be distorted by varying the horizontal and vertical size and axes of a graph.

Transparencies have several advantages: They can be produced quickly—in seconds with the right copying machine. They are often easier to create than other types of visuals, since you can copy professional-looking visuals from other sources instead of creating images from scratch. (Be sure to give credit to the original creator.) They can be projected to a large size for all members of a large audience to see. They are visible in a lighted room. Using special pens, you can draw on them as you speak, underlining key words, circling important numbers, completing graphs, and so on. After the presentation, you can erase your additions and reuse the same sheets in future presentations. They are easy to store and don't wear out like flip charts and poster boards.

Transparencies also suffer from several drawbacks: Most important, they require a projector that isn't always easy to find and may not work on the day of your presentation. (Many speakers have been thwarted by a burned-out light bulb.) In addition, the audience or speaker may have to be positioned in a special way so that the projector doesn't block anyone's view (see Figure 12-15 for room layouts). Finally, the projection screen may need to be mounted at an angle to prevent a "keystone" distortion of the image (see Figure 12-16).

Presentations using an overhead projector will be most effective when you remember several points:

- *Show transparencies only when you are discussing them.* Between transparencies, shut off the projector.
- *Never remove or replace images while the projector is on.* Position a transparency, and then turn on the machine. Turn it off, and then remove the sheet.

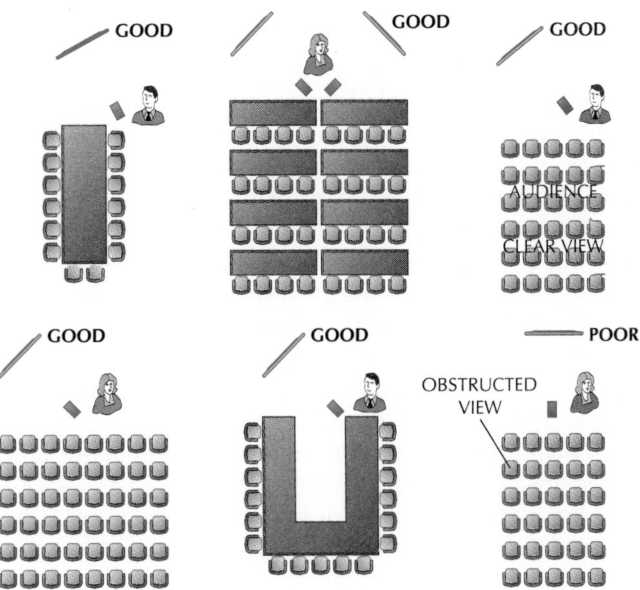

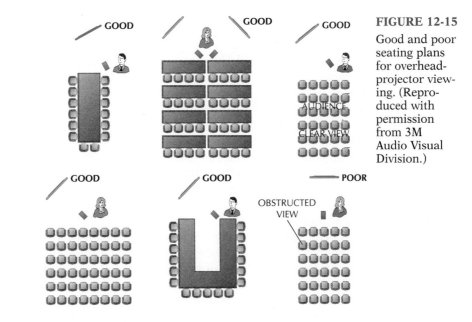

FIGURE 12-15 Good and poor seating plans for overhead-projector viewing. (Reproduced with permission from 3M Audio Visual Division.)

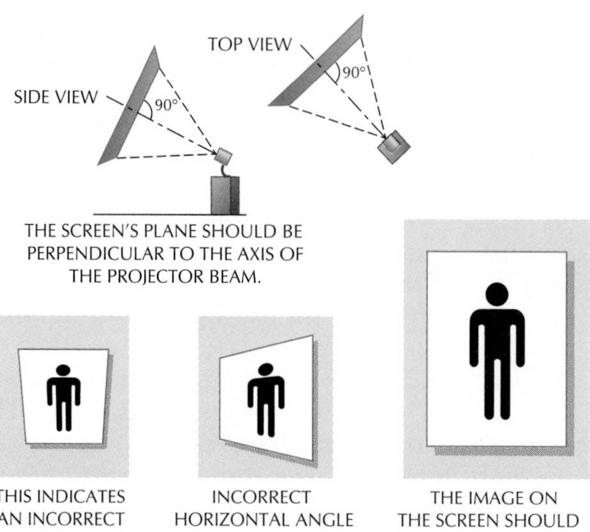
TOP VIEW
SIDE VIEW
90°
90°
THE SCREEN'S PLANE SHOULD BE PERPENDICULAR TO THE AXIS OF THE PROJECTOR BEAM.
THIS INDICATES AN INCORRECT VERTICAL ANGLE.
INCORRECT HORIZONTAL ANGLE WILL PRODUCE AN IMAGE LIKE THIS.
THE IMAGE ON THE SCREEN SHOULD LOOK LIKE THIS.

FIGURE 12-16
Proper viewing angles for overhead projector. (Reproduced with permission from 3M Audio Visual Division.)

- *Consider using a piece of paper or cardboard to cover the parts of a sheet you haven't discussed yet.* As you come to each point, move the cover to reveal the new information. This technique prevents your audience from getting ahead of you.
- *Face the audience as you speak.* Use a pointer to refer to the transparency as it rests on the glass stage of the projector; don't turn your back on the audience and point to the screen.

Slides. Although they are projected on a screen like overhead transparencies, slides have different uses and properties. They work best when you want to show an actual photographic image. In fact, they are often far superior to photos printed on paper since they can be easily seen by even a large audience. They are inexpensive and can be produced quickly—in an hour or a couple of days. They are easy to edit: you can add, delete, and rearrange them to suit the needs of a particular presentation.

New software programs and services make it easy to transfer computer-generated visuals onto slides so that they can be mixed with traditional photographs in a presentation. Companies with a high demand for this service can purchase slide recorders, which connect to a computer and produce transparencies almost immediately. Low-volume users who can't justify the cost of a slide recorder can send floppy disks containing their files to service bureaus that will convert the files into slides.[18]

The biggest drawback of slides is the need for a darkened room. While the slides are being shown, the speaker is only a shadowy figure to the audience. This setup makes it easy for minds to wander or for listeners to doze off. If you do use slides:

- *Keep the show brief.* The distraction factor will be smallest if you don't keep the room dark for a long time. Don't dwell on each slide. Everyone has suffered through a seemingly endless narrative of boring vacation slides, and the same abuses can occur in business presentations.
- *Use a remote-control device with a long cord.* Stand next to the screen during your show, not next to the projector. When you become a disembodied voice at the back of the room, you are inviting the audience to drift off.
- *Talk to your listeners, not to the screen.* Stand to one side, and use a pointer to direct their attention. Never turn your back on your audience.

Handouts. Handouts provide a permanent record of your ideas. Intricate features of a product, names and phone numbers, or "do's and don'ts" are easier to recall when your listeners have a printed record of them. Handouts also enable you to give your audience more details than you want to talk about in your presentation. You might, for instance, mention the highlights of a sales period or briefly outline the technical features of a new product and then refer your listeners to a handout for further information.[19]

You can use handouts to reduce or eliminate your listeners' need to take notes. If you put key ideas and figures on a handout, listeners' attention will be focused on you instead of on their notebooks—and you'll be sure their notes are accurate. Some speakers use an "electronic blackboard," a plastic write-and-wipe board that can produce handout-size copies of what you've written on the board.

The biggest problem with handouts is that they can be distracting. The activity that accompanies passing around papers interrupts the flow of your presentation. Once the handout is distributed, you'll have to compete with it for your audience's attention. For this reason, it's better to distribute handouts *after* you've finished speaking. If printed material has to be introduced during your presentation, tell your listeners when to begin referring to it and when to stop: "Let's take a look at the budget on the pink sheet in your folders." "Now that we've examined the budget, let me direct your attention to the chart up here."

Computerized Displays. You have several options for displaying images produced by a computer.

> Don't start with the idea, "I am going to give a slide talk; I am going to make a videotape; or I am going to put on a multimedia presentation."
>
> You don't start there! You start with your aim, your goal, your objective. What do you want to do with the talk? If it calls for slides, fine. If television is the best medium to make the point, okay. But don't go for the medium first and the message later.
>
> John R. Bonée, *A Few Age-Old Principles of Effective Oratory*

- The cheapest and easiest output device is the screen of your own computer, but its small size limits you to an audience of only a few people.
- You can buy a cheap interface that allows you to display computer output on an ordinary television set. The convenience of this setup is offset by the less-than-perfect reproduction of type and other thin lines, so be sure to check the image quality in advance. Also realize that images on ordinary-size television screens are still not large enough to be viewed by more than fifteen or twenty people.
- Liquid crystal display (LCD) panels connect to a computer and fit on an overhead projector. They allow the user to project images from the computer onto a large screen, where these images can be seen easily by an audience. The price of LCD panels is steadily dropping, even for color displays. As they become affordable, LCDs are likely to become a familiar and useful fixture in business presentations.
- If you are speaking in a large room, you may have the option of front- or rear-screen video projectors. These expensive devices operate like superlarge-screen TV projectors and are capable of displaying an enormous image.

With all computer-assisted displays, keep Murphy's Law in mind: Whatever can go wrong with the system probably will. Beware of compatibility problems. Test all parts of the system together, just as you plan to use it, ideally in the place where you will speak. A sophisticated display is worse than useless if it doesn't work when you are standing in front of an expectant audience.

Videotape. As the price of camcorders and videocassette players falls, the possibility of including videotape in presentations grows. Everyone is familiar with the attention-grabbing potential of television, and it is tempting to use that technology to boost the impact of your talks.

There are times when videotaped support is a plus. If you are illustrating action—the performance of an athletic team or the gestures of a speaker, for

If not properly used and appropriately timed, visual aids (anything from charts and graphs to elaborate multimedia shows) can work against you.

First, people have opinions on everything. If you're not careful you can find the conversation deflected toward a critique of your visual aids rather than holding it to what you are there to sell in the first place.

Second, if introduced too early in the presentation it can be distracting. All of a sudden everyone's playing with your visual aids while your sales strategy and game plan go out of the window.

Until you are ready to get to the "show" part of the show and tell, keep your visual aids *out of sight*. You don't want people waiting and wondering what you've got in that little black box.

Mark H. McCormack, *What They Don't Teach You at Harvard Business School* example—video may do the job better than any other medium. But despite the benefits of video, including televised segments can be risky. There is an enormous gap between the production quality you can achieve with a hand-held camcorder and the kind of sophistication that is possible with professional editing equipment. Common problems include segments that last too long, that lack the kind of narration and musical accompaniment that add continuity, and that are full of jerky images and awkward cuts between shots. The risk of using amateur videos containing flaws like these is that they will cast the rest of your message in an unprofessional light. This is why most business communication experts use only video programs that have been professionally prepared—usually at considerable expense. Computerized technology is making it increasingly possible to edit videos yourself, although mastering the software is far more challenging than learning word processing, database, or spreadsheet programs.[20]

Computer-Assisted Design of Visual Aids

A decade ago, most business speakers had few choices about how to design visuals. They could rely on their own talent and create them by hand—usually with amateurish results—or they could turn the job over to a professional graphic artist, who would produce impressive displays—usually at great cost. Now, through *computer-assisted design,* any businessperson with a personal computer, relatively inexpensive presentation software, and a decent printer can produce charts and graphs that approach the quality that used to be possible only from experts.

Presentation software helps speakers in many ways by enabling them to generate customized materials on an as-needed basis. Listed below are some of the things you can do with a good software program:

- Deliver an on-screen show with special effects such as smooth transitions between screens, animation, and synchronized timing that reveals each point as you raise it
- Create visuals in many formats, including slides, overhead transparencies, and screen output
- Organize a set of speaker's notes for yourself
- Prepare a variety of handouts for your audience, based on your speaking notes or displays
- Create "run-time" versions of your displays so that you can distribute copies of your presentation to people who may not have seen you speak
- Create charts, graphs, and tables[21]

Figure 12-17 illustrates some features of Aldus Persuasion, a leading presentation software program. Figure 12-18 illustrates how computer graphics can enhance the display of information.

As Table 12-2 shows, presentation software isn't the only means of creating and displaying computer-generated images. Even a word processing program can improve the quality of your visual exhibits. The range of computer-

CREATE AN OUTLINE OF THE PRESENTATION

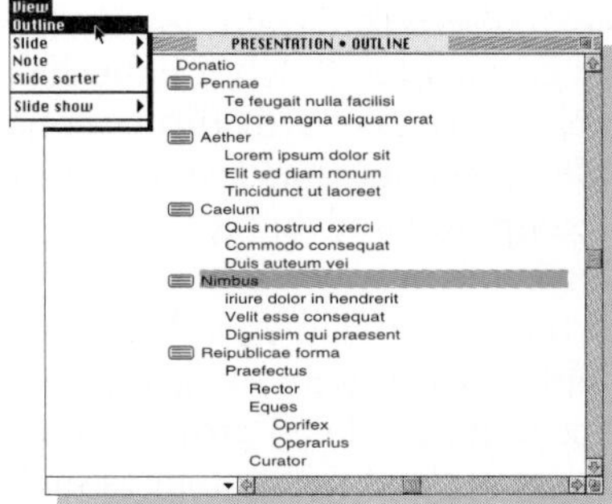

PREVIEW EACH "SLIDE" FROM THE ON-SCREEN PRESENTATION

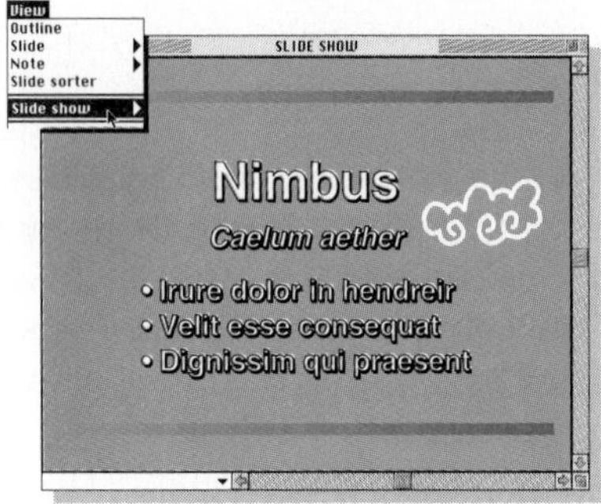

SORT THE ORDER OF EXHIBITS

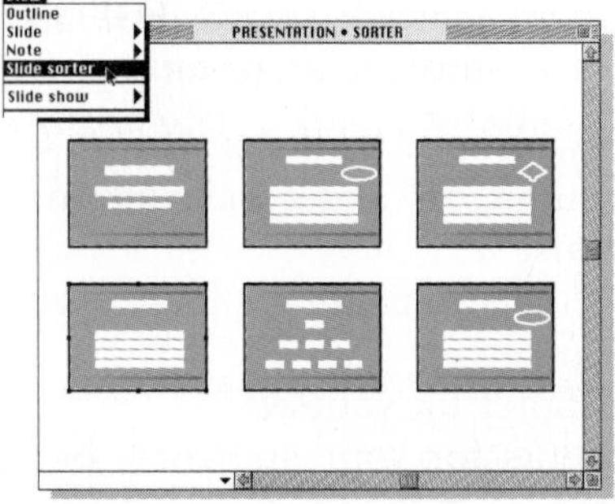

FIGURE 12-17 Presentation software allows speakers to turn material from an outline into a series of consistent, professional looking exhibits, which can be arranged easily using a slide sorter. The screens here are from Aldus Persuasion.

ized graphic displays is great. At its most basic, a beginner can use software programs like Lotus 1-2-3 and Microsoft Excel to turn spreadsheet numbers into a variety of charts—pie, bar, column, line, and so on. Specialized presentation software like Harvard Graphics, Aldus Persuasion, Microsoft Power Point, and Gold Disk's Astound make it especially easy to produce customized output.

Computer-assisted designs can often impress audiences in ways that low-tech exhibits cannot. One southern California real-estate development company wanted to convince a slow-growth-oriented city council that its proposed seven-story office building would not overwhelm its surroundings. The developers knew that the traditional architect's rendering would not convince the city council, so they hired a design consultant who used a set of computerized drawing, painting, and animation tools to create a more realistic vision of the completed product. Besides producing a better image, the computerized design proved more flexible. For example, the developers created customized versions of the drawing that showed the name of potential lessees on a sign across the building. As one of the building's planners put it, "I can show that image to Company X and ask, 'How would you like to have your company's name up there?' That's a very strong marketing tool."

Although computer-assisted design can be very effective, it isn't foolproof. Even basic charting programs—like their word processing and spreadsheet cousins—do take time to learn. If you are using one for the first time, prepare to invest an hour or two of study and practice before turning out a finished product. It's even better to get the help of a friend or co-worker who already is skilled with a design program. Such help can save you a great deal of the time and frustration you would otherwise experience in trial-and-error experimenting or leafing through an instruction book.

Once you have mastered a charting program, it is important to resist the temptation to overuse it. In most presentations, simplicity is a virtue. Just because it is *possible* to produce an elaborate visual full of detail doesn't mean that this sort of display will communicate your message effectively. For example, the three-dimensional chart in Figure 12-18 is probably as complex as a visual display should be—at least in an oral presentation. If it were any more complex, the figure would be hard to understand in the limited time available for viewing. Detailed visuals may be appropriate for written reports, but in oral talks simplicity is usually the best approach.

Rules for Using Visual Aids

Whether you are using handouts, poster boards, flip charts, transparencies, slides, or a chalkboard, be sure to follow the basic rules discussed in this section.[22]

> Occasionally designers seem to seek credit merely for possessing a new technology, rather than using it to make better designs. Computers and their affiliated apparatus can do powerful things graphically. . . . But at least a few computer graphics only evoke the response "Isn't it remarkable that the computer can be programmed to draw like that?" instead of "My, what interesting data." . . .
>
> The purpose of decoration varies—to make the graphic appear more scientific and precise, to enliven the display, to give the designer an opportunity to exercise artistic skills. Regardless of its cause, it is all non-data-ink or redundant data-ink, and it is often chartjunk. Graphical decoration . . . comes cheaper than the hard work required to produce intriguing numbers and secure evidence.
>
> Edward R. Tufte, *The Quantitative Display of Visual Information*

FIRST QUARTER SALES ($00)

	STORE #1	STORE #2	STORE #3
JAN	425	248	125
FEB	298	224	150
MAR	322	148	109

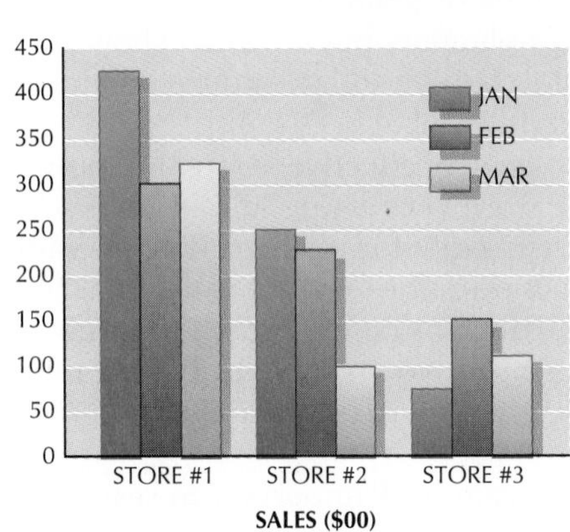

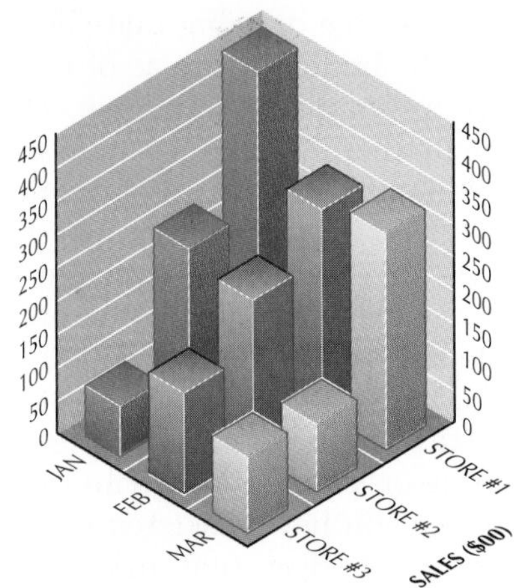

FIGURE 12-18 Computer graphics can increase the sophistication and clarity of displays. The same information becomes more understandable and visually interesting when it is enhanced by the use of charting software. Tables can be created with most word processing programs. Two- and three-dimensional charts can be generated from most programs with spreadsheet and charting capabilities, such as Microsoft Excel and Lotus 1-2-3.

TABLE 12-2 Options for Computer-Assisted Presentation Aids

Means of Creating Images
Word processing software
Drawing software
Presentation design software
Charting software (usually combined with spreadsheet or presentation design program)
Scanning software (for pictures, charts, or text)
Output
Paper handouts
Overhead-projection transparencies
35-millimeter slides
On-screen displays
Projected image from computer output

Selection. As with any part of your presentation, visual exhibits must be chosen with care.

Be Sure You Have a Reason for Using a Visual Aid. If your image doesn't explain a point better than words alone, don't use it. Visuals used for their own sake will distract your audience from the point you're trying to make. Douglas Vogel, a professor of management information systems at the University of Arizona, cites an example of how using animation without any purpose can backfire: "If the animation is improperly focused or too clever, people may only remember 'dancing cows' and not 'how milk may be good for you.' "[23]

Match the Sophistication of Your Visuals to the Audience. Presentations to important audiences—top bosses, key customers, and so on—usually require polished graphics. There are exceptions, however. For example, financial and scientific professionals are usually receptive to a "no-frills approach." Amy Ofsthun, product manager of Polaroid's Digital Palette film recorder, explains: "If they see color and exciting visuals, people feel the data is being massaged somehow. They don't trust the results."[24]

For routine talks, you can probably produce perfectly adequate exhibits on your own. Thanks to advances in computer graphics, you may even be spared the trouble of having to create figures from scratch. In any case, you shouldn't mix informal images with more formal ones any more than you would wear tennis shoes with a dressy outfit.

Design. Confusing or sloppy exhibits will be counterproductive. The simple guidelines below will help you create clear, neat images.[25]

Make Sure the Visual Is Large Enough to See. The visual that looks so clear on the desktop in front of you might be almost microscopic from where your listeners are seated. Avoid using items, drawings, or photographs that are so small you have to describe them or pass them around. Remember, a distracting or unclear visual is worse than no support at all.

Keep the Design of Your Visuals Simple. Show only one idea per exhibit and avoid unnecessary details. If an exhibit needs further explanation, supply it verbally. Remember that you are giving an oral presentation, not showing your audience a written report.

INVITATION TO INSIGHT

You can get a sense of how visual aids are used, ignored, and abused by attending a presentation of your choice in the community. Identify the visual support the speaker uses, and evaluate its effectiveness using the rules in this section. If you had been hired as a consultant, what advice would you give the speaker about the effectiveness of his or her visual exhibits?

Use Only a Few Words. Most exhibits are visual images, so you should avoid excessive text. Captions should contain only key words or phrases, not sentences. Omit subtitles. Never use more than twenty-five characters in a single line. Use simple typefaces. If a visual needs more explanation, supply it orally.

Use Only Horizontal Printing. Avoid vertical or diagonal wording. If necessary, place captions in margins to allow you to use a horizontal format.

Label All Items for Clear Identification. Make sure each exhibit has a descriptive title. Label each axis of a chart, each part of a diagram, and so on.

Presentation. The way you present your exhibits is as important as their design.

Don't Display a Visual Until You Are Ready for It. Once you have revealed an exhibit, the audience will try to make sense of it, whether or not you are ready to discuss it. This sort of preview invites confusion and lessens the impact of the point you want to make with the exhibit. In addition, it distracts your listeners from what you are saying now.

Remove a Visual after Discussing It. Leaving a visual on display after its usefulness is over draws away the attention of your audience. If you are using a flip chart, put blank sheets between the visuals. With an overhead projector, turn off the light between exhibits. Erase chalkboard visuals after you have referred to them.

Make Sure Your Visuals Will Work in the Meeting Room. Double-check the availability of easels, screens, and other equipment you'll need. Be sure that electrical outlets are in the right locations and extension cords are available if you will need them. Check sight lines from all audience seats. Be sure you can easily control lighting levels as necessary.

Practice Using Your Visuals. Rehearse setting up and removing visuals smoothly and quickly. Review the comments you'll make with each one. Be sure exhibits are arranged in the right order and lined up properly so that you can avoid the embarrassment of mixed-up charts or upside-down slides.

SUMMARY

Supporting material is vital in any presentation. It serves three purposes: to clarify the speaker's ideas, to make the material more interesting, and to offer proof. Several types of verbal support are available to a speaker: examples, stories (factual and hypothetical), statistics, comparisons (figurative and literal), and citations.

Visual aids are a common and important type of support in most business presentations. They can make a point more quickly and clearly than can words alone, add variety and interest, and boost a speaker's professional image. Visuals serve several functions: they can show how things look, how they work, or how they relate to one another, and they can highlight important information.

Speakers can use several types of visual aids: objects, models, photographs, diagrams, lists and tables, pie charts, bar and column charts, pictograms, and graphs. These visuals can be presented via a number of media: flip charts and poster-board displays, overhead transparencies, slides, chalkboard, handouts, computerized displays, and videotapes.

Computer-assisted design allows presenters to develop professional looking visual exhibits quickly and easily. Presentation software makes it possible to create on-screen slide shows, 35 millimeter slides and overhead transparencies, speaker's notes and handouts for an audience, and graphs and charts that can be printed out in large sizes. Presentation software takes some time to master, but the results can be worth the effort. Even basic word processing software can help presenters design clear, effective exhibits.

Whatever the medium, all visuals should follow the same basic rules. They should be easy to understand, purposeful, well suited to the point they illustrate and to the audience, and workable in the presentational setting. Speakers should be familiar with the visuals they use to avoid any unpleasant surprises when the time for delivery comes.

RESOURCES

Currid, C., *Make Your Point! The Complete Guide to Successful Business Presentations Using Today's Technology* (Rocklin, Calif.: Prima, 1995).

This book provides instructions for every step of developing and delivering a presentation, but its greatest strength is its guidelines for using computerized technology to develop visual exhibits.

Drew, J., "How to Develop and Deliver Powerful Presentations," in *Mastering Meetings: Discovering the Hidden Potential of Effective Business Meetings* (New York: McGraw-Hill, 1994).

There is much to recommend in this chapter, especially the ample and thoughtful advice on using visuals to enhance a presentation. Look for sound advice on creating, choosing, and using graphics to spice up your talks.

Lavin, M. R., *Business Information: How to Find It, How to Use It*, 2nd ed. (Phoenix, Ariz.: Oryx, 1992).

This is a compendium of business information resources and a list of strategies about how to locate the information you need. It contains chapters on business directories, corporate finances, investment information, statistical databases, marketing information, business law, and much more.

Raab, M. (ed.), *The Presentation Design Book: Projecting a Good Image with Your Desktop Computer* (Chapel Hill, N.C.: Ventana, 1990).

This book provides useful, often amusing advice about how to use personal computers to create clear, effective visual exhibits. It doesn't offer advice about specific programs; rather, it introduces design principles that are important when you are using any software package.

Vesper, J., and V. Ruggiero, "Using and Misusing Graphs," in *Contemporary Business Communication: From Thought to Expression* (New York: HarperCollins, 1993).

This chapter emphasizes that effective visual aids must be "judiciously chosen, carefully prepared, and joined to verbal explanations." The authors focus on the thinking process that must precede the choice of visuals.

Wilder, C., "Creating and Using Visuals," in *The Presentations Kit: 10 Steps for Selling Your Ideas* (New York: Wiley, 1994).

Practical information on creating and using flip charts, overheads, and slides is offered in this chapter. The discussion of the pros and cons of using LCD panels to display computer images is useful. A checklist for using visuals concludes the chapter.

CHAPTER 13

Delivering the Presentation

KEY TERMS

Extemporaneous Presentation / Impromptu Presentation / Manuscript Presentation / Memorized Presentation

In an age of instantaneous communication via telephone, computer, and fax, face-to-face presentations might seem like an anachronism. After all, presentations are enormous consumers of time: just scheduling a date when everyone can attend can be a major chore. Then the audience members have to travel to the location of the talk—sometimes across the hall, but just as often much farther afield. After the message is delivered, the speaker and audience have to finish up their business and get back to work. With all this effort, even a ten-minute talk to a five-person audience takes at least an hour of working time—much more than it would take to send the same message in writing or even over the telephone.

Despite their apparent inefficiency, presentations are still an important part of doing business—and with good reason. The potential advantages of speaking to an audience face-to-face are tremendous. You can control the attention of your audience instead of risking the chance that your message will be shuffled aside. You can share your enthusiasm about the message in a way that words on paper or spoken over the telephone can't match. If your listeners have questions or objections, you can address them directly.

In order to take advantage of these strengths, a presentation has to be well delivered. If you look sloppy, speak in a way that is hard to understand, or seem unenthusiastic, the face-to-face medium changes from an asset to a liability. Instead of leading the audience members to accept your message, poor delivery can cause them to doubt or even reject it. As communication consultant Roger Ailes puts it, "You become the message. People cannot distinguish between the words and who speaks them."[1]

The following pages will offer suggestions that can help you deliver your remarks in a way that makes your message clearer, more interesting, and more persuasive. They describe the various styles of delivery, offer tips for improving your visual and vocal performance, explain how to deal with questions from the audience, and give advice for dealing with the nervousness that often accompanies an important presentation.

TYPES OF DELIVERY

There are four ways to deliver a presentation. In most situations, though, two of these approaches are so disastrous that only uninformed speakers use them.

Manuscript Presentations

In ***manuscript presentations,*** speakers read their remarks word for word from a prepared statement. Manuscript speaking is common at annual companywide meetings, conventions, and press conferences. Yet few experiences are so boring as the average manuscript presentation.

The most dynamic and personable managers often try to conceal their nervousness at facing a large audience by reading from a script—and they turn into lifeless drones. Since most speakers are not trained at reading aloud, their delivery is halting and jerky. Even worse, a nervous speaker who relies too heavily on a manuscript can make serious mistakes without even knowing it. Management consultant Marilyn Landis describes one such disaster:

> I remember the president of a large corporation who followed his usual pattern of asking his public relations director to write a speech for him. Due to a collating error, the script contained two copies of page five. You guessed it. The president read page five twice—and didn't even realize it.[2]

Even when a speaker reads a report flawlessly, the presentation often sounds mechanical and lifeless. It may be possible to read an adventure story or an interesting newspaper article enthusiastically, but almost anyone's voice and manner will be flat when reading a financial report or a market analysis. One important ingredient of a speaker's credibility is sincerity, and it's difficult to seem sincere when reading.

To make things worse, the text of a manuscript presentation is often a copy of a written report—usually far too long and detailed for effective oral presentation. "I don't know why we have to sit through people reading a report that's been copied and distributed," one manager complained. "I can read it myself a lot faster."

In legal or legislative testimony, diplomatic speeches, or other situations in which a slight misstatement could have serious consequences, manuscript speaking may be your best means of delivery. Most presentations, however, do not fall into this category. A simple but important rule for most cases, then, is *don't read your presentation.*

Memorized Presentations

If speaking from a script is bad, trying to memorize that script is even worse. You probably have been subjected to a door-to-door salesperson's obviously memorized pitch for encyclopedias or carpet cleaning. If so, you know that the biggest problem of a ***memorized presentation***—one recited word for word from memory—is that it *sounds* memorized.

Never memorize! You cannot communicate with your audience if you're struggling to remember each word of a speech. And what happens if you forget?

"Studio One" was one of the most popular shows in the golden days of live television. During one memorable broadcast, the scene was the interior of an airplane cabin. The plane was at an altitude of 30,000 feet, flying over the mountains of Tibet. Three men were in the cabin talking when suddenly there was silence. One of the actors had forgotten his lines. There were no retakes, no stopping of the action. That was it. Millions of eager viewers were glued to their black-and-white screens, waiting to see what would happen next. What did the actor do? He got to his feet, in an airplane cabin 30,000 feet over the mountains of Tibet, and voiced this immortal line: "Well, here's where I get off." He left the set and walked into history.

If *you* memorize a speech and forget it anywhere along the line, you'll have to get off that plane at 30,000 feet over Tibet—and there's no parachute. But even if you do find your way back, when you memorize, the material controls you, rather than you controlling the material. *Master* your material, but don't memorize. Memorizing robs you of being natural.

Milo Frank, *How to Get Your Point Across in Thirty Seconds or Less*

It might seem that memorizing a presentation would help with your nervousness, but memorizing almost guarantees that "stage fright" will become a serious problem. Speakers who spend great amounts of time simply learning the words of a talk are asking for trouble. During the presentation, they must focus on remembering what comes next instead of getting involved in the meaning of their remarks. One worker described a personnel manager's habitual problems with memorized presentations:

> He'd start *reciting,* like a kid reciting a poem in school. If you interrupted him to ask a question, he'd stumble all over himself. Then he couldn't pick up again where he'd left off. He had to start over.

Sometimes it's necessary to memorize parts of a presentation since referring to notes at a critical moment can diminish your credibility. A salesperson is usually expected to know the major features of the product—how much horsepower it has, how much it costs, or how many copies per minute it delivers. A personnel manager might be expected to know, without referring to a brochure, the value of the employee's life insurance (if each employee's is the same) and how much the employee contributes to the premium. A co-worker would look foolish at a retirement dinner if she said, "Everybody knows about Charlie's contributions—" and then had to pause to refer to her notes. For such situations, you can memorize essential *parts* of a presentation.

Extemporaneous Presentations

An ***extemporaneous presentation*** is planned and rehearsed, but not word for word. If you prepare carefully and practice your presentation several times with a friend, a family member, or even a group of co-workers or subordinates, you have a good chance of delivering an extemporaneous talk that seems spontaneous and even effortless. Virtually every presentation you plan—a sales presentation, a talk at the local high school, a progress report to a management review board, a training lecture, an annual report to employees or the board of directors—should be delivered extemporaneously.

A good extemporaneous presentation should be carefully rehearsed, but it will never be exactly the same twice. The words will differ each time. The speaker might respond to an audience's nonverbal cues to explain a point more fully or to move on when the point seems clear. The important points, though, remain the same. The speaker uses notes for reminders of the order and content of ideas.

There is no single best format for speaking notes. Some speakers prefer abbreviated outlines, while others find that index cards with key words or phrases work best. Whatever form you use, speaking notes should possess the following characteristics.

Notes Should Be Brief. Overly detailed notes tempt a speaker to read them. Inexperienced salespeople who rely on a brochure, for instance, often wind up reading to their prospective customers. More experienced salespeople might be able to use the brochure's boldface headings as a guide.

Notes Should Be Legible. Your words shouldn't turn into meaningless scribbles when you need them. The writing on your notes should be neat and large enough to be read at a glance.

Notes Should Be Unobtrusive. Most audiences won't be offended if you speak from notes, as long as the notes aren't distracting. A sheet of $8\frac{1}{2}$- by 11-inch paper flapping in your hand can become a noisy irritation, as can shuffling several sheets of paper on a lectern. Some speakers avoid such problems by providing their listeners with a guide and then using the guide for their own notes.

Impromptu Presentations

Sooner or later you will be asked to give an ***impromptu presentation***—an unexpected, off-the-cuff talk. A customer might stop in your office and ask you to describe the new model you'll have next spring. At a celebration dinner, you may be asked to "say a few words." A manager might ask you to "give us some background on the problem" or to "fill us in on your progress." You may suddenly discover at a weekly meeting that your subordinates are unaware of a process they need to know about in order to understand the project you are about to explain.

While you may feel anxious at the thought of impromptu speaking, the experience needn't be as threatening as it seems. Most of the time, you will be asked to speak about a subject within your expertise—such as a current project, a problem you've solved, or a technical aspect of your training—which means you have thought about it before. Another reassuring fact is that most listeners won't expect perfection in off-the-cuff remarks.

Your impromptu presentations will be most effective if you follow these guidelines.[3]

Predict When You May Be Asked to Speak. Most impromptu speaking situations won't come as a complete surprise. You may be an "expert" on the subject under discussion or at least one of the people most involved in a situation. Or perhaps your knowledge of the person in charge suggests that impromptu remarks are to be expected. In any case, if you prepare yourself just in case you're asked to speak, your remarks will be better planned and delivered.

Accept the Invitation with Assurance. Try to look confident, even if you're less than delighted about speaking. If you stammer, stall, or look unhappy, your audience will doubt the value of your remarks before you say a word. Once asked, you're going to speak whether or not you want to. You might as well handle the situation well.

Present a Definite Viewpoint Early. Let the audience know your thesis at the outset: "I see several problems with that idea," or "From my experience with the Digitech project, I think our cost projections are low." If you aren't sure what your opinion is, present that thesis: "I'm not sure which approach we ought to take. I think we need to look at both of them closely before we decide."

Present Reasons, Logic, or Facts to Support Your Viewpoint. As with any presentation, your points will be clearer and more persuasive when you back them up with supporting material: statistics, examples, comparisons, and so forth. Of course, this information won't be as detailed as it would be if you had been able to prepare it in advance; but provide some evidence or explanation to support your points: "As I recall, the Digitech job ran 10 percent over estimate on materials and 15 percent over on labor."

Don't Apologize. Nobody expects a set of impromptu remarks to be perfectly polished, so it is a mistake to highlight your lack of knowledge or preparation. Remarks like "You caught me off guard" or "I'm not sure whether this is right" are unnecessary. If you really don't have anything to contribute, say so.

Don't Ramble On. Many novice speakers make the mistake of delivering their message and then continuing to talk: "So that's my point: I think the potential gains make the risk worthwhile. Sure, we'll be taking a chance, but look what we stand to win. That's why I think it's not just a matter of chance, but a calculated risk, and one that makes sense. We'll never know unless we try, and . . ."

The speaker needed only one sentence: "I think the risk is worth taking." Instead, he probably left the audience feeling bored and resentful. The safest way to avoid rambling is to use the few moments before you speak to sketch a mental outline of your main points. Then stick to it.

GUIDELINES FOR DELIVERY

Choosing the best method of delivery will help make your presentations effective, but it is no guarantee of total effectiveness. Your speeches will be better

INVITATION TO INSIGHT

With two or more classmates, try the various styles of delivery for yourself. Follow these steps:

1. Begin by choosing a paragraph of text on an appropriate business or professional topic. You can write the copy yourself or select an article from a newspaper, magazine, or some other publication.
2. Read the text to your listeners verbatim. Pay attention to your feelings as you deliver the comments. Do you feel comfortable and enthusiastic? How do your listeners describe your delivery?
3. Try to memorize and then deliver the segment. How difficult is it to recall the remarks? How effective is your delivery?
4. Now deliver the same remarks extemporaneously, rephrasing them in your own words. See whether this approach leaves you more comfortable and your listeners more favorably impressed.

if you also consider the visual and vocal elements of delivery: how you look, what words you use, and how you sound.

Visual Elements

A major part of good delivery is how a speaker looks. One manager illustrated this fact dramatically by commenting on the appearance of a trainer she had hired:

> I read an article on personnel management this guy had published in a trade journal. The ideas were terrific, and I thought he would be the ideal person to lead our annual retreat for top managers. I spoke with him over the phone, and he sent me a written plan for the weekend that looked as good as the article.
>
> That's why I was so surprised when I finally met this trainer. He couldn't look anybody in the eye, and he kept fidgeting and stammering all weekend long. What he said was fine, but he looked so bad that nobody took him seriously. I looked bad for choosing him, but I sure learned a lesson. I'll never put my reputation behind anybody again before I see how they operate in person.

You can improve your visual effectiveness by following several guidelines.

Dress Effectively. Appearance is important in any setting. How you dress is even more important when you get up to speak, however. You may be able to hide a rumpled suit behind your desk sometimes or get away with wearing clothes more casual than usual office norms dictate the day you move your office furniture—but not when you get up to give your financial report at the annual meeting or present your latest proposal to top management.

Dressing effectively doesn't always mean dressing up. If the occasion calls for casual attire, an overly formal appearance can be just as harmful as underdressing. Automotive consultant Barry Isenberg found that an informal appearance contributed to his success as a leading speaker. While waiting to speak to an audience of hundreds of auto wreckers at a day-long seminar, Isenberg looked on as an attorney dressed impeccably in a three-piece suit gave an organized talk on warranties. Despite the importance of the topic, the audience was obviously bored silly. Isenberg rushed upstairs to his hotel room and changed out of his business suit and into the attire of his listeners—casual pants and an open-neck shirt. When his turn to speak arrived, Isenberg moved out from behind the lectern and adopted a casual speaking style that matched his outfit. Afterward, a number of listeners told Isenberg he was the first speaker who seemed to understand their business.[4]

Step Up to Speak with Confidence and Authority. Employees are often surprised to discover that their forceful, personable superiors completely lose their effectiveness when they have to address a group of people—and show this before they say a word. Speakers who fidget with their hands or their clothing while waiting to speak, approach the podium as if they were about to face a firing squad, and then fumble with their notes and the microphone send the nonverbal message "I'm not sure about myself or what I have to say." An audience will discount even the best remarks with such a powerful nonverbal preface.

Your presentation begins the moment you come into the view of your listeners. Act as if you are a person whose remarks are worth listening to.

Get Set before Speaking. If you need an easel or projection screen, move it into position before you begin. If a lectern needs repositioning, do it before you begin your talk. The same goes for the other details that come with so many presentations: adjust the microphone, close the door, reset the air conditioner, rearrange the seating.

Just as important, be sure to position yourself physically before beginning. Usually out of nervousness, some speakers blurt out their opening remarks before they are set in their speaking position. A far better approach is to stand or walk to the position from which you will talk, get set, wait a brief moment (a "power pause"), and then begin speaking.

Establish and Maintain Eye Contact. A speaker who talks directly to an audience will be seen as more involved and sincere. Whether you're proposing an innovative new product line, reassuring your employees about the effects of recent budget cuts, or trying to convince a group of local citizens that your company is interested in curbing pollution, your impression on the audience can ultimately determine your success.

This kind of immediacy comes in great part from the degree of eye contact between speaker and listeners. Use the moment before you speak to establish a relationship with your audience. Look around the room. Get in touch with the fact that you are talking to real human beings: the people you work with, the potential customers who have real problems and concerns you can help with, and so on. Let them know by your glance that you are interested in them. Be sure your glance covers virtually everyone in the room. Look about randomly: a mechanical right-to-left sweep of the group will make you look like a robot. Many speech consultants recommend taking in the whole room as you speak. If the audience is too large for you to make eye contact with each person, choose a few people in different parts of the room, making eye contact with each one for a few seconds.

Begin without Looking at Your Notes. Make contact with the audience as you begin speaking. You can't establish a connection if you are reading from notes. You can memorize the precise wording of your opening statement, but it isn't really necessary. Whether you say "I have a new process that will give you more reliable results at a lower cost" or "My new process is more reliable and costs less" isn't critical: the important thing is to make your point while speaking directly to your listeners.

Stand and Move Effectively. The best stance for delivering a presentation is relaxed but firm. The speaker's feet are planted firmly on the ground, spaced at shoulder width. The body faces the audience. The head is upright, turning naturally to look at the audience.

Having good posture doesn't mean standing rooted to the ground. Moving about can add life to your presentation and help release nervous energy. You can approach and refer to your visual aids, walk away from and return to your original position, and approach the audience. Your actions should always be purposeful, though. Nervous pacing might make a speaker feel better, but it will turn listeners into distracted wrecks.

If you're addressing a small group, such as four or five employees or potential customers, it may be more appropriate to sit when you're delivering a presentation. Generally, the same rules apply in such cases. You should sit up straight and lean forward—lounging back in your chair or putting a foot up on the desk indicates indifference or even contempt. Sit naturally; your behavior should be as direct and animated as it would be if you were conversing with these people—which, in a way, you are.

Don't Pack Up Early. Gathering your notes or starting for your seat before concluding is a nonverbal statement that you're anxious to get your presentation finished. Even if you are, advertising the fact will only make your audience see the presentation as less valuable. Keep your attention focused on your topic and the audience until you are actually finished.

Move Out Confidently When Finished. When you end your remarks (or finish answering questions), move out smartly. Even if you are unhappy with yourself, don't shuffle off dejectedly or stomp away angrily. Most speakers are their own greatest critics, and there is a good chance the audience rated you more favorably than you did. If you advertise your disappointment, however, you might persuade them that you really were a flop.

Verbal Elements

The words you choose are an important part of your delivery. As you practice your presentation, keep the following points in mind.

> The truth is, no one can manufacture an image for anyone. If you want to improve or enhance yourself in some way, the only thing a consultant can do for you is to advise and guide you. We can point out assets and liabilities in your style and we then offer substitutions and suggestions to aid you. You have to want to improve and work at it. Most importantly, whatever changes you make have to conform to who you really *are*—at your best. All the grooming suggestions, all the speech coaching, all the knowledge about lighting, staging, and media training—everything popularly associated with "image-making"—won't work if the improvements don't fit comfortably with who you essentially are.
>
> Roger Ailes, *You Are the Message*

Use an Oral Speaking Style. Spoken ideas differ in structure and content from written messages. The difference helps explain why speakers who read from a manuscript sound so stuffy and artificial. When addressing your audience, your speech will sound normal and pleasing if it follows some simple guidelines:

- *Keep most sentences short.* Long, complicated sentences may be fine in a written document, where readers can study them until the meaning is clear, but in an oral presentation your ideas will be easiest to understand if they are phrased in brief statements. Complicated sentences can leave your listeners confused: "Members of field staff, who are isolated from one another and work alone most of the time, need better technology for keeping in touch with one another while in the field as well as with the home office." The ideas are much clearer when delivered in briefer chunks: "Members of the field staff work alone most of the time. This makes it hard for them to keep in touch with one another and with the home office. They need better means of technology to stay in contact."
- *Use personal pronouns freely.* Speech that contains first-person and second-person pronouns sounds more personal and immediate. Instead of saying "People often ask," say "You might ask." Likewise, say "Our sales staff found," not "The sales staff found."
- *Use the active voice.* The active voice sounds more personal and less stuffy than passive use of verbs. Saying "It was decided" isn't as effective as saying "We decided." Do not say "The meeting was attended by ten people"; say "Ten people attended the meeting."
- *Use contractions often.* Instead of saying "We do not expect many changes," say "We don't expect many changes." Rather than saying "I do not know; I will find out and give you an answer as soon as possible," say "I don't know; I'll find out and give you an answer as soon as possible."
- *Address your listeners directly.* Using direct forms of address makes it clear that you are really speaking to your listeners and not just reading from a set of notes. Personalized statements will keep an audience listening: "Frank, you and your colleagues in the payroll office are probably wondering how these changes will affect you"; "Ms. Diaz, it's a pleasure to have the chance to describe our ideas to you this morning."

Don't Emphasize Mistakes. Even the best speakers forget or bungle a line occasionally. The difference between professionals and amateurs is the way they handle such mistakes. The experts simply go on, adjusting their remarks to make the error less noticeable.

Usually, an audience won't even be aware of a mistake. If listeners don't have a copy of your speaking outline, they won't know about the missing parts; even if they notice that you have skipped a section in a brochure you're going over with them or in a prepared outline you've distributed after your speech for their reference, they'll assume you did it on purpose, perhaps to save time. If you lose your place in your notes, a brief pause will be almost unnoticeable—as long as you don't emphasize it by frantically pawing through your notes.

What about obvious mistakes—citing the wrong figures, mispronouncing a name, or trying to use equipment that doesn't work, for example? The best response here is again the least noticeable. "Let me correct that. The totals are for the first quarter of the year, not just for March," you might say and then move on. When equipment fails, adapt and move on: "The chart with those figures seems to be missing. Let me summarize it for you."

Use Proper Vocabulary, Enunciation, and Pronunciation. The language of a board of directors' meeting or a formal press conference is different from that of a factory workers' meeting or an informal gathering of sales representatives at a resort. It is important to choose language that is appropriate to the particular setting.

It is also important to pronounce your words correctly. Few mistakes will erode your credibility or irritate an audience as quickly as will mispronouncing an important term or name: the word is *scenario,* not "screenario," and the author of this book likes to be called "Adler," not "Alder." Enunciation—articulating words clearly and distinctly—is also important. "We are comin' out with a new data processin' system" makes the speaker sound ignorant to many people, even if the ideas are good.

Vocal Elements

As Table 13-1 shows, how you sound is just as important as what you say and how you look. Speakers' voices are especially effective at communicating their attitudes about themselves, their topics, and their listeners: enthusiasm or disinterest, confidence or nervousness, friendliness or hostility, respect or disdain. The following guidelines are important elements in effective communication.

Speak with Enthusiasm and Sincerity. If you don't appear to feel strongly about the importance of your topic, there's little chance the audience will. Yet professionals often seem indifferent when they present ideas they're deeply committed to.[5]

The best way to generate enthusiasm is to think of your presentation as sharing ideas you truly believe in. In the stress of making a presentation, you might forget how important your remarks are. To prevent this, remind yourself of why you are speaking in the moments before you speak. Thinking about what you want to say can put life back into your delivery.

Speak Loudly Enough to Be Heard. At the very least, a quiet voice makes it likely that listeners won't hear important information. In addition, listeners often interpret an overly soft voice as a sign of timidity or lack of con-

TABLE 13-1 Checklist for Effective Delivery

- *Visual elements*
  Dresses effectively
  Steps up to speak with confidence and authority
  Gets set before speaking
  Establishes and maintains eye contact
  Begins without looking at notes
  Stands and moves effectively
  Doesn't pack up early
  Moves out confidently when finished
- *Verbal elements*
  Uses an oral speaking style
  Doesn't emphasize mistakes
  Uses proper vocabulary, enunciation, and pronunciation
- *Vocal elements*
  Speaks with enthusiasm and sincerity
  Speaks loudly enough to be heard
  Avoids disfluencies

viction. ("She just didn't sound very sure of herself.") Shouting is offensive, too ("Does he think he can force his product down our throats?"), but a speaker ought to project enough to be heard clearly and to sound confident.

Avoid Disfluencies. Disfluencies are those stammers and stutters ("eh," "um," and so forth) that creep into everyone's language at one time or another. Other "filler words" are "ya know," "so," "okay," and so on. A few disfluencies will be virtually unnoticeable in a presentation; in fact, without them, the talk might seem overly rehearsed and stilted. An excess of jumbles, stumbles, and fillers, however, makes a speaker sound disorganized, nervous, and uncertain.

Disfluencies can be overcome with some concentration. One manager who found that her presentations were marred by "okays" asked an associate to tally the number of "okays" in her conversation. She then agreed to contribute a dime for each one to the Friday afternoon happy-hour fund, hoping the financial penalty would break her bad habit. The first week she was astonished to find that her bill was over $20, but after only a month her "okay" rate had dropped to a level where counting was hardly worth the effort. Once she was

INVITATION TO INSIGHT

Scan a current television guide, and select a program in which a speaker is making some sort of oral presentation. The subject matter is not important: the show can be educational, religious, political, or news-related.

1. Turn down the volume, and observe the speaker's visual delivery. Notice the effects of dress, posture, gesture, facial expression, and eye contact.
2. What do these aspects of delivery suggest about the speaker's status, enthusiasm, sincerity, and competence?

aware of the "okays" in her everyday conversation, she found she could control them in her more formal presentations, too.

Speaking on Camera

You don't have to be a television celebrity or a public figure to appear on video. Most of your video presentations are likely to be in-house productions such as training videos and videotapes of your remarks for people who couldn't be present to hear you in person. If the audience for a presentation is large, you might also find your image being broadcast on large monitors in an auditorium or in overflow rooms. And, as you read in Chapter 1, videoconferencing is becoming much more affordable and common, so you may appear on screen in that format. Finally, you might find yourself part of a broadcast program for community access or commercial stations: an interview, public information announcement, or panel discussion. Whatever the occasion, the following tips will help you look and sound good when on screen.

Clothing. Cool colors (blue and green) are better than warm colors (yellow and orange). Shades of blue photograph best. Pastels look better than brilliant or fluorescent shades. Most experts agree that white is the worst color to wear on screen. Even white trim can present problems for the camera. If you can find out what color the background will be, you can make a choice that will not clash or fade in. Avoid plaids, busy patterns, stripes, and polka dots: they may seem to shimmer on camera and detract from your face. Sharply contrasting colors such as large black and red stripes or a black blouse and beige jacket wouldn't be the best choice.

If you are wearing a suit or jacket, sitting on the coat tails may help keep the lines smoother in front and look less rumpled. Women may find it easier to choose a longer skirt than to be concerned about changing camera angles, chair placement, and heights.

Face, Eyes, and "Body Language." If you are being taped in front of a live audience, your delivery will probably seem natural to viewers watching you on screen. If you are taping without an audience, looking at the camera will make viewers feel like you are looking them in the eyes. Often, TelePrompTers will display your words on a screen next to the camera, so you can look at the camera while reading your script.

It's important to be emotionally expressive on camera. Since facial expressions and movements (or lack of them) are exaggerated, a low-key style of delivery may make you seem stiff, unenthusiastic, and insincere. It might seem hard to show emotion to a camera, especially without a live audience, so practice is important. Usually, sitting toward the edge of the chair gives you a comfortable body slant and helps you appear interested.

Hair. Hair that is out of place or needs constant attention becomes especially distracting on camera, where every movement is magnified. Be sure your hair is tied, clipped, sprayed, or gelled into place so that it doesn't need constant on-camera attention. Avoid constant movements to swoop your hair from your eyes.

Makeup. Camera angles and lighting may make you appear heavier or thinner, older or younger; the norm is that most people look heavier. While you may not be able to control camera angles, you can use makeup to even out skin tones, creating a more pleasing appearance. Powder helps absorb perspiration that may result from nervousness or hot lights. Don't worry: makeup that looks thick and artificial in person looks natural on camera.

Jewelry. Jewelry has several potential drawbacks. It may reflect light. If it is large enough, it may clang or jingle and create microphone noise. Finally, it can attract the audience's attention, distracting listeners from your message. ("What an unusual necklace she has on!" "Is that an earring he's wearing?")

Using Notes. If you must use notes, try to keep them flat on the podium and use them sparingly. Pause when you look at your notes, so that you are always making eye contact with the camera (and through it, with your audience) when you are speaking. Make your notes less obtrusive by printing them on light blue cards rather than white ones, which are more likely to cast a glare.

QUESTION-AND-ANSWER SESSIONS

The chance to answer questions on the spot is one of the biggest advantages of oral presentations. Whereas a written report might leave readers confused or unimpressed, your on-the-spot response to questions and concerns can win over an audience.

Audience questions are a part of almost every business and professional talk from sales presentations and training sessions to boardroom meetings. Sometimes question-and-answer sessions are a separate part of the presentation. Other times, they are mingled with the speaker's remarks. In any case, a skillful response to questions is essential.

When to Answer Questions

The first issue to consider is whether you should entertain questions at all. Sometimes you have no choice, of course. If the boss interrupts your talk to ask

INVITATION TO INSIGHT

Locate a television or radio program that involves an oral presentation on some subject. The content is not important. Interview shows are fine, but don't choose shows in which the characters are acting roles other than themselves.

See how closely the speakers you observe follow the "Speaking on Camera" guidelines in this section. How effective is their delivery? What does their example tell you about how you can appear most effectively on video?

for some facts or figures, you're not likely to rule the question out of order. But there may be cases when time or the risk of being distracted will lead you to say something like "Because we only have ten minutes on the agenda, I won't have time for questions. If any of you do have questions, see me after my presentation or during the break or lunch."[6] If your presentation does call for questions from the audience, you can control much about when they are asked.

During the Presentation. Speakers often encourage their listeners to ask questions during a talk. This approach lets you respond to the concerns of your listeners immediately. If people are confused, you can set them straight by expanding on a point; if they have objections, you can respond to them on the spot.

Dealing with your listeners' questions during a talk does have its drawbacks. Some questions are premature, raising points you plan to discuss later in your talk. Others are irrelevant and waste both your time and your listeners'. If you decide to handle questions during a talk, follow the guidelines below.

Allow for Extra Time. Answering questions sometimes occupies as much time as your planned talk. A fifteen-minute report can run a half hour or longer with questions. If your time is limited, keep your remarks brief enough to leave time for the audience to respond.

Promise to Answer Premature Questions Later. Don't feel obligated to give detailed responses to every question. If you plan to discuss the information requested by a questioner later in your talk, say, "That's a good question; I'll get to that in a moment."

After the Presentation. Postponing questions until after your prepared remarks lets you control the way your information is revealed. You don't have to worry about someone distracting you with an irrelevant remark or raising an objection you plan to answer. You also have much better control over the length of your talk, lessening the risk that you'll run out of time before you run out of information.

On the other hand, when you deny listeners the chance to speak up, they may be so preoccupied with questions or concerns that they miss much of what you say. For instance, you might spend half your time talking about the benefits of a product while your listeners keep wondering whether they can afford it. In addition, since most of the information people recall is from the beginning and the end of presentations, you risk having your audience remember the high price you mentioned during the question-and-answer session or the sticky question you couldn't answer rather than the high quality you proved in your presentation.

How to Manage Questions

Whether you handle them during or after a presentation, questions from the audience can be a challenge. Some are confusing. Others are thinly veiled attacks on your position: "How much time have you New York folks spent out here in the Midwest?" Still other questions are off the topic you're discussing: "Your talk about film projectors was very interesting. I wonder, do you ever teach classes on making films?" You can handle questions most effectively by following the suggestions below.

Start the Ball Rolling. Sometimes listeners may be reluctant to ask the first question. You can get a question-and-answer session rolling with your own remarks: "One question you might have is . . . ," or "The other day someone asked whether . . ." You can also encourage questions nonverbally by leaning forward as you invite the audience to speak up. You might even raise your hand as you ask for questions.

Anticipate Likely Questions. Put yourself in the position of your listeners. What questions are they likely to ask? Is there a chance that they will find parts of your topic hard to understand? Might some points antagonize them? Just as you prepare for an important exam by anticipating the questions that are likely to be asked, you should try to prepare responses to the inquiries you're likely to receive.

Clarify Complicated or Confusing Questions. Make sure you understand the question by rephrasing it in your own words: "If I understand you correctly, Tom, you're asking why we can't handle this problem with our present staff. Is that right?" Besides helping you understand what a questioner wants, clarification gives you a few precious moments to frame an answer. Finally, it helps other audience members to understand the question. If the audience is large, rephrase every question to make sure that it has been heard: "The gentleman asked whether we have financing terms for the equipment."

Treat Questioners with Respect. There's little to gain by antagonizing or embarrassing even the most hostile questioner. You can keep your dignity and gain the support of other listeners by taking every question seriously or even complimenting the person who asks it: "I don't blame you for thinking the plan is farfetched, Nora. We thought it was strange at first, too, but the more we examined it, the better it looked."

Keep Answers Focused on Your Goal. Don' let questions draw you off track. Try to frame answers in ways that promote your goal: "This certainly is different from the way we did things in the old days when you and I started out, Steve. For instance, the computerized system we have now will cut both our costs and our errors. Let me review the figures once more."

You can avoid offending questioners by promising to discuss the matter with them in detail after your presentation or to send them further information: "I'd be happy to show you the electrical plans, Peggy. Let's get together this afternoon and go over them."

Buy Time When Necessary. Sometimes you need a few moments to plan an answer to a surprise question. You can buy time in several ways. You can *rephrase the question:* "It sounds like everything about the project looks good to you except the schedule, Gene." You can *turn the question around:* "How would you deal with the situation and still go ahead with the project, Mary?" You can also *turn the question outward:* "Chris, you're the best technical person we have. What's the best way to save energy costs?"

Address Your Answer to the Entire Audience. Look at the person asking the question while he or she is asking it, but address your answer to everybody. This approach is effective for two reasons: First, it keeps all the audience members involved instead of making them feel like bystanders. Second, it can save you from getting trapped into a debate with hostile questioners. Most critics are likely to keep quiet if you address your response to the entire group. You may not persuade the person who has made a critical remark, but you can use your answer to gain ground with everybody else.

Follow the Last Question with a Summary. Since listeners are likely to remember especially well the last words they hear you speak, always follow the question-and-answer session with a brief restatement of your thesis and perhaps a call for your audience to act in a way that accomplishes your purpose for speaking. A typical summary might sound like this:

> "I'm grateful for the chance to answer your questions. Now that we've gone over the cost projections, I think you can see why we're convinced that this proposal can help boost productivity and cut overhead by almost 10 percent overnight. We're ready to make these changes immediately. The sooner we hear from you, the sooner we can get started."

SPEAKING WITH CONFIDENCE

If the thought of making a presentation leaves you feeling anxious, you are in good company. According to Irving Wallace and David Wallechinsky's *Book of Lists,* a sample of 3,000 Americans identified "speaking before a group" as their greatest fear, greater even than death.[7] This doesn't mean most people would rather die than give a speech, but it does show which event makes them more anxious.

Stage fright—or communication apprehension, as communication specialists call it—is just as much a problem for businesspeople as it is for the general population. Communispond, a New York communications consulting firm, surveyed 500 executives and found that nearly 80 percent listed stage fright as their greatest problem in speaking before a group, putting it ahead of such items as "handling hostile interrogators."[8]

If you get butterflies in your stomach at the thought of giving a speech, if your hands sweat and your mouth gets dry, if you feel faint or nauseated or have trouble thinking clearly, you might be comforted to know that most people, including famous performers, politicians, and business executives who frequently appear before audiences, experience some degree of nervousness about speaking. Although it is common, communication apprehension doesn't have to present a serious problem.

It is reassuring to know that, however anxious you feel, your apprehension isn't as visible as you might fear. In several recent studies, communicators have been asked to rate their own level of anxiety.[9] At the same time, other people gave their impression of the speaker's level of nervousness. In every case, the speakers rated themselves as looking much more nervous than the observers thought they were. Even when the anxiety is noticeable, it doesn't result in significantly lower evaluations of the speaker's effectiveness.

These research findings are good news for anxious speakers. It's reassuring to know that, even if you are frightened, your listeners aren't likely to recognize the fact or find it distracting. And knowing that the audience isn't bothered by your anxiety can actually reduce a major source of nervousness, leading you to feel more confident.

Accept a Moderate Amount of Nervousness

A certain amount of anxiety is not only normal but desirable. When the success of your new product line depends on how well you explain it to the sales force, the future of a new proposal depends on how convincingly you can present it to management, or your next promotion or raise depends on how successful your speech is at the annual meeting of the company board of directors, it is natural to feel nervous.

A certain amount of anxiety can even be an asset. One consultant says, "If I had a way to remove all fear of speaking for you, I wouldn't do it. The day you become casual about speaking is the day you risk falling on your face."[10] The threat of botching your presentation can lead to what Edward R. Murrow once called "the sweat of perfection," spurring you to do your best. And the adrenaline rush that comes as you stand up—your body's response to a threat-

ETHICAL CHALLENGE

Every speaker wants to appear confident and enthusiastic. But sometime during the course of your speaking career you are likely to face an audience when you do not feel self-assured or enthusiastic about your topic. How can you reconcile the ethical demand to be honest with the pragmatic reality that business communicators are sometimes obliged to present ideas they do not personally like?

You may choose to use the interviewing skills described in Chapters 6 and 7 of this book to ask experienced communicators how they face this challenge. On the basis of their answers and your own thoughts, develop a policy on how accurately your public demeanor should reflect your private misgivings.

ening situation—can make you appear more energetic, enthusiastic, and forceful than would be the case if you were more relaxed and casual.

A proper goal, then, is not to eliminate nervousness but to *control* it. As one experienced speaker put it, "The butterflies never go away; it's just that after a while they begin to fly in formation."

Speak More Often

Like many unfamiliar activities—ice skating, learning to drive a car, and interviewing for a job, to mention a few—the first attempts at speaking before a group can be unnerving. The first attempts at any new activity are bound to be awkward. One source of anxiety is lack of skill and experience. In addition, the very newness of the act is frightening. What is new is unknown, and we assume the unknown always contains some risk.

Since newness generates anxiety, one way to become a more confident speaker is to speak more. As with other skills, your first attempts should involve modest challenges with relatively low stakes. Speech courses and workshops taught in colleges, corporations, and some community organizations provide opportunities for a group of novices to practice before one another and a supportive instructor. Once on the job, it's a good idea to make a number of beginning presentations to small, familiar audiences about noncritical matters. One corporate executive who anticipated having to give a number of important speeches and presentations began calling small meetings of his subordinates more frequently. At these meetings, he presented new information and problems to them as a group rather than following his usual habit of dropping in on each of them individually. On one occasion, when he was preparing his department's strategic plan for the following year to top management, he called his subordinates together for a rehearsal: "My success at presenting the strategic plan will affect our budget and staff allowances for a full year," he told them, "so I want you to give me all the help you can."

Rehearse Your Presentation

Many presentational catastrophes come from inadequate rehearsal. Missing note cards, excessive length, clumsy wording, and confusing material can all be remedied if you practice in advance. As you add more and more technological aids to your presentation, the need for complete and careful rehearsal increases dramatically. Projector bulbs can burn out, extension cords can be too short, slides can be upside down or mixed up, and microphones can fail. It's better to find out these facts before you face a real audience.

Computer-assisted presentations can create the ultimate presentational nightmare, as a few examples illustrate.

> Multimedia producer Dave Mandala was scheduled to deliver a sophisticated presentation in Hungary. Just to be safe, he shipped himself twelve monitors instead of the eight he needed. He was horrified to open his metal-framed, cushioned packing cases to find that each one was filled with water.

Craig O'Connor, a telecommuting consultant, used his own equipment to deliver an important talk. Halfway through the presentation, O'Connor's personal calendar program flashed a message onto the two huge projection screens he was using, reminding him of his wife's request to pick up a package of feminine hygiene products on the way home.

Consultant Danny Cooper was scheduled to speak before a nationwide group of theater producers. He checked and tested his rental equipment before the talk began, and everything worked perfectly. The presentation began smoothly: His computerized images flashed impressively on the screen one after another. But to Cooper's increasing dismay, after a few minutes the projection panel he was using to display his images began to fade. After about 20 minutes, the panel projected pure white, and no amount of fiddling could bring back his images.[11]

Rehearsals can minimize catastrophes like these. They will also ensure that you are familiar with your material by the time you face your audience. As you practice your talk, follow the guidelines below.

Rehearse on Your Feet, before an Audience. Mental rehearsal has its place, but you won't know if your ideas sound good or if they fit into the available time until you say them aloud.

Expect Your Talk to Run 20 Percent Longer. Presentations almost always run longer in real time than during rehearsals. If you are speaking for ten minutes, rehearse for about eight. Even if your talk ultimately runs a bit short, nobody will mind.

Rehearse Three to Six Times. Fewer than three times may leave you feeling shaky about your content. More than six times can make your talk sound canned.

Pay Special Attention to Your Introduction and Conclusion. Audiences remember the opening and closing of a talk most clearly. The first and last moments of your presentation have special importance, so make sure you deliver them effectively in a way that makes every word count.

Rehearse in a Real Setting. If possible, rehearse in the room where you will actually speak. Make sure that you have all the equipment you will need and that it all works. The checklist in Table 13-2 can help you keep track of the materials you need.

Think Rationally about Your Presentation

Some speakers feel more apprehensive because of the way they *think* about the speech than because of the act of speaking.[12] This is why the executive mentioned above felt little fear about speaking before friends, co-workers,

TABLE 13-2 Speaking-Materials Checklist

Equipment Needed	Supplies
Overhead projector	Audiotapes or videotapes (blank or prerecorded)
Slide projector (with remote control)	Paper
Projection screen	Pencils, pens
Audiocassette recorder	Name cards
Video recorder (proper format)	Chalk, marking pens
Video camera (with connecting cable)	Handouts
Video monitor	Attendance list
Extension cord(s)	
Chalkboard	
Flip chart	
Easel	
Podium	

or subordinates but felt very anxious about delivering the same speech to top management—an audience of powerful strangers. In such cases, we think of the event differently. In the first case, the thought is "I know I'll be accepted," while in the second instance, the speaker thinks "They might not like what I'm saying."

Researchers have identified a number of irrational but powerful beliefs that lead to unnecessary apprehension.[13] Among these mistaken beliefs are the following three myths.

Myth: A Presentation Must Be Perfect. Whether you're addressing a meeting of potential clients worth millions of dollars to your company or a small group of trainees, your presentation must be clearly organized, well documented, and effectively delivered. Expecting it to be perfect, though, is a surefire prescription for nervousness and depression. A talk can be effective without being flawless. The same principle holds for other types of speaking errors. Most listeners won't notice if you omit a point or rearrange an idea or two.

Myth: It Is Possible to Persuade the Entire Audience. Even the best products don't sell to everyone, and even the most talented people don't win the full support of their audiences. Instead of expecting to persuade everyone, strive for and be satisfied with the support you need.

It is a mistake to expect one presentation to achieve everything you are seeking. Your first sales presentation might only convince a prospective customer to consider buying the furniture for a new office building from your company, or you may have to convince management to let you hire ten more staff members over five years, rather than all at once. If you think of your remarks as one step in a campaign to achieve your long-term goals, you will feel less pressure.

Myth: The Worst Will Probably Happen. Some pessimistic speakers make themselves unnecessarily nervous by dwelling on the worst possible outcomes. They imagine themselves tripping on the way to the podium, going blank, or mixing up their ideas. They picture the audience asking unanswerable questions, responding with hostility, or even laughing. Even though such disasters are unlikely, these daydreams take on a life of their own and may create a self-fulfilling prophecy: the fearful thoughts themselves can cause the speaker to bungle a presentation.

One way to overcome the irrational fear of failure is to indulge your catastrophic fantasies. Picture yourself fainting from terror, everyone falling asleep, or the boss firing you on the spot. Now imagine the best possible outcome: receiving a standing ovation or an immediate promotion to the vice-presidency. After thinking about these extremes, ask yourself how likely each is. Then think about what might *really* happen and realize that you have the ability to determine the outcome within that range of realistic possibilities.

SUMMARY

There are four types of presentational delivery: manuscript, memorized, extemporaneous, and impromptu. With rare exceptions, an extemporaneous style is the most effective, combining the enthusiasm that comes with spontaneity and the accuracy that comes from rehearsal. When an impromptu talk is necessary, it will be most effective if the speaker presents a clear thesis; supports it with reasons, logic, or facts; speaks without apologizing; and does not ramble on.

Good delivery involves a number of elements, including visual, verbal, and vocal ones. Most of these involve looking enthusiastic and confident and sounding well rehearsed and committed to both the topic and the audience. Speaking in front of a video camera calls for some special considerations regarding the way you appear, speak, and move.

Question-and-answer sessions are part of almost every presentation. They allow a speaker to respond to the concerns of an audience more quickly and completely than is possible in written documents. A speaker needs to decide whether to invite questions during or after the prepared part of a presentation. Handling questions during a talk permits a speaker to clarify points as they arise, although there is a risk of getting sidetracked by discussing irrelevant points or information that will come up later in a presentation. Responding to questions after the prepared segment of a talk lets the speaker keep control of both the available time and the way information is introduced. On the other hand, listeners who have to hold their questions may be too distracted to follow the speaker's other points carefully.

Anxiety about speaking is common and not always a problem. A manageable amount of anxiety causes a speaker to prepare carefully and contributes to an energetic presentation. A speaker can keep anxiety within tolerable limits by accepting it as a normal occurrence, being well prepared, and thinking rationally about the event. Rational thinking involves the realization that one need not be perfect in order to be effective, that no single presentation will fully persuade an entire audience, and that catastrophes are unlikely to occur.

RESOURCES

Paulson, L. R., "Coming Across on Video and TV," in *The Executive Persuader: How to Be a Powerful Speaker* (Napa, Calif.: SSI Publishing, 1991).

Whether you are preparing videotaped presentations or appearing live on camera, this chapter is full of practical details and techniques that will help you perform more effectively. The rest of the book is just as practical for more insight on presentational speaking.

Richmond, V. P., and J. C. McCroskey, *Communication: Apprehension, Avoidance, and Effectiveness,* 3rd ed. (Scottsdale, Ariz.: Gorsuch Scarisbrick, 1992).

This concise book is one of the best sources of material on communication anxiety. Causes and effects of apprehension about communicating in many contexts, not only the public speaking context, are addressed and the appendix provides multiple self-report instruments for readers to assess their communication apprehension.

Wilder, C., "Energizing Yourself," in *The Presentations Kit: 10 Steps for Selling Your Ideas* (New York: Wiley, 1994).

Focusing on the many ways speakers can use nonverbal channels to energize themselves and their presentations, this chapter shows how to add zest to your addresses. Some suggestions are also directed at speaking to audiences of other cultures.

CHAPTER 14

Informative, Group, and Special-Occasion Speaking

KEY TERMS

Briefings / Explanations / Interjections / Reports / Signposts / Training

The last four chapters provided a set of guidelines that will serve you well when planning and delivering any type of presentation. But certain speaking situations call for unique approaches, and this chapter will discuss several of them. In the following pages you will learn how to speak effectively when the goal is to inform an audience. You will see what it takes to make a presentation when you are part of a team. Finally, you will learn guidelines for speaking on special occasions: when welcoming a visitor or newcomer, when making an introduction, when presenting or accepting an award, and when offering tribute to a person or institution.

INFORMATIVE PRESENTATIONS

Informative presentations are a common type of communication at work. Consider a few examples: An office manager explains to employees how to use the company's new voice-mail system. A human resources specialist explains federal and state laws governing nondiscrimination in hiring to a committee that will be interviewing job candidates. The foreman of a construction job gives the client a report on the progress of the project. A corporate recruiter speaks to an audience of college students on the opportunities in his industry.

As these examples show, some informative messages are delivered informally, with the speaker and a few listeners gathered around a conference table or piece of equipment. These messages might be brief ones: to help people catch up on late-breaking developments or to explain simple procedures like how to operate the new fax machine. Other informative messages are delivered in formal settings; the audience might be large and the planning extensive. Management might explain how the acquisition of the company by a large corporation will affect operations. A professional trainer might lead a three-day workshop on new accounting procedures.

Whatever the setting, topic, and audience, delivering informative material in an effective way is important. Recent college graduates recognize this fact: when a group of alumni were asked to rate the importance of a wide array of speaking skills, informative speaking wound up at the top of the list.[1] Perhaps the reason that businesspeople see the value of good speaking skills is because many of the presentations they hear are awful. Almost half of the vice-presidents surveyed at the nation's top 1,000 corporations reported that they found the majority of business presentations "boring," and 40 percent admitted that they had dozed off at least once during a presentation.[2]

Applying the techniques of effective speaking that you have already learned in Chapters 10 through 13 will help keep your audience awake, alert, and informed. The material in the following pages offers even more advice about how to make sure your informative presentations are successful.

Most informative presentations fall into one of four categories: reports, briefings, explanations, and training. ***Reports*** describe the state of an operation. They are usually (but not always) given by subordinates to their superiors to keep them informed and help them make decisions. Some reports are frequent and informal, such as the daily accounting of sales volume that department heads give a sales manager. Others are more formal, such as the financial accounting that senior management presents at a stockholders' meeting or the final report that a project manager gives to his superior. In between is a range of reports, including a sales representative's progress report, a secretary's report to her boss on events that occurred while he was on a business trip, a market researcher's profile of a market segment, and a plant supervisor's report on workers' reaction to a new machine.

Briefings are short talks that inform a generally knowledgeable audience about a specific area in which new knowledge has been gleaned.[3] The executive chef of a restaurant might brief waiters about the details of a new menu. The account representative handling an advertising account might brief the agency's team about a client before an important meeting. Nurses and police officers attend briefings before each shift to bring them up to the moment on the current situation.

Explanations increase listeners' understanding of a subject. An orientation session for new workers falls into this category, as does a meeting in which a new employee-benefits package is introduced or a purchasing policy explained. When a firm faces a major change in its business fortunes—whether this means growth or cutbacks—wise managers gather their employees and explain how the change will affect each one of them. Sometimes explanations are aimed at audiences outside the company. A utility company representative describing the future of electrical rates to the Rotary Club meeting and a community official explaining the effects of new zoning ordinances on local industry are also giving explanations. The sample speech that follows this section explains to employees how the company's tax-reduction plan will increase their real income.

Training teaches listeners how to do something. It can be informal or highly structured, from the simple advice an experienced employee gives a newcomer about how to transfer a telephone call to a week-long seminar on accounting principles for managers of a company.

Successful businesses recognize the value of training. One measure of its importance is the amount of time and money that firms invest in training their employees. For example, at McDonald's, every person who takes an order or prepares food has received eighty hours of instruction.[4] On any given day, International Business Machines Corporation is training 22,000 of its employees somewhere in the world. This sort of training doesn't come cheap. The annual cost of this training for IBM is $1.5 billion, not counting the participants' time.[5]

Strategies for Effective Informative Speaking

Whether you're explaining how you want your office organized, how your division solved a problem, or how your organization works, getting your audience to listen and understand can be one of the hardest communication tasks to face. You can use the following techniques to make your presentations interesting and clear.

Cover Only Necessary Information. As an informative speaker, you will usually be far more knowledgeable about the topic than the audience to whom you speak. This knowledge is both a blessing and a potential curse. On the one hand, your command of the subject means that you can explain the topic thoroughly. On the other hand, you may be tempted to give listeners more information than they want or need.

If you cover your topic in too much detail, you are likely to bore—or even antagonize—your listeners. One personnel specialist made this mistake when briefing a group of staffers about how to file claims with a new health insurance carrier. Instead of simply explaining what steps to take when they needed care, he launched into a twenty-minute explanation of why the company chose the present carrier, how that company processed claims at its home office, and where each copy of the four-part claims form was directed after it was filed. By the time he got to the part of his talk that was truly important to the audience—how to get reimbursed for out-of-pocket expenses—the staffers were so bored and restless that they had a hard time sitting still for the information. Don't make a mistake like this in your presentations: as you plan your remarks, ask yourself what your listeners need to know, and tell them just that much. If they want more information, they will probably ask for it.

Besides boring your listeners, there is always the danger that when you overwhelm them with information, they'll become so confused that they'll give up trying to understand the material you are explaining. One office manager created this sort of short circuit in the minds of her staff when she explained the features of a new word processing system. "It will do everything," she gushed. For the next hour she described the wonders of the program: its ability to handle footnotes, prepare indexes, offset page margins for bound books, hyphenate words, create tables of contents, number paragraphs, outline ideas, perform mathematical functions, and print documents in over thirty-five typefaces. As her talk stretched on, the staff grew more distressed. As one worker later put it, "You have to walk before you can run. I wish she had started by showing us how to type up simple letters and memos. After we could do that, then maybe we would have been ready to learn about all the bells and whistles."

Link the Topic to the Audience. People will most likely listen to a speaker when they have a reason for doing so. Sometimes the intrinsic interest of the subject is reason enough to listen; for instance, most people would

> The trickiest report to give is a technical one for nontechnical people. A key industry problem today is that everyone is a specialist—at least everyone seems to be. Both society and industry have become so complicated that the generalist is obsolete. All of us who are technicians in our own field are now obliged to communicate our expertise to nontechnical people. . . . Today's executive must package his technical information in a way that can be understood by nontechnical people.
>
> John T. Molloy, *Molloy's Live for Success*

listen carefully to a session on the fringe benefits of their jobs because they know the benefits are worth something to them personally. On the other hand, most people probably aren't interested in a discussion of "how we design the financial structures for new projects."

What can you do with a subject that isn't intrinsically interesting? One way to boost interest is to show that listening will help the audience avoid punishment. ("Don't try to charge the company for anything you're not entitled to. If you do, you'll be put on probation, or you could lose your job.") A pleasanter and more effective alternative, however, involves demonstrating the payoffs that come from listening. Some important needs are physical health, safety from danger, financial security, friendship, job advancement, recreation, and respect from others.

A financial officer explaining new expense-account procedures, for instance, might begin by saying, "I want to make sure you get the company to reimburse you for all expenses you're entitled to. I also don't want you to spend your own money, thinking the company will pay you back, and then find out it won't." Expense reporting might be a tedious subject to many people, but the chance to save money (or to avoid losing money) would also interest most listeners.

Link the Familiar to the Unfamiliar. Research has shown that people have the best chance of understanding new material when it bears some relationship to information they already know.[6] Without a familiar reference point, listeners may have trouble understanding even a clear definition. Two examples illustrate how comparisons and contrasts with familiar information help make new ideas more understandable:

Confusing: Unlike magnetic media, a CD-ROM computer disk is a storage medium that can be read optically by a laser scanner.

More familiar: The best way to understand the difference between CD-ROM and floppy computer disks is to compare the two most common ways we can buy music recordings these days: audiotape cassettes and CDs. A floppy disk works much like an audiotape, while a

SKILL BUILDER

What needs or interests could you appeal to in each of the following presentations?

1. A briefing for employees on new performance appraisal procedures
2. A training program on listening skills for managers
3. A speech to local high school students on "Careers in ———" (You choose the topic.)
4. A report to the administration of a college on student attitudes toward business courses
5. A presentation promoting a one-day $50 "Dress for Success" seminar to students

CD-ROM disk is more like the CDs you can buy at the local music store. [If the listeners understand the difference between audiotapes and CDs, they will find it easier to understand the computer storage media.]

Confusing: Money-market funds are mutual funds that buy corporate and government short-term investments. [In order to understand this definition, the audience needs to be familiar with money-market funds and with corporate and government short-term investments.]

More familiar: Money-market funds are like a collection of IOUs held by a middleman. The funds take cash from investors and lend it to corporations and the government, usually for between thirty and ninety days. These borrowers pay the fund interest on the load, and that interest is passed along to the investors. [If the listeners understand IOUs and interest, they can follow this definition.]

Involve the Audience. Listeners who are actively involved in a presentation will understand and remember the material far better than will passive listeners.[7] There are three ways to involve the audience: having direct participation, using volunteers, and holding question-and-answer sessions.

Of these three methods, *direct participation* creates the greatest involvement. This approach is especially effective when you want the listeners to develop a skill or firsthand understanding. People will learn how to operate a particular machine, fill in a certain form, or perform a specified procedure much better with hands-on experience than they will if they are only told what to do. Sales training often involves simulated experiences in addition to lectures and reading assignments. For example, Lever Corporation trains its representatives to sell industrial cleaning equipment by teaching them to operate the machines themselves.[8] A variety of other tools involve the audience in a way that boosts both understanding and interest: quizzes, contests, and having trainees teach one another.

SKILL BUILDER

Describe how you could use familiar concepts to help introduce one of the following topics to a group of listeners who did not understand it. (If you are not familiar with any of the topics below, choose a concept that you do understand, and explain it in terms an audience will find familiar.)

1. Depreciation of business equipment
2. Computer operating system commands
3. Etiquette at a business meal
4. Stagflation
5. The life cycle of a product
6. A corporate balance sheet
7. Chapter 11 bankruptcy

Using *volunteers* can create interest and let even the nonparticipating listeners get a sense of how they might have responded if they had been chosen. For example, a sales representative who is demonstrating a new computer system might ask a member of the audience to provide a specific problem, which the speaker would then use to show how the system operates.

These methods are highly entertaining and very appropriate for training and explaining sessions, especially with a large audience. For day-to-day reports and briefings, however, they probably would be too much. In the latter cases, *question-and-answer sessions* are desirable, if not absolutely necessary.

Organizing Informative Messages

The way you structure your message will affect how well the audience understands it. All the principles you learned in Chapter 11 apply for reports, briefings, explanations, and training. Beyond these basic guidelines, two strategies will help make your ideas easy to follow.

Start with an Overall Picture. Every presentation needs an introduction. But when the goal is to inform listeners, a clear preview is especially important. Without an overview, your listeners can become so confused by your informational trees that they won't be able to see the conceptual forest. Orient the audience by sketching the highlights of your message in enough detail to help listeners see what they are expected to know and how you will explain it to them. In the following example, the vice-president of a corporation facing a major change began her remarks with a preview that addressed the biggest concern of her listeners and outlined the information she would be presenting:

> As you probably know by now, management has decided to move all our manufacturing operations to the new Texas plant. There have been a lot of rumors floating around about what that will mean for us here, and we want you to know the facts.
>
> The most important fact is that *no employee*—not a single person—will lose his or her job as a result of this move. There will, however, be some changes in what many of us will be doing and where we'll be doing it. That's what I'll be explaining here today. Specifically, everyone here will fit into one of three categories. Some of us will keep doing the same work at the same place. Others will be staying here, but will be retrained in new jobs. And some of us will be offered our same jobs in Texas—along with some pretty generous incentives to make the move.

SKILL BUILDER

Describe how you could involve the audience in a training session on each of the following topics:

1. How to deal with customer complaints
2. How to use a new voice-mail phone system
3. Whether to lease or buy a piece of equipment
4. How to fill out a new expense-account form

> You're probably wondering which of these categories you fit in, so let me explain.

An overview is also important when you're giving instructions or describing a process. This orientation helps listeners see where you're headed, as the next example shows:

> "This morning, we're going to learn about the new E-mail system. I'll start by spending a little time explaining how the system works. Then we'll talk about the four ways you can use the system. First I'll show you how you can send messages to any person or group of people in the company—instantly. Then we'll talk about how you can get messages others have sent you. After that you will learn how you can put items on the companywide bulletin board. Finally, I'll show you how you can take part in companywide electronic conversations about topics that interest you.
>
> "I'll spend about ten minutes describing each of these steps in detail, and after each description you'll get a chance to try out the system yourself. By the time we break for lunch, you should be able to use the system in a way that will save you time and hassles and keep you better informed about what you need to know to get your job done. You won't be an expert, but you'll know enough to make the system work.

Emphasize Important Points. Since an oral presentation doesn't allow listeners to stop the flow of information and review what's been said—which they could do if they were reading a report or listening to a tape—it is especially vital to highlight key points. You can use several techniques to emphasize important points.

Number Items. If you are covering several points in a presentation or listing steps in a process, identifying each one by number will keep listeners aware of where you are:

> "The first advantage of the new plan is . . ."
>
> "A second benefit the plan will give us is . . ."

Use Signposts. As their name implies, ***signposts*** tell listeners how a new piece of material relates to your topic. Transitions are a kind of signpost:

> "We've talked about the problems that are facing the office products division; now let's look at some solutions."

Individual words or phrases can also let an audience know how your next remarks fit into a presentation:

> "*Another* important cost to consider is our overhead."

"*Next,* let's look at the production figures."

"*Finally,* we need to consider changes in customer demand."

Use Interjections. ***Interjections*** are words or phrases thrown into a commentary to highlight the importance or placement of an idea:

"So what we've learned—*and this is important*—is that it's impossible to control personal use of office telephones."

"Now here's another feature—*perhaps the best of all*—that makes this such a terrific plan."

Use Repetition and Redundancy. Repeating words (repetition) or delivering an idea two or more times in slightly different words (redundancy) intensifies the message and increases the odds that your point will get across:

"Under the old system it took three weeks—*that's fifteen working days*—to get the monthly sales figures. Now we can get the numbers in just two days. That's right, *two days.*"

Add Internal Summaries and Previews. Unlike readers of a written document, people who listen to a presentation don't have the luxury of scanning a table of contents or rereading a paragraph to figure out how one part of your message relates to another. A way to help your audience stay oriented is to offer periodically an internal summary reviewing the important points you've covered:

"Now you can see that the problem grew from several causes: a shortage of parts, inexperienced maintenance people, and the overload of opening the new warehouse."

Like internal summaries, internal previews orient an audience—this time by alerting listeners to the upcoming points:

"You're probably wondering how all these changes will affect you. Well, some of them will make life much easier, and others will present some challenges. Let's look at three advantages first, and then we'll look at a couple of those challenges I mentioned."

In many cases, you can maximize the clarity of a presentation by combining an internal summary and a preview:

"You can see that we've made great progress in switching to the new inventory system. As I've said, the costs were about 10 percent more than we anticipated, but we see that as a one-time expense. I wish I could be as positive about the next item on the agenda—the customer service problems we've been having. Complaints have increased. We do believe we've finally identified the problem, so let me explain it and show you how we plan to deal with it."

Use Multiple Channels. Listeners are likely to understand and remember a message when you deliver it via more than one channel. You can present figures on an overhead projector or flip chart while you introduce them orally. You might then represent those numbers visually, using a chart or graph. If you're discussing a physical object, you might display photos of it on slides or even bring in the object itself to show your listeners. If you are illustrating a process, you might decide to play a brief videotape of it.

Using multiple channels has two advantages: First, it allows you to pick the most efficient medium to represent your ideas. Some concepts are best expressed in words, but others are much clearer when the audience can see, hear, or even touch them. Talking about a new line of clothing or a new food product isn't nearly as effective as giving your audience a firsthand look or taste, for example. Likewise, telling listeners in a training session how to deal with customer objections isn't nearly as effective as demonstrating the procedure for them or letting them handle a situation themselves.

Second, besides being clearer, multiple channels have the advantage of keeping your listeners interested. The variety of seeing images, hearing recordings, or handling a sample is likely to make an audience eager to learn more, while listening to even a good speaker talk for an extended period can lead to fatigue.

SAMPLE INFORMATIVE PRESENTATION

The following presentation is typical of informative talks given every business day. The personnel specialist in a medium-size company has gathered a group of staff members together to describe the features of a tax-reduction plan covering employee benefits. Notice how the speaker uses most of the strategies covered in this chapter to make her ideas clearer and to increase the attention of her audience.

There are only three means of description available to us—words, pictures, and numbers. The palette is limited. Generally, the best instructions rely on all three, but in any instance one should predominate, while the other two serve and extend. The key to giving good instructions is to choose the appropriate means.

If I were going to describe my office, I could tell you in words, but it would take forever. I could tell you in numbers, but you would be left without a sense of the texture of the environment; you would have statistics without context. Clearly, the most appropriate way to describe my office would be in pictures, with a few dimensions and words of explanation.

If I were going to describe a person, a picture could never convey the complexities of personality. Only words might possibly do this, with a picture to enhance the description.

If I were going to describe the tangible assets of a company, I would probably rely on numbers, i.e. gross sales, profitability, market share, because these would be the easiest to compare, and would help you understand a company in terms relative to others of its kind.

Richard Saul Wurman, *Information Anxiety*

The speaker's goal here is to help listeners decide whether they're interested enough in the benefits plan to attend a much longer meeting on the subject. She wisely chose this approach to avoid going into detail about the plan when some people might not be interested. By giving a short description of how the plan works, she can keep this introductory talk brief and simple.

[The promise of increasing take-home pay is a guaranteed attention getter.]

I know you're busy, but I don't think you'll mind taking a few minutes away from work this morning. You see, I'm here today to show you a way that you can increase the amount of money you take home each month

No, I'm not going to announce an across-the-board raise. But increasing your salary isn't the only way to boost your income. Another way that works just as well is to reduce your taxes. After all, every dollar less you pay in taxes is like having a dollar more in your pocket.

[An overall view of the plan is presented here.]

In the next few minutes, I'll explain the company's Flexible Benefits Plan. It's a perfectly legal option that lets you increase your real income by cutting the amount of taxes you pay, so that your income will grow even without a raise. I know this sounds too good to be true, but it really works! I've already signed up, and figure it will save me almost $2,000 a year. It can probably save you a lot, too.

[A brief transition alerts listeners to the first main point in the body of the presentation: the difference between before- and after-tax dollars.]

[The enlarged display of a familiar paycheck stub clarifies the unfamiliar concepts of before- and after-tax dollars.]

Before you can appreciate how the Flexible Benefits Plan works, you have to understand the difference between before-tax and after-tax dollars. [The speaker shows Exhibit 1 here.] Before-tax dollars are the amount that shows up every month in the "Gross Amount" box on our paychecks. But we don't get to spend our full salaries. There are several deductions: federal income tax withholding, social security (the amount in the "F.I.C.A." box), state tax withholding, and disability insurance premiums (the amount in the "S.D.I." box). What's left in the "Net Amount" box is our pay in after-tax dollars.

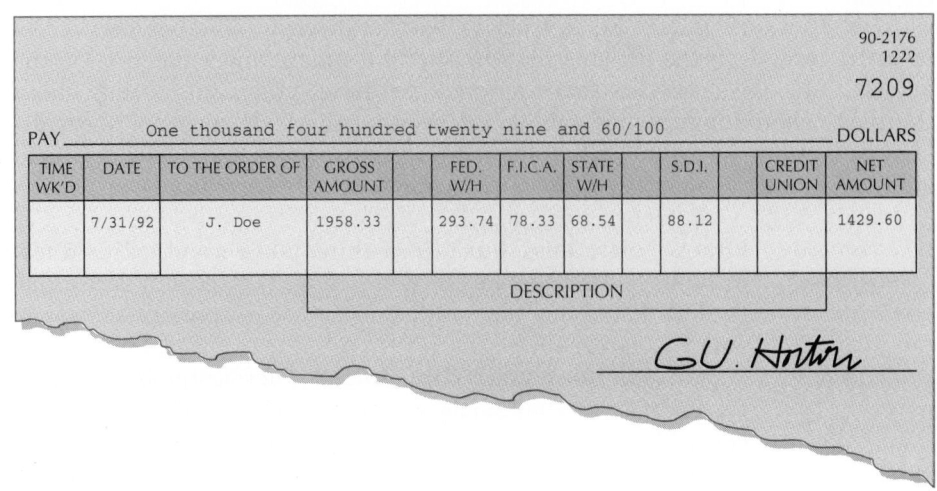

90-2176
1222

7209

PAY One thousand four hundred twenty nine and 60/100 DOLLARS

TIME WK'D	DATE	TO THE ORDER OF	GROSS AMOUNT		FED. W/H	F.I.C.A.	STATE W/H		S.D.I.		CREDIT UNION	NET AMOUNT
	7/31/92	J. Doe	1958.33		293.74	78.33	68.54		88.12			1429.60

DESCRIPTION

G.U. Horton

EXHIBIT 1 Paycheck Stub

[The speaker wisely avoids a complicated discussion of before- and after-tax dollars in different tax brackets.]

Once all those deductions are taken away from our pay, every before-tax dollar shrinks in value to about 73 cents. [The speaker shows Exhibit 2 here.] And that's in a low tax bracket. If your income is higher, then the difference between before- and after-tax dollars is even bigger. This means that it takes at least $136.33 in after-tax dollars to buy something that costs $100 in before-tax dollars.

[The visual display increases the clarity and impact of the difference between before- and after-tax dollars.]

EXHIBIT 2 Value of Before-and After-Tax Dollars

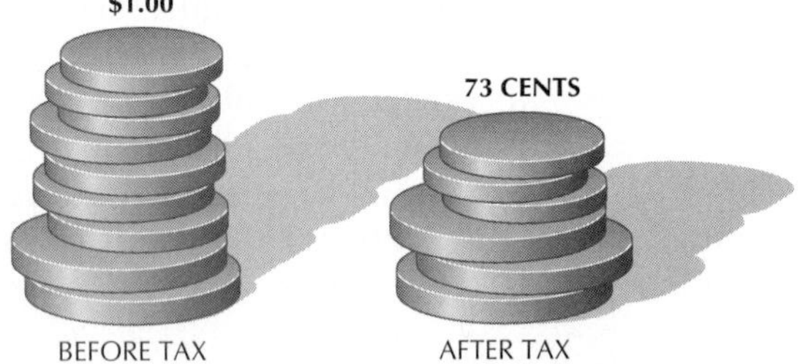

[*The transition here makes movement to the second part of body clear.*]

You can probably see now that it's better to buy things in before-tax dollars whenever you can. And that's what the Flexible Benefits Plan lets you do. Let me explain how it works.

[*An internal preview ori-*

The Flexible Benefits Plan is so great because it allows you to pay for some important items in before-tax dollars. The *ents the audience to the next two points.*]

plan lets you set aside pay in two categories: medical costs and dependent care. Let's cover each of these in detail so you can see which expenses are covered.

[*The speaker generates audience involvement by inviting listeners to consider their own expenses in following areas.*]

A look at the chart entitled "Allowable Medical Expenses" shows which items you can use under the Flexible Benefits Plan. [The speaker points to each item on Exhibit 3 as she discusses it.] As I cover these expenses, think about how much *you* spend in each area.

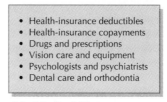

- Health-insurance deductibles
- Health-insurance copayments
- Drugs and prescriptions
- Vision care and equipment
- Psychologists and psychiatrists
- Dental care and orthodontia

EXHIBIT 3 Allowable Medical Expenses

[*The chart helps listeners understand which expenses are covered.*]

[*The hypothetical example helps show how the plan works in real life.*]

First we'll talk about health insurance deductibles and co-payments. Under our company's policy, you pay the first $300 of expenses for yourself and each dependent. You also make a $10 co-payment for each visit to a doctor. Let's say that you and one dependent have to pay the $300 deductible each year, and that you made five visits to the doctor. That's a total of $650 per year you could have covered under the plan.

[*A citation helps prove that the cost of medicines is considerable.*]

Drugs and prescriptions include every kind of medicine you buy, even if you buy it over the counter without a prescription. And, don't forget, the plan covers payments you make for everyone you claim as a dependent: your kids, maybe your spouse, and maybe even an older parent whom you're caring for. Here's an article from *Changing Times* magazine that says that a family of three spends an average of $240 per year on drugs. Maybe you spend even more. Whatever you do spend on medicine can be included in the plan, which means you will pay less for it than if you used after-tax dollars.

[*Examples of typical vision-care fees illus-*

Vision care and equipment include eyeglasses and contact lenses as well as any fees you or your dependents pay to optometrists or ophthalmologists. With a pair of reading glasses *trate the potential costs in this area.*]

costing at least $45 and a new set of contact lenses costing over $80, the money could really mount up.

Psychologists and psychiatrists are also covered, which means that any counseling you receive will cost a lot less.

Dental care and orthodontia are covered, too. If you or your dependents need major dental work, this can mean a lot. And if you're paying for your kids' braces, you can really save a bundle. We did some checking, and the average orthodontic treatment today runs about $3,500 over three years—or over $1,000 per year.

[*Comparing the unfamiliar benefits plan to the familiar notion of a discount helps make the advantages clear.*]

Nobody likes to spend money for medical expenses like these, but paying for them with before-tax dollars under the Flexible Benefits Plan is like getting a discount of 20 percent or more—clearly, a great deal.

[*Transition uses signposting to mark a shift to the second type of expense covered by the plan.*]

But medical costs aren't the only expenses you can include in the Flexible Benefits Plan. There's a second way you can boost your take-home pay: by including dependent care in the plan.

[*The example of potential savings under the plan is a guaranteed attention getter for working parents.*]

For most people, dependents are children. Any costs of caring for your kids can be paid for in before-tax dollars, meaning you'll pay a lot less. You can include day-care services, preschool fees, even in-home care for your child. We did some checking and found that keeping a child in preschool or day care in this area from 8:30 in the morning until 5 P.M. averages about $5,000 per year. By shifting this amount into the Flexible Benefits Plan, the real cost drops by over $1,000. Not bad for filling out a few forms!

[*A restatement of the thesis is combined with introduction of an example to support its claim.*]

When you combine the savings on health care and dependents, the potential savings that come from joining the Flexible Benefits Plan are impressive. Let's take a look at a typical example of just how much money the Flexible Benefits Plan can save. Your personal situation probably won't be exactly like this one, but you can still get a feeling for how good the plan is. [The speaker shows Exhibit 4.]

[*The chart provides a visual outline of the example. Without the exhibit,*

Let's suppose your salary is $23,500 and you have a spouse and one child. Let's say that your health and dependent expenses are pretty much like the ones we've been discussing here today. [The speaker points to "Salary Reductions" section of chart.] Your health-insurance deductibles and co-payments

	WITHOUT PLAN	WITH PLAN
GROSS SALARY	$23,500	$23,500
SALARY REDUCTIONS		
Health Care	0	650
Prescriptions and Drugs	0	240
Vision Care	0	60
Dental Care	0	180
Dependent Care	0	1,800
	$23,500	$20,570
TAXES		
Federal Income Tax @ 15%	3,525	3,085
State Income Tax @ 3.5%	764	720
FICA and SDI @ 8.15%	1,915	1,676
	$6,204	$5,481
AFTER-TAX EXPENSES		
Health Care	650	0
Prescriptions and Drugs	240	0
Vision Care	60	0
Dental Care	180	0
Dependent Care	1,800	0
Net Pay	$14,366	$15,089
ANNUAL SAVINGS $723		

EXHIBIT 4 Savings with Flexible Benefits Plan

the dollar amounts would be too confusing to follow.]

amount to $650, and you spend $240 over the year on prescriptions and drugs. Let's say that one person in your family needs one set of eyeglasses. You all get dental checkups, and you don't even have cavities! You spend $1,800 on child care—not bad these days.

If we look at the top third of the chart, it might seem that following the plan costs you more. After all, your salary would be $23,500 without the plan but only $20,570 with your expenses deducted from the plan.

[*As the speaker points to the "Annual Savings" line on the chart, the audience sees in real dollars the potential advantage of the plan.*]

But look what happens once we start to figure taxes. [The speaker points to "Taxes" section of chart.] Since your pay with the plan is less, you pay less in taxes. A little subtraction shows that the difference between the $6,204 you'd pay without the plan and the $5,481 you'd pay with it amounts to a savings of $723.

This is just a small example of how much you can save. If your expenses are higher—if you have more medical costs, for example—the advantage is even greater. As your salary goes up and you move into a higher tax bracket, the advantages grow, too. And don't forget that the savings I've been talking about are just for one year. As time goes by, your earning power will grow even more.

[In a restatement of the thesis the speaker returns to the main advantage of the plan.]

Now you can see why we're so glad to offer the Flexible Benefits Plan. It can boost your take-home pay even before you get a raise. It costs you nothing.

[Listeners are told what to do next if they are interested in the plan.]

If you're interested in learning more, we encourage you to read the booklet I'll hand out in a moment. It contains a worksheet that will help you estimate how much you stand to save under the plan. If the idea still interests you, please attend the workshop we'll be holding next Friday during the lunch hour in the third-floor meeting room. At that time, we can answer your questions and make an appointment for each of you to sign up at the personnel office. In the meantime, I'll be happy to answer any questions you have now.

GROUP PRESENTATIONS

Group presentations are a common feature in the working world. Sometimes the members of a group may be asked (or told) to present their information together. Other times team members choose to speak collectively, realizing that several presenters can be more effective than a single person.

Some group presentations are delivered to internal audiences. For example, a project team may be asked to give a status report to management, a computer support staff may introduce a new software package to users, and union representatives may brief members on negotiation progress. Other group presentations are delivered to external audiences. Sales teams make pitches to potential customers. Public officials explain their plans or actions to citizens. Representatives from health-care providers explain insurance benefits to employees. School officials inform parents about curriculum changes.

Group presentations can be effective for a variety of reasons. Hearing from several speakers can provide the variety that will keep audience members tuned in. For example, a sales pitch to a potential client would probably be strengthened by the contributions of experts in marketing, customer support, and product design. Besides adding interest, the perspectives of several people can give a more complete message than any single speaker could provide. It is easy to see how a presentation recruiting volunteers or soliciting donations to a worthy cause would be strengthened by the testimony of several people who have been involved. Sometimes presentation teams are balanced for gender, ethnicity, age, income level, or a variety of other factors in order to appeal to a wider audience.

Group presentations share many of the characteristics of successful individual presentations discussed in Chapters 10 to 13. They have a clearly defined goal. They are based on a solid analysis of the speaking situation. Their main points are clearly organized and backed up with a variety of interesting and clear supporting materials. And, of course, they are delivered effectively. But along with sharing these basic qualities, group presentations—at least successful ones—and solo performances differ in some important ways.

Like every other form of group activity, team presentations take time to develop. Just setting up meetings to plan the talk can be a challenge, especially when group members don't work in the same location. Once the members have come together, brainstorming and other discussions are rarely quick, and consensus isn't always easy to achieve. Organizing a group presentation can also be challenging, since you need to coordinate several speakers. Without this sort of coordination, some material may be repeated ("Mary already covered this, but I'll just go over it again since that's what I was going to talk about"), contradicted ("Tamiko talked about gross profits, but her numbers didn't include costs"), or left out entirely ("I thought Luis was going to cover that"). Stumbles like these make the entire group look unprofessional and inept. Furthermore, if the group isn't careful to control the length of individual segments, the whole presentation is likely to run over its scheduled time, irritating audience members. Overcoming challenges like these calls for careful planning.

Organizing a Group Presentation

There are two ways to decide who will say what in a group presentation: by task and by topic. The approach you take will depend on an analysis of the situation.

Organizing by Topic. In some cases, it makes sense to break the presentation into separate segments, with each speaker addressing one or more topics. Organizing by topic is a logical approach when different parts of the material call for special expertise. For instance, a press conference in which county department heads announce new approaches to cost cutting almost demands separate information from each person. Likewise, a sales presentation would profit from having topics like customer support, engineering, and production discussed by representatives from each of those departments.

Organizing by Task. Sometimes a presentation doesn't fall neatly into separate topics. In this case, it may make sense to assign speakers separate roles within the discussion of a topic. One role might be "spokesperson," whose job it is to introduce the main points. Other members might take the role of "example givers," offering details to support the spokesperson's claims. For example, a neighborhood association urging the city council to install a new traffic signal at a busy intersection might use a problem-solution plan. One person's job would be to describe the overall problem and the group's solution. After making each of these main points, that speaker would introduce several individuals to back up the points with a range of supporting details. This plan organizes the material clearly and provides an impressive array of speakers who are more likely to impress the council than a single presenter. A rough outline for this approach would look something like this:

1. *Spokesperson describes the problem:*
   "Lack of a traffic signal encourages speeding traffic, leading to several accidents and near misses. This situation risks lives and exposes the city to liability suits."
2. *Other speakers offer support:*
   Neighbor 1 cites police reports on the number of speeding tickets issued in the past year.
   Neighbor 2 describes hospital reports on injuries from accidents at the intersection.
   Neighbor 3 describes recent near misses.
   Neighbor 4 (an attorney) explains the city's exposure to lawsuits.
3. *Spokesperson suggests a solution:*
   "Installation of a new traffic signal will reduce or eliminate the problem in a cost-effective way."
4. *Other speakers offer support:*
   Person 1 compares the cost of a new signal to the cost of settling lawsuits arising out of future accidents at the intersection.
   Person 2 shows that funds are available in the city's street improvement fund.
   Person 3 presents a petition of neighbors requesting traffic control at the intersection (suggesting voter support for the signal).

Using Time Effectively

One of the biggest challenges in planning a group presentation is managing time. A smart team will make sure that members work on their own whenever possible and will use meetings to handle business that can profit from shared discussion. As Chapter 9 explained, some tasks are best handled in meetings. Anything that requires the support of every member or can benefit from creative thinking should be discussed collectively. This includes choos-

SKILL BUILDER

Imagine that you have been asked to develop a thirty-minute program for local employers designed to show that graduates of your school will make top-notch employees.

1. Formulate a specific purpose and thesis statement for the presentation.
2. Decide what speakers would be most effective for such a program.
3. Develop an organizational plan for the program, and assign speakers according to topic or task.
4. Map out an agenda for planning and rehearsing the program that uses the members' time most efficiently and effectively.
5. If time permits, rehearse and present the program.

ing the group's topic (if defining it is within your control), determining the group's overall approach, and assigning specific roles. At this time the group will need to consider questions such as:

- What order will we speak in?
- How much time will we each have?
- Do we want the "M.C." to introduce every speaker and provide transitions between segments, or do we want each speaker to provide a transition and introduce the next group member?

Once the overall plan is set, members can probably tackle the next stage on their own. Individuals or smaller groups can research and plan their own segments of the talk. There's little advantage to having two or more members dig through the same part of the library or interview the same person to gather information. Some team members can perform specialized jobs, such as making arrangements for the setup of the speaking room and creating visuals for all the presenters to ensure a consistent design.

After members finish their "homework," they can meet and assemble their results into a coherent plan. This is probably a good time to start rehearsing the presentation. At this point team members will need to decide logistical questions such as who will set up and operate any equipment used in the presentation and who will serve as timekeeper to keep speakers from talking too long. Running over the allotted time is a common problem for individual speakers, and in group presentations it can create serious problems.

Planning an Introduction, Conclusion, and Transitions

Every presentation needs an effective introduction, conclusion, and transitions connecting main points, but these elements are especially important in group presentations. They help listeners follow the overall plan and prevent confusion that can come when several speakers share the stage.

The following introduction was given by the representative of an architectural firm seeking to make the "short list" of candidates for a corporate design job. Notice how it gives listeners a clear introduction to who will be speaking and each member's role:

> Good morning, everybody. Most of you know that I'm Diana Salazar of KBS associates. My colleagues and I want to thank you for the chance to show how we can work with you on the design and construction of your company's regional service center.
>
> Architects like to design beautiful buildings, of course, and we know you like our work or we wouldn't be here today. But beauty alone isn't enough: We create designs that can be constructed on time and on budget. And we are committed to designing buildings that work well for our clients after they're finished. You and your customers are going to use this service center for many years, and it has to meet your needs long after your architects are gone.
>
> This morning we want to give you a picture of how we can work with you to design and build an outstanding service center. You'll meet some of the people

who will be involved with this project, and you'll see how KBS has handled some other important jobs over the past few years.

My colleague David Nguyen will begin by showing you samples of some work we've done for other clients: Edutech's corporate headquarters in Dallas, two service centers for the American Automobile Association, and the master plan for the Vista del Sol Center in Austin. David will also be sharing quotes from former clients to give you a feeling for what it would be like to work with KBS Associates. Next, Tom Lee will introduce you to representatives of some of the consultants who will be working with us and you on this job: Bill Whitcroft of Western Engineering, Joy Liebert of Energy Management Systems, and Leo Wang, who would be our liaison with local governing agencies. We are proud of this team, and we want you to get a sense of what it would be like to work with them. Finally, Sabrina Boldt will present some preliminary sketches for the service center, based on the program that the consultants developed with you over the last several months.

In our short time with you this morning, we want you to see that KBS is ready, willing, and able to tailor this project to your specific needs, just as we've done with other clients. So let's begin. David will start by showing you the kind of successful relationships we've built with clients in the last couple of years. David . . .

Like the introduction, transitions are an especially important way to help listeners follow the structure of a group presentation. Clear transitions help smooth the adjustment listeners need to make as they shift their attention from one speaker to another. There are two ways to handle transitions: A single master of ceremonies (probably the person who introduced the presentation) can make them, or each speaker can introduce the next person after summarizing his or her own section. Whichever method you choose, make sure the relationship between the preceding and following sections is clear.

The conclusion can be given by the same M.C. or by the final speaker. If you choose the latter approach, be certain that the wrap-up restates the group's overall thesis and main points and doesn't just review the most recent remarks.

Managing Audience Questions

The team also must consider how to manage questions from the audience. Will you invite them during each speaker's presentation, or will you encourage listeners to wait until everybody has finished? If you do have a question-and-answer session at the end of the program, one person should probably field queries and direct them to the team member best equipped to answer—perhaps the most knowledgeable person or the one who signals readiness to answer. Having several speakers talk at the same time—or, even worse, contradict one another—can make a group look unprofessional. The team member controlling the question period should also be prepared to provide a brief wrap-up before the group is finished, to make sure the presentation finishes on a clear, upbeat note instead of just petering out with a lame remark: "If there are no more questions, then I guess we're finished."

Delivering a Group Presentation

The potential for mix-ups and mistakes is especially great in group presentations. The key to minimizing problems is extensive rehearsal. Consider issues like the setup and position of speakers in advance to avoid last-minute bumbling. Will members speak while seated around a table? Will they sit in a row until it is each one's turn? Or will they come up from the audience? Choose the format that helps you make the best possible impression and avoid delays. Waiting for speakers to get from their chairs to the lectern greatly increases lag time, and the larger the room, the greater the distance. Sitting together at a table may provide a better and more cohesive look, as well as minimize delays. If the group does sit around a table, try to angle it so that the members of the team can comfortably see speakers as they present. However you set up the presentation, be sure speakers can rise and sit as necessary without bumping, banging, and clanging into equipment, the table, and each other.

In considering where to position team members when they are not speaking, think about how they will look to the audience. Remember that they will make an impression even when they aren't the principal focus of attention. When it is your turn to speak, be sure to talk to the audience, not your teammates. When you're not speaking, look at the speaker and listen with undivided attention. Even if you are bored because you've heard the remarks so often during rehearsal, or you are nervous about your upcoming turn, act like the ideas are fresh or interesting. Don't review your notes or let your eyes wander from the speaker, or you will encourage the audience to do the same.

SPECIAL-OCCASION SPEECHES

In business settings, there are many special speaking occasions and events, some of which you will quite likely be asked to participate in or be given a chance to volunteer for. You may be asked to give a welcome to guests touring your facility, introduce a speaker at a staff meeting or annual banquet, present an award to a retiring employee, or accept an award you've won. Perhaps you'll present a tribute to a member of a civic organization you belong to or bid farewell to a supervisor who was promoted out of your department. Keep in mind that every context is unique; you will want to adjust to the physical, social, chronological, and cultural context of each occasion. The following guidelines will help you feel confident and achieve your goals when delivering special-occasion remarks.

Welcoming Remarks

When you are welcoming someone, your remarks often set the tone for the whole event. Warmth and sincerity in words and behavior are important. Whether you are welcoming a special guest for a two-hour banquet or a group of permanent new employees, try to follow these guidelines:

- Say who you are (if the audience doesn't know) or on whose behalf you are speaking.
- Say who you are welcoming.
- Describe the occasion and the place to which someone or some group is being welcomed, if necessary.
- Thank the guest or group for coming, if they had a choice.
- Tell why the occasion is especially important or significant.

As you deliver your remarks, be sure to speak to the person or group you are welcoming. If appropriate, turn to the audience and invite your listeners to participate in the welcome by clearly stating or showing them how you want them to behave. The example below illustrates how this technique can be used with the guidelines to produce effective welcoming remarks:

> "The graphics department of Sizetec Corporation USA would like to welcome members of our Japanese plant's graphics department to our ribbon cutting of our new facility. We are honored that you took time to travel and be with us today because this expansion makes our department the largest Sizetec graphics department east of the Rockies. This is an exciting day for us, and we extend a warm welcome to you. [Turn to audience.] Please join me in a round of applause to welcome our Japanese guests."

Introductions

If you are asked to introduce someone, the most important goal is to be accurate. Inaccurate information will embarrass the speaker and confuse the audience. There are several steps you can take to ensure accuracy:

- Obtain a résumé or biographical information in writing ahead of time.
- If you can interview the speaker over the phone, try to get the information you need, but also ask the person to send or bring a résumé so that you can double-check your information. Be sure to get correct titles.
- Ask the person how he or she would like to be referred to (title and last name, first and last name, or first name only).
- Be sensitive to culture and gender differences. For example, members of many cultures prefer to be identified by formal titles (such as "director") that are not commonly used in the United States or Canada. The best way to use the right form of address is to check with the person.
- Strive for consistency if you are introducing more than one person. A common faux pas is referring to men as "Mr." or "Dr." while calling women by their first names.
- Check and practice the pronunciation of names, cities, and companies that you are unsure of.

A good introduction includes information the audience will want to know: who the person is, what his or her credentials are, why the person is present, and what he or she is going to talk about. Sometimes the questions will have been answered by previous speakers, in a written program, or by the nature of the gathering. Decide which information the audience needs. The following guidelines will be useful for most introductions:

- In describing who the person is, select the most interesting biographical information for your audience. It is best to give some general information and a few specifics, rather than rattling off long lists: "John has done training with many groups, including the Air Force, IBM, and Baxter Healthcare." Don't be vague ("John has done a lot of training for big groups") but don't burden the audience with too much time-consuming detail either ("John has done training for" followed by a list of twenty companies).
- Include the person's title and full name at least twice, preferably at the beginning and again at the end of the introduction. Throughout the introduction, refer to the person as he or she prefers. Sometimes the formal title ("President Ted Sanchez") is used at the beginning and end and the first name (if the person has expressed that preference) is used the rest of the time.
- If the speaker's topic is very familiar, you may only need to mention it. If the audience is unfamiliar with the topic, you may need to include more background information about the topic and explain why it is significant for the group.
- Include the title of the speech, if it is a formally titled speech.
- Showcase the person you are introducing, and be sure that you do not steal the show by making yourself the center of attention.

Notice how these points have been incorporated in this informative introduction:

> "Today, on this twentieth anniversary of the Sombra del Monte Parent Teacher's Association, I am delighted to be able to introduce to you Dr. Barbara Powdrell, our State Superintendent of Schools. In taking time to be with us tonight, Dr. Powdrell continues a tradition for which she is known: boosting and supporting parent involvement in the schools. Dr. Powdrell has been Superintendent of Schools for six years, and before that she was a midschool science teacher, a PTA president, and a vice-principal for curriculum at Sandia High School, as well as a member of various state education committees and initiatives. Dr. Powdrell will help empower each of us tonight as she speaks to us on 'Team Advocacy: Parents and Teachers Advocating Together.' Please join me in welcoming our State Superintendent of Schools, Dr. Barbara Powdrell."

Presentation of an Award

Sometimes persons may know they are recipients of awards, and at other times your presentation speech may be the first announcement. Depending on the situation, you will choose whether to let the audience (and winner) know who is receiving the award at the beginning of the speech or save that information until the end. For an effective presentation, follow this format:

- If everyone knows who is receiving the award, you might want to mention the person first. If it is a surprise, you might prefer to build suspense by withholding the name until the end.
- State the name and nature of the award.
- State the criteria for selection.
- Relate the way (or ways) in which the recipient meets the criteria, using specific examples.
- Make the presentation.
- Be sure that the person receiving the award—not you, the presenter—is the center of attention and focus.

As the speech below illustrates, this approach can serve as a framework for creating interesting, enthusiastic presentations:

> "'Success isn't measured by where you are, but by how far you've come from where you've started.' These words exemplify the spirit of the Most Improved Player Award. Each year, players have the privilege and difficult task of voting for the player they believe is the most improved. The winner of this award must have demonstrated to her teammates spirit and commitment and must have shown improvement and refinement in skills. This is not an easy task. Always spurring others on and never giving up even when we were down 14–7 against the Bulldogs, this year's winner went from being unable to stop a goal to stopping six goals in our last championship game. So, Mary Lee, it is with gratitude and delight that I present to you from your teammates the Most Improved Player Award."

Acceptance of an Award

When you are accepting an award, a few brief remarks are usually all that's necessary. Recollection of the long-winded speeches at the annual Academy Awards ceremony will help you appreciate the sentiment behind Marlene Dietrich's advice to Mikhail Baryshnikov when she sent him to accept her award from the Council of Fashion Designers: "Take the thing, look at it, thank them, and go."[9] This approach is probably too extreme, but brevity is certainly an important element of most acceptances. So, too, is gratitude. The following plan can help you organize your sincere gratitude in an effective way:[10]

1. Express your sincere gratitude (and surprise, if appropriate).
2. Acknowledge and show appreciation to contributors.

3. Describe how the reward will make a difference.
4. Say thank you again.

The following thank-you remarks, given by the head of a volunteer committee that had staged a profitable fund-raiser, illustrate how this simple approach can be sincere, easy, and effective:

> You have really surprised me today. When I said I'd help plan the auction, the last thing on my mind was an award. Raising scholarship money was our goal, and breaking last year's fundraising record was the only reward I'd hoped for. Getting this special thank-you is more than I had ever expected, and I am deeply honored.
>
> I'm also a little embarrassed to be singled out like this. We couldn't have broken that record without a tremendous amount of hard work by everybody. Chris and her committee rounded up an incredible bunch of auction items. Ben and his gang provided food and entertainment that we'll be talking about for years. Darnelle's publicity team brought in the donors. And Leo Morrell's talents as an auctioneer squeezed every last dollar out of those items. With wonderful people like this, how could we have gone wrong?
>
> I'm going to put this plaque in my office, right above my desk. Whenever I'm feeling tired and discouraged about human nature, it will remind me how generous and hard working people can be for a good cause. It will also remind me how lucky I am to know you all and have worked with you.
>
> So thanks again for this wonderful award. You're a great bunch of people, and I can hardly wait until we do it all again next year!

Tribute to a Person or Institution

When you are asked to give a speech of tribute, both chronological and topical approaches can be effective. You can follow the person's life or career chronologically and pay tribute to achievements and characteristics along the way, or you might choose some themes or traits from the person's life and or-

ETHICAL CHALLENGE

1. For each of the following situations, develop a presentation that would honor the person or group being presented without compromising your ethical principles:
   a. Welcoming members of the college administration to your class when you know that the real reason they're there is because they have received complaints about your instructor
   b. Introducing a guest speaker (who you don't like or respect) from your place of work to your class
   c. Presenting an achievement award to one fellow worker (or student) when you think someone else is more deserving
   d. Offering a tribute to a departing employee or student whom you are glad to see leave (Supply details from your personal experience.)
2. On the basis of the speeches you and your classmates present, develop a set of guidelines about how to deliver special-occasion speeches on personally distasteful topics in ways that honor the occasion without violating your ethical principles.

ganize around those topics. If you do choose to pay tribute along theme lines (bravery and commitment, for example), anecdotes and examples can illustrate your points.

Many of the guidelines for tributes parallel those for introductions: accuracy of names and details and sensitivity to culture, gender, and personal desires. Check your information with the person to whom tribute is being paid if possible or practical; if not, check with an extremely authoritative source. A sample tribute to an accountant who is leaving a firm is presented below. Of course, if the speaker had more time, each of the traits selected could be illustrated with more anecdotes that the audience would be familiar with.

> "Today is a day of celebration as we pay tribute to Joseph Begay. It is a privilege to speak for the management team here at Contrast Accounts and to honor Joe.
>
> "In thinking about Joe's accomplishments here, two words come to mind: commitment and community. Joseph is committed to doing a job well. He commands a tremendous measure of respect and esteem from colleagues in all of our departments. From Betty Murphy in Costs Analysis to Mike Burroughs in Media Relations, Joseph has earned our admiration for his commitment to quality work for our clients. Who else could have persuaded us to redo the entire Simpson account in less than two months? Who else could have enticed us with pizzas to get us to stay late and finish? Joe is committed to our clients and to our colleagues. The focal point of his work has been to help us all better understand the needs of members from various departments who populate our company. Joseph has helped us come together to look at specific ways we could meet the needs of diverse departments, and he has provided us with opportunities to give expression to our common frustrations and concerns which revolve around quality products for our clients.
>
> "Second only to his commitment is Joe's unique way of building community among us. It is because of Joe that over the past six years many of us first discovered our shared interests and commonalities across departments. The collective tasks he assigned to us created a bond and a basis for our common union. He showed us how to let our collective interests rise above our differences and then how to respect and work with our differences. I speak for many of us in saying I have increased admiration and regard for the wisdom and the work of our colleagues and for the intricate web of talents which contribute to Contrast Accounts' success. Through shared endeavors initiated by Joe we realized that we are not interchangeable parts but unique professionals with vision and expertise. Joe helped us all catch a glimpse of what community and connection can mean and how they can be achieved cross-departmentally.
>
> "I believe that because of Joe's commitment and creation of community, we are all richer, and Joe, I'd like to have you stand as we pay tribute to you and your endeavors here with a last round of applause."

SUMMARY

Informative presentations fall into one of four categories: reports, briefings, explanations, and training. In addition to following the guidelines for effective presentational speaking described earlier in this book, an informative speaker can benefit by using several techniques described in this chapter.

Covering only necessary information ensures that the audience cannot be distracted by extraneous material. Linking the topic to the interests and concerns of the audience offers listeners a reason to heed the presentation. Linking new or unfamiliar concepts to ideas that are familiar to the audience makes the material easier to understand. Finally, involving the audience is a way to keep attention high and increase understanding.

Following several organizational principles can increase comprehension. Beginning the presentation with an overall picture of the ideas to be covered gives listeners a frame of reference. Emphasizing important points helps achieve the speaking goal. Numbering items, signposting, using repetition and redundancy, and including internal summaries and previews are all ways to add emphasis. Using multiple channels to convey a message increases understanding.

Group presentations to both internal and external audiences are a common type of business and professional communication. They call for careful coordination of speakers to insure a coherent message and to convey an image of professionalism. Special attention should be devoted to insuring that each person clearly relates his or her segment to the overall group's message through clear transitions as well as introductions and conclusions of individual segments. The physical layout of speakers and how questions and answers will be managed are also important points to consider in advance of delivering the presentation.

RESOURCES

Allen, Steve, *How to Make a Speech* (New York: McGraw-Hill, 1986).

In this genuinely readable book, Steve Allen shares tricks of the trade from his forty years on the lecture circuit. He gives advice on using humor, dealing with stage fright, serving as toastmaster, delivering ad-lib remarks, and speaking on television and radio.

Osgood, Charles, *Osgood on Speaking: How to Think on Your Feet without Falling on Your Face* (New York: Morrow, 1988).

This short, simple, and very engaging book presents practical advice in a humorous manner. Example: "Sometime before you're due to speak, don't forget to take a leak."

Schloff, L., and M. Yudkin, *Smart Speaking: Sixty-Second Strategies* (New York: Henry Holt, 1991).

Organized around the questions and concerns of communicators, this book addresses such varied concerns as "I hate the way I sound on tape" to "I don't know how to handle idiotic, repetitive or hostile questions." A substantial part of the book is devoted to public speaking issues, but other communication topics are also covered, such as "I never remember people's names" and "People always interrupt me."

JOBS
WITH A
FUTURE
United Mine Workers
of America
SEAFARE
SUPPO

CHAPTER 15

Persuasive Presentations

KEY TERMS

Anchor / Comparative-advantages organizational plan / Credibility / Criteria-satisfaction organizational plan / Latitude of acceptance / Latitude of noncommitment / Latitude of rejection / Motivated-sequence organizational plan / Persuasion / Problem-solving organizational plan

Two partners are convinced that they have a winning idea for a new restaurant. They meet with a commercial loan officer from a local bank to seek financing for their project.

Faced with a wave of injuries, the foreman of a construction crew convinces his team members that they need to observe safety practices more carefully.

A local real-estate brokerage has merged with a nationwide chain. Ever since the news became public, rumors have swept the office about how the changes will affect pay, policies, and even job security. The owner has called a companywide meeting to reassure employees that the change will benefit them.

As part of a community-relations program, the electric company has started a community speakers' bureau. The bureau's director is speaking to a group of employees to recruit them as volunteers for the service.

A group of employees has grown increasingly disgruntled with the boss's policy on vacation scheduling. They have chosen a three-person delegation to present their grievances.

As these examples show, salespeople are not the only persuaders in business. At one time or another, everyone in an organization needs to influence the thinking or actions of others. When an issue is especially important, though, the persuasion frequently takes place in a presentation.

This chapter will give you information that can help you succeed in the persuasive presentations you will give in your career. It begins with a definition of persuasion, contrasting this form of communication with other methods of seeking change. After demonstrating that persuasion can be valuable and ethical, the chapter describes the types of persuasive presentations that commonly occur in business and professional settings. It then outlines a variety of strategies that can be used to present a message effectively. The chapter offers ways that speakers can maximize their credibility. Finally, the chapter presents four organizational patterns for developing persuasive messages.

ETHICAL PERSUASION DEFINED

Since persuasion often conjures up images of unscrupulous salespeople peddling worthless products to gullible consumers, it is important to begin our discussion with a definition of persuasion as an ethical and honorable form of communication. ***Persuasion*** is the act of motivating an audience, through communication, to voluntarily change a particular belief, attitude, or behavior.[1] This definition might seem long-winded, but it helps distinguish persuasion from other ways of influencing an audience.

To understand the nature of persuasion, imagine that the city council has announced its intention to turn a local athletic field and playground into a parking lot. The area's residents are understandably upset. Faced with this situation, the residents have four choices. First, they could accept the decision and do nothing to change it. This alternative is neither persuasive nor satisfying.

A second alternative would be to use coercion—forcing the council against its will to reverse its decision. The group could try to coerce a change by invading and disrupting a council meeting, demanding that the council promise to keep the park or face more demonstrations. Threatening to mount a recall campaign against any members who insist on supporting the parking lot would be another coercive approach. Although threats and force can change behavior, they usually aren't the best approach. The recipient of the threats can counterattack, leading to an escalating cycle of hostility. Threatened parties often dig in their heels and resist changing to save face or as a matter of principle, responding, "I'll be damned if I'll change just because you threaten me." Coercion also makes the instigator look bad.

A different approach to getting someone to change his or her mind involves manipulation—tricking the other party into thinking or acting in the desired way. A deceptive approach to the park-versus-parking-lot problem might be to present the council with a petition against the lot containing forged signatures that inflate the petition's size or to gain public sympathy by exaggerating the adverse effects of the project on certain groups—children, the elderly, and small-business owners, for example.

It is reassuring to know that, besides being ethical, honesty is also the best effective policy when it comes to changing the mind of an audience. A "boomerang effect" often occurs when receivers learn that they have been the target of manipulative communication. Faced with this discovery, they will often change their attitudes in the direction opposite that advocated by a speaker.[2] In other cases, speakers are viewed as more credible when they openly admit that they are trying to persuade an audience.

In mass communication, manipulation takes the form of propaganda: messages that use concealed means to sell the public an ideology. The ideology can be religious, political, or economic. Regardless of the subject, propaganda uses a wide array of techniques to impose a uniform system of beliefs on the public. The municipal-parking-lot issue is probably not big enough to generate a propaganda campaign by either the city or the neighbors. But when an issue is larger and more ideological, propaganda might come into play. The real-estate industry might, for instance, try to persuade the residents of the city that growth is good for them. Likewise, conservationists could promote the message that "small is beautiful." No matter what position one takes on an issue, propaganda can be used to gain converts. The key to this approach is manipulation of the audience.

A final way to achieve change is persuasion—communication that convinces the other person to act voluntarily in the desired way. The citizens' group could organize an appeal showing that the community sees keeping the park as more important than increasing the amount of available parking. It could describe the benefits of the park, bringing in local residents to testify about its importance to the community.

This chapter focuses on teaching the principles of persuasion. It doesn't instruct you on accepting the status quo: no guidance is needed on that alternative. You'll have to look elsewhere for advice on how to coerce others—at least blatantly. Finally, this isn't a chapter on how to deceive others into following your wishes. Manipulation can get results, but it raises serious ethical questions. What you'll learn in the following pages is how to make the best possible case for your position so that others will voluntarily choose to accept it.

The line between persuasion and coercion is sometimes fuzzy. While bald threats are clearly coercive, what about implied warnings? Consider the example of the city park: Speakers could remind the council that unhappy voters might remember the decision to close the park and choose other candidates in the next election. Approaches like this seem to have a coercive element even if they give the other party a choice of whether to comply.

On the other end of the scale, the boundary between persuasion and manipulation is also vague. If speakers compliment council members on their past concern for the environment and responsiveness to the voters before trying to persuade them to cancel the parking facility, are the speakers being persuasive or deceitful? If they stage an emotional but accurate series of pleas by children who will be forced to play in the street if the lot is built, are they being manipulative or merely smart?

By now, it should be clear that manipulation, persuasion, and coercion don't fall into three distinct categories. Rather, they blend into one another, like colors of the spectrum:

Coercion *Persuasion* *Manipulation*

The point where one method of gaining compliance stops and another begins will vary from situation to situation. Perhaps the best measures of whether a particular message is genuinely persuasive are (1) whether the recipient feels truly free to make a choice, and (2) whether the originator would feel comfortable if he or she were the recipient of the message instead of its sender.

ETHICAL CHALLENGE

Contrast an ethical persuasive approach to each of the following situations with coercive and manipulative alternatives:

1. A boss tries to get volunteers to work weekend hours.
2. A union representative encourages new employees to join the union.
3. An insurance agent tries to persuade a young couple to buy life and income protection policies.
4. The representative for a waste disposal company tries to persuade residents of a town that locating a regional recycling center nearby would be good for the community.

TYPES OF PERSUASIVE PRESENTATIONS

Most persuasive presentations in business fall into one of four categories: sales presentations, proposals, motivational speeches, and goodwill speeches.

Sales Presentations

Television commercials and direct-mail advertising might sell spaghetti sauce or commemorative medallions, but few people will spend large amounts of money on something unless it is sold personally. Salespeople make presentations about such diverse goods and services as real estate, insurance, merchandise packaging, telephone systems, advertising space, office furniture, heavy machinery, car-rental contracts, restaurant franchises, and many more.

Proposals

In an organization, the goal of most proposals is to persuade higher management. Many involve plans for a new program such as a new product line or an advertising campaign. Others involve requests for resources: additional staff, larger budgets, new equipment. Still others involve changes in policy or procedures: a new compensation plan or a change in the way a job is handled. Still others are personal requests for changes: a raise, involvement in a particular project, or a promotion. A developer seeking a zoning variation from the local planning committee, an account executive presenting a new campaign to a customer, and an executive proposing contract revisions to a union leader are also making proposals.

Motivational Speeches

At their worst, motivational speeches can combine the most oppressive elements of a bad sermon and a high school pep rally. On the other hand, when delivered effectively and at the proper time, such presentations can produce good results. A manager trying to persuade her subordinates to fill out a lengthy, time-consuming financial report by telling them it is essential for the good of the company will arouse only resentment if everyone knows that management reads only two lines on the reports (the gross margin and the pretax profit). The manager will probably be more successful at the same task if she agrees that the form is largely useless but says, "Look, you know how those financial guys are. They don't know anything about the market—they only know whether your numbers add up. We'll get a lot less interference from above if we give them the numbers they need to look good."

Goodwill Speeches

Representatives of organizations frequently speak to audiences to promote interest or support for their organizations. A corporate recruiter addressing graduating seniors and a bank economist explaining economic forecasts are making speeches of goodwill. So is the utility company's representative addressing the press after an accident in a nuclear power plant.

These goodwill speeches may seem informative, but they also try to change the attitudes or behavior of their listeners. The corporate recruiter is trying to encourage some students to apply for jobs with his company; the economist is trying to build the image of her institution as a leading business bank; and the utility-company representative is trying to soften negative reactions.

PERSUASIVE STRATEGIES

Whatever its nature and audience, a persuasive presentation should follow most of the guidelines described in Chapters 10 through 13 of this text. In addition, the presentation's effectiveness will be increased if it takes advantage of the following principles.

Appeal to the Needs of Your Audience

Asking for a promotion because you need the money isn't nearly as effective as demonstrating that you can help the company better in the new position. Asking for an assistant because you feel overworked isn't as likely to impress your boss as showing how the help will increase productivity or allow you to take on more business.

Perhaps the most important key to effective selling is identifying the prospect's needs and showing how the product can satisfy them. One organization's success at implementing this principle was featured in *Fortune* magazine:

> [At Lanier] a salesman does not merely sell hardware. He goes into an office, asks to see how the paperwork is handled, makes himself an overnight expert about the business involved, then prepares a plan for increasing its productivity by using a specific Lanier machine and disc. When he gives a demonstration, he programs the machine to churn out that prospect's actual paperwork.[3]

Even if the audience is not interested in or is unsympathetic to an idea, there is usually some way to link a proposal to the listeners' needs or values. A representative of an oil company speaking to residents of a coastal town where offshore drilling is being proposed could defend the move by showing how the local economy would benefit and how drilling platforms increase the abundance of marine life in the oceans, which in turn improves fishing.

Whenever possible, base your appeal on several needs. Listeners who are not reached by one appeal can still be persuaded by another. If you were try-

> Grant G. Gard tells salespeople "Don't start talking about yourself, your likes, your dislikes, or your achievements. Your prospect cares only about himself or herself and the things that affect him or her. Talk only in terms of the prospect's interests." The same principle applies to all persuasive communication: it's better to build an argument around the listener's needs than your own.
>
> Doug Harper, "Honing Your Professional Image," *Industrial Distribution*

ing to persuade co-workers to vote for separate smoking and nonsmoking areas in your building, for example, you might identify several needs for both smokers and nonsmokers and show how your proposal would fill each need:

NEED	SATISFACTION
Physical health	Separating smoking and nonsmoking areas will protect nonsmokers from cigarette smoke and may even help smokers cut down or quit smoking.
Comfort	Isolated smoking lounges will keep less ventilated parts of the building from getting unpleasantly smoky.
Friendship	Smokers won't annoy nonsmokers, and nonsmokers won't bother smokers about smoking in the separate lounges.

Have a Realistic Goal

Even the best presentation can't accomplish miracles. Asking audience members to accept an idea that they strongly oppose can backfire. Social scientists have refined this commonsense principle into *social judgment theory.*[4]

This theory helps speakers decide how to craft their arguments by identifying the range of possible opinions listeners might have about a speaker's arguments. (See Figure 15-1.) A listener's preexisting position is termed an ***anchor***. All the arguments a persuader might use to change the listener's mind cluster around this anchor point in three zones. The first area is the listener's ***latitude of acceptance***. As its name implies, this zone contains positions the listener would accept with little or no persuasion. By contrast, the ***latitude of rejection*** contains arguments that the listener opposes. Between the areas lies the ***latitude of noncommitment***, containing arguments that the listener neither accepts or rejects.

Research has demonstrated that speakers have the best chance of persuading an audience when their arguments fall within their listener's latitude of acceptance. An argument that lies within the latitude of noncommitment has a chance of reaching the audience, but an argument that lies within the receivers' latitude of rejection is likely to have a boomerang effect: rather than moving listeners toward the speaker's position, it will drive them further away.

Social judgment theory teaches a very practical lesson about how much to ask from your audience. The best chance for success comes when your plea is at the outer edge of the audience's latitude of acceptance. Arguments in the lis-

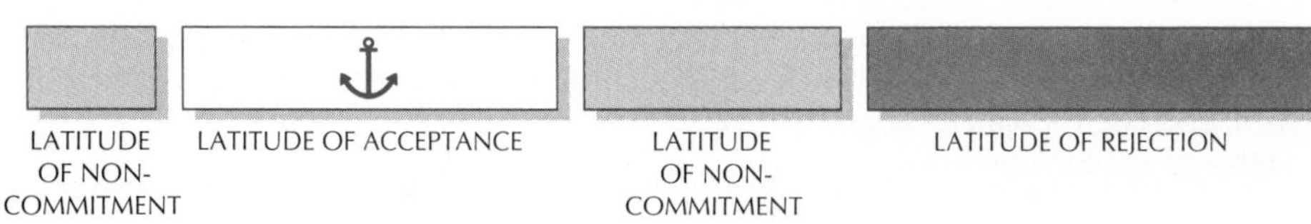

FIGURE 15-1 Range of responses to a persuasive appeal.

teners' latitude of noncommitment may not impress them, and those in the latitude of rejection will just strengthen their opposition.

Social judgment theory teaches that persuasion isn't a one-shot affair. In many cases your persuasive campaign will consist of many messages delivered over time, each one aimed at expanding your listeners' latitude of acceptance. An oil-company representative defending his company's proposal to start offshore drilling shouldn't expect his arguments about promoting business growth and increasing marine life to turn opponents into enthusiastic supporters. Rather than asking for their endorsement, his purpose might simply be to have them recognize that offshore drilling is "not all that bad." Similarly, a sales representative trying to sell furnishings for a new office building should not expect to make a $2 million sale on her first call; she might try only to make an appointment to present her proposal to a planning committee.

A human resources assistant at a medium-size company used the lessons of social judgment theory to choose a realistic goal in her campaign to persuade the corporation to set up a day-care center for the preschool-aged children of employees. Rather than ask her boss to authorize funds for the center—a goal she knew was unrealistic—she requested approval to conduct a feasibility study in which she would explore the ways that similar companies provided for child care. If the boss responded favorably to the center after seeing the results of this survey, she would present a full-blown proposal. If he still had doubts, her backup proposal was to suggest that the company subsidize tuition at a nearby child-care center—a plan closer to the boss's anchor point.

Focus Appeals on Critical Audience Segment

Sometimes one or two listeners have the power to approve or reject your appeal. Abraham Lincoln made this point clearly when his cabinet unanimously opposed one of his ideas. "The vote is eight to one against the plan," the president stated. "The motion carries." In cases such as this, it is important to identify the interests, needs, attitudes, and prejudices of the key decision makers and then focus your appeal toward them. For instance, if the office-furnishings sales representative finds that most of the members of the planning committee vote with the president, her presentation to the committee will be aimed at his apparent needs and interests. If she finds that the pres-

> My favorite applied social judgment story comes from a university development director I know who was making a call on a rich alumnus. He anticipated that the prospective donor would give as much as $10,000. He made his pitch and asked what the wealthy businessman would do. The man protested that it had been a lean year and that times were tough—he couldn't possibly contribute more than $20,000. The fund-raiser figured that he had seriously underestimated the giver's latitude of acceptance and that $20,000 was on the low end of that range. Without missing a beat he replied, "Trevor, do you really think that's enough?" The alumnus wrote a check for $25,000.
>
> Em Griffin, *A First Look at Communication Theory*

ident doesn't meet with the planning committee, she might try to get an appointment to speak with the president.

Defer Thesis with Hostile Audience

Usually, you state your thesis during the introduction of a presentation, but this rule may not be effective with skeptical or hostile listeners. If a manager seeking acceptance of changes in staffing thinks that the audience will respond favorably to her thesis ("Increased business has led us to open up several new positions, and we'd like you to apply for them"), she'll put the idea in the introduction of the speech. If she believes the thesis will not be received enthusiastically ("Declining business requires us to defer pay raises for the upcoming year") or if she believes an audience that hears the news too early will be too upset to accept—or even hear—the rationale behind the decision, she will present the thesis later in the speech.

A presentation with a deferred thesis still needs an introduction to capture the attention of the audience, demonstrate the importance of the topic, and orient the listeners to what will follow. In talks with a deferred thesis, the part of the introduction containing the preview carries the extra burden of setting up the thesis without stating it directly:

> "It's no secret that the recession and our industrywide slump in general have hurt the company. Today I want to tell you how management has tried to cope with these problems in a way that will protect our livelihoods as much as possible."

After the preview, the body of the presentation leads the audience members, step by step, to the point at which they are ready to understand and accept the speaker's thesis:

> "As you can see, given the problems we've faced, management's choice has been to either lay off personnel or defer pay raises. We hope you agree that our decision to defer raises is the best one under the circumstances and that you'll realize we still consider you valuable members of our team."

Present Ample Evidence to Support Claims

Chapter 12 outlined the types of support that can help you prove your claims: examples, stories, statistics, comparisons, and citations. When your goal is to persuade an audience, the generous use of support is especially important.

Research demonstrates that when an audience hears persuasive evidence backing up a persuasive claim, the chances increase that the influence of the message will last long after the presentation has concluded.[5] Furthermore, evidence supporting a claim makes listeners less likely to accept opposing viewpoints that they may hear after you have finished speaking.

The best evidence comes from credible sources. If your credibility on the subject is not high, be sure to cite others whose expertise and impartiality your listeners respect. For example, a prospective customer would expect a sales representative to praise a product he or she is trying to sell. But if the salesperson cites others who know the product and who don't have an interest in its sale, the message ("This product is excellent") becomes more persuasive. In this case, the testimony of other customers or of an independent testing service such as Consumers Union would be excellent evidence.

Consider Citing Opposing Ideas

Research indicates that it is generally better to mention and then refute ideas that oppose yours than to ignore them.[6] There are three situations when it is especially important to forewarn listeners about opposing ideas:

When the Audience Disagrees with Your Position. With hostile listeners, it's wise to compare their position and yours, showing the desirability of your thesis. If management has previously opposed products similar to the one you are about to propose, for instance, you'll need to bring up the managers' objections ("It's too risky, the capital outlay is too big, and the sales force can't sell it") and show how your proposal will meet their objections ("We can minimize the risk and the initial costs by limiting the first production run; if we put extra emphasis on advertising and show the salespeople how other companies have sold similar products very successfully in the last few years, they'll be more enthusiastic and more effective"). Similarly, if you're trying to sell an out-of-the-way plant location to a company that is planning to build its new plant in a more central location, you might show that transportation is as cheap and available in your location as in the central one or that savings on real-estate taxes and labor will allow the company to pay higher transportation costs. If you don't mention arguments that are already on their minds, your listeners may consider you uninformed.

When the Audience Knows Both Sides of the Issue. Well-informed listeners, even if they haven't made up their minds about an issue, will find a one-sided appeal less persuasive than a presentation that considers opposing arguments. Discussing these ideas shows that you are not trying to avoid them. Even if you refute the competition, considering it at all is more even-

SKILL BUILDER

What persuasive strategies described in this section might a speaker use in each of the following situations?

1. Persuading the loan officer at a local bank to lend you money for your proposed business venture
2. Encouraging local businesspeople to join a service club to which you belong
3. Convincing your boss to authorize a two-week leave of absence so that you can attend a relative's wedding across the country
4. Arguing that your suggestions for cutting costs are better than those proposed by your supervisor

handed than focusing exclusively on your plan and never acknowledging that alternatives exist.

An account executive at a full-service stock brokerage showed that he respected the knowledge and judgment of his listeners at an investment seminar when he discussed the alternatives to using the services of his firm:

> I know that most of you are familiar enough with the financial marketplace to be asking yourself "Why don't I save money and use a discount brokerage?" And that's a fair question. After all, discount firms charge you a much smaller commission for each transaction than full-service houses like mine. I'd like to suggest that the answer to the question of which kind of brokerage to use lies in the old saying "You get what you pay for." If you use a discount firm, you'll get limited service. Now, that may be all you want and all you need. But if you're looking for a source of financial support and attention, you'll get it at a full-service brokerage. Let me explain.

When the Audience Will Soon Hear Your Viewpoint Criticized or Another One Promoted. You will be better off defusing the opponents' thesis by bringing up and refuting their arguments than by letting them attack your position and build up theirs in its place. For example, a union organizer speaking to a group of plant workers might anticipate an argument from management this way:

> "The company representative will tell you that after we organized the Oregon plant, the people were out of work, on strike, for four months the next year. That's true. What the company probably won't tell you is that the people got strike pay from the union. The company also won't tell you that the people there were losing money every year before that because their wages weren't keeping up with inflation, and the strike got them guaranteed cost-of-living raises, plus life, health, and disability benefits and improved safety conditions."

Adapt to the Cultural Style of Your Audience

The cultural background of your listeners may affect the way they respond to various types of persuasive appeals.[7] The intensity of emotional appeals is

> Recently, I interviewed a scientist from Greece about his role in working with a group of international scientists who represent countries of the European Common Market. . . . The man I interviewed said that the team is having difficulties because of differences in presentation style. He said, "The Italians, Portuguese and Greeks present emotionally; the Germans are very linear and sequential; the French want the others to understand their presentation in French; and the English don't let us know their real agenda until the end of the presentation. Because of these cultural differences, we find it very hard to work together."
>
> Devorah A. Lieverman, *Public Speaking in the Multicultural Environment*

a good example. The traditional Euro-American ideal is to communicate without becoming too excited. By contrast, cultures in Latin America and the Middle East are generally more expressive, and their members respond more favorably to displays of emotion. An approach that would seem logical and calm to an audience in Seattle or Toronto might seem cold and lifeless to a group in Mexico City or Istanbul. Conversely, a Mexican or Turk speaker might seem overly excitable to a group in the United States or Canada.

The types of supporting material that are regarded as most persuasive also differ from one culture to another. Euro-American culture places a high value on data that can be observed and counted. Statistical data and eyewitness testimony are considered strong evidence. Communicators from other backgrounds are less impressed by these sorts of proofs. Arab speakers commonly rely on religious and national identification. They are more likely to use elaborate language, which would be considered flowery by other cultural standards. In some parts of Africa, for example, the words of a witness would be regarded with suspicion because members of that culture believe that people who speak out about a topic have a particular agenda in mind.

As Chapter 11 suggested, acceptable ways of organizing a message also vary. U.S. presenters are used to straightforward messages that introduce a thesis early in the presentation, develop it in the body, and summarize it in the conclusion. Japanese presenters rely less on a strong, direct close. Instead, they stress harmony with the audience, relying on this climate to generate acceptance of an idea.

Differences like these make it important to know the cultural preferences of your audience. Just because listeners come from a particular country or belong to a particular ethnic group doesn't mean they can be stereotyped, especially in a shrinking world where communication and travel blur national boundaries. Nonetheless, being sensitive to the attitudes of your listeners can help you avoid delivering a message that antagonizes, rather than persuades them.

MAXIMIZING SPEAKER CREDIBILITY

Winston Churchill once said that, when it comes to persuading, what matters most is who you are, then how you say what you want to say, and, finally, what you say. Even without taking this assertion literally, it is true that credibility is a powerful factor in persuasion. ***Credibility*** is the persuasive force that comes from the audience's belief in and respect for the speaker. Research shows that you can enhance your credibility in a variety of ways.[8]

Demonstrate Your Competence

Listeners will be most influenced by a speaker who they believe is qualified on the subject. You are more likely to believe career advice from a self-made millionaire than from your neighbor who has been fired from four jobs in three years. Similarly, the department staff is more likely to accept

> The bigger the prospect, the more likely they are to expect professionalism. My experience has been that when you don't get the business you are rarely, if ever, told the real reason or the complete reason you lost. The easy out is to tell you that it was price. But often the real reason is that you did a sloppy, disorganized, disjointed, and unprofessional job of telling your story. In the prospect's mind, the quality of your presentation is a mirror image of the quality of your company, your product, your service, and your people.
>
> David A. Peoples, *Presentations Plus*

the direction of a new manager who seems knowledgeable about the specific work of that department. Management is more likely to agree to take a risk on a new manufacturing material if the product manager seems to know the market very well. These are all examples of trusting someone's competence.

There are three ways to build perceived competence. The first is by demonstrating your *knowledge of the subject*. For example, the product manager might help to establish her credibility by citing statistics ("Our market research showed that 85 percent of the potential market is more concerned with maintenance costs than the initial cost of the product. A study published in the trade journal last month demonstrated that maintenance costs are often 80 percent of the cost of the equipment"). She could also remember facts ("Dorwald Associates tried something like this, although only in government markets, and it was pretty successful") and recent appropriate examples ("I was checking the records last week, and I realized that we could afford to replace the machines every five years on what we'd save on maintenance if we used plastic instead of metal").

A second way to demonstrate competence is by making your *credentials* known. These credentials could be academic degrees, awards and honors, or successful experiences ("I helped set up Hinkley's very profitable system a few years ago").

A third way to show your competence is through *demonstration of your ability*. A junior manager who bungles his figures will have a hard time convincing his superiors that he ought to be given more financial responsibility. A sales representative who reminds a customer that she has often solved problems by arranging emergency shipments will establish credibility for her claim that her company provides good service.

Earn the Trust of Your Audience

The most important ingredient of trustworthiness is *honesty*. If listeners suspect you are not telling the truth, even the most impressive credentials or grasp of the subject will mean little. For instance, a union leader gets little support from union members if they think that he's made a private agreement with management.

Impartiality is a second element of trustworthiness. We are more likely to accept the beliefs of impartial speakers than of those who have a vested interest in persuading us. A sales representative is hardly a neutral source of information about her product or her competition. She could, however, cite an independent journal's evaluation of a product.

Emphasize Your Similarity to the Audience

Audiences are most willing to accept the ideas of a speaker whose attitudes and behaviors are similar to their own. This persuasive ability exists even when the similarities are not directly related to the subject at hand. Thus, a subordinate may get a better hearing from the boss when both are golfers, have children of the same age, come from the same part of the country, or dress similarly. Customer-service representatives for farm machinery generally wear casual clothing and open-necked shirts to fit in with the people they visit. Many sales representatives begin conversations with prospects by mentioning a common interest—gardening, baseball, or a recent event that affects the customer's business.

Similarity in areas related to the speaker's topic is even more persuasive. This fact has led to the strategy of establishing *common ground* between speaker and listeners early in a presentation. A speaker who shows that he and the audience have similar beliefs will create goodwill that can make listeners willing to consider more controversial ideas later on. Notice, for example, how a business owner seeking a zoning variance based her appeal to the local architectural review board:

> Like you, I'm a strong believer in preserving the character of our town. As a businesswoman and a long-time resident, I realize beauty and lack of crowding are our greatest assets. Without them, our home would become just another overgrown collection of shopping malls and condominiums.
>
> Also, like you, I believe that change isn't always bad. Thanks to your efforts, our downtown is a more interesting and beautiful place now than it was even a few years ago. I think we share the philosophy that we ought to preserve what is worth saving and improve the town in whatever ways we can. I appreciate the chance to show you how this project will make the kind of positive change we all seek.

This speaker's chances of gaining acceptance for her proposal were in-

SKILL BUILDER

Credibility is a function of perceived competence, trustworthiness, similarity, and sincerity. How could a speaker's credibility be enhanced in each situation that follows?

1. A group of business students appeals to the Chamber of Commerce to sponsor an internship program for students seeking experience in local films.
2. A sales representative proposes a telecommunications system for an organization made up of 1,000 people.
3. A manager encourages subordinates to share their suggestions or complaints with her.

creased by her demonstrated support for the principles the board promotes. Of course, the board has to believe that the speaker is sincere. If they suspect she is just telling them what they want to hear, her credibility will shrink, not grow.

Increase Your Appeal to the Audience

Illogical as it may seem, listeners are more persuaded by speakers they find appealing in some way. This is especially true when listeners do not have a strong stake in the issue.[9] One source of attractiveness, of course, is *appearance*. Listeners are also attracted to speakers who are *complimentary*. Letting audience members know that you respect their accomplishments, value their judgment, or like them personally will predispose them toward accepting your viewpoint. An account executive addressing the marketing staff of a new company client, for instance, might begin by saying, "It's a great honor to work with you. I'm especially excited about working at Nordik because I know this staff has been primarily responsible for building Nordik's reputation for innovative, creative marketing campaigns."

Demonstrate Sincerity

Speakers perceived as believing strongly in their subjects are more persuasive than unenthusiastic ones. The audience reaction is usually "If this person cares so much about the idea, there must be something to it." Sincerity is only impressive if the audience *detects* it, however; unfortunately, some speakers don't show their enthusiasm and so reduce their effectiveness. A plant superintendent delivering a glowing report about the progress that his staff is making in solving an important problem, for example, could really be concerned about his job, which is dependent on the problem's being solved quickly. If his tension shows more than his enthusiasm, his superiors might suspect that the problem is still more serious than he claims.

ORGANIZING PERSUASIVE MESSAGES

Credibility may be important, but the way you structure your message also plays a major role in determining how successful you will be at persuading an audience. Chapter 11 discussed several patterns for organizing the body of a presentation. Of these, the problem-solution pattern is often appropriate in persuasive situations. The other plans described in the following pages can also work well. As Table 15-1 shows, there is no single best plan. The one you choose will depend on the topic and your audience's attitude toward it.

These are the fundamental selling truths. If you don't know your product, people will resent your efforts to sell it; if you don't believe in it, no amount of personality and technique will cover that fact; if you can't sell with enthusiasm, the lack of it will be infectious.

Mark H. McCormack, *What They Don't Teach You at Harvard Business School*

TABLE 15-1 Considerations for Choosing a Persuasive Organizational Plan

Organizational Plan	Considerations
Problem-solution	Most basic persuasive pattern. Use when audience needs convincing that a problem exists.
Comparative advantages	Use when audience is considering alternatives to your proposal. Show how your plan is superior to others. Defer thesis if audience will object to idea before hearing your reasoning.
Criteria satisfaction	Use when audience is not likely to consider alternative plans. Choose criteria important to your audience, and show how your plan meets them. If audience may be hostile to your plan, introduce criteria before discussing the plan.
Motivated sequence	Use when problem and solution are easy to visualize. Effective when seeking immediate audience reaction.

Problem-Solution

As its name suggests, a ***problem-solution*** plan first persuades the audience that something is wrong with the present situation and then suggests how to remedy the situation. This plan works especially well when your audience does not feel a strong need to change from the status quo. Since listeners have to recognize that a problem exists before they will be interested in a solution, showing them that the present situation is not satisfactory is essential before you present your idea. For example:

Thesis: Establishing a system of employee incentives can boost productivity.

I. Our level of productivity has been flat for over two years while the industry wide rate has climbed steadily in that period. *(Problem)*

II. Establishing an incentive system will give employees a reason to work harder. *(Solution)*

A problem-solution pattern might also be used to show how updating a computer system will solve problems with inventory monitoring, why a potential customer needs a personal financial advisor, or why a department needs additional staff.

The problem-solution approach is often effective, but it is not the best strategy for every situation. If your listeners already recognize that a problem exists, you may not need to spend much time proving the obvious. In such circumstances, you might touch on the problem in the introduction to your talk and devote the entire body to suggesting a solution. In this case, a topical plan might be the best approach—especially if the audience is likely to accept your recommendation without considering other alternatives. If you are competing against other ideas, however, a comparative-advantages plan may be a better organizational strategy.

Comparative Advantages

A ***comparative-advantages*** approach puts several alternatives side by side and shows why yours is the best. This strategy is especially useful when the audience is considering an idea that competes with the one you're advocating. Under this circumstance, ignoring alternative plans is a bad idea. A head-on comparison that supports your case is a far more effective plan. The manager of a health club used a comparative-advantages approach to encourage new members:

INTRODUCTION
When you decide to join a health club, you have several choices in the area. You might be tempted by the special introductory rates at some other clubs in town, but a feature-by-feature look shows that Nautilus 2000 is your best choice.

BODY
- I. The club is open longer every day than any other club in town.
- II. The club has more exercise machines than any other in town.
- III. The club has a wider variety of activities than any other in town: aerobics classes, swimming, saunas, massage, racquetball, and a snack bar.
- IV. The club's staff are all licensed fitness counselors—a claim than no other club in town can make.

CONCLUSION
When it comes to value for your dollar, Nautilus 2000 is your best health-club choice.

In the preceding example, the speaker made her thesis clear at the beginning of her presentation. A comparative-advantages approach also works well when you choose to defer your thesis. In this instance, you can build a case showing how your proposal is superior to the alternatives and then present your thesis as a conclusion. An insurance agent used this strategy to convince an audience to buy coverage:

INTRODUCTION
How should you spend your discretionary income?

BODY
There are several alternatives.
- I. You can spend it all on recreation, but that won't buy financial security for your family if anything happens to you.
- II. You can make investments to plan for the future, but there is always the risk of losing that money.
- III. More expensive housing is an option, but it risks placing you even more in debt.
- IV. Insurance guarantees your family an income if you die or are disabled.

CONCLUSION
At least some of your disposable income ought to be devoted to insurance. *(Deferred thesis)*

In this situation, deferring the thesis was a smart idea. If the speaker had started by praising the virtues of buying insurance, most listeners would have tuned out. Since very few people relish the thought of spending their discretionary income on something as intangible as more insurance coverage, they'd probably reject the idea unless they are led to the conclusion that it is the best choice.

Criteria Satisfaction

A ***criteria-satisfaction*** strategy sets up criteria for a plan that the audience will accept and then shows how your idea or product meets them. Unlike a comparative-advantages approach, a criteria-satisfaction plan does not consider alternative ideas. For this reason, it is a good approach when your audience isn't likely to think of alternative plans.

A venture capitalist used a criteria-satisfaction plan when seeking investors for a business project. Notice that he introduced each criterion and then showed how his project would satisfy it:

INTRODUCTION
Being in the right place at the right time can be the key to financial success. I'm here today to offer you a chance to reap substantial benefits from an extremely promising project. Like any investment, this project needs to be based on the sound foundation of a solid business plan, a talented management team, and adequate financing. Let me show you how the project meets all of these important requirements.

BODY

I. The first criterion is that the business plan must be solid. Extensive market research shows the need for this product. . . .

II. The second criterion is a talented management team. Let me introduce the key members of this management team and describe their qualifications. . . .

III. The third criterion is a solid, realistic financial plan. The following plan is very conservative yet shows strong potential for a substantial profit. . . .

CONCLUSION
Because it meets the conditions of a solid business plan, this project is worth your serious consideration.

In this example, the speaker introduced each criterion and then immediately showed how his plan satisfied it. A different approach is to present all the criteria first and then present your proposal. The strategy here is to gain the audience's acceptance first and boost your credibility. Having done this, you go on to show how your plan meets the criteria presented. With this approach, the thesis is deferred—which is especially smart when the audience may not be inclined to accept it without some powerful arguments.

A manager used a criteria-satisfaction plan with a deferred thesis to announce a wage freeze to employees—hardly a popular idea. If she had announced her thesis first ("A wage freeze is in your best interest"), the employees probably would have been too upset to listen thoughtfully to her arguments. By leading her audience through the reasons leading up to the freeze, she increased the chances that the employees would understand management's reasoning. Notice how the thesis is first presented in the middle of the body and is restated in the conclusion:

> You know that we've faced declining revenues for the past year. During these hard times, we need a policy that is best both for the company and for you, the employees. That's the only way we will be able to survive.
>
> BODY
>
> I. There are three important criteria for selecting a policy *(Introduces criteria first)*
>   A. It should be fair.
>   B. It should cause the least harm to employees.
>   C. It should allow the company to survive this difficult period without suffering permanent damage.
>
> II. A wage freeze is the best plan to satisfy these criteria. *(Satisfaction of criteria)*
>   A. It's fair.
>   1.
>   2.
>   B. It causes minimal harm to employees.
>   1.
>   2.
>   C. It will enable the company to survive.
>   1.
>   2.
>
> CONCLUSION
>
> A wage freeze is the best plan at this difficult time.

Motivated Sequence

The ***motivated-sequence*** approach is a five-step organizing scheme designed to boost the involvement and interest of the audience.[10] Regardless of the topic, the sequence of steps is the same:

1. *Attention:* Capture the attention of the audience by introducing the problem in an interesting manner.
2. *Need:* Explain the problem clearly and completely. Use a variety of supporting material to back up your claim, proving that the problem is serious. Ideally, make your listeners feel that the problem affects them in some way. Make them eager to hear a solution.

3. *Satisfaction:* Present your solution to the problem. Provide enough support to prove that the solution is workable and that it will, indeed, solve the problem.
4. *Visualization:* Describe clearly what will happen if your proposal is adopted so that the audience has a clear mental picture of how your proposal will solve the problem. You may also paint a verbal picture of what will happen if your proposal is *not* adopted. In either case, the key to success in this step is to paint a vivid picture of the outcomes, showing how your proposal will make a real difference.
5. *Action:* Call for a response by your audience. Explain what listeners can do to solve the problem.

The motivated-sequence plan provides a step-by-step approach for organizing a speech. It builds on the basic problem-solution plan: step 1 arouses the interest of listeners so that they will be more receptive to the topic: step 4 goes beyond simply providing a solution and helps the audience picture what a difference it will make; step 5 guides the audience on how to bring the solution about, making it easier for listeners to take the necessary steps and arousing them to act.

The motivated sequence works best when the problem that you present and the solution that you propose are easy to visualize. If your listeners can imagine the problem and see themselves solving it by following your plan, they'll be motivated to accept your reasoning. Recognizing this fact, a travel agent used the motivated sequence to capture the interest of audience members and show them the joys of cruising:

[*Attention*] Imagine yourself cruising in tropical waters . . . visiting foreign ports . . . dancing all night . . . dining on gourmet cuisine without worrying about the size of the check. These are just a few of the joys of cruising.

[*Need*] I'm sure everyone here would take a cruise if they could. But you're probably saying to yourself, "I can't afford it." You may be resigned to taking a vacation that costs plenty but doesn't give you the kind of special experience that's only possible on a vacation cruise.

[*Satisfaction*] I'm happy to say that you *can* afford it. Let me show you that cruising can be no more expensive than other, much-less-exciting vacations. . . .

[*Visualization*] What would a cruising vacation be like? Imagine yourself sailing on our ten-day "Sun and Sea Odyssey." Your trip would begin with a champagne bon voyage reception. . . .

[*Action*] A few reservations are still available for this winter's cruises. If you let me know that you are interested today, I'll send you a brochure describing the cruises in detail. Then we can discuss how to plan the vacation of your dreams at a price you can afford.

Because the motivated-sequence approach closes with an appeal to action, it is especially well suited to getting an immediate response to your proposal. Recognizing this fact, a fund-raiser used it to generate pledges for an urgent appeal:

[*Attention*] Here's a picture of the Myer family. Ted, the father, is a trained stonemason and proud of it. Anne, the mom, is a registered nurse. Little Chris is a normal kid who loves baseball and pizza. His teachers say he has a gift for math and languages.

[*Need*] Since this photo was taken, the Myers have had a run of terrible luck. Last year, Ted fell at work and wrenched his back. He's been unable to work ever since, and his disability insurance has almost run out. Three months after Ted's accident, Anne was diagnosed as having leukemia. She's undergoing treatment, and the doctors are optimistic; but she can't work now, and there's no telling when she will be able to return to her job. The Myers lived on their savings for six months, but now all the money is gone. Last week they had to move out of their apartment, and they have nowhere else to go. Nowhere, that is, except Transition House.

[*Satisfaction*] You can help provide temporary housing for the Myers and other neighbors who are in trouble by contributing to Transition House. Your donations will give these people a safe place to stay while they get back on their feet and save them from life on the street.

[*Visualization*] We're hoping to raise enough money tonight to give the Myer family a month at Transition House. During that time, Ted can finish training for a new career as a bookkeeper and get back to work. He hopes to become a CPA. Once he's on the job, the Myers will be able to find a new apartment so that Anne can fight for her health and Chris can stay in his same school, where he's doing so well.

SKILL BUILDER

What organizational plan would be best suited to the message in each of the following situations:

1. Showing a customer why leasing a car is a better choice then buying one
2. Convincing a charitable foundation to grant money to your job-training program for disadvantaged teenagers
3. Persuading a group of cost-conscious consumers of the advantages of shopping at a top-quality department store
4. Demonstrating the features of an expensive computer system
5. Persuading a group of long-time employees to accept a new affirmative-action hiring program.

[*Action*] What we need from you tonight is a donation. We're asking for anything you can afford: the price of an evening on the town or maybe a postponement of that new outfit you were thinking of buying. In just a moment, I'll be passing out pledge cards. . . .

At first glance, the motivated-sequence approach seems to depart from the basic introduction-body-conclusion pattern of organizing a presentation. A closer look shows that the plan does follow the same pattern:

INTRODUCTION
I. Attention

BODY
II. Need
III. Satisfaction
IV. Visualization

CONCLUSION
V. Action

By now, you can see that all of the organizational plans described in this chapter follow the same basic principles you learned in Chapter 11. Each has an introduction that captures the attention of your audience and gives members reasons to listen. Each has a body that is arranged in a pattern that is easy to follow and helps achieve the purpose of the presentation. Each has a conclusion that reinforces the thesis of the talk and leaves the audience motivated to accept it.

SAMPLE PERSUASIVE PRESENTATION

The following presentation demonstrates most of the persuasive principles covered in this chapter as well as the general guidelines about speaking to an audience introduced in Chapters 10 through 13. The purpose and approach are based on a sound audience analysis. As Figure 15-2 shows, the talk has a clear thesis and a clear, logical organizational structure. A variety of verbal and visual supports add interest, clarity, and proof.

The speaker's company, Ablex Technologies, manufactures sophisticated electronic components. One of its best customers is BioMedical Instruments (BMI), which produces a wide variety of sophisticated medical diagnostic instruments. The company's biggest contracts with BMI are for kidney-dialysis and blood-analyzer parts, which total almost $1 million per year.

Under a much smaller and older contract, Ablex also supplies BMI with parts for an x-ray unit. BMI doesn't make the unit anymore but is committed to furnishing current users with replacement parts until the machines drop out of use, and Ablex is obliged to supply BMI. Producing these x-ray parts is usually a problem: orders are small and sporadic, leading to delays and

Thesis
The proposed forecasting and purchasing agreement will allow both BMI and Ablex to better supply x-ray parts in a timely, affordable, and trouble-free manner.

Introduction

I. Our basically positive relationship with BMI has only one problem: the x-ray parts.

II. While a problem does exist, there is a solution
  A. The problem involves erratic orders for x-ray parts.
  B. Our solution has several benefits.

Body

I. Supplying x-ray parts has been a continuing headache.
  A. Orders for x-ray parts are irregular and unpredictable. *(line graph)*
  B. These irregular orders make it tough to ship orders to BMI in a timely way. *(example)*

II. Fortunately, there is a solution to the x-ray problem.
  A. Here's an outline of our plan.
  B. The plan has several advantages.
    1. Orders can be delivered more quickly. *(comparison chart)*
    2. Order is more flexible. *(examples)*
    3. Time can be saved in ordering and follow-up. *(example)*
    4. The unit cost is less than under current plan. *(column chart, comparison chart)*

Conclusion: By now you can see that there's a solution to the x-ray problem.

I. The plan has advantages for everyone involved.

II. We look forward to putting it into action soon.

FIGURE 15-2 Outline of sample presentation.

headaches for everyone concerned. The speaker is presenting a plan that offers a better way to handle the x-ray parts.

The audience is Mary Ann Hirsch, the buyer at BMI, and two production engineers. Although the purchasing director and the chief project engineer are not at the presentation, they will rely on the information gathered by their subordinates and, ultimately, will be the ones to approve or reject this idea—so in a way, they're part of the audience, too.

[*Introduction emphasizes the positive aspects of the relationship with the customer.*]

[*Brief sketch*

We've been involved in a long, positive relationship with BMI. The only troubles we've ever encountered have come from the x-ray parts. Even though they are only a small part of our business with you, they seem to involve the greatest headaches for you and us. The timing of these orders is impossible for you to predict, which makes it hard for us to get parts from our suppliers and deliver the product to you quickly. This leads to all sorts of problems: unhappy customers who have to wait for *of the problem establishes common ground: "We're in this together, and it's no good for either of us.*]

the equipment they ordered and time spent by people at both of our companies keeping in touch.

[*Preview lists the main advantages of the plan that will be proposed.*]

We think there's a better way to handle the x-ray problem. It'll reduce frustration, cut costs, and let all of us spend our time on more productive parts of our jobs. But before we talk about this new plan, let me review why the present arrangement for handling x-ray orders is such a headache.

[*Transition leads to the "Problem" section of the presentation.*]

[*Visual exhibit clearly demonstrates the unpredictable nature of customer orders.*]

The main problem we face is irregular orders. A look at the order history for the last year shows that there's no pattern—and no way to predict when customers will order replacement parts for their x-ray units. [The speaker shows Exhibit 1 here.]

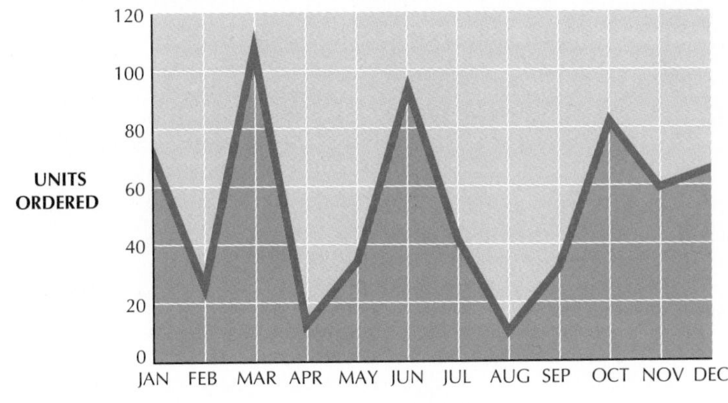

EXHIBIT 1 X-Ray Ordering Pattern

[*Example shows the problems flowing from irregular orders.*]

This unpredictable pattern makes it tough for us to serve you quickly. We have to order parts from our suppliers, which often can take a long time. For instance, in the February 17 order, it took six weeks for our suppliers to get us the parts we needed to manufacture the x-ray components you needed. Once we had the parts, it took us the usual four weeks to assemble them. As you said at the time, this delay kept your customer waiting almost three months for the components needed to get their equipment up and running, and that's poison for customer relations.

[*Transition leads to the second consequence of irregular orders: wasted time.*]

[*Example highlights amount of time wasted.*]

Delays like this aren't just bad for your relationship with customers, they also waste time—yours and ours. Mary Ann, do you remember how many phone calls and letters it took to keep track of that February order? In fact, every year we spend more time on these x-ray orders that involve a few thousand dollars than we do on the dialysis and blood-analyzer parts that involve around a million dollars annually. That's just not a good use of time.

[Transition leads to the "Solution" part of the presentation.] *[Solution is summarized concisely.]*

So we clearly have a situation that's bad for everybody. Fortunately, we believe there's a better way—better for you, us, and your customers. The plan involves your giving us an annual purchasing forecast for x-ray parts. Instead of waiting for your customers to place individual orders, you'd estimate the total sales likely to occur in a year. Then we would acquire enough parts from our suppliers to assemble those items so that we could have them ready quickly as your customers place orders.

[Advantages of solution are introduced and summarized in the chart.]

This simple plan has several advantages. They're summarized on this chart, but let me explain them in a little more detail. [The speaker shows Exhibit 2 here.]

- Quicker delivery
- Flexible ordering
- Fewer problems
- Lower cost

EXHIBIT 2 Advantages of Annual Forecasting for X-Ray Parts

[Strongest advantage to listeners is introduced first to get positive impression early.] *[Bar chart graphically demonstrates time saved.]*

The first advantage is that advance purchasing will speed up delivery of your orders. Instead of waiting for our suppliers to ship parts, we can begin to assemble your order as soon as you send it. You can get an idea of the time savings by looking at how much time this plan would have saved on the order you placed in February. [The speaker shows Exhibit 3.]

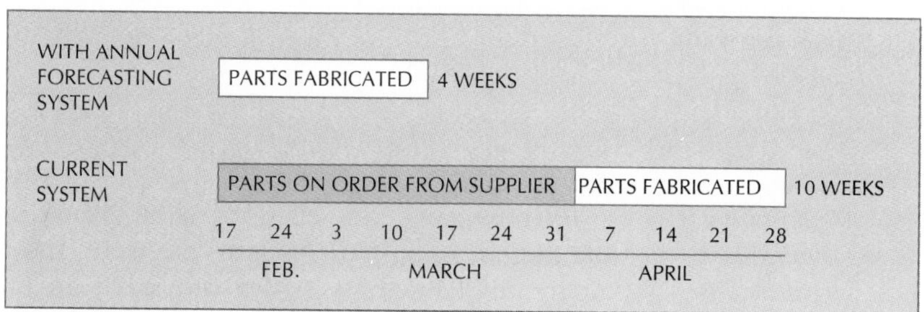

EXHIBIT 3 Annual Forecasting Speeds Delivery Time

[Transition leads to the second advantage

Besides being quick, the plan is flexible. If you wind up receiving more orders than you anticipated when you made your original forecast, you can update the plan every six months.

of the plan: flexibility.] [*Hypothetical example helps audience visualize this advantage.*]

That means we'll never run out of parts for the x-ray units. Suppose you projected 1,400 units in your original forecast. If you've already ordered 1,000 six months later, you could update your forecast at that point to 2,000 units and we'd have the parts on hand when you needed them.

[*Transition leads to anticipation of a possible listener objection: What if orders decrease?*] [*Credible authority is cited to support this point.*]

This semiannual revision of the forecast takes care of increases in orders, but you might be wondering about the opposite situation—what would happen if orders are less than you expected. The plan anticipates that possibility, too. We're willing to extend the date by which you're obliged to use your annual estimate of parts to eighteen months. In other words, with this plan you'd have eighteen months to use the parts you expected to use in twelve. That's pretty safe, since Ted Forester [BMI's vice-president of sales and marketing] predicts that the existing x-ray machines will be in use for at least the next six or seven years before they're replaced with newer models.

[*Internal review reminds listeners of previously introduced advantages and leads to identification of a third benefit: less wasted time.*]

Flexibility and speed are two good advantages, but there are other benefits of the plan as well. It can save time for both you and us. You know how much time we spend on the phone every time there's a surprise x-ray order, and I imagine you have to deal with impatient customers, too. Talking about delays is certainly no fun, and with this annual purchasing plan it won't be necessary since we can guarantee delivery within three weeks of receiving your order. Think of the aggravation that will avoid!

[*Second most important advantage is introduced last, where it is likely to be remembered by listeners.*]

By now, you can see why we're excited about this plan. But there's one final benefit as well: the plan will save you money. When we order our parts in larger quantities, the unit price is less than the one we face with smaller orders. We're willing to pass along the savings to you, which means that you'll be paying less under this plan than you are now. Notice how ordering a year's supply of parts drops the unit price considerably. [The speaker shows Exhibit 4.]

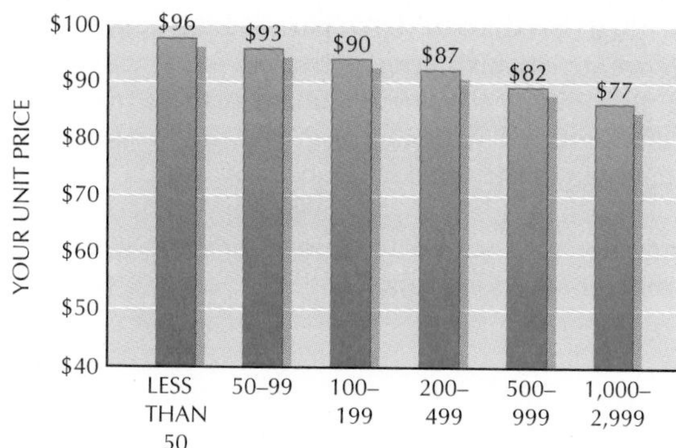

EXHIBIT 4 Annual Forecasting Reduces Unit Price

[Chart visually highlights cost savings.]

You can see that this plan is a real money saver. Compare the savings you could have realized on last year's order of 597 units if this plan had been in effect. [The speaker shows Exhibit 5.]

597 UNITS AT HIGHER UNIT PRICE	$55,506
597 UNITS AT VOLUME UNIT PRICE	45,969
FIRST YEAR SAVINGS	$ 9,537

EXHIBIT 5 One Year's Savings with Annual Forecasting Plan

[Conclusion reviews the plan's advantages and makes appeal to adopt it.]

So that's the plan. It's simple. It's risk-free. It's convenient. It's flexible. And along with all these advantages, it can cut your costs. We're prepared to start working with you immediately to put this plan into action. If we start soon, we'll never have to deal with x-ray headaches again. Then we can put our energy into the larger, more satisfying projects that are more rewarding for both of us.

SUMMARY

Persuasion is the act of motivating an audience, through communication, to voluntarily change a particular belief, attitude, or behavior. Unlike coercion on the one hand or manipulation on the other, it presents a message to an audience and allows the members to choose whether or not to accept it. Persuasive presentations are common in business and professional settings. Most take the form of sales presentations, proposals, motivational speeches, or goodwill speeches.

A variety of strategies maximize the chances of achieving a persuasive goal. Focusing the message on a key audience segment and defining a realistic goal are important. Demonstrating how the message can meet the needs of the audience is essential. Choosing the optimal placement for the thesis and deciding whether or not to discuss opposing ideas are important considerations. Citing ample evidence to support claims can make the message both persuasive and memorable, especially to audiences trained in the Euro-American tradition. In different cultures, other types of persuasive appeals may be more effective.

Speakers can enhance their credibility by demonstrating their competence, trustworthiness, and sincerity. Credibility is also enhanced when the speaker establishes common ground with the audience and when the audience views the speaker as personally attractive.

Four organizational plans are well suited to persuasive presentations: problem-solution, comparative advantages, criteria satisfaction, and motivated sequence. The choice of which organizational plan to use should be governed by the nature of the message and the attitudes of the audience toward the idea being proposed as well as by whether listeners are aware of and inclined to support opposing ideas.

RESOURCES

O'Keefe, D. J., *Persuasion: Theory and Research* (Newbury Park, Calif: Sage, 1990).

This book offers a comprehensive review of the findings about persuasion gleaned by social science research over the past decades. Separate chapters discuss the role of factors in the source (e.g., the speaker), the message, and the audience.

Reardon, K. K., *Persuasion in Practice* (Newbury Park, Calif.: Sage, 1990).

As the title suggests, this book discusses how persuasion operates in the "real world" beyond the laboratory. The chapter on persuasion in organizations is especially appropriate to business communicators.

Appendix

Format and Design of Written Business Messages

Just as your style of dress and grooming creates a first impression when you meet others face-to-face, the appearance of your written messages makes a powerful statement. A well-designed, well-executed piece of correspondence makes your message easier to understand and paints a flattering picture of you. Likewise, a shabby report, letter, or memo has the same effect as stained clothes or bad breath.

Because written messages are so important, entire books and academic courses are devoted to their study. This Appendix is no substitute for a thorough study of written communication. It does, however, provide some guidelines about the accepted design of typical business messages. The following suggestions reflect the most common standards for written communications. Many organizations have their own styles, which may vary in one or more ways from these basic rules. When you are writing on behalf of an organization, you will probably choose to follow its conventions.

GENERAL APPEARANCE

Regardless of the format and type of messages, most business correspondence should follow some basic guidelines.

Typing

Most business documents should be typewritten or created by a computer printer that has typewriter-quality or better output—not dot matrix. There are two reasons for this rule: First, high-quality print is easier to read than most handwriting, and the very least you can do for your readers is to make your ideas legible. Second, typing creates a businesslike impression that will serve you well in most situations. A typewritten message conveys more psychological weight than a handwritten one, just as a business suit creates more credibility than a casual outfit.

There are exceptions to the typing rule. A personal message—a letter of congratulations or condolence, for example—should probably be handwritten. It is usually acceptable to jot down a quick note to a colleague, and perhaps even your boss, rather than taking time to type it up. A longer or more formal message, however, ought to be typed. The culture of an organization usually offers clues about when handwritten notes are acceptable, so pay attention to how the successful people around you communicate. When in doubt, it is almost always best to use a typewriter or a computer.

All the benefits of a typewritten message will be lost if you do a sloppy job. A crisp, clear typeface is essential. This means using an electric or electronic typewriter, ideally with a carbon or plastic ribbon. Cloth ribbons and manual typewriters produce type that is somewhat fuzzy and uneven. Dot-matrix characters on lower-quality computer printers should be avoided whenever possible. The copy they produce can look rough and be difficult to read. Erasures on an important message are a taboo, since they create the same impression as food stains on your clothes.

A word processor with a good printer is the best way to produce neat messages, since it allows you to check and adjust your work before putting it on paper. Most business typewriters now have a key that will remove typographic errors quickly and easily. Even if your machine lacks this feature, you can buy correction film that will lift off or neatly cover up mistakes. Whatever equipment you use, make sure your work is meticulous.

The typeface you use also sends a message. The most common faces like Courier or Letter Gothic are usually the best to use. Using other businesslike, easily readable type styles may be a useful way to distinguish your message, but you should avoid using informal ones (e.g., script) or radically different typefaces that call more attention to the medium than the message.

Paper

The traditional dimensions for most business correspondence in the United States and Canada are 8½ by 11 inches, although some memorandum forms are smaller, and legal documents are usually printed on 8½- by 14-inch paper. White is the standard color for business paper, although neutral colors like light gray or tan are sometimes used. In some organizations, memos are typed on colored paper to make them easily identifiable. It is best to avoid brightly colored paper, since it is hard to read type or photocopy messages printed on them. It is also best to avoid slick or highly textured paper, since it can result in blurred type.

High-quality paper makes your messages look better and ensures that they will stand up under the reading, routing, filing, photocopying, faxing, and other punishments many documents receive. Choosing the right weight of paper is also important. Weight is measured in pounds (the weight of four 500-sheet reams). For reports and memos it is safest to use at least 20-pound paper, although 16-pound stock may do in a pinch. Stationery and résumés create the best effect when they are printed on at least 24-pound paper. The cotton content of paper is also a measure of its quality. Stock of at least 25 percent cotton has a better look and feel than the noncotton variety.

Spelling and Grammar

The content of your correspondence should match its high-quality appearance. Even a single error can stand out to readers, drawing their attention away from all the effective aspects of your message. A glaring mistake in an otherwise perfect document can have the same effect as a piece of food stuck between the teeth of an impeccably dressed and groomed person.

Spelling errors are easier to catch with spell-checker programs that now accompany most word processing computer programs, as well as many electronic typewriters. Don't assume that technology will correct all mistakes, however: if you carelessly type a word that is wrong for the situation but exists in the dictionary (*principle* instead of *principal* or *it's* where *its* is correct, for example), the spell-checker will not catch the error. Spell-checking software is also no help with most names. You will have to be sure that the letter to Ms. MacGregor doesn't leave your desk addressed to Ms. McGregor.

Grammar is just as important as spelling. Incorrect constructions can make you look ignorant or sloppy, leaving the reader to speculate about whether you may be as incompetent in other areas as you are in writing. Many word processing programs have a grammar-checking capability, but they are not foolproof. Careful reading can improve both grammar and syntax.

General Formatting Rules

Most documents should be laid out on the page so that they are easy to read and understand. Margins should be generous—at least an inch all around. The copy should be centered on the page, not crammed toward the top, bottom, or one side. Again, word processing software can make this task much easier than it would be on a typewriter.

The length of typed lines should be short enough to make the copy easily readable. If your typeface uses large type (12 points), each line should have a maximum of 60 characters. If you are using smaller (9 or 10 point) print, the line should be no more than 70 characters. On shorter pieces of correspondence, you can decrease the number of lines and increase the margins to create a better looking layout.

LETTERS

Business custom dictates the standard parts of business correspondence. The elements of a business letter aren't just a social nicety: each of them has a good reason for existing. Some elements should be included in every letter, while others might be included if they are appropriate.

Standard Elements

No matter what the business or topic, every business letter should contain the following elements:

1. Heading
2. Date
3. Inside address

4. Salutation
5. Body
6. Complimentary close
7. Signature block

These elements are illustrated in Figure A-1.

Heading. The heading of a letter shows its source: the organization's name, address, and phone number. Most organizations have printed letterhead that contains the heading. For personal correspondence, type this information (excluding your name) about 2 inches from the top of the first page.

Date. The date the letter is written should be typed at least one blank line beneath the bottom of the heading. The month should be spelled out completely, not abbreviated. The number of the day should be typed, and the full year should be included. The general format is month-day-year (January 15, 1992), although in the military and some other organizations the customary format is day-month-year (3 February 1992), without a comma separating the month and year. It is usually not considered correct to abbreviate a date by just typing its numerals.

Inside Address. The inside address identifies the recipient of the letter. It should be separated from the date by at least one blank line. The amount of space separating the inside address from the date should be adjusted to suit the length of the letter.

A courtesy title should precede the recipient's name. For men, "Mr." is correct unless the addressee merits a professional title such as "Doctor" or "Captain." Note that all professional titles should be spelled out, not abbreviated. For women who do not receive a professional title, "Ms." is generally the safest form of address. If, however, you know that the addressee prefers to be identified as "Mrs." or "Miss," you should use that title. It is always best to address your letter to a specific person. You can usually identify the name of the person you are seeking by telephoning the company and saying, "I will be sending some correspondence to the director of your customer-support division. Can you give me that person's name?" If you do not know the name of a specific person, it is acceptable to address the letter to the department or to a job title (e.g., "Director, Department of Human Resources").

If the addressee's organizational title is short, it can be included on the same line as his or her name: "Ms. Miranda Cortez, General Manager." If the recipient has a longer title, or if the title includes a department, this information can be displayed on a single line below the name.

Immediately following the addressee's name and title, separate lines should contain the name of his or her company, the street address or post office box number, and the city and state or province with proper zip or postal code. If you are writing internationally, the addressee's country should follow, typed in capital letters and occupying its own line.

FIGURE A-1 Block letter format.

Heading	8719 Weldon Drive Raleigh, NC 28328 (919) 555-9812
Date	January 12, 1996
Inside address	Claims Department Triton Health Insurance Co. P.O. Box 27212 Chicago, IL 60601
Attention line	Attention: Mr. Newsome
Salutation	Dear Mr. Newsome:
Subject line	Subject: Policy No. 27-445-8976-1
Body	Thank you for helping to clarify my questions about the delay in paying my claim for physical therapy arising from my recent tennis injury. As you requested in our phone conversation today, I am enclosing the following information: 1. A copy of the most recent statement from my physical therapist. 2. A letter from the personnel director at Carlton Industries verifying that I was a full-time employee at the time of my injury. It has been four months since I first filed my claim for these services. As you can imagine, I am anxious to be reimbursed for the expenses, as provided in my policy. If you need any further information, please write or phone me immediately.
Complimentary close	Sincerely, 
	Gregory Hsu
Signature block	Geoffrey Hsu
Enclosure line	Enclosures (2)
Copy line	Copy: Personnel Office, Carlton Industries

Salutation. The way you address the recipient should be governed by your relationship with that person. If you have not met, or if the relationship is a formal one, you should use his or her title and last name: "Dear Mr. Cooper." If you are on a first-name basis with the recipient, it is probably appropriate to use that form of address in your salutation: "Dear Marianne."

There is no agreed-upon salutation for letters when you do not know the recipient. The old-fashioned "Gentlemen:" may be inaccurate and sexist, so the alternative "Ladies and Gentlemen" is a better choice. Another option is "Dear Sir or Madam," although the formality suits some messages better than others. Generalized types of address such as "Dear Customer" are best for multiple mailings, since they sound impersonal. The old standby "To Whom It May Concern" is best suited to formal messages. Another alternative when you do not know who the recipient will be is to omit the salutation entirely, assuming that the title in the inside address will be sufficient to convey your message.

Body. The body of your letter will usually occupy the greatest space. It should be typed single-spaced, with a blank line separating it from the preceding and following parts of the letter. You should also separate each paragraph of the letter by a blank line.

Depending on the contents of the body, you may want to format some of the information it contains in a distinct manner: as a list, indented from the regular margins, underlined, or in bold type. Just be sure that the format you use is consistent within the letter. If an organization has its own style sheet for letter elements, be sure to follow it.

Complimentary Close. The complimentary close is a single word or phrase, separated from the body by a blank line. Your choice of close provides a way to create just the desired tone: there is a noticeable difference between the casual "Best regards" and the more formal "Very truly yours." Other traditional closes include "Sincerely" and "Cordially."

Signature Block. The signature block should be typed four lines below the complimentary close. At this point you should type your name, unless it is included on the letterhead. Your title, if any, can be included on the same line as your name or immediately below. If your name might leave doubt about your gender, you may include a title in the signature block (see Figure A-2). Women who prefer to be addressed by a specific title (e.g., "Mrs.") can add the desired title here.

Additional Letter Parts

In some letters you may have to include additional information that is not part of the standard elements. There are special ways of formatting this information that allow you to convey specific messages without cluttering up the body of the letter. It is unlikely that you will ever send a letter containing all of these elements, but sooner or later each of them will find its way into your correspondence.

Addressee Line. This line should be printed above the heading, separated by two blank lines. It is used to indicate any special handling the letter should receive. Common notifications include "URGENT," "CONFIDENTIAL," and "PERSONAL." The entire addressee notification should be typed in capital letters to emphasize its importance.

Attention Line. The attention line is a means of directing your letter to a specific department or position title when you do not know the name of the person your message is intended for. It can also be used to personalize a letter when you only know the last name of the recipient (see Figure A-1). Common attention lines take these forms:

ATTENTION: CREDIT DEPARTMENT

ATTENTION: Food Services Director

ATTENTION: Ms. James

The attention line may be placed within the inside address, just below the name of the company, or it may be typed two lines below the inside address. In either case, the form you use on the mailing envelope should match the form you use in the letter itself.

Subject Line. The subject line provides a clear indication of the topic of a letter, which is especially important when you are writing to an office that receives a high volume of mail. The subject line will increase the chances that your message will get the right sort of attention and that it will be easy to file and locate.

There are two possible positions for the subject line: It may be typed just below the salutation, separated by a blank line. Alternatively, it can be typed above the salutation, in the position that an addressee notation might go in another type of correspondence.

Reference Initials. When the person who types the letter is someone other than its composer, the initials of the typist are usually included below the signature block. If the writer's name is included in the signature block, only the typist's initials need appear as a reference. If the letter is written on behalf of a company and does not bear the signature of an individual sender, then the initials of both the writer (in capitals) and the typist (in lowercase letters) should be included. Either of the following forms is acceptable:

SWA:gh SWA/gh

Enclosure Line. An enclosure line indicates that materials accompany the letter itself. This serves as a useful check to make sure that anything that was supposed to be included in the mailing is, indeed, enclosed. It also provides a permanent record about any enclosed material.

The enclosure notation appears at the bottom of the letter, a line or two below the signature block and reference initials, if any. The notation may simply state "Enclosures" if the specific contents are described in the body of the letter. Or it may specify either the number of enclosures ("Enclosures: 2") or their actual contents ("Enclosure: Rate schedule").

Copy Line. A copy notation lets the addressee know who else will be receiving the letter. The notation should be set flush with the left margin, below any reference initials and enclosure notations. The following forms are commonly used to indicate a copy notation:

cc: Rebecca Haynes	pc: Rebecca Haynes
c: Rebecca Haynes	copy to Rebecca Haynes

Mailing Line. If the letter is sent by a means other than first-class mail (e.g., certified mail, special delivery, fax), it may be desirable to indicate this fact. The notation may be placed in either of two locations: at the top of the letter, just above the inside address; or below the signature block and any other notations described in this section.

Postscript. A postscript is traditionally an afterthought which occurs to the sender after the body is written but before the letter is sent. When taken in this sense, postscripts should be avoided: if a message is important enough to dignify with a letter, you should compose it thoughtfully. A second use for postscripts is to emphasize or separate an idea from the body of the letter. You might, for example, append personal congratulations for an accomplishment or thanks for a favor to the body of a businesslike message. Because of their "by the way" nature, postscripts are more appropriate when the sender and addressee have a familiar relationship than in a letter to a stranger.

Second-Page Heading. If a letter is longer than one page, a heading at the left margin top of the second and following sheets will help make your correspondence easy to identify. Subsequent pages should contain the name of the addressee, the page number, and the date. Each of these elements may be typed on its own line:

Mr. Eldon Press
July 22, 1996
Page 2

They may be combined on a single line set flush with the left margin:

Mr. Eldon Press, July 22, 1996, Page 2

Or they may be separated by tabs and centered on the page:

Mr. Eldon Press -2- July 22, 1996

Letter Formats

Most business letters follow one of two formats: the block format (see Figure A-1) and the modified-block format (see Figure A-2). The main differences between these styles are the placement of elements and the way they are indented. Either format is acceptable for a business letter, although some organizations may have a standard style that should be followed in any correspondence written on company letterhead.

In the block format, each element and paragraph is set flush with the left margin. In the modified-block format, the date, complimentary close, and signature block appear just to the right of the center of the page. In this format the first line of each paragraph in the body may also be indented five spaces, although this feature is not required.

Envelopes

The envelope that contains your letter will be the first thing the receiver sees, so it should look just as professional as the correspondence contained inside. In addition, a clearly addressed envelope minimizes the chances that your message will be lost on its way to the addressee.

The address on the envelope should match the content and style of the inside address on the letter it contains. Since the Postal Service routes mail by reading from the bottom of the address upward, your letter should start with the most specific information and add increasingly more general information on each succeeding line:

1. Name of the addressee
2. Department or group
3. Name of the organization
4. Name of the building or mail-stop number
5. Street address and suite number or post office box number
6. City, state, or province, and ZIP Code or Postal Code
7. Country (if the letter is being mailed overseas)

Most envelopes for business correspondence are "No. 10" size, which measures 9½ by 4¼ inches—just the right size to contain an 8½- by 11-inch piece of stationary folded in thirds. If your correspondence is too bulky to fit easily in such an envelope, don't try to cram it in. Instead, mail it in a larger envelope. Standard manila envelopes of varying sizes are available for this purpose at any stationery store. These oversize envelopes give you the advantage of sending your message without folding the paper. The address on a larger piece of correspondence will look most professional if you type it on a separate mailing label, which can then be attached to the envelope. If you use an envelope without the organization's return address printed on it, then type the necessary information neatly, as indicated in Figure A-3.

Folding the Letter

While the recipient isn't likely to notice that a letter is properly folded, a poorly folded one can create an unwelcome impression. For standard 8½ by

FIGURE A-2 Modified-block letter format.

Heading	*DDA* **DAVIS, DOYLE, ANSON ASSOCIATES** **300 Constance Street, Suite 1600** **Ft. Worth, Texas 76102**
Date	June 18, 1996
Addressee line	CONFIDENTIAL
Inside address	Ms. Rebecca Hovarth Managing Partner Batnett, Prince and Horton Advertising 1197 Century Avenue, Suite 479 Ft. Worth, TX 76102
Salutation	Dear Rebecca:
Body	Our search of the Dallas-Ft. Worth area revealed a large number of candidates for the creative director's position you intend to fill. The enclosed report profiles what we believe to be the top six candidates. I have spoken with each of the people on the list, and all of them are interested in talking further about a career move. As you requested, I have not disclosed the name of your agency to any of them, and I assured them that their interest in changing positions would be kept confidential. Once you have looked over the profiles, we can set up a meeting with the candidates who look promising. Please let me know as soon as you are ready to take the next step.
Complementary close	Best regards,
Signature block	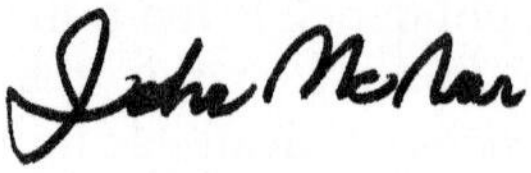 John W. McNair
Reference Initials	mjp
Enclosure line	Enclosure
Postscript	p.s. Thanks for sending the information about rafting in the Grand Canyon. If it isn't too late to make a reservation I'm going to give it a try this summer!

Jennifer Grasso
752 Crossfield St.
Denver, CO 80221

Mr. Gregory Larsen
Capitol Service Corp.
111 Dearborn St.
Orlando, FL 32805

FIGURE A-3 Envelope format.

11 stationery, fold the sheet (or sheets) in thirds. Begin by folding the bottom third upward and creasing it neatly. Then fold the top third downward, leaving a quarter inch or so of space between the top of the page and the first crease. Finally, insert the letter with the open end at the top and the loose flap facing out. When enclosing sheets in a large envelope, place the side with the type facing the rear of the envelope so that it is immediately visible when the receiver opens his or her mail.

MEMOS

It isn't necessary to type up an official memo for every message. When you need to send a quick note to an officemate, jotting a few words on a memo form, Post-it Note, or even a piece of scratch paper will probably do the job. But if your message will be filed for future reference, or if it will be read by a boss who may be judging the quality of your ideas, you should invest the time to type up a memo.

Format

Because they are used for internal messages, memos are usually not sent on the kind of top-quality paper that is used for letters. They may be typed on regular $8\frac{1}{2}$- by 11-inch paper or on half-size sheets measuring $5\frac{1}{2}$ by $8\frac{1}{2}$ inches. The paper size is usually standardized within the organization.

Every memo should contain the same basic elements:

1. Heading
2. Date
3. Addressee's name
4. Sender's name
5. Subject

Many businesses have preprinted memo forms, in which case adding this information is simply a matter of filling in the spaces. If you are creating a memo from scratch, it is acceptable either to use the format in Figure A-4 or to center the heading and set the date, addressee's name, sender's name, and subject line flush with the left margin.

Heading. Every memo should be identified by the heading "MEMO" or "MEMORANDUM," typed in capitals and centered at the top of the page.

Date. The date should indicate when the memo was sent, not when it was written. If the information in the memo changes before the memo is sent,

FIGURE A-4 Memo format.

MEMORANDUM

TO: Distribution*
FROM: K. Osgood
Director of Support Services

DATE: April 6, 1996
SUBJECT: Voice mail training

The new voice mail system is scheduled for installation on May 11. In order to have a smooth transition from our present phone system, all employees should receive training before installation day.

The following dates and times are available for training. All training will be conducted in the second-floor conference room. Please arrange to have everyone in your department attend one session.

Only 15 employees can be accommodated at each meeting, so please write or call Jane Finney at extension 327 to reserve spaces. Personnel who have not reserved times by April 19 will be scheduled into available slots.

Date	Time
April 27	9:00-10:30
	11:00-12:30
	1:00-2:30
April 2	8:30-10:00
	10:30-12:00
	1:00-2:30
May 4	9:00-10:30
	11:00-12:30
	1:00-2:30
May 8	1:00-2:30
	3:00-4:30

* Department heads
K. Fernandez
E. Washington

c: H. Wylie, Key Communications Corp.

the content should be adjusted and the date changed, if necessary. As with letters, the date should not be abbreviated.

The Addressee's Name. In a memo, it is usually not necessary to use a courtesy title like "Mr." or "Dr." with the addressee's name. You should include a courtesy title only if you would use the title when speaking to the addressee in person. In many organizations the accepted form is simply the addressee's first initial and last name (e.g., "J. Banducci").

If the memo is being sent to an entire group of people (e.g., department heads, sales representatives), simply indicate the category on the addressee line. If the memo is going to a large number of people who do not fit into an easy category, put the words "See distribution list," or simply "Distribution" accompanied by an asterisk, on the addressee line and list the names of all the addressees below the body of the memo (see Figure A-4).

The Sender's Name. Use the same format for your name as you do for the addressee's name, minus any courtesy titles. If the recipient does not know you, or if it would be helpful to add the weight of your position in the organization, include your department and/or your personal title (see Figure A-4). A memo doesn't contain a signature line, but you may add your initials next to your name on the "FROM" line.

The Subject of the Memo. The "SUBJECT" line helps the receiver identify the nature of your message quickly and makes it easier to file the memo. Try to keep the subject line brief. Instead of saying "Results of the survey you requested on customer satisfaction," simply type "Results of customer satisfaction survey."

Style

The style of most memos is short and to the point, although they should never be so brusque as to seem rude. Memos don't contain a salutation or complimentary close, and it isn't necessary to begin or conclude with the kind of niceties ("It was good to see you yesterday") you might use when writing a letter. It's likely that the recipient of your memo is a busy person who will appreciate receiving just the necessary facts.

The body of a memo should resemble a letter in appearance: single-spaced, with blank lines separating paragraphs. The same sort of lists and headings that are appropriate in letters can be used in memos. Ideally the memo will be no longer than one page, since lengthier ones may not get the kind of full reading you want. If your memo does require an additional page, the second page should be headed just like that in a letter. Other elements that can be used in business letters (reference initials, copy lines, enclosure line, etc.) are also appropriate in memos.

RÉSUMÉS

At some point during the employment process, you will almost certainly be asked to submit a *résumé*, a document that summarizes your background and qualifications. Résumés serve as a screening device, helping prospective employers decide which candidates' applications are worth further consideration.

A résumé won't get you hired, but it can put you on the "short list" of candidates to be considered—or cause you to be dropped from the running. As you read in Chapter 7, in competitive hiring situations, screening candidates is a process of *elimination* as much as *selection*. The people doing the hiring have more applications than they can handle, so they naturally look for ways of narrowing down the candidates to a manageable number. A good résumé can keep you in the running. A résumé can also be useful for presenting yourself to potential employers who might hire you for a job that hasn't been announced or even been created yet. (Figure A-5 shows a cover letter that would accompany a résumé of this sort.)

Besides listing your qualifications, a résumé offers tangible clues about the type of person you are. Are you organized? Thorough? How well can you present your ideas? Is your work accurate? After you have left the interview, your résumé will remain behind as a reminder of the way you tackle a job and of the kind of employee you are likely to be.

The most effective résumés are tailored to the interests and needs of a particular position and employer. This may not be practical, however, if you are applying to several firms at the same time. At the very least, your résumé should reflect the requirements of a field. For example, a medical technician should stress laboratory skills when applying for a job in a lab; but when a job opening is in a clinic, the same technician should emphasize experience that involves working with people. A résumé that encourages job offers focuses on the employer's needs—how you can help the employer.

Cover Letter

When mailed by itself, a résumé is usually incomplete. Whenever you send yours to a prospective employer, be sure to accompany it with a cover letter similar to the one on page 461. As you read in Chapter 7, a cover letter should include the following information:

- An introduction (or reintroduction) of yourself if the reader doesn't know (or remember) who you are. This paragraph should state your purpose for writing (e.g., in response to an advertisement, at the suggestion of a mutual acquaintance, as a result of your research) and describe your ability to meet the company's needs.
- A brief description of one or two of your most impressive accomplishments that are relevant to the job at hand. Remember: Don't just say you can help the organization. Offer some objective evidence that backs up your claim.

FIGURE A-5 Cover letter accompanying a résumé.

Reed College Box 4
3203 SE Woodstock Blvd.
Portland, OR 97202-8199
(503) 774-4406

April 28, 1996

Ms. Mary Chavez
General Manager
Triton Publishers
1187 Argonne Drive
Goleta, CA 93117

Dear Ms. Chavez:

I was motivated to write this letter after reading your advertisement for a production manager in the April 10 issue of Publisher's Weekly. As a soon-to-be college graduate I am not ready to apply for this position. Nonetheless, I was excited to learn about Triton Publishers, and hope you will consider me as a candidate for entry level editorial and production positions that might become open in late summer or early fall. As the enclosed resume suggests, I could bring to Triton a combination of academic training, work experience, and enthusiasm.

I will be graduating from Reed College at the end of May with a degree in English Literature. My experiences on the staffs of the college newspaper and literary magazine gave me a background in and appreciation for the challenges of producing high quality work on schedule. An internship in the marketing department of Oregon Public Broadcasting honed my appreciation for cultivating an audience. This summer I will be attending the Denver Publishing Institute, where I look forward to gaining a broader understanding and hands-on skill in most areas of publishing.

I will be returning to Santa Barbara around June 1, and would welcome the chance to meet with you to discuss how I might fit into Triton's plans. I will be phoning you soon in hope of arranging an appointment. In the meantime, I can be reached at the address above if you have any questions or need further information.

Thanks in advance for your consideration. I look forward to speaking with you soon.

Sincerely,

Serena West

Serena West

- A statement regarding the next step you hope to take—usually a request for an interview. Detail any information about limits on your availability (though you should keep these to an absolute minimum).
- A final, cordial expression of appreciation to the reader for considering you.

Appearance

Like every important business document, your résumé should be impeccable. Any mistakes or sloppiness here could cost you the job by raising doubts in an employer's mind. Because the design of résumés can be complicated, many candidates hire professional services to create them.

Whether you type the résumé yourself or have it done for you, the final product should reflect the professional image you want to create. It should meet these criteria:

- Be neat and error-free
- Contain plenty of white space to avoid crowding
- Be printed on heavyweight paper, either white or a light neutral color
- Be reproduced clearly on a high-quality printer or copy machine

Although you want to make yourself stand out from the crowd, be cautious about using unusual kinds of paper or typefaces. A novel approach may capture the fancy of a prospective boss, but it may be a turn-off. The more you know about the field and the organization itself, the better your decisions will be about the best approach.

Your résumé should almost never exceed two pages in length—and one is usually better. Employers are often unimpressed with longer résumés, which are hard to read and can seem padded—especially when they come from people with comparatively little job experience. A long résumé may even prompt your disqualification early in the selection process. One magazine editor admitted that when he was overwhelmed by 150 applicants for a job as his assistant, he laid out all the résumés on a table to sort. When he got tired of lifting the first pages to see what was on the second page, he threw out all the résumés that were longer than one sheet. Later, when his boss asked him how he was progressing, he was able to say, "Very well! I've already eliminated half of them."

Elements

While résumés can be organized in more than one way, they will almost always contain the same basic information.

Name, Address, and Phone Number. Make sure that the information allows an interested employer to reach you easily. If necessary, list both a permanent home address and a school address. If you are currently employed, list either your business phone number or another one where you can be reached during business hours.

Job or Career Objective. Most employers agree that a statement of professional objective should be included in a résumé. An effective statement consists of two parts: The first should announce your general goal and mention some important "demonstrated skills"—talents that will qualify you for the job. The second part should detail one or more specific areas in which you want to work. For example:

> A position in public relations using proven skills in writing, researching, and motivating. Special interests in radio and television programming.
>
> Entry-level position in design and development of microprocessor circuitry. Eventual advancement to position as project leader or technical manager.

Education. Employers are usually interested in learning about your academic training, especially education and training since high school, degrees earned, major fields of study, and dates you attended. Begin with your most recent education and work backward. If the information will be helpful and if space permits, you may consider listing notable courses you have taken. If your grade-point average is impressive, include it. Finally, note any honors you have earned. If you received awards for other accomplishments, consider listing all your achievements in a separate section entitled "Awards and Honors."

Experience. Every employer wants to know what kinds of work you have performed. By using the general title "Work Experience" instead of the more limited "Employment History," you can highlight a summer internship, delete a dishwashing job, group minor or similar jobs together, and include volunteer work or club activities that taught you marketable skills.

While you should list your former job titles, employers are really most interested in the kinds of duties you performed. They search this category for the answers to two questions: What can you do? What are your attributes as an employee? You can provide answers to these questions by accompanying your job title, name of employer, and city with a list of the duties you performed. There is no need to use complete sentences—phrases will do. Be sure to use very concrete language, including technical terminology, to describe the work you performed (see Figure A-6). Place this section either before or following the section on education, depending on which will be most important to an employer.

Special Interests and Aptitudes. Most employers want to know about special abilities that will make you a more valuable employee. These include community-service activities (cite offices you have held), languages you can write or speak, special equipment you can operate, hobbies, and so on. The

Susan Noji

Home Address and Phone	**University Address (until 6/7/96)**
1117 Palm Avenue	876 Wicker Avenue
Tucson, Arizona 85712	Redlands, California 92373
(602) 555-8957	(714) 682-4787

JOB OBJECTIVE	An entry-level position in broadcast media production using proven skills in videotape and film. Special interest in news, educational, and documentary programming.
EDUCATION	B.S., Western University (1993–96). Major in Broadcasting and Film, minor in Speech Communication. A.S. in General Studies, Pima Community College (1990–92). Degree granted "with honors."
WORK EXPERIENCE	1994-95: Technical director, Western University media productions: "Chumash Memories: An Oral History," "Women at Work," "Cocaine: Dreams and Nightmares." 1995: Production supervisor, Western University Media Services. Assisted in production of over forty instructional film and videotape programs for university faculty. 1993: Student summer intern, KRER-TV, Phoenix, Arizona. Assisted in production of news and public-affairs programming. 1990-91: Camera operator, sound technician, film editor, lighting technician, and prop crew for Pima College Media Services department.
SPECIAL SKILLS AND INTERESTS	Experienced in videotape productions and editing, including use of studio and portable cameras, remote broadcasting. Experienced in digital and online videotape editing . Familiar with super-8mm filming, including sound recording.
CERTIFICATION	F.C.C. Third Class Operator Permit.
REFERENCES	Available upon request.

FIGURE A-6 Standard chronological résumé featuring education and work experience.

key here is to include only information that the employer will find useful and that casts you in a favorable light.

Membership. If you belong to any organizations in your field, list them under "Memberships." Be sure to include any offices or committee appointments you have held. Membership in service and civic groups is usually less important, so include them only if you have held a major office.

Certification. Many professions and skilled trades offer people the opportunity to become officially certified by taking a competitive examination or by completing an advanced course of study. If you are certified or licensed in any occupational field, create a category in which to display that fact, even if it has only one entry.

References. This section always should be the last one in a résumé. Many experts suggest that you simply include the phrase "References available upon request" and supply the names only when and if you are asked. Employers rarely investigate references until you are under serious consideration, and including them on your résumé may waste precious space.

If you decide that your references will be impressive enough to merit listing, be sure to follow some basic guidelines. Choose only the three or four people who combine the best elements of familiarity with your work and a credible position. Recommendations from high-status people carry more weight, but a reference from a celebrity who barely knows you is not as good as one from an unknown who has worked closely with you. In any case, be sure to get permission beforehand from the people you list as references.

Types of Résumés

There are two approaches to organizing a résumé. Each has its own advantages, and the one you choose will probably depend on your past accomplishments.

Chronological Approach. The chronological approach (see Figure A-6) emphasizes your education and work experience. It is most effective when your education and work experience are clearly related to the job you are seeking.

Within the categories "Education," "Work Experience," and "Related Experience" (if you have such a section) list entries in reverse order, beginning with your most recent experience. Under each position, describe your responsibilities and accomplishments, emphasizing ways in which they prepared you for the job you are now seeking. If you are a recent graduate, listing your education first makes sense. Only cite your grades if they are especially strong.

Functional Approach. The functional approach (see Figure A-7) features the skills you bring to the job (organizer, researcher, manager, etc.) and provides examples of the most significant experiences that demonstrate these abilities. This approach is especially appropriate in the following instances:

When you are first entering the job market, or reentering it after an absence

When you have held a variety of apparently unrelated jobs

Patricia Schneider
909 Bird Ave.
Buffalo, NY 14213
(716) 416-7797

CAREER OBJECTIVE

A position as events coordinator for a successful catering firm, using demonstrated skills in event planning, menu planning, food preparation, and records management.

SKILLS AND EXPERIENCES

Event planning

- Principal planner for major nonprofit fundraisers, including American Heart Association's "Spring Fling" and "Run for Life."
- On-site team leader for 25+ weddings, anniversaries, and other occasions. Duties included menu planning, design and setup of food display and table/flower arrangements, serving, and cleanup for groups ranging from 40 to 250 guests.

Menu planning and food preparation

- Planned and prepared meals for a variety of catered events.
- Assistant restaurant chef, responsible for quality control and food preparation.

Records management

- Maintained daily tracking records of restaurant totals for food, liquor & wine sales.
- Balanced ledgers and assembled daily and monthly sales and expense totals.
- Developed database of current, past, and prospective clients for newsletters and special events promotion.

EMPLOYMENT HISTORY

1994-present — Blue Star Catering, Troy, NY: Team leader, chef, team member.

1992-1994 — Tyler Real Estate, Troy NY: Records management, reception, document preparation.

1991-1992 — Bernardi's Restaurant, Troy, NY: Assistant chef and bookkeeper.

EDUCATION

A.A. degree, Hudson Valley Community College, 1993

REFERENCES

Mr. A.L. Warren, Executive Director
American Heart Association
1165 Jefferson Ave.
Troy, NY 12181
(518) 986-4454

Ms. Jessica Ferrer, Owner
Blue Star Catering Co.
909 Cherry Lane
Troy, NY 12189
(518) 541-2364

FIGURE A-7 Functional résumé focusing on demonstrated skills.

- When you are changing careers or specialties
- When your past job titles don't clearly show how you are qualified for the position you are seeking

When you write a functional résumé, follow the "Skills" category immediately with a chronological "Work History" and a scaled-down "Education" section that lists only institutions, degrees, and dates. Either of the latter two categories may come first, depending on whether you gained most of your skills and experience in school or on the job.

Whatever format you choose, experts agree that strong résumés possess the same qualities:

- *They focus on the employer's needs.* If you understand what qualities (perseverance, innovation, ability to learn quickly) and skills (e.g., mastery of software, selling) an employer needs, you can focus your résumé on showing how you will fit the job.
- *They are concise.* A wordy, long-winded résumé sends the wrong message in a business environment where time is money and clarity is essential. Use simple, brief statements to describe yourself, and avoid verbose language.
- *They are honest.* Outright lies are obvious grounds for disqualification, of course. But getting caught exaggerating your qualifications will raise serious doubts about your honesty in other areas.

Glossary

Note: The number in parentheses at the end of each definition refers to the chapter in which the term is discussed.

A

Advising A type of listening in which the listener responds with ideas and suggestions about what the speaker should think or do. (4)

Agenda A list of topics to be covered in a meeting. Agendas also usually note the meeting's time, length, and location and the members who will attend. Complete agendas also provide background information and outcome goals. (9)

Analyzing A type of listening in which the listener responds with his or her insights about what is being said. (4)

Anchor A listener's preexisting position on an issue being advocated. (15)

Audioconferencing The holding of a conference among three or more geographically separated persons by means of simultaneous telephone connections. (1)

Authoritarian leadership style A leadership style in which the designated leader uses legitimate, coercive, and reward power to control members. (8)

Authority rule A group decision-making method in which a designated leader makes a final decision, either with or without consulting group members. (8)

B

Bar chart A chart consisting of horizontal bars that depict the values of several items in comparative terms. (12)

Bargaining orientation An approach to negotiation in which competitive communicators assume that one side's gains must be matched by the other side's losses. (5)

Biased language Any statement that seems to be objective but actually conceals the speaker's emotional attitude. (3)

Bona fide occupational qualification (BFOQ) A job requirement that is deemed reasonably necessary for the performance of a particular job. In employment interviewing, only questions exploring BFOQs are lawful. (7)

Brainstorming An approach to idea generation that encourages free thinking and minimizes conformity. (8)

Briefing An informative presentation that succinctly informs listeners about a specific task at hand. (14)

C

Cause-effect pattern An organizational arrangement which shows that events happened or will happen as a result of certain circumstances. (11)

Channel The method or medium used to deliver a message (e.g., face-to-face communication, written memos, or the telephone). (1)

Chronological context Factors involving time and timing that affect the transmission and reception of a message. (1)

Chronological pattern An organizational arrangement that presents points according to their sequence in time. (11)

Citations A type of support in which the speaker quotes or paraphrases authoritative or articulate sources. (12)

Claim A statement asserting a fact or belief. (11)

Closed questions Questions that restrict the interviewee's responses, usually to yes or no, a number or item from preselected items, or an either-or response. (6)

Co-culture A group that has a clear identity within the encompassing culture. (2)

Coercive power The ability to influence others that arises because one can impose punishment or unpleasant consequences. (8)

Cohesiveness The degree to which group members feel part of and want to remain with the group. (8)

Collectivist culture A culture with strong social frameworks in which members of a group (such as an organization) are socialized to care for one another and for the group. (2)

Column chart A visual exhibit consisting of vertical columns that depict the quantity of one or more items at different times; used to show changes in quantity over time. (12)

Communication climate A metaphor used to describe the quality of relationships in an organization. (5)

Communication networks Regular patterns or paths along which information flows in an organization. *See also* Formal communication networks and Informal communication networks. (1)

Comparative-advantages organizational plan An organizational strategy that puts several alternatives side by side and shows why one is the best. (15)

Comparisons A type of support in which the speaker shows how one idea is similar to another; may be figurative or literal. (12)

Compromise An orientation toward negotiation which assumes that each side needs to lose at least some of what it was seeking. (5)

Computer conferencing A form of technology that allows individuals to work on a single document via computer, making changes that can be viewed by other participants. (1)

Confirming messages Messages that express value toward other persons. (5)

Conflict phase The second of Aubrey Fisher's four group problem-solving phases; characterized by members' taking strong stands that result in conflict within the group. (8)

Connection power The ability to influence that arises because of one's connections and associations inside and outside the organization. (8)

Consensus A decision-making method in which the group as a whole makes a decision that each member is willing to support. (8)

Content messages The dimension of messages that focus upon the topic under discussion. *See also* Relational messages. (1)

Context The environment of physical, social, chronological, and cultural variables that surrounds any process of communication. (1)

Contingency approaches to leadership Leadership theories which assert that the most effective leadership style is flexible, changing as needed with the context. (8)

Counterfeit questions Utterances that appear to be questions but are actually statements, forms of advice, traps, or attacks on the speaker. (4)

Credibility The persuasive force that comes from the audience's belief in and respect for the speaker. (15)

Criteria-satisfaction organizational plan An organizational strategy that sets up standards (criteria) that the audience accepts and then shows how the speaker's idea or product meets the criteria. (15)

Cultural context Factors relating to the organizational or broader cultures of communicators that affect the transmission and reception of a message. (1)

Culture The set of values, beliefs, norms, customs, rules, and codes that lead people to define themselves as a distinct group, giving them a sense of commonality. (2)

D

Decoding The process of attaching meaning to words, symbols, or behaviors. (1)

Democratic leadership style A leadership style in which the designated leader encourages members to share decision making. (8)

Descriptive statements Statements that describe the speaker's perspective instead of evaluating the sender's behavior or motives. *See also* "I" language and "You" language. (5)

Designated leader A leader whose title indicates a leadership role, either by appointment or by group selection. (8)

Diagnostic interview An interview in which professionals (e.g., doctors and lawyers) gather information on their patients' or clients' needs. (7)

Direct question (in a group) A question addressed (by name) to a particular individual. (9)

Direct questions (in an interview) Straightforward questions that ask exactly what the interviewer wants to know. (6)

Disconfirming messages Messages that show a lack of valuing for other persons. (5)

Document conferencing *See* Computer conferencing.

Downward communication Communication that flows from superiors to subordinates. (1)

E

E-mail *See* Electronic mail.

Electronic mail (E-mail) A communication system whereby messages are exchanged via computer networks. (1)

Emergence phase The third of Aubrey Fisher's four group problem-solving phases; characterized by an end to conflict and emergence of harmony within the group. (8)

Emergent leader A leader chosen by the group, either officially or informally. (8)

Employment interview An interview designed to judge the qualifications and desirability of a candidate for a job. (7)

Encoding The intentional process of creating a message. (1)

Equivocal terms Words with more than one meaning. Equivocation can lead to unintentional misunderstandings. In contrast, *strategic ambiguity* is often used in business to promote harmony and soften the blow of unpleasant messages. (3)

Examples Brief illustrations that back up or explain a claim. (12)

Exit interview An interview designed to discover why an employee is leaving an organization. (7)

Expert opinion A decision-making method in which a single person perceived as an expert makes a decision for the group. (8)

Expert power The ability to influence that arises because of one's knowledge, ability, and expertise in a particular area. (8)

Explanation An informative presentation that increases listeners' understanding of a subject. (14)

Extemporaneous presentation A type of delivery in which the major ideas are planned and rehearsed but the speech is given spontaneously from notes. (13)

F

Factual questions Questions that ask for verifiable, factual information rather than opinion. (6)

Feedback The recognizable response of a receiver to a sender's message. (1)

Flip chart A large pad of paper, attached to an easel, that is used to create and/or display visuals. (12)

Formal communication networks Officially designated paths of communication designed by management to indicate who should communicate with whom. (1)

Functional roles Types of behavior that are necessary if a group is to do its job effectively. *See also* Task roles and Relational roles. (8)

Funnel sequence A sequence of interview questions that begins with a broad question and grows increasingly more specific. (6)

G

General purpose A broad indication of the purpose of a speech, generally to inform, persuade, or entertain. (10)

Graph A visual display that shows the correlation between two quantities. (12)

Groupthink A condition in which group members are unwilling to critically examine ideas because of their desire to maintain harmony. (8)

H

Hidden agenda A group member's personal goal that is not made public. (8)

High-context culture A culture that relies heavily on subtle, often nonverbal cues to convey meaning and maintain social harmony. (2)

High-level abstractions Terms that cover a broad range of possible objects or events without describing them in much detail. (3)

Highly scheduled interview An interview that consists of a standardized list of questions, sometimes in precise order and wording, as in research interviews. (6)

Horizontal (lateral) communication Communication in which messages flow between members of an organization who have equal power or responsibility. (1)

Hypothetical questions Questions that ask an interviewee how he or she might respond under certain circumstances. (6)

I

"I" language Language in which the communicator describes his or her feelings, needs, and behaviors without accusing others. (5)

Impromptu presentation A type of delivery in which the speaker has little or no preparation time before presenting his or her remarks. (13)

Indirect questions Questions that get at information the interviewer wants to know without asking for it directly. (6)

Individualistic culture A culture whose members are inclined to put their own interests and those of their immediate families ahead of social concerns. (2)

Informal communication networks Patterns of interaction that are based on proximity, friendships, and shared interests. (1)

Information power The ability to influence that arises because of one's access to otherwise obscure information. (8)

Interjection A word or phrase inserted into a presentation to highlight an idea's importance or placement. (14)

Interview A two-party somewhat structured conversation in which at least one person has a specific purpose. (6)

Inverted funnel sequence A sequence of interview questions that begins with specific, closed questions and introduces increasingly broader questions. (6)

Investigative interview An interview designed to discover the causes of an incident or problem. (7)

J

Jargon Specialized terminology used by members of a particular group. The word is used in a derogatory sense when applied to language that is overly obscure. (3)

L

Laissez-faire leadership style A leadership style in which the leader gives up power and transforms a group into a leaderless collection of equals. (8)

Lateral communication *See* Horizontal communication.

Latitude of acceptance The range of positions or arguments a person would accept with little or no persuasion. (15)

Latitude of noncommitment The range of positions or arguments a person neither accepts nor rejects. (15)

Latitude of rejection The range of positions or arguments a person opposes. (15)

Leading questions Questions that direct the interviewee to answer in a certain way, often by indicating the answer the interviewer wants to hear. (6)

Legitimate power The ability to influence that arises because of one's position (e.g., judge, elder, professor, president). (8)

Life-cycle theory of leadership An approach to understanding leadership which suggests that a leader's attention to tasks and relationships should vary depending on the organizational maturity of subordinates. (8)

Listen-and-tell performance appraisal style An approach to performance appraisal in which the interviewer (usually a supervisor) first listens to the subordinate and then gives feedback on the subordinate's performance. (7)

Lose-lose orientation An approach to negotiation in which one party's perceived loss leads to an outcome with negative consequences for the other parties. (5)

Low-context culture A culture that uses language primarily to express thoughts, feelings, and ideas as clearly and logically as possible. (2)

Low-level abstractions Highly specific statements that refer directly to objects or events that can be observed. (3)

M

Majority vote A decision-making method in which a vote is taken and the item with the most votes is the one accepted. (8)

Manuscript presentation A type of delivery in which the speaker reads word for word from prepared remarks. (13)

Meeting Any focused conversation that has a specific agenda; usually, but not always, scheduled in advance. (9)

Memorized presentation A type of delivery in which the speech is memorized and recited word for word from memory. (13)

Message Any symbol or behavior from which others create meaning or which triggers a response. (1)

Minority decision A decision-making method in which a few members make a decision for the whole group. (8)

Moderately scheduled interview A flexible interview in which major topics, their order, questions, and probes are planned but not rigidly adhered to. (6)

Motivated-sequence organizational plan An organizational strategy that presents a topic in terms of five sequential concepts: attention, need, satisfaction, visualization, and action. (15)

N

Negotiation Discussion of specific proposals for the purpose of finding a mutually acceptable agreement or settlement. (5)

Networks *See* Communication networks.

Noise Any factor that interferes with a message. Such factors are also called *barriers* or *interference. See also* Physical noise, Physiological noise, and Psychological noise. (1)

Nominal group technique (NGT) A five-phase method for giving group members' ideas equal chance at consideration. (9)

Nonscheduled interview An interview that consists of a topical agenda but no planned, specific questions. (6)

Nonverbal communication Communication that consists of messages sent by nonlinguistic means, either visually, physically, or vocally. (3)

Norms Informal rules about what behavior is appropriate in a group. Explicit norms are made clear by speaking about them or writing them out. Implicit norms are not openly discussed but are known and understood by group members. (8)

O

Open questions Questions that invite a broad, detailed response. *See also* Closed questions. (6)

Opinion questions Questions that seek the respondent's judgment about a topic. (6)

Organizational chart A drawing or model that shows the levels of authority and reporting relationships in an organization. (1)

Organizational culture A relatively stable picture of an organization that is shared by its members. (2)

Orientation phase The first of Aubrey Fisher's four problem-solving phases of groups; characterized by tentative statements and getting-acquainted types of communication. (8)

Overhead question A question directed at all members of a group, inviting a response from any member. (9)

P

Paralanguage Nonlinguistic vocal qualities such as rate, pitch, volume, and pauses. (3)

Paraphrasing Listening to another and restating what has been said in your own words. Both feelings and factual content can be paraphrased. (4)

Passive listening Listening characterized by a mixture of silence and prompts (e.g., "Uh-huh," "Really?," "Tell me more") that invite the speaker to keep going. (4)

Performance appraisal interview An interview, usually conducted by a superior, in which the quality of a subordinate's work is discussed. (7)

Persuasion The act of motivating an audience, through communication, to voluntarily change a particular belief. (15)

Physical context The environmental factors that affect the transmission and reception of a message. (1)

Physical noise Any external factor that interferes with communication (e.g., distracting sounds, walls, strong odors, someone standing in your way). (1)

Physiological noise Any physiological factor that interferes with communication (e.g., hearing disorders, speech impediments). (1)

Pictogram A visual support that employs an artistic or pictorial variation of a bar, column, or pie chart. (12)

Pie chart A round chart that is divided into segments to illustrate percentages of a whole. (12)

Power distance A measure of a culture's acceptance (high or low) of differences in authority. (2)

Primary questions Interview questions that introduce a new topic or a new area within a topic. *See also* Secondary questions. (6)

Problem-oriented messages Messages that aim at meeting the needs of both the sender and the other party. (5)

Problem-solution pattern (organizational plan) An organizational arrangement in which the speaker first convinces the audience that a problem exists and then presents a plan to solve it. (11, 15)

Problem-solving performance appraisal style An approach to performance appraisal in which the employee and manager work together to identify areas of concern and appropriate solutions. (7)

Psychological noise Any force within a receiver's mind that interferes with accurate encoding or decoding (e.g., prejudices, emotions, biases, defensiveness). (1)

Q

Questioning Listening responses that seek additional information from a speaker. *See also* Analyzing, Advising, Supporting, and Paraphrasing. (4)

R

Rapport talk Language that creates connections, establishes goodwill, and builds community; more typically used by women. (3)

Receiver Any person who perceives a message and attaches meaning to it, whether the message was intended for that person or not. (1)

Referent power The ability to influence because one is respected or liked by the group. (8)

Reflective-thinking sequence A seven-step problem-solving approach developed by John Dewey. (8)

Reinforcement phase The fourth of Aubrey Fisher's four group problem-solving phases; characterized by members' active endorsement of group decisions. (8)

Relational messages The dimension of messages that focus on how communicators feel about one another. *See also* Content messages. (1)

Relational roles Functional roles that help facilitate smooth interaction among members. (8)

Relay question In groups, a question asked by one member which the leader then addresses to the entire group. (9)

Relevancy challenge A request that asks a group member to explain how his or her seemingly off-track idea relates to the group task. (9)

Report An informative presentation that describes the state of an operation. (14)

Report talk Language that conveys information, facts, knowledge, and competence; more typically used by men. (3)

Research interview An interview designed to gather data on which to base a decision. (7)

Reverse question In groups, a question asked of the leader which the leader refers back to the person who asked it. (9)

Reward power The ability to influence that arises because one can induce desirable consequences or rewards. (8)

Rhetorical question A question with an obvious answer, which does not call for an overt response. (11)

Risky shift A type of harmful conformity in which groups take positions that are more extreme (on the side of either caution or risk) than the positions of individual members. (8)

Roles Patterns of behavior expected of individual group members. (8)

S

Self-directed work teams Groups that manage their own behavior to accomplish a task. (8)

Secondary questions Interview questions that seek additional information about a topic that is under discussion. *See also* Primary questions. (6)

Sender Any person who sends a message, whether intentionally or unintentionally. (1)

Signpost In presentations, a word, phrase, or sentence that tells listeners how new information relates to the topic. (14)

Sincere questions Requests for information that are genuinely meant to help the listener understand. *See also* Counterfeit questions. (4)

Social context Relational factors that affect the transmission and reception of a message. (1)

Spatial pattern An organizational arrangement that presents material according to its physical location. (11)

Specific purpose A concrete statement of what response a speaker is seeking as the result of his or her remarks. (10)

Statistics Numbers used to represent an idea. (12)

Stories Detailed descriptions of incidents that illustrate a point; may be factual or hypothetical. (12)

Style approach to leadership An approach to studying leadership based on the assumption that the designated leader's style of communication affects the group's effectiveness. (8)

Supporting A type of listening in which the listener responds with reassurance or comfort. (4)

Supporting material Material that backs up claims in a presentation. (12)

Survey interview An interview conducted with a number of people to gather information for conclusions, interpretations, or future action. (7)

T

Task roles Functional roles that are needed to accomplish a group's mission. (8)

Team A small, interdependent collection of people with a common identity who interact with one another, usually face-to-face over time, in order to reach a goal.

Tell-and-listen performance appraisal style An approach to performance appraisal in which the manager first describes his or her assessment and then listens to the employee's input. (7)

Tell-and-sell performance appraisal style An approach to performance appraisal in which the manager states his or her evaluation of the employee and then tries to persuade the employee of its accuracy. (7)

Thesis statement A single sentence that summarizes the central idea of a presentation. (10)

Topical pattern An organizational arrangement in which ideas are grouped around logical themes or divisions of the subject. (11)

Transparency A clear sheet used with an overhead projector to cast an image on a screen. (12)

Training An informative presentation that teaches listeners how to perform a task. (14)

Trait approach to leadership A leadership theory based on the belief that all leaders possess common traits that make them effective. (8)

Transition A statement used between parts of a presentation to help listeners understand the relationship of the parts to one another and to the thesis. (11)

Trigger words Terms that have such strong emotional associations that they set off an intense emotional reaction in certain listeners. (3)

Tunnel sequence A series of interview questions, all of equal depth. *See also* Funnel sequence, Inverted funnel sequence.

U

Uncertainty avoidance A measure of how accepting a culture is of a lack of predictability. (2)

Upward communication Communication that flows from subordinates to superiors. (1)

V

Videoconferencing The holding of a meeting or conference by means of audio and visual transmissions that enable two or more geographically separated persons to see, hear, and talk to each other. (1)

W

Win-win orientation A collaborative approach to negotiation which assumes that solutions can be reached that meet the needs of all parties. (5)

Work group A small, interdependent collection of people with a common identity who interact with one another, usually face-to-face over time, in order to reach a goal. (8)

Y

"You" Language Language that often begins with the word *you* and accuses or evaluates the other person. (5)

Notes

CHAPTER 1

1. D. B. Curtis, J. L. Winsor, and R. D. Stephens, "National Preferences in Business and Communication Education," *Communication Education* 38 (1989): 6–14.
2. I. N. Engleberg and D. R. Wynn, "DACUM: A National Database Justifying the Study of Speech Communication," paper presented at the Eastern Communication Association Convention, Washington, D.C., April 1994.
3. B. W. Bowman, "What Helps or Harms Promotability?" *Harvard Business Review* 42 (January–February 1964): 14.
4. D. Whetten and K. S. Cameron, *Developing Management Skills: Managing Conflict* (New York: HarperCollins, 1993), pp. 8–11.
5. T. W. Harrell and M. S. Harrell, "Stanford MBA Careers: A 20 Year Longitudinal Study," Graduate School of Business Research Paper No. 723 (Stanford, Calif., 1984).
6. S. Peterson, "Managing Your Communication: The Year 2000 and Beyond," *Vital Speeches of the Day* 61 (1995): 188–190.
7. T. Bailey, "Changes in the Nature and Structure of Work: Implications for Skill Requirements and Skill Formation," Columbia University Conservation of Human Resources Technical Paper No. 9 (November 1989).
8. J. Flanigan, "The Nation's Educational Crisis Is Also a Business Crisis," *Los Angeles Times* (Jan. 21, 1990): D1.
9. G. Goldhaber, *Organizational Communication,* 6th ed. (Dubuque, Iowa: Wm. C. Brown, 1993), p. 143.
10. A. S. Bednar and R. J. Olney, "Communication Needs of Recent Graduates," *Bulletin of the Association for Business Communication* (December 1987): 22–23.
11. See, for example, A. Petofi, "The Graphic Revolution in Computers," in *Careers Tomorrow: The Outlook for Work in a Changing World,* ed. E. Cornish (Bethesda, Md.: World Future Society, 1988), pp. 62–66.
12. "Harper's Index," *Harper's* (December 1994): 13.
13. T. Burghart, "A Spoonful of Concern," *Albuquerque Journal* (Dec. 5, 1994): 5.
14. F. S. Endicott, *The Endicott Report: Trends in the Employment of College and University Graduates in Business and Industry 1980* (Evanston, Ill.: Placement Center, Northwestern University, 1979).
15. Cited in V. V. Weldon, "The Power of Changing the Context," *Vital Speeches of the Day* 60 (1994): 217–219.
16. For a discussion of content and relational messages, see R. Adler and N. Towne, *Looking Out/Looking In,* 8th ed. (Ft. Worth, Tex.: Harcourt Brace, 1996), pp. 23–30.
17. For a discussion of the characteristics of networks, see P. R. Monge, "The Network Level of Analysis," in *Handbook of Communication Science,* ed. C. R. Berger and S. H. Chafee (Newbury Park, Calif.: Sage, 1987), pp. 239–270.
18. For a review of research on formal networks, see F. M. Jablin, "Formal Organization Structure," in *Handbook of Organizational Communication,* ed. F. Jablin, L. Putnam, K. Roberts, and L. Porter (Newbury Park, Calif.: Sage, 1987), pp. 389–419.
19. "Managers' Shoptalk," *Working Woman* (February 1985): 22.
20. D. Katz and R. Kahn, *The Social Psychology of Organizations,* 2nd ed. (New York: Wiley, 1978), p. 239.
21. T. J. Peters and R. H. Waterman, Jr., *In Search of Excellence: Lessons from America's Best-Run Companies* (New York: Harper & Row 1982), p. 267.
22. L. Schuster, "Wal-Mart Chief's Enthusiastic Approach Infects Employees, Keeps Retailer Growing," *Wall Street Journal* (Apr. 20, 1982): 21.
23. F. Rice, "Champions of Communication," *Fortune* (June 3, 1991): 111–120.
24. Adapted from Katz and Kahn, *The Social Psychology of Organizations,* p. 245.
25. L. Berkowitz and W. Bennis, "Interaction Patterns in Formal Service-Oriented Organizations," *Administrative Science Quarterly* 5 (1961): 210–222.
26. L. P. Stewart, A. D. Stewart, S. A. Friedley, and P. J. Cooper, *Communication between the*

Sexes: Sex Differences and Sex-Role Stereotypes, 2nd ed. (Scottsdale, Ariz.: Gorsuch Scarisbrick, 1990), p. 226.

27. G. Goldhaber, *Organizational Communication,* 6th ed. (Dubuque, Iowa: Wm. C. Brown, 1993), pp. 163–164.

28. D. O. Wilson, "Diagonal Communication Links within Organizations," *Journal of Business Communication* 29 (Spring 1992): 129–143.

29. Adapted from Goldhaber, *Organizational Communication,* pp. 174–175.

30. "Did You Hear It through the Grapevine?" *Training & Development* (October 1994): 20.

31. T. E. Deal and A. A. Kennedy, *Corporate Cultures: The Rites and Rituals of Corporate Life* (Reading, Mass.: Addison-Wesley, 1982), p. 86.

32. D. Krackhardt and J. R. Hanson, "Informal Networks: The Company behind the Chart," *Harvard Business Review* 71 (1993): 104–111.

33. R. M. Kanter, "The New Managerial Work," *Harvard Business Review* 67 (1989): 85–92.

34. J. B. Bush, Jr., and A. L. Frohman, "Communication in a 'Network' Organization," *Organizational Dynamics* 20 (Autumn 1991): 23–36.

35. E. M. Eisenberg and H. J. Goodall, Jr., *Organizational Communication: Balancing Creativity and Constraint* (New York: St. Martin's, 1993), p. 9.

36. T. J. Murray, "How to Stay Lean and Mean," *Business Month* (August 1987): 29–32.

37. R. H. Lengel and R. L. Daft, "The Selection of Communication Media as an Executive Skill," *Academy of Management EXECUTIVE* 11 (1988): 225–232.

38. M. Moeller, "Videoconferencing from the Desktop," *Presentations* (May 1994): 16–20.

39. "Meeters Want More for the Money," *Los Angeles Times* (Oct. 27, 1994): D4.

40. "Computer Support Can Enhance Meetings," *Meeting Management News* 2 (June 1993): 5. See also S. Barnes and L. M. Greller, "Computer-Mediated Communication in the Organization," *Communication Education* 43 (1994): 129–142.

41. J. F. Vesper and V. R. Ruggiero, *Contemporary Business Communication: From Thought to Expression* (New York: HarperCollins, 1993), p. 496.

42. "Are You Connected?" *Training & Development* (November 1994): 18.

43. Lengel and Daft, "The Selection of Communication Media," p. 229.

CHAPTER 2

1. E. Klein, "Tomorrow's Work Force," *D&B Reports* (January–February 1990): 30–35; and M. Riche, "America's New Workers," *American Demographics* (February 1988): 33–41.

2. L. Copeland, "Making the Most of Cultural Differences at the Workplace," *Personnel* (June 1988): 53.

3. J. Schacter, "Firms Begin to Embrace Diversity," *Los Angeles Times* (Apr. 17, 1988): A1.

4. S. Trenholm and A. Jensen, *Interpersonal Communication,* 2nd ed. (Belmont, Calif.: Wadsworth, 1992), p. 369.

5. E. Hall, *The Silent Language* (Greenwich, Conn.: Fawcett, 1959), p. 169.

6. L. A. Samovar and R. E. Porter, *Communication between Cultures,* 2nd ed. (Belmont, Calif.: Wadsworth, 1995), p. 11.

7. L. E. Boone, D. L. Kurtz, and J. R. Block, *Contemporary Business Communication* (Englewood Cliffs, N.J.: Prentice-Hall, 1994), p. 599.

8. T. Padgett and C. S. Lee, "Go South, Young Yanquis" *Newsweek* (Sept. 19, 1994): 48.

9. C. H. Deutsch, "Want to Sail to Top? Go Overseas," *Albuquerque Tribune* (Aug. 4, 1988): B7.

10. Boone, Kurtz, and Block, *Contemporary Business Communication,* p. 608.

11. J. Pacheco, "Proper Titles Are Big Part of Doing Business in Mexico," *Albuquerque Journal* (Mar. 6, 1995): 21.

12. Boone, Kurtz, and Block, *Contemporary Business Communication,* p. 603.

13. K. M. Glover, "Do's and Taboos," *Business America* 111 (Aug. 13, 1990): 5.

14. F. H. Katayama, "How to Act Once You Get There," *Fortune's Pacific Rim Guide* (1989): 87.

15. Padgett and Lee, "Go South," p. 48.

16. F. Trompenaars, *Riding the Waves of Culture* (Burr Ridge, Ill.: Irwin, 1994), p. 122.

17. Ibid., p. 123.

18. M. Park and M. Kim, "Communication Practices in Korea," *Communication Quarterly* 40 (1992): 398–404.

19. M. Miller, "A Clash of Corporate Cultures," *Los Angeles Times* (Aug. 15, 1992): A1, A8.

20. M. L. Lustig and J. Koester, *Intercultural Competence: Interpersonal Communication across Cultures* (New York: HarperCollins, 1993), pp. 14–17.

21. Ibid., p. 11.

22. P. R. Timm and B. D. Peterson, *People at Work: Human Relations in Organizations,* 4th ed. (Minneapolis/St. Paul, Minn.: West, 1993), p. 301.

23. Lustig and Koester, *Intercultural Competence,* p. 267.

24. C. Lauerman, "Do You Hear What I Hear?" *Chicago Tribune* (Nov. 5, 1985): sec. 5, pp. 1, 3, cited in L. S. Self and C. S. Carlson-Liu, *Oral Communication Skills: A Multicultural Approach* (Dubuque, Iowa: Kendall/Hunt, 1988), p. 80.

25. E. C. Condon, "Cross-Cultural Interferences Affecting Teacher-Pupil Communication in American Schools," *International and Intercultural Communication Annual* 3 (1976): 108–120, cited in Self and Carlson-Liu, *Oral Communication Skills,* p. 67.

26. Samovar and Porter, *Communication between Cultures,* p. 199.

27. K. G. Stone, "Disability Act Everyone's Responsibility in America," *Albuquerque Journal* (Feb. 19, 1995): H2.

28. D. O. Braithwaite and D. Labrecque, "Responding to the Americans with Disabilities Act: Contributions of Interpersonal Communication Research and Training," *Journal of Applied Communication Research* 22 (1994): 285–294. See also D. O. Braithwaite, " 'Just How Much Did That Wheelchair Cost?': Management of Privacy Boundaries by Persons with Disabilities," *Western Journal of Speech Communication* 55 (1991): 254–275.

29. E. Hall, *Beyond Culture* (New York: Doubleday, 1959).

30. M. Morris, *Saying and Meaning in Puerto Rico: Some Problems in the Ethnology of Discourse* (Oxford: Pergamon, 1981).

31. D. Locke, *Increasing Multicultural Understanding: A Comprehensive Model* (Newbury Park, Calif.: Sage, 1992), p. 140.

32. G. Thurmon, "Oral Rhetorical Practice in African American Culture," in *Our Voices: Essays in Culture, Ethnicity, and Communication: An Intercultural Anthology,* ed. A. Gonzalez, M. Houston, and V. Chen (Los Angeles: Roxbury, 1994) p. 82.

33. G. Hofsteide, *Culture's Consequences: International Differences in Work-Related Values* (Newbury Park, Calif.: Sage, 1980); and G. Hofsteide, "The Cultural Relativity of Organizational Practice and Theories," *Journal of International Business Studies* (Fall 1983): 75–89. For a summary of Hofsteide's research, see S. P. Robbins, *Organizational Behavior, Concepts, Controversies, and Applications,* 4th ed. (Englewood Cliffs, N.J.: Prentice-Hall, 1990), pp. 487–490.

34. "Formula for Success," *Financial World* (Dec. 8, 1992): 40.

35. G. Hofsteide, "Motivation, Leadership, and Organization: Do American Theories Apply Abroad?" *Organizational Dynamics* (Summer 1980): 55–60. See also Robbins, *Organizational Behavior,* p. 487.

36. See, for example, J. Dreyfuss, "Get Ready for the New Work Force," *Fortune* (Apr. 23, 1990): 165–181.

37. M. Marby, "Pin a Label on a Manager—and Watch What Happens," *Newsweek* (May 14, 1990): 43.

38. Copeland, "Making the Most of Cultural Differences," p. 60.

39. J. C. Pearson, L. Turner, and W. Todd-Mancillas, *Gender and Communication,* 3rd ed. (Madison, Wis.: Brown & Benchmark, 1995), pp. 153–157.

40. M. Houston, "When Black Women Talk with White Women: Why Dialogues Are Difficult," in Gonzalez, Houston, and Chen (eds.), *Our Voices,* p. 137.

41. "Past Tokenism," *Newsweek* (May 14, 1990): 37–43.

42. C. M. Kelly, *The Destructive Achiever: Power and Ethics in the American Corporation* (Reading, Mass.: Addison-Wesley, 1988), p. 159.

43. T. E. Deal and A. A. Kennedy, *Corporate Cultures: The Rites and Rituals of Corporate Life* (Reading, Mass.: Addison-Wesley, 1982), pp. 16–17.

44. E. C. Ravlin and C. L. Adkins, "A Work Values Approach to Corporate Culture: A Field Test of the Value of Congruence Process and Its Relationship to Individual Outcomes," *Journal of Applied Psychology* 74 (June 1989): 424–433.

45. A. Kennedy, "Back-Yard Conversations: New Tools for Quality Conversations," *Communication World* (November 1984): 26.

46. See, for example, E. M. Eisenberg and H. L. Goodall, Jr., *Organizational Communication: Balancing Creativity and Constraint* (New York: McGraw-Hill, 1992), pp. 182–187.

47. M. H. Brown, "Defining Stories in Organizations: Characteristics and Functions," in *Communication Yearbook 13,* ed. J. A. Anderson (Newbury Park, Calif.: Sage, 1990), pp. 162–190. See also P. Shockley-Zalabak and D. D. Morley, "Creating a Culture: A Longitudinal Examination of the Influence of Management and Employee Values on Communication Rule Stability and Emergence,"

Human Communication Research 20 (1994): 334–355.

48. T. J. Peters and R. H. Waterman, *In Search of Excellence: Lessons from America's Best-Run Companies* (New York: Harper & Row, 1982), p. 240. See also J. M. Byer and H. M. Trice, "How an Organization's Rites Reveal Its Culture," *Organizational Dynamics* (Spring 1987): 15.
49. Peters and Waterman, *In Search of Excellence,* pp. 244–245.
50. Adapted from Deal and Kennedy, *Corporate Cultures,* pp. 129–133.
51. F. Steele, *Physical Settings and Organizational Development* (Reading, Mass.: Addison-Wesley, 1973), p. 46.

CHAPTER 3

1. E. M. Eisenberg and S. R. Phillips, "Miscommunication in Organizations," in *Miscommunication and Problematic Talk,* ed. N. Coupland, H. Giles, and J. Wiemann (Newbury Park, Calif.: Sage, 1991), pp. 244–258.
2. M. Meyer and C. Fleming, "Silicon Screenings: The Marriage of Hollywood and Silicon Valley Gets Off to a Rocky Start," *Newsweek* (Aug. 15, 1994): 63.
3. M. Miller, "A Clash of Corporate Cultures," *Los Angeles Times* (Aug. 15, 1992): A1, A8.
4. J. S. Armstrong, "Unintelligible Management Research and Academic Prestige," *Interfaces* 10 (1980): 80–86.
5. "Up in Smoke," *Accountant's Journal* 66 (April 1987): 10.
6. See, for example, J. B. Bavelas, A. Black, N. Chovil, and J. Mullett, *Equivocal Communication* (Newbury Park, Calif.: Sage, 1990); and E. M. Eisenberg and H. L. Goodall, Jr., *Organizational Communication: Balancing Creativity and Constraint* (New York: St. Martin's, 1993), pp. 25–27.
7. D. Tannen, *You Just Don't Understand: Women and Men in Conversation* (New York: Morrow, 1990), p. 47. For a detailed summary of differences between male and female language use, see L. P. Stewart, A. D. Stewart, S. A. Friedley, and P. J. Cooper, *Communication between the Sexes: Sex Differences and Sex-Role Stereotypes,* 2nd ed. (Scottsdale, Ariz.: Gorsuch Scarisbrick, 1990); D. Tannen, *Talking from 9 to 5: How Women's and Men's Conversational Styles Affect Who Gets Heard, Who Gets Credit, and What Gets Done at Work* (New York: Morrow, 1994); and J. T. Wood, *Gendered Lives: Communication, Gender, and Culture* (Belmont, Calif.: Wadsworth, 1994), chap. 5.
8. See, for example, D. Geddes, "Sex Roles in Management: The Impact of Varying Power of Speech Style on Union Members' Perception of Satisfaction and Effectiveness," *Journal of Psychology* 126 (1992): 589–607.
9. *U.S. News & World Report* (Aug. 1, 1989): 50, reported in L. A. Samovar and R. E. Porter, *Communication between Cultures,* 2nd ed. (Belmont, Calif.: Wadsworth, 1995), p. 16.
10. N. Cooper, *Sexual Harassment in Employment* (Albuquerque: New Mexico Commission on the Status of Women), p. 5.
11. P. Lee, "EEOC: The Mill Grinds Slowly," *Los Angeles Times* (May 16, 1994): 5.
12. Summarized in J. K. Burgoon, D. B. Buller, and W. G. Woodall, *Nonverbal Communication: The Unspoken Dialogue* (New York: Harper & Row, 1989), pp. 155–156.
13. J. B. Stiff, J. L. Hale, R. Garlick, and R. G. Rogan, "Effect of Cue Incongruence and Social Normative Influences on Individual Judgments of Honesty and Deceit," *Southern Speech Communication Journal* 55 (1990): 206–229.
14. For a discussion of the principle "You can't not communicate nonverbally," see T. Clevenger, Jr., "Can One Not Communicate? A Conflict of Models," *Communication Studies* 42 (1991): 340–353.
15. P. Ekman, "Cross-Cultural Studies of Facial Expression," in *Darwin and Facial Expression,* ed. P. Ekman (New York: Academic Press, 1973).
16. N. Sussman and H. Rosenfeld, "Influence of Culture, Language and Sex on Conversational Distance," *Journal of Personality and Social Psychology* 42 (1982): 67–74.
17. V. P. Richmond and J. C. McCroskey, *Nonverbal Behavior in Interpersonal Relations,* 3rd ed. (Boston: Allyn and Bacon, 1995), p. 104.
18. See, for example, J. K. Burgoon, T. Birk, and M. Pfau, "Nonverbal Behaviors, Persuasion, and Credibility," *Human Communication Research* 17 (1990): 140–169.
19. See J. D. Rothwell, *In Mixed Company,* 2nd ed. (Ft. Worth, Tex.: Harcourt Brace Jovanovich, 1995), pp. 246–248.
20. S. Roan, "Overweight and Under Pressure," *Los Angeles Times* (Dec. 18, 1990): E1, E4.
21. R. M. Turk, "Strict Dress Codes Are Alive, Well in Laid-Back L.A.," *Los Angeles Times* (June 5, 1992): E1, E7.

22. "Computer Firm Boss Perot Ran Tight, Dressy Ship," *Albuquerque Journal* (June 6, 1992): A5.
23. R. E. Roel, "Corporate Dress Codes Increasingly in Dispute," *Newsday* (June 3, 1992): 12.
24. J. Matthews, "In Offices across America, Attire Is Changing," *Washington Post* (Jan. 31, 1994): 26.
25. D. Kunde, "Companies Ease Up on Strict Dress Codes," *Dallas Morning News* (Mar. 15, 1993): 16.
26. Richmond and McCroskey, *Nonverbal Behavior in Interpersonal Relations,* p. 244.
27. W. Wells and B. Siegel, "Stereotyped Somatypes," *Psychological Reports* 8 (1961): 1175–1178.
28. B. Hunter, "Are You Ready to Face '60 Minutes'?" *Industry Week* (Mar. 8, 1982): 74.
29. "Memos," *Industry Week* (Jan. 11, 1982): 11.
30. A. Mehrabian, *Silent Messages,* 2nd ed. (Belmont, Calif.: Wadsworth, 1981).
31. D. Borisoff and L. Merrill, *The Power to Communicate: Gender Differences as Barriers,* 2nd ed. (Prospect Heights, Ill.: Waveland, 1992), p. 48.
32. E. Hall, *The Hidden Dimension* (New York: Doubleday, 1969), pp. 113–125.
33. M. L. Knapp and J. A. Hall, *Nonverbal Behavior in Human Interaction,* 3rd ed. (Ft. Worth, Tex.: Harcourt Brace Jovanovich, 1992), pp. 127–130.
34. Ibid., p. 129.
35. Mehrabian, *Silent Messages,* p. 51.
36. D. Ogilvy, *Principles of Management* (New York: Ogilvy & Mather, 1968), p. 2.
37. J. E. McGrath and J. R. Kelly, *Time and Human Interaction* (New York: Guilford, 1989).
38. R. J. Schoenberg, *The Art of Being a Boss* (New York: New American Library, 1978), p. 36.
39. "Are You Really Ready to Change Jobs?" in "Fall Job Market," advertising supplement to the *Washington Post* (Sept. 28, 1986): 22.
40. "Coaching Football—Italian Style," *Thousand Oaks* (Calif.) *News Chronicle* (Jan. 4, 1990): 1, 20.
41. W. Griffitt, "Environmental Effects of Interpersonal Affective Behavior: Ambient Effective Temperature and Attraction," *Journal of Personality and Social Psychology* 15 (1970): 240–244.
42. T. Allen, "Meeting the Technical Information Needs of Research and Development Projects," M.I.T. Industrial Liaison Program Report No. 13-314 (Cambridge, Mass., November 1969).
43. F. Steele, *Physical Settings and Organizational Development* (Reading, Mass.: Addison-Wesley, 1973).
44. Ibid., p. 65.
45. P. Manning, *Office Design: A Study of Environment* (Liverpool, Eng.: Pilkington Research Unit, 1965), p. 474.
46. Research summarized in P. A. Andersen and L. L. Bowman, "Positions of Power: Nonverbal Influence in Organizational Communication," in *The Nonverbal Communication Reader,* ed. J. A. DeVito and M. L. Hecht (Prospect Heights, Ill.: Waveland, 1990) pp. 404–405.
47. Steele, *Physical Settings and Organizational Development,* p. 38.

CHAPTER 4

1. S. Covey, *The Seven Habits of Highly Effective People* (New York: Simon & Schuster, 1989).
2. J. Beels, "It's Time to Get Back to Basics," *Industrial Finishing* (May 1987): 28.
3. B. L. Harragan, "Career Advice," *Working Woman* (December 1985): 32.
4. K. K. Murphy, *Effective Listening: Hearing What People Say and Making It Work for You* (New York: Bantam, 1987), p. 74.
5. P. T. Rankin, "The Measurement of the Ability to Understand Spoken Language," *Dissertation Abstracts* 12 (1952): 847–848.
6. J. D. Weinrauch and J. R. Swanda, Jr., "Examining the Significance of Listening: An Exploratory Study of Contemporary Management," *Journal of Business Communication* 13 (February 1975): 25–32.
7. J. P. Kotter, "What Effective General Managers Really Do," *Harvard Business Review* 60 (1982): 156–167; and R. G. Nichols and L. A. Stevens, "Listening to People," *Harvard Business Review* 68 (1990) 95–102.
8. H. Mintzberg, "The Manager's Job: Folklore and Fact," *Harvard Business Review* 53 (July–August 1975): 49–61.
9. S. L. Becker and L. R. V. Ekdom, "That Forgotten Basic Skill: Oral Communication," *Association for Communication Administration Bulletin* 33 (1980): 12–15.
10. V. DiSalvo, D. C. Larsen, and W. J. Seiler, "Communication Skills Needed by Persons in Business Organizations," *Communication Education* 25 (1976): 269–275.
11. 10. *U.S. News & World Report* (May 26, 1980): 65.

12. D. H. Sweet, "Successful Job Hunters Are All Ears," *Managing Your Career* (New York: Dow Jones, 1993).

13. B. D. Sypher, R. N. Bostrom, and J. H. Siebert, "Listening, Communication Abilities, and Success at Work," *Journal of Business Communication* 26 (1989): 293–303.

14. D. P. Rogers, "The Development of a Measure of Perceived Communication Openness," *Journal of Business Communication* 24 (1987): 53–61.

15. S. Zurier, "Strictly for Salesmen," *Industrial Distribution* (August 1987): 47.

16. B. D. Ruben, *Communicating with Patients* (Dubuque, Iowa: Kendall/Hunt, 1992), p. 77. See also T. Peters and N. Austin, *A Passion for Excellence* (New York: Random House, 1985), pp. 16–20.

17. J. Brownell, "Listening in the Service Industries," in *Listening in Everyday Life: A Personal and Professional Approach,* ed. D. Borisoff and M. Purdy (Lanham, Md.: University Press of America, 1991), pp. 229, 256.

18. B. H. Spitzberg, "The Dark Side of Incompetence," in *The Dark Side of Interpersonal Communication* (Hillsdale, N.J.: Erlbaum, 1994), pp. 27–28.

19. R. G. Nichols, "Listening Is a 10-Part Skill," *Nation's Business* 75 (September 1987): 40.

20. R. G. Nichols, *Are You Listening?* (New York: McGraw-Hill, 1957), pp. 1–17.

21. See, for example, S. Golan, "A Factor Analysis of Barriers to Effective Listening," *Journal of Business Communication* 27 (1990): 25–36; and J. E. Hulbert, "Barriers to Effective Listening," *Bulletin for the Association for Business Communication* 52 (1989): 3–5.

22. A. Vangelisti, M. L. Knapp, and J. A. Daly, "Conversational Narcissism," *Communication Monographs* 57 (1990): 251–274.

23. P. F. Drucker, "Management Communications," in *Management—Tasks, Responsibilities, Practices* (New York: Harper & Row, 1974).

24. *Industrial Marketing* (April 1982): 108.

25. Borisoff and Purdy (eds.), *Listening in Everyday Life,* p. xiii.

26. S. Peterson, "Managing Your Communication: The Year 2000 and Beyond," speech delivered at the INC Conference, Chicago, Oct. 19, 1994, and printed in *Vital Speeches of the Day* (Jan. 1, 1995).

27. D. J. Schwartz, *The Magic of Thinking Big* (New York: Simon & Schuster, 1980), p. 78.

28. Ibid., p. 77.

29. T. D. Thomlison, "Intercultural Listening," in Borisoff and Purdy, eds., *Listening in Everyday Life,* p. 119.

30. M. Houston, "When Black Women Talk with White Women: Why Dialogues are Difficult," in *Our Voices: Essays in Culture, Ethnicity, and Communication: An Intercultural Anthology,* ed. A. Gonzalez, M. Houston, and V. Chen (Los Angeles: Roxbury, 1994), 133–139.

31. Thomlison, "Intercultural Listening," p. 117.

32. M. L. Lustig and J. Koester, *Intercultural Competence: Interpersonal Communication across Cultures* (New York: HarperCollins, 1993), p. 203.

33. L. D. Mare, "Ma and Japan," *Southern Speech Communication Journal* 55 (Spring 1990): 319–328.

34. J. C. Pearson, L. H. Turner, and W. Todd-Mancillas, *Gender and Communication,* 2nd ed. (Dubuque, Iowa: Wm. C. Brown, 1985), pp. 38–39.

35. D. Tannen, *You Just Don't Understand: Women and Men in Conversation* (New York: Morrow, 1990), p. 142.

36. C. A. Rategan, "He Said, She Said," *Current Health* 2 (September 1993): 6.

37. M. Booth-Butterfield, "She Hears . . . He Hears: What They Hear and Why," *Personnel Journal* (May 1984): 36–42.

38. D. Tannen, *Talking from 9 to 5* (New York: Morrow, 1994), p. 284.

39. D. J. McNerney, "Improve Your Communication Skills," *HR Focus* 71 (1994): 22. See also J. Procter, "You Haven't Heard a Word I Said: Getting Managers to Listen," *IEEE Transactions on Professional Communication* 37 (1994).

40. A. D. Wolvin and C. G. Coakley, "A Survey of the Status of Listening Training in Some Fortune 500 Companies," *Communication Education* 40 (1991): 152–165.

41. The typology that follows in the text was developed by R. F. Proctor II in R. B. Adler, L. B. Rosenfeld, and N. Towne, *Interplay: The Process of Human Communication,* 6th ed. (Ft. Worth, Tex.: Harcourt Brace Jovanovich, 1995), pp. 121–122.

42. D. Borisoff and D. A. Victor, *Conflict Management: A Communication Skills Approach* (Englewood Cliffs, N.J.: Prentice-Hall, 1989), p. 45.

43. K. A. Kiewra, N. F. DuBois, D. Christian, and A. McShane, "Note-Taking Functions and Techniques," *Journal of Educational Psychology* 83 (June 1991): 240–246.

44. Covey, *The Seven Habits,* p. 252.

CHAPTER 5

1. D. B. Curtis, J. L. Winsor, and R. D. Stephens, "National Preferences in Business and Communication Education," *Communication Education* 38 (1989): 6–14.
2. L. Iacocca and W. Novak, *Iacocca: An Autobiography* (New York: Bantam, 1984), p. 58.
3. Quoted by H. Sutton, "The CEO as Syndicated Columnist," *Across the Board* 24 (July–August 1987): 62.
4. E. Sieburg, "Confirming and Disconfirming Communication in an Organizational Setting," in *Communication in Organizations,* ed. J. Owen, P. Page, and G. Zimmerman (St. Paul, Minn.: West, 1976), pp. 129–149; and E. Sieburg and C. Larson, "Dimensions of Interpersonal Response," paper presented to the International Communication Association, Phoenix, Ariz., 1971.
5. J. Gibb, "Defensive Communication," *Journal of Communication* 11 (September 1961): 141–148.
6. "Nineteen Eighty-Nine Turkeys of the Year," *San Jose Mercury News* (Nov. 23, 1989), p. 1D.
7. L. Coser, *The Functions of Social Conflict* (New York: Free Press, 1956).
8. For more detailed descriptions of the approaches to conflict discussed in the text, see J. L. Hocker and W. W. Wilmot, *Interpersonal Conflict,* 4th ed. (Madison, Wis.: Brown & Benchmark, 1995), pp. 96–100.
9. D. Tannen, *Talking from 9 to 5* (New York: Morrow, 1994), p. 91.
10. For an extended discussion of the merits of indirectness, see ibid., pp. 78–106.
11. M. McCormack, *What They Don't Teach You at Harvard Business School* (New York: Bantam, 1984), pp. 152–153.
12. R. J. Burke, "Methods of Resolving Superior-Subordinate Conflict: The Constructive Use of Subordinate Differences and Disagreements," *Organizational Behavior and Human Performance* 5 (1970): 393–411.
13. R. Fisher and W. Ury, *Getting to Yes: Negotiating Agreement without Giving In* (Boston: Houghton Mifflin, 1981), p. 45.
14. S. R. Wilson and L. L. Putnam, "Interaction Goals in Negotiation," in *Communication Yearbook 13,* ed. J. A. Anderson (Newbury Park, Calif.: Sage, 1990), pp. 374–406.

CHAPTER 6

1. C. J. Stewart and W. B. Cash, Jr., *Interviewing: Principles and Practices,* 7th ed. (Dubuque, Iowa: Wm. C. Brown, 1994), p. 5.
2. Ibid., p. 1.
3. D. Harper, "Strictly for Salesmen," in a review of G. Gard, *Championship Selling,* in *Industrial Distribution* (May 1987): 122.
4. L. B. Andrews, "Mind Control in the Courtroom," *Psychology Today* 16 (March 1982): 70.
5. D. Deaver, in Shirley J. Shepherd, "How to Get That Job in 60 Minutes or Less," *Working Woman* (March 1986): 118.
6. Adapted from G. L. Wilson and H. L. Goodall, Jr., *Interviewing in Context* (New York: McGraw-Hill, 1991), p. 291.

CHAPTER 7

1. S. Moramarco, "What You Should Say about Yourself in a Job Interview," *Redbook* (August 1979): 50.
2. H. D. Tschirgi, "What Do Recruiters Really Look for in Candidates?" *Journal of College Placement* (December 1972–January 1973): 75–79.
3. "The Hidden Hurdle: Executive Recruiters Say Firms Tend to Hire 'Our Kind of Person,' " *Wall Street Journal* (May 12, 1979): 1.
4. R. N. Bolles, *What Color Is Your Parachute: A Practical Manual for Job-Hunters and Career-Changers* (Berkeley, Calif.: Ten Speed Press, 1995), pp. 20–21.
5. M. S. Granovetter, "The Strength of Weak Ties," *American Journal of Sociology* 78 (1973): 1360–1380.
6. E. M. Rogers, *Diffusion of Innovations,* 3rd ed. (New York: Free Press, 1983), p. 297.
7. T. H. Willard, "Computers Could Soon Tackle Personnel Tasks," *Los Angeles Times* (May 16, 1990): D3.
8. R. W. Eder and G. R. Ferris (eds.), *The Employment Interview: Theory, Research, and Practice* (Newbury Park, Calif.: Sage, 1989).
9. H. A. Medley, *Sweaty Palms: The Neglected Art of Being Interviewed* (Belmont, Calif.: Wadsworth, 1978), p. 1.
10. R. S. Wyer and T. K. Scrull, "Human Cognition in Its Social Context," *Psychological Review* 93 (1990): 322–339; and R. Guilford, C. F. Ng, and M. Wilkinson, "Nonverbal Cues in the Employment Interview: Links between Applicant Qualities and Interviewer Judgment," *Journal of Applied Psychology* 70 (1985): 735.

11. D. B. Goodall and H. L. Goodall, Jr., "The Employment Interview: A Selective Review of the Literature with Implications for Communications Research," *Communication Quarterly* 30 (Spring 1982): 116–122.
12. Medley, *Sweaty Palms,* p. 19.
13. C. L. Cooper, "No More Stupid Questions," *Psychology Today* 26 (May–June 1993): 14–15.
14. S. Silverstein and N. R. Brooks, "And Be Sure to Mention Your Favorite Subject: You," *Los Angeles Times* (Mar. 1, 1993): D3.
15. Medley, *Sweaty Palms,* p. 164.
16. M. B. Dickson, *Supervising Employees with Disabilities: Beyond ADA Compliance* (Menlo Park, Calif.: Crisp, 1993), p. 107.
17. M. Z. Sincoff and R. S. Goyer, *Interviewing* (New York: Macmillan, 1984), p. 80.
18. J. K. Springston and J. Keyton, "So Tell Me, Are You Married?: When the Interviewee Knows You're Asking an Illegal Question," *Proceedings of the 1988 Annual National Conference of the Council of Employee Responsibilities and Rights* 2 (1988): 177–186.
19. J. Woo, "Job Interviews Post Risk to Employers," *Wall Street Journal* (Mar. 11, 1992): B1, B5.
20. C. W. Downs, G. P. Smeyak, and E. Martin, *Professional Interviewing* (New York: Harper & Row, 1980), p. 167.
21. K. Blanchard, "Rating Managers on Performance Reviews," *Today's Office* 22 (August 1987): 6–11.
22. C. O. Longenecker, "Truth or Consequences: Politics and Performance Appraisals," *Business Horizons* 27 (November–December 1989): 169–182.
23. G. L. Wilson and H. L. Goodall, *Interviewing in Context* (New York: McGraw-Hill, 1991), p. 181.
24. L. Iacocca and W. Novak, *Iacocca: An Autobiography* (New York: Bantam, 1984).
25. N. R. F. Maier, *The Appraisal Interview: Objectives, Methods, and Skills* (New York: Wiley, 1958).
26. J. L. Pearce and L. W. Porter, "Responses to Formal Performance Appraisal Feedback," *Journal of Applied Psychology* 71 (1986): 211–218.

CHAPTER 8

1. C. Lazzareschi, "Being Part of the Team at Work," *Los Angeles Times* (Sept. 12, 1994): pt. 2, p. 13.
2. R. Reich, *Tales of a New America* (New York: Time Books, 1987), p. 126.
3. M. V. Redmond, "A Plan for the Successful Use of Teams in Design Education," *Journal of Architectural Education* 17 (May 1986): 27–49.
4. D. L. Welles, Jr., and S. H. Hartley, "Teamwork and Cooperative Learning: An Educational Perspective for Business," *Quality Management Journal* (July 1994): 30.
5. T. J. Peters and R. H. Waterman, Jr., *In Search of Excellence: Lessons from America's Best-Run Companies* (New York: Harper & Row, 1982), p. 211.
6. Ibid., pp. 13–14.
7. "Hewlett-Packard Uses Barrier Meetings to Speed Production and Improve Quality," *Meeting Management News* 5 (June 1993): 1–2.
8. For a more detailed discussion of the advantages and drawbacks of working in groups, see S. A. Beebe and J. T. Masterson, *Communicating in Small Groups: Principles and Practices,* 4th ed. (New York: HarperCollins, 1994), pp. 8–11. See also J. D. Rothwell, *In Mixed Company: Small Group Communication,* 2nd ed. (Ft. Worth, Tex.: Harcourt Brace Jovanovich, 1995), pp. 72–75.
9. D. J. Rachman and M. H. Mescon, *Profile Kit for Business Today,* 4th ed. (New York: Random House, 1990), profile 2.
10. See, for example, J. R. Katzenbach and D. K. Smith, "The Discipline of Teams," *Harvard Business Review* 86 (March–April 1993): 111–120.
11. Peters and Waterman, *In Search of Excellence,* p. 32.
12. E. Bormann, *Small Group Communication: Theory and Practice* (New York: Harper & Row, 1990).
13. Rothwell, *In Mixed Company,* pp. 200–201.
14. K. Lewin, R. Lippitt, and R. K. White, "Patterns of Aggressive Behavior in Experimentally Created Social Climates," *Journal of Social Psychology* 10 (1939): 271–299.
15. L. L. Rosenbaum and W. B. Rosenbaum, "Morale and Productivity Consequences of Group Leadership Style, Stress, and Type of Task," *Journal of Applied Psychology* 55 (1971): 343–358.
16. R. R. Blake and J. S. Mouton, *The New Managerial Grid* (Houston, Tex.: Gulf, 1985).
17. F. E. Fiedler, *A Theory of Leadership Effectiveness* (New York: McGraw-Hill, 1967).
18. P. Hersey and K. Blanchard, *Management of Organizational Behavior,* 4th ed. (Englewood Cliffs, N.J.: Prentice-Hall, 1982); and K. Blanchard, "Selecting a Leadership Style

That Works," *Today's Office* 23 (September 1988): 14.

19. Rothwell, *In Mixed Company,* pp. 200–201.
20. R. S. Wellins, W. C. Byham, and J. M. Wilson, *Empowered Teams: Creating Self-Directed Work Groups That Improve Quality, Productivity, and Participation* (San Francisco: Jossey-Bass, 1991), p. 3.
21. B. Dumaine, "Who Needs a Boss?" *Fortune* (May 7, 1990): 52–60.
22. Ibid.
23. J. Solomon, "When Are Employees Not Employees? When They're Associates, Stakeholders . . ." *Wall Street Journal* (Nov. 9, 1988): B1.
24. Katzenbach and Smith, "The Discipline of Teams," pp. 111–114.
25. The discussion of the first five types of power is adapted from the work of J. R. P. French and B. Raven, "The Bases of Social Power," in *Studies in Social Power,"* ed. D. Cartwright (Ann Arbor: University of Michigan, Institute for Social Research, 1959). Information power was introduced by B. Raven and W. Kruglanski, "Conflict and Power," in *The Structure of Conflict,* ed. P. G. Swingle (New York: Academic Press, 1975), pp. 177–219. Connection power was introduced by Hersey and Blanchard, *Management of Organizational Behavior,* p. 179.
26. S. T. Loh, "You Say the Boss Is How Old?" *Los Angeles Times* (Mar. 1, 1993): pt. 2, pp. 9–10.
27. Bormann, *Small Group Communication.* For a succinct description of Bormann's findings, see Rothwell, *In Mixed Company,* pp. 191–194.
28. Adapted from M. Z. Hackman and C. E. Johnson, *Leadership: A Communication Perspective* (Prospect Heights, Ill.: Waveland, 1991), pp. 125–126.
29. M. Zey (ed.), *Decision Making: Alternatives to Rational Choice Models* (Newbury Park, Calif.: Sage, 1992).
30. See R. Y. Hirokawa, "Group Communication and Problem-Solving Effectiveness: An Investigation of Group Phases," *Human Communication Research* 9 (1983): 291–305; Edward R. Marby and Richard E. Barnes, *The Dynamics of Small Group Communication* (Englewood Cliffs, N.J.: Prentice-Hall, 1980), p. 78; Norman R. F. Maier and Robert A. Maier, "An Experimental Test of the Effects of 'Developmental' vs. 'Free' Discussions on the Quality of Group Decisions," *Journal of Applied Psychology* 41 (1957): 320–323; and Ovid L. Bayless, "An Alternative Model for Problem-Solving Discussion," *Journal of Communication* 17 (1967): 188–197.
31. J. Dewey, *How We Think* (New York: Heath, 1910).
32. See, for example, Zey (ed.), *Decision Making.*
33. B. A. Fisher, "Decision Emergence: Phases in Group Decision Making," *Speech Monographs* 37 (1970): 53–66. See also M. S. Poole and J. Roth, "Decision Development in Small Groups. IV: A Typology of Group Decision Paths," *Human Communication Research* 15 (1989): 232–256.
34. M. S. Poole and J. Roth, "Decision Development in Small Groups. V: Test of a Contingency Model," *Human Communication Research* 15 (1989): 549–589. See also E. M. Eisenberg and H. L. Goodall, Jr., *Organizational Communication: Balancing Creativity and Constraint* (New York: St. Martin's, 1993), pp. 267–268.
35. B. Day, "The Art of Conducting International Business," *Advertising Age* (Oct. 6, 1990): 48.
36. Eisenberg and Goodall, *Organizational Communication,* p. 264.
37. L. Browning, "Reasons for Success at Motorola," paper presented at the conference of the International Communication Association, Miami, May 1992.
38. Some sequences of escalating penalties for nonconformity have been described in the literature. See, for example, J. R. Wenberg and W. Wilmot, *The Personal Communication Process* (New York: Wiley, 1973); and T. D. Daniels and B. K. Spiker, *Perspectives on Organizational Communication,* 2nd ed. (Dubuque, Iowa: Wm. C. Brown, 1991), p. 237.
39. I. L. Janis, *Victims of Groupthink* (Boston: Houghton Mifflin, 1972), p. 9.
40. Adapted from E. G. Bormann, *Discussion and Group Methods,* 2nd ed. (New York: Harper & Row, 1975), pp. 176–195. See also P. Adler and P. Adler, "Intense Loyalty in Organizations: A Case Study of College Athletics," *Administrative Science Quarterly* 33 (1988): 401–418.
41. Janis, *Victims of Groupthink,* p. 9.
42. D. G. Myers and H. Lamm, "The Group Polarization Phenomenon," *Psychological Bulletin* (July 1976): 602–627.
43. S. P. Robbins, *Organizational Behavior: Concepts, Controversies, and Applications,* 4th ed. (Englewood Cliffs, N.J.: Prentice-Hall, 1990), p. 289.

44. A. Osborn, *Applied Imagination* (New York: Scribner's, 1959). See also F. Hurt, "Better Brainstorming," *Training & Development* (November 1994): 57–59.

CHAPTER 9

1. D. Tannen, *Talking from 9 to 5* (New York: Morrow, 1994), p. 276.
2. D. Colemon, "The Electronic Rorschach," *Psychology Today* 17 (February 1983): 35–43.
3. P. Sandwich, "Better Meetings for Better Communication," *Training & Development* (January 1992): 29–30.
4. D. Cole, "Meetings That Make Sense," *Psychology Today* 23 (May 1989): 14–15.
5. D. Tyson, "Meetings Cited as Time Wasters," *Los Angeles Times* (Sept. 4, 1989): pt. 4, 2–3.
6. In J. H. Boren, *The Bureaucratic Zoo: The Search for the Ultimate Mumble* (McLean, Va.: EPM Publications, 1976).
7. F. Williams, *Executive Communication Power: Basic Skills for Management Success* (Englewood Cliffs, N.J.: Prentice-Hall, 1983), p. 65.
8. From *Six Secrets to Improve Your Future Business Meetings* (Austin, Tex.: 3M Visual Systems) and S. De Wine, *The Consultant's Craft: Improving Organizational Communication* (New York: St. Martin's, 1994), p. 162.
9. C. Allard, "Trust and Teamwork: More Than Just Buzzwords," *En Route* (August 1992): 41.
10. A. L. Wiley, "The Quest for Quality," *Technical Communication* (January–March 1993): 165.
11. C. O. Steele, "Make Your Meetings More Productive," *Black Enterprise* 24 (March 1994): 76.
12. De Wine, *The Consultant's Craft,* p. 165.
13. *Leading Meetings,* vol. 1 (Great Neck, N.Y.: Xerox Learning Systems), pp. 15–17.
14. Tannen, *Talking from 9 to 5,* p. 290.
15. A. L. Delbercq, A. H. Van de Ven, and D. H. Gustafson, *Group Techniques for Program Planning: A Guide to Nominal Group and Delphi Processes* (Glenview, Ill.: Scott, Foresman, 1975), pp. 7–16.
16. L. N. Loban, "Questions: The Answer to Meeting Participation," *Supervision* (January 1972): 11–13.
17. M. McMaster and J. Grinder, *Precision: A New Approach to Communication* (Beverly Hills, Calif.: Precision Models, 1980), pp. 70–73.
18. *Leading Meetings,* vol. 1, p. 50.
19. 3M Management Institute, "Meeting Quality: A Chicken-Egg Question?" *Meeting Management News* 4 (June 1992): 2–3.
20. Allard, "Trust and Teamwork," p. 41.
21. *Leading Meetings,* vol. 2, pp. 41–45.

CHAPTER 10

1. D. Z. Meilach, "Even the Odds with Visual Presentations," *Presentations* (November 1994): 51.
2. L. Tuck, "Profiling the Presentation Professional," *Presentation Products* (November 1992): 35–42.
3. J. P. Wright, *On a Clear Day You Can See General Motors* (New York: Avon, 1979), p. 96.
4. H. M. Boettinger, *Moving Mountains, or The Art of Letting Others See Things Your Way* (New York: Collier, 1969), p. 6.
5. "The Conference Board," *Across the Board* 24 (September 1987): 7.
6. H. Hamashige, "Speech! Speech!" *Los Angeles Times* (Nov. 1, 1994): D1.
7. D. R. Seibold, S. Kudsi, and M. Rude, "Does Communication Training Make a Difference?: Evidence for the Effectiveness of a Presentation Skills Program," *Journal of Applied Communication Research* 21 (May 1993): 111–129.
8. R. L. Spiro and B. A. Weitz, "Adaptive Selling: Conceptualization, Measurement, and Nomological Validity," *Journal of Marketing Research* 24 (1990): 61–69.
9. J. T. Molloy, *Molloy's Live for Success* (New York: Bantam, 1985), p. 16.
10. *Los Angeles Times* (Oct. 21, 1993): F1.
11. Cited in *This Just In* (Mar. 19, 1995), Internet: archie@netcom.com.
12. B. E. Bradley, *Fundamentals of Speech Communication: The Credibility of Ideas,* 6th ed. (Dubuque, Iowa: Wm. C. Brown, 1991), pp. 58–61.
13. Meilach, "Even the Odds," p. 3.
14. "The Gray Flannel Sideshow," *Presentations* (November 1993): 50.
15. H. L. Marsh, "Summary Membership Remarks," speech delivered at a meeting of the New York Chapter of the Institute of Internal Auditors, New York, May 13, 1983.

CHAPTER 11

1. For a discussion of research supporting the value of organization, see B. E. Bradley, *Fundamentals of Speech Communication: The Credibility of Ideas,* 6th ed. (Dubuque, Iowa: Wm. C. Brown, 1991), pp. 181–183.
2. Adapted from C. L. Bovée and J. T. Thill, *Business Communication Today,* 2nd ed. (New York: Random House, 1989), pp. 89–90.

3. *Los Angeles Times* (Jan. 18, 1992): A18.
4. For a discussion of nonlinear organizing patterns, see C. Jaffe, *Public Speaking: A Cultural Perspective* (Belmont, Calif.: Wadsworth, 1995), pp. 188–191; and M. W. Lustig and J. Koester, *Intercultural Competence* (New York: HarperCollins, 1993), pp. 219–221.
5. "Presentation Planning: Draw a Logic Tree," *Meeting Management News* (April 1993): 1–2.
6. Based on an outline in W. A. Mambert, *Presenting Technical Ideas: A Guide to Audience Communication* (New York: Wiley, 1968), pp. 163–164.
7. The uppermost limit of items people can usually recall from their short-term memory is seven. For oral presentations, however, limiting the number of main points to five increases the odds that listeners will retain them. For a summary of research supporting this conclusion, see G. Rodman, *Public Speaking in the Media Age* (Ft. Worth, Tex.: Harcourt Brace Jovanovich, 1996), chap. 8.
8. R. Moran, "Tips on Making Speeches to International Audiences," *International Management* 44 (1989): 74.
9. P. Preston, *Communication for Managers* (Englewood Cliffs, N.J.: Prentice-Hall, 1979), p. 24.
10. N. L. Reding, "Leading American Agriculture into the 21st Century," speech delivered at the commencement ceremony of the College of Agriculture, University of Missouri, Columbia, May 14, 1983, and reprinted in *Executive Speaker* 4 (September 1983): 6.
11. "Errors Are Common in Credit Reports, Small Study Suggests," *Wall Street Journal* (May 27, 1991): B7.
12. J. R. Bonée, "Making Love in Public: Bank Marketing and Public Relations," speech delivered at the Bank Administrative Institute, Elgin, Ill., Apr. 12, 1983, and reprinted in *Executive Speaker* 4 (August 1983): 7.
13. Quoted in J. W. Robinson, *Winning Them Over* (Rocklin, Calif.: Prima, 1987), p. 279.
14. D. M. Roderick, "A Most Ingenious Paradox," speech delivered at the National Press Club, Washington, D.C., and reprinted in *Executive Speaker* 5 (January 1984): 4.
15. *Executive Speechwriter Newsletter* 8 (1993): 3.

CHAPTER 12

1. L. Poole, "A Tour of the Mac Desktop," *Mac World* 1 (February 1984): 16.
2. C. Spangenberg, "Basic Values and the Techniques of Persuasion," *Litigation* (Summer 1977): 64.
3. H. Anderson, "Day Care: Big Hit at the Office," *Los Angeles Times* (May 21, 1989): 30–33.
4. J. Lawlor, "Offbeat Perks Can Perk Up Workers," *USA Today* (Aug. 17, 1992): 2B.
5. J. Applegate, "Best, Worst Small-Business Names of 1994," *Los Angeles Times* (Apr. 12, 1994): D3.
6. Ibid.
7. C. J. Silas, "Natural Gas: The Bureaucratic Muddle," speech delivered in January 1983, and reprinted in *Executive Speaker* 4 (May 1983): 6.
8. A. Rooney, "Sales vs. Service," *Executive Speechwriter Newsletter* 14 (May 1989): 5.
9. J. D. Ong, "Workplace 2000: Managing Change," speech delivered at the National Alliance of Business Conference, Atlanta, Mar. 25, 1988, and reprinted in *Executive Speaker* 8 (November 1988): 6.
10. "Making Time and Money Real," *Executive Communication Report* 3 (March 1987), developed by *Small Business Report,* 203 Calle del Oaks Mount, Monterey, CA 93940.
11. T. G. Labrecque, "A Radical Approach to Banking Reform: Legalize Competition," speech delivered at the University of Richmond Business School, Feb. 12, 1987, and reprinted in *Executive Speaker* 8 (August 1987): 5.
12. S. J. Diamond, "Some Airlines Ads Mislead without Lying," *Los Angeles Times* (June 13, 1991): E1.
13. P. Saffo, "Compute: IBM Is Refocusing on Revising Home PCs," *Los Angeles Times* (June 25, 1990): D4.
14. J. Levy and R. Miller, "Taking the Guesswork Out of Networking," *Today's Office* 24 (January 1990): 9–10.
15. J. D'Arcy, "Getting Technical," *Presentations* (December 1994): 37.
16. "Paper Work Is Avoidable (If You Call the Shots)," *Wall Street Journal* (June 17, 1977): 24.
17. D. R. Vogel, G. W. Dickson, and J. A. Lehman, "Driving the Audience Action Response," *Computer Graphics World* 5 (August 1986): 25–28. See also D. R. Vogel, G. W. Dickson, and J. A. Lehman, *Persuasion and the Role of Visual Presentation Support: The UM/3M Study* (Austin, Tex.: 3M Corporation, 1986): 1–20.

18. D. Z. Meilach,"Control Your Own Slides," *Presentation Products* (March 1993): 25–32.
19. For more suggestions on how to use handouts, see R. W. Pike, "Handouts: A Little Charity to Your Audience Goes a Long Way," *Presentations* (May 1994): 31–35.
20. L. Sherman, "Digital Video Moves Out of the Trenches," *Presentation Products* (March 1993): 32–40.
21. C. Currid, *Make Your Point! The Complete Guide to Successful Business Presentations Using Today's Technology* (Rocklin, Calif.: Prima, 1995).
22. For more information on using visual aids effectively, see S. M. Kosslyn and C. Chabris, "The Mind Is Not a Camera, The Brain Is Not a VCR: Some Psychological Guidelines for Designing Charts and Graphs," *Aldus Magazine* (September–October 1993): 33–36.
23. L. Tuck, "Improving Your Image with LCD Panels," *Presentations* (January 1994): 32.
24. L. Pearson, "The Medium Speaks," *Presentation Products* (June 1993): 55–56.
25. See, for example, L. Tuck, "Using Type Intelligently," *Presentations* (April 1994): 30–32; and S. Hinkin,"Not Just Another Pretty Face: 10 Tips for the Most Effective Use of Type," *Presentations* (January 1995): 34–36.

CHAPTER 13

1. R. Ailes, "You Are the Message," *Executive Communications* (January 1988): 1.
2. M. Landis (Houser), "Taking the Butterflies Out of Speechmaking," *Creative Living* 9 (Spring 1980): 19.
3. Adapted from L. Fletcher, *How to Design and Deliver a Speech,* 4th ed. (New York: Harper & Row, 1990), pp. 347–351.
4. J. Grossman, "Resurrecting Auto Graveyards," *Inc.* (March 1983): 73–80.
5. W. L. Haynes, "Public Speaking Pedagogy in the Media Age," *Communication Education* 38 (1990): 89–102.
6. P. J. Stella, "Are There Any Questions?" *Presentations* (November 1994): 12.
7. I. Wallace and D. Wallechinsky, *Book of Lists* (New York: Bantam, 1977), p. 469.
8. "The Speaker May Look Calm but Survey Confirms Jitters," *Los Angeles Times* (Sept. 13, 1981): pt. 5, p. 13.
9. See, for example, R. R. Behnke, C. R. Sawyer, and P. E. King, "The Communication of Public Speaking Anxiety," *Communication Education* 36 (April 1987): 138–139; J. Burgoon, M. Pfau, T. Birk, and V. Manusov, "Nonverbal Communication Performance and Perceptions Associated with Reticence," *Communication Education* 36 (April 1987): 119–130; and K. L. McEwan and G. Devins, "Increased Arousal in Emotional Anxiety Noticed by Others," *Journal of Abnormal Psychology* 92 (November 1983): 417–421.
10. J. C. Humes, *Talk Your Way to the Top* (New York: McGraw-Hill, 1980), p. 135.
11. D. Pogue, "Panic on the Podium," *Mac World* (January 1995): 97–98.
12. M. J. Beatty and M. H. Friedland, "Public Speaking State Anxiety as a Function of Selected Situational and Predispositional Variables," *Communication Education* 38 (1990): 142–147.
13. See, for example, A. Ellis, *A New Guide to Rational Living* (North Hollywood, Calif.: Wilshire Books, 1977); and A. Beck, *Cognitive Therapy and the Emotional Disorders* (New York: International Universities Press, 1976).

CHAPTER 14

1. J. R. Johnson and N. Szczupakiewicz, "The Public Speaking Course: Is It Preparing Students with Work Related Public Speaking Skills?" *Communication Education* 36 (1987): 133.
2. Reported in *Presentation Products* 2 (August 1989): 8.
3. R. Verderber, *Essentials of Informative Speaking: Theory and Contexts* (Belmont, Calif.: Wadsworth, 1991), p. 201.
4. R. E. Wilkes, "Mortgage Megatrends," speech delivered at a meeting of the Austin Association of Professional Mortgage Women, Austin, Tex., Sept. 15, 1987, and reprinted in *Executive Speaker* 9 (1988): 9.
5. E. Graham, "High-Tech Training," *Wall Street Journal* (Feb. 9, 1990): R16.
6. Research summarized in T. H. Leahey and R. J. Harris, *Human Learning,* 2nd ed. (Englewood Cliffs, N.J.: Prentice-Hall, 1989), p. 203.
7. K. Blanchard, "Managers Must Learn to Teach," *Today's Office* 22 (October 1987): 8–9.
8. "How Lever's 'Hands-On' Demos Ignited Rep Enthusiasm," *Business Marketing Digest* 18 (Third Quarter 1993): 29–32.
9. C. Osgood, *Osgood on Speaking: How to Think on Your Feet without Falling on Your Face* (New York: Morrow, 1988), p. 39.
10. Adapted from G. C. Gard, "Accepting an Award: How to Be Gracious and Effective in 30 Seconds," *Toastmaster* (November 1988): 20.

CHAPTER 15

1. Adapted from R. B. Adler and G. Rodman, *Understanding Human Communication,* 5th ed. (Ft. Worth, Tex.: Harcourt Brace Jovanovich, 1994), pp. 499–502.
2. M. Burgoon and M. D. Miller,"Communication and Influence," in *Human Communication: Theory and Research,* ed. G. L. Dahnke and G. W. Clatterbuck (Belmont, Calif.: Wadsworth, 1990), pp. 233–234.
3. "At Lanier a Better Mousetrap Isn't Quite Enough," *Fortune* (Feb. 26, 1979): 74, 76.
4. D. J. O'Keefe, "Social Judgment Theory," in D. J. O'Keefe, *Persuasion: Theory and Research* (Newbury Park, Calif.: Sage, 1990).
5. M. Burgoon and J. K. Burgoon, "Message Strategies in Influence Attempts," in *Communication and Behavior,* ed. G. J. Hanneman and W. J. McEwen (Reading, Mass.: Addison-Wesley, 1975), p. 153.
6. M. Allen, "Determining the Persuasiveness of Message Sidedness: A Prudent Note about Utilizing Research Summaries," *Western Journal of Communication* 57 (1993): 98–103. See also M. Allen, J. Hale, P. Mongeau, S. Berkowitz-Stafford, S. Stafford, W. Shanahan, P. Agee, K. Dillon, R. Jackson, and C. Ray, "Testing a Model of Message Sidedness: Three Replications," *Communication Monographs* 57 (1990): 275–291.
7. For more information on cultural differences in styles of persuasion, see M. L. Lustig and J. Koester, *Intercultural Competence: Interpersonal Communication across Cultures* (New York: HarperCollins, 1993), pp. 226–229; and D. A. Lieberman, *Public Speaking in the Multicultural Environment* (Englewood Cliffs, N.J.: Prentice-Hall, 1994), p. 16.
8. For a detailed review of credibility, see S. Trenholm, *Persuasion and Social Influence* (Englewood Cliffs, N.J.: Prentice-Hall, 1989), pp. 179–201. See also L. Beason, "Strategies for Establishing an Effective Persona: An Analysis of Appeals to Ethos in Business Speeches," *Journal of Business Communication* 28 (1991): 326–346.
9. O'Keefe, *Persuasion,* pp. 95–129. See also "Elaboration Likelihood Model," in E. M. Griffin, *A First Look at Communication Theory,* 2nd ed. (New York: McGraw-Hill, 1994), pp. 238–248.
10. B. E. Gronbeck, K. German, D. Ehninger, and A. H. Monroe, *Principles of Public Speaking,* 12th brief ed. (New York: HarperCollins, 1995), pp. 244–255.

Acknowledgments

Pages 108, 159, 433: From *What They Don't Teach You in Harvard Business School* by Mark McCormack. Copyright © 1984 by Book Views, Inc. Used by permission of Bantam Books, a division of Bantam Doubleday Dell Publishing Group, Inc.

Page 67 Table: From *Organizational Behavior: Theory and Practice* by Steven Altman, Enzo Valenzi, and Richard M. Hodgetts. Copyright © 1985 by Harcourt Brace Jovanovich, Inc., reproduced by permission of the publisher.

Pages 107, 122, 214, 301: From *Iacocca: An Autobiography* by Lee Iacocca with William Novak. Copyright © 1984 by Lee Iacocca. Used by permission of Bantam Books, a division of Bantam Doubleday Dell Publishing Group, Inc.

Index

D

E